The Decision-Making Skillbook

Donald L. Barnes
Kenneth Miller

J. Weston Walch, Publisher
Portland, Maine

Name ______________________________

Class ______________________________

1 2 3 4 5 6 7 8 9 10

ISBN 0-8251-1609-0

J. Weston Walch, Publisher

P. O. Box 658 • Portland, Maine 04104-0658

Printed in the United States of America

Contents

To the Teacher . . . vii

Introduction to the Skillbook . . . vii

Recognizing Problems Associated with Decision Making . . . viii

How the Brain Responds to Changing Stimuli . . . ix

To the Student . . . xi

Part I: Knowing Yourself . . . 1

Introducing Yourself . . . 3

Looking Ahead . . . 5

Taking Responsibility . . . 6

Goals . . . 8

Your Favorite Things . . . 10

What Bothers You Most? . . . 12

How Much Control Do You Have? . . . 14

Comparing Heroes—Teenagers and Adults . . . 16

Avoiding Problem Situations . . . 17

Knowing Your Likes and Dislikes . . . 18

Values . . . 20

Good Sportsmanship . . . 21

Words of Wisdom: Do You Agree with Them? . . . 22

Dealing With Persuasive Advertisements . . . 23

Choosing a Girlfriend or Boyfriend Carefully . . . 24

What You Want to Do and What You Ought to Do Are Sometimes Different . . . 25

Things Worth Fighting For . . . 26

Group Pressures . . . 27

Comparing Views—Teenagers and Parents . . . 28

Part II: Dealing With Everyday Stresses and Tensions . . . 31

Risk Takers and Security Seekers . . . 33
Stress Is a Natural Part of Life . . . 34
Problems That Often Upset or Frighten Young People . . . 34
How Do *You* Deal With Stress? . . . 38
Making and Keeping Friends . . . 38

Part III: Story Problems: Making Choices . . . 43

Everything but the Evidence . . . 45
Dick's Dilemma . . . 46
When Do You Protect a Friend? . . . 48
Just for Fun . . . 50
Winners and Losers . . . 52
Giving Personal Advice . . . 54
The Wallet . . . 55
It's Nice to Be Liked, But This Is Too Much! . . . 56
Gary Chooses a Friend . . . 58
The Kid with the Terrible Temper . . . 59
When You're Not Included . . . 60
The Biggest Bragger in Town . . . 62
How Do You Deal With Personal Threats? . . . 64
Mom Defends Her Boy . . . 66
If Only I'd Known! . . . 68
Getting to Know You . . . 70

Albert Runs the Show . . . 72

Too Good to Be True . . . 74

When There's No Easy Answer . . . 76

Just for Jess . . . 78

It's Terrible to Be Left Out . . . 80

A Chance for Recognition . . . 82

Changing Schools Is a Moving Experience . . . 84

Secrets Are Hard to Keep . . . 86

Best Friends . . . 88

Rosa Has a Great Imagination! . . . 90

Choosing a Class President . . . 92

Lonely People Sometimes Need You . . . 94

Alice's Friend . . . 96

Last Chance Charlie . . . 98

When Friends Don't Care . . . 100

Michael Faces a Challenge . . . 102

Protecting a Friend . . . 104

What Are Friends For? . . . 106

Notes . . . 107

To the Teacher

Introduction to the Skillbook

This book has been designed specifically for middle school/junior high students, gifted pupils in the upper elementary grades, and special classes with school guidance counselors. There are almost five hundred opportunities for students to respond on the pages that follow.

The situations presented in this book are typical of those which students face in their daily lives. The problems are not simplistic; there are no easy answers to most of the dilemmas. They involve conflicts with peers and adults, problems in setting personal priorities (goals, personal expectations), an analysis of personal likes and dislikes, and surveys of peer pressures and family and school responsibilities. There is a special section which focuses on fundamental strategies students utilizing this book may employ in coping with everyday tensions and stresses.

We have field-tested these activities and exercises with a broad cross section of sixth, seventh, and eighth graders to make certain that the case studies and checklists are easily understood, interesting to students, and unambiguous. Many of the participants in the field-testing commented that they enjoyed the exercises and wished we would bring in additional activities. In many homes, children do not have a chance to participate in important decision-making activities. Parents have neither the time nor the inclination to ask for their opinions. These exercises offer a welcome opportunity for many to try their wings and develop greater confidence in their personal ability to cope effectively with problem-solving situations.

You will note that several of the earlier exercises require students to examine their response patterns and make judgments about their individual concerns and priorities. They can learn a good deal about themselves through follow-up discussions. Teachers who use these books in their classrooms should maintain an open-minded attitude, stressing the fact that we are all changing from day to day and week to week. Our decision-making skills, attitudes, and priorities should also be evolving as we grow and mature.

Many of the later exercises are didactic. They utilize a systematic question format that teaches students how to confront and methodically determine how various decisions of a main character in a story situation will affect others.

Recognizing Problems Associated with Decision Making

The types of decisions we make from day to day and week to week determine, to a large degree, the quality of our lives. If we make carefully reasoned judgments which take into account a variety of key factors in each situation, we may be pleased with the results. If, on the other hand, we make hasty, ill-conceived choices, we may find the consequences distressing.

There are a number of commonly occurring factors which interfere with thoughtful decision making:

A. The first of these factors is our *preference for rapid results.* Most of us find it discomforting to live with perplexing dilemmas over an extended period of time. We want to quit ourselves of our problems as quickly as possible and move on to other matters. In this era of instant foods and five-minute car washes, it is logical to assume that personal and social problems will lend themselves to similar kinds of quick fixes and rapid resolutions. Unfortunately, individual values, personal priorities, and worthwhile insights do not occur overnight. These important dimensions of living are crafted, like the work of a great sculptor, through a series of carefully reasoned strategic decisions. In most instances the quality of the final outcome is directly related to the amount of effort and creative talent expended in its preparation.

B. A second difficulty arises from the fact that we are *emotional beings*, easily provoked and frequently inclined toward irrational responses. When we feel we have been abused, we want to even the score, not seek a just solution. When we feel we have been overlooked or left out, we often want to be compensated for our suffering. Being included as an afterthought is not enough. We have a strong tendency to believe that someone must pay when we have been wronged. In many instances, this demand for retribution simply tips the scales unjustly in the opposite direction, and the search for a fair solution is once more aborted.

   Numerous authors, including Thomas Harris who developed transactional analysis, have tried to convince us that it is important to examine social conflicts and social situations rationally and seek solutions which are fair to all those involved. We are urged to transcend our personal biases and selfish motivations as well as our penchant for using demeaning comments which depreciate the worth of others. Instead, we are asked to treat others as valued colleagues in a common search for mutually satisfying resolutions.

C. Thirdly, there are always problems related to the effective use of knowledge. In this brief summary we will only touch on four of the more obvious problems in dealing with information: personal versus public knowledge, facts versus values and opinions, hidden or unstated assumptions, and difficulties in determining the relevance of information. Since decision making basically rests upon the validity of information and the manner in which we sort and use it, the judgments we ultimately reach can be no more reliable than the data we have used in fabricating our conclusions.

   1. We need to help students recognize the difference between personal and public knowledge. When a friend tells us about a dream or feelings he or

she has about a classmate, there is no way we can observe these experiences directly. Likewise, people who have seen a vision can only tell us about it; we cannot witness the vision ourselves. On the other hand, there are many events which can be observed by more than one person. If your friend tells you that there is a penguin in the refrigerator, you can go check it for yourself. It is important for students to recognize that we can have more confidence in our observations when they have been checked by others.

2. When dealing with information, it is important for students to recognize that *facts* tell us *what actually happened*. Facts do not tell us what ought to happen. Speculations about how we should conduct our national affairs or how people should lead their personal lives are value judgments. They are statements about what is thought to be desirable in particular situations. Value judgments are extremely important in the conduct of human affairs, but they are not facts. We have an unfortunate habit of confusing statements of fact with statements of value; therefore, we frequently find ourselves in the embarrassing position of trying to defend a statement of value as though it were a statement of fact.

3. In many instances in everyday life people provide us with information that contains hidden assumptions. For example, we may be told that Hitler's decision not to invade England cost him the war. It is crucial for students to recognize that there is an important hidden assumption in the statement. It assumes that if Hitler had invaded England, he would have been victorious. A student may suggest that everyone get together after the ball game to celebrate the victory. There is a similar assumption behind this statement.

   Teachers need to help students learn to check on the reasonableness or logic of an assumption. We can reasonably assume that the sun will rise in the east tomorrow morning. We may also accept the assumption that we will have food to eat tomorrow. If, on the other hand, we assume that a friend will win the state lottery, we must recognize that these expectations are much more remote. In the last analysis, assumptions really rest upon probabilities.

4. Finally, it is important to recognize that information may be related to a given topic, yet not be relevant to the solution of the problem. Relevant information doesn't automatically solve the problem, but it is clearly useful in the search for a solution. If, for example, you are trying to locate a safe place to cross a river, and your uncle tells you that this particular stream is considered to be one of the most beautiful in the nation, your uncle's comments are about the river, but they do not contribute to the resolution of the problem.

How the Brain Responds to Changing Stimuli

In recent years, researchers have begun to unravel the problem-solving intricacies of the human brain. Studies conducted by Richard Granger at the University of California (Irvine) and Ralph Linsker at the Thomas J. Watson Research Center in Yorktown Heights, New York, demonstrate that even though the brain's neural networks are laid down prior to birth, the connections between neurons can rearrange themselves at almost any time during the life of an individual. These neural networks actually adapt and change in response to new experiences. The neurons form specialized clusters as more adequate responses to problems evolve.

This intricate, adaptive capacity of the brain permits each of us to develop problem-solving strategies. The magnificent machinery, the *basic ingredients* are there; all we have to do as teachers is add the water and a measure of patience. The water in this case is made up of challenging episodes and events tailored to provoke thoughtful responses and, ultimately, well-crafted solutions to important problems.

Lawrence Kohlberg and his colleagues at Harvard University have demonstrated repeatedly that students can be assisted in making more prudent, reflective judgments when given ample opportunities to analyze and discuss problematic situations. We are hopeful that this series of activities will contribute to this effort. Each episode in this book should serve as a springboard for class discussion. As students discover that their peers have formed quite different opinions from their own, their individual worlds will be extended and enriched.

To the Student

Welcome to the world of decision making. This is your chance to compare your opinions with those of your friends on a large number of interesting, practical, everyday topics. As you read through the stories of normal problems and the checklists describing school and family pressures, you will feel right at home. Many of the situations described are difficulties which you and your friends are already facing. In fact, most of the problems were suggested by boys and girls like yourselves. These are not easy problems. If there were simple answers to these conflicts, people would have agreed on how to handle them long ago.

If you can remember your early years, you will quickly realize that things were simpler then. You didn't have to make a lot of big decisions. You didn't have to choose your friends, decide which groups and organizations to join or figure out how to pay for things you wanted. The important decisions were made for you.

You have probably enjoyed the increasing freedoms you have been given as you have grown older. It is fun to feel that you are having a chance to make more of your own plans and run your affairs. You may feel that you are more in charge of your life. Parents and teachers usually value the suggestions of teenagers more than they do the recommendations of younger children. They know that as you get older, you can make wiser choices. You are often able to anticipate problems before they occur, and your suggestions normally take into account the welfare of other people.

Unfortunately, good decision-making skills don't develop overnight. They take time, effort, and practice. We face so many kinds of situations that there aren't any really simple answers or clever ways of handling all of them. Each new problem requires thoughtful consideration and careful reasoning. If, however, you can become really good at decision making, you will be much more valuable to yourself and to your friends and family. You will also be a freer person. You will be freer because you don't have to go to others constantly for answers to your problems. You will be freer because the solutions you develop will be your own. The answers you offer will represent your own thinking rather than the thinking of others.

It is very important that we all respect the privacy of others. There is a real difference between showing sympathetic concern for others and prying into their affairs. The problem situations and checklists included in this book are not embarrassing, and they do not require you to share private information about yourself or others.

Students your age in other schools who have helped plan these situations have really enjoyed talking about these everyday problems. They have been surprised at the many ways their friends have viewed the same difficulties. We hope you will find them intriguing as well as informative.

PART I

Knowing Yourself

Introducing Yourself

How you view yourself is important in helping you develop a unique individual identity. You have strong feelings about what you are capable of doing, what you want to be, and how you fit into the world around you. These and other feelings about yourself all contribute to making you what you are. Can you identify some of these feelings? If you can, you will have a better understanding of your uniqueness.

In the space below complete a letter of introduction describing yourself to someone you have never met. Your letter should be 100–150 words.

My name is ______________________________. I am presently in the ________ grade at ______________________ School. My favorite subjects are ______________________________________. I am also very good at ____.

Physically, I am ______________________. I have ______________ eyes and ______________ hair. I particularly like to ______________________ ______________________________, and I get the greatest happiness from ____.

After I graduate from high school, I would like to ______________________ ______________________________. My single most important ambition is to ______________________________________. My single greatest fear is that ____ ____.

If I could change one thing about myself I would ______________________. People who know me think I am ______________________________. If you could get to know me I think you would like me because I am ______________ ______________________.

(continued

Introducing Yourself *(continued)*

What other things would you like to say about yourself?

____

____

____

____

____

____

Using the letter of introduction which you just wrote, make a short list of your characteristics.

________	________	________
________	________	________
________	________	________
________	________	________
________	________	________
________	________	________
________	________	________

Look at the list which you just prepared. Are there characteristics which you wish you had included but failed to mention? If so, here's your chance to list them below.

________	________	________
________	________	________
________	________	________
________	________	________
________	________	________
________	________	________
________	________	________

Looking Ahead

Setting goals is an important part of your life. Goals give purpose to what you are doing. Most people change their goals as they grow older.

Think about the statements below and how they relate to the goals you have set in your life. By completing each statement you will be able to figure out how your goals may change as you grow older. Following each completed statement, list three things which you can do to make sure you achieve the goal.

1. When I graduate from high school I plan to ______________

   a. ______________________________

   b. ______________________________

   c. ______________________________

2. In 10–15 years I hope to be employed as ______________

   a. ______________________________

   b. ______________________________

   c. ______________________________

3. When I am a young adult I would like to spend my spare time doing ______________________________

   a. ______________________________

   b. ______________________________

   c. ______________________________

4. By the time I am thirty I hope to have completed ______________

   ____

   a. ______________________________

   b. ______________________________

   c. ______________________________

5. As an older adult I hope my greatest accomplishment will be

   ____

   a. ______________________________

   b. ______________________________

   c. ______________________________

Taking Responsibility

An important part of growing up is taking responsibility. Look at the situations below and check the column that tells how often you take responsibility in each situation.

	All the Time	Most of the Time	Some-times	Never
1. If I walk in the house and see mud tracked on the floor, I clean it up.	____	____	____	____
2. I do my homework with-out being told.	____	____	____	____
3. I keep my room clean.	____	____	____	____
4. When I see the garbage can is full, I take it out.	____	____	____	____
5. If the lawn needs mow-ing, I cut the grass.	____	____	____	____
6. If I see my father or mother working at some-thing, I will help without being asked.	____	____	____	____
7. If I see some trash in our yard, I will pick it up.	____	____	____	____
8. If I see someone has dropped something and failed to notice, I will call it to that person's atten-tion.	____	____	____	____
9. If I find something which has been lost, I will try to see that it is returned to its owner.	____	____	____	____
10. If I find something which is not in its proper place, I will put it where it belongs.	____	____	____	____

(continued)

Taking Responsibility *(continued)*

	All the Time	Most of the Time	Some-times	Never
11. If a friend is in trouble for something he didn't do, I will come to his defense.	____	____	____	____
12. If I have told my parents I will be home at a specific time, I will be on time.	____	____	____	____
13. If I promised a friend I would do something for her, I will keep my word.	____	____	____	____
14. If my teacher has given me an assignment to do, I will have it completed on time.	____	____	____	____
15. If I see someone trying to open a door with both arms loaded with packages, I will open the door for the person.	____	____	____	____

What do these answers say about your willingness to take responsibility?

____

____

Do you have more marks in the first two columns (all or most of the time) than you have in the last two columns (sometimes or never)?

____

____

After looking at those things which you seldom do, which three areas do you think you might be able to improve in the near future?

____

____

Goals

A goal represents something we want to achieve. Whether we are aware of it or not, we all set goals many times each day. Below are opportunities for you to state goals which are worthwhile.

Complete the following sentences:

1. In the area of artistic skills, I would really like to begin to learn to

____

____

2. If I could do something useful with my friends, I would

____

____

3. If I had my wishes, this weekend I would really like to

____

____

4. When I get home from school, my parents expect me to

____

____

5. Within the next few weeks, I plan to buy

____

____

6. If I have time to myself this evening, I want to

____

____

(continued)

Goals *(continued)*

7. While I have some skills in this area, I really want to improve in

____

____

8. In order to be a better student, my teachers would like me to

____

____

9. I know I could be a better friend if I would

____

____

10. Regarding my work in school, my parents would like me to

____

____

11. In looking over the ten items above, does it appear my interest in improvement focuses mainly on mental skills, social skills, or physical skills?

____

____

12. In which of the areas above am I likely to have the quickest success?

____

____

Your Favorite Things

Everyone has special things which they really enjoy or like to do. It may be a favorite song or picture or just sitting in a chair watching birds in the yard. What are your special things? The questions below will help you to identify some of your favorites.

1. What is your favorite subject in school?

   ____

2. What is your favorite thing to do when you have spare time?

   ____

   ____

3. List your hobbies or any special collections that you may have.

   ____

   ____

4. What is your favorite book?

   ____

5. What is your favorite movie?

   ____

6. Who is your favorite television or movie star?

   ____

7. Who is your favorite musical recording star or music group?

   ____

8. What is your favorite radio station?

   ____

9. What is your favorite food?

   ____

(continued)

Your Favorite Things *(continued)*

10. What is your favorite television program?

____

11. What do the ten things you listed have in common?

____

____

12. Are you more like other people or do you tend to be different?

____

____

13. Do the choices you made seem to indicate that your favorites are like the choices of your friends? (Put an X beside your answer and explain why you chose it.)

_____ This seems to be true because _______________

____

____

____

____

____

_____ This does not seem to be true because _______________

____

____

____

____

____

14. Circle the words below which describe your favorite things.

exciting   adventurous   quiet   staid   colorful

What Bothers You Most?

Many times during the course of every day we run into situations which may disturb us. The nature of the things which bother us helps to identify the values we hold and how we apply them in our actions with our friends.

Place a check mark in the column that indicates how much each of the following situations would bother you.

	Very Much	Some	Not at All
1. Your friends tease you about something you did.	______	______	______
2. People around you act obnoxiously.	______	______	______
3. Someone tells a lie about you.	______	______	______
4. You see someone cheat on a test.	______	______	______
5. You are unable to keep a promise you made to a friend.	______	______	______
6. Two of your friends get into a fight.	______	______	______
7. Your friends don't want to do what you want to do.	______	______	______
8. One of your friends starts picking on a smaller child.	______	______	______
9. Your teacher accuses a friend of something she didn't do.	______	______	______
10. Your friends go to the mall without asking you to go along.	______	______	______

(continued)

What Bothers You Most? *(continued)*

	Very Much	Some	Not at All
11. A friend walks out of a store with you with something he hasn't paid for.	________	________	________

Are the things which would bother you "Very Much" hurtful to you personally (designed to do damage to you), or are they things which are unfair but don't hurt you directly?

____

____

____

____

Are the things which would bother you "Some" hurtful to you personally (designed to do damage to you), or are they things which are unfair but don't hurt you directly?

____

____

____

____

Regarding the items you marked "Not at All," why do you think these things would not bother you?

____

____

____

____

How Much Control Do You Have?

Part of growing up is learning to deal with our fears and the various situations in which we find ourselves. How we cope with our fears and the situations we face helps us to develop a degree of control over our life.

Listed below are some everyday situations. Identify the degree of control you think you can exercise over each situation and the reason why you have that degree of control.

	Much Control	Some Control	No Control
1. In setting aside specific time to do my homework	______	______	______
Reason: ______________________________			
2. In buying a new family car	______	______	______
Reason: ______________________________			
3. In going to a movie within walking distance	______	______	______
Reason: ______________________________			
4. In deciding whether to take piano lessons	______	______	______
Reason: ______________________________			
5. In deciding whether to go out for the baseball team	______	______	______
Reason: ______________________________			
6. In being given babysitting responsibilities for a younger brother or sister	______	______	______
Reason: ______________________________			
7. In picking out new clothes	______	______	______
Reason: ______________________________			

(continued)

How Much Control Do You Have? *(continued)*

	Much Control	Some Control	No Control
8. In deciding where our family goes on vacation	______	______	______
Reason: ______________________________			
9. In deciding what we have for dinner	______	______	______
Reason: ______________________________			
10. In picking out television programs to watch	______	______	______
Reason: ______________________________			
11. In selecting books I will read	______	______	______
Reason: ______________________________			
12. In deciding how late I can stay out	______	______	______
Reason: ______________________________			
13. In making a decision about whether I can stay home alone	______	______	______
Reason: ______________________________			
14. In making a decision on how I will spend my money	______	______	______
Reason: ______________________________			
15. In deciding whether I can have friends over after school	______	______	______
Reason: ______________________________			

Over what kinds of situations like those listed above would you like to have more control?

____

____

____

Comparing Heroes—Teenagers and Adults

Ask three friends your own age to choose one person from the following list whom they admire and would prefer for a best friend. Put a check mark beside their choices.

________	A Leading Political Figure	________	An Actress
________	A Judge	________	A Doctor
________	An Olympic Gold Medal Winner	________	A Magician
________	A Veterinarian	________	A Scientist
________	A Race Car Driver		

Now ask some adults whom you know really well the same question and mark their choices below.

________	A Leading Political Figure	________	An Actress
________	A Judge	________	A Doctor
________	An Olympic Gold Medal Winner	________	A Magician
________	A Veterinarian	________	A Scientist
________	A Race Car Driver		

How do adults' heroes differ from heroes selected by your age group?

____

____

____

____

____

____

Avoiding Problem Situations

Try listing the ways you can be tactful when you are refusing to participate in activities which you feel are wrong.

Now tell how you would handle the following situation:

You have been invited to a party at the home of a classmate. Some of your close friends have told you that the party will not be closely supervised and will be "wild." You know this family has many valuable possessions which could be destroyed if the party gets out of control. You are afraid you might be held responsible for any damages which might occur.

What would you do? Here are some things to think about.

1. How can you bow out gracefully? What kinds of words or statements would you use to avoid hurting the feelings of the ones who are going ahead and participating?
2. Would you make up an excuse or would you tell them exactly how you feel?
3. Would you purposely schedule another activity during the same time so there would be a reason for you to be absent?
4. Would you plan a future time to get together with your friends when you could enjoy a different activity with them?

Explain how you would deal with the situation.

Knowing Your Likes and Dislikes

Everyone has likes and dislikes. Understanding the kinds of things we like and dislike and the reasons why we like or dislike them can help us to know ourselves better. You should be able to explain why you like or dislike something. That way you can be sure your feelings are really yours and that you are not just following the feelings of your friends. Filling in the blanks below can help you to clarify some of your likes and dislikes. You may find words in the following list that you want to use.

harsh	open	peppy	new
boring	loud	friendly	quiet
spicy	familiar	cool	long
sentimental	natural	traditional	

Complete each sentence by listing three terms that describe what you dislike:

1. I dislike music that is ____________ ____________ ____________

2. I dislike books that are ____________ ____________ ____________

3. I dislike movies that are ____________ ____________ ____________

4. I dislike people who are ____________ ____________ ____________

5. I dislike foods that are ____________ ____________ ____________

6. I dislike teachers who are ____________ ____________ ____________

(continued)

Knowing Your Likes and Dislikes *(continued)*

Complete each sentence by listing three terms that describe what you like:

7. I like music that is ______ ______ ______

8. I like books that are ______ ______ ______

9. I like movies that are ______ ______ ______

10. I like people who are ______ ______ ______

11. I like foods that are ______ ______ ______

12. I like teachers who are ______ ______ ______

Do you tend to like more things than you dislike?

______

Do your likes relate more to things than to people?

______

Do your dislikes relate more to things than to people?

______

Make a list of the descriptive words which you used more than once in each list.

______

______

______

Values

Values represent those things which we feel are particularly important to us. Eight things which people find valuable are listed below. Put a *1* beside the item in the list which is most important to you. Put a *2* beside the item which is second in importance, and continue until you have numbered all items *1* through *8*.

_____ Having many friends
_____ Good family life
_____ Freedom to do what I want
_____ Doing things for people
_____ Doing things which are exciting
_____ Good health
_____ Having a sense of accomplishment
_____ Good reputation

1. List two things that you are presently doing in your life that help strengthen your number 1 choice.

____

____

2. List two things that you are presently doing in your life that help strengthen your number 2 choice.

____

____

3. List two things that you are presently doing in your life that help strengthen your number 3 choice.

____

____

4. To what extent do you think your first three choices would agree with the choices of your friends?

____

____

5. Which of your choices might your friends find it most difficult to agree with, and why?

____

____

Good Sportsmanship

Coaches often point out that good sportsmanship is very important. They sometimes even dismiss a player from a team for poor sportsmanship. If you were a baseball coach, which kinds of poor sportsmanship would you consider serious enough for you to dismiss a player from a game?

Put a *1* beside the incident below you consider the most serious, a *2* beside the incident which you consider the second most serious, and continue until all seven incidents have been rated.

_____ a. Arguing with the umpire about a decision

_____ b. Calling players on the other team terrible names

_____ c. Claiming you're safe when you really know you are out

_____ d. Arguing with other players about the score

_____ e. Pushing in front of other players so you get to bat sooner

_____ f. Taking equipment that doesn't belong to you after you lose

_____ g. Hitting or pushing other players when there are disagreements

Incidents *a* and *d* describe situations which disrupt the game; *b*, *e*, and *g* describe incidents which show mistreatment of other players; and *c* and *f* show incidents of dishonesty. Looking at how you rated the seriousness of these incidents, are you more concerned with disrupting the game, mistreating other players, or being dishonest?

____

____

____

____

____

Words of Wisdom: Do You Agree with Them?

You have probably heard a great many words of wisdom or pieces of advice. Some of them are listed below. After each piece of advice, write your reaction. Do you agree with it? Do you disagree with it? Put a check mark beside the answer you agree with. Then explain your answer.

1. Honesty always pays.

_____ I agree with this because ______________________________

_____ I do not agree with this because ______________________________

2. Kindness is always important.

_____ I agree with this because ______________________________

_____ I do not agree with this because ______________________________

3. We should always search for the fairest possible solutions to problems.

_____ I agree with this because ______________________________

_____ I do not agree with this because ______________________________

4. If you feel like saying something mean, keep quiet. You'll be better off.

_____ I agree with this because ______________________________

_____ I do not agree with this because ______________________________

5. Never limit yourself to just one friend.

_____ I agree with this because ______________________________

_____ I do not agree with this because ______________________________

6. Even though things seem unfair, they will even out in the end.

_____ I agree with this because ______________________________

_____ I do not agree with this because ______________________________

Dealing With Persuasive Advertisements

We are all faced with an assortment of cleverly worded advertisements every day. Billboards, newspapers, magazines, TV and radio programs, as well as clerks and salespeople try hard to persuade us to buy special products. The writers who think up advertising slogans and catchy phrases know how to appeal to our basic interests and concerns. They realize that we like to feel important, so they tell us their products will make us glamorous. They know that we want to feel confident and proud of our purchases, so they tell us their products are well made, tested, and reliable. The people who dream up the ads have discovered that we are a bit lazy, so they tell us that their products are easy to use. Some advertisers have figured out that we like to think of ourselves as kindly and considerate. They urge us to send cards and gifts that they offer.

We can call these advertising techniques by the following names:

1. *Glamorous You* (emphasizing how attractive you'll be)
2. *Top Quality* (messages that focus on reliability of the item)
3. *Easy-to-Use* (products that require little effort on our part)
4. *Showing You Care* (products that reflect kindness, interest in others)

See if you can recall or find two or three advertisements that use each one of these techniques. List the product beside each technique.

1. Glamorous You ______________________________

   ____

2. Top Quality ______________________________

   ____

3. Easy-to-Use ______________________________

   ____

4. Showing You Care ______________________________

   ____

Which technique is most effective on persons in your age group?

____

Choosing a Girlfriend or Boyfriend Carefully

Everyone knows that people choose girlfriends and boyfriends for different reasons. Which of the traits below would you consider most important in selecting a girlfriend or boyfriend? Put a check mark beside your three highest choices and explain your answers.

He or she . . .

_____ is really good looking.

This is important to me because ______________________________

____

_____ is smart and will probably be very successful in everything he or she tries.

This is important to me because ______________________________

____

_____ is a very gentle person who knows how to care about others.

This is important to me because ______________________________

____

_____ is always pleasant or upbeat.

This is important to me because ______________________________

____

_____ is always loyal and doesn't say things behind my back.

This is important to me because ______________________________

____

_____ is really physically fit and good at sports.

This is important to me because ______________________________

____

_____ really knows what to do in social situations. He or she's cool.

This is important to me because ______________________________

____

What You Want to Do and What You Ought to Do Are Sometimes Different

You have probably heard people describe some of the things *they'd like to do*. These may be glamorous or exciting or they may be things that will hurt others (like evening the score when you have felt wronged). Often the things we like to do best are activities that will put us in the spotlight.

On the other hand, we know that there are things *we ought to do*. These may be jobs around the house, caring for a younger brother or sister, or helping the elderly couple across the street. There are also tests to take at school and assignments to be completed for class.

Life seems to be a mixture of interesting and uninteresting things. Sometimes we are told that we should finish our jobs first and then go out to play. We can then play without a sense of guilt because we have taken care of our responsibilities.

List four responsibilities which you have in or around your house.

____

____

____

____

List four things you like to do with your free time.

____

____

____

____

On the lines below, describe how you manage your responsibilities and free time. Do you have a plan that you follow?

____

____

____

____

Things Worth Fighting For

We all know that it is sometimes best to ignore little problems. We also know that there are some important problems that we cannot ignore. We must do something about them. Which of the following problems would you probably ignore? Explain your answers.

1. The man next door beats his dog quite often. What would you do?

   ____ Ignore it. ____ Do something about it.

   Explain your answer. ______________________________

2. The three-year-old next door can't find her toy. What would you do?

   ____ Ignore it. ____ Do something about it.

   Explain your answer. ______________________________

3. The baby across the street is choking and crying. What would you do?

   ____ Ignore it. ____ Do something about it.

   Explain your answer. ______________________________

4. A small boy is picking flowers from a garden that doesn't belong to his family. What would you do?

   ____ Ignore it. ____ Do something about it.

   Explain your answer. ______________________________

5. Some older children are teasing their younger brothers and sisters. What would you do?

   ____ Ignore it. ____ Do something about it.

   Explain your answer. ______________________________

6. A neighborhood girl took three cents off the counter in your kitchen when your mom was not looking. What would you do?

   ____ Ignore it. ____ Do something about it.

   Explain your answer. ______________________________

In looking over your answers, did you tend to ignore those situations in which a person or animal might lose its life or suffer serious injury?

____ Yes ____ No

Group Pressures

Students your age are often influenced by others. They want to dress alike in many cases. They may also develop personal habits (smoking, cutting classes, hanging out at places downtown) that they would not normally choose if it were not for the influences of their friends. Everyone wants to be accepted. It is uncomfortable to be considered odd or to be left out. It is fun to belong!

Sometimes we want to fight against certain group expectations which we find unacceptable. We may want to get to know new students rather well before we agree to do many things with them. That way we may be able to avoid embarrassing predicaments. We may want to go over the details of a plan before we agree to join in.

What types of group pressures do you feel are most influential in your school?

____

____

____

____

____

____

____

How do students deal with these pressures in your school?

____

____

____

____

____

____

____

Comparing Views—Teenagers and Parents

Write your answers to the six questions below. Then get your parents or guardians to answer the same six questions on the next page.

Your Answers

1. Should teenage students be responsible for setting aside a specific time each school day for studying?

   ____ Yes ____ No

2. Should teenagers call their parents if they are going to be late getting home?

   ____ Yes ____ No

3. Should teenagers stop seeing friends who are not acceptable to their parents?

   ____ Yes ____ No

4. Should teenagers contribute money they earn to help with the purchase of large items (like a ten-speed bike)?

   ____ Yes ____ No

5. Should teenagers be paid for work they do around their homes?

   ____ Yes ____ No

6. Should teenagers join an organization (like a dance club) because their parents think it will be a valuable experience?

   ____ Yes ____ No

(continued)

Comparing Views—Teenagers and Parents *(continued)*

Your Parents' Answers

1. Should teenage students be responsible for setting aside a specific time each school day for studying?

    _____ Yes _____ No

2. Should teenagers call their parents if they are going to be late getting home?

    _____ Yes _____ No

3. Should teenagers stop seeing friends who are not acceptable to their parents?

    _____ Yes _____ No

4. Should teenagers contribute money they earn to help with the purchase of large items (like a ten-speed bike)?

    _____ Yes _____ No

5. Should teenagers be paid for work they do around their homes?

    _____ Yes _____ No

6. Should teenagers join an organization (like a dance club) because their parents think it will be a valuable experiennt?

    _____ Yes _____ No

In what areas do you agree?

____

____

In what areas do you disagree?

____

____

How do you work out agreements in those areas of disagreement?

____

____

PART II

Dealing With Everyday Stresses and Tensions

Risk Takers and Security Seekers

Have you ever noticed that some two- and three-year-olds like to take chances, while others from the same age group carefully avoid new situations? We call the ones who like to take chances **risk takers**. These children seem to have a lot of self-confidence. They're willing to try almost anything. They climb on furniture, mingle easily with strangers, and volunteer quickly when the nursery school teacher asks for help. The other children (who avoid new situations) are called **security seekers**. They don't seem to have much self-confidence, they stay close to their parents, and they seem happiest and most comfortable in familiar surroundings.

We don't know why some children are bold and others are timid but we do know that the amount of self-confidence children have definitely affects their outlook on the world. If children are filled with self-doubts, they will worry more from day to day and experience much more stress. They may be burdened by a variety of fears and anxieties. More secure children, on the other hand, anticipate fewer problems and difficulties.

The level of anxiety that children have and their attitude toward new experiences tend to stay with them throughout their lives. Studies conducted at Yale University show that fearful children tend to grow up to be fearful adults, and preschoolers who seek novel experiences continue to seek out and enjoy new experiences when they are grown.

Which of the following career opportunities would a **risk taker** most likely choose? Put a check mark beside your three choices.

____ 1. Factory Worker	____ 4. Teacher
____ 2. Paratrooper	____ 5. Airline Pilot
____ 3. Firefighter	____ 6. Farmer

(Did you choose 2, 3 and 5? These are good answers.)

Regardless of whether you are a risk taker or a security seeker, you can learn to manage many of the stress situations in your life. Researchers have found that the fears we experience can be classified into three categories:

1. There are **fears of physical injury or loss**. We may worry about being kidnapped or having surgery. We may also be fearful of losing a parent through divorce or death.

2. There are **fears associated with natural or supernatural dangers**. We may worry about ghosts, storms, fires, or haunted places.

3. There are also **social fears**. School tests and examinations may cause us anxieties, or we may dread getting up in front of groups. We may also be fearful of new social situations—moving to a strange community or meeting people for the first time.

Stress Is a Natural Part of Life

Despite our wishful thinking, there are no "super kids" who can overlook or set aside all of the stresses of life. You may have friends who appear to be calm and confident all of the time. If, however, you could crawl into their heads, you would find plenty of worries and frustrations. They may have learned to look cool when you're around them, but they can't help but wonder from time to time how things will turn out for them in the future. Tragedies can strike anywhere without warning. The cool kids are bound to worry about serious injuries or illness, the possibilities of devastating fires, or the social problems that may face them in a new school.

Problems That Often Upset or Frighten Young People

Studies by psychologists show that students your age are worried most about things that may happen at home or at school. At school, students are most afraid of getting poor grades or failing tests, being held back a grade, being made fun of, or being accused of bad behavior such as lying or stealing. At home, students are worried about losing a parent, noticing increased conflict between their parents, and facing problems with family finances (which may result from changes in parents' employment or added financial burdens). Among all of the *physical* problems that students face, they are most fearful of going blind or having to enter the hospital for major surgery.

Rate these sources of stress from *1* to *9* as you see them. Put a *1* beside your greatest source of stress, a *2* beside the second most important source of stress, continuing until you have rated them all.

____ Getting poor grades

____ Not being promoted

____ Being teased by others

____ Going blind

____ Being accused of lying, stealing

____ Not having enough money

____ Losing a parent

____ Noticing increased conflict at home

____ Facing major surgery

These are real problems, of course, but it is important to recognize that many of the problems you may face in school can be reduced through careful planning and thoughtful decision making. Tensions that could easily dominate your thinking for a whole day or ruin an otherwise pleasant week at school can be dealt with intelligently and systematically. Sometimes you can do something to reduce the problem itself; sometimes you can do something to change your attitude or your reaction to the problem.

There are at least ten strategies you should keep in mind when you are facing stressful situations:

1. **Try to decide whether the problem can be avoided.** Students can sometimes change their daily routines so that they are less likely to be faced with bothersome problems. They can ask to change their seats in class or move to other tables in the cafeteria to avoid being hassled. By setting things up ahead of time and getting to places early, they can frequently gain greater personal control over uncomfortable social situations.

   There is no reason for you to accept the taunts and insults of other students. The intelligent thing to do is to plan your day so that you reduce the frustrating encounters with those who make you feel inadequate. Feelings of inadequacy increase stress.

2. **Don't be afraid to express your concerns.** If the driver of a car in which you are riding is going too fast, let that person know that you are worried. The driver has no right to risk your life! If your classmates leave you with all of the clean-up duties following a party, speak up. People need to share responsibilities as well as fun. You are likely to feel much less stress when you believe that things are fair and equitable. You can help reduce tensions by seeing to it that duties are shared equally. A duty chart can often help keep things straight.

3. **Make certain that you really prepare for classroom assignments, tests, and other school responsibilities.** It is natural to put things off, but it is shortsighted and foolish to do so. Throwing things together at the last moment usually results in poor work. Get your assignments done and then have fun. If students use their energies preparing assignments instead of worrying, they would experience a lot less tension. When you are unprepared, you anticipate failure, and the expectation of failure increases stress.

4. **When a problem becomes an obsession and you can't get it off your mind, don't panic!** Remind yourself that you have faced problems all your life, and you are still here. Problems tend to fade with time. Frustrations that appeared overwhelming a few short weeks ago may seem minor as you look back on them later.

5. **Avoid making decisions when you are tired and upset.** You are likely to overreact. When you are worn-out and distressed, it is very difficult to see things in the proper light. Problems normally appear much larger than they really are. Try to get a good night's rest and work out possible solutions in the morning.

6. **Establish a close personal relationship with at least one person.** Everybody needs a really good friend, one who cares about them and knows how to keep a secret. When you feel pressured, misunderstood, or abused, it is very comforting to share your frustrations with a close friend. It may be your mother or father, a neighbor, a sister, or someone at school. In any case, a caring friend who knows how to listen can be of great help when you need to unload your feelings.

7. **Exercise.** Thousands of people have found that unused energies stored up while you are worrying can add to your nervousness and anxiety. Releasing this pent-up energy can help reduce tension and change the way you view the entire situation. The body's reaction to highly stressful situations is known as the "fight or flight" response. When this happens, quantities of adrenaline are released into the blood. This stimulates the liver to provide the body with stored carbohydrates for extra energy. The heart beats faster, the breathing rate increases, and there is greater muscle tension. The body is ready for action. If there is no opportunity to act, this frustrated readiness may cause a headache, upset stomach, or other forms of physical irritability. When you exercise, you may not be solving the problem, but you are diverting your energies from self-destructive tensions to something that is both constructive and exhilarating.

8. **Use relaxation techniques to reduce your inner frustrations and anxieties.** Even the Ancients knew the value of relaxation, and people throughout the world have used relaxation exercises for thousands of years. Sometimes people start with their fingers and toes and gradually relax their whole bodies; sometimes they relax to soothing music or practice quiet breathing exercises. One psychologist has suggested that students breathe slowly and calmly through imaginary holes in their feet. First you have to imagine small holes dotting the bottoms of your feet. Next, as you inhale, you try to feel cool air flowing up through these imaginary holes into your stomach. You hold the air in your stomach for a few seconds and then push the stressed air down through your body and out through the imaginary holes in your feet. During these kinds of relaxation exercises, your mind takes charge of your body.

9. **Set high personal goals, but don't try to do everything at once.** Some students, as well as adults, make plans that are far too complicated and demanding. They accept too many responsibilities at a time and then find themselves overwhelmed. Their failure to meet these many obligations results in feelings of frustration, tension, and guilt.

   Most people can accomplish more than they are now doing, but Father Time will not let you or anyone else care for an unlimited number of tasks at once. If you have lines to learn for a play plus band or athletic practices in addition to regular school assignments, you may not want to accept additional responsibilities. It is generally better to do a few things well than accept a lot of responsibilities and do them haphazardly. Too many demands on your time will add to your frustrations and stress.

10. **Finally, learn to look for humor in difficult situations.** A boy who had recently lost his foot in an accident was asked how things were going. He looked down at his missing foot and replied cheerfully, "Oh, I can't kick." It was true. He really couldn't kick. Another student who was badly beaten in a tennis match explained that he really played the match to show what a good loser he could be, and he had to avoid a victory so that he could demonstrate his newly developed good-loser attitudes. He was joking, of course, but it was far better than crying and complaining.

    Disappointments are never fun, but there are often humorous ways of looking at them. Kids tell funny stories about living through storms, missing the bus, or getting lost, even though the experiences were not very humorous at the time.

How Do *You* Deal With Stress?

You have dealt with stress on many, many occasions. Have you ever used any of these techniques? Rate techniques from *1* to *10* according to how effective you think they might be in reducing your stress. Put a *1* beside the one you think would be most helpful, a *2* beside the second most useful technique, continuing until you have rated them all.

______ Avoid the problem.

______ Prepare carefully for responsibilities.

______ Express your concerns to those involved.

______ Remind yourself that your problems will gradually become less worrisome.

______ Avoid making decisions when you are tired and upset.

______ Establish a close relationship with someone you can trust.

______ Use relaxation techniques.

______ Get good exercise.

______ Don't complicate your life with too many responsibilities.

______ Add a dash of humor.

Making and Keeping Friends

Having a close friend you enjoy and trust can be the most valuable source of comfort in frustrating situations. If you can share your troubles with a sympathetic person who really cares about you, your problems will seem less overwhelming and more manageable. In many instances, just talking about your feelings with a close friend may allow you to get them off your mind and help straighten out your thinking about the difficulties you face.

Unfortunately, you can't just pick up a friend when you are faced with a problem. A friend is not someone you simply call during an emergency, like a firefighter, who rushes in, puts out a fire, and leaves. Good friendships last through sad times as well as good times. Building a good, solid friendship can't happen overnight because it takes time for you to learn to know and trust someone else. The other person also has to learn to know and trust you.

You will seldom find a friend who is perfect. Any friend is going to say and do things that you don't like now and then. You are going to have to overlook things they do that turn you off. Real friends, however, accept each other as they are, not simply as they want to be. There will be times when a good friend is more of a problem than a help, but if you truly value your friendship, you will learn to overlook the bad times and concentrate instead on the many ways you can be helpful to each other.

Friendships may at first look like lucky associations that people simply fall into. Although they often begin as very casual encounters, if they are to grow stronger and develop, they will require careful, thoughtful attention. Strong friendships have at least ten things in common:

1. **Good friends usually choose each other because of *what the other person is like* rather than *who the other person is.*** It may be tempting to choose a cheerleader or an outstanding athlete as a friend because it will give you a chance to join the "in" crowd. A friendship based on prestige, however, is not as genuine as one in which the other person knows you like him or her *as a person* and not simply as someone who has a special position at school.

2. **You have to *be a friend* in order to *have a friend.*** This means that you have to be truly concerned about your friend's happiness. You need to notice when your friend needs cheering up, and you need to listen patiently when he or she has problems to share with you. It isn't easy to listen. It is often more fun to tell about yourself. If you want a companion to know you really care, however, you will need to be a sympathetic listener. Just talking about a problem may be a great help to a friend who is trying to sort out feelings and ideas.

3. **Good friends learn to share feelings in honest and thoughtful ways.** This is not easy. You can be honest and cruel with friends and make them miserable. This is a good way to destroy the friendship. You can also be unwilling to talk honestly about your feelings and end up shutting your friend out of your life. The trick is to learn to share ideas openly so that your companion really knows how you feel, and yet to express your thoughts in ways that do not hurt your friend's feelings or cause a break in your relationship.

4. **One of the best ways to build a friendship is to lend a helping hand when your friend has jobs to do or other responsibilities.** When you provide help, you are reminding your friend that you are willing to share the unexciting tasks as well as the enjoyable times together. Real friendships are not turned on and off. They include the difficult chores as well as the happy times. In fact, you really need your friends more during down times than you do when things are going well.

5. **Good friends try to avoid serious arguments.** Important disagreements often tear friendships apart. If a friend really wants to study or go to the movies and those activities don't appeal to you, go along with his or her plans and perhaps your friend will fit in with your plans the next time. It is natural to feel differently about activities, but if you are going to do lots of things together, someone will need to be flexible and understanding. Many good friends learn to take turns doing first what one companion wants to do and then the other.

6. **If you are a gracious loser and a modest winner, friendships can survive.** It is not likely that you and your friends will enjoy the same number of successes and honors. It may be difficult to accept the fact that things don't often even out. When you receive a great deal more recognition than your friend, it may strain your relationship, but your reaction to your achievement is even more important. If you are not boastful, and you quickly think of other things to talk about, your friend will probably appreciate your thoughtfulness.

7. **Forgiveness is a very important part of friendship.** You have probably known people who carry grudges forever. They can never seem to forget a thoughtless act, and they are not happy until they have done something to their friend to even the score. Good friends, however, learn to forget and forgive. They learn to overlook the petty little off-the-cuff remarks that can quickly lead to a breakdown of communications. Sometimes the offending partner will need to ask the other person for forgiveness. If you have a lot of personal pride, this is hard to do.

8. **Good friends praise each other for their successes.** It is often difficult to compliment people when they do well. It is more natural to be envious. We all wish that we were the one who is getting the praise. However, friends need to know that you are happy about their successes. If you truly care about them, you want them to achieve as much as they can. If you support them in their victories, they will be more likely to cheer for you when you excel in something later.

9. **Really good friends know how to keep an important secret.** If you share your inner thoughts with someone you care about and later find out that everyone in class has been told, it is terribly embarrassing. You feel hurt and betrayed. You will probably decide then and there that you won't share your feelings again. Since friendships are built on trust, it is not likely that a friendship could survive many such disappointments. When you share your deepest thoughts, you have to be absolutely confident that you will not be betrayed by friends, and that jokes about you will not be circulated around the school.

10. **Finally, good friends are loyal.** They look for the best in those they care about, and they don't say mean things about each other. They are not two-faced. They don't say one thing to your face and then make negative comments about you to others. It is great to know that your friends are loyal. It is devastating to find out that they are ridiculing you behind your back. Above all else, you need to feel that you can have complete confidence in the things your friends will say about you when you are apart.

As you look around and see friends who are splitting up, what seems to cause most of the difficulties? Put a *1* beside the statement below that tells what causes most breakups, a *2* beside the second-most common cause, continuing until you have marked them all.

_____ The friends involved chose someone who was very popular rather than someone who could be a real friend.

_____ The friends you have observed were not sympathetic enough. They couldn't be good listeners for each other.

_____ The friends turned each other off because they did not know how to talk to each other in a pleasant manner.

_____ The friends broke up because they were not willing to help each other when there were jobs to be done.

_____ The friends argued too much. They couldn't get along.

_____ One of the friends had more successes than the other, and the pair broke up.

_____ One of the friends was offended, and the other could not forgive and forget.

_____ The friends broke up because of envy. One friend could not compliment and support the other.

_____ One or both of the friends could not keep an important secret and there was a sense of betrayal.

_____ One or both of the friends were disloyal. They said mean things behind each other's backs.

PART III

Story Problems: Making Choices

Everything but the Evidence

Things in room 22 had been disappearing all week long. Jimmy had "lost" his new watch. Tiffany thought she had put lunch money in her desk, but it was gone when she went to get it. Sara couldn't find her new scarf. The teacher, Mr. Roberts, was missing some valuable science equipment.

Jimmy, Tiffany, and Sara never paid much attention to the problem until their own things began disappearing. It made them very angry. They finally concluded that someone was stealing.

All the students thought that they knew who the thief was, but no one could prove it.

How would you deal with the problem? Rank the choices listed below, starting with the best course of action. Number *1*, in your opinion, is the best solution and number *10* is the least effective.

______ Tell the teacher you think you know who took your property.

______ Take something from the thief so he or she will know how it feels.

______ Tell your friends and others in your class not to talk to or associate with the person who you think stole the items.

______ Talk to your principal about the problem.

______ Talk to your parents.

______ Threaten to beat up the person you suspect.

______ Talk to the suspect and try to find out why he or she is stealing.

______ Try to help the person who seems to be stealing.

______ Set a trap to catch the thief.

______ Keep things hidden, locked up, or under guard until the thief quits taking things.

Explain why you think your number 1 choice is best.

____

____

____

Dick's Dilemma

Scouting meant a great deal to Dick. He joined in all of the activities at the weekly scout meetings. The other fellows in the troop were fun to be around.

Mr. Majors, the troop leader, had announced that on the last Saturday of the month he would drive the boys to the zoo in East Hampton. The boys were to meet at Mr. Major's house at 9 A.M. that Saturday.

At breakfast on Saturday morning Dick's mother asked him if he would be responsible for his six-year-old brother, Timmy, while she went shopping. Dick readily agreed. A few minutes after his mother left, the telephone rang. It was Mr. Majors asking whether he was ready to go to the zoo. Dick immediately realized his mistake.

Dick's mind went numb. He tried to think of ways to get out of his responsibility. Could he possibly leave Timmy home alone? Could he get Mrs. James next door to look in on Timmy? Could he take Timmy along? Could he take Timmy on his bicycle to his aunt a mile away and still be ready to join his friends on the trip? After checking the clock, Dick realized that there wasn't time to make other arrangements. He had to leave Timmy or stay and care for him.

1. Based on the story, describe two ways that Dick can deal with the problem.

   a. ____

   ____

   b. ____

   ____

2. If Dick leaves Timmy, what will Dick gain?

   ____

   ____

   ____

   ____

(continued)

Dick's Dilemma *(continued)*

3. If Dick stays with Timmy, what will Dick gain?

4. If Dick leaves Timmy, how will this affect Timmy?

5. If Dick stays with Timmy, how will this affect Timmy?

6. Looking at what Dick gains by staying with Timmy and how it will affect Timmy if he stays, would it be better for Dick to stay with Timmy or go to the zoo?

When Do You Protect a Friend?

Although Sue and Karen were as different as night and day, they were close friends. Sometimes Karen said things that weren't true. Sometimes she borrowed things from other people without asking. Sue's mother said that Karen was a "little disorganized."

Late Friday afternoon on their way home from school the girls found a new bicycle lying near the sidewalk. "Let's take a ride," Karen suggested. When Sue refused, Karen hopped on the bike, laughed, and waved good-bye as she rode off.

Tuesday morning Sue noticed a police officer near the outside gate leading to the main entrance of the school. The officer was talking to the principal. Sue heard the officer remark, "We found Sara Brown's bike, but it was damaged beyond repair. Someone saw a girl riding it near the river, but we have no additional information."

Sue was shocked and confused. She knew the bike the police officer had found was probably the one Karen had taken. Sue wondered whether she should tell the principal what she knew or go to class and forget what she had overheard.

1. Based on the story, describe two ways that Sue could deal with this problem.

   a. ____

   ____

   b. ____

   ____

2. If Sue tells the principal, what will Sue gain?

   ____

   ____

   ____

   ____

   ____

(continued)

When Do You Protect a Friend? *(continued)*

3. If Sue does *not* tell the principal, what will Sue gain?

4. If Sue tells the principal, how will this affect Karen?

5. If Sue does *not* tell the principal, how will this affect Karen?

6. Looking at what Sue gains by telling the principal and what happens to Karen if Sue tells the principal, would it be fairer to tell the principal or not?

Just for Fun

A number of the seventh graders had been frightening the elementary children on the playground across the street from the middle school. For two weeks they had been bringing rubber spiders and throwing them at the smaller children. A few days later they had a live snake. The seventh graders loved to hold the snake out towards the younger ones and watch them run and scream. When the playground supervisors chased the seventh graders away, the older students began accosting the little children on the way to school.

Beth watched from the school entrance across the street where she and some of her friends were talking. Beth was really upset. She felt that the seventh graders had no right to tease the little children. Her younger sister, Hannah, was one of the first graders they liked to tease most. Beth had tried to protect Hannah on two occasions, but that only made things worse. When she forced the older kids to stop, they tried even harder the next day to frighten Hannah and her first-grade classmates. Beth was becoming concerned. Hannah had been waking up at night screaming. It seemed that her frightening experiences were really affecting her.

Beth realized that she could seek help from her teachers or the school principal. She wondered if she should.

1. Based on the story, describe two ways that Beth could deal with this problem.

   a. ______________________________

   ____

   b. ______________________________

   ____

2. If Beth tells the principal or the teachers, what will Beth gain?

   ____

   ____

   ____

   ____

(continued)

Just for Fun *(continued)*

3. If Beth does *not* tell the principal or the teachers, what will Beth gain?

____

____

____

____

4. If Beth tells the principal or the teachers, how will this affect the seventh graders?

____

____

____

____

5. If Beth does *not* tell the principal or the teachers, how will this affect the seventh graders?

____

____

____

____

6. Looking at what Beth gains by telling the principal and how this affects the seventh graders, would it be best to tell the principal or not tell the principal?

____

____

____

____

____

____

Winners and Losers

Jane thought her special day would never come. For weeks she had watched preschoolers coming and going from the Little Haven Nursery School. They were cute! They were the kinds of children you'd love to teach. Jane even knew a few of them by name because their older brothers and sisters were in her classes.

Now, finally, Jane was to have a chance to help in the nursery school. Ms. Thompson, the woman who ran the school, talked with Jane for thirty minutes before school. She seemed most interested in seeing that none of the children were injured and that they had equal opportunities to do things.

When eight o'clock arrived and the children tumbled in, it appeared that everyone had a favorite place to go. Coats and mittens were thrown on the floor next to boots and galoshes. Closet doors were almost torn off their hinges as a sea of little hands reached for pull toys, wagons, puzzles, jump ropes, and huge rubber balls. Jane quickly realized that her Saturday morning job was not going to be easy. The adorable little tots who she thought would be competing to hold her hand didn't even notice her.

At eleven o'clock Ms. Thompson asked Jane to take four of the older children outside. She gave Jane a kickball and two bases. Two of the children didn't seem interested in playing kickball. It wasn't long before Jane knew why. The two who didn't want to play couldn't kick the ball when their team was up, and they couldn't catch the ball when they were in the field. Jane realized very quickly that the two good players were going to be up all morning! Jane didn't know what to do. She thought about switching the players so that there would be one good player and one poor player on each team. The good players, however, didn't want to switch, and Jane was worried that they would dislike her if she insisted on reorganizing the teams.

1. Based on the story, describe two ways that Jane could deal with this problem.

   a. ____

   ____

   b. ____

   ____

(continued)

Winners and Losers *(continued)*

2. If Jane does *not* switch the players around, what will she gain?

3. If Jane switches the players around, what will she gain?

4. If Jane does *not* switch the players around, how will this affect the players?

5. If Jane switches the players around, how will this affect the players?

6. Looking at what Jane gains by *not* switching the players around and how it affects the players if she does *not* switch them, would it be wiser to switch the players or not?

Giving Personal Advice

You're a newspaper columnist who tries to help people with nagging problems. Write your reply to each of the following requests for assistance.

Dear Pat:

We have some kids in the neighborhood who hang around our house after school, and they never seem to know when to go home. We get ready to sit down to dinner, and they don't take the hint and leave. My sister and I like them, but we don't want them around all the time! What should we do?

All in the Family

____

____

____

Dear Pat:

I live in a mobile home park with my family. Our neighbor to the east lives very close. She is an elderly lady, and she is constantly watching what my friends and I are doing. We can't do anything without her knowing about it. Mom says not to worry, but I don't think neighbors should be so nosy. What should we do?

Shadowed

____

____

____

Dear Pat:

We live on the fourth floor of a big apartment building. It seems that everyone has kids in our project. Our next-door neighbors are nice, but they think they own the halls. They leave their bikes and roller skates as well as boxes of outside toys on both sides of their door. The rest of us can barely get through to the elevator. It's a mess! What should I do?

Boxed In

____

____

____

The Wallet

On Monday, Carol was walking home from school dreaming about a new ten-speed bike. What a breeze it would be getting to and from school on a new bike! She kicked an object on the ground. "Hey," she said to herself, "it's a wallet!" Carol remembered what her mother had always said: "Leave things alone which don't belong to you." Carol, however, was curious about the wallet.

Carol stooped over and picked up the wallet. She opened it and found five twenty-dollar bills and several credit cards. Here was the answer to her dreams! But should she really keep the wallet?

Below are eight choices for Carol. Place a *1* beside the best choice, and *2* by the next best, continuing until you have numbered them all.

______ Hide the wallet nearby until you can decide what to do.

______ Call a police officer. Ask the police officer to take the wallet.

______ Take the wallet home and tell your parents you found it.

______ Leave the wallet on the sidewalk and hope the person who lost it will come back and find it.

______ Find the name of the owner in the wallet and call him or her on the phone.

______ Keep the money and throw the wallet in a trash can.

______ Go through the neighborhood and ask people if they know to whom the wallet belongs.

______ Take the wallet home and tell your parents a friend gave it to you.

Explain why you think your number 1 choice is best.

____

____

____

____

____

____

____

____

It's Nice to Be Liked, But This Is Too Much!

Jason had a problem. Ms. Black, his teacher, was always complimenting him. She said so many nice things about him that the other kids were convinced that he was the teacher's pet. Jason wanted to do good work in school, but he didn't relish the thought of being considered "Mister Perfect."

Jason guessed from the very first day in class that Ms. Black might favor him. Ms. Black had mentioned in front of the whole class that she was especially happy to have Jason because she had had his brother two years earlier, and she knew Jason was from a fine family.

When there were special jobs to do, Ms. Black usually called on Jason. He sometimes wished that he could become invisible. He liked Ms. Black, but being treated in a special way all the time was losing him friends and making him the target of cruel comments and jokes.

On one dreadful day, Ms. Black told Jason in front of the other students that he had a smile just like his brother Tom's. That did it! His classmates started calling him "Smiley" during the noon hour and after school. It was awful!

Jason's mother knew Ms. Black very well, and Jason wondered if he might ask his mom to discuss the problem with Ms. Black. He hated to get his mom involved, and he hated to make a big deal of the problem with Ms. Black. After all, she wasn't trying to embarrass him.

1. Based on the story, describe two ways Jason could deal with the problem.

   a. ____

   ____

   ____

   b. ____

   ____

   ____

(continued)

It's Nice to Be Liked, But This Is Too Much! *(continued)*

2. If Jason asks his mom to talk with Ms. Black, what will he gain?

____

____

____

3. If Jason does *not* ask his mom to talk with Ms. Black, what will he gain?

____

____

____

4. If Jason asks his mom to talk with Ms. Black, how will this affect Ms. Black?

____

____

____

5. If Jason does *not* ask his mom to talk with Ms. Black, how will this affect Ms. Black?

____

____

____

6. Looking at what Jason gains by asking his mom to talk with Ms. Black and how his mom's talk will affect Ms. Black, would it be better for Jason to talk with his mother or not?

____

____

____

____

____

Gary Chooses a Friend

Gary's mother has told him that he cannot associate with Todd, the new boy from Centerville. Gary likes Todd and wants to be with him. They both like sports, and Todd is always there ready to do things. No matter what Gary has planned, Todd fits right in.

During the noon hours at school, there is free time in the gym, but on several occasions the other guys in the gym have not let Todd join in the games. On Tuesday Gary felt so sorry for Todd that he quit the game himself and left with his new-found friend. They didn't leave the building, but Gary knew that this would get him in trouble with his mother.

Gary and His Mother Know Different Things About Todd.

Gary's mother has not met Todd. She has drawn her conclusions about him from things she has heard.

Gary has been with Todd on many occasions. They are in several classes together, and Todd has proven to be a trusted friend.

What Gary's Mother Knows	What Gary Knows
Todd's father has an alcohol problem.	Todd's mother is dead, and he lives with his father.
Todd has been in reform school.	Todd told Gary that he was sent to reform school when his father was out of work and he had to steal food from a bakery.
Other mothers who have children at school have forbidden their boys to associate with Todd.	Todd was so upset that he started to cry when the other boys refused to let him play.

In your opinion, was Gary right in leaving the gym with Todd?

____

____

How can this problem be resolved so that the people involved will be fairly treated?

____

____

____

The Kid with the Terrible Temper

Brad recently entered Washington Junior High, and he's having difficulty with his classmates. There's less fighting at Washington than at his old school. Things are quieter and everyone seems to get along really well. At Washington no one wants to argue. Despite this, every time someone looks at Brad wrong, he is ready to fight.

Many of the boys have tried to make friends with Brad. They have invited him to join them at lunch, and they have asked him to play on their teams after school. Brad gets along fine until there is a little difference of opinion. Then the sparks fly! Brad won't give an inch, and he always wants to settle every difference of opinion with his fists.

The boys are getting tired of Brad's temper. One of them, Jerry Johnson, wants to talk to Brad. Brad sits next to Jerry in two classes. Jerry is tired of Brad's unfriendly stares. In addition, he's afraid of avoiding him for fear of irritating Brad. Jerry's not looking forward to the "talk." Brad is likely to be unhappy. He may even challenge him to a fight.

1. Do junior high students have any responsibility to try to help a hotheaded kid like Brad?

   ____

   ____

2. What would you do to try to help Brad? Check the best idea or add your own.

_____ Ignore Brad's outbursts.

_____ Tell Brad he is wrecking his own chances.

_____ Give Brad a lot of praise.

_____ Think of things that will give Brad a chance for recognition.

_____ Don't invite Brad to anything until he cleans up his act.

_____ Try to get an adult to help Brad.

Add a suggestion of your own.

____

____

____

____

____

When You're Not Included

Janice was pleased to get an invitation to Mary's birthday party. She couldn't wait for Saturday to come. Finally, it arrived! Janice went and had a super time! Then Cindy Thomas asked if she was "sleeping over." Janice hesitantly said, "No." She began to feel a lump in her throat. She realized the other girls were trying to keep the slumber party a secret. She was terribly embarrassed when her mother came to pick her up. She was the only one that was not staying! As she walked dejectedly down the walk, she could hear shrieks of laughter as the other three girls pulled out their sleeping bags. It was a long trip home. Janice was confused. Why hadn't they asked her to stay?

Janice wondered if she should find a new set of friends who would include her in all their activities.

1. Based on the story, describe two ways Janice could deal with the problem.

   a. ____

   ____

   ____

   b. ____

   ____

   ____

2. If Janice finds a new set of friends, what will Janice gain?

   ____

   ____

   ____

   ____

   ____

   ____

(continued)

When You're Not Included *(continued)*

3. If Janice stays with her present friends, what will Janice gain?

4. If Janice finds a new set of friends, how will this affect Cindy and her group?

5. If Janice stays with her present friends, how will this affect Cindy and her group?

6. Looking at what Janice gains by finding a new set of friends and how this affects Cindy and her group, would it be better to find new friends or not?

The Biggest Bragger in Town

Terry has been a real pain since fifth grade. He is always bragging. No matter what someone else has done, Terry has done it better. If someone tells about a camping trip, Terry tells about a better trip he's made. If a kid describes a model plane he's proud of, Terry has an even better one he isn't even using any more.

The more Terry brags, the less others like him. The less his buddies like him, the more he tries to impress them. He always has a story about himself to tell.

The neighborhood gang was really disgusted with Terry. They wished they could find some way to put him in his place. One day while jumping street curbs on his bike, Terry bragged about the tremendous jumps he had done earlier. He said he could easily jump over three barrels.

Tom knew where he could find some barrels, but couldn't decide whether to set them up and dare Terry. Tom was worried about what might happen to Terry if they called his bluff. It was time, however, that somebody did something about his bragging.

1. Based on the story, describe two ways that Tom can deal with the problem.

   a. ____

   ____

   b. ____

   ____

2. If Tom sets up the barrels for Terry to jump, what does Tom gain?

   ____

   ____

   ____

   ____

(continued)

The Biggest Bragger in Town *(continued)*

3. If Tom does *not* set up the barrels for Terry to jump, what does Tom gain?

4. If Tom sets up the barrels for Terry to jump, how does this affect Terry?

5. If Tom does *not* set up the barrels for Terry to jump, how does this affect Terry?

6. Looking at what Tom gains by *not* setting up the barrels and how not setting up the barrels affects Terry, would it be wiser to set up the barrels or not?

How Do You Deal With Personal Threats?

Bob and Rosita were ninth graders. They had both been sick and had lost out on a lot of school. Now it was time to make up the science test they had missed. The teacher agreed to let them take the test while the other students were out of the room.

Bob was worried about taking the test because he hadn't studied for it. When Mrs. Allen handed out the exam, he was sure he couldn't pass it. Part way through the test, Mrs. Allen was called out of the room. When Bob was sure she was out of sight, he left his seat and went to the pencil sharpener. As he returned, Bob saw the answer sheet on Mrs. Allen's desk. Quickly he took the sheet and returned to his seat. In a few minutes he finished the test and returned it and the answer sheet to Mrs. Allen's desk.

Rosita saw what Bob had done and said, "I know you cheated and I'm going to tell Mrs. Allen." Bob's eyes narrowed. He scowled at Rosita and warned, "If you say a word about this, I'll get you after school." Rosita knew he meant it and wondered what she should do.

1. Based on the story, describe two ways Rosita could deal with the problem.

   a. ____

   ____

   b. ____

   ____

2. If Rosita does *not* tell Mrs. Allen about the cheating, what will Rosita gain?

   ____

   ____

   ____

   ____

   ____

(continued)

How Do You Deal With Personal Threats? *(continued)*

3. If Rosita does tell Mrs. Allen about the cheating, what will Rosita gain?

____

____

____

____

____

4. If Rosita does *not* tell Mrs. Allen about the cheating, how will this affect Bob?

____

____

____

____

____

5. If Rosita does tell Mrs. Allen about the cheating, how will this affect Bob?

____

____

____

____

____

6. Looking at what Rosita gains by *not* telling and how *not* telling will affect Bob, would it be better to tell or not?

____

____

____

____

____

Mom Defends Her Boy

Danny was just sick about the way things were going. His mom appeared at school and went on and on about Rick Jackson. It seemed as though she would never stop talking. "Somebody's got to stop that boy!" she was shouting. "Rick's pestering everybody in the neighborhood. And he loves to pick on little guys like Danny."

Mrs. Green, Danny's teacher, was obviously concerned. "I didn't realize that Danny was being picked on," she replied. "He's never complained to me!" Mrs. Green looked at Danny. "How long has this been going on?" she asked. Danny could only shake his head and look at the floor.

Danny hadn't said anything about the problem because he wanted to do things with the guys in the neighborhood. After all, most of them were nice to him. He hated to quit the gang just because of Rick. Maybe the time had come to find new friends. It was a hard decision.

1. Based on the story, describe two ways Danny could deal with the problem.

   a. ____

   ____

   ____

   b. ____

   ____

   ____

2. If Danny quits the gang because of Rick, what does Danny gain?

   ____

   ____

   ____

   ____

(continued)

Mom Defends Her Boy *(continued)*

3. If Danny does *not* quit the gang, what does Danny gain?

____

____

____

____

____

4. If Danny quits the gang because of Rick, how does this affect the rest of the gang?

____

____

____

____

____

5. If Danny does *not* quit the gang because of Rick, how does this affect the rest of the gang?

____

____

____

____

____

6. Looking at what Danny gains if he quits the gang and how his quitting will affect the rest of the gang, would it be best to quit the gang or not?

____

____

____

____

____

If Only I'd Known!

Adam was always putting things off until the last minute. He was late in finishing his science fair project, he was the last one to learn his lines for the play, and he was the next-to-last one in his social studies class to finish his map.

Adam knew he was usually late getting tasks done, but he liked to do lots of things.

In the spring Adam started a dog-grooming business. He had four regular customers. Adam usually groomed the dogs after school, unless he played ball; then he groomed them on Saturday.

During the past week there had been time to groom some of the dogs, but somehow Adam left all the jobs until Saturday. Just as he was getting the clippers out, Adam's dad came home with free tickets to a Pirates game. Adam had never seen the Pirates play. He wanted to go! He called three friends and asked them to groom the dogs, but they each had plans. Adam had promised all of his customers that their dogs would be groomed once a week.

Adam obviously has a problem. He can skip the game and disappoint himself or he can skip the grooming and disappoint his customers. He wants to avoid both, of course. He knows there will be other Pirates games, but he also knows that the dogs won't suffer if they aren't groomed.

1. Based on the story, describe two ways Adam could deal with the problem.

   a. ______________________________

   ____

   b. ______________________________

   ____

2. If Adam skips the game and grooms the dogs, what does he gain?

   ____

   ____

   ____

(continued)

If Only I'd Known! *(continued)*

3. If Adam goes to the game and does *not* groom the dogs, what does he gain?

4. If Adam skips the game and grooms the dogs, how does this affect his customers?

5. If Adam goes to the game and does *not* groom the dogs, how does this affect his customers?

6. Looking at what Adam gains by grooming the dogs and how grooming the dogs affects his customers, would it be wiser to groom the dogs or go to the game?

Getting to Know You

Tim had just moved to Greensburg. In fact, he had been attending Lincoln School just a few days. On the fourth day he was there, Bill Bobbitt and his friends asked Tim to eat lunch with them. That made Tim really happy. Bill was a big wheel at school!

It wasn't long, however, before Tim began to see that belonging to Bill's gang had some real drawbacks. Bill and his friends were always in trouble! They pestered people in the halls and on the school bus, and they were always acting up in class. Mrs. Jordon and the other teachers began to frown when they saw Tim in class. It seemed that they were expecting him to be a troublemaker too, simply because he hung around with Bill and his friends.

There were some other kids in the class whom Tim really wanted to get to know. Jack had some airplane models and Ted's hobby was the same as Tim's, science. On the other hand, it was a lot more exciting to be with Bill and his friends. Tim had a hard choice.

1. Based on the story, describe two ways that Tim could deal with the problem.

   a. ______________________________

   ____

   ____

   b. ______________________________

   ____

   ____

2. If Tim gets out of Bill's gang, what will Tim gain?

   ____

   ____

   ____

   ____

(continued)

Getting to Know You *(continued)*

3. If Tim stays in Bill's gang, what will Tim gain?

4. If Tim gets out of Bill's gang, how will this affect Bill and his friends?

5. If Tim stays in Bill's gang, how will this affect Bill and his friends?

6. Looking at what Tim gains from getting out of Bill's gang and how getting out of the gang affects Bill, what do you think is the best thing to do?

Albert Runs the Show

Albert had been a real problem for the Tigers all year. He loved to boss people around. He just had to have his way, not just part of the time, but all of the time! He wanted to pitch every game. He even served as umpire, calling players out or safe. He insisted on telling everybody where to play. As soon as he walked onto the field, there was trouble.

The Tigers had just nine players. They needed everybody available when they played. Albert knew this. Any time he didn't get his way, he'd threaten to quit. If he quit, everybody knew the Tigers would not have enough players to enter the city play-offs.

On Saturday, things went very much as usual. The team showed up for a game with the Albany Bears. Albert began bossing people around. He had not been playing first base, but on Saturday he decided he wanted to play that position. Tom, who usually played first base, got mad. Albert, true to form, threatened to quit if he couldn't play first base. Tom was faced with a real decision. Should he give in to Albert or insist on his own rights to play first base?

1. Based on the story, describe two ways that Tom could deal with the problem.

   a. ______________________________

   ____

   ____

   b. ______________________________

   ____

   ____

2. If Tom gives in to Albert, what will Tom gain?

   ____

   ____

   ____

   ____

(continued)

Albert Runs the Show *(continued)*

3. If Tom does *not* give in to Albert, what will Tom gain?

4. If Tom gives in to Albert, how will this affect the team?

5. If Tom does *not* give in to Albert, how will this affect the team?

6. Looking at what Tom gains by *not* giving in to Albert and how *not* giving in affects the rest of the team, would it be best to give in or *not* give in?

Too Good to Be True

Robert had the best entry in the school hobby show, and he had a beautiful blue ribbon to show for it. His entry was an eye-catching model of an ornate Spanish galleon. His classmates were really impressed! There was a lot of intricate detail—tiny windows with shutters that opened, miniature brass cannons, and very realistic rigging. His friends all thought Robert had done a great job. Robert decided to let them believe that, but it wasn't really true. Robert's dad had constructed the model while he was recovering from surgery.

Things had not gone well for Robert during the year. His grades were down, and he seldom got any recognition. It really felt good now to have his classmates congratulating him.

Just before school was to be dismissed, Mrs. Allen told the students with hobby show projects that they would have an opportunity to explain how they had planned and created their entries. Robert had a deep sinking feeling inside. How he wished he had acknowledged from the very beginning that he had not constructed the galleon himself!

1. Based on the story, describe two ways Robert could deal with the problem.

   a. ____

   ____

   b. ____

   ____

2. If Robert tells the class that his dad made the model, what will Robert gain?

   ____

   ____

   ____

   ____

(continued)

Too Good to Be True *(continued)*

3. If Robert does *not* tell the class that his dad made the ship, what will Robert gain?

____

____

____

____

4. If Robert tells the class the truth, how will this affect his friends?

____

____

____

____

5. If Robert does *not* tell the class the truth, how will this affect his friends?

____

____

____

____

6. Looking at what Robert gains from *not* telling that his dad made the model and how his friends are affected by not knowing the truth, would it be fairer to admit he didn't make it or fairer to let them think he did make it?

____

____

____

____

____

____

When There's No Easy Answer

The thermometer outside the kitchen window registered three above zero. That's cold, thought Jan as she got ready to deliver her morning papers. Jan had 50 customers, and on cold mornings when she couldn't ride her bicycle, it took her more than an hour to make her rounds.

As she wrapped her papers and stuffed them into her big canvas bag, Jan regretted that she hadn't finished her math homework the night before. There was still time. She'd hurry with the papers and finish the math before breakfast.

Less than an hour later Jan was nearly finished. She had only five customers to go. She could then head for home and complete her math while her mom fixed breakfast. As she rounded the corner, she saw a car stalled in the middle of the street. It was Mr. Zimmerman, the elderly man who walked with a cane. His car was out of gas.

I'd like to help Mr. Zimmerman, thought Jan, but if I do, I won't have time to do my homework assignment. She hated to think what Mrs. Roberts would say if she hadn't completed her assignment.

"It's his own fault for running out of gas," Jan muttered to herself. "The station is only a half mile down the street. Surely Mr. Zimmerman can walk that far, even on a cold morning like this . . . can't he?" As she walked down the street, Jan wondered what to do.

1. Based on the story, describe two ways that Jan could deal with the problem.

   a. ____

   ____

   b. ____

   ____

2. If Jan does *not* help Mr. Zimmerman, what will she gain?

   ____

   ____

   ____

(continued)

When There's No Easy Answer *(continued)*

3. If Jan helps Mr. Zimmerman, what will she gain?

____

____

____

____

4. If Jan helps Mr. Zimmerman, how will this affect Mr. Zimmerman?

____

____

____

____

5. If Jan does *not* help Mr. Zimmerman, how will this affect him?

____

____

____

____

6. Looking at what Jan gains by *not* helping Mr. Zimmerman and how her help would affect Mr. Zimmerman, would it be fairer to help him or not?

____

____

____

____

____

Just for Jess

Jess was happy as a lark. When he arrived at his seat in the classroom that morning, he found an invitation on his desk. The note was from several of his classmates asking him to join them on a camping trip. This was the first time he'd been included in any out-of-school activity. Why were they asking him now? Nobody seemed to like him. In fact, he had been so lonely that he drowned his feelings with food. As a result, he had gained a good deal of weight, and this gave the kids something else to tease him about.

Cindy, who had been standing near Jess when he read the note, rushed off to tell the others that the trick had worked. Everyone was amazed that Jess actually believed that he had been invited. Actually, there was no camping trip. The whole thing had been made up.

At first, Cindy thought it was hilarious. But later, when Jess told her that he was planning to buy a sleeping bag with his savings, Cindy had second thoughts. She knew that Jess's family had little money, and she hated to see him spend his limited savings on something he would never use. Cindy also hated to tell Jess the truth. The other kids in the gang would be furious with her.

1. Based on the story, describe two ways that Cindy could deal with the problem.

   a. ____

   ____

   b. ____

   ____

2. If Cindy tells Jess that it is a trick, what will Cindy gain?

   ____

   ____

   ____

   ____

(continued)

Just for Jess *(continued)*

3. If Cindy does *not* tell Jess that it is a trick, what will Cindy gain?

4. If Cindy does tell Jess that it is a trick, how will it affect Jess?

5. If Cindy does *not* tell Jess that it is a trick, how will it affect Jess?

6. Looking at what Cindy will gain by *not* telling Jess and how *not* telling will affect Jess, would it be fairer to tell Jess or not to tell Jess?

It's Terrible to Be Left Out

Jed couldn't keep the tears from welling up in his eyes. His friend, Rob, wanted to help, but the more he talked about it, the worse Jed felt.

"I know how terrible you must feel," Rob whispered. "Everyone on the team thought the coach would choose you. He must be crazy to let Tom swim the breaststroke!"

When the coach had announced the date and place for the state swim meet for boys 13 and under, Jed assumed that he would be swimming the breaststroke. He even told his family that he would be swimming the individual event.

When the coach chose Tom Timmons, the new boy from Springfield, to swim the breaststroke, Jed could hardly believe it. Coach Robertson told Jed he could swim on the relay team, but that offered little consolation.

"I may quit the team," he told Rob. "I'd rather not swim at all than be on the relay team."

"I don't know whether you should do that or not," Rob commented. "We need you on the relay team. Of course, if you say you won't swim at all, the coach may have to change his mind and let you swim the breaststroke."

Jed left Rob and headed towards home. He knew it would be embarrassing to have to tell his family and friends that he had been replaced by another boy. He wondered if he should make up a story and tell his mom and dad that he urged the coach to put the new boy in. Jed didn't know what to do.

1. Based on the story, describe two ways Jed can deal with the problem of talking to his parents.

   a. ____

   ____

   ____

   b. ____

   ____

   ____

(continued)

It's Terrible to Be Left Out *(continued)*

2. If Jed tells his parents the truth about what happened, what does Jed gain?

____

____

____

3. If Jed tells his parents that he urged the coach to put in the new boy, what does Jed gain?

____

____

____

4. If Jed tells his parents the truth about what happened, how will this affect his parents?

____

____

____

5. If Jed tells his parents that he urged the coach to put in the new boy, how will this affect his parents?

____

____

____

6. Looking at what Jed gains by telling the truth and how telling the truth affects his parents, would it be fairer to tell the truth or not?

____

____

____

7. In everyday life, people often don't do what is fair. Why is this true?

____

____

____

A Chance for Recognition

Ralph didn't do very well in school. He never answered in class or offered suggestions. In fact, no one paid very much attention to him. He was naturally quiet and seemed to avoid opportunities to socialize. Even teachers had a tendency to overlook him.

Then, Ralph seemed to change into a new person. No one knew quite what happened. Ralph had gotten a new watch, and he insisted on showing it to everyone in sight. There was no way to get Ralph to stop talking about his new acquisition. Even though most of the students realized that Ralph didn't have other special things to be proud of, it didn't keep them from feeling that Ralph was gradually driving them up the wall.

On Friday Ralph announced that he was planning to bring in another prized possession—a large model car his older brother had made while he was in the service. The car was an exact replica of the old Bearcat that some of the students had seen in a classic car magazine. The students wanted to see the model, but they wondered if they would ever survive all the bragging that would go with it. One student suggested that Jimmy Lee talk to Ralph and tell him that people were getting tired of his constant bragging.

1. Based on the story, describe two ways that Jimmy Lee could deal with the problem.

   a. ______________________________

   ____

   b. ______________________________

   ____

2. If Jimmy Lee tells Ralph how the students feel, what does Jimmy Lee gain?

   ____

   ____

   ____

   ____

(continued)

A Chance for Recognition *(continued)*

3. If Jimmy Lee does *not* tell Ralph how the students feel, what does Jimmy Lee gain?

____

____

____

____

4. If Jimmy Lee tells Ralph how the students feel, how will it affect Ralph?

____

____

____

____

5. If Jimmy Lee does *not* tell Ralph how the students feel, how will it affect Ralph?

____

____

____

____

6. Looking at what Jimmy Lee gains by telling Ralph how the students feel, and how being told affects Ralph, would it be fairer to tell him or not?

____

____

____

____

Changing Schools Is a Moving Experience

Jack lived in a small town near the ocean. He loved the beaches and the tourists who came in the summer. His family had moved there when he was two years old. Now, eleven years later, he was about to enter the eighth grade. Jack had lots of friends, really good friends, and the school he attended was almost new. He loved basketball. He played as a seventh grader, and he was looking forward to being in the starting five during the coming season.

One morning at the breakfast table, Jack's dad told everybody that he was being transferred, and the family would be moving to a large city in another state. Jack was angry and terribly disappointed. He didn't like big cities, and he knew that leaving his friends would be very hard.

His first week at his new school confirmed his worst expectations. The school was much older and dingier than the school he had attended, and the students didn't seem as friendly.

"I really hate this school," Jack said at the dinner table that night. "Why can't we move back where all my friends are?"

Jack's mother asked him if he was really trying to make new friends. Jack didn't answer. He was too busy thinking back over the great times he used to have with his old friends at the beach and during practices in the gym.

Jack's disappointment deepened the next day when he learned that his new school didn't even have organized sports. There was no basketball team! He felt like telling the kids in the new school exactly what he thought about the place, but something inside of him told him that he ought to keep his thoughts to himself.

1. Based on the information in the story, describe two ways that Jack could deal with this problem.

   a. ____

   ____

   b. ____

   ____

(continued)

Changing Schools Is a Moving Experience *(continued)*

2. If Jack tells his friends at the new school he hates the school, what will he gain?

____

____

____

3. If Jack does *not* tell his friends that he hates the new school, what will he gain?

____

____

____

4. If Jack tells his friends at the new school that he hates the school, how will this affect them?

____

____

____

5. If Jack does *not* tell his friends at the new school that he hates the school, how will this affect them?

____

____

____

6. Looking at what Jack has to gain by telling his new friends he hates the school and what happens to them if he tells them he hates the school, would it be fairer to complain or not?

____

____

____

Secrets Are Hard to Keep

"We're going to move," sobbed Jinny to Mr. James, her teacher. "Dad lost his job and now we can't afford to live in our house."

Pam wasn't a nosy person, but she couldn't help but overhear Jinny's conversation with Mr. James.

In the lunchroom Pam spotted Carol and blurted, "I've got something to tell you about Jinny." As she began to tell Carol about Jinny's dad, several other kids stopped to listen. Pam felt uncomfortable telling what she had overheard but she continued anyway.

After school, Pam saw several of her classmates talking to Jinny. "Where does your dad work?" one of the boys asked. Jinny's face turned red. She left without answering.

Pam felt bad, because she didn't mean to hurt Jinny. It hadn't occurred to her that some of the kids would tease Jinny about her father's unemployment. Pam wondered what she could do to make amends.

1. Based on the story, describe two ways Pam could deal with the problem.

   a. ____

   ____

   ____

   b. ____

   ____

   ____

2. If Pam admits to Jinny that she told others, what will Pam gain?

   ____

   ____

   ____

   ____

(continued)

Secrets Are Hard to Keep *(continued)*

3. If Pam doesn't admit that she told others, what will Pam gain?

____

____

____

____

4. If Pam admits to Jinny that she told, how will it affect Jinny?

____

____

____

____

5. If Pam doesn't admit that she told others, how will it affect Jinny?

____

____

____

____

6. Looking at what Pam gains by admitting she told and what Jinny gains by learning that Pam told, would it be wiser to tell or not?

____

____

____

____

Best Friends

Sally had been selected by the physical education teacher to manage the equipment room. Her responsibility involved keeping the area neat and checking out equipment. Sally was given the key to the room and warned to keep the area locked when she was out of the room for any length of time. She was also told not to loan the key to anyone for any reason. Sally felt really good about her responsibility.

Ann is Sally's best friend. After class one day, Ann asked Sally to get the volleyballs out for her, but Sally didn't have time between classes to get the balls. When Ann heard this, she asked Sally for the key to the room. She promised to get it back to her right away. Ann explained that the teacher would never know the difference. Sally couldn't decide what to do.

1. Based on the story, describe two ways Sally could deal with this problem.

   a. ______________________________

   ____

   ____

   b. ______________________________

   ____

   ____

2. If Sally gives Ann the key, what will she gain?

   ____

   ____

   ____

   ____

   ____

(continued)

Best Friends *(continued)*

3. If Sally doesn't give Ann the key, what will she gain?

4. If Sally gives Ann the key, how will it affect Ann?

5. If Sally doesn't give Ann the key, how will it affect Ann?

6. Looking at what Sally gains by giving the key and at what happens to Ann, would it be fairer to give Ann the key or not give Ann the key?

Rosa Has a Great Imagination!

Rosa had a habit of making things up. She was so convincing that her classmates usually believed her. In fact, the whole class believed her! At first she thought it was fun. Now, as she got up to talk before the class, she knew that make-believe stories have an odd way of coming back to haunt you.

Rosa's parents were separated. Nine months out of the year, Rosa lived with her mother in an apartment on Anderson Street. But when summer arrived, she went to her father's ranch in Arizona.

The ranch was great! Rosa rode horses and helped with the cattle. Her father, however, was so busy that he seldom had time to go places with her. When she arrived each summer, her father would meet her at the airport and take her out to eat. And the day she went back to the city, he would always buy her a present. At other times, he didn't pay much attention to her.

When summer came to a close, Rosa returned to Anderson Street. At school she heard lots of stories her friends told about their family trips. Rosa wished she had a family to tell about.

Not long after returning to school, Rosa was looking through travel magazines in the school library. They described fascinating places, like England and Germany. When Rosa's friends asked what she had done that summer, she made up something terrific. Remembering the exciting travel magazines she had looked at, she told her classmates that she and her father had gone to England!

When the class began studying England, Mr. Thomas asked Rosa to tell all the things she could remember about her trip to England.

Rosa was now in front of the class, shaking from head to toe. What should she do?

1. Based on the story, describe two ways that Rosa could deal with this problem.

   a. ____

   ____

   b. ____

   ____

(continued)

Rosa Has a Great Imagination! *(continued)*

2. If Rosa tells the truth, what will she gain?

____

____

____

3. If Rosa does *not* tell the truth, what will she gain?

____

____

____

4. If Rosa tells the truth, how will this affect her friendships?

____

____

____

5. If Rosa does *not* tell the truth, how will this affect her friendships?

____

____

____

6. Looking at what Rosa gains by telling the truth and what happens to her friendships if she tells the truth, would it be wiser to tell the truth or not tell the truth?

____

____

____

7. In everyday life people sometimes don't tell the truth. Why is this?

____

____

____

Choosing a Class President

Jerry and Carla were asked to nominate people for class president. As they glanced through the list of kids in the room, they stopped at Tina's name. Tina had lots of ideas, and she never said mean things about other people.

"I really like Tina," said Carla, "but she looks terrible! She puts on too much makeup, and she wears odd clothes. Sometimes she wears things that don't even fit her."

"You're right," agreed Jerry, "but she is one of the most thoughtful people we have in class. She would always treat people fairly."

"Do you think we could get her to use less makeup and wear some decent clothes?" Carla asked.

"We couldn't. It would be embarrassing for us and her," replied Jerry. "She goes around with high school girls, and she must know by now how she looks. My mother says it is wrong for eighth graders to try to look like movie actresses!"

"Yes," Carla agreed, "and what would the teachers think if we nominated Tina?"

1. Based on the story, describe two ways that Jerry and Carla could deal with this problem.

   a. ____

   ____

   b. ____

   ____

2. If they do *not* nominate Tina, what will they gain?

   ____

   ____

   ____

   ____

(continued)

Choosing a Class President *(continued)*

3. If they do nominate Tina, what will they gain?

4. If they do *not* nominate Tina, how will this affect Tina?

5. If they do nominate Tina, how will this affect Tina?

6. Looking at what Jerry and Carla gain by not nominating Tina and what happens to Tina if she is not nominated, would it be fairer to nominate her or not to nominate her?

7. In everyday life people often do not do what is fair. Why is this true?

Lonely People Sometimes Need You

Rudy always took the newspaper to Grandpa Thompson's home last before heading for home. Grandpa Thompson's was at the end of his route. Rudy liked Grandpa Thompson. He was often waiting for him near the front gate with a candy bar. In addition, he usually asked Rudy about the things he was doing—about his plans for the summer and his hobbies.

The thing that Rudy didn't like about Grandpa was his never-ending stories about his boyhood in California. Rudy never asked to hear about Grandpa's boyhood, but he couldn't get away.

After Grandpa's wife died in October, Rudy noticed that Grandpa was lonelier than ever. He would often join Rudy halfway along his route and walk along with him as he delivered the papers. Grandpa seemed to have all day, and Rudy often was late getting his papers to his customers. Rudy didn't want to complain, but customers were unhappy.

1. Based on the story, describe two ways Rudy could deal with the problem.

   a. ____

   ____

   ____

   b. ____

   ____

   ____

2. If Rudy doesn't stop to visit with Grandpa, what will Rudy gain?

   ____

   ____

   ____

   ____

   ____

(continued)

Lonely People Sometimes Need You *(continued)*

3. If Rudy does stop to visit Grandpa, what will Rudy gain?

4. If Rudy doesn't stop to visit with Grandpa, how will it affect Grandpa?

5. If Rudy does stop to visit with Grandpa, how will it affect Grandpa?

6. Look at what Rudy gains and what happens to Grandpa, would it be fairer to stop to talk with Grandpa or not stop to visit with Grandpa?

Alice's Friend

Alice wanted to be nice to Susan, but she often wished that she had never made friends with her.

In spite of the fact that Susan had a slight physical disability, she was mainstreamed into the P.E. class. When she first started coming to class, she seemed lonely and upset. She really needed a friend, and Alice wanted to help. Alice stood next to Susan and talked to her. She even chose Susan for her team.

Alice didn't mind helping Susan, but before long Susan was looking for her everywhere she went. She waited for Alice outside the school cafeteria. She waited for her before school. She even came to Alice's house after school was out.

Alice's other friends didn't care for Susan. In addition to being physically awkward, Susan didn't speak clearly. After a while, Alice's friends stopped seeking Alice out. They didn't call her or include her in their activities. Alice didn't know what to do. She really liked Susan, but she certainly didn't want to lose her other friends.

1. Based on the story, describe two ways Alice could deal with the problem.

   a. ______________________________

   ____

   b. ______________________________

   ____

2. If Alice doesn't keep Susan for a friend, what will Alice gain?

   ____

   ____

   ____

   ____

(continued)

Alice's Friend *(continued)*

3. If Alice keeps Susan for a friend, what will Alice gain?

____

____

____

____

4. If Alice doesn't keep Susan for a friend, how will it affect Susan?

____

____

____

____

5. If Alice keeps Susan for a friend, how will it affect Susan?

____

____

____

____

6. Looking at what Alice gains by not keeping Susan as a friend and what happens to Susan if she does keep her as a friend, would it be fairer to keep Susan as a friend or not keep her as a friend?

____

____

____

____

7. In everyday life, people often don't do what is fair. Why is this true?

____

____

____

____

Last Chance Charlie

The score was tied, and there were just three minutes remaining in the final game of the community basketball play-offs. Charlie Johnson had practiced hard all season, but he was still the seventh man on the team. Coach Stafford had not played him at all. The games during the season were too close to risk using an unseasoned player. This championship meant a lot to the team, but to Charlie it meant a great deal more. It was his only hope! This was the last game and his last chance to participate.

As the last quarter rolled on, Charlie's hopes were fading fast. Then it happened! Romano Tibbs, the star forward, fouled out. Coach Stafford had to go to his bench. He had two subs, Charlie and Tim Linson. Tim was a first year man with some game experience. Charlie was in his last game, had no playing experience, and had no chances to play in the future.

1. Based on the story, describe two ways Coach Stafford could deal with the problem.

   a. ____

   ____

   ____

   b. ____

   ____

   ____

2. If Coach Stafford doesn't put Charlie Johnson in, what will the coach gain?

   ____

   ____

   ____

   ____

   ____

(continued)

Last Chance Charlie *(continued)*

3. If Coach Stafford does put Charlie Johnson in, what will the coach gain?

4. If Coach Stafford puts Charlie in, how will it affect Tim Linson?

5. If Coach Stafford doesn't put Charlie in, how will it affect Tim Linson?

6. Looking at what Charlie gains and what happens to Tim Linson, would it be fairer to put Charlie in or not put him in?

When Friends Don't Care

"Terri, please let me borrow a quarter," Candy pleaded as they stood in the school lunch line. "I have one in my jacket, but I don't want to leave and lose my place."

"Okay," agreed Terri.

Terri waited all day for Candy to pay back the quarter she borrowed, but Candy always seemed to be busy. "She's just forgotten," thought Terri. "I don't want to bug her." Still, her tiny allowance didn't go far. Some kids, like Candy, were getting five dollars a week.

Weeks went by. Finally, Terri got up enough courage to mention the loan.

"Oh Terri, I forgot!" Candy explained. "I'll bring the quarter tomorrow."

The next day Candy seemed to have forgotten again. During the noon hour Terri saw her buying gum for Jane and Erin. Candy saw Terri looking at her. Then she whispered something to the other two girls. Cheeks burning, Terri asked her teacher if she could go back to her homeroom.

In the homeroom, Terri noticed two new pencils on Candy's desk. An idea occurred to her.

"Candy's been so mean lately, and anyway, she really owes me. Besides, she has enough money to buy more. A quarter doesn't mean anything to her, but it means a lot to me."

1. Based on the story, describe two ways Terri could deal with the problem.

   a. ____

   ____

   b. ____

   ____

(continued)

When Friends Don't Care *(continued)*

2. If Terri takes Candy's new pencils, what will Terri gain?

3. If Terri does *not* take Candy's new pencils, what will Terri gain?

4. If Terri takes Candy's new pencils, how will this affect Candy?

5. If Terri does *not* take Candy's new pencils, how will this affect Candy?

6. Looking at what Terri gains by taking Candy's new pencils and how taking the pencils affects Candy, would it be wiser to take them or not?

Michael Faces a Challenge

Miss Johnson, the science teacher, asked Michael if he would be willing to serve as the general chairman of the science fair. It was a real honor, but Michael knew that it was a huge job. He would have to get dependable helpers and see that everything went smoothly. He would have to see that there were enough exhibits to make the fair worth coming to. He'd have to convince his classmates to enter. He would have to see that there were enough electrical outlets and tables, entry forms, and judges. Above all, he would have to make sure that the students who entered projects understood and followed the rules. In previous years there were misunderstandings and hurt feelings.

Michael had lots of interests. He liked to play basketball after school. He enjoyed going to movies with his friends, and he really liked the new chess club that Mr. Anderson had organized. Michael knew that he would have to give these up if he accepted the general chairmanship of the science fair. There were very few, if any, students in Michael's class who could or would organize the fair. In fact, there might not be a fair if Michael did not agree to take charge. It wasn't an easy thing to decide.

1. Based on the story, describe two ways that Michael can deal with this problem.

   a. ____

   ____

   b. ____

   ____

2. If Michael accepts the science fair job, what will he gain?

   ____

   ____

   ____

   ____

(continued)

Michael Faces a Challenge *(continued)*

3. **If Michael does *not* accept the science fair job, what will he gain?**

4. **If Michael accepts the science fair job, how will this affect Miss Johnson?**

5. **If Michael does *not* accept the science fair job, how will this affect Miss Johnson?**

6. **Looking at what Michael gains by accepting the science fair job and how it affects Miss Johnson if he does *not* accept the job , would it be best to take the job or not?**

Protecting a Friend

José had just seen his golden retriever, Mike, hit by a speeding truck. He wept silently as he thought about his injured friend. Nothing else seemed to matter now. He couldn't do his school assignments. At home, he stared blankly at the TV screen. José knew that Mike would get better, but he worried about the future. Would it happen again?

Mike was a big dog, and José knew that he probably belonged in the country where there were fields and woods. There he could run and play safely away from the city traffic. José also knew that if he gave Mike to a farmer that he would seldom, if ever, get to see him again. It was a tough decision. José had raised Mike from the time he was a puppy. He knew what Mike liked, and he took good care of him. He wasn't at all sure that a new owner would take care of Mike in the same way.

José didn't know if he could protect Mike from the heavy traffic if he stayed in town. Dogs like Mike who want to run often have a way of getting away when you least expect it.

1. Based on the story, describe two ways that José can deal with this problem.

   a. ____

   ____

   ____

   b. ____

   ____

   ____

2. If José gives Mike to a farmer, what will José gain?

   ____

   ____

   ____

   ____

   ____

(continued)

Protecting a Friend *(continued)*

3. If José keeps Mike in town, what will José gain?

4. If José gives Mike to a farmer, how will this affect Mike?

5. If José keeps Mike in town, how will this affect Mike?

6. Looking at what José gains by giving Mike to the farmer and how giving Mike away will affect Mike, would it be best to send Mike away or not?

What Are Friends For?

Nancy was finishing up her take-home quiz when her best friend, Majorie, called. Marjorie wanted Nancy to read her the answer over the phone. Nancy was hesitant. A part of her wanted to help Marjorie; another part of her really rebelled at the thought. Do you help a friend in need? Do you stick with the rules against cheating? Nancy was confused. She made up a quick excuse and promised Marjorie that she would call her back in an hour. In the meantime, Nancy thought about her problem. She even listed reasons for and against helping. Check the reasons you think are best.

1. Nancy should help because . . .

   ______ a. if she doesn't, Marjorie will think she is a pretty unreliable friend.

   ______ b. Marjorie will do something for her sometime in return.

   ______ c. Majorie has had a difficult year. She has been absent all week and must pass the test for the year.

   ______ d. her friends won't think she's cool if she doesn't help.

   ______ e. following the rules of her gang is very important, and giving help to anyone in trouble at school is one of the rules.

2. Nancy should not help because . . .

   ______ a. the rules of the school prohibit cheating.

   ______ b. everyone agrees that cheating is not fair.

   ______ c. if she is caught her teachers and her parents will think she is bad.

   ______ d. Nancy has a younger sister. This will set a bad example for her.

   ______ e. Nancy could help Marjorie study instead of giving the answers.

3. Can you think of a better way of dealing with this situation?

   ____

   ____

   ____

   ____

Notes

Notes

Notes

Notes

Notes

The American Economy in the Twentieth Century

Gene Smiley
Marquette University

COLLEGE DIVISION South-Western Publishing Co.
Cincinnati Ohio

Sponsoring Editor: Jack Calhoun
Production Editor: Shelley Brewer
Production House: Impressions, A Division of Edwards Brothers, Inc.
Cover Design: Joe Devine
Cover Photos: FPG International
Photo Editor: Jennifer Mayhall
Photo Researcher: Alexandra Truitt
Sponsoring Representative: Don Waller

1 2 3 4 5 6 7 8 9 D 0 2 1 9 8 7 6 5 4 3

Printed in the United States of America

Library of Congress Cataloging-in-Publication Data

Smiley, Gene,
The American economy in the twentieth century / Gene Smiley.
p. cm.
Includes bibliographical references and index.
ISBN 0-538-83238-X
1. United States—Economic conditions—1918–1945 2. United States—Economic conditions—1945– I. Title.
HC106.S673 1993
330.973'09—dc20 93-26323
CIP

I(T)P

International Thomson Publishing

South-Western Publishing Co. is an ITP Company. The ITP trademark is used under license.

This book is printed on acid-free paper that meets Environmental Protection Agency standards for recycled paper.

Chapter opening photo credits
1: Archive photos 2: Library of Congress 3: Library of Congress 4: Texaco Archives 5: Library of Congress 6: Library of Congress 7: Library of Congress 8: Library of Congress 9: UPI/Bettman Newsphotos 10: © Fernando Bueno/The Image Bank 11: Photographic Archives, University of Louisville 12: UPI/Bettman Newsphotos 13: UPI Bettman Newsphotos 14: The Bettman Archive 15: D&D Still Media Records Center 16: Reuters/Bettman

Preface

I have long been bothered by the relative paucity of material on the twentieth century United States in most American economic history textbooks, especially on the causes of the Great Depression and performance of sectors of the economy in the postwar period. For various reasons for the better part of a decade my courses have concentrated on the twentieth century American economy. To augment the text material, in 1983 I began including a handout on the causes of the Great Depression. By 1990 this had been revised several times and expanded until I was distributing handouts on most of the period from 1914 through the Second World War. And I intended to develop similar handouts on the postwar American economy. In 1990, with the support of South-Western Publishing, I began the process of developing the rest of what became this textbook.

The textbook is not intended to teach basic principles of economics, rather I have assumed that students using this book already understand these concepts. However, to make it as accessible as possible I have chosen not to include analytical models (graphical or algebraic) and statistical estimating equations. The most difficult chapter is clearly chapter 7 on the causes of the Great Depression where I have assumed that the instructor can supply the necessary models on which the analyses are based. Where possible I have tried to incorporate recent work to keep the presentation up-to-date. I have also incorporated what is sometimes called "old-fashioned" economic history of a descriptive nature to provide the student with the institutional setting within which events and economic activity occurred. Chapter 6, on monetary and fiscal policies and the New Deal, and chapter 7, on the causes of the Great Depression, both include summaries of recent research. Chapter 8, on the 1940s, includes recent research questioning the magnitude of the recovery during World War II as well as the source of this recovery, and quite recent research on the postwar boom and its causes. Chapter 9 considers, among other topics, the postwar rise of public sector unionism. Chapter 10 discusses the meat crisis of the 1970s and the farm debt crisis of the 1980s. Chapter 12 includes discussions of the price controls and the gasoline crises of the 1970s. I have included coverage of interwar and postwar communications markets, an area which I think is too often not discussed. These discussions include consideration of the rise of radio and television broadcasting and networks, and the development of the telecommunications network and the fall of AT&T in the 1970s and 1980s. Another area which I think is given inadequate coverage is retail trade developments and I have briefly discussed this in both the interwar and postwar periods. Finally, in chapter 16 I have spent more space than is normal in discussing the distribution of income—an important topic in my opinion.

Any author incurs an immense debt. My initial interest in economics was spurred by Anthony Costantino at the University of Iowa. Samuel Williamson and Joseph A. Swanson, who were at the University of Iowa at the time, guided my interest in economic history. Murray Rothbard, Gerald P. O'Driscoll, Roger Garrison, and Israel Kirsner later introduced me to Austrian economics. James Keefe at South-Western Publishing Company supported the development of this book while Shelley Brewer and Sandy Ridenhour shepherded the book through its production schedule. Gregory Everitt of Impressions had the unenviable task of copyediting my writing. There were a number of economic historians who read and commented on parts or all of this text at various stages. They were: Hugh Aitken (Amherst College), Martin Bronfenbrenner (Duke University), Louis Cain (Loyola University-Chicago), Leonard Carlson (Emory University), Lowell Gallaway (Ohio University), John Hanson (Texas A&M University), William K. Hutchison (Miami University-Ohio), Richard H. Keehn (University of Wisconsin-Parkside), David Klingaman (Ohio University), James J. McClain (University of New Orleans), Clark Nardinelli (Clemson University), Paul O'Connor (Onondaga Community College), Thomas Ulen (University of Illinois), and Richard K. Vedder (Ohio University). The text is far better for their comments. In fact, I expect that many will have difficulty recognizing the finished product after the crude drafts they viewed. I was not able to incorporate all of their suggestions, and I am the only person who can be held responsible for the shortcomings of this textbook. I must also thank all of the students in my economic history classes who were subjected to various early versions of this. Finally, I thank my wife and daughters to whom I devoted too little attention while writing this textbook.

Gene Smiley
Milwaukee, Wisconsin
July, 1993

Contents

1 The American Economy Prior to 1920 **1**
The American Economy at the Turn of the Century 2
The American Economy During the First World War 4
American War Preparations 5
Economic Mobilization: The Command Economy 5
Agriculture and Industry during the War 7
Labor during the War 8
Financing the War 9
The United States at the End of the First World War 10

2 American Economic Growth, Population Changes, and Labor Force Developments, 1920–1940 **14**
An Overview of American Economic Growth, 1920–1940 15
The Twenties 17
The Great Depression, 1929–1933 19
The Recovery of 1933–1937 21
The 1937–1938 Depression 22
The Interwar American Economy 23
Population Growth 23
Labor Force Growth 26
Labor Unions in the Interwar Period 28

3 Developments in Agriculture and Manufacturing, 1920–1940 **35**
Agriculture 36
A Declining Sector 38
Technological Improvements in Agricultural Production 40
Federal Agricultural Programs in the Interwar Period 43
Manufacturing 46
Manufacturing's Importance 46
Productivity Developments 48
Competition, Monopoly, and the Government 50
Interwar Manufacturing 54

4 Developments in Energy, Transportation and Communications: 1920–1940 **62**
The Energy Industries 63
Coal 63
Petroleum 67

Electricity 69
Energy in the Interwar American Economy 71
Transportation 72
Railroads 72
Trucks and Buses 73
Airlines 75
Transportation in the Interwar American Economy 76
Communications 77
Telegraph and Telephones 77
Newspapers 80
Radio 81
Communications in the Interwar American Economy 83

5 Developments in Finance and Domestic and International Trade: 1920–1940 89
Domestic Trade 90
Department Stores 90
Mail Order Firms 90
Chain Stores 91
Self-Service Policies 91
Shopping Centers and Supermarkets 92
Retailing in the Interwar Period 93
International Trade 93
War Debts and War Reparations 94
Tariffs and Trade Barriers in the Interwar Period 94
Commodity and Service Trade in the Interwar Period 95
War Debts and Reparations in the Depression 95
The End of the Gold Exchange Standard 96
International Trade and the Interwar American Economy 98
Banking and Finance 99
Banking 99
Securities Markets 101
Other Financial Institutions 102
The Great Bull Market 102
Financial Markets in the Interwar American Economy 106

6 The Role of Government, 1920–1940: Monetary and Fiscal Policies and the New Deal 113
The Evolution of Monetary Policy 114
Problems in Policy Formulation and Control 115
Federal Reserve Policies from 1920 to 1940 115
The 1920–1921 Depression 117
The Great Depression 118
The 1937-1938 Depression 121

Monetary Policy in the Interwar Period 122
Fiscal Policy in the 1920s and 1930s 122
The 1920s 123
The 1930s 123
The New Deal 125
The Creation of the New Deal 126
Financial Reform and Recovery 127
Relief for the Unemployed 128
Farm Relief 129
Industrial Reform 130
Politics and the Allocation of Federal Funds 133
The New Deal: An Assessment 134

7 What Caused the Great Depression? 145
The Austrian Explanation of the Great Depression 148
Criticisms of the Austrian Explanation 150
The Keynesian Explanation 151
Excess Capacity and Saturation in the Automobile Market 152
Housing Overinvestment in the Twenties 154
An "Unexplained" Decline in Consumption Spending 155
The Magnitude of the Initial Decline 156
The Absence of Equilibrating Adjustments 158
The Monetarist Explanation 158
The Onset of the Depression in 1929 159
The Effects of Panics and Bank Failures 159
Could the FED Have "Put Out the Fire" in Late 1930? 161
Criticisms of the Monetarists' Explanation 163
Disruptions in the International Sector 165
The Great Depression: An Assessment 170

8 The American Economy During the 1940s 183
The Second World War 184
Administrative Changes During the War 184
Mobilizing the Population 187
Expanding Production 188
Financing the War 191
Wage and Price Controls 194
World War II and the Recovery from the Thirties 197
The Postwar Boom 199
Some Other Postwar Changes 200
Demobilization and Reconversion 201
Postwar International Developments 203
Was it a Postwar Boom or "The Great Depression of 1946?" 204
The United States at the End of the 1940s 206

9 American Economic Growth, Population Changes, and Labor Force Developments, 1950 to the Present 212

Postwar Economic Growth 213
An Overview of the American Economic Growth, 1950–1990 214
The 1960s 216
The 1970s 217
The 1980s 218
The Postwar American Population 220
Mortality 220
Fertility 221
Causes of the Baby Boom and Bust 222
Immigration 222
The Postwar American Labor Force 223
Occupations 223
Unemployment 224
Productivity and Wages 225
Postwar American Labor Unions 230
Union Developments Since World War II 230
Public Sector Unionism 231
Causes of Declining Union Membership 232

10 Developments in Agriculture, 1950 to the Present 235

An Overview of Post-World War II Agriculture 236
Technological Change in Agriculture 238
Machinery 240
Fertilizers, Herbicides, and Insecticides 241
Genetics and Modern Breeding 242
The Meat Crisis of 1973 242
The Farm Debt Crisis of the 1980s 245
Federal Farm Programs 250

11 Developments in Manufacturing, 1950 to the Present 258

Manufacturing's Importance: Size, Growth and Location 259
Productivity Developments 263
Research and Development 264
Patents 266
The Materials Revolution 267
Managerial Developments 267
Manufacturing Productivity Changes in the Postwar Period 268
Competition, Monopoly and Government 269
Mergers 269
Postwar Antitrust Policy 272
Industrial Concentration and Economic Performance 274

12 Developments in Energy and Transportation, 1950 to the Present 281
Energy 282
Petroleum 282
Natural Gas 288
Coal 290
Electricity 291
Energy in the Postwar American Economy 293
Transportation 294
Freight Traffic 294
Passenger Traffic 296
Transportation in the Postwar American Economy 299

13 Developments in Communications and Finance, 1950 to the Present 304
Communications 305
Mass Communications 305
Interpersonal and Business Communications 310
Communications Changes in the Postwar American Economy 316
Financial Markets 316
Banking 316
Credit Cards 321
Insurance 322
Securities Markets 322
Changes in Financial Markets in the Postwar American Economy 326

14 Developments in Domestic & International Trade, 1950 to the Present 333
Domestic Trade 334
Shopping Centers 335
Supermarkets 335
Department, Specialty, and Chain Stores 336
Discount Stores 337
Developments in Domestic Trade in the Postwar American Economy 338
International Trade 339
Merchandise and Service Trade 341
Exchange Rates 344
Trade Policies 347
Developments in International Trade in the Postwar American Economy 351

15 Government and the Post War American Economy 355
The Growth of Government 356
Stabilization Policies 365
The Late 1940s and 1950s 366

The 1960s 368
The 1970s 369
The 1980s 372
Social Policies 374
Social Security 375
Eliminating Poverty and Welfare 377
Businesses: The New Regulation 380
Government and the Economy: A Personal Assessment 382

16 The American Achievement 391
The Distribution of Income 392
The Functional Distribution of Income 393
The Size Distribution of Income 395
The United States' Place in the World Economy 413

CHAPTER 1

The American Economy Prior to 1920

THE AMERICAN ECONOMY AT THE TURN OF THE CENTURY

In the twentieth century the United States has dominated global economic activity. From the turn of the century into the 1970s, our manufacturing and service industries were the marvels of the world; firms and countries wishing to obtain the most advanced technologies in television, telecommunications, or computers, for example, immediately thought of the United States. To many observers that edge was lost sometime during the 1970s, and some of the dynamism in our economy disappeared during the following decades. But prior to that, even during the Great Depression, the United States set the standards.

In 1914, on the eve of the First World War, the United States was the world's preeminent industrial power, responsible for over half of the world's industrial output. It was a dynamic, growing, and (by the standards of the time) high-wage economy, and this land of opportunity's siren call had been answered by millions of immigrants. The flood of immigrants which began in 1840 continued through 1920 as an average of 1,000 immigrants entered the United States each day over that 80 year period. These immigrants augmented a growing industrial labor force. Though conditions in the ghettoes of the eastern and midwestern industrial cities sometimes fit the gloomy portraits drawn for this period, most of the new arrivals could remember far worse. And here, they realized, existed an opportunity to move upward and improve themselves.

The farmers were also optimistic. With the end of the regional expansion of agriculture at the turn of the century, the increases in agricultural production slowed down; at the same time demand rose with the increases in the export of American foodstuffs. As a result, farm prices and farm incomes rose, and by the mid-1920s American farmers would view 1910 to 1914 as the golden age of American agriculture.

Businesses had also changed. In many firms the heroic owner/entrepreneur of the nineteenth century was being replaced by technical specialists and managers, and ownership was being divided and subdivided through shares of corporate stock. Frederick Taylor and others were creating a new science of management to bring rigor and rationality to the administration and organization of production in the new big companies. Business associations were being formed to protect and advance their interests against those of labor unions, politicians, and other businesses, as illustrated by the formation in 1912 of the U.S. Chamber of Commerce. As the 1920s approached, more and more business leaders came to believe that logical, careful planning could not only stabilize and ensure the growth of their firms but also stabilize and control the entire economy.

A new era of financial affairs had also dawned. The New York Stock Exchange had been fully transformed into an industrial stock market; it created a national market for industrial securities and helped to solidify the development of a national capital market for the larger firms. The financial leaders, such as J. P. Morgan, had risen to a position of prominence much to the dismay of industrial leaders like Henry Ford.

In the years leading up to 1914, those who were dissatisfied with business behavior generally turned to government intervention to correct the perceived wrongs of the marketplace.[1] The failure of state granger laws to control the railroads led to the

Interstate Commerce Act of 1887, though this was, at first, not a very effective control. Concern about the rise of business monopolies brought on the Sherman Antitrust Act of 1890. The Elkins Act of 1903, the Hepburn Act of 1906, and the Mann-Elkins Act of 1910 dramatically expanded the powers of the ICC and allowed it to truly control the railroads. The Standard Oil and American Tobacco decisions of 1911 established the "rule of reason" in controlling monopolistic behavior, and the 1914 Clayton and FTC Acts specified the types of behavior that businesses could and could not engage in and also provided for a federal agency to administer the provisions of the acts.

There were other reactions to the excesses of big business in the late nineteenth century. One early indication of this came in the labor relations between large firms and their workers. As firms grew larger, they became increasingly impersonal, with more layers of middle-level managers and supervisors between the owners/executives and the workers. Industrial workers pushed for shorter hours and better (mainly safer) working conditions and resisted wage cuts often attempted by firms due to the general fall in prices. Workers organized two short-lived unions, the National Labor Union (1866–72) and the Knights of Labor (1878–86), and finally the skilled craftsworker's trade unions were organized into the American Federation of Labor, which continued through the interwar period. For the most part court decisions went against laborers and labor unions before 1914.

In 1913 Senator Arsene Pujo released his committee's report condemning a "money monopoly" in the United States. The committee, after several years of study, concluded that the powerful bankers of the nation's financial centers, such as J. P. Morgan, James Stillman, and George Baker, controlled the nation's credit, exacting excessive interest charges. And by their presence on the boards of a number of large corporations, the Pujo Committee also found that these bankers effectively brought about the monopolistic behavior of those businesses.

One result of the committee's activities was an impetus for the passage of a law creating a central bank to control the stock of money and credit in the United States. Concern with the "money monopoly" led to the creation of 12 regional central banks rather than one, and industrialists and farmers as well as bankers were to be represented on these Federal Reserve Boards. By providing a lender of last resort and a new national currency in the form of the Federal Reserve Note, it was hoped that banking crises would be forever ended.

The industrial transformation and expansion of the American economy in the postbellum period had created great disparities in income and wealth. As a means of reducing income inequality and as a fresh source of federal revenue, the Civil War income tax was revived in 1894. After lengthy deliberations and with some hesitation, the Supreme Court ruled that one part of the tax was unconstitutional and, therefore so was the entire tax.[2] The continued growth of the federal government and concern with reducing income inequality finally led to calls to amend the constitution to allow a federal income tax. Adroit channeling of pension outlays and military spending to states where there was a record of opposition to the income tax allowed the amendment to be ratified in 1913.[3] Immediately Congress began consideration of a revenue bill to use this new tax. The Underwood Tariff included the new income tax with, in retrospect, very low but slightly progressive rates on the highest income recipients.

The enactment of a federal income tax opened the door to a much more important role for the federal government in redistributing income, while the laws strengthening the regulatory powers of the Interstate Commerce Commission and the 1914 amendments that enlarged and strengthened the 1890 Sherman Antitrust Act forecast the federal government's emergence as a regulatory agency. These developments were leading the United States further away from the classical liberal concept of government as a "nightwatchman."

THE AMERICAN ECONOMY DURING THE FIRST WORLD WAR

In 1914 Europe erupted into war as various military alliances inexorably drew the nations into battle. Few people, including Americans, were untouched by the war. Though the United States did not enter the war until April of 1917, in the nearly three year interval there was a huge increase in foreign, mainly Allied, demand for some American manufactures and foodstuffs. U.S. exports of chemicals, dyes, drugs, iron and steel, munitions, meat, wheat, and flour all rose enormously. Farm prices and farm incomes rose dramatically. Munitions manufacturers, such as Du Pont, experienced dramatic increases and their firms undertook great expansion projects.[4] Overall, however, the economy did not expand during this period. As Table 1.1 shows, the real per capita GNP achieved in 1913 was not reached again until 1918. Unemployment was higher in 1914 and 1915 than in 1913, but it had virtually disappeared by 1918. Driven by the rising export demand and increases in the stock of money, price inflation began increasing in 1916 and was still quite high in 1920.

This enormous expansion in American exports further increased the export surplus. In the 19th century the United States had periodically imported large amounts of capital and became a debtor nation. But for the ten years prior to 1914 the United States had an export surplus of about $400 to $500 million a year. This export of capital had started the transformation of the United States from a debtor nation to a creditor nation. The onset of the First World War accelerated this trend as Allied nations, particularly Great Britain and France, collected the American assets their citizens owned and sold them in the United States to obtain the dollars needed to buy American products. By 1917 the U.S. export surplus reached $3.5 billion, and the United States had been fully transformed from a debtor to a creditor nation.[5]

As the Allied governments ran out of the dollars they needed to buy American goods, they asked for permission to borrow in the United States. President Wilson was reluctant to approve this because the United States was officially neutral, but he finally gave in. J. P. Morgan and other investment banking houses then began to sell large amounts of British, French, and Russian bonds to American private investors. With the entrance of the United States into the war, the government floated the First Liberty Loan of 1917. From this and subsequent loans, $10 billion was made available to the Allied governments, and private lending to the Allies stopped.

Table 1.1 Selected Economic Statistics, 1913–1922

Year	Real GNP per Capita (1)	Per-cent Unem-ployed (2)	Rate of Price Change CPI (3)	WPI (4)	Money Stock, M2 (5)	Federal Government Outlays as percent of GNP (6)	Active Duty Military Personnel (7)
1913	$1,351	4.3%	2.4%	1.1%	$15.73	1.81	154,914
1914	1,267	7.9	1.3	−2.2	16.39	1.88	165,919
1915	1,238	8.5	1.0	1.7	17.59	1.87	165,919
1916	1,317	5.1	7.3	20.9	20.85	1.48	179,376
1917	1,310	4.6	16.1	31.8	24.37	3.24	643,833
1918	1,471	1.4	16.1	10.9	26.73	16.57	2,897,167
1919	1,401	1.4	13.9	5.5	31.01	21.96	1,172,602
1920	1,315	5.2	14.7	10.9	34.80	6.95	343,302

Source: *Historical Statistics of the United States: Colonial Times to 1970* (Washington: U.S.G.P.O., 1976). Col. (1) 1958=100. Cols. (3) and (4) 1967=100. Col (5) billions of current dollars.

American War Preparations

Although the United States did not enter the war until April of 1917, it had been clear that war was coming; preparations had begun well before then. In 1916 Congress passed the National Defense Act to expand the armed forces. The Shipping Act of 1916 organized and formed the Merchant Marine, which was to be controlled by the U.S. Shipping Board. A Naval Consulting Board composed of private experts and businessmen was established, and from this a Committee on Industrial Preparedness was spun off. In 1916 this committee was changed to the Council for National Defense. It was fully funded by the federal government and for all practical purposes was an official federal government agency.[6]

Economic Mobilization: The Command Economy

With the entrance of the United States into the First World War, the federal government passed a number of acts to mobilize resources for war. These acts transformed much of the economy from a market-based into a "command economy."[7] The primary control legislation for this command economy was the Lever Food and Fuel Control Act, which provided for the power to federally license businesses, requisition commodities, take over factories directly, and even fund the infant Federal Bureau of Investigation. This act also gave the government the power to establish minimum crop prices, especially for wheat, and authorized "meatless" days so that the nation could conserve meat.

The Food and Fuel Production Act established the U.S. Fuel Administration to control the output of coal and fix its price. The War Industries Board was established on July 8, 1917, to make priority allocations in manufacturing, fix prices, and coordinate government purchases of manufactured products. However, it did not initially prove as successful as was hoped; in the spring of 1918, Bernard Baruch was named to head the WIB, and it was given more power to coordinate war industries. The only power it did not have was the power to fix prices. The U.S. Grain Corporation was organized to buy food and other commodities, fix prices, and store surpluses. The U.S. Housing Corporation used government money to supply housing for defense workers. The Emergency Fleet Corporation was created to organize shipyards, materials, and labor to build a huge fleet of ships. The War Finance Corporation used federal funds to underwrite bank loans to private industry.

The government's control of the economy went far beyond anything previously considered in the United States. The start of war found U.S. rail transportation in a chaotic state. The increased activity had used up all of the excess capacity, and there was a general surge in the flow of freight traffic toward the major East Coast ports. Complicating matters were attempts by various government agencies to give each of their shipments the highest priority for quick transport to the coast. Freight cars and loaded and unloaded freight piled up at key junctions such as the rail yards in Pittsburgh. Attempts at cooperation by competing railroads drew letters warning of antitrust action from the Attorney General.[8]

The railroads also faced financial problems. The Adamson Act of 1916 had forced the railroads to offer an eight-hour day with no drop in daily pay to avert a threatened nation wide strike by rail unions. Because of inflation caused by the war, rail labor unions demanded wage increases while shippers expressed their strong opposition. The ICC, which had not approved rate increases after the passage of the Adamson Act, could not find a way to mediate among the conflicting demands.

On December 26, 1917, President Wilson issued a proclamation enabling the federal government to take the reins of the nation's railroads. His son-in-law, William G. McAdoo, was appointed director of the newly created United States Railroad Association (USRA). The USRA was able to coordinate shipments and train movements and clear the freight car logjams in East Coast ports because it was no longer hampered by the antitrust laws against cooperative action; as well the USRA and McAdoo had the power to assign priorities to the different federal agencies demanding priority shipments. The USRA increased wages for railway workers several times, including one increase of nearly 40 percent. They ordered 100,000 new freight cars and 2,000 new locomotives for the various railroads. The result was an enormous increase in railroad outlays, especially in labor expenses, and increasing amounts of federal subsidies to keep the railroads operating.

In 1918 the federal government assumed command over the nation's telegraph and telephone systems, placing them under the jurisdiction of the Postmaster General.[9] One of the justifications for government takeover of the telephone system was that it could be operated more efficiently that way. But within weeks the Postmaster General instituted service connection charges, which state public service commissions had blocked in the past. Rates were sharply increased—long distance charges went up 20 percent—in spite of protests. A Supreme Court ruling confirmed that the Postmaster General had the power to order such rate hikes. When the telephone systems were returned to private ownership, it was found that government operation had resulted in a deficit of more than 13 million dollars of which 4 million came from AT&T's surplus and the rest from the Treasury. Everyone was glad to see the government get out of the operation of the telephone system. Congressman James B. Atwell of Louisiana, who had proposed the original resolution for federal takeover of the telephone and telegrah systems, introduced another resolution apologizing to the American people and to Congress for what he had done. John Brooks said, "The ghost of government ownership was laid; agitation for it disappeared in popular and orthodox political circles."[10]

The government's need for large numbers of uniform items led to a further move toward standardization in production. The production of uniforms during the Civil War had led to the first systematic measurements for clothing, shoes, hats, and so on; the First World War pushed this much further. "One of the most effective ways of increasing the quantities of necessary manufactures was found to be the standardization of products and the reduction in the number of sizes and designs."[11] The standardization was first pushed in the production of weapons and munitions and then extended to consumer goods. To preserve steel, the steel in women's steel-boned corsets was eliminated. The amount of thread per spool was increased. The types of typewriter ribbons were reduced from 150 to 56, and the number and sizes of plows reduced from 376 to 76. George Soule argues that "Everything from baby carriages to coffins was standardized and simplified. Altogether 1,241 savings of this kind were effected."[12]

Agriculture and Industry During the War

Although there was some increase in agricultural production during the war, most of the increase occurred during the prewar period from 1914 to 1917. The overall index of agricultural output actually shows a slight decline from 100 in 1914 and 1915 to 92 and 96 in 1916 and 1917, respectively. The index of agricultural output rose to 101 in 1918. What continued to rise at a faster rate were the prices of agricultural products. With the rising prices, boards, such as the Sugar Equalization Board, were established to attempt to control and stabilize the prices of agricultural commodities. Wholesale food prices at the beginning of 1917 were 50 percent above the 1913 levels; by August of 1917 they were 80 percent above 1913 levels. The physical volume of food exports in 1917–18 was 77 percent greater than the yearly average for 1914–17, and the 1919 volume was 51 percent greater than that for 1918.

The increases in the prices and output of agricultural commodities varied. The greatest gains came in the prices of grains, especially wheat and rye, and in hog prices. Cotton gained the least. Controlling prices created coordination problems. For example, an important ingredient in cooking was lard (or hog fat). Initially hog production—particularly lard production—began to fall. It was found that the price of corn had risen more than hog prices, and farmers were therefore decreasing hog production and selling off their stocks. To increase pork and lard production, the price of hogs relative to the price of corn had to be raised. The Food Administration could not directly set the prices for hogs; however, it could significantly influence these prices, because about 30 to 40 percent of all pork produced in the United States was purchased for the army, navy, Belgian Relief, and the Red Cross by the Food Administration. These officials obtained an agreement from the meapacking companies that if they (the packers) received higher prices from the Food Administration, they would pass these on in the form of higher hog prices to farmers. Although the process did not work smoothly and required numerous adjustments, it was successful in raising hog prices relative to corn prices and thereby increasing pork and lard production.

Like agriculture, most of the increase in manufacturing had occurred by the time the United States entered the war. The sectors that grew more were those associated with war production, such as the steel and munitions industries. Products that had formerly been imported from Germany, such as dyestuffs and chemicals, accounted for another growth area. Automobile production and sales had been growing rapidly as Ford's mass-production assembly line techniques allowed it to lower prices and expand production from 460,000 cars in 1913 to 1,750,000 in 1917; however, war demands reduced automobile production in 1917 and 1918. Associated with the rising use of the car were expansions in the number of oil wells, refineries, petroleum pipelines, gasoline stations, and automobile garages. The production of rubber products, particularly automobile tires, also rose sharply. From 1914 to 1917, state and local governments undertook considerable paved road construction, most of which was financed by bond sales.

For the most part after 1917, the gains that occurred in industrial output were in products associated with the war, and these were largely offset by declines in the production of other products. There was a rise in manufacturing construction and investment in machinery and equipment, but these were more than offset by the dramatic declines in housing construction.

With the onset of war, the U.S. Shipping Board established the Merchant Marine and moved to increase American shipping capacity to offset the reduction in British shipping. The existing shipyards in the United States mobilized to produce more cargo ships, and production rose from 384,899 tons in 1916 to 821,115 tons in 1917 and 2,602,153 tons in 1918. To increase production more rapidly, new government shipyards were constructed in Wilmington, North Carolina; Newark, New Jersey; and Bristol and Philadelphia, Pennsylvania. Bureaucratic red tape slowed progress; and the first ships from the new yards were launched on December 18, 1918, just as President Wilson sailed for Europe to discuss the terms of peace. Though the Merchant Marine's size had been increased, most of the ships created during the war were not well suited to the commercial requirements of peacetime.

Labor During the War

In the late nineteenth century and the first decade of the twentieth, labor unions and other labor representatives had systematically called for restrictions on immigration into the United States. Though many reasons were presented, the overriding concern was to reduce the expansion of the labor force and raise wages. From 1905 through 1914, an average of one million immigrants a year entered the United States. With the onset of the war in Europe, immigration dramatically declined. From 264,000 immigrants in 1916, the number declined to 81,000 in 1917 and 41,000 in 1918. The combination of the dramatic reduction of immigration and an increased demand for labor led to rising real wages. During the war the federal government required that firms with government contracts establish an eight-hour day, something that labor had long called for. This and the excess demand for labor led to the general establishment of the eight-hour day and 44-hour week by the end of the First World War. The establishment of Selective Service and the compulsory draft helped reduce the supply of and augmented the excess demand for labor.[13]

There was a shift in migration within the United States as well. The rising demand for labor in industrial activity led to a migration of workers from the farms to the cities, which caused the farm population to fall much more rapidly than previously. Women entered the labor force in relatively large numbers to move into retail and commercial employment as men were drawn into the war and into the factories. Labor recruiters also turned to the south to recruit blacks, both from the rural areas and from the southern cities. The first large migrations of poor southern blacks and whites to northern cities occurred during the First World War and led to increases in southern wage rates, though southern wages fell in the 1920s.[14] This exodus from the South led to racial tensions in the North as bloody race riots occurred in East St. Louis in 1917 and in Chicago in 1919.

Unions received an important boost as the federal government encouraged firms to recognize unions and promoted bargaining between firms and unions to reduce labor strife and increase output. In 1918 the War Labor Board was created to adjudicate labor disputes. During the war, it handled 1500 compulsory arbitration cases. The War Labor Policies Board was created to establish general policies and guidelines on hours, wages, and working conditions. Though there were 6,000 strikes during the war, most were of very short duration.[15]

The result was that both the nominal and real wages of laborers rose. Salaried workers found it much more difficult to get their salaries adjusted, and salaries generally rose less than wages. Interest rates and rates of return on capital generally did not increase as much as the rate of price inflation did, so real interest income from capital (bonds, stocks, profit, and so on) generally fell, leading to a trend toward equalization in the personal distribution of income during the war.

Financing the War

The federal government relied upon a combination of borrowing and taxes to finance the war effort. About one third of the costs of the war were raised through current taxation, with the rest financed through borrowing or future taxation. The total cost of the war was $35.5 billion, of which $9.5 billion was lent to the governments of Allied nations. In all, $24 billion was borrowed through bond issues, of which about 71 percent was subscribed to by individuals and the remaining 29 percent subscribed to by financial institutions. The First Liberty Loan was issued in April of 1917. There were three more Liberty Loan issues, with coupon interest rates ranging from 3.5 to 4.5 percent. The last bond issue was in 1919, after the war had ended, and was called the Victory Liberty Loan issue.

The relative amount raised through current taxation was much larger than in previous wars. Prior to 1914 the federal government had relied mainly on tariffs for revenue.

The new individual and corporate income taxes allowed the government to raise additional revenue by dramatically increasing income taxes and broadening the base of those who paid them. By 1913 the maximum individual income tax rate was 7 percent on taxable incomes of over $1,000,000. In 1918 the maximum rate was 77 percent on taxable incomes of over $1,000,000, and individuals with taxable incomes of $6,000 faced a higher tax rate, 13 percent, than any individual at any income level had faced in 1913.

The United States at the End of the First World War

The United States emerged from the First World War as the strongest economic power in the world. Virtually overnight it had been transformed from a debtor to a creditor nation, a position it retained until the early 1980s. The flow of gold to pay for war-related exports had left the United States holding the majority of the world's monetary gold stock. These changes would bring about the adoption of an altered form of the gold standard in the twenties.

With the end of the war, President Wilson moved quickly to end the federal boards that had controlled the economy during the war, although some industrialists and bureaucrats wished to see them continued. In 1919 the Commerce Department attempted to establish a government-private arrangement to fix prices, but Wilson quickly squashed this.[16] The government also pulled back from its support of labor unions, and strike losses, particularly in the steel industry in 1919, led to a loss of union membership. But permanent changes had occurred. Membership in the Industrial Workers of the World (IWW) had dwindled due to its pronounced anti-war position, while the American Federation of Labor (AFL) which had supported the war, was considerably strengthened. When the New Deal adopted the analogy of the depression as war and resurrected war-era institutions to combat the depression, some of the AFL unions were ready to seize this opportunity to revitalize the labor movement. And laborers could see the wage gains that had been made during the war when immigration was choked off; when immigration increased sharply in 1919, there was a much stronger and more concerted movement to get Congress to limit immigration. As a result, America's open door to immigrants ended in 1921.

The war had given the U.S. government the opportunity to dramatically increase its new personal and corporate income taxes. By 1919 the upper 30 percent of all income earners were subject to income taxes. Though the rates were lowered in the twenties as the federal government ran continued budget surpluses, the maximum marginal rate was 25 percent, far higher than the 7 percent of 1913. With the onset of the depression, just as during the First World War, the rates were increased dramatically. By the end of the twenties, many states had followed the federal government's lead and adopted personal income taxes. As Jonathan Hughes has stated, the income tax rates and yields of 1918 were "the initial yield of the Sixteenth Amendment. It was the small beginning of a fiscal revolution that would change the American economy beyond the wildest dreams of those who pushed for the Sixteenth Amendment as a needed social reform."[17]

In the opinions of most observers, the Federal Reserve System had also passed its first test. It had made it much easier for the government to finance the war, though one of the costs was a much higher rate of price inflation. Indeed, in 1919, when the federal government needed to sell the last Liberty Loan issue, "the Fed" was pressured into keeping interest rates low to facilitate bond sales. To do this, the stock of money was allowed to grow rapidly, setting off an inflationary boom. Once the Fed adopted a much more restrictive monetary policy with the end of the federal government's bond sales in late 1919, this boom collapsed. But, to most observers the Fed had shown that it could control monetary affairs and therefore, many hoped, the business cycle as well.

Finally, there were many who had been impressed with the wartime controls. Many industrialists liked being sheltered from price competition. Others believed that careful planning and centralized coordination would work for the economy as well as it worked for big businesses and believed that the First World War demonstrated this. When the Great Depression engulfed the economy at the beginning of the thirties, proposals to resurrect wartime control boards appeared. Roosevelt compared fighting the depression to fighting a war, and the old controls boards were resurrected and given new names. For example, the War Industries Board became the National Recovery Administration and the United States Grain Corporation became the Commodity Credit Corporation.[18] Many of the people who had served on war boards were recycled to serve on New Deal agencies. In a sense the First World War was a training ground for Roosevelt's New Deal programs of the thirties, and the lessons learned in 1917 and 1918 would not be forgotten in the prosperous twenties.

SELECTED REFERENCES

Brooks, John. *Telephone: The First Hundred Years.* New York: Harper and Row, 1975.

Bruchey, Stuart. *Growth of the Modern American Economy.* New York: Dodd Mead and Company, 1975.

Davis, Lance E., Richard A. Easterlin, William N. Parker et al. *American Economic Growth: An Economists' History of the United States.* New York: Harper and Row, 1972.

Faulkner, Harold U. *The Decline of Laissez Faire, 1897–1917.* New York: Holt, Rinehart, and Winston, 1951.

Fearon, Peter. *War, Prosperity and Depression: The U.S. Economy, 1917–1945.* Lawrence, KS: University of Kansas Press, 1987.

Fogel, Robert W. and Stanlley L. Engerman, eds. *The Reinterpretation of American Economic History.* New York: Harper and Row, 1971.

Hawley, Ellis W. *The Great War and the Search for a Modern Order: A History of the American People and Their Institutions, 1917–1933.* New York: St. Martin's Press, 1979.

Higgs, Robert. *The Transformation of the American Economy, 1865–1914.* New York: John Wiley & Sons, 1971.

__________. *Crisis and Leviathan: Critical Episodes in the Growth of American Government.* New York: Oxford University Press, 1987.

Hughes, Jonathan. *The Governmental Habit: Economic Controls from Colonial Times to the Present.* New York: Basic Books, 1977.

__________. *American Economic History*, 3d ed. Glenview, IL: Scott, Foresman and Company, 1990.

Lebergott, Stanley. *The Americans: An Economic Record.* New York: W. W. Norton, 1984.

Lee, Susan Previant and Peter Passell. *A New Economic View of American History.* New York: W. W. Norton, 1979.

Porter, Glenn. *The Rise of Big Business, 1860–1910.* New York: The Thomas Y. Crowell Co., 1973.

Rosenberg, Nathan. *Technology and American Economic Growth.* New York: Harper Torchbooks, 1972.

Soule, George. *Prosperity Decade: From War to Depression, 1917–1929.* New York: Holt, Rinehart, and Winston, 1947.

Taylor, George Rogers. *The Transportation Revolution, 1815–1860.* New York: Holt, Rinehart, and Winston, 1951.

Walton, Gary and Hugh Rockoff. *The History of the American Economy*, 6th ed. Englewood Cliffs, NJ: Prentice-Hall, 1990.

NOTES

1. However, there are those who argue that much of the Progressive Era's legislation to regulate business was inspired by businesses wishing to escape from the reins of competition rather than by the Progressive Era reformers. In particular, see Gabriel Kolko, *The Triumph of Conservatism: A Reinterpretation of American History, 1900–1916* (New York: The Free Press, 1963). Much of this discussion is drawn from the following studies: Robert H. Wiebe, *The Search for Order: 1877–1920* (New York: Hill and Wang, 1967); Ellis W. Hawley, *The Great War and the Search for a Modern Order: A History of the American People and Their Institutions, 1917–1933* (New York: St. Martin's Press, 1979), chapter 1; Stanley Lebergott, *The Americans: An Economic Record* (New York: W. W. Norton and Co., 1984), chapter 31; and Charles H. Hession and Hyman Sardy, *Ascent to Affluence: A History of American Economic Development* (Boston: Allyn and Bacon, Inc., 1969), chapter 22.
2. See Robert Higgs, *Crisis and Leviathan: Critical Episodes in the Growth of American Government* (New York: Oxford University Press, 1987). Other sources for this discussion of the federal income tax are as follows: Bennett D. Baack and Edward John Ray, "Special Interests and the Adoption of the Income Tax in the U.S.," *The Journal of Economic History*, 45 (September 1985): 607–26; Jonathan Hughes, *The Governmental Habit: Economic Controls from Colonial Times to the Present* (New York: Basic Books, 1977); Roy G. and Gladys C. Blakey, *The Federal Income Tax* (New York: Longmans, Green and Company, 1940); Jonathan Hughes, *American Economic History*, 2d ed. (Glenview, IL: Scott, Foresman and Co., 1987), chapter 23; and Lebergott, *The Americans: An Economic Record*, chapter 31.
3. Baack and Ray, "Special Interests and the Adoption of the Income Tax in the U.S."
4. Most of the material on the first World War comes from the following sources: Harold U. Faulkner, *The Decline of Laissez Faire, 1897–1917* (New York: Holt, Rinehart, and Winston, 1951), chapters 12 and 13; George Soule, *Prosperity Decade: From War to Depression, 1917–1929* (New York: Holt, Rinehart, and Winston, 1947), chapters 1–3; Peter Fearon, *War, Prosperity, & Depression: The U.S. Economy, 1917–1945* (Lawrence, KS: University of Kansas Press, 1987), chapter 1.

5. Cleona Lewis, *America's Stake in International Investments* (Washington, D.C.: The Brookings Institution, 1938), 352.
6. George Soule, *Prosperity Decade: From War to Depression, 1917–1929*, 10–12.
7. For a discussion of this see Jonathan Hughes, *American Economic History*, 2d ed. (Glenview, IL: Scott, Foresman, and Co., 1987), chapter 23. This concept is developed in more detail in Jonathan Hughes, *The Governmental Habit: Economic Controls from Colonial Times to the Present* (New York: Basic Books, 1977); and in Ronald Radosh and Murray N. Rothbard, eds., *A New History of Leviathan: Essays on the Rise of the American Corporate State* (New York: Dutton, 1972).
8. Much of this discussion of the railroads up to 1920 is drawn from K. Austin Kerr, *American Railroad Politics, 1914–1920* (Pittsburgh: University of Pittsburgh, 1968).
9. Soule, *Prosperity Decade*, 33 and 42.
10. John Brooks, *Telephone: The First Hundred Years* (New York: Harper and Row, 1975), 159.
11. Soule, *Prosperity Decade*, 17.
12. Ibid.
13. See Soule, *Prosperity Decade*, 36–38; and Robert Higgs, *Crisis and Leviathan: Critical Episodes in the Growth of American Government* (New York: Oxford University Press, 1987), chapter 7.
14. See Gavin Wright, *Old South, New South: Revolutions in the Southern Economy Since the Civil War* (New York: Basic Books, 1986), 201–202.
15. Soule, *Prosperity Decade*, 65–67.
16. Robert F. Himmelberg, "The War Industries Board and the Antitrust Question in 1918," *The Journal of American History*, 52, (June 1965), 59–74.
17. Hughes, *American Economic History*, 414.
18. For a discussion of this see William E. Leuchtenberg, "The New Deal and the Analogue of War," in John Braeman et al., *Change and Continuity in Twentieth Century America* (New York: Harper and Row, 1967).

CHAPTER 2

American Economic Growth, Population Changes, and Labor Force Developments, 1920–1940

AN OVERVIEW OF AMERICAN ECONOMIC GROWTH, 1920–1940

Few decades in American history present such dramatic contrasts as the 1920s and 1930s. The 1920s, after the recovery from the 1920–21 depression, were a decade of growth and prosperity. In fact George Soule titled his well known book on the economic history of the 1920s *Prosperity Decade*.[1] The twenties are often depicted as a decade of flamboyant and frivolous fun, of open roadsters, speakeasies, and the Charleston. Americans were the richest people in the world, and in this decade they realized it and began to enjoy it. In 1929 this new era ended. It seems likely that the collapse of the booming stock market in late October of 1929 will, in popular perception, forever mark the end of the prosperous twenties and the onset of the thirties, the "depression decade" as Broadus Mitchell calls it.[2]

As Figure 2.1 shows, a sharp depression opened the 1920s. This contraction was severe but short, and by latc 1922 the economy was once again operating near full employment. Minor recessions occurred in 1923–24 and 1927–28, though these were hardly noticeable in the midst of the real growth of the decade. From the cyclical peak in 1923 to the cyclical peak in 1929, total real GNP grew 3.38 percent per year, while

Fig. 2.1 Real GNP Per Capita and the Rate of Unemployment for the United States, 1920–1940

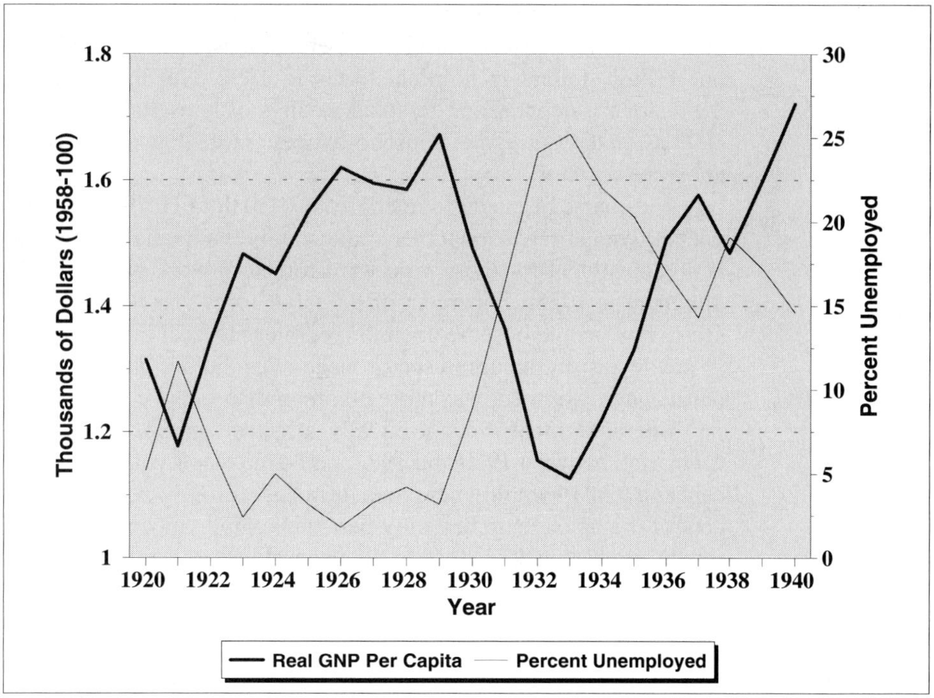

Source: *Historical Statistics of the United States: Colonial Times to 1970* (Washington, D.C.: U.S. Government Printing Office, 1976).

real GNP per capita grew 2 percent per year. Consumption purchases grew at a rate of 3.72 percent per year, gross private domestic investment grew at 0.75 percent per year, and the government purchases of goods and services grew at a rate of 5.5 percent per year.

The economic contraction that is called the Great Depression began in the middle of 1929 and continued through the first quarter of 1933. It is without parallel in the history of the United States. The depression of the 1870s lasted somewhat longer, from 1873 to 1878, but most economic historians now believe that price declines played a more important role in that contraction than declines in real output and employment. The 1893–96 depression is generally conceded to have been the second most severe contraction, but the highest nonfarm unemployment rate then was 32 percent in 1894, while the nonfarm unemployment rate was over 36 percent in 1932 and nearly 38 percent in 1933. (And this rate would have been much higher if it also counted those who could only find part-time employment.) The recovery was much more rapid in the 1890s. In the Great Depression of the thirties, the recovery began in the second quarter of 1933 and continued slowly until 1937 when another depression occurred. It was 1942 before the unemployment rate dropped to 5 percent, a level commonly used to indicate full employment.

Nominal GNP fell 46.1 percent from 1929 to 1933 while real GNP fell 30.5 percent over the same years. The largest declines occurred between 1929 and 1930 (9.9 percent), and 1931 and 1932 (14.8 percent). Prices also fell sharply. (See Figure 2.2.) Real consumption expenditures fell 21.7 percent between 1929 and 1933. Gross private domestic investment fell 86.9 percent between 1929 and 1932 and was less than one billion dollars in nominal terms in 1932. Net investment was negative at the depths of the depression. Personal savings of households were negative in 1932 and 1933 as, in the aggregate, households spent more than they received in income for two consecutive years.

The course of unemployment from 1930 through 1941 is shown in Figure 2.1. The unemployment rate shown there counts only the totally unemployed individuals; there is no adjustment for those who were forced to work part-time. At the peak of unemployment in 1933, 25 percent of the labor force was totally unemployed. In the rural sector few people became unemployed; instead, real income dropped to extraordinarily low levels. In the urban sector wage rates did not drop as sharply, and complete or partial unemployment was more common than in the countryside.

Unemployment did not equally affect all groups or all cities. For example, in Cincinnati between 1929 and 1932, part-time employment rose from 5.27 to 18.85 percent and total unemployment rose from 5.94 to 18.32 percent. In Philadelphia 19.9 percent of the labor force had only part-time employment in 1933, while 46 percent was totally unemployed. In Buffalo the unemployment rate, weighted to include those who were employed only part-time, rose from 7.9 percent in 1929 to 31.2 percent in November of 1932. Large cities with a concentration of heavy industries, such as steel and automobile production, had much higher unemployment rates—often 40 or 50 percent.[3] Finally, as would be expected at a time when the number of individuals seeking employment was increasingly larger than the number of jobs employers could offer, other types of job rationing became much more important. Employers could choose not

Fig. 2.2 Real Rates of Price Changes in the Consumer Price Index and the Wholesale Price Index, and the Stock of Money, 1920–1940

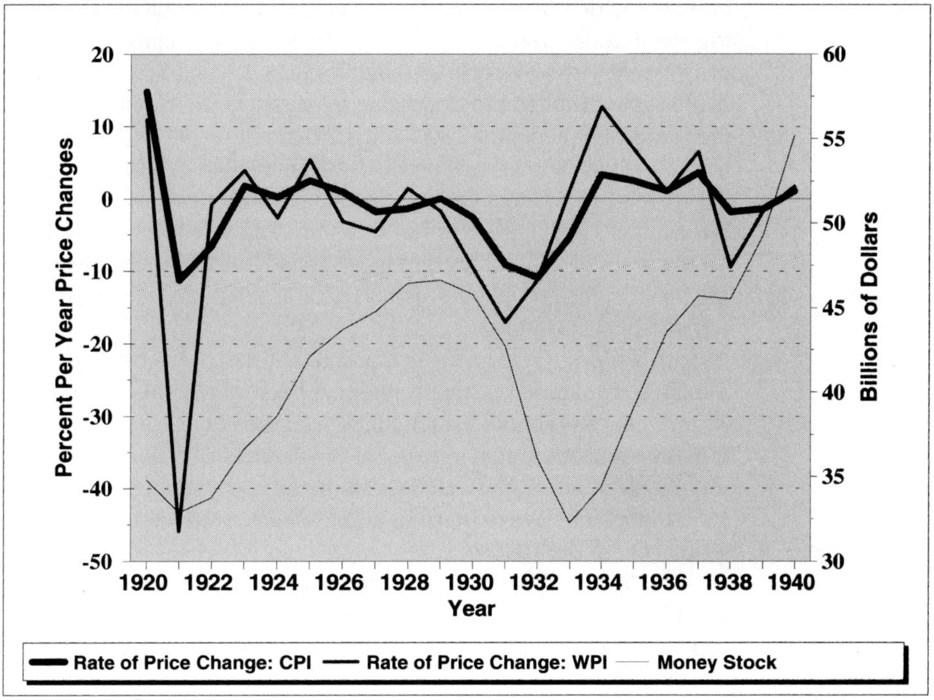

Source: *Historical Statistics of the United States: Colonial Times to 1970* (Washington, D.C.: U.S. Government Printing Office, 1976).

to hire the very young or old; they could hire men rather than women; and, at low cost, they could discriminate against nonwhites. As a result, unemployment rates for the young, the old, women, and nonwhite workers were much higher than reported unemployment rates for the total labor force.

The recovery from the Great Depression is generally judged to have been slow because full employment was not reached during the thirties. From 1933 to 1937, the rate of unemployment fell from 25.2 to 14.3 percent; the unemployment rate in early 1937 was likely considerably less than 14.3 percent because a short but severe depression began around May of 1937.[4] The 1937–38 depression increased the unemployment rate from 14.3 to 19.1 percent. As late as 1940, 14.6 percent of the labor force was still unemployed.

The Twenties

It is frequently asserted that there is a tradeoff between inflation and unemployment—that to have a growing, highly active economy, the society's inhabitants must be willing to pay the price of some inflation. However, the decade of the twenties contradicts this assertion. This was a relatively modern period. Although the essential urban-industrial nature of the society was in place, with high levels of employment and real economic growth, prices were virtually constant and, in fact, tended to decline slightly during the decade. Between 1923 and 1929 real per capita GNP grew 12 percent, while prices were virtually constant. (See Figures 2.1 and 2.2.) After the end of the 1920–21 depression, the unemployment rate remained quite low at less than 4 percent except for the peaks of 5 percent in 1924 and 4.2 percent in 1928. There was a high rate of capital formation that helped raise productivity and led to a more rapid growth of real incomes. The federal government contracted from its wartime and depression size as its outlays fell from 4.3 and 3.5 percent of GNP in 1922 and 1923, respectively, to 3.0 percent in 1926 and 1927 and 3.1 percent in 1928 and 1929. The rising productivity and continuing real income growth during the 1920s accelerated changes in the consumption habits of American consumers.

In 1965, W. W. Rostow proposed that the 1920s marked the onset of a consumer durables revolution.[5] Though this had been a generally accepted axiom in economic history, in 1967 Harold Vatter challenged the idea.[6] He pointed out that there was actually little data presented to support this assertion. Vatter's examination of the evidence did not show any significant rise in the ratio of durables to total consumption. In constant dollars the ratio rose from about 9 percent in the late nineteenth century to about 11 percent in the 1920s.[7]

Though it does not appear that the consumption shift toward durable goods was of much magnitude, there does seem to have been some small shift. More important than this was the change in the character of the durable goods being purchased. The most obvious change, which Vatter suggests may have given rise to the idea of a consumer durables revolution, was the automobile as production rose from 1,746,000 in 1917 to 4,587,000 in 1929, an increase of 13.1 percent per year. This rapid adoption of the automobile by Americans initiated a number of other changes such as traffic jams, increasing calls for improved (or paved) roads, and new recreational pursuits.

An important force in this period was the electrification of the household. In 1920, 47.4 percent of the urban and nonfarm households, 1.6 percent of the farms, and 34.7 percent of all dwellings had electric service. In 1930, 84.8 percent of all urban and nonfarm households, 10.4 percent of farm households, and 68.2 percent of all American dwellings had electric service. As a result there was a rapid expansion in the production and purchase of household electric appliances such as mechanical washing machines, electric ranges, refrigerators, radios, clocks, lighting, toasters, and fans.

With the increasing real incomes and leisure time there was an expanding demand for new and existing services. The twenties saw a huge increase in movie patronage and major league basball and college football attendance. The growth in the consumption of these services was associated with the rise of the automobile as a means of rapid, comfortable, and relatively cheap personal transportation. America became a nation of people on the move, and the demand for other types of recreational activities much more closely linked with the automobile as a means of transportation exploded. The American countryside became dotted with gasoline stations, hot dog and hamburger stands, and cabin camps (as the early motor hotels were called) to cater to the automobile traffic.

These changes in consumer purchases were accomplished by changes in the methods of making purchases of durable goods. The rapid rise of consumer installment credit in the 1920s allowed consumers to borrow the purchase price of a durable good while savings were realized after the purchase by paying off the debt. Though installment credit existed as early as the 1850s, it had been relatively unimportant. During the first two decades of the twentieth century, however, installment credit for consumer durables gradually became much more respectable. Estimates suggest that by the late twenties, nearly two thirds of the new car sales and three fourths of the furniture were sold "on time." Installment credit grew much faster than noninstallment credit—in 1919, 30.3 percent of all credit outstanding was installment credit, compared with 66.3 percent in 1941. Installment credit to purchase automobiles, though somewhat less than credit on consumer goods such as furniture and other household appliances, grew faster during the interwar period. Noninstallment credit outstanding as a share of consumer credit declined as a result of a dramatic drop in consumer borrowing through charge accounts.

The Great Depression, 1929–1933

The Great Depression brought about a profound transformation of the role of government in the economy. Though governmental power had been expanding for decades, the depression spawned a huge number of new rules and regulations designed to allow the government to direct and stabilize private economic activity. The government assumed the primary responsibility of caring for the aged, disabled, and unemployed. As a result of the Great Depression, what occurred was little short of a social revolution in American society in terms of the relationships between individuals, business, and the government.

Through the summer and early fall of 1930, the character of the contraction was not particularly unusual though many noted that it appeared to be more severe than any contraction since that of 1920–21. In November of 1930, there was a series of bank failures in the southeastern states, and in December of 1930 the private Bank of the United States failed. By the end of 1930, the depression had overtaken all of the developed countries. There was a renewed banking panic and a flurry of bank failures from March to June of 1931 in the United States and an avalanche of bank panics and failures in Europe from May through July of the same year. Countries abandoned the gold standard and began to withdraw gold from the financial centers in London. Britain left the gold standard on September 21, 1931, and the pressure to convert financial assets into gold shifted to New York. The Federal Reserve System took steps to stop the gold drain and keep the United States on the gold standard. But there was another flurry of bank failures, and the decline in economic activity intensified in late 1931 and early 1932. By the late summer of 1932, there were signs that the trough of the depression had been reached; in fact, in most European countries the depression ended in 1932 or earlier. In late 1932 there were renewed bank failures. The number of failures grew sharply in January, 1933, and states began declaring "banking holidays." President Roosevelt took office on March 6, 1933, and using emergency Presidential powers granted by

Congress, he declared a nationwide banking holiday that was extended to a week or more in some areas. This final convulsive banking panic in early 1933 marked the end of the Depression.

This description and these statistics cannot adequately convey the complexity and character of the Great Depression. It is difficult for those who did not live through the era to fully grasp the extraordinary human suffering and frustration the contraction brought about. But the following brief descriptions can provide a more graphic impression.

The automobile industry was concentrated in and around Detroit. In 1929 total new car production was 4,587,000 but by 1933 had dropped to 1,573,512 new cars. General Motors' production between 1929 and 1933 shrank from 1,482,189 to 652,063 new cars. Chrysler's production fell from 375,249 to 245,058 in 1931 but then rose to 399,829 in 1933. The Ford's production fell the most, from 1,435,856 new cars in 1929 to 325,560 new cars in 1933.[8] The fall in automobile production meant that thousands of auto workers were laid off and entire plants shut down.

Firms supplying the automobile industry, such as producers of tires or steel and manufacturers of electrical equipment, found their sales falling and so laid off workers. As Lester Chandler writes, "Detroit was virtually impoverished."[9] By early 1933 roughly 51 percent of Detroit's labor force was totally unemployed, and many of the employed worked only part-time. Tax revenues fell, tax delinquencies were up, and attempts to provide a subsistence level of relief to the most needy caused the city to head toward bankruptcy. A similar scene existed in most other large cities. Across the United States, services normally provided by governments were being reduced. School expenditures were cut and whole programs eliminated, library hours and services were slashed, and medical and hospital services provided by government were curtailed.

The incidence of illness and malnutrition increased, and the number of the homeless multiplied. "Hoovervilles," the ramshackle huts of the destitute, arose in many American cities.[10] Others among the unemployed and homeless—men, women, and entire families—wandered the United States; these were the "Nomads of the Depression" as David A. Shannon terms them. One estimate suggested that there were 1,250,000 homeless; another estimate said that there were 25,000 families and 200,000 homeless men and boys. By the end of 1931, it was thought that as many as 1,200 homeless people were arriving in California each day. Railroad officials in Kansas City reported that 1,500 individuals a day passed through on the freight trains, and the Missouri Pacific Railroad officially counted 186,028 transients, or trespassers, on their trains in 1931, up from 13,875 in 1929.[11]

The Soviet government advertised for 6,000 skilled workers and its American office was deluged by 100,000 applications. Jury duty had often been considered something to be avoided in the twenties. But during the depression the "Halls of Justice" were crowded, and it was rare to hear of an absence because jurors were paid $4 for each day they served. Shining shoes became a common occupation of the unemployed, and shoe shiners from all walks of life and all ages multiplied.[12] At the same time that malnutrition and hunger were ravaging the United States, farmers were destroying crops because prices were too low. In Montana, wheat prices were often too low to make it worthwhile to harvest some of the crop. In Oregon's Willamette Valley, thousands of bushels of apples went to waste because only absolutely flawless apples could be sold. In Oregon, thousands of ewes were killed by sheep ranchers because the price they brought was insufficient to pay the cost of shipping them to market. In the South cotton rotted in the fields because, given the price paid by the cooperatives, the planters could not pay wages high enough for the pickers to purchase food.[13]

In what came to be known as the "shame of Anacostia Flats," unemployed veterans, who gathered between May and July in 1932 at Washington, D.C., to demand early payment of war bonuses were driven out by the army, and their shacks were destroyed. In the same year Milo Reno led farmers in Iowa to organize a Farmers' Holiday Association and this spread to other states. Their goal was to stop the shipment of food to market for 30 days or until the cost of production was received. Shannon reports that one article described the situations as follows:

> Omaha, Council Bluffs, and Des Moines were blockaded as well as Sioux City. In all these cities numerous deputies were sworn in to help the respective sheriffs. The Governor of Iowa ordered the roads cleared. Trucks attempted to rush through the lines of picketing farmers. A few trucks were escorted through the farmers' line by armed deputies.
>
> The armed deputies at James, ten miles out of Sioux City, started to convoy a fleet of thirty trucks through the lines. Guns were pointed. The farmers stood fast. Before an audience of bystanders the trucks were turned back. No shots were fired.
>
> On another highway, farmers bared their breasts, daring the armed deputies to shoot. The deputies did not take the dare.
>
> At Council Bluffs there were sixty arrests. A thousand farmers marched on the jail. The prisoners were hastily released on nominal bail.[14]

The U.S. economy was in its darkest hour. There was starvation amid bountiful resources. The nation's factories, land, minerals, forests, and laborers still existed, but much of these resources were unemployed. The knowledge of how to produce commodities and services was still there and people continued to desire them, but the intricate market coordination that made the demands effective and employed the resources and knowledge was failing. There were rumblings of social discontent across the nation.[15]

The Recovery of 1933–1937

Franklin Delano Roosevelt assumed the presidency in March of 1933 during the nadir of the depression. The continuing banking crisis had culminated in nationwide runs on banks. Roosevelt's first act as president was to use emergency powers to close the nation's banks. All banks were closed a week or more; then "sound" banks were allowed to reopen, weak ones merged into strong ones, and bankrupt ones dissolved. Nearly a quarter of all banks disappeared.

Though the depression came to an end with this final convulsive tremor of the financial system, the American economy was farther from full resource employment than ever before. Roosevelt had been elected by an overwhelming majority, and he took this landslide as a mandate from the American people "to do something" about the depression. The election brought in a huge Democratic majority in Congress who were anxious to act. Lester Chandler argues that Roosevelt's problem was often to keep Congress from "enacting unwanted mandatory measures."[16]

Over the next seven years Roosevelt's administration implemented what came to be called the New Deal. This haphazard amalgam of programs and policies was intended to restore the health of the American economy. Some of the programs were intended to provide immediate relief to the destitute, homeless, and unemployed; other programs aimed at restructuring and reform. Taxes were increased several times in an attempt to provide more equality in the distribution of income because Roosevelt believed that one of the defects of American society was too great a concentration of wealth in the hands of too few.

Measured by its ability to bring about a level of economic activity that fully employed Americans and restored high levels of income, Roosevelt's New Deal must be judged an abject failure. It was 1940 before real per capita income equaled or exceeded the level of 1929. In other words, the 1930s were a decade with no growth, the longest such period in the annals of American history. The Roosevelt administration was successful at its goal of getting prices to rise as the rise in the consumer price index averaged 2.6 percent a year between 1934 and 1937.

With the end of the banking crisis in early March of 1933, industrial production quickly rose until June of 1933 and then was stagnant. As Michael Weinstein points out, "After June 1933 industrial production reached a plateau that was not finally surpassed until more than a year and a half later."[17] On May 27, 1935, the Supreme Court ruled that the National Industrial Recovery Act, one of the early cornerstones of Roosevelt's New Deal, was unconstitutional. Industrial production increased 15 percent in the last half of 1935, and then rose 19 percent during 1936. From December of 1936 to the peak in May of 1937, industrial production rose only 3.6 percent, with most of this smaller increase occurring in January and February of 1937.

The 1937–1938 Depression

From May through July, industrial production was almost constant. It declined 1 percent from July to August and 3.2 percent from August to September. Between September and December, industrial production fell 27 percent, a precipitous decline. The contraction continued until the trough in May of 1938, when industrial production was 39.1 percent lower than one year earlier. Though the depression ended in May of 1938 industrial production did not surpass the May 1937 level until October of 1939.

The 1937–38 depression was about as short as the 1920–21 depression but was also very severe, and it ended a recovery that had never came close to reaching full employment. Though the index of industrial production suggests that the depression began in June, it was a violent stock market crash beginning in mid-August of 1937 that really caught the public's attention. From a Dow-Jones average of 190.38 on August 14, stock prices fell sharply and continuously until reaching a low of 97.46 on March 31, 1938, a decline of 48.8 percent over that seven month period.[18] Though annual averages understate the magnitude of the changes, unemployment rose from an average of 14.3 percent in 1937 to 19.1 percent in 1938, and real per capita GNP dropped by 6 percent. Consumer prices fell 2 percent, while wholesale prices fell over 9 percent. The recovery from the 1937–38 depression was slow, and unemployment still averaged 14.6 percent in 1940. It was 1942 before the United States once again reached full employment.

The Interwar American Economy

Interest in the performance of the interwar American economy has always focused on its schizophrenic nature, with the prosperity of the twenties contrasted with the devastating contraction of the thirties. And this is as it should be, because the Great Depression is one of those defining events that ushered in dramatic societal and economic changes. In later chapters we will examine the government's attempts to control the economy in the twenties and resurrect it in the thirties. We will also look at explanations of how the Great Depression could have occurred.

But a fascination with the Great Depression as a whole, must not lead us to ignore the important changes in individual sectors of the American economy that took place at this time. Agriculture had its own problems throughout the interwar period. Manufacturing innovations, many of which were related to the rise of electric utilities and the electrification of the nation, continued even during the depressed thirties. New institutions to distribute goods and services to consumers reduced the costs of making transactions. Long distance telephone services brought new conveniences to businesses and consumers while the radio provided a startling innovation in home entertainment. Trucks and airlines began to compete seriously with the nation's railroads. We will briefly examine these sectors before we look at the big picture of the interwar economy.

First, however, we need to examine changes in the interwar American population and labor force.

POPULATION GROWTH

The growth rate of the American population, which had been declining since the end of the Revolutionary War, continued to decline during the twenties and thirties. As can be seen in Figure 2.3, from an annual rate of increase of 1.85 and 1.93 percent in 1920 and 1921, respectively, population growth rates fell to 1.23 percent in 1928 and 1.04 percent in 1929. The 1930s saw a dramatic decline in the growth rate of the American population: between 0.6 and 0.8 per year from 1931 through 1940.

These changes in the overall growth rate were linked to the birth and death rates of the resident population and a decrease in foreign immigration. Though the crude death rate changed little during the period, the crude birth rate fell sharply into the early 1930s. (See Figure 2.4.) There are several explanations for the decline in the birth rate during this period. First, there was an accelerated rural-to-urban migration. Urban families have always had fewer children than rural families because urban children do not

Fig. 2.3 The Level and Rate of Growth of the United States' Resident Population

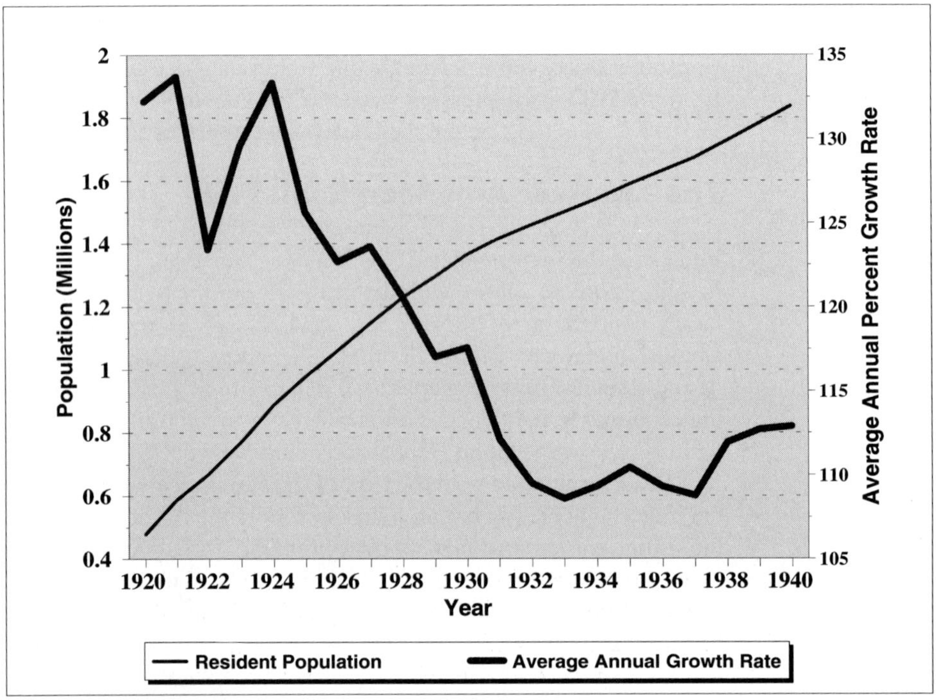

Source: *Historical Statistics of the United States: Colonial Times to 1970* (Washington, D.C.: U.S. Government Printing Office, 1976).

augment family incomes as rural children do. Second, the period also saw continued improvement in women's job opportunities and rise in their labor force participation rates. Third, with the depression of the thirties, individuals waited longer before marrying and had fewer children. Divorces rose as families were torn apart due to the dismal prospects brought on by the depression.

Immigration also fell sharply. In 1917 the federal government finally began to limit immigration and in 1921 an immigration act limited the number of prospective citizens of any nationality entering the United States each year to no more than 3 percent of that nationality's resident population as of the 1910 census. A new act in 1924 lowered this to 2 percent of the resident population at the 1890 census and more firmly blocked entry for people from central, southern, and eastern European nations. Though the limits were relaxed slightly in 1929, the depression and sluggish recovery in the 1930s slowed immigration to a mere trickle.

The American population continued to move during the interwar period. Table 2.1 shows regional population shares and shifts from 1920 to 1940. Two regions experienced the largest losses in population shares, New England and the Plains. For New England this was a continuation of a long-term trend. The population share for the

Fig. 2.4 Immigration Into the United States and Crude Birth and Death Rates for the Resident Population

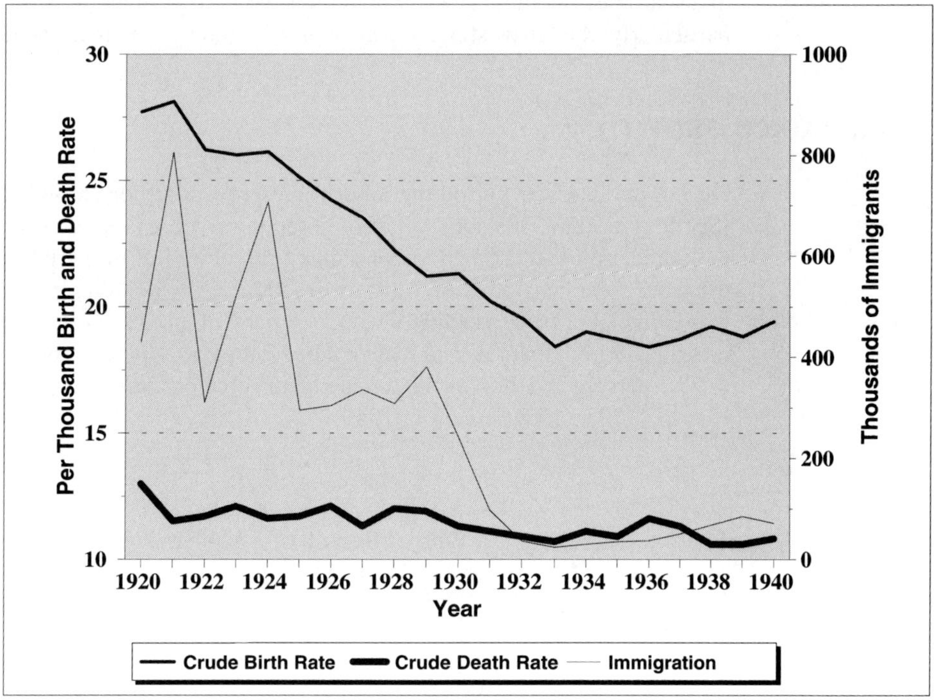

Source: *Historical Statistics of the United States: Colonial Times to 1970* (Washington, D.C.: U.S. Government Printing Office, 1976).

Table 2.1 Regional Population Shares and Shifts, 1920–1940.

Region	1920	1930	1940	Change 1920–1940
New England	7.0%	6.7%	6.4%	−0.6
Middle Atlantic	23.1	23.3	23.0	−0.1
Great Lakes	20.3	20.6	20.2	−0.1
Southeast	23.0	22.2	22.9	−0.1
Plains	11.9	10.8	10.3	−1.6
Southwest	7.0	7.4	7.4	+0.4
Mountain	2.4	2.2	2.2	−0.2
Far West	5.3	6.8	7.5	+2.2

New England: ME, NH, VT, MA, RI, CT. Middle Atlantic: NY, NJ, PA, DL, MD, DC. Great Lakes: OH, IN, IL, MI, WI. Southeast: VA, WV, KY, TN, NC SC, GA, FL, AL, MS, AK, LA. Plains: MN, IA, MO, ND, SD, NE, KS. Southwest: OK, TX, AZ, NM. Mountain: MT, ID, WY, UT, CO. Far West: WA, OR, CA, NV.

Source: Harvey S. Perloff, Edgar S. Dunn, Jr., Eric E. Lampard, and Richard F. Muth, *Regions, Resources and Economic Growth* (Lincoln: University of Nebraska Press, 1960), Table 1, p. 12.

Plains region had been rising through the nineteenth century. In the interwar period its agricultural base, combined with the continuing shift from agriculture to industry, led to a sharp decline in its share. The regions gaining population were the southwest and, particularly, the far west. California began its rapid growth at this time.

LABOR FORCE GROWTH

During the interwar period the labor force grew at a more rapid rate than population. (See Figure 2.5.) This somewhat more rapid growth came from the declining share of the population less than 14 years old and therefore not in the labor force. In contrast, the labor force participation rates, or fraction of the population aged 14 and over that was in the labor force, declined from 54.3 percent in 1920 to 52.4 percent in 1940. This was due entirely to a fall in the male labor force participation rate (84.6 percent in 1920 to 79.1 percent in 1940) as the female labor force participation rate rose from 22.7 percent in 1920 to 25.8 percent in 1940.

Fig. 2.5 The Level and Rate of Growth of the American Labor Force

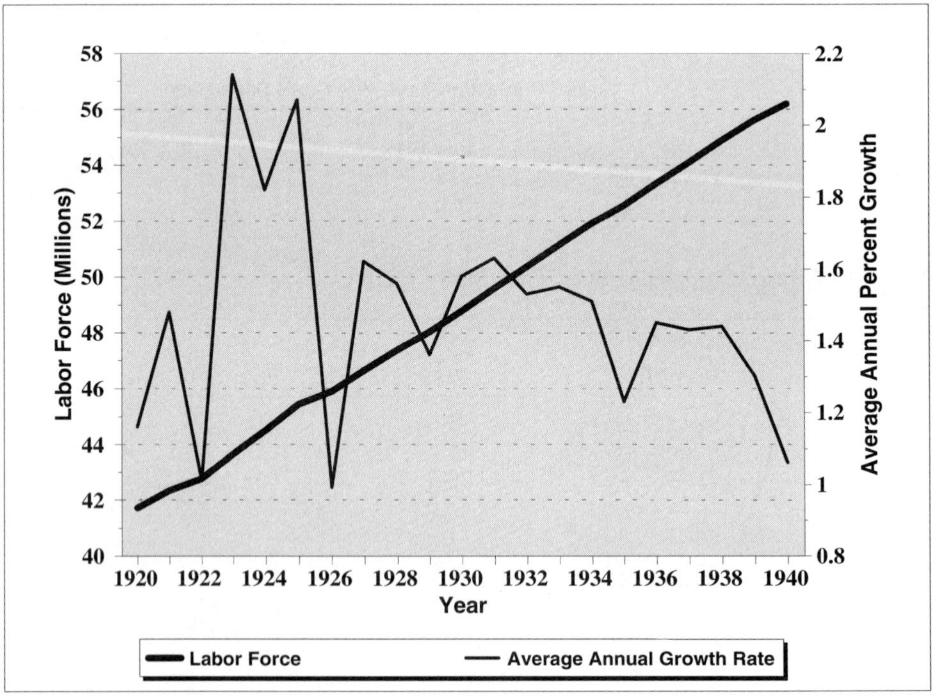

Source: *Historical Statistics of the United States: Colonial Times to 1970* (Washington, D.C.: U.S. Government Printing Office, 1976).

Earnings for laborers varied considerably during the interwar period. Figures 2.6 and 2.7 present relative average annual earnings for nine broad sectors, which are shown as a percentage of the mean average annual earnings for the nine sectors. The annual earnings reflect variations in both pay and hours worked. As can be seen annual earnings for workers in manufacturing, mining, and construction fell sharply during the Great Depression. Other workers—especially those in communications, public utilities, and government—saw their relative earnings rise during the depression.

Figure 2.8 presents average weekly earnings for 25 manufacturing industries. For these industries male skilled and semi-skilled laborers generally commanded a premium of 35 percent over the earnings of unskilled male laborers during the twenties. Unskilled males received on average 35 percent more than females during the twenties. Between 1934 and 1940, the differential between male unskilled laborers and male skilled and semiskilled laborers remained at 35 percent, while the differential between male unskilled laborers and female laborers declined to 28 percent. These earnings increased sharply after 1933 and this is at least partly due to the post-1933 success of labor unions at organizing industrial workers.

Fig. 2.6 Annual Earnings for Selected Sectors as a Percent of Mean Annual Earnings for Nine Sectors

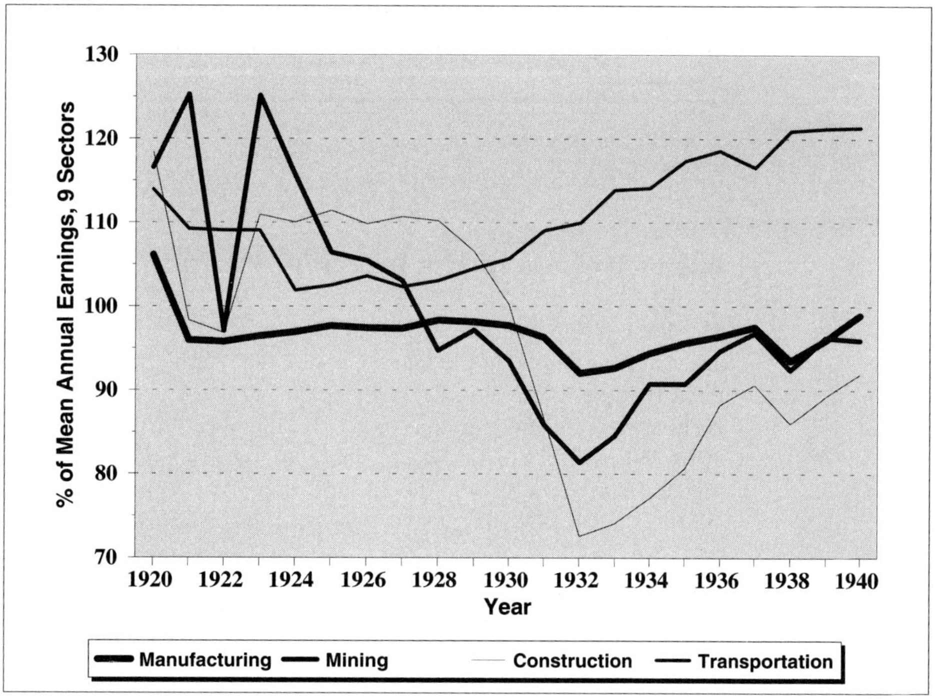

Source: *Historical Statistics of the United States: Colonial Times to 1970* (Washington, D.C.: U.S. Government Printing Office, 1976).

Fig. 2.7 Annual Earnings for Selected Sectors as a Percent of Mean Annual Earnings for Nine Sectors

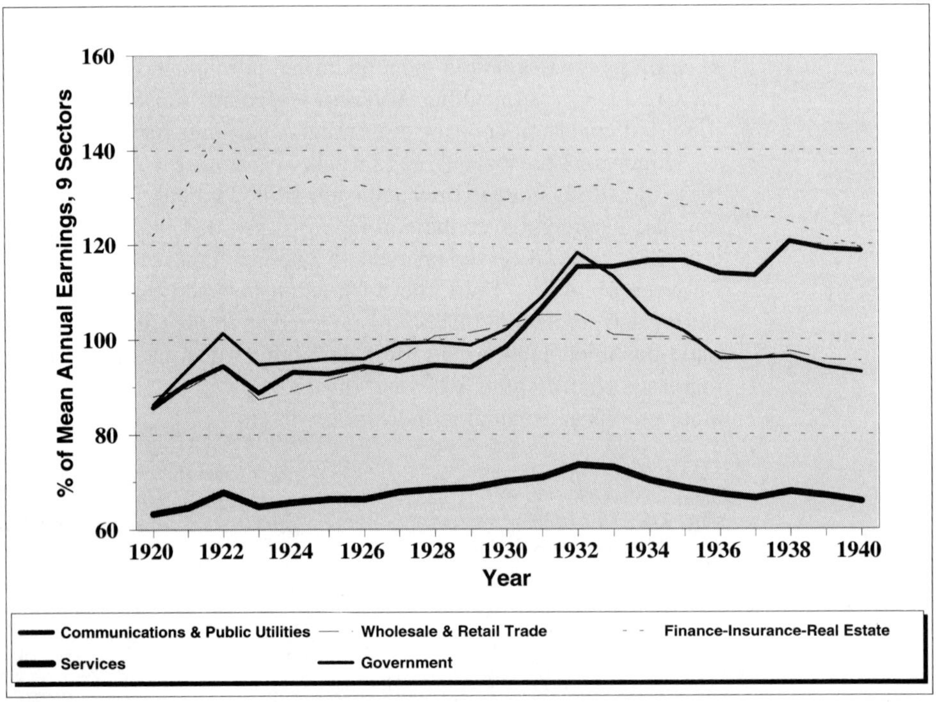

Source: *Historical Statistics of the United States: Colonial Times to 1970* (Washington, D.C.: U.S. Government Printing Office, 1976).

Labor Unions in the Interwar Period

The First World War solidified the dominance of the American Federation of Labor among labor unions in the United States. The rapid growth in union membership fostered by federal government policies during the war ended in 1919. A committee of AFL craft unions undertook a successful membership drive in the steel industry during 1919. When U.S. Steel refused to bargain, the committee called a strike, the failure of which was a sharp blow to the unionization drive.[19] In the same year, the United Mine Workers undertook a large strike and also lost. These two lost strikes and the 1920–21 depression took the impetus out of the union movement and led to severe membership losses that continued through the twenties. (See Figure 2.9.)

Under Samuel Gompers's leadership, the AFL's "business unionism" had attempted to promote the union and collective bargaining as the sole answers to the workers' concerns with wages, hours, and working conditions. The AFL officially opposed any government actions that would have diminished worker attachment to unions by providing competing benefits.[20] As Lloyd Ulman points out, the AFL, under Gompers's

Fig. 2.8 Real Average Weekly Earnings for Production Workers in 25 Manufacturing Industries

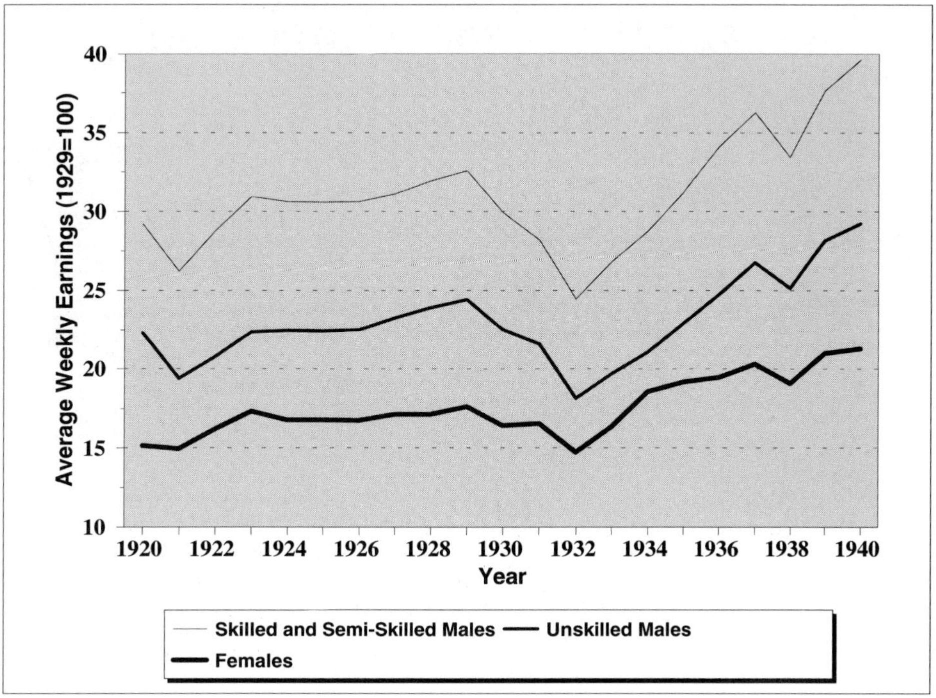

Source: *Historical Statistics of the United States: Colonial Times to 1970* (Washington, D.C.: U.S. Government Printing Office, 1976).

direction, differentiated on the basis of whether the statute would or would not aid collective bargaining.[21] After Gompers's death, William Green led the AFL in a policy change as the AFL promoted the idea of union-management cooperation to improve output and promote greater employer acceptance of unions. But Irving Bernstein concludes that, on the whole, union-management cooperation in the twenties was a failure.[22]

To combat the appeal of unions in the twenties, firms used the "yellow-dog" contract requiring employees to swear they were not union members and would not join one; the "American Plan" promoting the open shop and contending that the closed shop was un-American; and welfare capitalism. The most common feature of welfare capitalism was the creation of a management-controlled company union; other aspects included personnel management to handle employment issues and problems, the doctrine of "high wages," company group life insurance, old-age pension plans, stock-purchase plans, and more.

Until the late thirties the AFL was essentially a voluntary association of independent national craft unions. It had been created on two principles: the autonomy of the national unions and the exclusive jurisdiction of the national union.[23] Individual union

Fig. 2.9 Union Membership

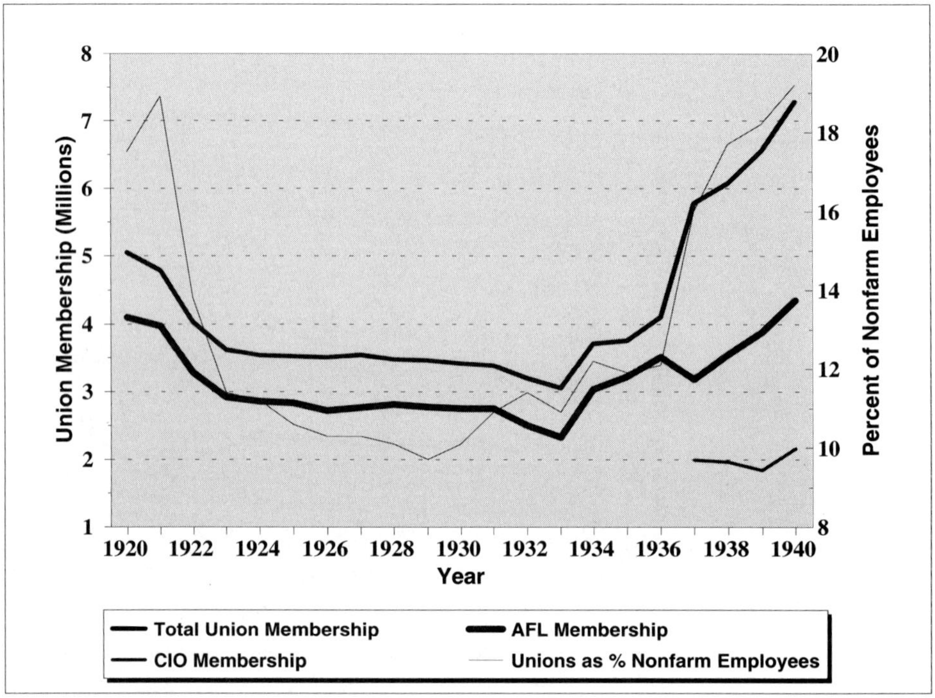

Source: *Historical Statistics of the United States: Colonial Times to 1970* (Washington, D.C.: U.S. Government Printing Office, 1976).

members were not, in fact, members of the AFL; rather, they were members of the local and national union, and the national was a member of the AFL. Representation in the AFL gave dominance to the national unions, and, as a result, the AFL had little effective power over them. The craft lines, however, had never been distinct and increasingly became blurred. The AFL was constantly mediating jurisdictional disputes between member national unions.

The 1933 passage of the National Industrial Recovery Act (NIRA) made the promotion of unionism a federal government policy, and the legions of unskilled and semiskilled workers in American industry were the target. John L. Lewis and the leaders of the essentially industrial unions in the AFL wanted to move quickly. Lewis, in particular, expanded the United Mine Workers (UMW) membership dramatically, as did David Dubinsky with the International Ladies Garment Workers Union (ILGWU) and Sidney Hillman with the Amalgamated Clothing Workers Union (ACWU).[24]

At the AFL convention in October of 1933, a resolution was offered to prevent the inclusion in the AFL of any Federal Labor Union[25] that included members over whom a member national craft union might have jurisdiction. Without much AFL support and in the face of company unions and violent, largely unsuccessful strikes, by 1935 the Federals in rubber, textiles, and automobiles had largely withered away.

Section 7a of the NIRA had been largely unsuccessful in promoting unionization. New York's Senator Wagner authored a National Labor Relations Bill that became law on July 5, 1935. The National Labor Relations Act, or Wagner Act, has been called labor's Magna Carta because it established labor's right to organize freely and engage in collective bargaining and abridged employers' right to resist unionism. This was largely accomplished by outlawing company unions, outlawing employer discrimination against union members, and requiring firms to bargain collectively with unions. The act provided a mechanism for employees to elect their bargaining agent and established the National Labor Relations Board (NLRB) to hear and decide on unfair labor practices, determine the collective bargaining unit, and conduct elections. Though employers continued to sharply resist union organization, the battle was now fought on dramatically different terms. The NLRB had legal powers.

Because of the AFL's continued reluctance to organize workers in unorganized industries, John L. Lewis and the leaders of several other minority industrial unions in the AFL formed a Committee for Industrial Organization (CIO) following the November 1935 AFL convention. Because this was considered "dual unionism," the AFL expelled the CIO unions in November of 1937. They then formed a rival federation, the Congress of Industrial Organizations.

In 1936 the new CIO moved aggressively to organize under the Wagner Act. Financed largely by the UMW, and, to a lesser extent, the ACWU and ILGWU, the CIO's drive led to success in 1937 in organizing GM, Chrysler, U.S. Steel, and other, smaller steel companies. U.S. Steel, the very epitome of antiunion sentiment and activity in previous decades, capitulated in March of 1937 without a strike. In the automobile industry the United Automobile Workers (UAW) concentrated on GM, which was larger and not as aggressively antiunion as Ford. At GM the sit-down strike, later to be ruled unlawful, emerged as a major and powerful union tactic. Once GM signed on February 11, 1937, Hudson, Packard, Studebaker, and Chrysler quickly signed agreements. The CIO also undertook successful organizing drives among dock workers, the rubber firms, electrical manufacturers, textile firms, and the sawmill industry.

However, neither Ford nor "Little Steel" (composed of Bethlehem, Republic, Youngstown Sheet and Tube, Inland, National (or Weirton), and ARMCO) signed agreements in 1937 or 1938. Little Steel developed a strategy to fight unionization where they granted the same wages and hours as U.S. Steel did in its agreement: 10 cents an hour increase to 62.5 cents per hour and time and a half after 8 hours a day or 40 hours a week. They then used a combination of propaganda, public relations, and force in successfully fighting off unionization. With Little Steel paying the same wages and having the same hours as U.S. Steel, some of the organizing momentum was lost. Strikes against firms in the declining economy of the last half of 1937 failed.

Having failed in 1937 at organizing Little Steel and Ford through membership drives and strikes, the Steel Workers' Organizing Committee (SWOC) and the UAW brought charges of unfair labor practices by these firms before the NLRB, which in 1938 and 1939 found the firms guilty. The firms' appeals delayed the final rulings until mid-1941. In 1941 and 1942 the SWOC undertook the last steel organizing drives and finally unionized Little Steel. With Ford employees overwhelming choosing the UAW affliated with the CIO in 1941, Ford entered into bargaining. In 12 days the negotiations were over, and Ford had yielded far more to the UAW than even GM or Chrsyler had.

With the capitulation of Little Steel and Ford, the great union organizing drives of the late thirties ended.

SELECTED REFERENCES

Anderson, Benjamin M. *Economics and the Public Welfare: A Financial and Economic History of the United States, 1914–1946.* Indianapolis: Liberty Press, 1979 reprint of 1949 edition.

Bernstein, Irving. *The Lean Years: A History of the American Worker, 1920–1933.* Boston: Houghton Mifflin Co., 1960.

__________. *The Turbulent Years: A History of the American Worker, 1933–1941.* Boston: Houghton Mifflin Co., 1970.

Brody, David. *Labor in Crisis: The Steel Strike.* Philadelphia: J. B. Lippincott Co., 1965.

Brunner, Karl, ed. *The Great Depression Revisited.* Boston: Martinus Nijhoff Publishing, 1981.

Chandler, Alfred D., Jr. *Giant Enterprise: Ford, General Motors, and the Automobile Industry.* New York: Harcourt, Brace, and World, Inc., 1964.

Chandler, Lester V. *America's Greatest Depression, 1929–1941.* New York: Harper and Row, 1970.

Darby, Michael. "Three-and-a-Half Million U.S. Employees Have Been Mislaid: Or, and Explanation of Unemployment, 1934–1941." *Journal of Political Economy*, Vol. 84 (February 1976), pp. 1–16.

Fearon, Peter. *War, Prosperity & Depression: The U.S. Economy, 1917–1945.* Lawrence, KS: The University of Kansas Press, 1987.

Mitchell, Broadhus. *Depression Decade: From New Era Through New Deal, 1929–1941.* New York: Holt, Rinehart, and Winston, 1947.

Shannon, David A., ed. *The Great Depression.* Englewood Cliffs, NJ: Prentice-Hall, 1960.

Soule, George. *Prosperity Decade: From War to Depression, 1917–1929.* New York: Holt, Rinehart, and Winston, 1947.

Ulman, Lloyd. *The Rise of the National Trade Union.* Cambridge, MA: Harvard University Press, 1955.

__________. "The Development of Trades and Labor Unions." *American Economic History.* Edited by Seymour E. Harris. New York: McGraw-Hill, 1961.

Vatter, Harold. "Has There Been a Twentieth-Century Consumer Durables Revolution?" *The Journal of Economic History*, 27 (March 1967): 1–16.

Weinstein, Michael. *Recovery and Redistribution Under the NIRA.* Amsterdam: North Holland Publishing Co., 1980.

NOTES

1. George Soule, *Prosperity Decade: From War to Depression, 1917–1929* (New York: Holt, Rinehart, and Winston, 1947).
2. Broadhus Mitchell, *Depression Decade: From New Era Through New Deal, 1929–1941* (New York: Rinehart and Co., 1947).

3. Lester V. Chandler, *America's Greatest Depression, 1929–1941* (New York: Harper and Row, 1970), chapter 3.
4. Michael Darby has argued that this overstates the "correct" unemployment rate because these figures count as unemployed all those who were employed on federal work-relief projects. Using figures revised to exclude those employed on such projects, Darby found that unemployment would have declined to 5 percent in 1938 if the 1937–38 depression had not occurred. Michael Darby, "Three-and-a-Half Million U.S. Employees Have Been Mislaid: Or, an Explanation of Unemployment, 1934–1941," *Journal of Political Economy,* 84 (February 1976): 1–16.
5. W. W. Rostow, *The Stages of Economic Growth: A Non-Communist Manifesto* (New York: Cambridge University Press, 1965), chapter 6.
6. Harold Vatter, "Has There Been a Twentieth-Century Consumer Durables Revolution?" *The Journal of Economic History*, 27 (March 1967): 1–16.
7. Ibid., 8–11.
8. Alfred D. Chandler, Jr., ed., *Giant Enterprise: Ford, General Motors, and the Automobile Industry* (New York: Harcourt, Brace, and World, Inc., 1964), 3.
9. Chandler, *America's Greatest Depression,* 44.
10. David A. Shannon, ed., *The Great Depression* (Englewood Cliffs, NJ: Prentice-Hall, 1960), chapter 9. The quotation is from page 14.
11. Ibid., chapters 27–31.
12. Ibid., chapters 6–7.
13. Ibid., chapter 13.
14. Ibid., 124.
15. For a flavor of this discontent, see Shannon, *The Great Depression*, chapters 43–50.
16. Chandler, *America's Greatest Depression,* 133.
17. Michael Weinstein, "Some Macroeconomic Impacts of the National Industrial Recovery Act, 1933–1935," in Karl Brunner, ed., *The Great Depression Revisited* (Boston: Martinus Nijhoff Publishing, 1981), 262–81. See also Michael Weinstein, *Recovery and Redistribution Under the NIRA* (Amsterdam: North Holland Publishing Co., 1980).
18. Benjamin M. Anderson, *Economics and the Public Welfare: A Financial and Economic History of the United States, 1914–1946* (Indianapolis: Liberty Press, 1979 reprint of 1949 edition), 430–31.
19. David Brody, *Labor in Crisis: The Steel Strike* (Philadelphia: J. B. Lippincott Co., 1965).
20. Competing government benefits included government-sponsored unemployment insurance, minimum wage proposals, maximum hours proposals, and social security programs.
21. Lloyd Ulman, "The Development of Trades and Labor Unions," chapter 14 in Seymour E. Harris, ed., *American Economic History* (New York: McGraw-Hill Book Co., 1961). See also Lloyd Ulman, *The Rise of the National Trade Union* (Cambridge, MA: Harvard University Press, 1955).
22. Irving Bernstein, *The Lean Years: A History of the American Worker, 1920–1933* (Boston: Houghton Mifflin Co., 1960).
23. Ulman, "The Development of Trades and Labor Unions."
24. See Irving Bernstein, *The Turbulent Years: A History of the American Worker, 1933–1941* (Boston: Houghton Mifflin, 1970), particularly chapter 8. Most of the following discussion of unions in the thirties draws upon Bernstein's detailed history.
25. The Federal Labor Union was the chief method of bringing in unorganized workers in new industries. It was attached directly to the AFL. Once the workers were organized, the process of deciding which workers were to belong to which member national craft union

could take place, and the Federal Labor Union would be dismantled. Craft unions were not anxious to pursue this strategy because skill classifications were ambiguous, and this threatened to dilute the membership of the unions, weakening their bargaining power.

CHAPTER 3

Developments in Agriculture and Manufacturing, 1920–1940

AGRICULTURE

The onset of the First World War in Europe brought unprecedented prosperity to American farmers. As agricultural production in Europe declined, the demand for American agricultural exports rose, leading to rising farm product prices and incomes. In response to this, American farmers expanded production by moving onto marginal farmland, such as Wisconsin cutover property on the edge of the woods and hilly terrain in the Ozark and Appalachian regions. They also increased output by purchasing more machinery, such as tractors, plows, mowers, and threshers. The price of farmland, particularly marginal farmland, rose in response to the increased demand, and the debt of American farmers increased substantially.

This expansion of American agriculture continued past the end of the First World War as farm exports to Europe and farm prices initially remained high. However, agriculture production in Europe recovered much faster than most observers had anticipated. Even before the onset of a short depression in 1920, farm exports and farm product prices had begun to fall. During the depression, farm prices virtually collapsed. From 1920 to 1921, the consumer price index fell 11.3 percent, the wholesale price index fell 45.9 percent, and the farm products price index fell 53.3 percent.[1]

Average net income per farm fell over 83 percent in current dollars and, though rising in the twenties, never recovered the relative levels of 1919 and 1920. Farm mortgage foreclosures rose and stayed at historically high levels for the entire decade of the 1920s. As Figure 3.1 shows, the value of farmland and buildings fell throughout the twenties and, for the first time in American history, the number of cultivated acres actually declined as farmers pulled back from the marginal farmland brought into production during the war. Rather than indicators of a general depression in agriculture in the twenties, these were the results of the financial commitments made by overoptimistic American farmers during and directly after the war. The foreclosures were generally on second mortgages rather than on first mortgages as in the early 1930s.[2]

The onset of the Great Depression in 1929 plunged American agriculture into a severe depression. The prices of some farm products had weakened in 1928 and 1929, and this had provided the impetus for the Hawley-Smoot Tariff of early 1930. The combination of the domestic depression and contracting world trade sharply decreased farm exports, and farm product prices plummeted, as the parity price ratio fell from 92 in 1929 to 67 in 1931. The average value per acre of farmland and buildings fell from $49.25 in 1929 to $29.28 in 1933, and gross and net farm income fell 54 and 66.8 percent from 1929 to 1932, respectively. Average net income per farm fell from $945 in 1929 to $304 in 1932. Farm mortgage foreclosures, which had been historically high at 14.7 per thousand in 1929, rose to an astounding 38.8 per thousand in 1933. (See Figures 3.1 to 3.3.)

Many farmers fiercely protested the depressed prices and the mortgage foreclosure crisis. Milk was dumped into the streets rather than sold at the prevailing low prices, and "holidays," or strikes, during which no agricultural products were to be brought to market and sold, were declared. As the depression continued, more and more farmers became delinquent on their mortgages, and the number of foreclosures soared.

Fig. 3.1 The Average Value per Acre of Farmland and Buildings and the Realized Gross Farm Parity Ratios

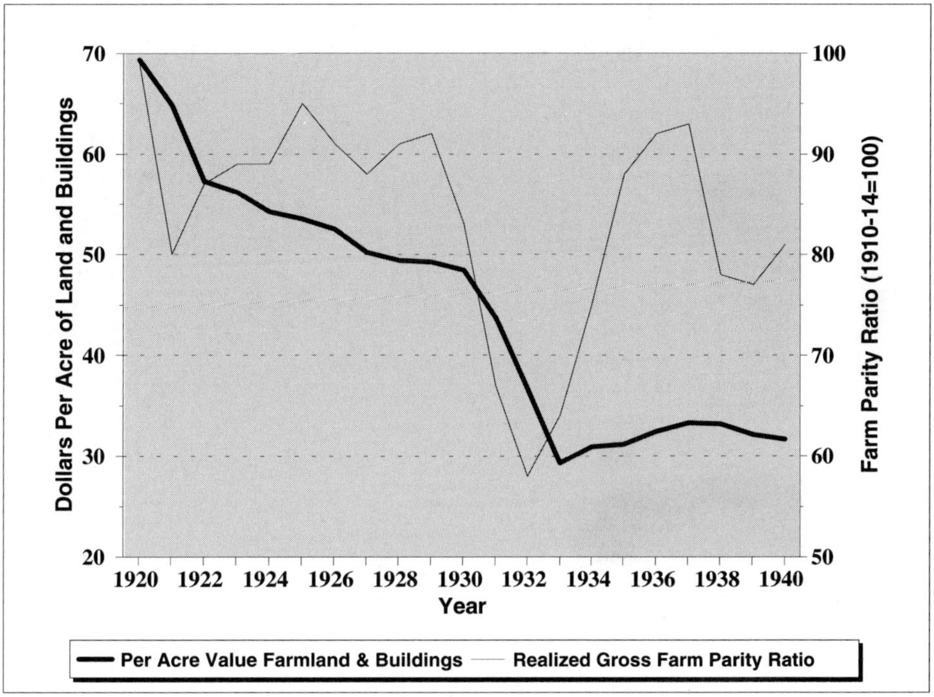

Source: *Historical Statistics of the United States: Colonial Times to 1970* (Washington, D.C.: U.S. Government Printing Office, 1976).

Sporadic incidents of violence began to accompany the foreclosure sales in late 1932 and 1933, and farmers stopped a few sales.[3]

The economic distress in the farming sector led 25 states to enact farm foreclosure moratoria between 1932 and 1934.[4] The constitutionality of this legislation was upheld by the Supreme Court in 1934 when it ruled in favor of the Minnesota statute.[5] Lee Alston's research indicates that this assistance came at the expense of the creditors (who were prohibited from foreclosing) as well as prospective borrowers. Private lenders reacted to the moratoria by rationing mortgage loans through a tightening of eligibility requirements and by raising mortgage interest rates more in states where moratoria had been enacted.[6]

The federal government soon developed more direct ways to alleviate the farmers' distress. The Roosevelt administration's first step in 1933 was to attempt to reduce the supply of some agricultural products through the "plow-up" and "kill" campaigns.[7] Over 6,000,000 pigs and 220,000 soon-to-farrow sows were destroyed to reduce the potential oversupply of pork.[8] About one quarter of the cotton crop, or 10,000,000

Fig. 3.2 The Average Net Income per Farm and the Ratio of Farm to Nonfarm Incomes

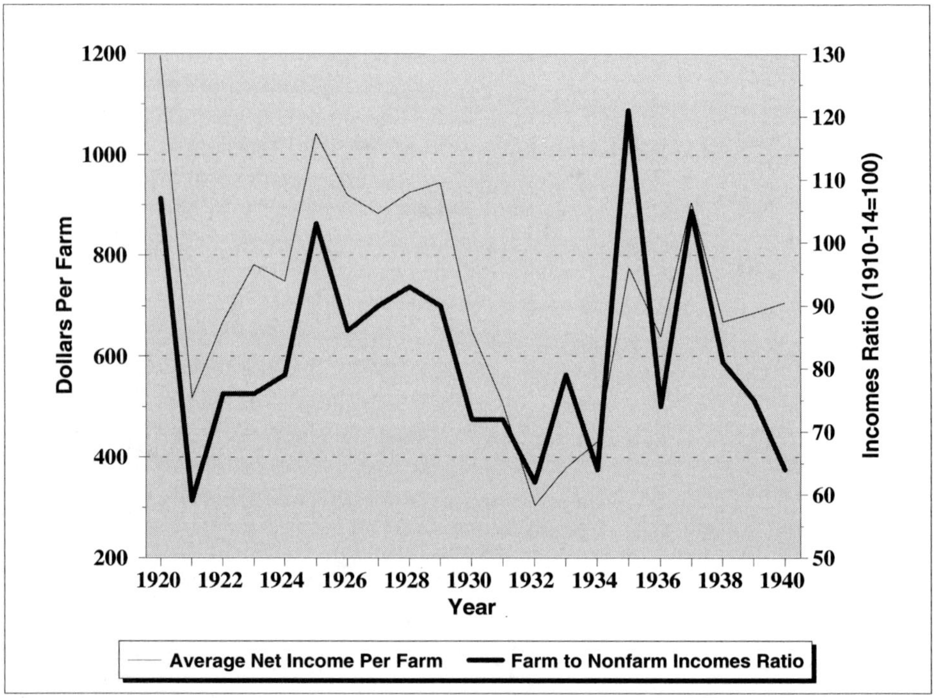

Source: *Historical Statistics of the United States: Colonial Times to 1970* (Washington, D.C.: U.S. Government Printing Office, 1976), and H. Thomas Johnson, "Postwar Optimism and the Rural Financial Crisis of the 1920's," *Explorations in Economic History*, 11 (Winter 1973–74): 173–192.

acres, were plowed under, as were 12,000 acres of tobacco. In California the growers were paid to let cling peaches rot in the orchard.[9] Two Agricultural Adjustment Acts attempted to raise prices by limiting production and imposing price supports, though the severe droughts of 1934 and 1936 probably had more effect in temporarily raising prices.[10]

A Declining Sector

A major difficulty in analyzing the interwar agricultural sector lies in separating the effects of the 1920–21 and 1929–33 depressions from those that arose because agriculture was in decline overall. Economic growth as a whole plus rising productivity in farming required a shift of resources, particularly labor, out of agriculture. The market induces labor to voluntarily move from one sector to another through income differentials, suggesting that even in the absence of the effects of the depressions, farm incomes would have been lower than nonfarm incomes so as to bring about this migration.

Fig. 3.3 Farm Mortgage Foreclosure Rates

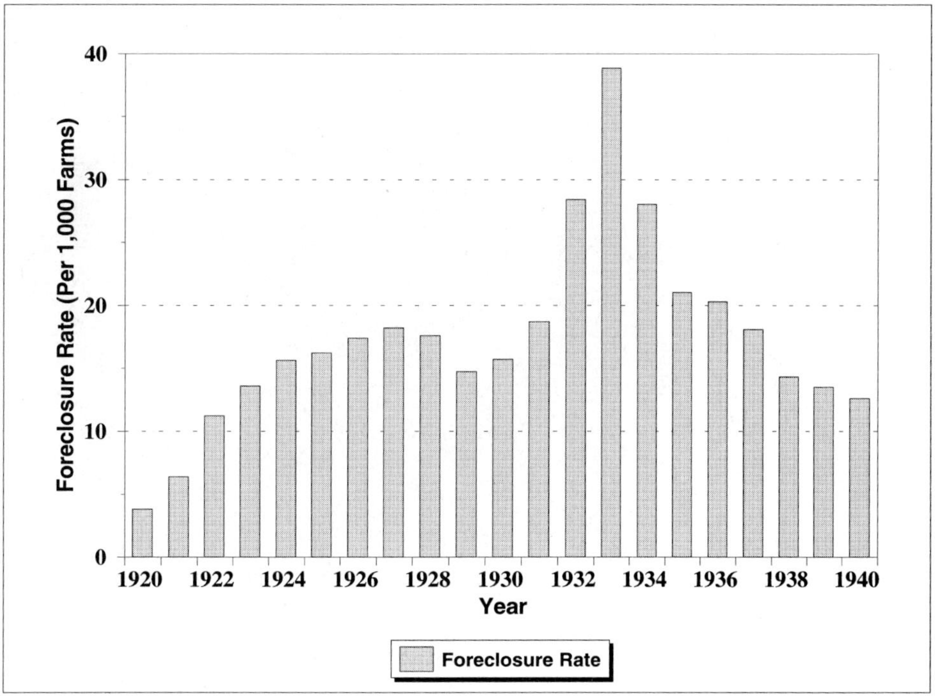

Source: Lee J. Alston "Farm Foreclosures in the United States During the Interwar Period," *The Journal of Economic History,* 43 (December 1983): 885–904.

Farm employment fell throughout the interwar period—especially after 1935. There was little change in the number of farms during the 1920s but as people moved back to the farms during the depression, the number of farms increased. After 1936 the number of farms once again began to fall. The average farm size was roughly constant from 1919 through 1926 at about 144 to 145 acres. In 1927 farm sizes began to increase; by 1940 the average farm had grown to 174 acres. (See Figure 3.4.)

The continuous substitution of tractor power for horse and mule power released hay and oats acreage to grow crops for human consumption. Though cotton and tobacco continued as the primary crops in the south, the relative production of cotton continued to shift to the west as production in Arkansas, Missouri, Oklahoma, Texas, New Mexico, Arizona, and California increased. As quotas reduced immigration and incomes rose, the demand for cereal grains declined, and the demand for fruits, vegetables, and dairy products grew. Refrigeration and faster freight shipments expanded the milk sheds further from metropolitan areas. Wisconsin and other North Central states began to ship cream and cheeses to the Atlantic Coast. Due to transportation improvements, specialized truck farms and the citrus industry became more important in California and Florida.[11]

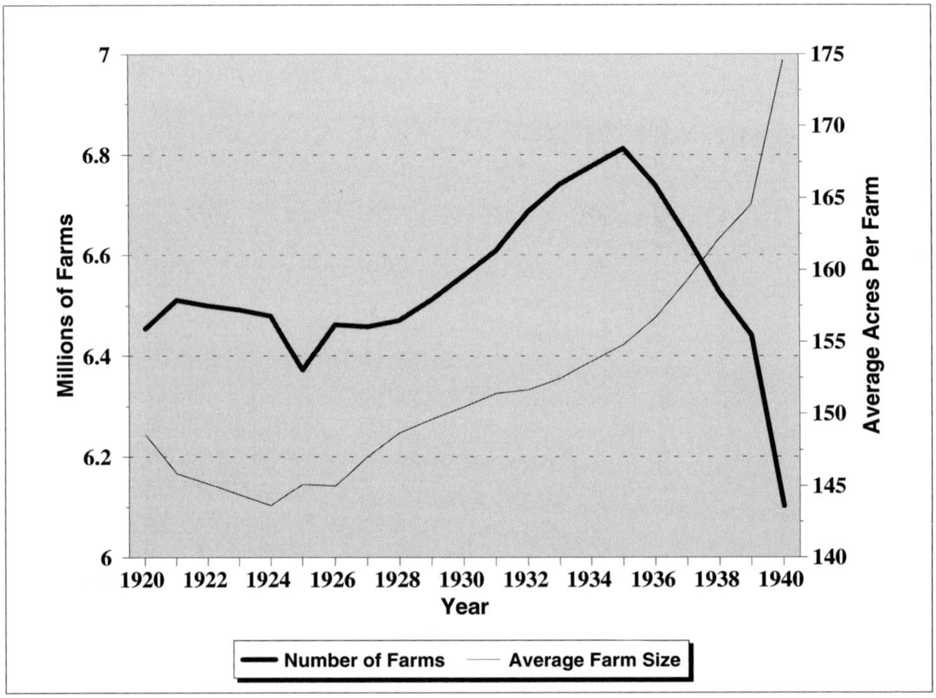

The decline of the agricultural sector in the interwar period was closely related to the highly inelastic income elasticity of demand for many farm products, particularly cereal grains, pork, and cotton. As incomes grew, the demand for these staples grew much more slowly. At the same time, rising land and labor productivity was increasing the supplies of staples, causing real prices to fall.

Table 3.1 presents selected agricultural productivity statistics for these years. Those data indicate that there were greater gains in labor productivity than in land productivity (or per acre yields). Per acre yields in wheat and hay actually decreased between 1915–19 and 1935–39. These productivity increases, which released resources from the agricultural sector, were the result of technological improvements in agriculture.

Technological Improvements in Agricultural Production

In many ways the adoption of the tractor in the interwar period symbolizes the technological changes that occurred in the agricultural sector. This changeover in the power source that farmers used had far-reaching consequences and altered the organization of the farm and the farmers' lifestyle. The adoption of the tractor was land saving (by

Table 3.1 Selected Agricultural Productivity Statistics, 1915–1939. (Annual Averages)

	Labor-Hours Per Unit							Per Acre Yield			
Period	Wheat 100 (Bush.) (1)	Corn 100 (Bush.) (2)	Cotton (Bales) (3)	Hay (Tons) (4)	Milk (Cwt) (5)	Beef (Cwt) (6)	Hogs (Cwt) (7)	Wheat (Bush.) (8)	Corn (Bush.) (9)	Cotton (Lbs.) (10)	Hay (Tons) (11)
1915-19	98	132	299	10.4	3.7	4.5	3.6	13.9	25.9	168	1.25
1920-24	90	122	296	10.2	3.6	4.5	3.5	13.8	26.8	155	1.22
1925-29	74	115	268	9.8	3.3	4.3	3.3	14.1	26.3	171	1.22
1930-34	70	123	252	9.5	3.4	4.3	3.2	13.5	23.0	184	1.08
1935-39	67	108	209	9.1	3.4	4.2	3.2	13.2	26.1	226	1.24
Percent Change 1915-19 to 1935-39	−31.6	−18.2	−30.1	−12.5	−8.1	−6.7	−11.1	−5.0	0.8	34.5	−0.8

Source: *Historical Statistics of the United States: Colonial Times to 1970* (Washington: U.S. Government Printing Office, 1976).

releasing acreage previously used to produce crops for workstock) and labor saving. At the same time it increased the risks of farming because farmers were now much more exposed to the marketplace. They could not produce their own fuel for tractors as they had for the workstock. Rather, this had to be purchased from other suppliers. Repair and replacement parts also had to be purchased, and sometimes the repairs had to be undertaken by specialized mechanics. The purchase of a tractor also commonly required the purchase of new complementary machines; therefore, the decision to purchase a tractor was not an isolated one.[12]

The gasoline-powered tractor had been improving since its introduction in 1892. Generally the improvements involved making it lighter, more powerful, and more dependable through replaceable parts, higher grade steel, ball and roller bearings and many other changes. These also reduced the need for frequent routine maintenance. The introduction of the two-cylinder engine made the large, heavy flywheel less important, but it remained on tractors because it provided a source of versatile belt power for washing machines, grinding mills, power saws, water pumps, and so on.

The first small tractor, the Fordson, appeared in 1917. In 1922 International Harvester introduced a row-crop tractor with small tricycle front wheels and width-adjustable rear wheels so that tractors could plant, cultivate, and harvest row crops such as corn. It also pioneered the power takeoff that allowed implements to operate at constant speeds independently of the speed at which the tractor and implement were moving. Power was transferred from the tractor engine to the implement through drive shafts with universal joints. In 1929 Allis-Chalmers introduced a rubber-tire tractor. The rubber tires with large raised cleats dug flexibly into the earth, giving better traction and pulling power and allowing it to travel on surfaced roads, something that tractors with spade lug metal tires could not do. Rubber-tired tractors were more comfortable, faster, decreased fuel consumption by 10 to 20 percent, and reduced repair costs.

These changes resulted in more and more farmers purchasing and using tractors, but the rate of adoption varied sharply across the United States. By 1940, 50 to 60 percent of the farms in the North Central states had tractors. Adoption was slower in California, where in 1939 only 33 percent of the farms used tractors, and much slower in the south.[13] This relatively slow adoption rate seems puzzling because studies showed that farming costs were lower with tractors than horses or mules for most of the relevant farm sizes in the thirties.[14] However, there were some rational reasons why farmers were reluctant to adopt a tractor-based technology.

The costs associated with the tractor involved cash outlays, whereas much of the costs associated with horses and mules were opportunity costs not involving cash. During the depression, many farmers reduced their risks by sticking with horses and mules whose fuel they could provide.[15] As mentioned, the change to tractor power involved a considerable increase in the commercialization of the farm. In the south many farms were too small to utilize a tractor.[16] The smaller size of farms and lag in mechanization in the south reflected the annual labor contract implicit in the sharecropping or share tenancy arrangement. Mechanization would have required consolidating the small tenant farms, and hiring labor, but with very thin labor markets and an extremely seasonal demand, plantation owners found it was much easier to establish yearly labor contracts through sharecropping arrangements.[17] There was a rapid resumption of tractor purchases beginning in 1934 as the New Deal programs reduced farmers' debt burdens and guaranteed production costs and crop prices, freeing farmers from the strategies of minimizing cash outlays for safety against price collapses and thereby making investment in the more efficient tractors more attractive.[18]

In the cornbelt the purchase of a tractor was also dependent on the development of hybrid seed corn and mechanical corn pickers.[19] In the late 1930s hybrid seed corn was perfected and began to be marketed by commercial seed companies. The rate of adoption of hybrid seed corn was determined by its profitability, so it was adopted most quickly by farmers in the corn belt where more corn was planted and the increase in production and profits was largest.[20] Though experiments dated back to the 1890s it took until the 1930s to create varieties that "stood straight on strong root systems and produced ears at a uniform height on strong shanks" and ripened more uniformly so that mechanical corn pickers could be used.[21]

The first practical pickers dated from the early 1900s, but the early machines were far from satisfactory and were used only by the very large farms. In the late 1920s and early 1930s two-row corn pickers were developed that operated off of the power take-off. The Great Depression slowed sales, but by 1937 sales of these mechanical corn pickers surpassed the sales figures of the late 1920s.[22]

The tractor, corn picker, and hybrid seed corn came together to raise labor and land productivity in corn production in the late 1930s. As Allan Bogue notes, "Not until the development of the general-purpose tractor with power take-off did an efficient mechanical picker become possible. That machine, however, was not cost efficient for some Corn Belt farmers until hybrid corn minimized the loss of grain experienced in mechanical picking."[23]

These changes in corn belt farming also brought on other changes. Because the tractor, mechanical corn picker, and hybrid seed corn were labor saving, they allowed an individual farmer to farm more land, and farm sizes began to increase to take advantage of this. In addition the use of "itinerant or local labor" during the picking season diminished sharply because of the mechanical picker's ability to pick all of the farmer's corn.[24]

These changes were, by no means, limited to corn production. Tractor development helped alter grain harvesting as the binder was improved and quickly was adapted to the power takeoff in the early 1920s. Milking machines first appeared in 1905 and continued to be developed and adopted during the interwar period. Estimates suggested that on dairy farms these machines saved an average of 28 hours of labor per cow per year.

Technological innovations in plants and animals also raised productivity. Hybrid seed corn increased yields from an average of 40 bushels per acre to 100 to 120 bushels per acre. New varieties of wheat were developed from the hardy Russian and Turkish wheat varieties which had been imported. The U.S. Department of Agriculture's Experiment Stations took the lead in developing wheat varieties for different regions. For example, in the Columbia River Basin new varieties raised yields from an average of 19.1 bushels per acre in 1913–22 to 23.1 bushels per acre in 1933–42.[25] New hog breeds produced more meat[26] and new methods of swine sanitation sharply increased the survival rate of piglets.[27]Artificial insemination of dairy cattle developed in the late 1930s, allowing bulls of proven ability to impregnate many more cows. This contributed to an average increase of nearly 14 percent in milk production per cow between 1937 and 1947.[28] An effective serum for hog cholera was developed,[29] and the federal government led the way in the testing and eradication of bovine tuberculosis and brucellosis. The development and use of sulfa drugs in the late 1930s helped control animal bacterial infections.[30] Prior to the Second World War, a number of pesticides to control animal disease were developed, including cattle dips and disinfectants. By the mid-1920s a vaccine for "blackleg," an infectious, usually fatal disease that particularly struck young cattle, was completed. The cattle tick, which carried Texas Fever, was largely controlled through inspections.[31]

These productivity developments began to come together in the late thirties. The increasing adoption of the tractor and other implements allowed farmers to farm increasingly larger farms, and farm employment began to fall more swiftly. The new hybrid varieties of seed corn, wheat, and other grains began raising yields more rapidly at the very end of the thirties. These changes were the initial results of a revolution in agricultural productivity that would come to fruition after the Second World War.

Federal Agricultural Programs in the Interwar Period

Though there was substantial agricultural discontent in the period from the Civil War to late 1890s, the period from then to the onset of the First World War was relatively free from overt farmers' complaints. In later years farmers dubbed the 1910–14 period as agriculture's "golden years" and used the prices of farm crops and farm inputs in that period as a standard by which to judge crop and input prices in later years. The problems which arose in the agricultural sector during the twenties once again led to insistent demands by farmers for government to alleviate their distress.

Though there were increasing calls for direct federal government intervention to limit production and raise farm prices, this was not used until Roosevelt took office. Rather, there was a reliance upon the traditional method to aid injured groups—tariffs, and upon the "sanctioning and promotion of cooperative marketing associations."[32] In 1921 Congress attempted to control the grain exchanges and compel merchants and stockyards to charge "reasonable rates," with the Packers and Stockyards Act and the Grain Futures Act. In 1922 Congress passed the Capper-Volstead Act to promote agricultural cooperatives and the Fordney-McCumber Tariff to impose high duties on most agricultural imports. The Cooperative Marketing Act of 1924 did not bolster failing cooperatives as it was supposed to do.[33]

Twice between 1924 and 1928 Congress passed "McNary-Haugan" bills, but President Calvin Coolidge vetoed both. The McNary-Haugan bills proposed to establish "fair" exchange values (based on the 1910–14 period) for each product and to maintain them through tariffs and a private corporation that would be chartered by the government and could buy enough of each commodity to keep its price up to the computed fair level.[34] The revenues were to come from taxes imposed on farmers. The Hoover administration passed the Hawley-Smoot tariff in 1930 and an Agricultural Marketing Act in 1929. This act committed the federal government to a policy of stabilizing farm prices through several nongovernment institutions but these failed during the depression.

Under Roosevelt's new Democratic administration, there was a change in the federal government's agricultural policies. The Agricultural Adjustment Act of 1933 was a resurrected form of the McNary-Haugan bills. Its purpose was to restore "parity prices" such as had existed in 1910–14. The AAA required the department of agriculture to determine the total acreage of major crops and then subdivide this into first state and then individual farm allotments on the basis of each farm's recent history. Farmers were paid to cut acreage through a "benefit payment" or an "adjustment payment"; the payments were financed by a processing tax imposed on the first processors of any product. In 1936 the AAA was declared unconstitutional because the processing tax was an attempt to regulate intrastate agricultural production, a power reserved for the states. Congress then passed the Soil Conservation and Domestic Allotment Act to replace it. This act changed the basis for making acreage allotments so that soil conservation was being encouraged. The act attempted to restore parity prices by reducing crop production rather than acreage, but 1937 production levels were still quite high.

In 1938 a new (or second) Agricultural Adjustment Act was passed. New acreage allotments were created while maintaining the Soil Conservation and Domestic Allotment Act. A Commodity Credit Corporation (CCC) had been established in 1933 to make nonrecourse loans on agricultural commodities. If the price of the commodity fell, the farmer let the CCC take title to the stored commodity, thus canceling the debt and the interest owed. If the price rose, the farmer sold the commodity, paid back the debt and interest, and kept the profit. The loan rate became, in effect, the minimum price. From 1933 to 1937 the CCC carried out its operations with only vague price objectives. The new AAA of 1938 increased the power of the CCC and made it mandatory that loans be extended on corn, wheat, and cotton at rates between 52 and 75 percent of parity. The AAA also established a Federal Crop Insurance Corporation, under which farmers were insured for an amount up to a specific percentage of their normal yield.

Marketing quotas became important after 1936. With these the secretary of agriculture was empowered to set upper limits on the quantities to be sold of certain crops. If the current supply of a basic commodity exceeded a "reserve supply," a referendum was held. If two thirds of the qualified producers approved, a quota was assigned to each grower, and farmers who marketed amounts in excess of the quota were subject to a penalty or a fine on the excess sold. After 1937 marketing agreements also became a part of the federal government's agricultural policies. They were implemented primarily in the production of fruits and vegetables and in the chief milk-producing areas. The marketing agreements were made between the producers and processors of the agricultural products, and the contractual agreement was refereed by a representative of the department of agriculture. The marketing agreement set minimum prices, total quantities to be marketed, and the allotments of marketings among producers.

In an effort to stimulate the demand for agricultural commodities in the late 1930s the federal government implemented a food stamp plan for low-income families, a school lunch program allowing public schools to purchase surplus food commodities at subsidized prices, and an export subsidy program.

The Results of Agricultural Programs. Generally these programs addressed the supply of agricultural commodities because not much could be done with demand. For most agricultural products the demand was both price and income inelastic. If the supply of wheat, corn, rye, cotton, and so on, could be reduced, the inelastic demand would cause the total revenues received by farmers to increase as the price increased. The problem had always been to get the farmers to cooperate in reducing output because each individual farmer had a strong incentive to expand production to take advantage of the higher price due to the reduced supply from other farmers. The programs used different methods in an attempt to achieve this. The AAA's approach was to use the Commodity Credit Corporation to guarantee farmers minimum prices as long as they reduced output. Marketing quotas forced farmers to market no more than their assigned quotas, whereas marketing agreements also required producers to limit production. The CCC and marketing agreements could accumulate inventories when necessary to implement the minimum prices.

The programs, however, were not effective. Surpluses began to accumulate at a startling rate, and if the Second World War had not intervened, the government would have had to face the programs' internal contradictions in the 1940s. As it was, these were only postponed to the 1950s.

The ultimate aim of the programs was to raise the incomes of the *existing number* of farmers up to a targeted level and reduce the variability of agricultural prices and farm incomes. If successful, the programs would have largely maintained the existing farm population. However, as we have seen, the long decline of the agricultural sector required a reallocation of resources out of agriculture. The federal agricultural programs were incompatible with these trends, especially as agricultural productivity gains began to accelerate at the end of the thirties.

MANUFACTURING

Agriculture was not the only sector experiencing difficulties in the interwar period. Other industries, such as textiles, boots and shoes, and coal mining, also experienced trying times, particularly in the twenties. However, at the same time that these industries were declining, other industries, such as electrical appliances, automobiles, and construction, were growing rapidly. With the crushing depression of the thirties, all of these sectors experienced varying degrees of contraction. The simultaneous existence of growing and declining industries has been common to all eras because economic growth and technological progress never affect all sectors in the same way. In general, in manufacturing there was a rapid rate of growth of productivity during the twenties, and, to a lesser extent, in the thirties. The rise of real wages due to immigration restrictions and the slower growth of the resident population spurred this. Transportation improvements and communications advances were also responsible. These developments brought about differential growth in the various manufacturing sectors in the interwar United States.

Manufacturing's Importance

Because of the historic pattern of economic development in the United States, the northeast was the first area to really develop a manufacturing base. In the late nineteenth century and twentieth century, the other regions began to create manufacturing bases, resulting in a relative westward and southern shift of manufacturing activity. As Table 3.2 shows, this trend continued in the 1920s as the New England and Middle Atlantic regions' shares of manufacturing employment fell while all of the other regions—excluding the West North Central region—gained. The depressed 1930s altered this as the Eastern areas—the New England, Middle Atlantic, East North Central, South Atlantic, and East South Central regions—gained while all other lost shares of manufacturing employment.

Table 3.3 presents data on the relative sizes of broadly defined industries in the interwar period and ranks those industries by their relative sizes in 1939.[35] As can be seen there was considerable variation in the growth of the industries and shifts in their ranking during the period. The largest broadly defined industries are, not surprisingly, food and kindred products; textile mill products; those producing and fabricating primary metals; machinery production; and chemicals. When industries are more narrowly defined, the automobile industry, which ranked third in manufacturing value added in 1919, ranked first by the mid-1920s and held its lead except for a few years during the nadir of the Great Depression.

Table 3.2 Regional Manufacturing Employment.

Region	Shares of Manufacturing Employment 1920	1930	1940
New England	12.73%	10.48%	11.10%
Middle Atlantic	29.74	28.15	28.73
East North Central	24.74	25.59	27.90
West North Central	7.51	7.11	5.28
South Atlantic	9.37	10.37	11.96
East South Central	4.08	4.48	4.60
West South Central	4.59	5.40	3.83
Mountain	1.77	1.81	0.97
Pacific	5.45	6.61	5.62

Sources: Harvey S. Perloff, Edgar S. Dunn, Jr., Eric E. Lampard, and Richard F. Muth, *Regions, Resources, and Economic Growth* (Baltimore: The Johns Hopkins Press, 1960).

Table 3.3 Manufacturing Value Added: Selected Industries and Years. (Millions of Constant Dollars*)

Rank	Industry	1921	1929	1939	Percent Inflation Adjusted Growth 1921–39
1	Food and Kindred Products	$2,120	$3,340	$3,485	72.94%
2	Primary Metal Industries	n.a.	n.a.	2,169	n.a.
3	Machinery, Except Electrical	n.a.	n.a.	2,037	n.a.
4	Chemicals and Allied Products	834	1,737	1,819	101.22
5	Textile Mill Products	1,824	2,321	1,818	22.91
6	Transportation Equipment	n.a.	n.a.	1,773	n.a.
7	Printing and Publishing	1,306	2,233	1,765	53.35
8	Fabricated Metal Industries	n.a.	n.a.	1,401	n.a.
9	Apparel and Other Textile Products	1,408	1,927	1,386	21.66
10	Electrical Equipment and Supplies	547	1,389	941	77.49
11	Paper and Allied Products	392	782	888	105.01
12	Stone, Clay, and Glass Products	605	1,054	856	57.94
13	Lumber and Wood Products	853	1,322	731	7.80
14	Petroleum and Coal Products	430	829	697	71.54
15	Leather and Leather Products	610	774	583	18.71
16	Furniture and Fixtures	347	615	418	41.85
17	Rubber and Plastics Products N.E.C.	327	539	406	44.88
18	Tobacco Manufactures	n.a.	n.a.	350	n.a.
19	Instruments and Related Products	189	301	333	79.88

*Value-added dollar figures deflated by the GNP Implicit Price Deflator, 1958=100. N.E.C. indicates Not Elsewhere Classified.

Source: Historical Statistics of the United States: Colonial Times to 1970 (Washington, D.C.: U.S. Government Printing Office, 1976).

Productivity Developments

Technological changes during the twenties and thirties tended to raise the productivity of the existing capital through replacement of critical types of capital equipment with superior equipment and through changes in management methods.[36] Some changes, such as the standardization of parts and processes and the reduction of the number of styles and designs, raised the productivity of both capital and labor. Modern management techniques, first introduced by Frederick W. Taylor, were introduced on a wider scale.

One of the important forces contributing to mass production and increased productivity was the transfer to electric power.[37] By 1929 about 70 percent of manufacturing activity relied on electricity, compared to roughly 30 percent in 1914. An increasing number of factories were buying their power from electric utilities. In 1909, 64 percent of the electric motor capacity in manufacturing establishments used electricity generated on the factory site; by 1919, 57 percent of the electricity used in manufacturing was purchased from independent electric utilities.[38]

The shift from coal to oil and natural gas and from raw unprocessed energy in the forms of coal and waterpower to processed energy in the form of internal combustion fuel and electricity increased thermal efficiency. After the First World War energy consumption relative to GNP fell, there was a sharp increase in the growth rate of output per labor-hour, and the output per unit of capital input once again began rising. In manufacturing, steam provided 80 percent of the mechanical drive capacity in 1900, but electricity provided over 50 percent by 1920 and 78 percent by 1929.[39]

Warren Devine, Jr. reports that at the time the most important result of the adoption of electricity was that it would be an indirect "lever to increase production."[40] There were a number of ways in which this occurred. Electricity brought about an increased flow of production by allowing new flexibility in the design of buildings and the arrangement of machines. In this way it maximized throughput. Electric cranes were an "inestimable boon" to production because with adequate headroom they could operate anywhere in a plant, something that mechanical power transmission to overhead cranes did not allow. Electricity made possible the use of portable power tools that could be taken anywhere in the factory. Electricity brought about improved illumination, ventilation, and cleanliness in the plants, dramatically improving working conditions. It improved the control of machines since there was no longer belt slippage with overhead line shafts and belt transmission, and there were less limitations on the operating speeds of machines. Finally, it made plant expansion much easier than when overhead shafts and belts had been relied upon for operating power.

The mechanization of American manufacturing accelerated in the 1920s, and this led to a much more rapid growth of productivity in manufacturing compared to earlier decades and to other sectors at that time. There were several forces that promoted mechanization. One was the rapidly expanding aggregate demand during the prosperous twenties. Another was the technological developments in new machines and processes, of which electrification played an important part. Finally, Harry Jerome and, later, Harry Oshima both suggest that the price of unskilled labor began to rise as immigration sharply declined with new immigration laws and falling population growth.[41] This accelerated the mechanization of the nation's factories

Technological changes during this period can be documented for a number of individual industries. In bituminous coal mining, labor productivity rose when mechanical loading devices reduced the labor required from 24 to 50 percent. The burst of paved road construction in the twenties led to the development of a finishing machine to smooth the surface of cement highways, and this reduced the labor requirement from 40 to 60 percent. Productivity in road construction was further increased by mechanical pavers that spread centrally mixed materials. These replaced the roadside dump and wheelbarrow methods of spreading the cement.[42] The glass in electric light bulbs was made by new machines, which cut the number of labor-hours required for their manufacture by nearly half. New machines to produce cigarettes and cigars, for warp-tying in textile production, and for pressing clothes in clothing shops also cut labor-hours. The Banbury mixer reduced the labor input in the production of automobile tires by half, and output per worker of inner tubes increased about four times with a new production method.[43] However, as Daniel Nelson points out, the continuing advances were the "cumulative process resulting from a vast number of successive small changes."[44] Because of these continuing advances in the quality of the tires and in the manufacturing of tires, between 1910 and 1930 "tire costs per thousand miles of driving fell from $9.39 to $0.65."[45]

John Lorant has documented other technological advances that occurred in American manufacturing during the twenties.[46] For example, the organic chemical industry developed rapidly due to the introduction of the Weizman fermentation process. In a similar fashion, nearly half of the productivity advances in the paper industry were due to the "increasingly sophisticated applications of electric power and paper manufacturing processes," especially the fourdrinier paper-making machines. As Avi Cohen has shown, the continuing advances in these machines were the result of evolutionary changes to the basic machine.[47] Mechanization in many types of mass-production industries raised the productivity of labor and capital. In the glass industry, automatic feeding and other types of fully automatic production raised the efficiency of the production of glass containers, window glass, and pressed glass.[48] Giedion reported that the production of bread was "automatized" in all stages during the 1920s.[49]

Though not directly bringing about productivity increases in manufacturing processes, developments in the management of manufacturing firms, particularly the largest ones, also significantly affected their structure and operation. Alfred D. Chandler, Jr., has argued that the structure of a firm must follow its strategy.[50] Until the First World War most industrial firms were centralized, single-division firms even when becoming vertically integrated. When this began to change the management of the large industrial firms had to change accordingly.

Because of these changes in the size and structure of the firm during the First World War, E. I. du Pont de Nemours and Company was led to adopt a strategy of diversifying into the production of largely unrelated product lines. The firm found that the centralized, divisional structure that had served it so well was not suited to this strategy, and its poor business performance led its executives to develop between 1919 and 1921 a decentralized, multidivisional structure that boosted it to the first rank among American industrial firms.

General Motors had a somewhat different problem. By 1920 it was already decentralized into separate divisions. In fact, there was so much decentralization that those divisions essentially remained separate companies and there was little coordination between the operating divisions. A financial crisis at the end of 1920 ousted W. C. Durant and brought in the du Ponts and Alfred Sloan. Sloan, who had seen the problems at GM but had been unable to convince Durant to make changes, began reorganizing the management of the company. Over the next several years Sloan and other GM executives developed the general office for a decentralized, multidivisional firm.

Though facing related problems at nearly the same time, GM and du Pont developed their decentralized, multidivisional organizations separately. As other manufacturing firms began to diversify, GM and du Pont became the models for reorganizing the management of the firms. In many industrial firms these reorganizations were not completed until well after the Second World War.[51]

Competition, Monopoly, and the Government

The rise of big businesses, which accelerated in the postbellum period and particularly during the first great turn-of-the-century merger wave, continued in the interwar period. Between 1925 and 1939 the share of manufacturing assets held by the 100 largest corporations rose from 34.5 to 41.9 percent.[52] As a public policy, the concern with monopolies diminished in the 1920s even though firms were growing larger. But the growing size of businesses was one of the convenient scapegoats upon which to blame the Great Depression. The Roosevelt administration's first response was to take advantage of the large size of firms by establishing government-organized and -directed cartels under the umbrella of the NIRA. Failing this, the New Dealers then began an attack to break up the larger firms by using the antitrust laws.

However, the rise of large manufacturing firms in the interwar period is not so easily interpreted as an attempt to monopolize their industries. Some of the growth came about through vertical integration by the more successful manufacturing firms. Backward integration was generally an attempt to ensure a smooth supply of raw materials where that supply was not plentiful and was dispersed and firms "feared that raw materials might become controlled by competitors or independent suppliers."[53] Forward integration was an offensive tactic employed when manufacturers found that the existing distribution network proved inadequate. Livesay and Porter suggested a number of reasons why firms chose to integrate forward. In some cases they had to provide the mass distribution facilities to handle their much larger outputs; especially when the product was a new one. The complexity of some new products required technical expertise which the existing distribution system could not provide. In other cases "the high unit costs of products required consumer credit which exceeded financial capabilities of independent distributors."[54] Forward integration into wholesaling was more common than forward integration into retailing. The producers of automobiles, petroleum, typewriters, sewing machines, and harvesters were typical of those manufacturers which integrated all the way into retailing.[55]

In some cases, increases in industry concentration arose as a natural process of industrial maturation. In the automobile industry, Henry Ford's invention in 1913 of the moving assembly line—a technological innovation that changed most manufacturing—lent itself to larger factories and firms. Of the several thousand companies which had produced cars prior to 1920, 120 were still doing so then, but Ford and General Motors were the clear leaders, together producing nearly 70 percent of the cars. During the twenties, several other companies, such as Durant, Willys, and Studebaker, missed their opportunity to become more important producers, and Chrysler, formed in early 1925, became the third most important producer by 1930. Many went out of business and by 1929 only 44 companies were still producing cars.

The Great Depression decimated the industry. Dozens of minor firms went out of business. Ford struggled through by relying on its huge stockpile of cash accumulated prior to the mid-1920s, while Chrysler actually grew. By 1940, only eight companies still produced cars—GM, Ford, and Chrysler had about 85 percent of the market, while Willys, Studebaker, Nash, Hudson, and Packard shared the remainder. The rising concentration in this industry was not due to attempts to monopolize. As the industry matured, growing economies of scale in factory production and vertical integration, as well as the advantages of a widespread dealer network, led to a dramatic decrease in the number of viable firms.[56]

It was a similar story in the tire industry. The increasing concentration and growth of firms was driven by scale economies in production and retailing and by the devastating effects of the depressions in the thirties. Although there were 190 firms in 1919, 5 firms dominated the industry—Goodyear, B. F. Goodrich, Firestone, U.S. Rubber, and Fisk, followed by Miller Rubber, General Tire and Rubber, and Kelly-Springfield. During the twenties, 166 firms left the industry while 66 entered. The share of the 5 largest firms rose from 50 percent in 1921 to 75 percent in 1937. During the depressed thirties, there was fierce price competition, and many firms exited the industry. By 1937 there were 30 firms, but the average employment per factory was 4.41 times as large as in 1921, and the average factory produced 6.87 times as many tires as in 1921.[57]

The steel industry was already highly concentrated by 1920 as U.S. Steel had around 50 percent of the market. But U.S. Steel's market share declined through the twenties and thirties as several smaller firms competed and grew to become known as Little Steel, the next six largest integrated producers after U.S. Steel. Jonathan Baker has argued that the evidence is consistent with "the assumption that competition was a dominant strategy for steel manufacturers" during the depression. However, the initiation of the National Recovery Administration (NRA) codes in 1933 required the firms to cooperate rather than compete, and Baker argues that this constituted a training period; from 1935 to 1939 the firms were cooperating in price and output policies. Thus the behavior in the steel industry became more monopolistic in the late 1930s after federal policies had initially forced this to occur.[58]

Mergers. A number of the larger firms grew by merger during this period, and the second great merger wave in American industry occurred during the last half of the 1920s.[59] Figure 3.5 shows two series on mergers during the interwar period. The FTC series included many of the smaller mergers, but not their value. The series constructed by Carl Eis only includes the larger mergers and ends in 1930, but it also includes their value.

This second great merger wave coincided with the stock market boom of the twenties and has been called "merger for oligopoly" rather than merger for monopoly.[60] The second merger wave created many larger firms that ranked below the industry leaders. Much of the activity in the second merger wave occurred in the banking and public utilities industries.[61] In manufacturing and mining, the effects on industrial structure were less striking. Eis found that while mergers took place in almost all industries, they were concentrated in a smaller number of them, particularly petroleum, primary metals, and food products.[62]

Government Policy. The federal government's antitrust policies toward business varied sharply during the interwar period. In the 1920s there was relatively little activ-

Fig. 3.5 Mergers in Manufacturing and Mining

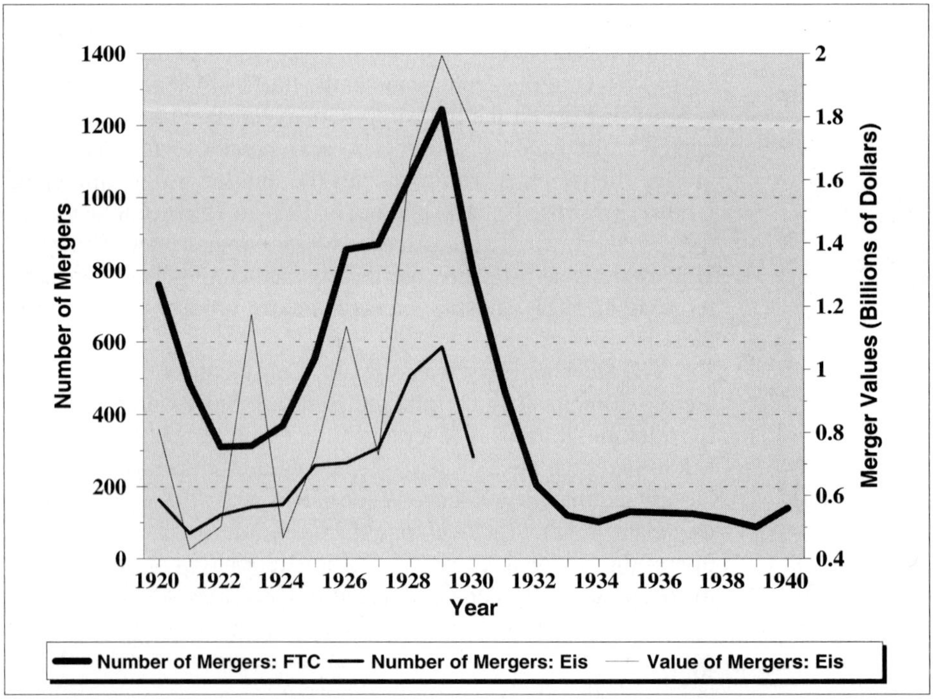

Source: *Historical Statistics of the United States: Colonial Times to 1970* (Washington, D.C.: U.S. Government Printing Office, 1976).

ity by the Justice Department, but after the Great Depression the New Dealers tried to take advantage of big business to make business exempt from the antitrust laws and cartelize industries under government supervision. Failing that, the Roosevelt administration moved to break up big business by an expanded application of the antitrust laws.

With the passage of the FTC and Clayton Acts in 1914 to supplement the 1890 Sherman Act, the cornerstones of American antitrust law were complete. Though minor amendments were later enacted, the primary changes after that came in the enforcement of the laws and in swings in judicial decisions. Their two primary areas of application were in the areas of overt behavior, such as horizontal and vertical price-fixing, and in market structure, such as mergers and dominant firms.

Price-fixing continued to be considered illegal throughout the period, but there was no major judicial activity regarding it in the 1920s other than the Trenton Potteries decision in 1927. In that decision 20 individuals and 23 corporations were found guilty of conspiring to fix the prices of bathroom bowls. The evidence in the case suggested that the firms were not very successful at doing so, but the court found that they were guilty nevertheless; their success, or lack thereof, was not held to be a factor in the decision.[63] Though criticized by some, the decision was precedent setting in that it prohibited explicit pricing conspiracies per se.[64]

The Justice Department had achieved success in dismantling Standard Oil and American Tobacco in 1911 through decisions that the firms had *unreasonably* restrained trade. These were essentially the same points used in court decisions against the Powder Trust in 1911, the thread trust in 1913, Eastman Kodak in 1915, the glucose and cornstarch trust in 1916, and the anthracite railroads in 1920.[65] The criterion of an *unreasonable* restraint of trade was used in the 1916 and 1918 decisions that found the American Can Company and the United Shoe Machinery Company innocent of violating the Sherman Act; it was also clearly enunciated in the 1920 U.S. Steel decision.[66] This became known as the *rule of reason standard* in antitrust policy.

Merger policy had been defined in the 1914 Clayton Act to prohibit only the acquisition of one corporation's *stock* by another corporation. Firms then shifted to the outright purchase of a competitor's assets. A series of court decisions in the twenties and thirties further reduced the possibilities of Justice Department actions against mergers. "Only fifteen mergers were order dissolved through antitrust actions between 1914 and 1950, and ten of the orders were accomplished under the Sherman Act rather than Clayton Act proceedings."[67]

During the Great Depression, big businesses and their behavior came to be widely viewed as one of its major causes. Once Roosevelt took office in 1933, his administration moved to address the problem.[68] The first attempt was the National Recovery Administration which was formed by Title I of the National Industrial Recovery Act (NIRA) signed on June 16, 1933, where industry codes—enacted to bring about a rational order for cooperative behavior—became monopolistic devices to organize industry cartels. Ellis Hawley says, "The practical effect of the NRA, then, was to allow the erection, extension, and fortification of private monopolistic arrangements, particularly for groups that already possessed a fairly high degree of integration and monopoly power."[69]

Within a short time, dissension within the NRA and external criticism was rife. Small businesses criticized the NRA codes as having been drawn up by and protective of big businesses at the expense of small businesses. In some industries the codes became objects of great internal dispute, while in others they were so complex as to be unenforceable. Compliance with the codes varied sharply among industries. Labor, the planners, and the antitrusters all condemned the NRA. By early 1935 there was growing doubt that Congress would vote to extend the two-year charter of the NIRA. The Supreme Court's *Schecter* decision in May of 1935, which ruled the NIRA unconstitutional, made congressional action on extending the NIRA a moot point.

With the NRA dead and facing a rising chorus of criticism from industrialists and their organizations, the Roosevelt administration's strategies toward business began to change. National economic planning disappeared, except for a few industries such as coal and crude oil production. In transportation, planning via the federal government's regulatory agencies was extended to the airline and interstate trucking industries.[70]

As Roosevelt's war of words with big business continued, his administration's policies began to swing toward the programs that the antitrusters proposed as a means to reestablish a competitive economy. During 1936 and the first part of 1937, this trend slowly developed in several directions. New laws were drafted to control banks and financial institutions, to control the securities markets via the SEC, and to raise taxes to redistribute income. Under Robert Jackson, the Antitrust Division of the Justice Department began to initiate more antitrust cases. With the depression of 1937–38 the anti-big business attitude in Washington increased, and the antitrust program began to grow more rapidly. In speeches in late 1937 and early 1938, Jackson attacked big business as causing the 1937 contraction through their monopolistic pricing tactics. In 1938 Congress created the Temporary National Economic Committee to examine the monopoly question, and the committee commissioned a number of academic studies of various aspects of monopoly power in the United States.

In March of 1938, Roosevelt appointed Jackson to a loftier position, and Thurman Arnold left the Yale Law School to head the Antitrust Division. Under Arnold the number of antitrust cases initiated rose from 5, 7, and 10 cases in 1936, 1937, and 1938, respectively, to 31 in 1939, 65 in 1940, and 71 in 1941.[71] Much of Arnold's antitrust program was aimed at bringing about price flexibility because he had become convinced that inflexible prices were the major cause of the contractions and the slow recovery—an assumption of dubious validity. Hawley argues that Arnold's antitrust campaign made no real effort to alter the underlying economic structures or break up going concerns, and, as a result, the "program had little success in achieving its avowed goals."[72]

Interwar Manufacturing

American manufacturing bore the brunt of the economic turbulence in the interwar period. Exuberant and growing in the twenties, it was the epitome of the business orientation of American society. The depression's downturn fell like a sledgehammer on manufacturing, and this was where the fingers pointed when the government and other groups searched for an easy explanation of the contraction. It neither deserved the applause of the twenties nor the scorn of the thirties, but the sheer size and visibility of the firms made it an easy target.

During the New Deal, manufacturers were in a quandary as to which strategies to pursue as the administration vacillated between programs. From a formal promotion of cartels, the administration moved to regulation and then to a stated desire to break up large businesses, though its actions never fully followed its words. The Wagner Act forced manufacturing firms to recognize and bargain with labor unions, thus permanently changing labor-management relations. The most important result of the Jackson-Arnold antitrust initiative of the late thirties, the Alcoa decision overturning the rule of reason, would not occur until 1945, but it would then influence antitrust activity well into the 1970s.

On the whole, American manufacturing at the end of the thirties still was the envy of the world. It would not be until the 1960s and 1970s that foreign manufacturing of such basic products as steel, automobiles, and electrical appliances would overtake America's lead.

SELECTED REFERENCES

Adams, Walter, ed. *The Structure of American Industry*, 5th ed. New York: Macmillan Publishing Co., 1977.

Alston, Lee J. "Farm Foreclosures in the United States During the Interwar Period." *The Journal of Economic History*, 43 (December 1983): 885–904.

__________. "Farm Foreclosure Moratorium Legislation: A Lesson from the Past." *American Economic Review,* 74 (June 1984): 445–457.

Ankli, Robert. "Horses vs. Tractors on the Corn Belt." *Agricultural History*, 54 (January 1980): 134–148.

__________ and Alan L. Olmstead. "The Adoption of the Gasoline Tractor in California." *Agricultural History*, 55 (July 1981): 213–230.

Baker, Jonathan B. "Identifying Cartel Pricing Under Uncertainty: The U.S. Steel Industry, 1933–1939." *The Journal of Law and Economics*, 32 (October 1989): S47–76.

Barger, E. L. et al. *Tractors and Their Power Units*. New York: John Wiley & Sons, 1952.

Bernstein, Michael A. *The Great Depression: Delayed Recovery and Economic Change in America, 1929–1939*. New York: Cambridge University Press, 1987.

Bogue, Allan G. "Changes in Mechanical and Plant Technology: The Corn Belt, 1910–1940." *The Journal of Economic History*, 43 (March 1983): 1–26.

Breit, William and Elzinga, Kenneth. *The Antitrust Casebook: Milestones in Economic Regulation*, 2d ed. Chicago: The Dryden Press, 1989.

Chandler, Alfred D., Jr. *Strategy and Structure: Chapters in the History of the American Industrial Enterprise*. Cambridge, MA: The M.I.T. Press, 1962.

__________. *Giant Enterprise: Ford, General Motors, and the American Automobile Industry*. New York: Harcourt, Brace, and World, 1964.

__________. *The Visible Hand: The Managerial Revolution in American Business*. Cambridge, MA: the Belknap Press Harvard University Press, 1977.

Chandler, Lester V. *America's Greatest Depression.* New York: Harper and Row, 1970.

Clark, Sally. "New Deal Regulation and the Revolution in American Farm Productivity: A Case Study of the Diffusion of the Tractor in the Corn Belt, 1920–1940." *The Journal of Economic History*, 51 (March 1991): 105–15.

Cohen, Avi. "Technological Change as Historical Process: The Case of the U.S. Pulp and Paper Industry, 1915–1940." *The Journal of Economic History*, 44 (September 1984): 775–79.

Davis, Lance E.; Richard A. Easterlin, William N. Parker, et al. *American Economic Growth: An Economist's History of the United States*. New York: Harper and Row, 1972.

Devine, Warren D., Jr. "From Shafts to Wires: Historical Perspectives on Electrification." *The Journal of Economic History*, 43 (June 1983): 347–372.

Eis, Carl. "The 1919–1930 Merger Movement in American Industry." *The Journal of Law and Economics*, XII (October 1969): 267–96.

French, Michael J. "Structural Change and Competition in the United States Tire Industry, 1920–1937." *Business History Review*, 60 (Spring 1986): 28–54.

__________. *The U.S. Tire Industry*. Boston: Twayne Publishers, 1991.

Fricke, Ernest B. "The New Deal and the Modernization of Small Business: The McCreary Tire and Rubber Company, 1930–1940." *Business History Review*, 56 (Winter 1982): 559–76.

Giedion, Simon. *Mechanization Takes Command*. New York: Oxford University Press, 1948.

Gray, Roy Burton. *Development of the Agricultural Tractor in the United States,* 2 volumes. Washington: U.S Government Printing Office, 1954.

Griliches, Zvi. "Hybrid Corn: An Exploration in the Economics of Technological Change." *Econometrica*, 25 (October 1957): 502–22.

__________. "Research Costs and Social Returns: Hybrid Corn and Related Innovations." *Journal of Political Economy*, 66 (October 1958): 419–31.

__________. "Hybrid Corn and the Economics of Innovation." *Science*, 132 (July 1960): 257–80.

Hawley, Ellis W. *The New Deal and the Problem of Monopoly: A Study in Economic Ambivalence*. Princeton: Princeton University Press, 1966.

Higgs, Robert. "The Boll Weevil, the Cotton Economy, and Black Migration, 1910–1930." *Agricultural History*, 50 (April 1976): 335–50.

__________. *Crisis and Leviathan: Critical Episodes in the Growth of American Government*. New York: Oxford University Press, 1987.

Historical Statistics of the United States: Colonial Times to 1970. Washington: U.S. Government Printing Office, 1976.

Hoffman, Elizabeth and Gary D. Liebcap. "Institutional Choice and the Development of U.S. Agricultural Policies in the 1920s." *The Journal of Economic History*, 51 (June 1991): 397–412.

Jerome, Harry. *Mechanization in Industry*. New York: National Bureau of Economic Research, 1934.

Johnson, H. Thomas. "Postwar Optimism and the Rural Financial Crisis." *Explorations in Economic History*, 11 (Winter 1973–74): 173–92.

Jones, Fred R. and William H. Aldred. *Farm Power and Tractors*, 5th ed. New York: McGraw-Hill, 1979.

Lagenfeld, James. "Comment on Baker." *The Journal of Law and Economics*, 32 (October 1989): S77–82.

Livesay, Harold C. and Patrick G. Porter. "Vertical Integration in American Manufacturing, 1899–1948." *The Journal of Economic History*, 29 (September 1969): 494–500.

Lorant, John. "Technological Change in American Manufacturing During the 1920s." *The Journal of Economic History*, 33 (June 1967): 243–47.

Markham, Jesse. "Survey of the Evidence and Findings on Mergers." In *Business Concentration and Price Policy*, National Bureau of Economic Research. Princeton: Princeton University Press, 1955.

McCraw, Thomas K. and Forest Reinhardt. "Losing to Win: U.S. Steel's Pricing, Investment Decisions, and Market Share, 1901–1938." *The Journal of Economic History*, 49 (September 1989): 592–620.

Mitchell, Broadus. *Depression Decade: From New Era Through New Deal, 1919–1941*. New York: Rinehart and Company, 1947.

Musoke, Moses S. "Mechanizing Cotton Production in the American South: The Tractor, 1915–1960." *Explorations in Economic History*, 18 (October 1981): 347–75.

Nelson, Ralph L. *Merger Movements in American Industry, 1895–1956*. Princeton: Princeton University Press, 1959.

Nelson, Daniel. "Mass Production and the U.S. Tire Industry." *The Journal of Economic History*, 48 (June 1987): 329–40.

Oshima, Harry T. "The Growth of U.S. Factor Productivity: The Significance of New Technologies in the Early Decades of the Twentieth Century." *The Journal of Economic History*, 44 (March 1984): 161–70.

Perloff, Harvey S., Edgar S. Dunn, Jr., Eric E. Lampard, and Richard F. Muth. *Regions, Resources, and Economic Growth*. Baltimore: The Johns Hopkins Press, 1960.

Posner, Richard A. *Antitrust Law: An Economic Perspective*. Chicago: The University of Chicago Press, 1976.

Rae, John B. *The American Automobile Industry*. Boston: Twayne Publishers, 1984.

Scherer, Frederick M. and David Ross. *Industrial Market Structure and Economic Performance*, 3d ed. Boston: Houghton Mifflin, 1990.

Schlebecker, John T. *Whereby We Thrive: A History of American Farming, 1607–1972*. Ames, IA: The Iowa State University Press, 1975.

Shannon, David A. *The Great Depression*. Englewood Cliffs, NJ: Prentice-Hall, 1960.

Shepherd, James. "The Development of New Wheat Varieties in the Pacific Northwest." *Agricultural History*, 54 (January 1980): 52–63.

Soule, George. *Prosperity Decade: From War to Depression: 1917–1929*. New York: Holt, Rinehart, and Winston, 1947.

Stigler, George J. "Monopoly and Oligopoly by Merger." *American Economic Review*, 40 (May 1950): 23–34.

Weiss, Leonard W. *Cast Studies in American Industry*, 3d ed. New York: John Wiley & Sons, 1980.

Wendel, C. H. *Encyclopedia of American Tractors*. Sarasota, FL: Crestline Publishing Co., 1979.

Whatley, Warren. "Southern Agrarian Labor Contracts as Impediments to Cotton Mechanization." *The Journal of Economic History*, 87 (March 1987): 45–70.

Wood, Charles. "Science and Politics in the War on Cattle Diseases: The Kansas Experience, 1900–1940." *Agricultural History*, 54 (January 1980): 82–92.

NOTES

1. Calculated from *Historical Statistics of the United States: Colonial Times to 1970* (Washington, D.C.: U.S. Government Printing Office, 1976), Series E-40, E-42, and E-135.
2. H. Thomas Johnson, "Postwar Optimism and the Rural Financial Crisis," *Explorations in Economic History*, 11 (Winter 1973–74): 173–92. See also Lee J. Alston, "Farm Foreclosures in the United States During the Interwar Period," *The Journal of Economic History*, 43 (December 1983): 885–904.

3. Some farmers tried unsuccessfully to prevent a sale in Ashland County, Wisconsin, in December of 1932, but others were successful in stopping a sale in LeMars, Iowa, the next week and several more in the following weeks. In other cases farmers bid very low prices for a farm, stopping all other bidders, and then returned the farm to its original owner. For example, Lester Chandler reports that a farm in Shelby, Nebraska, that had been mortgaged for $4,100 was purchased by neighbors for $49.50 and then given back to the owner. Chandler, *America's Greatest Depression*, 65.
4. Lee J. Alston, "Farm Foreclosure Moratorium Legislation: A Lesson from the Past," *American Economic Review*, 74 (June 1984): 446.
5. It did not seem to bother the majority that this decision was in direct conflict with the Contracts Clause which prohibited government interference with valid contracts. For a discussion of this decision see Robert Higgs, *Crisis and Leviathan: Critical Episodes in the Growth of American Government* (New York: Oxford University Press, 1987): p. 180–83.
6. Ibid., 451–56.
7. Broadhus Mitchell, *Depression Decade: From New Era through New Deal, 1929–1941* (New York: Rinehart & Company, Inc., 1947) 191–97; Chandler, *America's Greatest Depression*, 218.
8. Chandler, *America's Greatest Depression*, p. 218.
9. Mitchell, *Depression Decade*, 190.
10. The production of crops such as wheat, corn, and cotton fell sharply, in fact, the United States imported wheat in 1935 and 1936. Beef production fell because of the loss of pasturage and feed grains. Because of the decrease in production, farm prices rose sharply and carryovers fell. Though production rose in 1937, prices remained high enough to provide farm incomes roughly equal to those received in the years from 1924 to 1929. Chandler, *America's Greatest Depression*, 217–18. Mitchell, *Depression Decade*, 202.
11. William N. Parker, "Agriculture," chapter 11 in Lance E. Davis, Richard A. Easterlin, William N. Parker, et al., *American Economic Growth: An Economist's History of the United States* (New York: Harper and Row, 1972), 376–82; Soule, *Prosperity Decade*, 235–40; Mitchell, *Depression Decade*, 217–20.
12. This and the following discussion draws upon these sources. Roy Burton Gray, *Development of the Agricultural Tractor in the United States*, 2 vols. (Washington, D.C.: U.S. Government Printing Office, 1954); Fred R. Jones and William H. Aldred, *Farm Power and Tractors*, 5th ed. (New York: McGraw-Hill, 1979); E. L. Barger et al., *Tractors and Their Power Units* (New York: John Wiley and Sons, 1952); C. H. Wendel, *Encyclopedia of American Tractors* (Sarasota, FL: Crestline Publishing Co., 1979); John T. Schlebecker, *Whereby We Thrive: A History of American Farming, 1607–1972* (Ames, IA: The Iowa State University Press, 1975).
13. The data come from the following studies. Robert E. Ankli, "Horses vs. Tractors on the Corn Belt," *Agricultural History*, 54 (January 1980): 134 and 147. Robert E. Ankli and Alan L. Olmstead, "The Adoption of the Gasoline Tractor in California," *Agricultural History*, 55 (July 1981): 215. Moses S. Musoke, "Mechanizing Cotton Production in the American South: The Tractor, 1915–1960," *Explorations in Economic History*, 18 (October 1981): Table 5, p. 264.
14. Ankli, "Horses vs. Tractors on the Corn Belt," and Ankli and Olmstead, "The Adoption of the Gasoline Tractor in California."
15. Sally Clarke, "New Deal Regulation and the Revolution in American Farm Productivity: A Case Study of the Diffusion of the Tractor in the Corn Belt, 1920–1940," *The Journal of Economic History*, 51 (March 1991): 105–15.

16. Ankli, "Horses vs. Tractors on the Corn Belt," 146–47; Ankli and Olmstead, "The Adoption of the Gasoline Tractor in California," 229; and Musoke, "Mechanizing Cotton Production in the American South," 366.
17. Warren Whatley, "Southern Agrarian Labor Contracts as Impediments to Cotton Mechanization," *The Journal of Economic History*, 87 (March 1987): 45–70.
18. Clarke, "New Deal Regulations and the Revolution in American Farm Productivity," 116.
19. Allan G. Bogue, "Changes in Mechanical and Plant Technology: The Corn Belt, 1910–1940," *The Journal of Economic History*, 43 (March 1983): 1–26.
20. Zvi Griliches, "Hybrid Corn: An Exploration in the Economics of Technological Change," *Econometrica*, 25 (October 1957): 501–22; "Research Costs and Social Returns: Hybrid Corn and Related Innovations," *Journal of Political Economy*, 66 (October 1958): 419–31; and "Hybrid Corn and the Economics of Innovation," *Science*, 132 (July 1960): 257–80.
21. Bogue, "Changes in Mechanical and Plant Technology," 10–12.
22. Ibid., 16–17.
23. Ibid., 21.
24. Ibid.
25. James Shepherd, "The Development of New Wheat Varieties in the Pacific Northwest," *Agricultural History*, 54 (January 1980): 62.
26. Schlebecker, *Whereby We Thrive*, 267–68.
27. Bogue, "Changes in Mechanical and Plant Technology," 2.
28. Schlebecker, *Whereby We Thrive*, 267–68.
29. Bogue, "Changes in Mechanical and Plant Technology," 2.
30. Ibid., 267–74.
31. Charles Wood, "Science and Politics in the War on Cattle Diseases: The Kansas Experience, 1900–1940," *Agricultural History*, 54 (January 1980): 82–92.
32. Elizabeth Hoffman and Gary D. Liebcap, "Institutional Choice and the Development of U.S. Agricultural Policies in the 1920s," *The Journal of Economic History*, 51 (June 1991): 377.
33. Ibid., 399–408.
34. This was similar to what the federal government had done during the First World War.
35. The rankings by production workers (not shown here) are very similar to those by value added.
36. George Soule, *Prosperity Decade: From War to Depression: 1917–1929* (New York: Holt, Rinehart, and Winston, 1947), chapter 7. John Lorant, "Technological Change in American Manufacturing During the 1920s," *The Journal of Economic History*, 33 (June 1967): 243–47. Warren D. Devine, Jr., "From Shafts to Wires: Historical Perspective on Electrification," *The Journal of Economic History*, 43 (June 1983): 347–72. Harry T. Oshima, "The Growth of U.S. Factor Productivity: The Significance of New Technologies in the Early Decades of the Twentieth Century," *The Journal of Economic History*, 44 (March 1984): 161–70.
37. Devine, "From Shafts to Wires."
38 Devine, "From Shafts to Wires," 369.
39. Devine, "From Shafts to Wires," 349.
40. Ibid., 364. The rest of the discussion of these indirect effects draws upon this part of Devine's study.
41. Harry Jerome, *Mechanization in Industry* (New York: National Bureau of Economic Research, 1934): 367; and Oshima, "The Growth of U.S. Factor Productivity."
42. Soule, *Prosperity Decade*, 129.

43. Jerome, *Mechanization in Industry*, 368–69.
44. Daniel Nelson, "Mass Production and the U.S. Tire Industry," *The Journal of Economic History*, 48 (June 1987): 331–32.
45. Nelson, "Mass Production and the U.S. Tire Industry," 331.
46. Lorant, "Technological Change in American Manufacturing," 243–45.
47. Avi Cohen, "Technological Change as Historical Process: The Case of the U.S. Pulp and Paper Industry, 1915–1940," *The Journal of Economic History*, 44 (September 1984): 775–99.
48. Lorant, "Technological Change in American Manufacturing," 243–45.
49. Simon Giedion, *Mechanization Takes Command* (New York: Oxford University Press, 1948): 192.
50. Alfred D. Chandler, Jr., *Strategy and Structure: Chapters in the History of the American Industrial Enterprise* (Cambridge, MA: The M.I.T. Press, 1962). Chandler's analysis of the development of the management of American business was later expanded and further developed in *The Visible Hand: The Managerial Revolution in American Business* (Cambridge, MA: Harvard University Press, the Belknap Press, 1977).
51. See chapter 7, "The Spread of the Multidivisional Structure," in Chandler, *Strategy and Structure*.
52. Albert W. Niemi, Jr., *U.S. Economic History*, 2d ed. (Chicago: Rand McNally Publishing Co., 1980), table 19–2, p. 336.
53. Harold C. Livesay and Patrick G. Porter, "Vertical Integration in American Manufacturing, 1899–1948," *The Journal of Economic History*, 29 (September 1969): 496.
54. Ibid., 498.
55. Ibid., 498–99.
56. This discussion of the interwar automobile industry is drawn from the following studies. Alfred D. Chandler, Jr., *Strategy and Structure: Chapters in the History of Indutrial Enterprises* (Cambridge, MA: M.I.T. press, 1962); Alfred D. Chandler, Jr., *Giant Enterprise: Ford, General Motors, and the American Automobile Industry* (New York: Harcourt, Brace, and World, 1964); John B. Rae, *The American Automobile Industry* (Boston: Twayne Publishers, 1984); Michael A. Bernstein, *The Great Depression: Delayed Recovery and Economic Change in America, 1929–1939* (New York: Cambridge University Press, 1987).
57. This discussion of the tire industry is drawn from the following studies. Michael J. French, "Structural Change and Competition in the United States Tire Industry, 1920–1937," *Business History Review*, 60 (Spring 1986): 28–54; Michael J. French, *The U.S. Tire Industry* (Boston: Twayne Publishers, 1991); Daniel Nelson, "Mass Production and the U.S. Tire Industry," *The Journal of Economic History*, 48 (June 1987): 321–28; Ernest B. Fricke, "The New Deal and the Modernization of Small Business: The McCreary Tire and Rubber Company, 1930–1940," *Business History Review*, 56 (Winter 1982): 559–76.
58. Jonathan B. Baker, "Identifying Cartel Pricing Under Uncertainty: The U.S. Steel Industry, 1933–1939," *The Journal of Law and Economics*, 32, no. 2, Pt. 2 (October 1989): S71. Also see the following studies: James Lagenfeld, "Comment on Baker," *The Journal of Law and Economics*, 32, no. 2, Pt. 2 (October 1989): S77-S82; Thomas K. McCraw and Forest Reinhardt, "Losing to Win: U.S. Steel's Pricing, Investment Decisions, and Market Share, 1901–1938," *The Journal of Economic History*, 49 (September 1989): 593–620; Leonard W. Weiss, "Oligopoly—Steel," *Case Studies in American Industry*, 3d ed. (New York: John Wiley & Sons, 1980); Walter Adams, "The Steel Industry," *The Structure of American Industry*, 5th ed., edited by Walter Adams (New York: Macmillan Publishing Co., 1977).

59. This section draws primarily upon the following studies: Carl Eis, "The 1919–1930 Merger Movement in American Industry," *The Journal of Law and Economics*, XII (October 1969): 267–96; Jesse W. Markham, "Survey of the Evidence and Findings on Mergers," *Business Concentration and Price Policy*, National Bureau of Economic Research (Princeton: Princeton University Press, 1955), 141–212; Ralph L. Nelson, *Merger Movements in American Industry, 1895–1956* (Princeton: Princeton University Press, 1959); Frederick M. Scherer and David Ross, "Mergers: History, Effects, and Policy," *Industrial Market Structure and Economic Performance*, 3d ed. (Boston: Houghton Mifflin Company, 1990).
60. George J. Stigler, "Monopoly and Oligopoly by Merger," *American Economic Review*, 40 (May 1950): 23–34.
61. Markham, "Survey of the Evidence and Findings on Mergers," 168–69.
62. Eis, "The 1919–1930 Merger Movement," 296.
63. Scherer and Ross, *Industrial Market Structure and Economic Performance*, 319–20. See also William Breit and Kenneth Elzinga, *The Antitrust Casebook: Milestones in Economic Regulation*, 2d ed. (Chicago: The Dryden Press, 1989): 24–27.
64. For a criticism see Richard A. Posner, *Antitrust Law: An Economic Perspective* (Chicago: University of Chicago Press, 1976): 40–41 and 76.
65. Scherer and Ross, *Industrial Market Structure and Economic Performance*, 452.
66. Ibid., 453.
67. Ibid., 175.
68. This section on New Deal policies toward big business draws primarily on Ellis W. Hawley, *The New Deal and the Problem of Monopoly: A Study in Economic Ambivalence* (Princeton: Princeton University Press, 1966).
69. Ibid., 479.
70. Ibid., chapters 8–14.
71. Posner, "A Statistical Study of Antitrust Enforcement," 366.
72. Hawley, *The New Deal and the Problem of Monopoly*, 489.

CHAPTER 4

Developments in Energy, Transportation and Communications: 1920–1940

THE ENERGY INDUSTRIES

The search for energy and new ways to translate it into heat, light, and motion has been one of the unending themes in economic history. From whale oil to coal oil to kerosene to electricity, the search for better and less costly ways to light our lives, heat our homes, and move our machines has consumed much time and effort. The energy industries responded to those demands and the consumption of energy materials (coal, oil, gas, and fuel wood) as a percent of GNP rose from about 2 percent in the latter part of the nineteenth century to about 3 percent in the twentieth.

Changes in the energy markets that had begun in the nineteenth century continued. Processed energy in the forms of petroleum derivatives and electricity continued to become more important than "raw" energy, such as that available from coal and water. The evolution of energy sources for lighting continued; at the end of the nineteenth century, natural gas and electricity, rather than liquid fuels began to provide more lighting for streets, businesses, and homes.

In the twentieth century the continuing shift to electricity and internal combustion fuels increased the efficiency with which the American economy used energy. These processed forms of energy resulted in a more rapid increase in the productivity of labor and capital in American manufacturing. From 1899 to 1919, output per labor-hour increased at an average annual rate of 1.2 percent, whereas from 1919 to 1937 the increase was 3.5 percent per year. The productivity of capital had fallen at an average annual rate of 1.8 percent per year in the 20 years prior to 1919, but it rose 3.1 percent a year in the 18 years after 1919.[1] As we saw in the previous chapter, the adoption of electricity in American manufacturing initiated a rapid evolution in the organization of plants and rapid increases in productivity in all types of manufacturing.

The change in transportation was even more remarkable. Internal combustion engines running on gasoline or diesel fuel revolutionized transportation. Cars quickly grabbed the lion's share of local and regional travel and began to eat into long distance passenger travel, just as the railroads had done to passenger traffic by water in the 1830s. Even before the First World War cities had begun passing laws to regulate and limit "jitney" services and to protect the investments in urban rail mass transit. Trucking began eating into the freight carried by the railroads.

These developments brought about changes in the energy industries. Coal mining became a declining industry. As Figure 4.1 shows, in 1926 the share of petroleum in the value of coal, gas, and petroleum output exceeded bituminous coal, and by the thirties its share was more than twice as large. Anthracite coal's share was much smaller and declined in the thirties, while natural gas and LP (or liquified petroleum) gas were relatively unimportant. These changes, especially the declining coal industry, were the source of considerable worry in the twenties.

Coal

One of the industries considered to be "sick" in the twenties was coal, particularly bituminous, or soft, coal. Income in the industry declined, and bankruptcies were frequent.

Fig. 4.1 Percentage Shares of the Real Output of Energy Materials

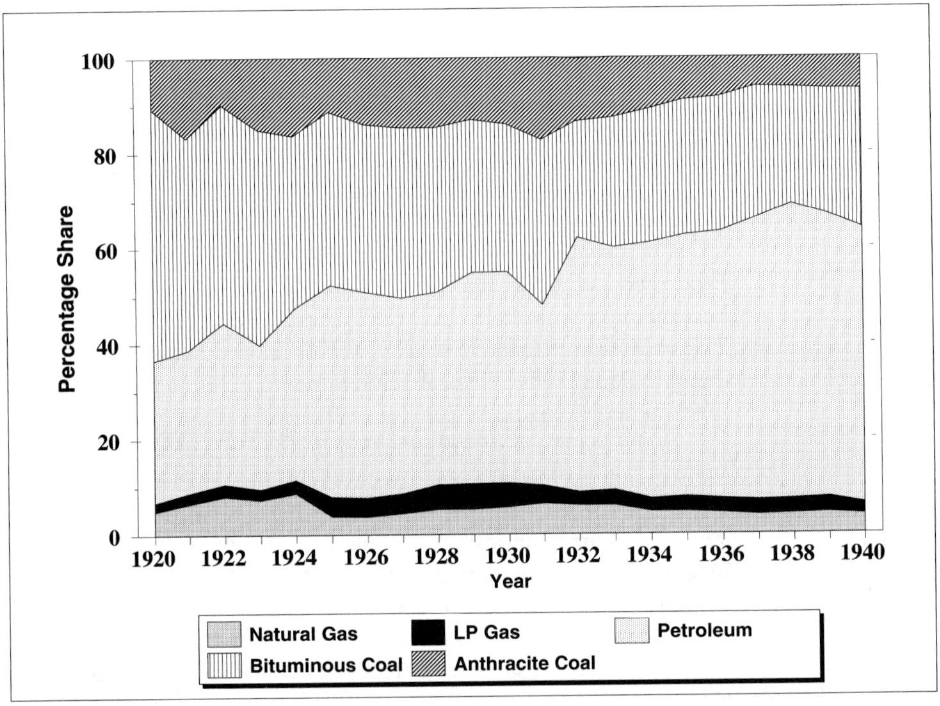

Source: *Historical Statistics of the United States: Colonial Times to 1970* (Washington, D.C.: U.S. Government Printing Office, 1976).

Strikes frequently interrupted production. The majority of the miners "lived in squalid and insanitary houses, and the incidence of accidents and diseases was high."[2]

The number of operating bituminous coal mines declined sharply from 1923 through 1932. Though there was a brief recovery in the number of bituminous coal mines and the value of their output from 1932 to 1936, the number of mines again fell from 1936 to 1940. Anthracite (or hard) coal output was much smaller and, though not declining during the twenties, steadily declined during the thirties. Real coal prices rose sharply from 1919 to 1923, and bituminous coal prices fell sharply from then to 1925. During the depression, real prices rose as current coal prices failed to fall as much as prices in general did. Although bituminous coal prices remained relatively constant from 1934 on, anthracite coal prices fell during that period. (See Figure 4.2.)

Coal mining employment plummeted during the twenties and the Great Depression, falling nearly 40 percent. Annual earnings, especially in bituminous coal mining, also fell because of dwindling hourly earnings and, from 1929 on, a shrinking workweek. Current and real earnings rose sharply after 1933 as a result of the New Deal programs and the trend toward unionization in the industry. (See Figures 4.3.)

Fig. 4.2 Real Retail Price Indexes for Anthracite and Bituminous Coal

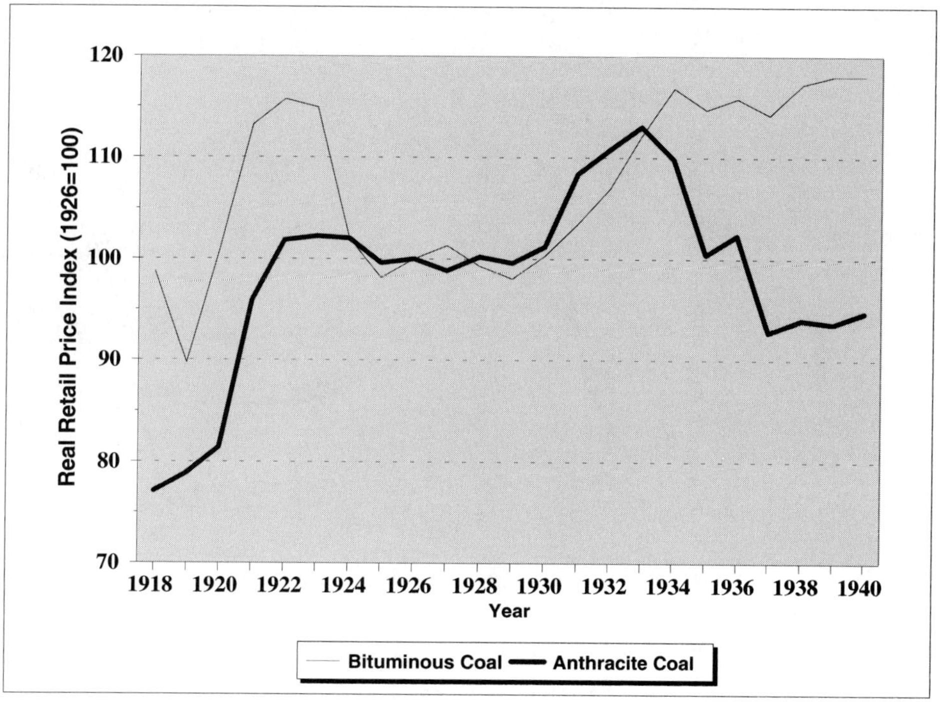

Source: *Historical Statistics of the United States: Colonial Times to 1970* (Washington, D.C.: U.S. Government Printing Office, 1976).

The sources of these changes are to be found in the increasing supply due to productivity advances in coal production and in the decreasing demand for coal. The demand fell as industries began turning from coal to electricity and because of productivity advances in the use of coal to create energy in steel, railroads, and electric utilities.[3] In the generation of electricity, larger steam plants employing higher temperatures and steam pressures continued to reduce coal consumption per kilowatt hour from 3 pounds in 1929 to 1.3 pounds by 1945. Similar reductions were found in the production of coke from coal for iron and steel production and in the use of coal by the steam railroad engines.[4] All of these factors reduced the demand for coal.

Productivity advances in coal mining tended to be labor saving. Mechanical cutting accounted for 60.7 percent of the coal mined in 1920 and 78.4 percent in 1929. By the middle of the twenties, the mechanical loading of coal began to be introduced. Between 1929 and 1939, output per labor-hour rose nearly one-third in bituminous coal mining and nearly four-fifths in anthracite, as more mines adopted machine mining and mechanical loading and strip mining expanded.

Fig. 4.3 Average Hourly Earnings and Average Weekly Hours Worked in Bituminous Coal Mining

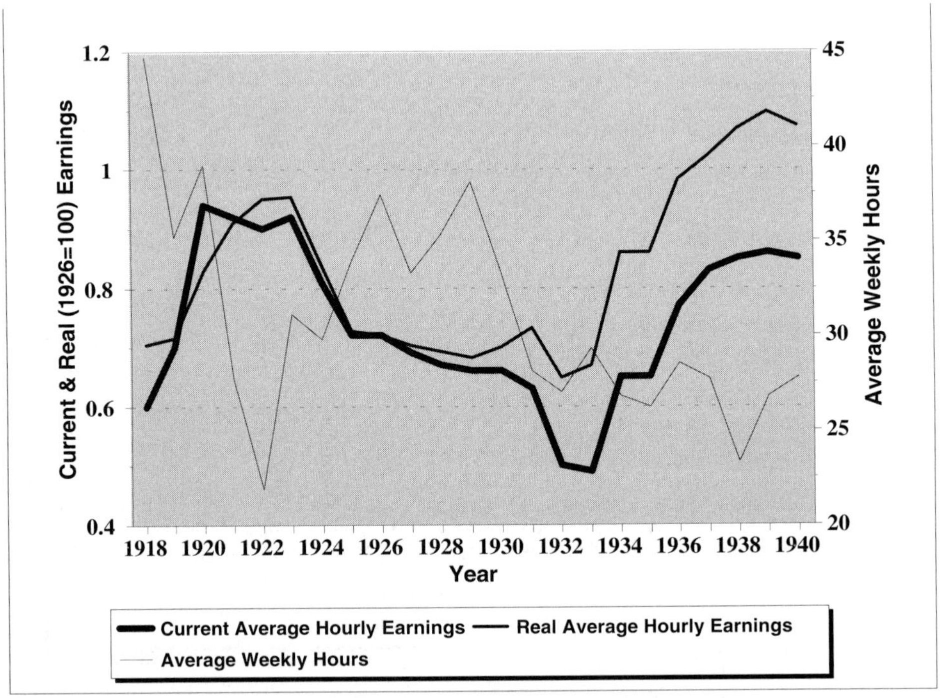

Source: *Historical Statistics of the United States: Colonial Times to 1970* (Washington, D.C.: U.S. Government Printing Office, 1976).

The increasing supply and falling demand for coal led to the closure of mines that were too costly to operate. A mine could simply cease operations, let the equipment stand idle, and lay off employees. When bankruptcies occurred, the mines generally just turned up under new ownership with lower capital charges. When demand increased or strikes reduced the supply of coal, idle mines simply resumed production. As a result, the easily expanded supply largely eliminated economic profits. The federal government intervened and tried to stabilize the coal industry in the thirties. Two acts were passed: the Guffy-Snyder Act and the Guffy-Vinson or Bituminous Coal Conservation Act of 1937. These attempted to set up procedures to require minimum prices and establish fair trade practices (or, in other words, stop price competition). They were not very successful, and the Guffy-Vinson Act expired in 1943.[5]

The average daily employment in coal mining dropped by over 208,000 from its peak in 1923, but the sharply falling real wages suggests that the supply of labor did not fall as rapidly as the demand for labor. Soule notes that when employment fell in coal mining, it meant fewer days of work for the same number of men. Social and cultural characteristics tended to tie many to their home region. The local alternatives were few, and ignorance of alternatives outside the Appalachian rural areas, where most bituminous coal was mined, made it very costly to transfer out.[6]

Petroleum

In contrast to the coal industry, the petroleum industry was growing throughout the interwar period.[7] By the thirties, crude petroleum dominated the real value of the production of energy materials. As Figure 4.4 shows, the production of crude petroleum increased by a factor of three between 1920 and 1940, while real petroleum prices, though highly variable, tended to decline.

The growing demand for petroleum was driven by the growth in demand for gasoline as America became a motorized society. The production of gasoline surpassed kerosene production in 1915. Kerosene's market continued to contract as electric lighting replaced kerosene lighting. The development of oil burners in the twenties began a switch from coal toward fuel oil for home heating, and this further increased the grow-

Fig. 4.4 Petroleum Production and the Real Average Wellhead Price per Barrel of Petroleum

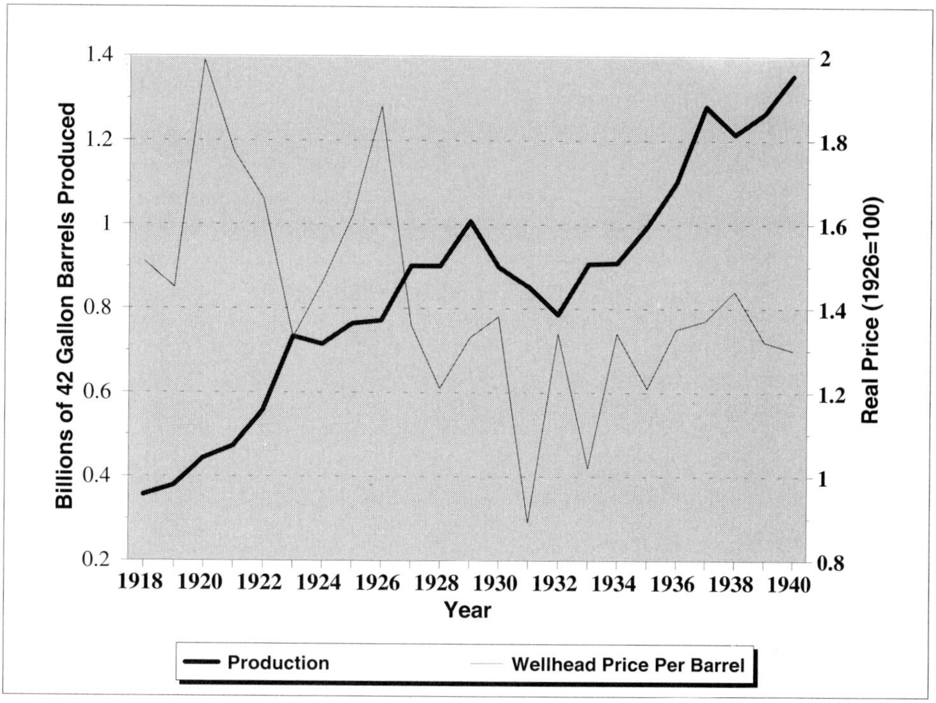

Source: *Historical Statistics of the United States: Colonial Times to 1970* (Washington, D.C.: U.S. Government Printing Office, 1976).

ing demand for petroleum. The growth in the demand for fuel oil and diesel fuel for ship engines (and, at the end of the thirties, the new diesel-electric locomotives) also increased petroleum demand. But it was the growth in the demand for gasoline that drove the petroleum market.

The decline in real prices prior to 1934 shows that supply was growing even faster than demand. The discovery of new fields in the early twenties increased the supply of petroleum and led to falling prices. In 1926, more new fields were discovered in Texas, California, and Oklahoma, and these were in production by 1927. This led to another sharp rise in production and drop in prices.

The supply of gasoline increased more than the supply of crude petroleum. In 1913 a chemist at Standard Oil of Indiana introduced the cracking process to refine crude petroleum; until that time it had been refined by distillation or unpressurized heating. In the heating process, various refined products such as kerosene, gasoline, naphtha, and lubricating oils were produced at different temperatures. It was difficult to vary the amount of the different refined products produced from a barrel of crude. The cracking process used pressurized heating to break heavier components down into lighter crude derivatives; with cracking, it was possible to increase the amount of gasoline obtained from a barrel of crude from 15 to 45 percent. In the early twenties, chemists at Standard Oil of New Jersey improved the cracking process, and by 1927 it was possible to obtain twice as much gasoline from a barrel of crude petroleum as in 1917. In the mid-1930s, catalytic cracking was introduced, which further increased the gasoline yield from a barrel of crude and allowed refiners to vary the yield of several products.

The petroleum companies also developed new ways to distribute gasoline to motorists that made it more convenient to purchase. Prior to the First World War, gasoline was commonly purchased in one-or five-gallon cans and the purchaser used a funnel to pour the gasoline from the can into the car. Then "filling stations" appeared, which specialized in filling cars' tanks with gasoline. These spread rapidly, and by 1919 gasoline companies were beginning to introduce their own filling stations or contract with independent stations to exclusively distribute their gasoline. Increasing competition and falling profits led filling station operators to expand into other activities such as oil changes and other mechanical repairs. The general name attached to such stations gradually changed to "service stations" to reflect these new functions.

Though the petroleum firms tended to be large, they were highly competitive, trying to pump as much petroleum as possible to increase their share of the fields. This, combined with the development of new fields, led to an industry with highly volatile prices and output. Firms desperately wanted to stabilize and reduce the production of crude petroleum so as to stabilize and raise the prices of crude petroleum and refined products. Unable to obtain voluntary agreement on output limitations by the firms and producers, governments began stepping in. Led by Texas, which created the Texas Railroad Commission, oil-producing states began to intervene to regulate production. Such laws were usually termed *prorationing laws* and were quotas designed to limit each well's output to some fraction of its potential. The purpose was as much to stabilize and reduce production and raise prices as anything else, although generally such laws were passed under the guise of conservation. Although the federal government supported such attempts, not until the New Deal were federal laws passed to assist this. In 1935 the Connally Act forbid, but could not fully stop, the shipment in interstate commerce of "hot oil" (crude petroleum produced in excess of state conservation laws' prorationing quotas).

Electricity

By the mid 1890s the debate over the method by which electricity was to be transmitted had been won by those who advocated alternating current. The reduced power losses and greater distance over which electricity could be transmitted more than offset the necessity for transforming the current back to direct current for general use. Widespread adoption of machines and appliances by industry and consumers then rested on an increase in the array of products using electricity as the source of power, heat, or light and the development of an efficient, lower cost method of generating electricity.

General Electric, Westinghouse, and other firms began producing the electrical appliances for homes and an increasing number of machines based on electricity began to appear in industry. The problem of lower cost production was solved by the introduction of centralized generating facilities that distributed the electric power through lines to many consumers and business firms.

Though initially several firms competed in generating and selling electricity to consumers and firms in a city or area, by the First World War many states and communities were awarding exclusive franchises to one firm to generate and distribute electricity to the customers in the franchise area. The electric utility industry became an important growth industry and, as Figure 4.5 shows, electricity production and use grew rapidly.[8]

The electric utilities increasingly were regulated by state commissions charged with setting rates so that the utilities could receive a "fair return" on their investments. Disagreements over what constituted a "fair return" and the calculation of the rate base led to a steady stream of cases before the commissions and a continuing series of court appeals. Generally these court decisions favored the reproduction costs basis.[9] Because of the difficulty and cost in making these calculations, rates tended to be in the hands of the electric utilities which, it has been suggested, did not lower rates adequately to reflect the rising productivity and lowered costs of production. Whether or not this increased their monopoly power is still an open question, but it should be noted, that electric utilities were hardly price-taking industries prior to regulation.[10] The utilities argued that a more rapid lowering of rates would have jeopardized their profits.[11]

The depression stalled the growth in electricity use. As prices fell sharply through 1933, nominal rates were much slower to fall, resulting in sharp increases in real electricity rates. (See Figure 4.6.) This and the slow recovery of incomes caused the growth in usage and in the wiring of new homes and farms to largely cease from 1929 through 1935. As a recovery stimulus and in order to promote the electric utility industry, Roosevelt proposed the creation of the Tennessee Valley Administration (TVA). In addition, the TVA was aimed at revitalizing a poverty-ridden region and developing a

Fig. 4.5 Average Annual Electricity Use per Residential Customer

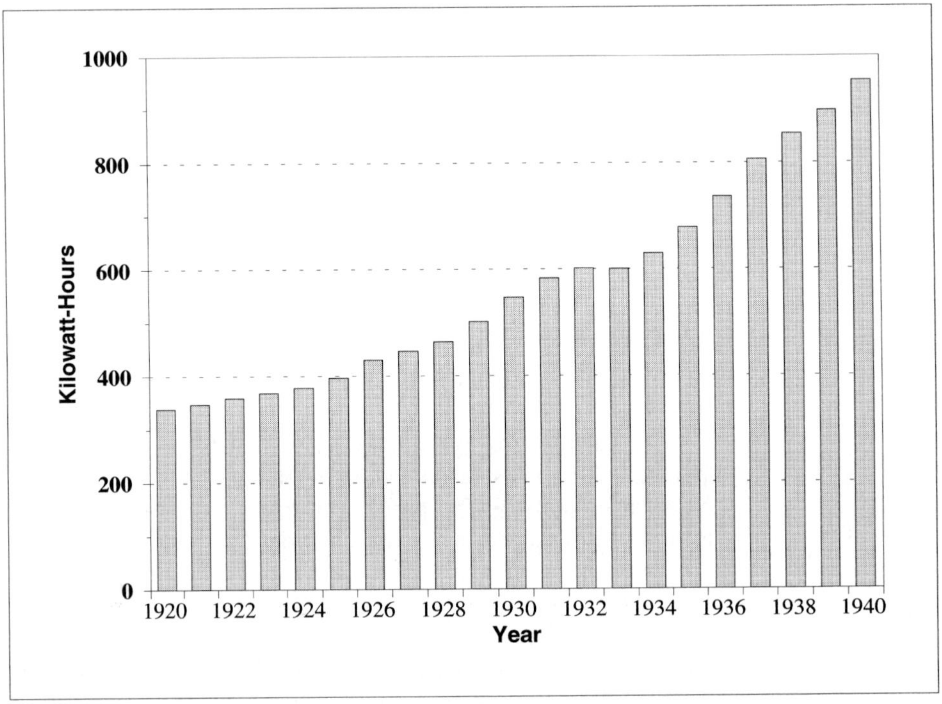

Source: *Historical Statistics of the United States: Colonial Times to 1970* (Washington, D.C.: U.S. Government Printing Office, 1976).

yardstick by which to measure the costs of generating electricity and determining fair electric rates for utilities. The TVA dwarfed all other such projects and became a prototype for similar projects in the West later in the decade. Private power companies all over the United States bitterly opposed the TVA. Besides providing low-cost electricity for the Tennessee River valley's farmers and citizens, the dams controlled the catastrophic flooding that periodically hit the valley.[12]

Farms were slower to gain electric power. The problem with bringing electricity to farmers was one of costs. In the cities, the densely packed population meant that the costs per customer of constructing the distribution network (poles, lines, transformers, and so on) were relatively low. Because of the much greater distances between farms, the cost per customer of constructing the distribution network was much higher. In the late thirties the federal government established the Rural Electrification Administration to make allotments to rural cooperatives to bring electricity to the nation's farmers.[13] Most of these allotments were made in 1939, 1940, and 1941.[14]

Fig. 4.6 Current and Real Prices for Residential Electricity Use

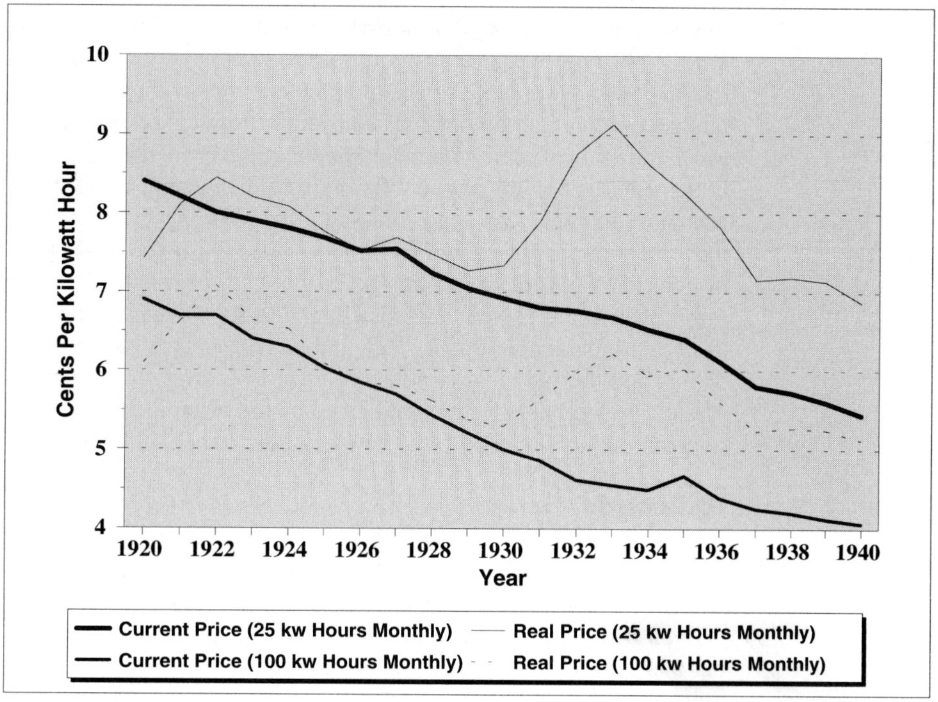

Source: *Historical Statistics of the United States: Colonial Times to 1970* (Washington, D.C.: U.S. Government Printing Office, 1976).

Energy in the Interwar American Economy

The changes in the energy industries had far-reaching consequences. The coal industry faced a continuing decline in demand. Even in the growing petroleum industry, the periodic surges in the supply of petroleum caused great instability. In manufacturing, as described in the previous chapter, electrification contributed to a remarkable rise in productivity. The transportation revolution brought about by the rise of gasoline-powered trucks and cars changed the way businesses received their supplies and distributed their production as well as where they were located. The suburbanization of America and the beginnings of urban sprawl were largely brought about by the introduction of low-priced gasoline for cars. As we will see later in this chapter, America's love affair with the radio in the interwar period transformed mass entertainment, and electrification played a crucial role in this. However, we first need to examine interwar transportation, because the rise of gasoline powered cars and trucks brought about a decline in the demand for other forms of transportation.

TRANSPORTATION

The American economy was forever altered by the dramatic changes in transportation after 1900. Following Henry Ford's introduction of the moving assembly production line in 1914, automobile prices plummeted, and by the end of the 1920s nearly every family owned an automobile. The advent of low-cost personal transportation led to an accelerating movement of population out of the crowded cities to more spacious homes in the suburbs and the automobile set off a decline in intracity public passenger transportation that has yet to end. Massive road-building programs facilitated the intercity movement of people and goods. Trucks increasingly took over the movement of freight in competition with the railroads. In the last half of the 1930s, commercial airlines began their rapid growth and contributed to the further erosion of the railroads' share of intercity passenger traffic. New industries, such as gasoline service stations, motor hotels, and the rubber tire industry, arose to service the automobile and truck traffic. These developments were complicated by the turmoil caused by changes in the federal government's policies toward transportation in the United States.

Railroads

With the end of the First World War, a debate began as to whether the railroads, which had been taken over by the government, should be returned to private ownership or nationalized. The voices calling for a return to private ownership were much stronger, but doing so fomented great controversy. Many in Congress believed that careful planning and consolidation could restore the railroads and make them more efficient. There was continued concern about the near monopoly that the railroads had on the nation's intercity freight and passenger transportation. The result of these deliberations was the Transportation Act of 1920, which was premised on the continued domination of the nation's transportation by the railroads—an erroneous presumption.

The Transportation Act of 1920 presented a marked change in the Interstate Commerce Commission's ability to control railroads.[15] The ICC was allowed to prescribe exact rates that were to be set so as to allow the railroads to earn a fair return, defined as 5.5 percent, on the fair value of their property. The ICC was authorized to make an accounting of the fair value of each regulated railroad's property; however, this was not completed until well into the 1930s, by which time the accounting and rate rules were out of date. To maintain fair competition between railroads in a region, all roads were to have the same rates for the same goods over the same distance. With the same rates, low-cost roads should have been able to earn higher rates of return than high-cost roads. To handle this, a recapture clause was inserted: any railroad earning a return of more than 6 percent on the fair value of its property was to turn the excess over to the ICC, which would place half of the money in a contingency fund for the railroad when it encountered financial problems and the other half in a contingency fund to provide loans to other railroads in need of assistance.

In order to address the problem of weak and strong railroads and to bring better coordination to the movement of rail traffic in the United States, the act was directed to encourage railroad consolidation, but little came of this in the 1920s. In order to facilitate its control of the railroads, the ICC was given two additional powers. The first was the control over the issuance or purchase of securities by railroads, and the second was the power to control changes in railroad service through the control of car supply and the extension and abandonment of track. The control of the supply of rail cars was turned over to the Association of American Railroads. Few extensions of track were proposed, but as time passed, abandonment requests grew. The ICC, however, trying to mediate between the conflicting demands of shippers, communities and railroads, generally refused to grant abandonments, and this became an extremely sensitive issue, particularly after 1932.

As indicated above, the premises of the Transportation Act of 1920 were wrong. Railroads experienced increasing competition during the 1920s, and both freight and passenger traffic were drawn off to competing transport forms. Both railroads and inland and intercoastal water carriers carried much less freight during the Great Depression, while intercity trucking and oil pipelines continued to carry more. Passenger traffic exited from the railroads much more quickly. As the network of all-weather surfaced roads increased, people quickly turned from the train to the car. Harmed even more by the move to automobile traffic were the electric interurban railways that had grown rapidly just prior to the First World War.[16] Not surprisingly, during the 1920s few railroads earned profits in excess of the fair rate of return.[17]

The crisis in the railroad industry caused by the plummeting freight and passenger traffic during the Great Depression led to the Emergency Transportation Act of 1933, an attempt to stave off the collapse of the railroads. The recapture clause was repealed and the ICC was instructed to set rates according to a number of objectives that included the generation of revenues sufficient to allow the railroads, under efficient and honest management, to be able to provide service.[18]

As railroad bankruptcies multiplied from 1932 to 1934, the railroads pointed to the unregulated trucks and buses as the culprits of the worsening state of the railroads.

Trucks and Buses

The use of trucks to deliver freight began shortly after the turn of the century.[19] Before the outbreak of war in Europe, White and Mack were producing trucks with as much as 7.5 tons of carrying capacity. Most of the truck freight was carried on a local basis, and it largely supplemented the longer distance freight transportation provided by the railroads. However, truck size was growing. In 1915 Trailmobile introduced the first four-wheel trailer designed to be pulled by a truck tractor unit. During the First World War, thousands of trucks were constructed for military purposes, and truck convoys showed that long distance truck travel was feasible and economical. The use of trucks to haul freight grew, and by 1929 intercity trucking accounted for more than 1 percent of the ton-miles of freight, an amount that had been growing by over 18 percent per year since 1925.

The railroads argued that the trucks and buses provided "unfair" competition and believed that if they were also regulated, then the regulation could equalize the conditions under which they competed. As early as 1925, the National Association of Railroad and Utilities Commissioners issued a call for the regulation of motor carriers in general. In 1928 the ICC called for federal regulation of buses and in 1932 extended this call to federal regulation of trucks.

Most states had began regulating buses at the beginning of the 1920s in an attempt to reduce the diversion of urban passenger traffic from the electric trolley and railway systems. However, most of the regulation did not aim to control intercity passenger traffic by buses. As the network of surfaced roads expanded during the twenties, so did the routes of the intercity buses. In 1929 a number of smaller bus companies were incorporated in the Greyhound Buslines, the carrier that has since dominated intercity bus transportation.

With the depression, intercity trucking and buslines suffered along with the railroads. Entry into intercity trucking was extremely easy, and the result was a highly competitive market. Many truckers were sympathetic to the call to regulate interstate trucking because they thought that this could control the entry into trucking and stabilize—even raise—trucking rates and earnings by, of course, stopping rate-cutting.

With the intense competition and low profits during the depression and calls from both truckers and railroads for regulation, Congress moved toward regulating interstate trucking. In 1935 it passed the Motor Carrier Act as part of the Interstate Commerce Act. The authority to regulate interstate trucking was given to the Interstate Commerce Commission. The regulation focused on the common carriers which required terminals where less than carload lots could be combined for truck shipments. Common carriers were required to have a certificate of convenience and necessity.[20] The rates were regulated in much the same way as were railroad rates. As in railroads, the ICC was granted the authority to control consolidations and securities issuance, though most interstate trucking firms were not large enough to issue securities.

The existing common carriers were to be "grandfathered" (or given an automatic license) at the time the Motor Carrier Act became law resulting in over 89,000 applications. There was a simple reason for this. Grandfathered trucking firms did not have to show that they were providing a service that fulfilled a necessity and was a public convenience. Firms applying after that for a license had to show that they were "fit, willing, and able" to provide the interstate trucking services they proposed. Because generally the firm already had to be providing these trucking services to show this and such services could not be provided without the ICC license, this catch-22 clause effectively stopped the entry of new common carrier trucking firms.

Firms were assigned very specific routes to reduce the competition between ICC-licensed carriers, and they had to specify the service to be rendered, including the commodities to be carried. Existing firms also found it difficult to get extensions of their routes. The method of determining rates was much the same as for the railroads. In fact, the ICC began to move to equalize rates as much as possible between trucks and railroads so that neither had a competitive edge.

A complaint of the railroads was that interstate trucking competition was unfair because it was subsidized while railroads were not. All railroad property was privately owned and subject to property taxes, whereas truckers used the existing road system and therefore neither had to bear the costs of creating the road system nor pay taxes upon it. Beginning with the Federal Road-Aid Act of 1916, small amounts of money were provided as an incentive for states to construct rural post roads.[21] However, through the First World War most of the funds for highway construction came from a combination of levies on the adjacent property owners and county and state taxes. The monies raised by the counties were commonly 60 percent of the total funds allocated, and these primarily came from property taxes. In 1919 Oregon pioneered the state gasoline tax, which then began to be adopted by more and more states. A highway system financed by property taxes and other levies can be construed as a subsidization of motor vehicles, and one study for the period up to 1920 found evidence of substantial subsidization of trucking.[22] However, the use of gasoline taxes moved closer to the goal of users paying the costs of the highways. Neither did the trucks have to pay for all of the highway construction because automobiles jointly used the highways. What the gasoline taxes collected from trucks needed to cover were the extra costs involved in constructing the highways so as to accommodate the larger and heavier trucks which is what gasoline taxes aimed at.

Airlines

Though their history can be dated back to 1914, the nation's airlines only began to provide significant competition for the railroads' passenger traffic in the late 1930s.[23] Air travel in the 1920s was subsidiary to the air mail service which the Post Office contracted for. The 1925 Kelly (or Air Mail) Act and the 1926 Air Commerce Act, creating the Bureau of Commerce to control airline and airport development, initiated the modern era of airlines in the United States. The primary purpose of the Air Mail Act was to provide the subsidy to create domestic airlines. Most of the early airlines were organized as extensions of aircraft producers and were a way to sell their planes. In the late 1920s and early 1930s there was a series of mergers from which evolved the nuclei of the four dominant airlines through the 1970s.

United Airlines grew out of William E. Boeing's company. Eastern Airlines grew out of a merger of several producers, including the Curtiss-Wright Aircraft and Engine Company and several small carriers. TWA was formed by a merger of competing airlines in the western United States. American Airlines grew out of the Aviation Company, AVCO, which had combined Fairchild, an aircraft producer, and, 12 small airlines. These 4 airlines became the dominant trunk carriers. The regional carriers, such as Northwest, Braniff, Western, Continental, Northeast, National, and Delta, were also initially created to obtain mail contracts.

Postmaster General Walter Folger Brown forced some of these mergers in the early 1930s (primarily through his awarding of contracts) to fit his vision of a nationwide airline system.[24] Such a policy was bound to make enemies, and by 1933 such charges were being printed in the newspapers. Hearings were held, Brown was suspended and all air mail contracts were suspended. The Army Air Corps began carrying the mail but there were numerous crashes and rising costs. Congress quickly passed the Air Mail Act of 1934, which prohibited carriers that were party to the W. F. Brown route manipulations from bidding on the air mail routes. It also mandated a separation of aircraft producers and air carriers. United Air Lines, American Airlines, Transcontinental and Western Airlines, Eastern Airlines, and others were created from the former firms.

By 1933 a revolution in aircraft was underway. In 1932 Boeing created the Boeing 247 for United Airways. The plane could carry 10 passengers and a stewardess and was faster. Unable to purchase the plane, TWA asked Donald Douglas's company to design a bigger, faster aircraft. The plane—shortly to become the DC-3—could comfortably carry 21 passengers and fly at 170 miles per hour. It was the first plane to make passenger service alone a profitable business. By 1940, 80 percent of all scheduled airliners were DC-3s.[25] The overseas airline, Pan American Airways, developed a fleet of amphibious planes—Sikorskys and the 1939 Boeing B-314—which could carry many more fare paying passengers. By 1940 Pan Am was generally called the world's greatest airline.[26]

The Air Mail Act of 1934 was essentially a stop-gap measure with overlapping and confusing duties divided between the Post Office, Bureau of Commerce, and ICC. To end this the Civil Aeronautics Act was passed in 1938. It created a new body, the Civil Aeronautics Authority (CAA), to control the airlines rather than giving these powers to the ICC. The CAA was created with five appointed members, no more than three of whom could come from the same political party. President Roosevelt found this unsatisfactory, and in 1940 legislation was passed creating a Civil Aeronautics Board (CAB) which was more independent and replaced the CAA.[27]

The CAA and CAB were charged with three main tasks: they were to control service and entry, rates and earnings, and ensure safe operations. The existing airlines and routes were grandfathered. New routes and route extensions were denied if they would harm any existing carriers "contrary to the public interest." This froze the existing trunk route system and stopped the entry of new trunk (or national) airlines. The CAB also set rates and eliminated rate competition.

Transportation in the Interwar American Economy

The American economy occupies a vast geographic region. Because economic activity occurs over most of the country, falling transportation costs have been crucial to knitting American firms and consumers into a unified market. Throughout the nineteenth century the railroads played this crucial role. Because of the size of the railroad companies and their importance in the economic life of Americans, the federal government began to regulate them. But, by 1917 it appeared that the railroad system had achieved some stability, and it was generally assumed that the post-First World War era would be an extension of the era from 1900 to 1917.

Nothing could have been further from the truth. Spurred by public investments in highways, cars and trucks voraciously ate into the railroad's market, and, though the regulators failed to understand this at the time, the railroad's monopoly on transportation quickly disappeared. As the depression enveloped the United States, the highly competitive trucking industry suffered. The government's response was to assume that this was due to the structure of the trucking industry and could be corrected with an extension of regulation to interstate trucking. And, of course, the regulation would also reduce the competitive pressures on the railroads. If regulation was to be extended to interstate trucking and buses, then it certainly should be extended to the oil pipelines, which were carrying much of the nation's petroleum, and to natural gas pipelines. The infant airlines had largely been created by federal air mail contracts and also required government action. By 1940, when the government extended the ICC's control to domestic water transportation, all types of public interstate transportation of freight and passengers were regulated by the federal government. This pervasive government influence had already shaped domestic transportation and would continue to do so in the years following the Second World War.

COMMUNICATIONS

Communications had joined with transportation developments in the nineteenth century to tie the American economy together more completely. The telegraph had benefited by using the railroads' right-of-ways, and the railroads used the telegraph to coordinate and organize their far-flung activities. As the cost of communications fell and information transfers sped, the development of firms with multiple plants at distant locations was facilitated. The interwar era saw a continuation of these developments as the telephone continued to supplant the telegraph and the new medium of radio arose to transmit news and provide a brand new entertainment source.

Telegraph and Telephones

Telegraph domination of business and personal communications had given way to the telephone as long distance telephone calls between the east and west coasts with the new electronic amplifiers became possible in 1915.[28] The number of telegraph messages handled grew in the twenties, but dropped 39 percent between 1929 and 1933. Overall, the number of telegraph messages handled grew 20.7 percent between 1920 and 1940.

In contrast, the number of local telephone conversations grew 64.5 percent between 1920 and 1940, while the number of long distance conversations grew 67.6 percent over the same period. (See Figure 4.7.) There were three times as many long distance telephone calls as telegraph messages handled in 1920, and six times as many in 1940. And the number of local telephone conversations was about 30 times larger in 1940 than it had been in 1920.

The twenties were a prosperous period for the AT&T and its 18 major operating companies.[29] The number of daily local telephone conversations increased 45 percent, while the number of daily long distance conversations increased 78 percent. As Figure 4.8 shows, the share of all households with a telephone rose from 35 percent to nearly 42 percent. In cities across the nation, AT&T consolidated its system, gained control of many operating companies, and virtually eliminated its competitors.[30] It was able to do

Fig. 4.7 Average Daily Local and Toll Telephone Conversations

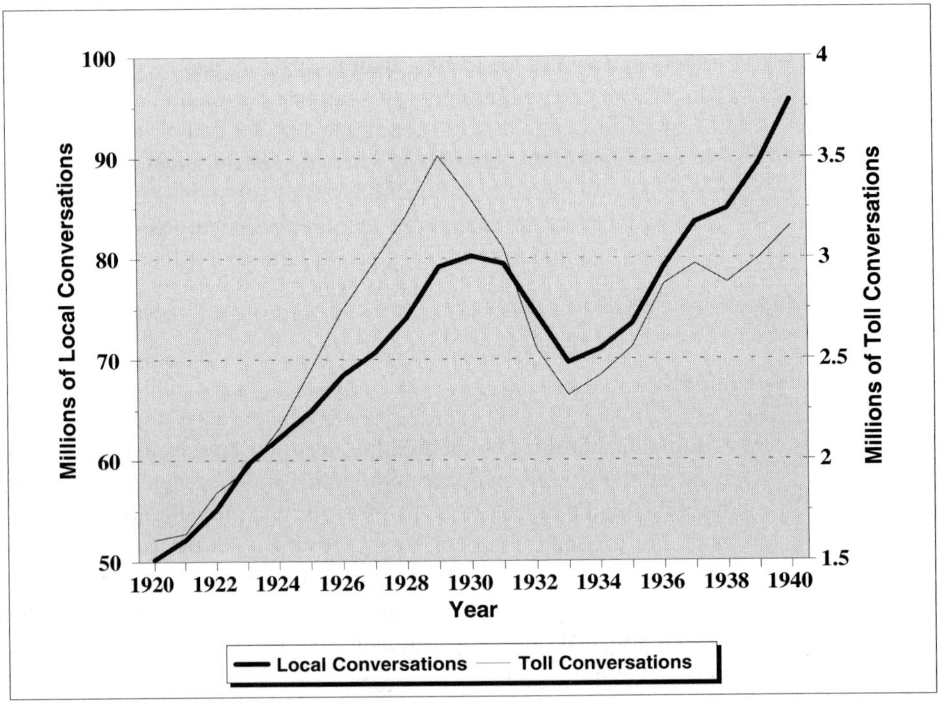

Source: *Historical Statistics of the United States: Colonial Times to 1970* (Washington, D.C.: U.S. Government Printing Office, 1976).

this because in 1921 Congress passed the Graham Act exempting AT&T from the Sherman Act in consolidating competing telephone companies. By 1940, the non-Bell operating companies were all small.

The depression hit telephone use hard. In the rural areas this decline was even worse and actually began in the twenties.[31] In 1920, 39 percent of American farms had telephones, and this percentage, surprisingly enough, was higher than for city households, of which only 34 percent had telephones. By 1930, only 34 percent of farm households had telephones; by 1940 this percentage had fallen even further, to 25 percent.[32]

The decline in telephone use during the Great Depression is not too difficult to understand. Lengthy hearings by state public service commissions on requests for rate changes typcially delayed rate changes for several years. During the depression falling prices led to sharp increases in real telephone rates and telephone use correspondingly declined.[33]

But this does not explain the decline in telephone use on the farms during the twenties and the recovery from the Great Depression. Rising telephone rates explain part of the decline in rural use. The imposition of connection fees during the First World War

Fig. 4.8 The Number of Telephones and the Percent of Households with Telephones

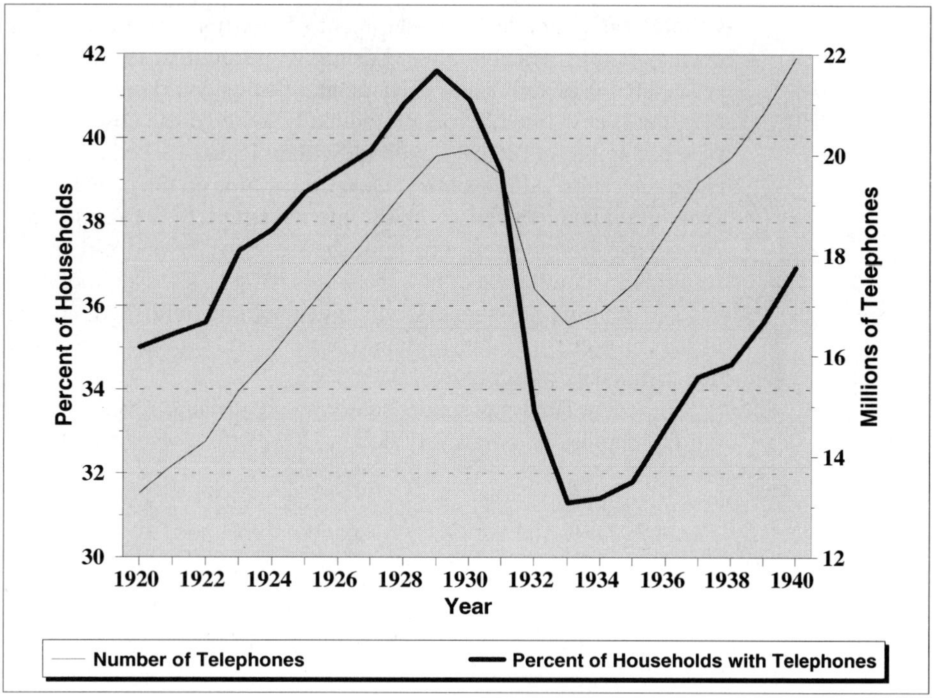

Source: *Historical Statistics of the United States: Colonial Times to 1970* (Washington, D.C.: U.S. Government Printing Office, 1976).

made it more costly for new farmers to hook up. As AT&T gained control of more and more operating systems, telephone rates were increased. AT&T also began requiring as a condition of interconnection that independent companies upgrade their systems to meet AT&T standards. Most of the small mutual companies that had provided service to farmers had operated on a shoestring—wires were often strung along fenceposts, and phones were inexpensive "whoop and holler" magneto units. Upgrading to AT&T's standards raised costs, forcing these companies to raise rates.

However, it also seems likely that during the 1920s there was a general decline in the rural demand for telephone services.[34] One important factor in this was the dramatic decline in farm incomes in the early twenties and again during the Great Depression. The second reason was a change in the farmers' environment. Prior to the First World War, the telephone eased farm isolation and provided news and weather information which was otherwise hard to obtain. After 1920 automobiles, surfaced roads, movies, and the radio loosened the isolation and the telephone was no longer as crucial.

Newspapers

Othmar Merganthaler's development of the linotype machine in the late nineteenth century had irrevocably altered printing and publishing. This machine which quickly created a line of soft, lead-based metal type that could be printed, melted down and then recast as a new line of type, dramatically lowered the costs of printing. Previously, all type had to be set by hand, with individual letters picked out to construct words, lines, and paragraphs. After printing, each line of type on the page had to be broken down and each individual letter placed back into its compartment for use in the next printing job. Newspapers often were not published every day and did not contain many pages, resulting in a multitude of newspapers in most cities. The linotype machine lowered the costs of printing newspapers, which began to be published more regularly and to grow in size. A process of consolidation of daily and Sunday newspapers began that continues to this day. (See Figure 4.9.)

By early 1933 newspaper sales and advertising revenue, like everything else during the depression, were way down. However, newspapers placed the primary blame

Fig. 4.9 Daily and Sunday Newspapers Published

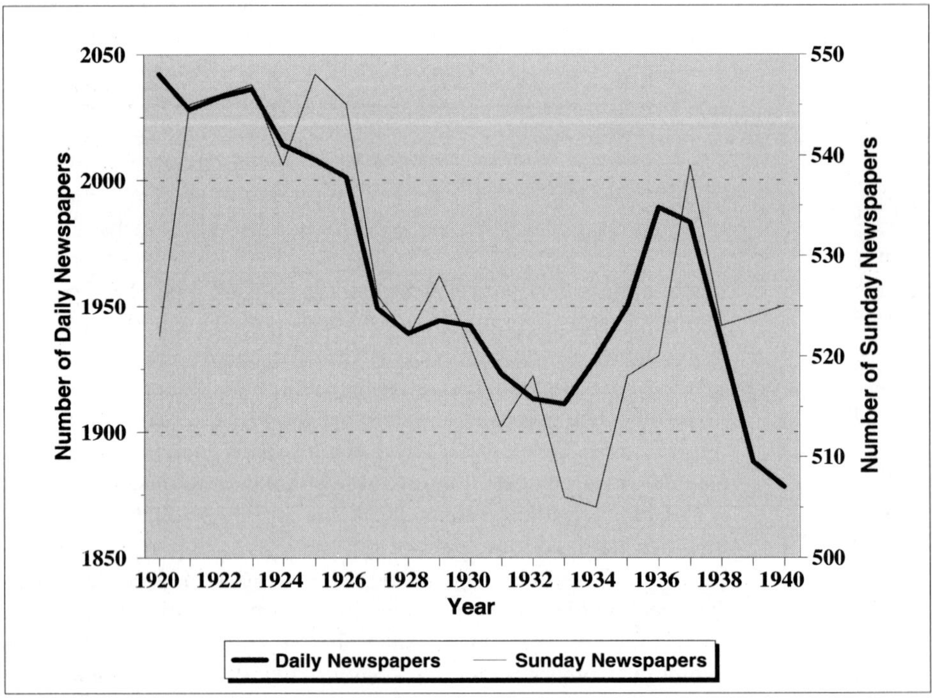

Source: *Historical Statistics of the United States: Colonial Times to 1970* (Washington, D.C.: U.S. Government Printing Office, 1976).

for their troubles on the new medium of radio, which had continued to expand during the depression. Newspapers had been providing news to the radio stations, as had the wire services—Associated Press (AP), United Press (UP), and the International News Service (INS). They believed that if they and the wire services stopped providing news reports to the radio stations and networks, consumers and advertisers would have to turn back to the newspapers, and in 1933 such an agreement was reached. By the fall of 1933, the NBC and CBS radio networks were successfully developing their own news organizations. A new agreement was reached to provide limited news clips to the networks and radio stations. In response several radio news services were started, of which the most successful was Transradio. This led the three major wire services to cancel their agreement and begin directly supplying wire news services to the radio stations and the networks, the same as to the newspapers.[35] With the recovery after 1933, the number of newspapers and newspaper circulation and advertising revenues began to recover.

Radio

For city families as well as farm families, radio became the new source of news and entertainment.[36] It soon took over as the prime advertising medium and in the process revolutionized advertising. By 1930 more homes had radio sets than had telephones, and by 1940 over 81 percent of all households had a radio set. The social power of radio was vividly demonstrated on Halloween of 1938 when Orson Welles's Mercury Theater Players broadcast H. G. Wells's fantasy, *The War of the Worlds*, as a mock news report. The result was panic in many places as the broadcast was believed to be a real news event. More importantly, the radio networks sent news and entertainment broadcasts all over the country. The isolation of rural life, particularly in many areas of the plains, was forever broken by the intrusion of the "black box," as radio receivers were often called. The radio began a process of breaking down regionalism and creating a common culture in the United States.

The potential demand for radio became clear with the first regular broadcast of Westinghouse's KDKA in Pittsburgh in the fall of 1920.[37] Because the Department of Commerce could not deny a license application there was an explosion of stations all broadcasting at 360 meters and signal jamming and interference became a serious problem.[38] By 1923 the Department of Commerce had gained control of radio over the Post Office and the Navy and began to arbitrarily disperse stations on the radio dial and deny licenses creating the first market in commercial broadcast licenses.[39] In 1926 a U.S. District Court decided that under the Radio Law of 1912 Herbert Hoover, the secretary of commerce, did not have this power. New stations appeared and the logjam and interference of signals worsened. A Radio Act was passed in January of 1927 creating the Federal Radio Commission (FRC) as a temmporary licensing authority. Licenses were to be issued in the public interest, convenience, and necessity.[40] A number of broadcasting licenses were revoked; stations were assigned frequencies, dial locations, and power levels. The FRC created 24 clear-channel stations with as much as 50,000 watts of broadcasting power, of which 21 ended up being affiliated with the new national radio networks. The Communications Act of 1934 essentially repeated the 1927 act except that it created a permanent, seven-person Federal Communications Commission (FCC).

Local stations broadcast and initially created the radio programs. The expenses were modest, and stores and companies operating radio stations wrote this off as indirect, goodwill advertising. Several forces changed all this. In 1922, AT&T opened up a radio station in New York City, WEAF (later to become WNBC). AT&T envisioned this station as the center of a radio toll system where individuals could purchase time to broadcast a message transmitted to other stations in the toll network using AT&T's long distance lines and an August, 1922 broadcast by a Long Island realty company became the first conscious use of direct advertising.

Though advertising continued to be condemned, the fiscal pressures on radio stations to accept advertising began rising. In 1923 the American Society of Composers and Publishers (ASCAP), began demanding a performance fee anytime ASCAP-copyrighted music was performed on the radio, either live or on record. By 1924 the issue was settled, and most stations began paying performance fees to ASCAP. AT&T decided that all stations broadcasting with non AT&T transmitters were violating their patent rights and began asking for annual fees from such stations based on the station's power. By the end of 1924, most stations were paying the fees. All of this drained the coffers of the radio stations, and more and more of them began discreetly accepting advertising.[41]

RCA became upset at AT&T's creation of a chain of radio stations and set up its own toll network using the inferior lines of Western Union and Postal Telegraph, because AT&T, not surprisingly, did not allow any toll (or network) broadcasting on its lines except by its own stations. AT&T began to worry that its actions might threaten its federal monopoly in long distance telephone communications. In 1926 a new firm was created, the National Broadcasting Company (NBC), which took over all broadcasting activities. When NBC debuted in November of 1926, it had two networks: the Red, which was the old AT&T network, and the Blue, which was the old RCA network.[42] Radio networks allowed advertisers to direct advertising at a national audience at a lower cost. Network programs allowed local stations to broadcast superior programs that captured a larger listening audience and in return received a share of the fees the national advertiser paid to the network.

In 1927 a new network, the Columbia Broadcasting System (CBS) financed by the Paley family began operation.[43] The success of NBC's two networks and of CBS induced others to enter. Ed Wynn, a famous comedian, unsuccessfully attempted to start the Amalgamated Broadcasting Network in 1934, and another network proposed in the same year by George McClelland never got off the ground. The Mutual Broadcasting System, also started in 1934 by the *Chicago Tribune* and the R. H. Macy Company, did survive, but it always had a minor role compared to CBS and NBC.[44] In 1941, as a result of the FCC's 1938 probe of monopoly in broadcasting, NBC agreed to dispose of one of its two networks. The assets of the two NBC networks were separated and, because the Red network was the stronger, the Blue network was put on the auction block. Edward J. Noble acquired the Blue network in 1943 along with eight stations and renamed it the American Broadcasting Company (ABC), while the NBC's simply became NBC.[45]

In the late thirties two new technologies were developed. FM (or frequency modulation) radio signals which provided static-free reception compared to the AM (or amplitude modulation) radio signals, was developed by E. H. Howard, while RCA developed electronic television.[46] When they presented their proposals to the FCC in 1936, both used the same frequencies. Demonstrations of both FM radio and television were prepared and presented at the end of the 1930s, but the conflict over frequency assignments and then the Second World War stopped further development of these technologies.

Communications in the Interwar American Economy

Communications developments in the interwar era present something of a mixed picture. By 1920 long distance telephone service was in place, but rising rates slowed the rate of adoption in the period, and telephone use in rural areas declined sharply. Though direct dialing was first tried in the twenties, its general implementation would not come until the postwar era, when other changes, such as microwave transmission of signals and touch-tone dialing, would also appear. Though the number of newspapers declined, newspaper circulation generally held up. The number of competing newspapers in larger cities began declining, a trend that also would accelerate in the postwar American economy. Both television and FM radio had made an initial appearance, but they would have to wait for the postwar era to make their moves toward entertainment supremacy. Through 1948, AM radio reigned supreme as the entertainment and news medium. Since its commercial birth in the early twenties, AM radio had irrevocably altered the social lives of Americans bringing all corners of the United States much closer together.

SELECTED REFERENCES

Barnouw, Eric. *A Tower in Babel: A History of Broadcasting in the United States: Vol. I—to 1933.* New York: Oxford University Press, 1966.

__________. *The Golden Web: A History of Broadcasting in the United States: Vol. II—1933 to 1953.* New York: Oxford University Press, 1968.

Bright, Arthur A., Jr. *The Electric Lamp Industry: Technological Change and Economic Development from 1800 to 1947.* New York: Macmillan, 1947.

Brown, D. Clayton. *Electricity for Rural America: The Fight for the REA.* Westport, CT: The Greenwood Press, 1980.

Bryant, Keith L., Jr., and Henry C. Dethloff. *A History of American Business.* Englewood Cliffs, NJ: Prentice-Hall, 1983.

Chandler, Alfred D., Jr. *Strategy and Structure: Chapters in the History of the American Industrial Enterprise.* Cambridge: The M.I.T. Press, 1962.

__________. *The Visible Hand: The Managerial Revolution in American Business.* Cambridge: Harvard University Press Belknap Press, 1977.

Chester, Giraud, and Garnet R. Garrison. *Radio and Television: An Introduction.* New York: Appleton-Century Crofts, 1950.

Daley, Robert. *An American Saga: Juan Trippe and His Pan American Empire.* New York: Random House, 1980.

Davies, R. E. G. *A History of the World's Airlines.* London: Oxford University Press, 1964.

Dearing, Charles L., and Wilfred Owen. *National Transportation Policy.* Washington: The Brookings Institution, 1949.

Devine, Warren D., Jr. " From Shafts to Wires: Historical Perspectives on Electrification." *The Journal of Economic History* 43 (June 1983): 347–72.

Eckert, Ross D., and George W. Hilton. "The Jitneys." *The Journal of Law and Economics* 15 (October 1972): 293–326.

Fischer, Claude. "The Revolution in Rural Telephony, 1900–1920." *Journal of Social History* 21 (1987): 221–38.

__________. "Technology's Retreat: The Decline of Rural Telephony in the United States, 1920–1940." *Social Science History*, Vol. 11 (Fall 1987), pp. 295–327.

Garnet, Robert W. *The Telephone Enterprise: The Evolution of the Bell System's Horizontal Structure, 1876–1900.* Baltimore: The Johns Hopkins University Press, 1985.

Hadwiger, Don F., and Clay Cochran. "Rural Telephones in the United States." *Agricultural History* 58 (July 1984): 221–38.

Herbst, Anthony F., and Joseph S. K. Wu. "Some Evidence of Subsidization of the U.S. Trucking Industry, 1900–1920." *The Journal of Economic History* 33 (June 1973): 417–33.

Hilton, George W., and John Due. *The Electric Interurban Railways in America.* Stanford: Stanford University Press, 1960.

Hunter, Louis C. "Industry in the Twentieth Century." Chapter 37 in *The Growth of the American Economy* 2d ed. Edited by Harold F. Williamson. Englewood Cliffs, NJ: Prentice-Hall, 1951.

Keller, Robert. "Factor Income Distribution in the United States During the 20's: A Reexamination of Fact and Theory." *The Journal of Economic History* 33 (March 1973): 252–95.

Kelly, Charles J., Jr. *The Sky's the Limit: The History of the Airlines.* New York: Coward-McCann, 1963.

Lipartito, Kenneth. *The Bell System and Regional Business: The Telephone in the South, 1877–1920.* Baltimore: The Johns Hopkins University Press, 1989.

MacDonald, Forrest. *Insull.* Chicago: University of Chicago Press, 1962.

McCraw, Thomas K. *TVA and the Power Fight, 1933—1937.* Philadelphia: J. B. Lippincott, 1971.

Mitchell, Broadhus. *Depression Decade: From New Era through New Deal, 1929–1941.* New York: Rinehart and Co., 1947.

Morris, Lloyd. *Not So Long Ago.* New York: Random House, 1949.

Mosco, Vincent. *Broadcasting in the United States: Innovative Challenge and Organizational Control.* Norwood, NJ: Ablex Publishing Corp., 1979.

Moulton, Harold G. et al. *The American Transportation Problem.* Washington: The Brookings Institution, 1933.

Norton, Hugh S. *Modern Transportation Economics.* Columbus, OH: Charles E. Merrill Books, Inc., 1963.

Passer, Harold C. *The Electrical Manufacturers, 1875–1900.* Cambridge: Harvard University Press, 1953.

Pusateri, C. Joseph. *A History of American Business*, 2d ed. Arlington Heights, IL: Harlan Davidson, 1988.

Rae, John B. *Climb to Greatness: The American Aircraft Industry, 1920–1960.* Cambridge: The M.I.T. Press, 1968.

Rezneck, Samuel. "Mass Production and the Use of Energy." Chapter 38 in *The Growth of the American Economy* 2d ed. Edited by Harold F. Williamson. Englewood Cliffs, NJ: Prentice-Hall, 1951.

Rosen, Philip T. *The Modern Stentors: Radio Broadcasters and the Federal Government, 1920–1934.* Westport, CT: The Greenwood Press, 1980.

__________. "Government, Business, and Technology in the 1920s: The Emergence of American Broadcasting." In *American Business History: Case Studies.* Edited by Henry C. Dethloff and C. Joseph Pusateri. Arlington Heights, IL: Harlan Davidson, 1987.

Sampson, Roy J., and Martin T. Ferris. *Domestic Transportation: Practice, Theory, and Policy,* 4th ed. Boston: Houghton Mifflin Co., 1979.

Soule, George. *Prosperity Decade: From War to Depression, 1917–1929.* New York: Rinehart and Co., 1947.

Temin, Peter. *The Fall of the Bell System.* New York: Cambridge University Press, 1987.

Williamson, Harold F. et al. *The American Petroleum Industry: The Age of Energy, 1899–1959.* Evanston, IL: Northwestern University Press, 1963.

NOTES

1. Warren D. Devine, Jr., "From Shafts to Wires: Historical Perspectives on Electrification," *The Journal of Economic History* 43 (June 1983): 347–72.
2. George Soule, *Prosperity Decade: From War to Depression, 1917–1929* (New York: Rinehart and Co.) 175.
3. Robert Keller, "Factor Income Distribution in the United States During the 20's: A Reexamination of Fact and Theory," *The Journal of Economic History* 33 (March 1973): 252–95.
4. Samuel Rezneck, "Mass Production and the Use of Energy," chapter 38 in Harold F. Williamson, ed., *The Growth of the American Economy*, 2d ed., (Englewood Cliffs, NJ: Prentice-Hall, 1951), 735–36.
5. Louis C. Hunter, "Industry in the Twentieth Century," chapter 37 in Williamson, *Growth of the American Economy*, 711.
6. Soule, *Prosperity Decade*, 178.
7. The discussion in this section is drawn from the following sources: Louis C. Hunter, "Industry in the Twentieth Century," chapter 37 in Williamson, *The Growth of the American Economy*; Alfred D. Chandler, Jr., *Strategy and Structure: Chapters in the History of the American Industrial Enterprise* (Cambridge: The M.I.T. Press, 1962), chapter 4; Alfred D. Chandler, Jr., *The Visible Hand: The Managerial Revolution in American Business* (Cambridge: Harvard University Press Belknap Press, 1977); Keith L. Bryant, Jr., and Henry C. Dethloff, *A History of American Business* (Englewood Cliffs, NJ: Prentice-Hall, Inc., 1983); Harold F. Williamson et al., *The American Petroleum Industry: The Age of Energy, 1899–1959* (Evanston, IL: Northwestern University Press, 1963).
8. Some of this information is drawn from the following sources: Arthur A. Bright, Jr., *The Electric Lamp Industry: Technological Change and Economic Development from 1800 to 1947* (New York: Macmillan, 1947); Harold C. Passer, *The Electrical Manufacturers, 1875–1900* (Cambridge: Harvard University Press, 1953).
9. George Soule, *Prosperity Decade*, 183; Robert Keller, "Factor Income Distribution in the United States During the 1920's: A Reexamination of Fact and Theory," *The Journal of Economic History* 33 (March 1973): 252–95.

10. Lloyd J. Mercer, "Comment on Papers by Scheiber, Keller, and Raup," *The Journal of Economic History* 33 (March 1973): 291–95.
11. Soule, *Prosperity Decade*, 183.
12. See Thomas K. McCraw, *TVA and the Power Fight, 1933–1937* (Philadelphia: J. B. Lippincott, 1971).
13. The creation and development of the Rural Electrification Administration is discussed extensively in D. Clayton Brown, *Electricity for Rural America: The Fight for the REA* (Westport, CT: The Greenwood Press, 1980).
14. Broadhus Mitchell, *Depression Decade: From New Era through New Deal, 1929–1941* (New York: Rinehart and Co., 1947), 222–23.
15. Most of the following information comes from the following sources: Hugh S. Norton, *Modern Transportation Economics* (Columbus, OH: Charles E. Merrill Books, Inc., 1963), chapters 10 and 11; Roy J. Sampson and Martin T. Farris, *Domestic Transportation: Practice, Theory, and Policy,* 4th ed, (Boston: Houghton Mifflin Company, 1979), chapters 20–22; Charles L. Dearing and Wilfred Owen, *National Transportation Policy* (Washington: The Brookings Institution, 1949).
16. On the history of the electric interurban railways see George W. Hilton and John Due, *The Electric Interurban Railways in America* (Stanford: Stanford University Press, 1960).
17. Harold G. Moulton et al., *The American Transportation Problem* (Washington: The Brookings Institution, 1933), 89.
18. Norton, *Modern Transportation Economics*, 195.
19. The following discussion draws on several sources: Keith L Bryant, Jr., and Henry C. Dethloff, *A History of American Business* (Englewood Cliffs, NJ: Prentice-Hall, Inc., 1983), chapter 8; Sampson and Farris, *Domestic Transportation*, chapter 2, 4, and 21; Norton, *Modern Transportation Economics*, chapters 10 and 11; and Dearing and Owen, *National Transportation Policy*.
20. Contract carriers (under contract to a single firm to carry one specified type of freight), private carriers, local trucking, newspaper trucks, U.S. mail trucks, and state and local government trucks did not have to be licensed or have permits.
21. The following data and information comes from Dearing and Owen, *National Transportation Policy*, chapter 6.
22. Anthony F. Herbst and Joseph S. K. Wu, "Some Evidence of Subsidization of the U.S. Trucking Industry, 1900–1920," *The Journal of Economic History* 33 (June 1973): 417–33.
23. Most of this discussion is taken from the following sources: R. E. G. Davies, *A History of the World's Airlines* (London: Oxford University Press, 1964); John B. Rae, *Climb To Greatness: The American Aircraft Industry, 1920–1960* (Cambridge, MA: The MIT Press, 1968); Dearing and Owen, *National Transportation Policy*; Sampson and Farris, *Domestic Transportation*. For additional information, see Robert Daley, *An American Saga: Juan Trippe and His Pan American Empire* (New York: Random House, 1980), and Charles J. Kelly, Jr., *The Sky's the Limit: The History of the Airlines* (New York: Coward-McCann, 1963).
24. Ibid., 123–30.
25. Rae, *Climb to Greatness*, chapter 4.
26. Davies, *A History of the World's Airlines*, chapter 9.
27. Ibid., chapter 10.
28. Western Union's telegraph empire was the great communications monopoly in the 1870s. But its refusal to join Theodore Vail's new telephone venture was a mistake. By 1909 Bell Telephone was much larger and purchased Western Union, though the Justice Department

objected and the two firms were separated.

29. The following is drawn from the following sources: Peter Temin, *The Fall of the Bell System* (New York: Cambridge University Press, 1987); John Brooks, *Telephone: The First Hundred Years* (New York: Harper and Row, 1975); Robert W. Garnet, *The Telephone Enterprise: The Evolution of the Bell System's Horizontal Structure, 1876–1900* (Baltimore: The Johns Hopkins University Press, 1985); Kenneth Lipartito, *The Bell System and Regional Business: The Telephone in the South, 1877–1920* (Baltimore: The Johns Hopkins University Press, 1989).
30. In 1945, Philadelphia, the last two-system city, became a one-system city. Brooks, *Telephone*, 160.
31. This discussion draws upon the following sources: Don F. Hadwiger and Clay Cochran, "Rural Telephones in the United States," *Agricultural History* 58 (July 1984): 221–38; Claude Fischer, "The Revolution in Rural Telephony, 1900–1920," *Journal of Social History* 21 (1987): 5–26; Claude Fischer, "Technology's Retreat: The Decline of Rural Telephony in the United States, 1920–1940," *Social Science History* 11 (Fall 1987): 295–327.
32. Fischer, "Technology's Retreat," 297.
33. In 1931 the Wisconsin Public Service Commission, under the direction of David E. Lilienthal, set out to change the basic procedures and reduce the delays. These changes filtered down to other state public service commissions and in 1933 regulators generally began to order rate reductions. Brooks, *Telephone*, 188–189.
34. This discussion draws upon Fischer, "Technology's Retreat," 300–20.
35. Erik Barnouw, *The Golden Web: A History of Broadcasting in the United States: Vol. II—1933 to 1953* (New York: Oxford University Press, 1968), 18–22.
36. This section primarily draws upon the following sources: Erik Barnouw, *A Tower in Babel: A History of Broadcasting in the United States: Vol. I-to 1933* (New York: Oxford University Press, 1966); Erik Barnouw, *The Golden Web: A History of Broadcasting in the United States: Vol. II-1933 to 1953* (New York: Oxford University Press, 1968); Giraud Chester and Garnet R. Garrison, *Radio and Television: An Introduction* (New York: Appleton-Century-Crofts, Inc., 1950); and, Philip T. Rosen, "Government, Business, and Technology in the 1920s: The Emergence of American Broadcasting," in Henry C. Dethloff and C. Joseph Pusateri, *American Business History: Case Studies* (Arlington Heights, IL: Harlan Davidson, Inc., 1987). Also see, Lloyd Morris, *Not So Long Ago* (New York: Random House, 1949); Philip T. Rosen, *The Modern Stentors: Radio Broadcasters and the Federal Government, 1920–1934* (Westport, CT: Greenwood Press, 1980); Vincent Mosco, *Broadcasting in the United States: Innovative Challenge and Organizational Control* (Norwood, NJ: Ablex Publishing Corporation, 1979); C. Joseph Pusateri, *A History of American Business*, 2d ed. (Arlington Heights, IL: Harlan Davidson, 1988); Keith L. Bryant, Jr., and Henry C. Dethloff, *A History of American Business* (Englewood Cliffs, NJ: Prentice-Hall, Inc., 1983).
37. The excitement and rising sales of Westinghouse receivers caused the RCA group, composed of General Electric; RCA; AT&T; and AT&T's subsidiary, Western Electric, to bring Westinghouse into the patent pool they had set up. The intention was to have GE and Westinghouse manufacture receivers that were all to be sold through RCA under its label and have Western Electric manufacture all transmitting equipment that AT&T would sell. Barnouw, *A Tower in Babel*, 67–74 and 80–81.
38. Ibid., chapter 3.

39. Rosen, "Government, Business, and Technology in the 1920s: The Emergence of American Broadcasting."
40. The FRC was to be composed of five members, each with a one year term, after which the powers were to revert back to the secretary of commerce. Later amendments extended the commission's tenure, and the powers were never returned to the secretary of commerce.
41. Barnouw, *A Tower in Babel*, 114–21 and 176.
42. Ibid., 181–91.
43. The United Independent Broadcasters, was formed in 1927. AT&T initially said that no new long distance lines would be available for three years, but after one of the founders went to Washington with checks for $1,000 and $10,000, lines suddenly became available. The Columbia Phonograph Record Company initially agreed to back the new network, which was renamed the Columbia Phonograph Broadcasting System; however, the firm shortly backed out of its commitment. The Paley family of Philadelphia then took over the network and renamed it the Columbia Broadcasting System. Barnouw, *A Tower in Babel*, 201 and 219–24.
44. Barnouw, *The Golden Web*, 31–2.
45. Ibid., 168–72 and 187–88.
46. Edwin Howard Armstrong was one of the great geniuses in the development of radio. Experimental work on television with mechanical transmission of pictures dated to the early twenties. Vladimir Zworykin directed RCA's research on this, though an isolated genius from Idaho, Philo T. Farnsworth, had taken out patents on electronic television broadcasting as early as 1930 and 1931, a date prior to RCA and Zworykin's patents.

CHAPTER 5

Developments in Finance and Domestic and International Trade: 1920–1940

DOMESTIC TRADE

Suppose that each time we wanted to discover the price of or purchase a good we had to travel to the producer's site. In such cases the cost of purchasing each good would be much higher than its price at the producer's location. Of course, this does not happen because a complex network of wholesale and retail firms exists to lower the costs of distributing goods and to lower the costs of negotiating transactions. Though we sometimes overlook the role of these intermediaries, they have, in fact, played an important role in improving efficiency in the economy.

In the nineteenth century, a complex array of wholesalers, jobbers, and retailers had developed, but changes in the postbellum period reduced the role of the wholesalers and jobbers and strengthened the importance of the retailers.[1] The appearance of the department store in the major cities and the rise of mail order firms in the postbellum period changed the retailing market.

Department Stores

A department store is a combination of specialty stores organized as departments within one general store. A. T. Stewart's huge 1846 dry goods store in New York City is often referred to as the first department store.[2] R. H. Macy started his dry goods store in 1858 and Wanamaker's in Philadelphia opened in 1876. By the end of the nineteenth century, every city of any size had at least one major department store.[3] Until the late twenties the department store field was dominated by independent stores, though some department stores in the largest cities had opened a few suburban branches and stores in other cities. In the interwar period department stores accounted for about 8 percent of retail sales.[4]

The department stores relied on a "one-price" policy, which Stewart is credited with beginning. In the antebellum period and into the postbellum period, it was common not to post a specific price on an item; rather, each purchaser haggled with a sales clerk over what the price would be. Stewart posted fixed prices on the various dry goods sold, and the customer could either decide to buy or not buy at the fixed price. The policy dramatically lowered transactions costs for both the retailer and the purchaser. Prices were reduced with a smaller markup over the wholesale price, and profits were generated by a large sales volume and a quicker turnover of the store's inventory.

Mail Order Firms

What changed the department store field in the twenties was the entrance of Sears Roebuck and Montgomery Ward, the two dominant mail order firms in the United States.[5] Both firms had began in the late nineteenth century and by 1914 the younger Sears Roebuck had surpassed Montgomery Ward. Both located in Chicago due to its central location in the nation's rail network and both had benefited from the advent of Rural Free Delivery in 1896 and low cost Parcel Post Service in 1912.

In 1924 Sears hired Robert C. Wood, who was able to convince Sears Roebuck to open retail stores. Wood believed that the declining rural population and the growing urban population forecast the gradual demise of the mail order business; survival of the mail order firms required a move into retail sales. By 1925 Sears Roebuck had opened 8 retail stores, and by 1929 it had 324 stores. Montgomery Ward quickly followed suit. Rather than locating these in the central business district (CBD), Wood located many on major streets closer to the residential areas. These moves of Sears Roebuck and Montgomery Ward expanded department store retailing and provided a new type of chain store.

Chain Stores

Though chain stores grew rapidly in the first two decades of the twentieth century, they date back to the 1860s when George F. Gilman and George Huntington Hartford opened a string of New York City A&P stores exclusively to sell tea.[6] Stores were opened in other regions and in 1912 their first "cash-and-carry" full-range grocery was opened. Soon they were opening 50 of these stores each week and by the 1920s A&P had 14,000 stores. They then phased out the small stores to reduce the chain to 4,000 full-range, supermarket-type stores. A&P's success led to new grocery store chains such as Kroger, Jewel Tea, and Safeway.

Prior to A&P's cash-and-carry policy, it was common for grocery stores, produce (or green) grocers, and meat markets to provide both home delivery and credit, both of which were costly. As a result, retail prices were generally marked up well above the wholesale prices. In cash-and-carry stores, items were sold only for cash; no credit was extended, and no expensive home deliveries were provided. Markups on prices could be much lower because other costs were much lower. Consumers liked the lower prices and were willing to pay cash and carry their groceries, and the policy became common by the twenties.

Chains also developed in other retail product lines. In 1879 Frank W. Woolworth developed a "5 and 10 Cent Store," or dime store, and there were over 1,000 F. W. Woolworth stores by the mid-1920s.[7] Other firms such as Kresge, Kress, and McCrory successfully imitated Woolworth's dime store chain. Dry goods (J.C. Penney's in 1901), drugs (Walgreen's in 1909), shoes, jewelry, cigars, and other lines of merchandise also began to be sold through chain stores.[8]

Self-Service Policies

In 1916 Clarence Saunders, a grocer in Memphis, Tennessee, built upon the one-price policy and began offering self-service at his Piggly Wiggly store. Previously, customers handed a clerk a list or asked for the items desired, which the clerk then collected and the customer paid for. With self-service, items for sale were placed on open shelves among which the customers could walk, carrying a shopping bag or pushing a shopping cart. Each customer could then browse as he or she pleased, picking out whatever was desired. Saunders and other retailers who adopted the self-service method of retail selling found that customers often purchased more because of exposure to the array of products on the shelves; as well, self-service lowered the labor required for retail sales and therefore lowered costs.

Two other innovations in retailing that began in the interwar period were not destined to become major forces in retail developments until after the Second World War. These innovations were planned shopping centers and supermarkets.

Shopping Centers and Supermarkets

The ultimate cause of both of these innovations was the widening ownership and use of the automobile. By the 1920s, as the ownership and use of the car began expanding, population began to move out of the crowded central cities toward the more open suburbs. When General Robert Wood set Sears off on its development of urban stores, he located these not in the CBD but as free-standing stores on major arteries away from the CBD with sufficient space for parking. The supermarkets developed in the 1930s followed a similar practice.[9]

At about the same time, a few entrepreneurs began to develop shopping centers. Yehoshua Cohen says, "The owner of such a center was responsible for maintenance of the center, its parking lot, as well as other services to consumers and retailers in the center."[10] Perhaps the earliest such shopping center was the Country Club Plaza built in 1922 by the J. C. Nichols Company in Kansas City, Missouri. Other early shopping centers appeared in Baltimore and Dallas. By the mid-1930s the concept of a planned shopping center was well known and was expected to be the means to capture the trade of the growing number of suburban consumers.[11] However, the depressed 1930s and controls on production and investment during the Second World War retarded the development of planned shopping centers.

According to Malcolm McNair and Eleanor May, "The food supermarket was perhaps the single most important innovation in retail distributive institutions in the entire period from 1850 to the present."[12] Most grocery stores, including the chains, operated small stores, and it was not uncommon for them to slip back from self-service to full service.[13] Chains had reduced markups from the 30 percent common in the small independent stores, but these were still relatively high, often as much as 20 percent.

The supermarkets that evolved in the 1930s took full advantage of the prior one-price, cash-and-carry, self-service developments and the widened market areas made possible by the automobile.[14] Michael Cullen's first King Kullen store was opened in August, 1930, in Jamaica, New York, and within two years he had eight such stores which he called "The Price Wreckers."[15] In December of 1932, Roy Dawson (a former associate of Clarence Saunders in Memphis) and Robert Otis opened the Big Bear (to sell groceries and other merchandise) in Elizabeth, New Jersey. Dawson and Otis advertised their store as "The Big Bear, The Price Crusher," and within a short time customers were driving up to 100 miles to shop at the Big Bear.[16] The chains and independents tried to stop wholesalers from selling to the Big Bear and newspapers from accepting the Big Bear's advertising.[17] In spite of these impediments, customers flocked to the Big Bear. Other low-priced supermarkets began opening and by the mid-

1930s were cutting into the business of the chain grocery stores.[18] The chains began to respond by developing larger stores that emulated the supermarkets. Rom Markin reports that "Between the year 1934–1937, A & P closed 933 of its 4,306 units in 38 cities, replacing them with 204 supermarkets."[19]

Retailing in the Interwar Period

By the twenties and thirties these developments in pricing and sales had brought about a remarkable transformation in retail selling as mass retailers in chains and department stores lowered the costs of selling products, lowered the cost of transactions for consumers, and facilitated the development of national brands and the advertising that came to accompany such sales. In particular, the innovations pioneered by the early supermarkets—large stores, high volume, high turnover, reduced cost and markups, and catering and responding to the growing use of the automobile—were to influence the development of discount stores, department stores, and shopping centers after the Second World War.

INTERNATIONAL TRADE

In the twenties a gold exchange standard was developed to replace the gold standard of the prewar world. Under a gold standard, each country's currency carried a fixed exchange rate with gold, and the currency had to be backed up by gold. As a result, all countries on the gold standard had fixed exchange rates with all other countries. Adjustments to balance international trade flows were made by gold flows. If a country had a deficit in its trade balance, gold would leave the country, forcing the money stock to decline and prices to fall. Falling prices made the deficit countries' exports more attractive and imports more costly, reducing the deficit. Countries with a surplus imported gold, which increased the money stock and caused prices to rise. This made the surplus countries' exports less attractive and imports more attractive, decreasing the surplus. Most economists who have studied the prewar gold standard contend that it did not work as the conventional textbook model says, because capital flows frequently reduced or eliminated the need for gold flows for long periods of time. However, there is no consensus on whether fortuitous circumstances, rather than the gold standard, saved the international economy from periodic convulsions or whether the gold standard as it did work was sufficient to promote stability and growth in international transactions.[20]

In the twenties it was argued that there was a "shortage" of fluid monetary gold to use for the gold standard, so some method of "economizing" on gold had to be found. To do this, two basic changes were made. First, most nations other than the United States stopped domestic circulation of gold. Second, the "gold exchange" system was created. Most countries held their international reserves in the form of U.S. dollars or British pounds and international transactions used dollars or pounds, as long as the United States and Great Britain stood ready to exchange their currencies for gold at fixed exchange rates. However, the overvaluation of the pound and the undervaluation of the franc threatened these arrangments. The British trade deficit led to a capital outflow, higher interest rates, and a weak economy. The French trade surplus led to the importation of gold which they did not allow to expand the money supply.[21]

Economizing on gold by no longer allowing its domestic circulation and by using key currencies as international monetary reserves was really an attempt to place the domestic economies under the control of the nations' politicians and make them independent of international events. Unfortunately, in doing this the politicians eliminated the equilibrating mechanism of the gold standard but had nothing with which to replace it. The new international monetary arrangements of the twenties were potentially destabilizing because they were not allowed to operate as a price mechanism promoting equilibrating adjustments.

War Debts and War Reparations

There were other problems with international economic activity in the twenties. As previously mentioned because of the war the United States was abruptly transformed from a debtor to a creditor on international accounts. Though the United States did not want reparations payments from Germany, it did insist that Allied governments repay American loans. The Allied governments then insisted on war reparations from Germany.[22] These initial reparations assessments were quite large. The Allied Reparations Commission collected the charges by supervising Germany's foreign trade and by internal controls on the German economy, and it could increase the reparations if it was felt that Germany could pay more. The treaty allowed France to occupy the Ruhr after Germany defaulted in 1923.[23]

Ultimately, this tangled web of debts and reparations, which was a major factor in the course of international trade, depended upon two principal actions. First, the United States had to run an import surplus or, on net, export capital out of the United States to provide a pool of dollars overseas. Germany then had either to have an export surplus or else import American capital so as to build up dollar reserves—that is, the dollars the United States was exporting. In effect, these dollars were paid by Germany to Great Britain, France, and other countries who then shipped them back to the United States as payment on their U.S. debts. If these conditions did not occur, (and note that the "new" gold standard of the twenties had lost its flexibility because the price adjustment mechanism had been eliminated) disruption in international activity could easily occur and be transmitted to the domestic economies.

Tariffs and Trade Barriers in the Interwar Period

In the wake of the 1920–21 depression Congress passed the Emergency Tariff Act, which raised tariffs, particularly on manufactured goods. The Fordney-McCumber Tariff of 1922 continued the Emergency Tariff of 1921, and its protection on many items was extremely high, ranging from 60 to 100 percent *ad valorem*.[24] As farm product prices fell at the end of the decade a tariff bill was introduced into Congress. Special interests succeeded in gaining additional (or new) protection for most domestically produced commodities. In spite of widespread condemnation by economists President Hoover signed the Hawley-Smoot Tariff in June, 1930 and rates rose sharply. With the signing of the tariff, other nations (Spain, Switzerland, Canada, Italy, Cuba, Mexico, France, Australia, and New Zealand) raised their duties or reduced quotas on American exports.[25] In 1934 President Roosevelt proposed the Reciprocal Trade Act. The act was passed and renewed in 1937 and 1940. Through executive action, reciprocal reductions in tariffs were negotiated with several countries, however, the reductions were generally small and primarily lowered redundant or ineffective duties.[26]

Commodity and Service Trade and Capital Flows in the Interwar Period

Following the First World War, the U.S. government actively promoted American exports, and in each of the postwar years through 1929, the United States recorded a surplus in its balance of trade. (See Figure 5.1.) However, the surplus declined in the 1930s as both exports and imports fell sharply after 1929. (See Figure 5.2.) From the mid-1920s on finished manufactures were the most important exports, while agricultural products dominated American imports.

The majority of the funds that allowed Germany to make its reparations payments to France and Great Britain and hence allowed those countries to pay their debts to the United States came from the net flow of capital out of the United States in the form of direct investment in real assets and investments in long- and short-term foreign financial assets. After the devastating German hyperinflation of 1922 and 1923, the Dawes Plan reformed the German economy and currency and accelerated the U.S. capital outflow.[27] (See Figure 5.3.) American investors began to actively and aggressively pursue foreign investments, particularly loans[28] and in the late twenties there was a marked deterioration in the quality of foreign bonds sold in the United States.[29]

The system, then, worked well as long as there was a net outflow of American capital, but this did not continue. In the middle of 1928, the flow of short-term capital began to decline. In 1928 the flow of "other long-term" capital out of the United States was 752 million dollars, but in 1929 it was only 34 million dollars. Though arguments now exist as to whether the booming stock market in the United States was to blame for this, it had far-reaching effects on the international economic system and the various domestic economies.[30]

War Debts and Reparations in the Depression

As the worldwide depression and contraction in international trade reduced the ability of Germany to make reparations payments and European countries to make debt payments to the United States, governments agreed to an intergovernmental debt moratorium. At a 1931 conference President Hoover made a statement (the "Hoover-Laval communique") that seemed to tie reparations payments and war debts together—if one were canceled, then the other would be too. In June and July of 1932, agreements

Fig. 5.1 The United States Balance of Payments on Goods and Services

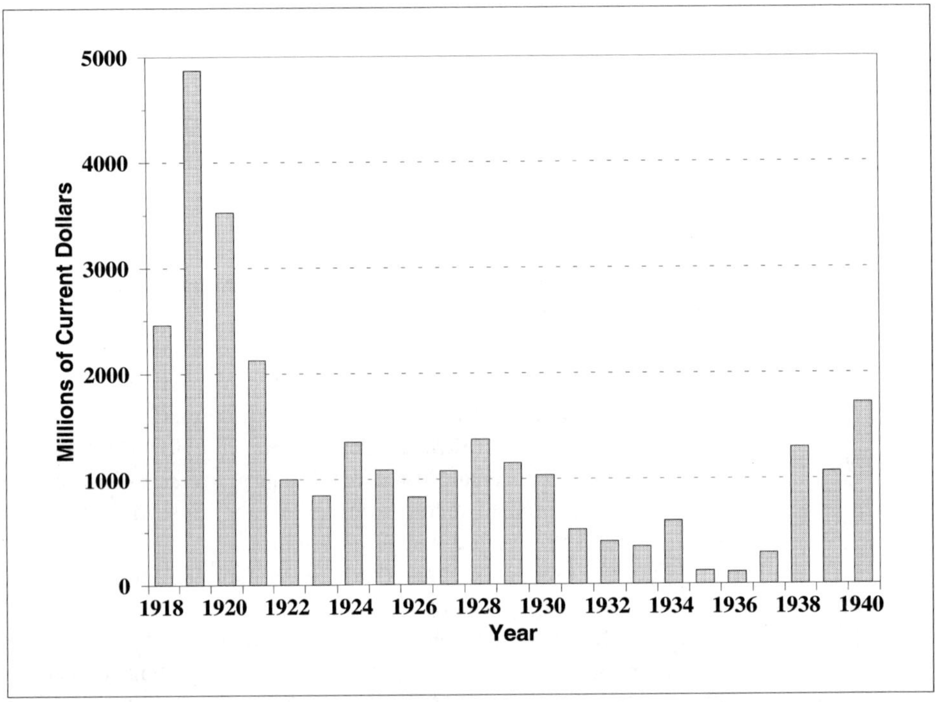

Source: *Historical Statistics of the United States: Colonial Times to 1970* (Washington, D.C.: U.S. Government Printing Office, 1976).

essentially wiped out the reparations payments. In December of 1932, Britain and France then presented notes requesting deferments of the war debt payments and a review of the entire war debt issue.[31] The United States insisted that the issues were separate and demanded the debt payments. Only Britain, Finland, Czechoslovakia, Italy, and Lithuania paid their war debt installments. In June of 1933, some countries made their payments in silver at artificially high prices while others defaulted. The process was repeated in December of 1933: after that the defaults were complete, and no more payments were made.

The End of the Gold Exchange Standard

The gold exchange standard developed in the twenties was unable to withstand the worldwide depression of the early 1930s. The initial cracks in the international monetary arrangements appeared in central Europe. In May of 1931, there were runs on Austria's largest bank and Austrian banks closed. With Austrian assets frozen, the rising liquidity demands hit banks in other countries. German banks closed in mid-July, followed by Rumanian and Hungarian banks. Private investors, banks, and govern-

Fig. 5.2 Exports and Imports as a Percent of Gross National Product

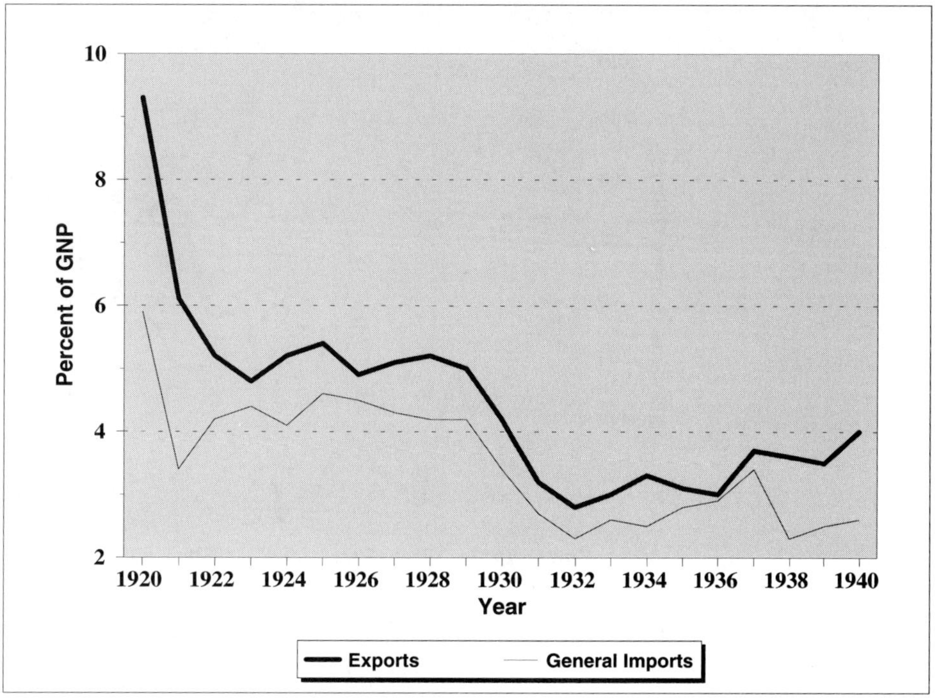

Source: *Historical Statistics of the United States: Colonial Times to 1970* (Washington, D.C.: U.S. Government Printing Office, 1976).

ments began attempting to convert their British currency and financial assets into gold, and on September 21, 1931, Great Britain left the gold standard.[32]

With Britain off gold, central banks and foreign holders of dollars began converting their dollar assets into gold since they expected the United States also to abandon the gold standard. To stop the gold drain, but remain on the gold standard, the Federal Reserve System raised the discount rate from 1.5 to 3.5 percent between October 9 and October 16. The gold drain ceased as foreign investors were induced to hold their U.S. financial assets due to the sharp increase in real interest rates.

On March 6, 1933, President Roosevelt issued a presidential proclamation prohibiting banks from paying out gold and gold certificates, and all transactions in gold and foreign exchange were placed under the control of the secretary of the treasury.[33] On April 5, 1933, he issued an executive order requiring the public to surrender all gold certificates and gold, with some minor exceptions.[34] The federal government redeemed these at the official price of $20.67 per fine ounce.

At the same time the Roosevelt Administration begin to devalue the dollar. From an initial mint price of $20.67 per fine ounce of gold, the dollar began to fall, and finally, in

Fig. 5.3 Net United States Capital Flows

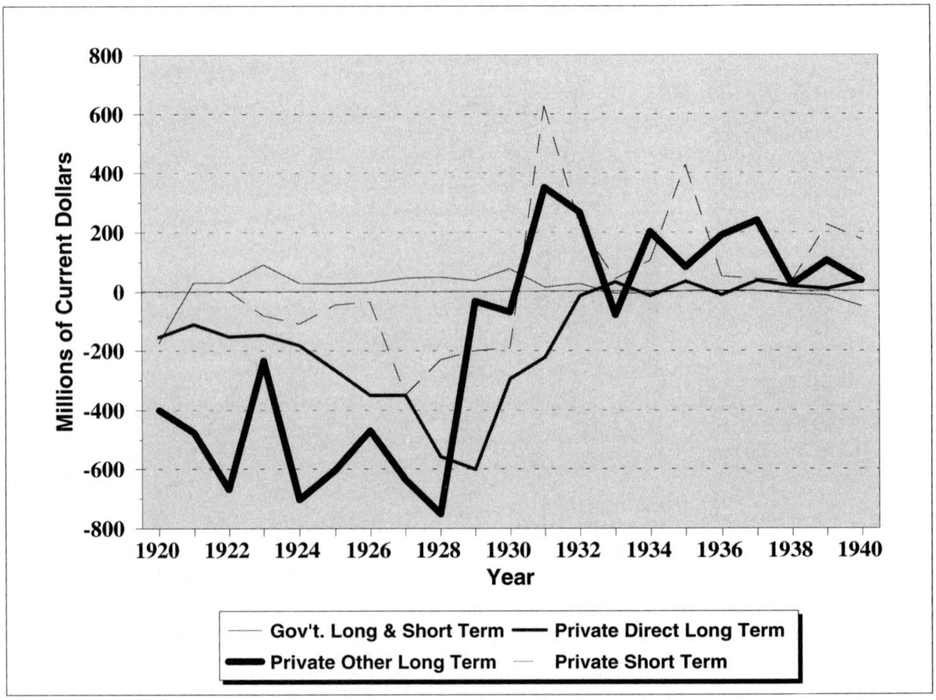

Source: *Historical Statistics of the United States: Colonial Times to 1970* (Washington, D.C.: U.S. Government Printing Office, 1976).

the Gold Reserve Act of 1934, the value was fixed at $35 per fine ounce of gold. The nationalization of all gold—completed on December 28, 1933—was ratified by this act, and the domestic redeemability of currency in gold or gold certificates was ended.[35]

One purpose of the devaluation of the dollar was to raise prices and stimulate exports. Because it raised the domestic price of imported goods and lowered the price of American exports, it effectively amounted to a very large increase in protective tariffs. The American devaluation set off a competitive devaluation by a number of countries. The regime of fixed exchange rates that developed out of the Great Depression would be incorporated into new international monetary arrangements in the Bretton Woods agreements following the Second World War.

International Trade and the Interwar American Economy

International trade and investment played an important role in the behavior of the interwar American economy. In the twenties, foreign markets provided an outlet for our growing industrial production, and overseas investment opened up new opportunities for expansion. Helped by our initiation of "beggar-thy-neighbor" policies in the late twenties and early thirties, the United States was caught in the spiraling contraction of world trade that disrupted the world's industrial economies.

We still have important, unanswered questions about international trade and the Great Depression. For example, to what extent did the Hawley-Smoot tariff, passed in early 1930, cause the contraction in international trade? Or was the contraction the result of, rather than a cause of, the Great Depression? Was the gold standard, as it was reconstituted in the twenties, a major, if not *the* major, force in bringing on a worldwide depression? We will examine these issues at length in Chapter 7.

BANKING AND FINANCE

In the twenties commercial banks became "department stores of finance."[36] Banks opened up installment (or personal) loan departments, expanded their mortgage lending, opened up trust departments, undertook securities underwriting activities, and offered safe deposit boxes. These changes were a response to growing competition from other financial intermediaries. Businesses, stung by bankers' control and reduced lending during the 1920–21 depression, began relying more on retained earnings and stock and bond issues to raise investment and, sometimes, working capital. This reduced loan demand. The thrift institutions, after good growth in the twenties, did not grow in the thirties. The stock market boom of the twenties was matched by its collapse and failure to recover in the thirties. However, the nation's commercial banks were the most important financial institutions and played the principal role in the supply of money in the United States as well as being key financial intermediaries.

Banking

There were two broad classes of commercial banks; those that were nationally chartered and those that were nonnationally chartered. Only the national banks were required to be members of the Federal Reserve System. (See Figure 5.4.) Most banks were unit banks because national regulators and most state regulators prohibited branching. However, in the twenties a few states began to permit limited branching; California even allowed statewide branching.[37] The bulk of the assets of all commercial banks were held by the Federal Reserve member banks, even though most banks were not members. A high bank failure rate in the 1920s has usually been explained by "overbanking" or too many banks located in an area, but H. Thomas Johnson makes a strong argument against this.[38] (See Figure 5.5.)

Prior to the twenties, the main assets of commercial banks were short-term business loans, made by creating a demand deposit or increasing an existing one for a borrowing firm. As business lending declined in the 1920s, commercial banks vigorously moved into new types of financial activities. As banks purchased more securities for their earning asset portfolios and gained expertise in the securities markets, larger ones established investment departments and by the late twenties were an important force in the underwriting of new securities issued by nonfinancial corporations.

The onset of the depression devastated banking as panics and continued withdrawals forced more and more banks to close. Major banking panics occurred in 1930,

Fig. 5.4 Commercial Banks in the United States

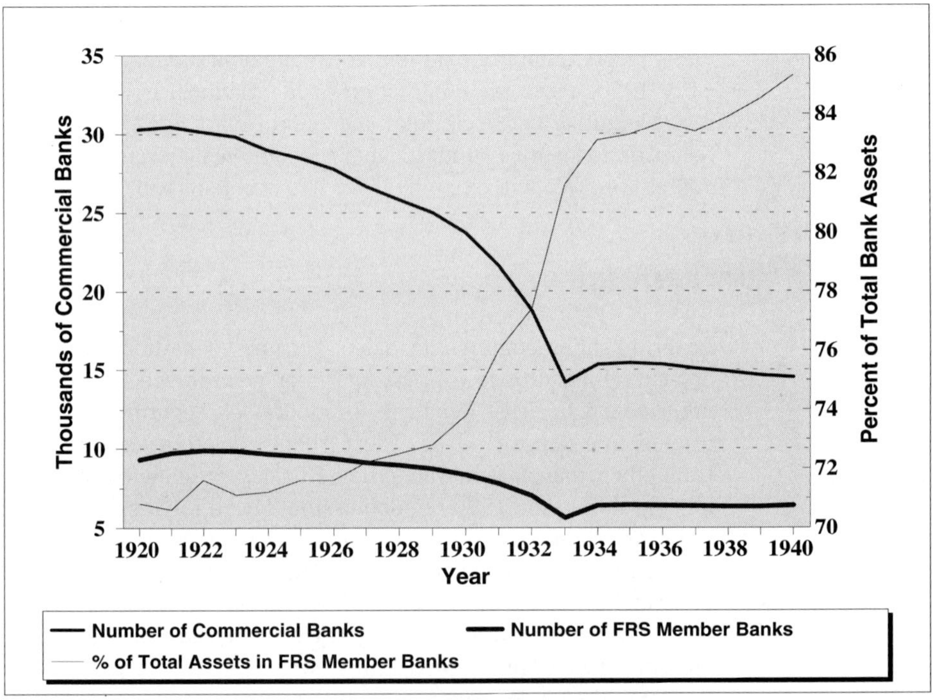

Source: *Historical Statistics of the United States: Colonial Times to 1970* (Washington, D.C.: U.S. Government Printing Office, 1976).

1931, and 1933, but in between depositors continued to reduce their deposits. In 1931, over 10.5 percent of the banks suspended operations, and in 1933 over 28 percent suspended business. Between 1929 and 1933 the number of banks fell from 24,970 to 14,207, or by 43 percent. Though more nonmember banks suspended operations than member banks, 35.6 percent of the member banks closed.

Having passed through the fires of the panics of the early thirties, banks became very cautious. They accumulated large excess reserves as a "Maginot Line" of defense against further banking panics and purchased large quantities of highly liquid federal government securities. Loans as a share of all assets dropped sharply, though some of this decline was certainly due to the weak business loan demand. Demand deposits as a share of all deposits rose as time deposit rates fell, and an increasing number of banks simply refused to accept time deposits.[39] The huge buildup of excess reserves led the Federal Reserve System to attempt to reduce these through a doubling of the required reserve ratio between August of 1936 and May of 1937. Banks quickly built up new excess reserves to replace most of those which the Fed eliminated.[40]

The depressed thirties brought about innovations in bank lending. Banks accepted a wider range of collateral and provided more short- and intermediate-term lending for

Fig. 5.5 Bank Suspensions

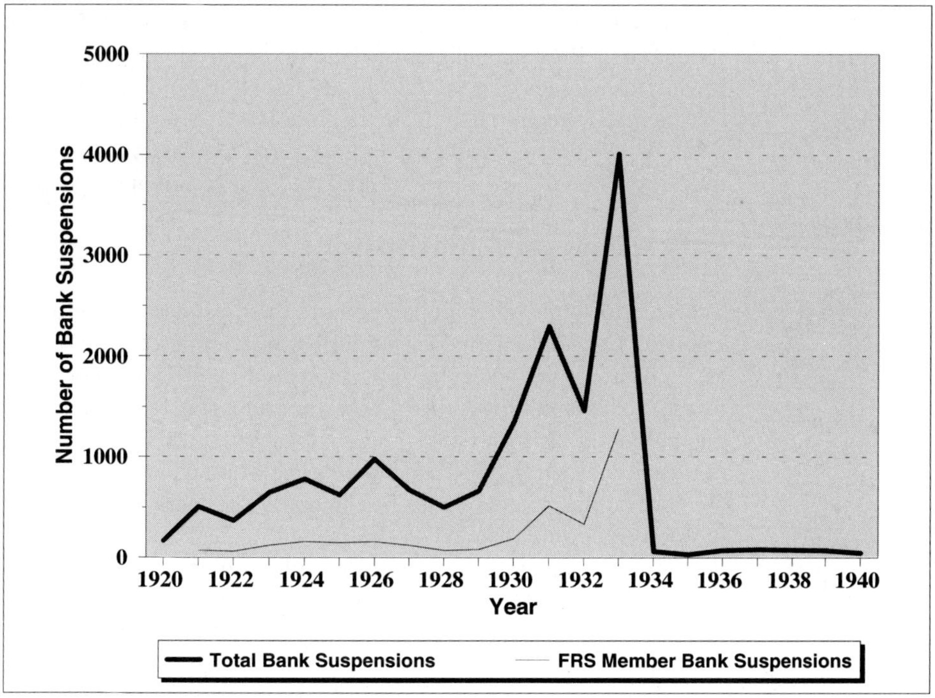

Source: *Historical Statistics of the United States: Colonial Times to 1970* (Washington, D.C.: U.S. Government Printing Office, 1976).

businesses. The installment loan, pioneered for consumer credit, was extended to business firms so that longer maturity loans were available.[41] Consumer lending and the purchase of consumer installment paper also grew.[42] Finally, the depression and New Deal brought in the end of "free banking," whereby a bank would be issued a charter as long as it was able to meet certain objective requirements. The Banking Act of 1935 required the comptroller of the currency and the Federal Deposit Insurance Corporation (FDIC) to consider the prospective profitability of new and existing banks as well as the convenience and needs of the community to be served by the proposed bank.[43] The rationale was to be certain that "overbanking" did not occur, but, by making the entry of new banks much more difficult (and arbitrary), it helped create monopoly rents for existing banks.

Securities Markets

There was a dramatic expansion in new corporate securities in the twenties—especially common and preferred stock. The number of shares exchanged on the New York

Stock Exchange (NYSE) increased at a rate of 26 percent per year from 1923 to 1929. Almost as quickly as the New York securities market expanded in the twenties, it contracted in the depression. After an aborted recovery in 1933, the activity continued to slide, and in 1940 the number of shares exchanged was less than one fifth of the number in 1929. Issues of corporate bonds and notes held up well between 1930 and 1932 and then fell precipitously from 1932 to 1933. After 1934 the issuance of bonds and notes by businesses recovered and averaged almost as much as in the last half of the twenties, whereas new issues of preferred and common stocks plunged in the thirties.

Other Financial Institutions

The securities market exhibited perhaps the most dramatic growth of the noncommercial bank financial intermediaries during the twenties, but others also grew rapidly. The assets of life insurance companies increased by 10 percent a year from 1921 to 1929; by the late twenties they were a very important source of funds for construction investment. Mutual savings banks and savings and loan associations (thrifts) operated in essentially the same types of markets. The Mutual savings banks were concentrated in the northeastern United States. As incomes rose, personal savings increased, and housing construction expanded in the twenties, there was an increasing demand for the thrifts' interest earning time deposits and mortgage lending.

The assets of mutual savings banks rose during the depression and then were constant (in real terms) throughout the rest of the thirties. Savings and loan associations' assets grew until 1932 and then dropped through 1937, remaining at this lower level until the end of the decade. Though small relative to the other financial intermediateis, the Postal Savings System provided a safe place for the small funds of lower income people, particularly recent immigrants, and its deposits increased sharply during the contraction. The major growth came in the life insurance industry. The assets of life insurance companies had been growing during the twenties, and this growth was almost as fast during the thirties—9.6 percent a year in the twenties compared to 7.2 percent a year in the thirties. As a result, the life insurance companies became a more important factor in long-term financing in the thirties.

The Great Bull Market

The late twenties boom in the American economy was rapid, highly visible, and dramatic. Skyscrapers were being erected in most major cities, the automobile manufacturers produced over four and a half million new cars in 1929; and the stock market, like a barometer of this prosperity, was on a dizzying ride to higher and higher prices. "Playing the market" seemed to become a national pastime.[44]

The Dow-Jones index hit its peak of 381 on September 3 and then slid to 320 on October 21. In the following week the stock market "crashed," with a record number of shares being traded on several days. At the end of Tuesday, October, 29th, the index stood at 230, 96 points less than one week before. On November 13, 1929, the

Dow-Jones index reached its lowest point for the year at 198—183 points less than the September 3 peak.[45]

The path of the stock market boom of the twenties can be seen in Figure 5.6. Sharp price breaks occurred several times during the boom, and each of these gave rise to dark predictions of the end of the bull market and speculation. Until late October of 1929, these predictions turned out to be wrong. Between those price breaks and prior to the October crash, stock prices continued to surge upward. In March of 1928, 3,875,910 shares were traded in one day, establishing a record. By late 1928, five million shares being trade a day was a common occurrence.

New securities, from rising merger activity and the formation of holding companies, were issued to take advantage of the rising stock prices.[46] Stock pools, which were not illegal until the 1934 Securities and Exchange Act, took advantage of the boom to temporarily drive up the price of selected stocks and reap large gains for the members of the pool.[47] Another factor commonly used to explain both the speculative boom and the October crash was the purchase of stocks on small margins. However, contrary to popular perception, margin requirements through most of the twenties were

Fig. 5.6 Standard and Poor's Common Stock Price Index

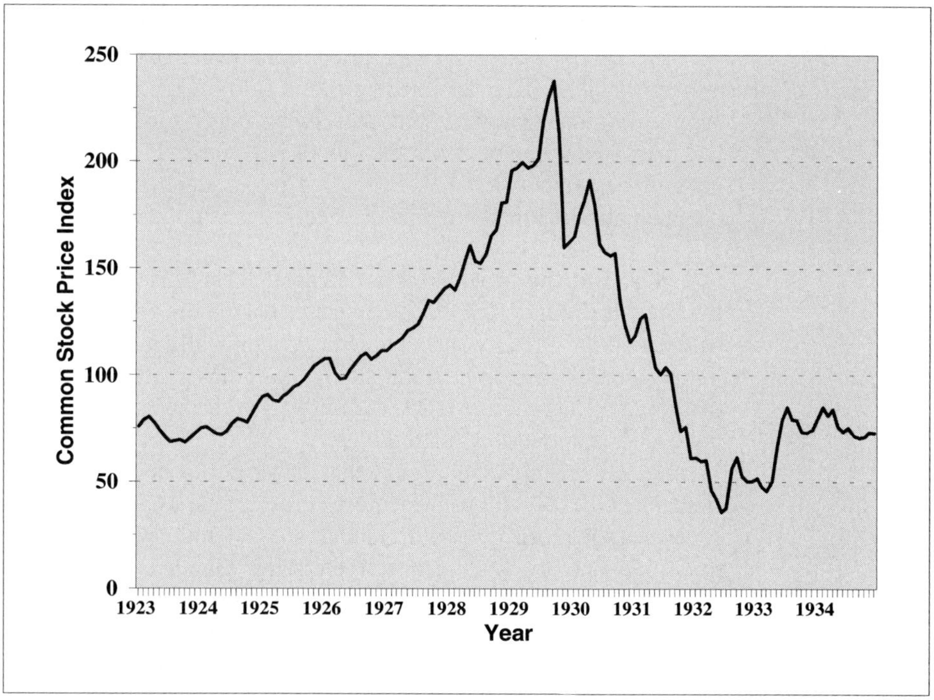

Source: *Historical Statistics of the United States: Colonial Times to 1970* (Washington, D.C.: U.S. Government Printing Office, 1976).

essentially the same as in previous decades. Brokers, recognizing the problems with margin lending in the rapidly changing market, began raising margin requirements in late 1928, and by the fall of 1929, margin requirements were the highest in the history of the New York Stock Exchange.[48] Even so, during the crash, as investors could not provide additional margin, brokers' sold the stock at the market and these forced sales helped drive prices even lower.

The crash began on Monday, October 21, as the index of stock prices fell 3 points on the third-largest volume in the history of the New York Stock Exchange. After a slight rally on Tuesday, prices began declining on Wednesday and fell 21 points by the end of the day bringing on the third call for more margin in that week. On Black Thursday, October 24, prices initially fell sharply, but rallied somewhat in the afternoon so that the net loss was only 7 points, but the volume of thirteen million shares set a NYSE record. Friday brought a small gain which was wiped out on Saturday. On Monday, October 28, the Dow Jones index fell 38 points on a volume of nine million shares—three million in the final hour of trading. Tragic Tuesday, October 29, brought declines in virtually every stock price. Manufacturing firms, which had been lending large sums to brokers for margin loans, had been calling in these loans and this accelerated on Monday and Tuesday. The big Wall Street bank increased their lending on call loans to offset some of this loss of loanable funds. The Dow Jones Index fell 30 points on a record volume of nearly sixteen and a half million shares exchanged. Black Thursday and Tragic Tuesday wipied out entire fortunes.

Though the worst was over, prices continued to decline until November 13, 1929, as brokers cleaned up their accounts and sold off the stocks of clients who could not supply additional margin. After that, prices began to slowly rise and by April of 1930 had increased 96 points from the low of November 13, "only" 87 points less than the peak of September 3, 1929. From that point, stock prices resumed their depressing decline until the low point was reached in the summer of 1932.

Why Did the Stock Market Crash? There is a long tradition that insists that the Great Bull Market of the late twenties was an orgy of speculation that bid the prices of stocks far above any sustainable or economically justifiable level creating a *bubble* in the stock market. John Kenneth Galbraith observed that "The collapse in the stock market in the autumn of 1929 was implicit in the speculation that went before."[49] But not everyone has agreed with this.

In 1930 Irving Fisher argued that the stock prices of 1928 and 1929 were based on fundamental expectations that future corporate earnings would be high.[50] More recently, Murray Rothbard, Gerald Gunderson, and Jude Wanniski have argued that stock prices were not too high prior to the crash.[51] Gunderson suggested that prior to 1929, stock prices were where they should have been and that when corporate profits in the summer and fall of 1929 failed to meet expectations, stock prices were written down.[52] Wanniski argued that political events brought on the crash. The market broke each time news arrived of advances in congressional consideration of the Hawley-Smoot tariff. However, the virtually perfect foresight that Wanniski's explanation requires is unrealistic.[53] Charles Kindleberger and Peter Temin examined common stock yields and price-earnings ratios and found that the relative constancy did not suggest that stock prices were bid up unrealistically high in the late twenties.[54] Gary Santoni and Gerald Dwyer also failed to find evidence of a bubble in stock prices in 1928 and 1929.[55] Gerald Sirkin found that the implied growth rates of dividends required to justify stock prices in 1928 and 1929 were quite conservative and lower than post-Second World War dividend growth rates.[56]

However, examination of after-the-fact common stock yields and price-earning ratios can do no more than provide some *ex post* justification for suggesting that there was not excessive speculation during the Great Bull Market. Each individual investor was motivated by that person's *subjective expectations* of each firm's *future* earnings and dividends and the *future* prices of shares of each firm's stock. Because of this element of subjectivity, not only can we never accurately know those values, but we can also never know how they varied among individuals. The market price we observe will be the end result of all of the actions of the market participants, and the observed price may be different from the price almost all of the participants expected.

In fact, there are some indications that there were differences in 1928 and 1929. Yields on common stocks were somewhat lower in 1928 and 1929. In October of 1928, brokers generally began raising margin requirements, and by the beginning of the fall of 1929, margin requirements were, on average, the highest in the history of the New York Stock Exchange. Though the discount and commercial paper rates had moved closely with the call and time rates on brokers' loans through 1927, the rates on brokers' loans increased much more sharply in 1928 and 1929.[57] This pulled in funds from corporations, private investors, and foreign banks as New York City banks sharply reduced their lending. These facts suggest that brokers and New York City bankers may have come to believe that stock prices had been bid above a sustainable level by late 1928 and early 1929. White created a quarterly index of dividends for firms in the Dow-Jones index and related this to the DJI. Through 1927 the two track closely, but in 1928 and 1929 the index of stock prices grows much more rapidly than the index of dividends.

The qualitative evidence for a bubble in the stock market in 1928 and 1929 that White assembled was strengthened by the findings of J. Bradford De Long and Andre Shleifer.[58] They examined closed-end mutual funds, a type of fund where investors wishing to liquidate must sell their shares to other individual investors allowing its fundamental value to be exactly measurable.[59] Using evidence from these funds, De Long and Shleifer estimated that in the summer of 1929, the Standard and Poor's composite stock price index was overvalued about 30 percent due to excessive investor optimism.[60]

There are several reasons for the creation of such a bubble. First, fundamentals become difficult to assess when there are major industrial changes, such as the rapid changes in the automobile industry, the new electric utilities, and the new radio industry.[61] Eugene White suggests that "While investors had every reason to expect earnings to grow, they lacked the means to evaluate easily the future path of dividends."[62] Second, participation in the stock market widened noticeably in the twenties. The new investors were relatively unsophisticated, and they were more likely to be caught up in the euphoria of the boom and bid prices upward.[63] New, inexperienced commission sales personnel were hired to sell stocks.

These observations were strengthened by the experimental work of economist Vernon Smith. In a number of experiments over a three year period using students and Tucson businessmen and businesswomen, bubbles developed as inexperienced investors valued stocks differently and engaged in price speculation. As these investors in the experiments began to realize that speculative profits were unsustainable and uncertain, their dividend expectations changed, the market crashed, and ultimately stocks began trading at their fundamental dividend values. These bubbles and crashes occurred repeatedly, leading Smith to conjecture that there are few regulatory steps that can be taken to prevent a crash.[64]

Though the bubble of 1928 and 1929 made some downward adjustment in stock prices inevitable, as Barsky and De Long have shown, changes in fundamentals govern the overall movements. And the end of the long bull market was almost certainly governed by this. In late 1928 and early 1929 there was a striking rise in economic activity, but a decline began somewhere between May and July of that year. By the middle of August, the rise in stock prices had slowed down as better information on the contraction was received. As this information was assessed, the number of speculators selling stocks increased, and the number buying decreased. With the decreased demand, stock prices began to fall, and as more accurate information on the nature and extent of the decline was received, stock prices fell more. The late October crash made the decline occur much more rapidly, and the margin purchases and consequent forced selling of many of those stocks contributed to a more severe price fall. The recovery of stock prices from November 13 into April of 1930 suggests that stock prices had been driven too low during the crash.

Financial Markets in the Interwar American Economy

There can be no question about the crucial role of financial institutions in the interwar economy. There is now nearly universal agreement that the 1929 stock market crash did not cause the Great Depression. Instead, the initial downturn in economic activity was a primary determinant of the ending of the 1928–29 stock market bubble. But it is clear that the long, dreary decline of the stock market during the thirties made it more difficult for businesses to raise capital for modernization and expansion. We also understand the crucial role that the near collapse of the banking system had in extending and intensifying the Great Depression. We will be examining these issues in the next two chapters.

SELECTED REFERENCES

Aldcroft, Derek H. *From Versailles to Wall Street, 1919–1929*. Berkeley: The University of California Press, 1977.

Allen, Frederick Lewis. *Only Yesterday*. New York: Harper and Sons, 1931.

Bishop, Jerry E. "Stock Market Experiment Suggests Inevitability of Booms and Busts." *The Wall Street Journal*, 17 November, 1987.

Brown, William A., Jr. *The International Gold Standard Reinterpreted, 1914–1934*, 2 vols. New York: National Bureau of Economic Research, 1940.

Bucklin, Louis P. *Competition and Evolution in the Distributive Trades*. Englewood Cliffs, NJ: Prentice-Hall, 1972.

Cochran, Thomas C. *200 Years of American Business*. New York: Delta Books, 1977.

Cohen, Yehoshua S. *Diffusion of an Innovation in an Urban System: The Spread of Planned Regional Shopping Centers in the United States, 1949–1968*. Chicago: The University of Chicago, Department of Geography, Research Paper No. 140, 1972.

Chandler, Alfred D., Jr. *Strategy and Structure: Chapters in the History of Industrial Enterprise*. Cambridge: The M.I.T. Press, 1962.

__________. *The Visible Hand: The Managerial Revolution in American Business*. Cambridge: Harvard University Press, Belknap Press, 1977.

Clewett, Richard C. "Mass Marketing of Consumers' Goods." Chapter 40 in *The Growth of the American Economy*. 2d ed. Edited by Harold F. Williamson. Englewood Cliffs, NJ: Prentice-Hall, 1951.

De Long, J. Bradford, and Andre Shleifer. "The Stock Market Bubble of 1929: Evidence from Closed-end Mutual Funds." *The Journal of Economic History* 51 (September 1991): 675–700.

Eichengreen, Barry, ed. *The Gold Standard in Theory and History*. New York: Metheun, 1985.

Emmet, Boris, and John E. Jeuck. *Catalogues and Counters: A History of Sears Roebuck and Company*. Chicago: University of Chicago Press, 1950.

Fisher, Irving. *The Stock Market Crash—and After*. New York: Macmillan, 1930.

Friedman, Milton, and Anna J. Schwartz. *A Monetary History of the United States, 1867–1960*. Princeton: Princeton University Press, 1963.

Galbraith, John Kenneth. *The Great Crash*. Boston: Houghton Mifflin, 1954.

Gideonse, Max. "Foreign Trade, Investments, and Commercial Policy." Chapter 41 in *The Growth of the American Economy*. 2d ed. Edited by Harold F. Williamson. Englewood Cliffs, NJ: Prentice-Hall, 1951.

Gunderson, Gerald. *An Economic History of America*. New York: McGraw-Hill, 1976.

Higgs, Robert. *Crisis and Leviathan: Critical Episodes in the Growth of American Government*. New York: Oxford University Press, 1987.

Kindleberger, Charles. *The World in Depression, 1929–1939*. Berkeley: The University of California Press, 1973.

Klebaner, Benjamin J. *Commercial Banking in the United States: A History*. New York: W. W. Norton and Co., 1974.

Johnson, H. Thomas. "Postwar Optimism and the Rural Financial Crisis." *Explorations in Economic History* 11 (Winter 1973–74): 173–92.

Lewis, Cleona. *America's Stake in International Investments*. Washington: The Brookings Institution, 1938.

Marburg, Theodore. "Domestic Trade and Marketing." Chapter 26 in *The Growth of the American Economy*. 2d ed. Edited by Harold F. Williamson. Englewood Cliffs, NJ: Prentice-Hall, 1951.

Markin, Rom J. *The Supermarket: An Analysis of Growth, Development, and Change*. Rev. ed. Pullman, WA: Washington State University Press, 1968.

McNair, Malcolm P., and Eleanor G. May. *The Evolution of Retail Institutions in the United States*. Cambridge, MA: The Marketing Science Institute, 1976.

Mintz, Ilse. *Deterioration in the Quality of Foreign Bonds Issued in the United States, 1920–1930.* New York: National Bureau of Economic Research, 1951.

Peak, Hugh S., and Ellen F. Peak. *Supermarket Merchandising and Management.* Englewood Cliffs, NJ: Prentice-Hall, 1977.

Rockwell, Llewellyn H., Jr., ed. *The Gold Standard: An Austrian Perspective.* Lexington, MA: Lexington Books, 1985.

Rothbard, Murray N. *America's Great Depression.* Kansas City: Sheed and Ward, 1963.

Santoni, Gary, and Gerald Dwyer. "Bubbles vs. Fundamentals: New Evidence from the Great Bull Markets." In *Crises and Panics: The Lessons of History.* Edited by Eugene N. White. Homewood, IL: Dow Jones/Irwin, 1990.

Sirkin, Gerald. "The Stock Market of 1929 Revisited: A Note." *Business History Review* 49 (Fall 1975): 233–41.

Smiley, Gene. "Some Austrian Perspectives on Keynesian Fiscal Policy and the Recovery in the Thirties." *Review of Austrian Economics* 1 (1987): 145–79.

__________, and Richard H. Keehn. "Margin Purchases, Brokers' Loans and the Bull Market of the Twenties." *Business and Economic History.* 2d series. 17 (1988): 129–42.

Sobel, Robert. *The Entrepreneuers: Explorations Within the American Business Tradition.* New York: Weybright and Talley, 1974.

__________. *Panic on Wall Street.* New York: Truman Talley Books, 1988.

Soule, George. *Prosperity Decade: From War to Depression, 1917–1929.* New York: Rinehart and Co., 1947.

Temin, Peter. "The Beginning of the Depression in Germany." *Economic History Review.* 24 (May 1971): 240–48.

__________. *Did Monetary Forces Cause the Great Depression?* New York: W. W. Norton, 1976.

Thomas, Gordon, and Max Morgan-Witts. *The Day the Bubble Burst.* Garden City, NY: Doubleday, 1979.

Wanniski, Jude. *The Way the World Works.* New York: Simon and Schuster, 1978.

White, Eugene N. "The Stock Market Boom and Crash of 1929 Revisited." *The Journal of Economic Perspectives.* 4 (Spring 1990): 67–83.

__________. "When the Ticker Ran Late: The Stock Market Boom and Crash of 1929." In *Crises and Panics: The Lessons of History* Edited by Eugene N. White. Homewood, IL: Dow Jones/Irwin, 1990.

NOTES

1. There are several sources presenting an overview of the development of wholesale and retail distribution in American history. Thomas C. Cochran, *200 Years of American Business* (New York: Delta Books, 1977); Alfred D. Chandler, Jr., *The Visible Hand: The Managerial Revolution in American Business* (Cambridge: The Harvard University, the Belknap Press, 1977); Theodore Marburg, "Domestic Trade and Marketing," chapter 26 in *The Growth of the American Economy*, 2d ed., ed. Harold F. Williamson, (Englewood Cliffs, NJ: Prentice-Hall, Inc., 1951); Richard C. Clewett, "Mass Marketing of Consumers' Goods," ch. 40 in Williamson, *The Growth of the American Economy.*
2. For the history of A. T. Stewart's store, see Harry E. Resseguie, "Alexander Turney Stewart and the Development of the Department Store, 1823–1876," *Business History Review* 39 (Autumn 1965): 301–22; and Robert Sobel and David B. Sicilia, *The Entrepreneurs: An*

American Adventure (Boston: Houghton Mifflin Co., 1986).

3. In addition to the references cited above, see the following: Joseph H. Appel, *The Business Biography of John Wanamaker, Founder and Builder* (New York: The Macmillan Company, 1930); Susan Porter Benson, *Counter Cultures: Saleswomen, Managers, and Customers in American Department Stores, 1890–1940* (Urbana, IL: University of Illinois Press, 1986); Robert Hendrickson, *The Grand Emporiums: The Illustrated History of America's Great Department Stores* (Briarcliff Manor, NY: Stein and Day, 1979); Ralph W. Hower, *History of Macy's of New York, 1858–1919* (Cambridge: Harvard University Press, 1946); Robert Sobel, *The Entrepreneurs: Explorations With the American Business Tradition* (New York: Weybright and Talley, 1974).
4. Clewett, "Mass Marketing," 769.
5. The following discussion is adapted from these sources: Boris Emmet and John E. Jeuck, *Catalogues and Counters: A History of Sears Roebuck and Company* (Chicago: University of Chicago Press, 1950); Chandler, *Strategy and Structure*, chapter 5; and Chandler, *The Visible Hand*, chapter 7.
6. For a discussion of chain stores as they were viewed in the thirties, see Theodore N. Beckman and Herman C. Nolen, *The Chain Store Problem: A Critical Analysis* (New York: McGraw-Hill Book Co., 1938). On chain stores in general, see Godfrey M. Lebhar, *Chain Stores in America, 1859–1962* (New York: Chain Store Publishing Corp., 1963). The history of the A&P can be found in Roy J. Bullock, "The Early History of the Great Atlantic & Pacific Tea Company," *Harvard Business Review* 11 (April 1933): 289–93, and Roy J. Bullock, "A History of the Great Atlantic & Pacific Tea Company Since 1878," *Harvard Business Review* 12 (October 1933): 59–69.
7. John Kennedy Winkler, *Five and Ten: The Fabulous Life of F. W. Woolworth* (New York: R. M. McBride and Company, 1940).
8. Norman Beasley, *Main Street Merchant: The Story of the J. C. Penney Company* (New York: Whittlesey House, 1948).
9. Yehoshua S. Cohen, *Diffusion of an Innovation in an Urban System: The Spread of Planned Regional Shopping Centers in the United States 1949–1968* (Chicago: The University of Chicago, Department of Geography, Research Paper No. 140, 1972), 27.
10. Ibid., 27.
11. Ibid., 28.
12. Malcolm P. McNair and Eleanor G. May, *The Evolution of Retail Institutions in the United States* (Cambridge, MA: The Marketing Science Institute, 1976), 27.
13. Paul H. Nystrom, *Economics of Retailing*, vol. 1, 3d ed. (New York: The Ronald Press Company, 1930), 111, as cited in Louis P. Bucklin, *Competition and Evolution in the Distributive Trades* (Englewood Cliffs, NJ: Prentice-Hall, 1972), 86.
14. Rom J. Markin, *The Supermarket: An Analysis of Growth, Development, and Change*, rev. ed. (Pullman, WA: Washington State University Press, 1968), 10.
15. Ibid., 11.
16. Louis P. Bucklin, *Competition and Evolution in the Distributive Trades* (Englewood Cliffs, NJ: Prentice-Hall, 1972), 86. The average gross margin on grocery sales was 12.1 percent, allowing prices to average about 10 percent lower than at the chain stores and conventional independent grocers. Markin, *The Supermarket: An Analysis of Growth, Development, and Change*, 12.
17. Hugh S. Peak and Ellen F. Peak, *Supermarket Merchandising and Management* (Englewood Cliffs, NJ: Prentice-Hall, 1977), 17.
18. Ibid., 17.

19. Ibid., 15.
20. The debate on the prewar gold standard is discussed in Derek H. Aldcroft, *From Versailles to Wall Street, 1919–1929* (Berkeley: University of California Press, 1977), chapter 7. The prewar and interwar gold standards are discussed in a number of papers in Barry Eichengreen, ed., *The Gold Standard in Theory and History* (New York: Metheun, 1985); and in Llewellyn H. Rockwell, Jr., ed., *The Gold Standard: An Austrian Perspective* (Lexington, MA: Lexington Books, 1985). The interwar gold standard is considered in some detail in William A. Brown, Jr., *The International Gold Standard Reinterpreted, 1914–1934*, 2 vols. (New York: National Bureau of Economic Research, 1940).
21. For a discussion of these problems see Aldcroft, *From Versailles to Wall Street*, chapter 7; and George Soule, *Prosperity Decade: From War to Depression: 1917–1929* (New York: Holt, Rinehart, and Winston, 1947), chapter 12.
22. Charles Kindleberger, *The World in Depression, 1929–1939* (Berkeley: University of California Press, 1973), 34. The following discussion draws upon Soule, *Prosperity Decade*, chapter 12; Aldcroft, *From Versailles to Wall Street*, chapter 4; and Kindleberger, *The World in Depression*, chapters. 1 and 2.
23. Soule, *Prosperity Decade*, 260.
24. Max Gideonse, "Foreign Trade, Investments, and Commercial Policy," chapter 41 in Harold F. Williamson, ed., *The Growth of the American Economy*, 2d ed. (Englewood Cliffs, NJ: Prentice-Hall, Inc., 1951), 790–91.
25. Kindleberger, *The World in Depression*, 131–135.
26. Ibid., 236–38.
27. Ibid., 263–64.
28. Lewis, *America's Stake in International Investments.*
29. Ilse Mintz, *Deterioration in the Quality of Foreign Bonds Issued in the United States, 1920–1930* (New York: National Bureau of Economic Research, 1951).
30. Kindleberger believes that it did, while Peter Temin argues that it did not. See Kindleberger, *The World in Depression*, 60–76; and Peter Temin, "The Beginning of the Depression in Germany," *Economic History Review* 24 (May 1971): 240–48.
31. Kindleberger, *The World in Depression*, 195–96. This discussion also draws upon Gideonse, "Foreign Trade, Investments, and Commercial Policy," 791.
32. Kindleberger, *The World in Depression*, 149–50. The following discussion is based upon Kindleberger, 148–51, and Milton Friedman and Anna J. Schwartz, *A Monetary History of the United States, 1867–1960* (Princeton: Princeton University Press, 1963), 313–22.
33. This discussion is drawn from Friedman and Schwartz, *A Monetary History of the United States*, 462–83.
34. Individuals were allowed to keep rare coins, reasonable amounts for use in industry and the arts could be retained, and a maximum of $100 in gold coin and certificates for each person could also be kept. (Friedman and Schwartz, *A Monetary History of the United States*, 463.)
35. A gold clause specified that the contractual obligations could be discharged by a specified payment of ounces of fine gold rather than simply in dollars. It was a procedure by which the parties could contract against unexpected price inflation or price deflation. These actions were threatened by the gold clauses contained in many contracts. On June 5, 1933, Congress abrogated the gold clauses in all obligations. This was challenged in the courts since the constitutional guarantee of due process of law prohibited arbitrary legislative impairment of valid contracts. In early 1935 the Supreme Court upheld this action. Chief Justice Hughes ". . . simply took for granted that a constitutional delegation of power to Congress must necessarily override a constitutional protection of individual rights." Robert

Higgs, *Crisis and Leviathan: Critical Episodes in the Growth of American Government* (New York: Oxford University Press, 1987), 186.

36. Benjamin J. Klebaner, *Commercial Banking in the United States: A History* (New York: W. W. Norton and Co., 1974), chapter 12.
37. Ibid., 126.
38. H. Thomas Johnson, "Postwar Optimism and the Rural Financial Crisis," *Explorations in Economic History* 11 (Winter 1973–74): 173–92.
39. Klebaner, *Commercial Banking in the United States*, 111. At the end of the 1930s over 400 banks simply refused to accept time deposits.
40. See Gene Smiley, "Some Austrian Perspectives on Keynesian Fiscal Policy and the Recovery in the Thirties," *Review of Austrian Economics* 1 (1987): 145–79.
41. Klebaner, *Commercial Banking in the United States*, 147–48.
42. Ibid., 151.
43. Ibid., 157–58.
44. Though the general impression is that there was widespread speculation in stocks in 1928 and 1929, Allen estimates that no more than one million individuals held stock on margin in the summer of 1929, while other estimates suggest that there were no more than 600,000 active margin accounts. [See Allen, *Only Yesterday*, 260; and Robert Sobel, *Panic on Wall Street* (New York: Truman Talley Books, 1988), 356.] Soule estimates that all the shares of stock in American corporations were held by no more than nine million individuals in 1929. [George Soule, *Prosperity Decade: From War to Depression, 1917–1929* (New York: Rinehart and Co., 1947), 293–94.]
45. Frederick L. Allen, *Only Yesterday* (New York: Harper and Sons, 1931), 266.
46. Although there is still debate as to which was the causal factor, there seems to be good reason to believe that the booming stock market stimulated merger activity rather than vice versa. When the companies were merged, new securities were issued; in a period of rapidly rising stock prices, this could easily be translated into substantial profits for the owners of the firms being merged as well as the merger promoters. The formation of holding companies, especially utility holding companies, and investment trusts fed more securities into the growing market. For example, see George Soule's discussions of the investment banking house of Dillon, Read, and Company; the Van Sweringen Brothers' empire of railroads; and Samuel Insull's public utility holding company, in *Prosperity Decade*, 298–304.
47. Michael Meehan, the "Radio" broker at post 12 of the New York Stock Exchange, was one of the most successful arrangers of stock pools. In early March of 1928, he had successfully run a pool in RCA stock. In January and February of 1929, he directed a pool in Anaconda Copper stock. In March of 1929, to celebrate the anniversary of his RCA pool one year before, he arranged another pool in RCA stock. The total amount contributed by the members of the pool was $12,683,000. A few days before the pool began operation, "paid" tips on the financial health of RCA appeared in New York City papers. On March 12, 1929, the pool members surreptitiously began buying and selling RCA shares and bidding up its price. On March 18 the pool members began selling off the shares they had purchased, and the price of RCA dropped 22 percent between March 16 and March 23. The pool was enormously profitable for its participants because the net profit was nearly $5,000,000 on the initial total of $12,683,000, or a return of 39 percent in one week. [Gordon Thomas and Max Morgan-Witts, *The Day the Bubble Burst* (Garden City, NY: Doubleday, 1979), chapter 8.]
48. Gene Smiley and Richard H. Keehn, "Margin Purchases, Brokers' Loans and the Bull Market of the Twenties," *Business and Economic History*, 2d series, 17 (1988): 129–42.

49. John Kenneth Galbraith, *The Great Crash* (Boston: Houghton Mifflin, 1954), 174.
50. Irving Fisher, *The Stock Market Crash—and After* (New York: Macmillan, 1930).
51. Murray N. Rothbard, *America's Great Depression* (Kansas City: Sheed and Ward, 1963), chapter 4; Gunderson, *An Economic History of America* (New York: McGraw-Hill Book Co., 1976), chapter 16; Jude Wanniski, *The Way the World Works* (New York: Simon and Schuster, 1978), 125.
52. Gunderson, An Economic History of America, 473.
53. Wanniski, *The Way the World Works*, 125. Neither does Wanniski provide an explanation why stock prices peaked at the beginning of September and then began falling. Wanniski argued that the market broke because transactors *anticipated* the June 16, 1930, signing of the tariff. And tariffs are another form of a tax wedge driven between transactors in market transactions, reducing economic activity and efficiency and causing output, income, and profits to fall.
54. Charles P. Kindleberger, *The World in Depression, 1929–1939* (Berkeley: University of California Press, 1973), chapter 5; Peter Temin, *Did Monetary Forces Cause the Great Depression?* (New York: W. W. Norton, 1976), 42–5. The yield is the yearly dividend divided by the average of the monthly stock prices during the year and is comparable to an interest rate. The earnings are the firms' net earning rather than just dividends paid out to shareholders so that the implicit rates of return are higher than the yields reported in Figure 5.14.
55. Gary Santoni and Gerald Dwyer, "Bubbles vs. Fundamentals: New Evidence from the Great Bull Markets," in *Crises and Panics: The Lessons of History*, ed. Eugene N. White (Homewood, IL: Dow Jones/Irwin, 1990).
56. Gerald Sirkin, "The Stock Market of 1929 Revisited: A Note," *Business History Review* 49 (Fall 1975): 233–41.
57. Eugene N. White, "The Stock Market Boom and Crash of 1929 Revisited," *The Journal of Economic Perspectives* 4 (Spring 1990): 75–6. Eugene N. White, "When the Ticker Ran Late: The Stock Market Boom and Crash of 1929," in *Crises and Panics: The Lessons of History*, ed. Eugene N. White (Homewood, IL: Dow Jones/Irwin, 1990).
58. J. Bradford De Long and Andre Shleifer, "The Stock Market Bubble of 1929: Evidence from Closed-end Mutual Funds," *The Journal of Economic History* 51 (September 1991): 675–700.
59. Ibid., 677.
60. Ibid., 695.
61. White, "The Stock Market Boom and Crash of 1929 Revisited," 77–8.
62. Ibid., 77.
63. Women investors were a new group that was specially catered to. Frances D. McMullen, "Women and the Ticker Tape—A Year After the Crash," *The Women's Journal*, November 1930, as cited in White, "The Stock Market Boom and Crash of 1929 Revisited," 78.
64. Jerry E. Bishop, "Stock Market Experiment Suggests Inevitability of Booms and Busts," *The Wall Street Journal*, 17 November, 1987.

CHAPTER 6

The Role of Government, 1920–1940: Monetary and Fiscal Policies and the New Deal

Laissez-faire explanations of the role of government in an economic system portray it as a "nightwatchman" who simply stands guard on the economy to protect life and property and provide those public goods that the private market fails to supply or supplies in inefficient quantities, such as fire and police protection, highway construction and maintenance, and public health services.

There is a good reason why this description seems to fall short of what governments in the United States and other advanced countries undertake. They are not, in fact, laissez-faire governments, and by the above standards hardly any government has ever been laissez-faire. Governments at all levels have always exercised some economic and social regulation and over time have moved further away from the nightwatchman image of government.

The analysis of government activities in the interwar period focuses on the Federal Reserve System's policies and the New Deal. Throughout the period the new Federal Reserve System was in the process of developing U.S. monetary policy. Fiscal policy, as a separate tool for macroeconomic policy, was not really known or used, and the New Deal policies were much broader than macroeconomic stabilization.

We begin our survey of government in the interwar American economy by examining the development and implementation of monetary policy.

THE EVOLUTION OF MONETARY POLICY

In the 1913 Federal Reserve Act fear of the "money trust" and their monopoly power caused Congress to create 12 central banks. The role of the Federal Reserve Board, located in Washington, D.C., was to coordinate the policies of the district banks; it was composed of five presidential appointees and the current secretary of the treasury and comptroller of the currency. All national banks had to become members, and any state bank meeting the qualifications could elect to do so.

The act specified fixed reserve requirements on demand and time deposits, all of which had to be on deposit in the district bank.[1] Commercial banks were allowed to rediscount commercial paper and given Federal Reserve currency. Initially, each district bank set its own rediscount rate. To provide additional income when there was little rediscounting, the district banks were allowed to engage in open market operations that involved the purchasing and selling of federal government securities, short-term securities of state and local governments issued in anticipation of taxes, foreign exchange, and domestic bills of exchange. The district banks were also designated to act as fiscal agents for the federal government. Finally, the Federal Reserve System provided a central check clearinghouse for the entire banking system.

The Banking Act of 1935 changed the Federal Reserve Board's name to the Board of Governors and changed the titles of the district officers to president and vice-president to indicate the more powerful role of the Board of Governors in Washington, D.C. The secretary of the treasury and comptroller of the currency were removed from the Board of Governors and the Federal Open Market Committee. The Fed was authorized to issue its currency on any collateral acceptable to it, vary the reserve requirements on demand and time deposits, and set maximum interest rates paid on time deposits. Finally, the Board of Governors was given the power to set margin requirements on loans granted by member and nonmember banks on stock purchases.

Problems in Policy Formulation and Control

When the Federal Reserve System was originally set up, it was believed that its primary role was to be a lender of last resort to prevent banking panics and become a check-clearing mechanism for the nation's banks. Both the Federal Reserve Board and the Governors of the District Banks were bodies established to jointly exercise these activities. The division of functions was not clear, and a struggle for power ensued, mainly between the New York Federal Reserve Bank, which was led by J. P. Morgan's protege, Benjamin Strong, through 1928, and the Federal Reserve Board. By the thirties the Federal Reserve Board had achieved dominance.

There were really two conflicting criteria upon which monetary actions were ostensibly based: the Gold Standard and the Real Bills Doctrine. The Gold Standard, as described in Chapter 5, was supposed to be quasi-automatic, with an effective limit to the quantity of money. However, the Real Bills Doctrine (which required that all loans be made on short-term, self-liquidating commercial paper) had no effective limit on the quantity of money. The rediscounting of eligible commercial paper was supposed to lead to the required "elasticity" of the stock of money to "accommodate" the needs of industry and business. Actually the rediscounting of commercial paper, open market purchases, and gold inflows all had the same effects on the money stock.

Federal Reserve Policies from 1920 to 1940

During the First World War, the Fed kept discount rates low and granted discounts on banks' customer loans used to purchase V-bonds in order to help finance the war. In 1919, after the war's end, the Fed continued to keep the discount rate low to facilitate the Treasury's final drive to sell war bonds. Raising the discount rate would have driven interest rates and bond yields up while sending bond prices down. This policy brought on a rapid increase in the stock of money and in the rate of price inflation. Between November of 1919 and June of 1920, the discount rate was raised from 4 to 7 percent ending the inflation, contracting the stock of money, and setting off the 1920–21 depression.

By 1921 the district banks began to recognize that their open market purchases had effects on interest rates, the money stock, and economic activity. For the next several years, economists in the Federal Reserve System discussed how this worked and how it could be related to discounting by member banks.[2] A committee was created to coordinate the open market purchases of the district banks. With these tools the Federal Reserve System was given credit for smoothing the minor contractions in 1923–24 and 1927. Many felt that the Fed was now able to eliminate the business cycle.

During the stock market boom of the late 1920s the Federal Reserve Board preferred to use "moral suasion" rather than raise discount rates to lessen member bank borrowing. The New York City district bank insisted that moral suasion would not work unless backed up by literal credit rationing. Rates were not raised until August of 1929 by which time the contraction had already begun. In late October the stock market crashed, and America slid into the Great Depression.

As banks reduced their discounting in 1930, the stock of money declined. Though the Fed decreased discount rates, no open market operations were undertaken. There was a banking crisis in the southeast in November and December of 1930, and in its wake the public's holding of currency relative to deposits and banks' reserve ratios began to rise. The stock of money continued to decline during 1931, and discount rates were again reduced, and some open market purchases were made.[3]

When Great Britain left the gold standard on September 21, 1931, foreign holders of dollars turned to the United States to obtain gold. To stem the gold outflow, the New York bank's discount rate was raised from 1.5 to 2.5 percent on October 9 and then to 3.5 percent on October 16. The gold outflow stopped, but in the following months there was an acceleration in the decline in the money stock and an increase in bank suspensions.[4] The Fed made open market purchases from April through June of 1932.

The publication of the names of banks borrowing from the Reconstruction Finance Corporation and president-elect Roosevelt's refusal to deny that he was considering devaluing the dollar initiated new panics and, for the first time, there were specific demands to convert deposits and currency into gold. The flow of gold out of the United States also increased and the Fed's response was to increase the discount rate, again unaccompanied by open market operations. In early March of 1933, the New York bank's gold reserve dropped below the required percentage, and the reserve requirements were suspended for 30 days.[5] With the banking panic now nationwide, President Roosevelt declared a nationwide banking holiday when he assumed office on March 6, 1933.

Following the end of the depression discounting disappeared because the discount rate remained above the commercial paper and treasury bill rates and banks accumulated large excess reserves. The Fed did not undertake open market purchases because it worried about the possibility of future inflation due to the growing accumulation of excess reserves in banks, and to sell on the open market would have deprived district banks of most of their income earning assets. The money stock did expand as gold flowed into the United States after Roosevelt's devaluation of the dollar, however, in 1937 the Treasury sterilized these gold inflows to stop the expansion of the stock of money.[6]

The Fed concluded that the excess reserves were due to a lack of loan demand. Worried that banks would draw down the excess reserves and fuel inflation when loan demand increased, the Fed, after considerable study, decided to use its new powers to alter reserve requirements.[7] Between August 1, 1936, and May 1, 1937, the reserve requirements for demand and time deposits were doubled, eliminating much of the excess reserves. The money stock then began to fall, and the 1937–38 depression began. Reserve requirements were lowered slightly in April of 1938, and between then and the beginning of the Second World War in Europe, the Fed did not change the reserve requirements or discount rate or engage in open market operations.

With this overview of Federal Reserve System monetary policies in the interwar period, we to turn our attention to the three most important policy episodes: the 1920–21 depression, the Great Depression, and the 1937–38 depression.

The 1920–21 Depression

The final Victory Loan had not been floated when the Armistice was signed in November of 1918: in fact, it took until October of 1919 for the government to fully sell this last loan issue. The Treasury, with the secretary of the treasury sitting on the Federal Reserve Board, persuaded the Federal Reserve System to maintain low interest rates and discount the Victory bonds until this last issue had been floated. As a result, during this period the money supply grew rapidly and prices rose sharply.

A shift from a federal deficit to a surplus and supply disruptions due to steel and coal strikes in 1919 and a railroad strike in early 1920 may have contributed to the end of the boom.[8] But the consensus is that the Fed's monetary policy was the main determinant of the end of the expansion and inflation and the beginning of the subsequent contraction and severe deflation.[9] When the Fed was released from its informal agreement with the Treasury in November of 1919, it raised the discount rate from 4 to 4.75 percent. Benjamin Strong (the governor of the New York bank) was beginning to believe that the time for strong action was past and that the Federal Reserve System's actions should be moderate. However, the Federal Reserve Board increased the discount rate from 4.75 to 6 percent in late January of 1920 and to 7 percent on June 1, 1920. By the middle of 1920, economic activity and employment were rapidly falling, and prices had began their downward spiral. The Federal Reserve System kept the discount rate at 7 percent until May 5, 1921, when it was lowered to 6.5 percent. By June of 1922, the rate had been lowered yet again to 4 percent.

The Federal Reserve System authorities received considerable criticism then and later for their actions. Milton Friedman and Anna Schwartz contend that the discount rate was raised too much too late and then kept too high for too long, causing the decline to be more severe and the price deflation to be greater. In their opinion the Fed acted in this manner due to the necessity of meeting the legal reserve requirement with a safe margin of gold reserves. Elmus Wicker, however, argues that the gold reserve ratio was not the main factor determining the Federal Reserve policy in the episode.[10] Rather, the Fed knowingly pursued a deflationary policy because it felt that the money supply was simply too large and prices too high. To return to the prewar parity for gold required lowering the price level, and there was an excessive stock of money because the additional money had been used to finance the war, not to produce consumer goods. Finally, the outstanding indebtedness was too large due to the creation of Fed credit.

Whether statutory gold reserve requirements to maintain the gold standard or domestic credit conditions were the most important determinant of Fed policy is still an open question, though both certainly had some influence. Regardless of the answer to that question, the Federal Reserve System's first major undertaking in the years immediately following the First World War demonstrated a poor choice of policy.

The Great Depression

At the time, and for years afterward, the monetary authorities contended that they had pursued an "easy money" policy during the Great Depression but that monetary policy alone had been virtually powerless to stop or moderate the contraction and continuing financial crises. In 1963 Friedman and Schwartz demonstrated that monetary policy generally was not expansive during the Great Depression. They argue that events of the twenties indicate that the Fed had learned how to use the "tools" available to pursue the appropriate monetary policy and had moderated and promoted the recoveries from the mild contractions of 1923–24 and 1926–27. Therefore, monetary policy in 1929–33, in addition to being "inept," was also inconsistent with that of the twenties.[11]

According to Friedman and Schwartz, the Fed could have acted aggressively to offset the drain of currency from the banking system and the rise in the reserve ratios so that the stock of money would not have fallen. If the high powered money (currency in the nonbanking public's hands and reserves of commercial banks) and money stock had been kept constant between October of 1929 and October of 1930, they believe that there would have been no banking crisis in the fall of 1930, which in their opinion was what turned a mere recession into the protracted and deep Great Depression.[12] The banking crisis began the increases in the public's holding of currency relative to deposits and the banks' reserve ratios, and these were the direct forces causing the stock of money to begin falling.[13] Open market purchases during 1931 would have offset the currency drains and reserve buildup and in September offset the discount rate increases to stop the gold outflow.[14] And, they maintain, the start of an aborted recovery in the summer of 1932 was due to the Fed's open market purchases.

What could explain the ineptness of monetary policy during the Great Depression compared to the twenties? Friedman and Schwartz argue that it was the untimely death of Benjamin Strong, the forceful and powerful governor of the New York bank until 1928. With his death there was a shift of power within the Federal Reserve System to individuals who had neither his experience nor his understanding.[15] Their thesis is that Strong would have seen the onset of the liquidity crisis in late 1930 and provided the liquidity the financial system needed. But the lack of leadership and consensus after his death allowed for indecision and tentative actions. The failure to act decisively to stop or mitigate the first such crisis in late 1930 made it even less likely that the Federal Reserve System authorities would act to stem future crises.

Two other studies supported Friedman and Schwartz's contention that the Fed had learned how to exercise monetary policy in the decade prior to the Great Depression's onset. Jeffrey Miron's study found that during the twenties the Fed reduced the seasonal variation in interest rates and, at the same time, reduced the frequency of financial panics.[16] Paul Trescott found that in the twenties the Fed effectively countered disturbances to bank reserves, and undertook dynamic policy to increase banks' reserves over time. According to his calculations, if the Fed had continued its 1924–29 policy regime, its open market holdings would have increased by $1,047 million rather than the actual $148 million. Trescott blamed much of this on the loss of the New York bank's influence when the Open Market Committee was reconstituted in January 1930.[17]

However, not everyone agrees with Friedman and Schwartz's explanation. Elmus Wicker asserts that monetary policy pursued during the twenties was consistent with that pursued from 1929 through 1933.[18] The quality and efficiency of monetary policy did not deteriorate quickly after Strong's death because his understanding of open market operations and monetary policy was not as profound as Friedman and Schwartz claim. For example, one of Strong's guideposts in open market purchases was simply to get the New York and Chicago member banks out of debt to the Fed, and this partly explains the easy money policy of 1924 and 1927. In June of 1930 the five person (not the reconstituted) Open Market Committee voted against additional market purchases because, following Strong's approach, the New York and Chicago member banks had no indebtedness. Wicker also asserts that international considerations were often more important than domestic price stability, and these provide the consistent link between monetary policy in the twenties and the Great Depression. In 1924 and 1927 monetary policy to achieve international objectives also tended to promote and accelerate domestic recovery, but in 1931 the two conflicted, and international considerations were dominant.

In 1924 the Open Market Investment Committee decided to purchase securities to build up the Fed's portfolio so as to be able to check any future inflation arising from the gold imports. In 1927 the interest rate differential between New York and London was reduced to slow down the flow of gold into the United States.[19] However, in 1930 the reasons for pursuing an easy money policy did not exist because the international gold standard was not threatened and there was no concern about future inflation. In late 1931 when the gold outflow was making it difficult for the United States to continue on the gold standard, the Fed acted to raise U.S. interest rates above those in Europe to reverse the gold flow. Under Wicker's explanation, monetary policy in the Great Depression was consistent with that in the twenties because it was primarily determined by international considerations.

Karl Brunner and Alan Meltzer provide another explanation for monetary policy in the twenties and early thirties.[20] They suggest that monetary policy from 1922 to 1933 was consistent but inappropriate because it focused on the wrong variables. The Burgess-Riefler doctrine was an attempt to explain how open market operations in conjunction with traditional discounting affected economic activity.[21] Central bank discounting affected market rates by changing the discount rate and inducing banks or dealers to borrow from or repay the central bank.[22] But if banks borrowed for profit, they could subvert open market operations. When the Fed reduced reserves, the banks could borrow to replenish reserves and then repay the borrowing when the Fed sold securities to increase reserves. The Fed staff argued that banks did not borrow for profit, doing so only when they needed to and then with great reluctance; to ensure this the Fed imposed restrictions on member bank discounting and undertook a "campaign to convince the bankers that bankers were reluctant to borrow from the Reserve banks and anxious to repay as quickly as possible."[23] In this manner the classical theory of central bank operations still held, and the Fed could use market interest rates—particularly short term rates—as the key indicator of monetary policy. Falling rates were a sign of an expansionary policy, whereas rising rates were a sign of a restrictive policy.

Short-term rates declined more after the 1929 peak than after the 1923 or 1926 peaks, and by the summer of 1930 they were at the lowest levels in over a decade. Because of this, Fed officials believed that monetary policy was extremely easy and there was no need to produce increased ease. Therefore, Brunner and Meltzer argue that monetary policy during the Great Depression was consistent with that in practice during the twenties. David Wheelock's analysis largely agrees with Brunner and Meltzer in finding that there was no significant change in Fed policy between the twenties and early thirties and that the flawed policy was guided primarily by interest rates and bank debt.[24]

In another study Mark Toma found that the Fed was not able to use monetary policy to stabilize the economy during the twenties. He argued that unique conditions at that time allowed the private banking system to react to open market operations in a way that eliminated any lasting effects on Federal Reserve credit. The close of the decade brought on an environment where the Fed's monetary policy could, and did, influence Federal Reserve credit. As Friedman and Schwartz, Wicker, Brunner and Meltzer, and others have demonstrated, the information and timing problems inherent in using discretionary monetary policy make it possible for such policies to be destabilizing as well as stabilizing and, Toma argues, this is what occurred in the Great Depression.[25]

Whether Fed policy from 1929 to 1933 was or was not consistent with policy in the twenties, there is general agreement among these studies that it was a major contributor to the banking failures and the length and severity of the contraction. The reasons offered range from a change in leadership at the Fed—a change to leaders without the requisite skill and knowledge—to the assertion that Fed officials were simply using the wrong tools through the twenties and the Great Depression. Were the authorities in the Federal Reserve System that irrational and inept?

Two analyses argue that the Fed officials were neither inept nor irrational—they did understand what they were doing. Gary Anderson, William Shughart, and Robert Tollison maintain that the Fed pursued what was a restrictive policy because it provided important benefits to member banks.[26] By 1929 there were more nonmember banks than member banks, though member banks, on average, were much larger. Small, state-chartered banks, away from the financial centers, were less able to weather the storm of the depression. From 1930 to 1933, 80 percent of the bank failures were among nonmember banks. The result was that the Fed had better control of monetary matters when more of the banks were members of the system, and, once the worst of the contraction passed, member bank profitability rose. Though this does not prove that regulators were captured by the regulated and operated for their mutual benefits rather than those of the economy in general, Anderson and his colleagues do say, "We do know the path that was chosen and that, contrary to the conventional wisdom, this path had a rationally-motivated, interest-group basis."[27]

This regulatory capture thesis was given stronger support by Gerald Epstein and Thomas Ferguson.[28] Contrary to Friedman and Schwartz, Epstein and Ferguson argue that prior to 1932 the Fed was concerned about the small amount of gold available to back up open market purchases. In addition, they contend that officials also expressed faith that wage reductions would revive prosperity and supported the idea of the real bills doctrine. This mindset limited their actions prior to 1932.

The increases in the discount rates in the fall of 1931, aimed at stemming the gold outflow, had caused bond prices to plummet, and the bond price collapse had threatened the solvency of many banks that had been increasing their holdings of short-term federal government securities all through the depression. By early 1932 the banks had largely recovered from the crisis of the previous fall. In early 1932 Congress passed the Glass-Steagall Act, which allowed government securities to secure Federal Reserve notes. This freed up one billion dollars in gold for export. Facing considerable pressure from Congress, where many bills had been proposed to increase the stock of money, and now having what they considered to be sufficient free gold, the Fed began open market purchases on a large scale, about $100,000,000 a month.

Opposition to this arose from several regional reserve banks, particularly Chicago's McDougall and Boston's Young. These bankers were worried about the rising animosity of bankers in their regions. Yields on short-term government securities had fallen from 3.4 percent in November of 1929 to 0.34 percent. Because banks were holding a much larger amount of these securities, it placed a severe squeeze on their earnings.[29] Regional reserve banks that had less free gold also began to object to the open market purchases. The British and French, upset at the open market purchases, began to withdraw their deposits from New York City banks to the detriment of the deposits and earnings in those banks, and New York banks began objecting to the Fed's purchases.[30]

The result was a rising chorus of demands to end the open market purchases. The Fed heeded these requests, and virtually no purchases were made after June of 1932. Epstein and Ferguson also argue that this makes it easier to understand why the authorities of the Federal Reserve System were so concerned with inflation after 1935 and refused to undertake open market purchases. They quote Governor Norris of Philadelphia: "Further increases in excess reserves would adversely affect bank earnings, and incur the risk of disturbance which might arise from eliminating interest on deposits." They indicate that many bankers supported the increases in reserve requirements that the Fed enacted in 1936 and 1937 because their earnings were closely tied to the rates on the government securities that made up large percentages of all bank portfolios.[31]

The 1937–1938 Depression

Banks accumulated reserves after mid-1933. Because banks were not borrowing through the discount window and the Fed could not sell securities through the open market to reduce high-powered money, when it decided to act it used its new tool of variations in required reserve ratios. Arguing that the excess reserves represented inadequate loan demand and were not desired by the banks, in July of 1936 the Fed announced that reserve requirements would be increased and began to do so in August. By May 1, 1937, the reserve ratios had doubled and were at their legal maximum.

Industrial production gradually declined from May until September. Between September and December, industrial production plunged 27 percent. The contraction continued until the trough in May of 1938, when industrial production was 39.1 percent lower than one year earlier. The 1937–1938 depression was quite severe and ended a recovery that had never come close to reaching full employment.[32] Unemployment rose from an annual average of 14.3 percent in 1937 to 19.1 percent in 1938, and real per capita GNP dropped by 6 percent. Consumer prices fell 2 percent, while wholesale prices fell over 9 percent.

Within a few years the explanations offered for the depression centered on the Federal Reserve System's doubling of member banks' reserve requirements in the eight months prior to May, 1937, and a sharp reduction in the federal government's budget deficit. In 1949 Benjamin Anderson argued that neither of these views were correct.[33] Rather, he wrote that a rapid rise in real wages in 1937, due primarily to a surge in labor union activity after the Wagner Act and the 1936 elections, reduced businesses' profits, leading firms to contract production and reduce investment expenditures.

However, Anderson's view places him in the minority; the spending and money views have dominated. Kenneth Roose, E. Cary Brown, and Larry Peppers argue that fiscal policy was the primary factor.[34] Federal expenditures fell in 1937 as the 1936 veterans bonus payments ended, while taxes rose with the new social security taxes. Friedman and Schwartz claim that monetary factors were the dominant force bringing on the contraction.[35] Banks had built up large amounts of excess reserves because required reserves could not be used in a banking crisis, and, with the banking panics and runs of the depression deeply imprinted in their memories, the excess reserves were desired. As bankers began to restore those wiped out by the doubling of reserve requirements, the stock of money declined; setting off the contraction. Several recent studies have supported this.[36]

Monetary Policy in the Interwar Period

The studies referred to above disagree on a number of points, but they do agree on one thing; during times of stress, Federal Reserve System authorities made monetary policy decisions that frequently brought on contractions or intensified already existing ones. *If* the goal of monetary policy was macroeconomic stability, then these were certainly poor policy decisions. It is not very satisfying to be unable to say exactly why such policies were pursued. Unfortunately, facts rarely fit neatly into one explanation or another. It is almost certainly the case that there was *some* ineptness in making monetary policy decisions, *some* inexperience, *some* determination of policy by international considerations, and *some* determination of policy by how it affected member banks. We just do not know the relative importance of each of these factors.

FISCAL POLICY IN THE TWENTIES AND THIRTIES

As a tool to promote stability in aggregate economic activity, fiscal policy is largely a post-Second World War phenomenon. Prior to 1930 the federal government's spending and taxing decisions were largely based on the perceived "need" for government-provided public goods and services.

The 1920s

Though the fiscal policy concept had not been developed, this does not mean that during the twenties no concept of the government's role in stimulating economic activity existed. Herbert Stein points out that in the twenties Herbert Hoover and some of his contemporaries shared two ideas about the proper role of the federal government.[37] The first was that federal spending on public works could be an important force in reducing unemployment during a depression.[38] The other was the idea that the right type of tax cut (on higher income tax rates) could actually increase the government's revenues by stimulating savings and productive investment. Both concepts fit the ideas held by Hoover and others of his persuasion that the U.S. economy of the twenties was not the result of laissez-faire workings but of "deliberate social engineering."[39]

Federal government expenditures fell sharply after the end of the First World War, while the higher tax rates imposed during the war created a large surplus that was used to reduce the federal debt. The Mellon tax cuts of the twenties slashed tax rates such that the top marginal personal income tax rate fell from 73 percent in 1921 to 25 percent in 1925. Even though tax rates were slashed, the budget surpluses continued undiminished through the twenties, and these were used to reduce the federal debt by 25 percent in that decade.

Recent research has shown that the reason the budget surpluses did not decline with the massive tax cuts was not because of a huge spurt in economic activity.[40] Rather, the sharply dropping tax rates induced wealthy individuals to shift assets from nontaxable activities to higher return taxable activities. The paradoxical result was that the federal income taxes collected rose, and taxpayers with the highest incomes bore a greater share of the tax burden even though they received huge tax cuts in the twenties.

The 1930s

By default the federal government pursued deficit spending in the depression and recovery of the thirties. For some years economists maintained that the federal government unknowingly pursued an expansionary fiscal policy, but E. Cary Brown's 1956 reexamination of fiscal policy in the thirties concluded that expansionary fiscal policy was not used.[41] Expansionary tendencies of the federal government were offset by the contractionary policies of state and local governments.

However, only the federal government is sufficiently free from budget constraints to actively pursue a fiscal policy designed to stabilize the economy at high employment. In 1973 Larry Peppers improved Brown's estimates of tax receipts and examined federal fiscal policy.[42] Federal fiscal policy was not very expansionary during the period because relative to 1929 it would have generated full-employment surpluses in 1933 and from 1937 on.

The full-employment surplus has limitations because it tends to overstate the effect of tax rate changes and convey inaccurate information when the economy is operating well below full-employment.[43] A more accurate measure of fiscal policy for both periods of low and higher unemployment rates is the weighted standardized surplus, which differs from the weighted full-employment surplus by the level of GNP at which fiscal policy is measured.[44] Thomas Renaghan has examined fiscal policy during the thirties using this measure.[45] Figure 6.1 shows his estimates. Federal fiscal policy became much more deflationary in 1932 with Hoover's revenue act and the end of the 1931 veterans' bonus payments. In the last half of the thirties, federal fiscal policy was consistently expansionary.

Stein has termed the move to expansionary fiscal policies in 1931 and 1936 "fiscal stimulation by inadvertence."[46] In both years the federal government's autonomous expenditures increased sharply because bonus payments to veterans were passed over presidential vetoes. But most of the other changes in fiscal policy were associated with tax changes. In 1932 massive increases in personal income tax rates, increases in estate tax rates, a gift tax, and new and increased excise taxes were enacted. The National Recovery Administration imposed higher liquor excise and processing taxes, and the

Fig. 6.1 Federal Surpluses or Deficits as Measures of Fiscal Policy in the 1930s

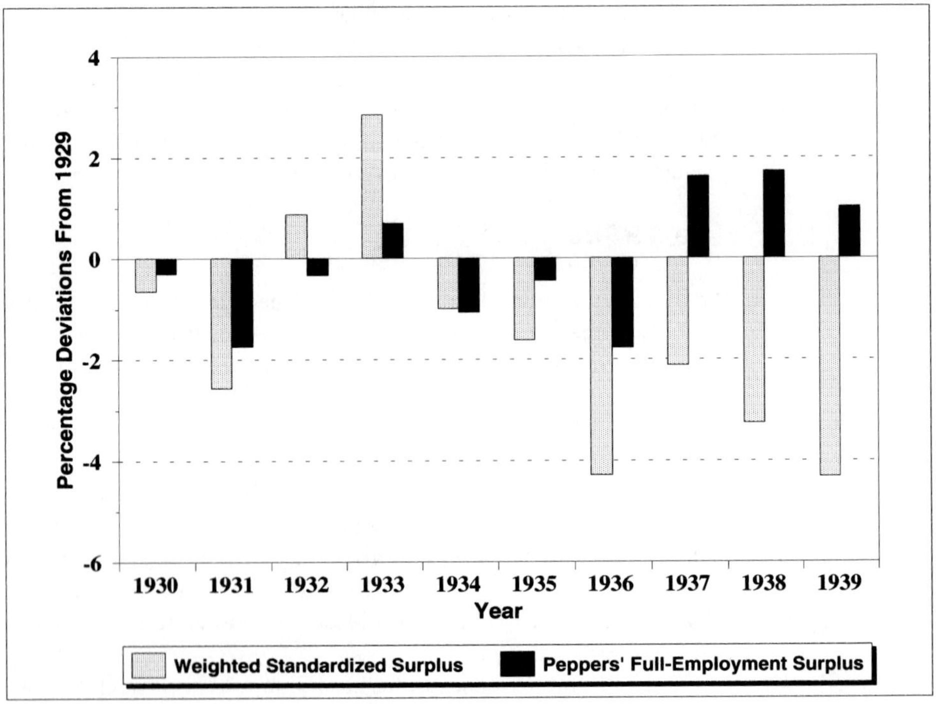

Source: Thomas M. Renaghan, "A New Look at Fiscal Policy in the 1930s," *Research in Economic History* 11 (1988): 171–83.

Revenue Act of 1934 raised individual surtax rates. The Revenue Act of 1935 was passed to correct the "maldistribution" of income by placing higher tax rates on wealthy individuals and corporations, and Social Security taxes were imposed though they did not become very large in the thirties.

It is often suggested that in 1938 Roosevelt finally turned to expansionary fiscal policy as the means to promote recovery, but Stein asserts that it was not the administration's policy to use fiscal means to whatever amount was felt necessary to achieve full employment. "Fiscal policy did not have an unlimited, residual role of doing whatever all other means in combination failed to do."[47] Rather, Roosevelt's expenditures were geared to provide jobs and relief for the neediest cases while economizing on regular expenditures.[48] Taxes were increased to provide revenue for the spending programs and for the redistribution that was part of the New Deal's programs of spending, taxation, and reform.

THE NEW DEAL

The New Deal was Roosevelt's controversial set of programs to restructure industries, redistribute income, and bring recovery to the American economy. One of the more telling criticisms of the New Deal is that in spite of—or perhaps because of—all it did, the recovery was very slow; full employment was not restored prior to 1941.

A number of explanations for the slowness of the recovery have been offered. Seymour Harris and Paul Sweezy argue that it was due to the increasing inequality in the distribution of income.[49] Vladimir Timoshenko, W. Arthur Lewis, and Charles Kindleberger suggest that it was due to a general shift in the terms of international trade away from primary products toward industrial products.[50] Others, such as Adolf Berle and Gardiner Means, assert that the increasing market power of the larger firms had made prices downwardly inflexible and generally noncompetitive creating persistent market disequilibriums.[51] Alvin H. Hansen, Paul Baran and Paul Sweezy, Michael Kalecki, David Weintraub, and Josef Steindl suggest that in the thirties the United States had entered an era of secular stagnation.[52] Joseph Schumpeter, Simon Kuznets, Moses Abramovitz, and Richard Easterlin argue that various regular cycles reached their nadir in the late twenties and thirties, causing the slow recovery from the contraction.[53] Michael A. Bernstein proposes that, due to changing consumer tastes, technologies, and the skewed income distribution, industrial investment was unable to rise sufficiently to move the economy toward full employment.[54]

More recently Robert Lucas and Leonard Rapping used an "anticipations-search" model to explain the high unemployment rates of the thirties.[55] Though their model did well for 1930 to 1933, its estimates, unlike what actually occurred, showed an unemployment rate falling to the natural rate by 1937 at the latest.[56] Michael Darby's reexamination found that unemployment data in the thirties included all those employed at federal government work-relief projects. Because these people were not searching for a job, he contends, the anticipations-search model holds that they should not be counted as unemployed.[57] Using corrected data, Darby's reestimate finds a marked movement toward full employment with an estimated natural rate of unemployment for the decade of 8.65 percent, well below the average of 13.1 percent for the decade but above estimates of about a 5 percent natural unemployment rate for other decades in this century. J. R. Kesselman and N. E. Savin argue that evidence from the thirties indicates that there was an excess demand for private sector jobs, which is inconsistent with an anticipations-search model where workers are assumed to be voluntarily unemployed while searching for a job.[58] Their reestimate also finds a relatively high estimate of the natural rate of unemployment.[59]

In general these recent studies have found that there was a movement toward the natural unemployment rate after 1933, but the estimates were that this rate was 8 percent or higher. Kesselman and Savin believe this indicates that the natural rate hypothesis was not appropriate for the thirties, whereas Darby attributes this to the effects of the National Industrial Recovery Act and other New Deal programs of the Roosevelt administration. We now turn to that topic.

The Creation of the New Deal

In March of 1933, Franklin Delano Roosevelt assumed the office of the president of the United States. It was the nadir of the depression, and the continuing banking panic had culminated in nationwide runs on banks. Though the depression ended with this final convulsive tremor of the financial system, the American economy was further from full employment than at any time in its history. Roosevelt had been elected by a large majority, receiving 59 percent of the popular vote and 89 percent of the electoral votes. He took this landslide as a mandate from the American people "to do something" about the depression. The election also brought in a huge Democratic majority in Congress who were anxious to act.[60]

The response of the Roosevelt administration was the creation of what came to be called The New Deal. Drawing upon war as an analogy for the efforts to combat the depression, policies to restore economic activity were referred to as the war on depression, and war-era agencies were resuscitated.[61] The early New Deal saw a flurry of programs enacted and put into effect with great haste in order to "do something." In the famous first "hundred days" of the Roosevelt administration, it guided to congressional approval no less than 15 major laws covering a diverse range of topics.[62] Many of the programs were found to be inconsistent, and by 1935 several major ones were found unconstitutional.

Apparently the Roosevelt administration saw the cause of the depression to be neither a failure in the market economy nor a failure of governmental policy but a result of "failures" in particular sectors of the economy—that is "basic structural problems." Many of the New Deal reform measures were not designed to promote recovery and were even inimical to it. Roosevelt's advisors wanted to reform the system to bring about "fair returns to all and the final elimination of privilege based on private selfishness."[63] Rexford Tugwell, one of the architects of the early New Deal, wanted major structural changes in both government and the private economy. He welcomed centralizing tendencies and wanted a "concern of interests" which to him "meant a collective cooperative system, without divisive private interests."[64] According to Paul Conkin, Tugwell believed that the "allocation of resources, priorities in production, profits, wages, prices—all should be determined by government in behalf of the whole nation, not the more powerful or persuasive interest groups."[65] Tugwell was willing to plunge ahead with his program even if some lost their "existing freedom and much of their existing income" because he believed that freedom in the American society had become freedom for just a few. Roosevelt probably never grasped the staggering implications of Tugwell's concept of a strongly centralized economy, a politically explosive issue. "As Tugwell conceded, Roosevelt could not be induced to think and act outside of a political context."[66]

Here we will briefly consider the major New Deal acts and then examine in somewhat more detail the National Recovery Administration.[67]

Financial Recovery and Reform

One of Roosevelt's first priorities had to be the banking system. With the banks closed, barter, local government's scrip, coined tokens, and Canadian and Mexican money were used for transactions. On March 9, 1933, Congress passed the Emergency Banking Bill.[68] The bill confirmed Roosevelt's closing of the banks and developed procedures for reopening, merging, or liquidating them; it authorized the Reconstruction Finance Corporation to put banks on a sound basis by subscribing to new issues of a bank's preferred stock, allowed the Federal Reserve System to issue new currency backed only by the government securities held, and authorized discounting on a much wider range of assets.

The Banking Act of June 16, 1933, was an attempt to reform the nation's banking system and cure the perceived weaknesses of the private banks. It directed the Federal Reserve System to supervise and control all foreign transactions. The payment of interest on demand deposits was forbidden, and the Fed was directed to set the maximum rate of interest that could be paid on time and savings deposits. Commercial and investment banking were separated so that banks could not use volatile short-term deposits to purchase securities. Finally the Banking Act of 1933 created the Federal Deposit Insurance Corporation to provide temporary insurance for the deposits of commercial banks.

The Federal Farm Mortgage Corporation and the Home Owners Loan Corporation of 1933 were temporary institutions to handle the existing debt crisis and provide additional credit to stave off foreclosures, postpone payments, and scale down debts. New programs for the agricultural sector included banks for farm cooperatives, federal land banks, production credit associations, and the Commodity Credit Corporation, which guaranteed private loans on farm commodities to provide farm price supports. Twelve Federal Housing Administration banks were created to provide credit to the savings and loan associations, which made the bulk of long-term home mortgages.

The majority of the other financial programs were designed to reform the financial sector and eliminate what the administration perceived as flaws or weaknesses. The Securities Act of May 27, 1933, was followed by the Securities and Exchange Act of

June 6, 1934, which established the Securities and Exchange Commission and gave the Fed the power to set margin requirements. The Banking Act of 1935 made the Federal Deposit Insurance Corporation and Federal Savings and Loan Insurance Corporation permanent, and reorganized the Federal Reserve System to reduce political pressures and centralize authority.

Finally, the Roosevelt administration devalued the dollar in terms of gold and outlawed ownership of gold by private citizens. The administration apparently followed the advice of Professor George W. Warren, who contended that devaluing the dollar in terms of gold would cause prices to rise and help bring back prosperity, a dubious assumption at best.

Relief for the Unemployed

In the aftermath of the depression, unemployment was numbingly high. Many of these workers had been unemployed for very long periods and were dependent upon relief. One third of all of the relief cases were in the four northern industrial states of New York, Pennsylvania, Ohio, and Illinois. An October, 1933, estimate indicated that 10 percent of the population was dependent upon relief as of that date.[69]

Much of the relief of the unemployed was directed by Harry Hopkins and consisted of two types: direct relief and work relief. The administration saw a serious unemployment problem looming for the winter of 1933–34 and created the Civil Works Administration to provide immediate employment for up to four million unemployed, but it drew much criticism and was quickly wound down after the spring of 1934. The Federal Emergency Relief Act of May 12, 1933 provided both direct and work relief. Direct money grants were given to states that would provide additional funds. The act also created and administered a number of public works programs, such as the Civil Works Service Program, the Emergency Education Program, and the Women's Work Program.

The Roosevelt administration was convinced that the federal government should withdraw from providing relief for the unemployed needy and that, for the most part, this should be turned over the state and local governments, which, they believed, were better able to administer such relief. The federal government's proper role was to centralize work relief projects. As a result Congress replaced the Federal Emergency Relief Act with the Works Progress Administration in 1935. This program undertook a number of local public works construction projects to provide employment. Other projects employed artists to paint and decorate public buildings, and writers to develop local histories and local guide books. Theater and music projects were initiated to employ actors and actresses and musicians.

The Public Works Administration was begun in the summer of 1933 as the second part of the National Industrial Recovery Act, and it continued until mid-1941. It undertook a number of large-scale projects such as the construction of highways, dams (the Hoover and Grand Coulee Dams), public buildings, and harbor improvements. The Civilian Conservation Corps was created on April 5, 1933. Its military style camps for young men were run in the national parks and forests. The National Youth Administration was started in June of 1935 to provide an out-of-school program and a student work program. Finally, in the form of longer term, more permanent relief, the Social Security Act was passed on August 14, 1935. This provided both unemployment insurance and old-age insurance. Passed at the same time but separate from the Social Security program was a program of special assistance to the needy aged, dependent children, and the blind.

Farm Relief

Because agriculture was a price-taking industry, prices had fallen dramatically and in the process driven incomes to extraordinarily low levels. Foreclosures on farm mortgages were common, and some states had declared farm foreclosure moratoriums. The problem was not to provide work for the agriculturally unemployed but to raise prices so as to generate incomes that would allow the farmers to meet their current debt obligations and provide an adequate standard of living.

The New Deal began a set of farm programs that, in altered form, continue today.[70] The basic approach of the programs was to raise farmers' incomes by raising farm prices, a prospect that was not enthusiastically supported by the food processors. The farm programs began with the first Agricultural Adjustment Act passed on May 12, 1933. Using the concept of "parity," the Agricultural Adjustment Act attempted to provide farmers with the same purchasing power as was possible in the "golden" period of 1910–14 (or 1919–24 for tobacco and potatoes). There were several devices used to accomplish this. Production controls were imposed on the amount of farm commodities produced, benefit programs designed to pay farmers to take land out of production were created, nonrecourse loans to provide minimum (or support) prices for farm commodities were developed, and direct government purchases of farm commodities (such as milk—a program which continues today) were instituted.

Roosevelt wanted the program to be voluntary and administered in a decentralized manner, preferably by the farmers in each district, but neither characteristic was realized. Some farmers and legislators were quite willing to use large taxes to force farmers to cooperate. Neither did the decentralization of the administration of the Agricultural Adjustment Act work. As would be expected, power tended to be concentrated in the hands of the largest and wealthiest farmers, the Farm Bureau, and the Government Extension Service.

Individual farmers were assigned production allotments, and they could then individually enter into agreements to reduce production to those allotments. If they signed the agreement and reduced production, they received benefit payments using funds from a processing tax levied on the first processing of the product for domestic use. The first Agricultural Adjustment Act also allowed the secretary of agriculture to enter into marketing agreements with farmers, processors, and distributors to fix marketing quotas, prohibit price-cutting, and fix and maintain prices. Because this was clearly illegal under existing laws, the act granted exemptions from the antitrust laws for participants. In addition to these supply-restricting programs, the Commodity Credit Corporation made nonrecourse loans to farmers at predetermined prices; if prices dropped below the set price, farmers simply defaulted on the loan, or, in effect, sold the commodities to the government at the loan price.

The programs spawned by the first Agricultural Adjustment Act had a short life. The A. L. Schecter Company, a poultry processor of Long Island, New York, initiated a lawsuit charging that the Agricultural Adjustment Act was unconstitutional. On January 6, 1936, the Supreme Court declared the processing tax unconstitutional because farm production was intrastate, not interstate, commerce. The Roosevelt administration and Congress quickly reacted by approving the Soil Conservation and Domestic Allotment Act, which attempted to restrict acreage in production and promote soil conservation. Commodity Credit Corporation nonrecourse loans were still used to augment demand, and the Federal Surplus Relief Corporation also purchased large amounts of farm commodities.

The second Agricultural Adjustment Act was passed on February 16, 1938, and embodied the "ever normal granary" concept of Henry Wallace. The carryover of farm commodities from year to year showed great variation, and it was felt that at least part of the reason for this was inflexible price supports, so the support measures were made flexible to smooth out this carryover. The second Agricultural Adjustment Act was not a radical departure from the preceding farm programs, and its programs are still in evidence today.

Industrial Reform

The programs for the unemployed and the farm sector were primarily for relief, though some reform measures were included. In contrast, the New Deal financial programs were as much about reform as relief, and its industrial programs were almost all aimed at "reforming" the industrial structure of the American economy. The first such attempt came through the National Recovery Administration, and after the Supreme Court ruled this unconstitutional, there was a move toward an application of the antitrust laws to this end.

The National Recovery Administration was one of two parts of the National Industrial Recovery Act passed on June 16, 1933. Chandler reports that Roosevelt described the program as one that would promote a great cooperative movement to begin employing the unemployed, "to shorten the working week, to pay a decent wage for a shorter week, and to prevent unfair competition and disastrous overproduction."[71] To do so, of course, required that the act exempt participating industries from the antitrust laws.

The "blue eagle" became the symbol of the National Recovery Administration, and firms engaging in manufacturing, mining, wholesaling, retailing, and services were urged to join it. In fact, it was suggested that it was undemocratic and un-American not to belong to the National Recovery Administration or to patronize a noncooperating firm. Code authorities were established in each of the covered industries, and they formulated codes of "fair competition" that covered firms' output, product or service prices, trade practices, wages, hours and conditions of work, and collective bargaining. The codes were examined by the National Recovery Administration and if approved, which they usually were, became binding upon cooperating firms and, in fact, achieved the force of law. The National Recovery Administration and the industry associations could resort to the courts for enforcement of the codes if necessary, though this option was rarely used.

Between July 9 and July 20 in 1933, 209 national industry codes were submitted, but it was felt that this was not fast enough and industries were asked to submit to a blanket code until the individual industry codes had been formulated and approved by the National Recovery Administration. The emphasis of the blanket code was on shortening the workweek, supporting wage rates, and minimizing price increases. The emphasis of the individual industry codes tended to be on increasing the product prices for the firms. The National Recovery Administration called for three boards to formulate the codes: a trade association board, a labor advisory board, and a consumer advisory board. When the consumer advisory board existed, it had little influence. The labor and trade association boards had conflicting objectives, and the trade association board tended to dominate.

During the National Recovery Administration's short life, there were constant conflicts between firms in various industries as well as between labor and the industries. Conflicts quickly arose over the wage policies and requirements of the industry codes. Firms argued over the minimum wage level, what the traditional skilled labor wage differentials were, and the traditional (or previous) wage differentials between firms for the same type of labor. Labor wanted the same weekly pay with reduced hours of work. Attempts to make wage rates uniform over regions brought sharp protests from the lower wage producers. The result was that bitter struggles ensued over the wage provisions of the National Recovery Administration's industry codes of self regulation.

The main purpose of the trade practice provisions of the codes was to raise product prices. To do so, the codes generally established minimum prices above the prevailing market prices so that the minimum prices tended to become the actual prices. Uniform cost accounting procedures were accompanied by prohibitions against selling at any price below "full cost," and open price systems required publication of a price list for all competitors to see as well as prior notification of price changes. Some code authorities could reject any price they considered unfair. The production limitations of the National Recovery Administration's codes included the following: limitations on the number of hours a machine or plant could be operated, maximum production quotas for individual firms, restrictions on the production capacity for individual firms, and limitations on the inventories a firm could carry.

From the beginning, compliance was poor, and it continued to deteriorate. The complexity of the structure of prices in any industry made detections of price violations difficult, and, like any cartel it was generally profitable to violate the price restrictions, especially if other firms adhered to the industry code prices. The enforcement procedures also tended to be inadequate. The National Recovery Administration wanted to minimize the number of court cases it brought and leave the enforcement of the codes to the individual associations as much as possible. This was an attempt to promote self-regulation and was not particularly successful.

By the spring of 1935, the National Recovery Administration was in disarray and widely criticized for promoting monopolistic practices and allowing the industry associations to be dominated by the large firms. Labor disputes and firm noncompliance were increasing. The issue was settled on May 27, 1935, when the Supreme Court ruled the National Industrial Recovery Act unconstitutional.

Some provisions of the National Recovery Administration were extended in the National Labor Relations Act of 1935 (or Wagner Act) and the Fair Labor Standards Act of June 25, 1938. The latter said there was to be no use of child labor (with a few exceptions), and set a maximum workweek and minimum wages. Finally, the federal government continued to sanction trade associations to limit output and set prices in the petroleum and coal industries due to "special conditions" there.

The court destruction of the National Industrial Recovery Act, new congressional pressures, largely from ardent labor supporters such as Senator Richard Wagner, and attacks from "conservative" business organizations, such as the National Association of Manufacturers, the American Farm Bureau, and the Liberty League, induced the Roosevelt administration to form a new labor policy and a new accord with "working people" for political support. To that point the New Deal reforms had accomplished few of their objectives. To Roosevelt the answer for this was simple. Men of power and other Republican "dupes" opposed it because they were evil. "Economic royalists, with a monopoly of power, they were not content with a repaired and honest capitalism. Instead, they wanted to drive on with their plutocracy and bring down upon the heads of good men of power the inevitable revolution."[72] The campaign was quite different from the 1932 campaign, with bitter attacks at organized money and the economic tyranny of big business.

New advisors helped usher in a program of "de-centralization" of wealth, location, and control.[73] There was a move to establish more competitive markets by reducing monopoly power through a more vigorous application of the antitrust laws and new legislation. There was a move to protect small businesses from the predations of larger ones in the Robinson-Patman Act in 1936 and the Miller-Tydings Act in 1937. The Robinson-Patman Act limited the price concessions that manufacturers could grant to the large (chain) buyers while not doing so for smaller (local) stores. The Miller-Tydings Act exempted manufacturers' resale price agreements, or "fair trade agreements" negotiated as a condition of selling their products, from prosecution under the Sherman Act.

The attacks by "big business" on the administration's policies and the 1937–38 depression moved Roosevelt's administration to accelerate its attack on "monopolies." Big business provided a convenient scapegoat upon which to blame the 1937 contraction. As a result the Temporary National Economic Committee was established in 1938 and charged with discovering and exposing price-fixing and other monopolistic behavior that had helped bring on the contraction in the previous year.

From 1935 to 1937, the antitrust attack on "big business" was largely ineffective. However, the antitrusters had a broader and more positive program as their goal. In 1937, under the leadership of Robert Jackson, the Antitrust Division of the Justice

Department undertook several major cases. The so-called Madison oil cases were among the more publicized; they arose from continued complaints from independent jobbers that the major oil companies conspired to rig prices. The famous ALCOA case was also initiated by Jackson's Antitrust Division in 1937, as was an investigation into financing by the automobile companies.

In 1938 Thurman Arnold, head of the Yale Law School, was appointed to head the Antitrust Division. Arnold's selection came about because he had the support of the number of influential New Dealers, and these people convinced Roosevelt—who had an ambivalent attitude toward antitrust—to nominate Thurman Arnold.[74] Under Arnold's direction, antitrust activity began to expand in 1938 and 1939 and continued to expand into the early 1940s, though none of his cases had thc effect of breaking up big business.

Politics and the Allocation of Federal Funds

The depression had touched all corners of the United States, though not with equal severity. And the New Deal economic agencies had operated in virtually every area of the nation. However, recent work has found that, not surprisingly, politics played an important role in deciding how to allocate federal funds among the states.

In 1969 Leonard Arrington used data prepared for Roosevelt's 1940 presidential campaign and found extremely large disparities in the per capita New Deal agricultural expenditures between states. He concludes that the main determinant of expenditure patterns was an attempt to restore the predepression farm incomes and not to reform the agricultural sector. Don C. Reading extended the analysis to see whether the geographic allocation of per capita New Deal spending was consistent with Roosevelt's announced goals of relief, recovery, and reform.[75] He concludes that it was more important to restore the predepression levels of real per capita income than to equalize real per capita income across the states.

Neither Arrington nor Reading closely examined the political determinants in allocating New Deal spending, but Gavin Wright[76] and Gary Anderson and Robert Tollison[77] have. Wright finds that about 80 percent of the state-by-state variation in per capita New Deal spending can be explained by political variables. Anderson and Tollison include the influence of Congress in these decisions because the tenure of the senators and representatives involved in the appropriations process was an important factor in how the federal funds were allocated. Together they argue that the location of New Deal spending was influenced by political motives, largely the reelection of Roosevelt and other Democrats.

John Joseph Wallis softens this criticism somewhat by concluding that reform attempts may have been thwarted by conservative state governments not wishing to see change. States with higher incomes and less in need of reform were more cooperative with federal officials and received more grants. Though Wallis restores some of the credibility of the traditional view of the New Deal, it is clear from these studies that politics played an important role in allocating federal funds among the states.

The New Deal: An Assessment

Conclusions about the effects of the New Deal programs and particularly the National Recovery Administration, vary widely. The noted historian Arthur Schlesinger, Jr. strongly approves of Roosevelt and the New Deal programs.[78] In *Business Cycles*, Joseph A. Schumpeter also reaches a generally favorable conclusion on the New Deal programs as a whole because of their psychological effects in restoring broken morale.[79] Writing in 1935, a group of Brookings Institution economists reached a generally adverse opinion of the New Deal.[80] They felt that boosting costs and prices was not the correct method of restoring purchasing power and suggested that the "retarding effect of the National Recovery Administration had been substantial." Lester Chandler is also generally critical of the New Deal and of the National Recovery Administration in particular.[81] He believes that the psychological boosts of the NRA quickly began to fade as the recovery proved to be slow and conflicts developed in the industries under National Recovery Administration codes. "After its initial stage, the National Recovery Administration probably did impede recovery."[82] Ellis Hawley suggests that the National Recovery Administration had been a disillusioning and frustrating experience that few wished repeated.[83] Though there was some economic recovery, he is not sure this can be credited to the National Recovery Administration. Paul Conkin says that by 1936 the New Deal had "failed to fulfill even the minimal dream of most of the varied reformers" as well as promote recovery.[84] Michael Darby also believes that the National Recovery Administration slowed recovery and caused unemployment rates to be higher than they otherwise would have been.[85] Though the above conclusions are not unanimous, most suggest that the New Deal, particularly the National Recovery Administration, impeded recovery rather than promoting it.

Examination of the National Recovery Administration codes and rules provides an indication of why this occurred. The emphasis by the firms was on raising prices and profits—not on increasing output. Labor wanted higher wages with shorter workweeks which would tend to relatively reduce output—and not restore it. The National Recovery Administration codes, with the ultimate force of law behind them, tried to eliminate price competition and product competition through standardization. Establishment of minimum prices generally above the prevailing prices restricted the operation of the pricing system in guiding resources into their most valuable uses and providing information on conditions in the markets. The production codes were all aimed at limiting output either through limits on the hours that machines or plants could operate, limits on the amount of output that a firm could produce, limits on inventories, or limits on production capacity. These production limits discouraged firms from expanding production and hiring additional labor and also discouraged investment in plant and equipment either to expand or modernize. Certainly the disputes that arose between firms in industries over wages, prices, output standards, fair practices, and market shares only discouraged and slowed recovery and expansion of production. After being confronted with entirely new institutional constraints in the summer of 1933 in the form of the National Recovery Administration, these constraints were sharply altered in May of 1935 when it was ruled unconstitutional. The Wagner Act of 1935 required further adjustments as company unions were ruled illegal and the

National Labor Relations Board was created to enforce the act's impetus to unionization. In 1938 the Fair Labor Standards Act created minimum wage and maximum hours legislation for businesses. These new labor market conditions certainly slowed restoration of production and employment. Confronted with these facts about the New Deal, logic suggests that it must have retarded the recovery from the Great Depression, and Darby's analysis suggesting that the natural rate of unemployment during the thirties was over 8.5 percent supports this.

The agricultural programs can be similarly criticized. The first and second Agricultural Adjustment Acts (and the Soil Conservation and Domestic Allotment Act that came in between them) failed to recognize the diverse characteristics of farmers and crops around the United States. The programs conflicted with other international and domestic New Deal policies. The attempt to raise domestic prices for agricultural products was inconsistent with the push to increase agricultural exports to reduce crop surpluses and was also inconsistent with a fixed exchange rate standard. Industrial policies, primarily the National Recovery Administration, attempted to raise the prices of manufactured products, but this was inconsistent with real increases in farm product prices to achieve parity ratios. Industries that used unprocessed agricultural products as inputs, such as the food processors and the cotton textile industry, were adversely affected by real increases in agricultural product prices, and their recovery was made more difficult. Finally, the general thrust of the agricultural policies was to reduce acreage and production so as to raise farm incomes. In practice most of the benefits favored the larger owner-operators over renters, share-croppers, and small-scale operators. The policies missed the fundamental point that the decline in farm incomes was due to a drop in the demand for agricultural products caused by the contraction, not because of overproduction in a highly competitive industry. The coercive attempts to reduce the acreage under cultivation and thus reduce production presented fundamental conflicts with the individual freedom that Americans had always prized.

Several recent studies attempt more precise evaluations of the effects of the New Deal programs. Wallis and Benjamin have developed a model to examine the impact of the postdepression federal government relief programs on private employment.[86] It has been suggested that the federal relief programs produced lower private employment in the thirties. Wallis and Benjamin do not find this to be the case. Though individuals did respond to the federal relief benefits, they responded by moving between relief and nonrelief unemployment. They qualify this by noting that their empirical versions of the theoretical constructs are flawed: "It would not surprise us if the improvements in measurement, particularly of wages and benefits, would yield significantly different conclusions from those we have suggested here."[87]

Michael Weinstein's extensive study provides quantitative estimates of the retardation of the recovery due to the enactment of the National Industrial Recovery Act.[88] The National Recovery Administration codes raised wages in the midst of massive unemployment and a slow recovery, and this "wage inflation" led to a continuing "price inflation" that was aided by the increased monopoly power of code industry firms and contributed to a stagnation in economic activity from 1933 to 1935. It was because of this that "after June 1933 industrial production reached a plateau that was not finally surpassed until more than a year and a half later."[89] In the second half of

1935, after the nullification of the National Industrial Recovery Act, industrial production spurted and rose 15 percent, or at a 27 percent annual rate of increase.

Weinstein estimates that the monetary expansion (due to the flow of gold into the United States) would have brought about an 8 percent annual rise in real output in the absence of mandated wage and price increases. Though crude, this estimate is incomplete because it does not include the effects of the National Industrial Recovery Act's production and investment prohibitions or the act's effects on business expectations. Businesses were further discouraged from investing by the new capital market regulations generated by the Securities and Exchange Act, the government's entry into the utility industry through the TVA, the continued tax increases (particularly the undistributed corporate profits tax) and rhetoric about the need to equalize incomes.

The New Deal, with its huge swings in programs and policies and its new laws, altered the environment within which business firms operated. It abruptly and dramatically altered the institutional framework within which private business decisions were made, not just once but several times. Though the analytical work necessary to provide quantitative estimates of the retarding effects of the entire New Deal on the recovery from the Great Depression has not been undertaken and clearly would be quite difficult, it seems likely that this retardation was substantial.

SELECTED REFERENCES

Abramovitz, Moses. "The Nature and Significance of Kuznets Cycles." *Economic Development and Cultural Change* 9 (April 1961): 225–48.

Anderson, Barry L., and James L. Butkiewicz. "Money, Spending, and the Great Depression," *Southern Economic Journal* 47 (October 1980): 388–403.

Anderson, Benjamin M. *Economics and the Public Welfare: A Financial and Economic History of the United States, 1914–1946.* Indianapolis: Liberty Press, 1979; reprint of 1949 edition.

Anderson, Gary M., William F. Shughart, II, and Robert D. Tollison. "A Public Choice Theory of the Great Depression." *Public Choice* 59 (October 1988): 3–23.

__________, William F. Shughart, II, and Robert D. Tollison. "Public Choice Theory of the Great Contraction: Further Evidence." *Public Choice* 67 (December 1990): 277–83.

__________, and Robert D. Tollison. "Congressional Influence and Patterns of New Deal Spending, 1933–1939." *The Journal of Law and Economics* 34 (April 1991): 161–75.

Arrington, Leonard. "The New Deal in the West: A Preliminary Statistical Inquiry." *Pacific Historical Review* 38 (August 1969): 311–16.

__________. "Western Agriculture and the New Deal." *Agricultural History* 44 (October 1970): 337–53.

Baran, Paul A. and Sweezy, Paul M. *Monopoly Capital: An Essay on the American Economic and Social Order.* New York: Monthly Review Press, 1966.

Bernstein, Michael A. *The Great Depression: Delayed Recovery and Economic Change in America, 1929–1939.* New York: Cambridge University Press, 1987.

Boughton, James M., and Elmus R. Wicker. "The Behavior of the Currency-Deposit Ratio During the Great Depression," *Journal of Money, Credit, and Banking* 11 (November 1979): 405–18.

Brown, E. Cary. "Fiscal Policy in the Thirties: A Reappraisal." *American Economic Review* 46 (December 1956): 857–79.

Brunner, Karl, and Allen Meltzer. "What Did We Learn from the Monetary Experience of the United States in the Great Depression?" *Canadian Journal of Economics* 1 (May 1968): 334–48.

Chandler, Lester V. *America's Greatest Depression, 1929–1941.* New York: Harper and Row, 1971.

Coelho, Philip R. P. and Santoni, G. J. "Regulatory Capture and the Monetary Contraction of 1932: A Comment on Epstein and Ferguson." *The Journal of Economic History* 51 (March 1991): 182–89.

Conkin, Paul. *The New Deal*, 2 ed. Arlington Heights, IL: AHM Publishing Co., 1975.

Darby, Michael. "Three-and-a-Half Million Employees Have Been Mislaid: Or, An Explanation of Unemployment, 1934–1941." *Journal of Political Economy* 84 (February 1976): 1–16.

Easterlin, Richard A. *Population, Labor Force, and Long Swings in Economic Growth: The American Experience*. New York: National Bureau of Economic Research, 1968.

Epstein, Gerald and Thomas Ferguson. "Monetary Policy, Loan Liquidation, and Industrial Conflict: The Federal Reserve and Open Market Operations of 1932." *The Journal of Economic History* 44 (December 1984): 957–84.

Epstein, Gerald and Thomas Ferguson. "Answers to Stock Questions: Fed Targets, Stock Prices, and the Gold Standard in the Great Depression." *The Journal of Economic History* 51 (March 1991): 190–200.

Fearon, Peter. *War, Prosperity, & Depression.* Lawrence, KS: University of Kansas Press, 1987.

Friedman, Milton and Anna J. Schwartz. *A Monetary History of the United States, 1867–1960.* Princeton: Princeton University Press, 1963.

Gandolfi, Arthur. "Stability of the Demand for Money During the Great Contraction, 1929–1933." *Journal of Political Economy* 82 (September/October 1974): 969–84.

Gordon, Robert Aaron. *Economic Instability and Growth: The American Record.* New York: Harper and Row, 1974.

Gordon, Robert J. and James A. Wilcox. "Monetarist Interpretations of the Great Depression: An Evaluation and Critique." *The Great Depression Revisited.* Edited by Karl Brunner. Boston: Martinus Nijhoff, 1981.

Hansen, Alvin H. "Economic Progress and the Declining Population Growth." *American Economic Review* 29 (March 1939): 1–15.

__________. *Full Recovery or Stagnation?* New York: W. W. Norton, 1941.

Harris, Seymour. *Saving American Capitalism: A Liberal Economic Program.* New York: Alfred Knopf, 1948.

Hawley, Ellis. *The New Deal and the Problem of Monopoly, 1933–1939.* Princeton: Princeton University Press, 1965.

Huberman, Douglas A. "An Alternative to 'A Public Choice Theory of the Great Contraction.'" *Public Choice* 67 (December 1990): 257–68.

Hughes, Jonathan. "Roots of Regulation: The New Deal." *Regulatory Change in an Atmosphere of Crisis: Current Implications of the Roosevelt Years.* Edited by Gary M. Walton. New York: Academic Press, 1979.

Kalecki, Michael. *Studies in Economic Dynamics.* London: George Allen and Unwin, 1943.

__________. *Theory of Economic Dynamics: An Essay on Cyclical and Long-Run Changes in Capitalist Economy.* New York: Monthly Review Press, 1968.

__________. *Studies in the Theory of Business Cycles, 1933–39.* New York: Augustus M. Kelly, 1969.

Keehn, Richard H. and Gene Smiley. "The U.S. Bank Failures, 1932–1933: A Provisional Analysis." *Essays in Business and Economic History: Selected Papers from the Business and Economic Historical Society Meetings, 1987* 6 (1988): 136–56.

Kesselman, Jonathan R. and N. E. Savin. "Three-and-a-Half Million Workers Never Were Lost." *Economic Inquiry* 16 (April 1978): 205–25.

Kindleberger, Charles P. *The World in Depression, 1929–1939*. Berkeley: University of California Press, 1973.

Kuznets, Simon P. "Long Swings in the Growth of Population and in Related Economic Variables." *Proceedings of the American Philosophical Society* 201 (February 1958): 25–52.

Leuchtenberg, William E. "The New Deal and the Analogue of War." *Change and Continuity in Twentieth Century America*. Edited by John Braeman et al. New York: Harper and Row, 1967.

Lewis, W. Arthur. *Economic Survey, 1919–1939*. London: George Allen and Unwin, Ltd., 1949.

Lothian, James R. "Comments on 'Monetarist Interpretations of the Great Depression.' " *The Great Depression Revisited*. Edited by Karl Brunner. Boston: Martinus Nijhoff, 1981.

Lyon, LeVerett S., Paul T. Homan, Lewis L. Lorwin, George Terborgh, Charles L. Dearing, and Leon C. Marshall. *The National Recovery Administration: An Analysis and Appraisal*. Washington: The Brookings Institute, 1935.

Lucas, Robert E., Jr. and Leonard A. Rapping. "Unemployment in the Great Depression: Is There a Full Explanation?" *Journal of Political Economy* 80 (January/February 1972): 186–91.

Means, Gardiner C. "Price Inflexibility and the Requirements of a Stabilizing Monetary Policy." *Journal of American Statistical Association* 30 (June 1935): 401–13.

__________, and Adolf Berle. *The Modern Corporation and Private Property*. New York: Harcourt, Brace, and World, 1968.

Miscamble, Wilson D. "Thurman Arnold Goes to Washington: A Look at Antitrust Policy in the Later New Deal." *Business History Review* 56 (Spring 1982): 295–304.

Miron, Jeffery. "Financial Panics, the Seasonality of the Nominal Interest Rate, and the Founding of the Fed." *American Economic Review* 76 (March 1986): 125–40.

Peppers, Larry. "Full-Employment Surplus Analysis and Structural Change: The 1930s." *Explorations in Economic History* 10 (Winter 1973): 197–210.

Pilgrim, John. "The Upper Turning Point of 1920: A Reappraisal." *Explorations in Economic History* 11 (Spring 1974): 271–98.

Reading, Don C. "New Deal Activity and the States, 1933 to 1939." *The Journal of Economic History* 33 (December 1973): 792–810.

Renaghan, Thomas M. "A New Look at Fiscal Policy in the 1930s." *Research in Economic History* 11 (1988): 171–83.

Roose, Kenneth D. *The Economics of Recession and Revival*. New Haven: Yale University press, 1954.

__________. "The Production Ceiling and the Turning Point of 1920." *American Economic Review* 48 (June 1958): 348–56.

Samuelson, Paul, and Everett E. Hagen. *After the War—1918–1920*. Washington: National Resources Planning Board, 1943.

Santoni, G. J., and Norman T. Van Cott. "The Ruthless Fed: A Critique of the AST Hypothesis." *Public Choice* 67 (December 1990): 269–75.

Schlesinger, Arthur M., Jr. *The Age of Roosevelt*. 3 vols. Boston: Houghton Mifflin, 1964.

Schumpeter, Joseph A. *Business Cycles: A Theoretical, Historical, and Statistical Analysis of the Capitalist Process*. 2 vols. New York: McGraw-Hill, 1939.

Smiley, Gene. "Some Austrian Perspectives on Keynesian Fiscal Policy and the Recovery in the Thirties." *Review of Austrian Economics* 1 (1987): 145–80.

Soule, George. *Prosperity Decade: From War to Depression, 1917–1929*. New York: Rinehart and Co., 1947.

Stein, Herbert. *The Fiscal Revolution in America*. Chicago: University of Chicago Press, 1969.
Steindl, Josef. *Maturity and Stagnation in American Capitalism*. New York: Monthly Review Press, 1979.
Sullivan, Lawrence. *Prelude to Panic: The Story of the Bank Holiday*. Washington: Statesman Press, 1936.
Sweezy, Paul. *The Theory of Capitalist Development*. New York: Monthly Review Press, 1968.
Timoshenko, Vladimir P. *World Agriculture and the Depression*, Michigan Business Studies. Vol. 5. Ann Arbor: University of Michigan Press, 1933.
Toma, Mark. "The Policy Effectiveness of Open Market Operations in the 1920s." *Explorations in Economic History* 26 (January 1989): 99–116.
Trescott, Paul B. "Federal Reserve Policy in the Great Contraction: A Counterfactual Assessment." *Explorations in Economic History* 19 (July 1982): 211–20.
__________. "The Behavior of the Currency-Deposit Ratio During the Great Depression: Comment," *Journal of Money, Credit, and Banking* 16 (August 1984): 969–83.
__________. "Bank Failures, Interest Rates, and the Great Currency Outflow in the United States, 1929–1933," *Research in Economic History*, Vol. 11 (1988), pp. 49–80.
Wallis, John Joseph and Daniel K. Benjamin. "Public Relief and Private Employment in the Great Depression." *The Journal of Economic History* 41 (March 1981): 97–102.
__________. "Employment, Politics, and Economic Recovery During the Great Depression." *The Review of Economics and Statistics* 69 (August 1987): 516–20.
__________. "The Birth of the Old Federalism: Financing the New Deal, 1932–1940." *The Journal of Economic History* 44 (March 1984): 139–59.
Weintraub, David. "Effects of Current and Prospective Technological Developments Upon Capital Formation." *American Economic Review* 29 (March 1939, Supplement): 32.
Wheelock, David C. "The Strategy, Effectiveness, and Consistency of Federal Reserve Monetary Policy 1924–1933." *Explorations in Economic History* 26 (October 1989): 453–76.
Wicker, Elmus. "Federal Reserve Monetary Policy, 1922–1933: A Reinterpretation." *Journal of Political Economy* 73 (August 1965): 325–43.
__________. *Federal Reserve Monetary Policy, 1917–1933*. New York: Random House, 1966.
__________. "A Reconsideration of Federal Reserve Policy During the 1920–1921 Depression." *The Journal of Economic History* 26 (June 1966): 223–38.
Wilson, Thomas. *Fluctuations in Income and Employment*, third edition. New York: Pitman Publishing, 1948.
Wright, Gavin. "The Political Economy of New Deal Spending: An Econometric Analysis." *Review of Economics and Statistics* 56 (February 1974): 30–8.

NOTES

1. Until 1917 one third of the reserves could be in vault cash and the rest on deposit in the district bank.
2. Milton Friedman and Anna J. Schwartz, *A Monetary History of the United States, 1867–1960* (Princeton: Princeton University Press, 1963), 253.
3. Ibid., 313–314.
4. Ibid., 317.
5. The final banking panic is discussed in Richard H. Keehn and Gene Smiley, "U.S. Bank Failures, 1932–1933: A Provisional Analysis." *Essays in Business and Economic History: Selected Papers from the Business and Economic Historical Society Meetings, 1987* 6 (1988): 136–56.

6. The Treasury had to buy the gold that flowed into the United States. Normally the Treasury issued gold certificates that the Fed purchased by printing notes or crediting the Treasury's deposits at the Fed. The Treasury then paid for the gold with Federal Reserve notes or a check on its Fed deposits. When the Treasury sterilized the gold inflow in 1937, it paid for the gold with receipts from securities issued and sold to the general public rather than to the Fed.
7. Their study indicated that the excess reserves were widely distributed geographically and among banks so that few banks would individually face mechanical difficulties in adjusting to higher reserve requirements.
8. See the following studies: Paul Samuelson and Everett E. Hagen, *After the War—1918–1920* (Washington: National Resources Planning Board, 1943); Thomas Wilson, *Fluctuations in Income and Employment*, 3d ed. (New York: Pitman Publishing, 1948); Robert Aaron Gordon, *Economic Instability and Growth: The American Record* (New York: Harper and Row, 1974); John Pilgrim, "The Upper Turning Point of 1920: A Reappraisal," *Explorations in Economic History* 11 (Spring 1974): 271–98. Kenneth D. Roose, "The Production Ceiling and the Turning Point of 1920," *American Economic Review* 48 (June 1958): 348–56.
9. Pilgrim, "The Upper Turning Point"; and Milton Friedman and Anna J. Schwartz, *A Monetary History of the United States, 1867–1960* (Princeton: Princeton University Press, 1963), chapter 5. Also see George Soule, *Prosperity Decade: From War to Depression, 1917–1929* (New York: Rinehart and Co., 1947), 89.
10. Elmus Wicker, "A Reconsideration of Federal Reserve Policy During the 1920–21 Depression," *The Journal of Economic History* 26 (June 1966): 223–38.
11. Friedman and Schwartz, *A Monetary History*, 407–19.
12. Ibid., 393. Brunner and Meltzer have argued similarly. See Karl Brunner and Allen Meltzer, "What Did We Learn from the Monetary Experience of the United States in the Great Depression?" *Canadian Journal of Economics* 1 (May 1968): 334–48.
13. Several studies had found that the demand for currency in this period prior to the final banking panic in early 1933 was primarily determined by banking failures, not interest rates on deposits. [See Barry L. Anderson and James L. Butkiewicz, "Money, Spending, and the Great Depression," *Southern Economic Journal* 47 (October 1980): 388–403; and Arthur Gandolfi, "Stability of the Demand for Money During the Great Contraction, 1929–1933," *Journal of Political Economy* 82 (September/October 1974): 969–84.] James Boughton and Elmus R. Wicker found that over the 1921–33 period deposit interest rates was quite important in determining the demand for currency while banking failures were not. [James M. Boughton and Elmus R. Wicker, "The Behavior of the Currency-Deposit Ratio During the Great Depression," *Journal of Money, Credit, and Banking* 11 (November 1979): 405–18.] However, as Paul Trescott has shown Boughton and Wicker's empirical estimates were quite sensitive to the period used. If estimates exclude the years prior to 1924, deposit interest rates become unimportant and banking failures become much more important. [Paul Trescott, "The Behavior of the Currency-Deposit Ratio During the Great Depression: Comment," *Journal of Money, Credit, and Banking* 16 (August 1984): 969–83.] In a more extensive analysis of the demand for currency during the Great Depresssion, Trescott found that the analysis *must* be disaggregated by region because of the sharply different experiences in different regions. If this is not done, then the aggregation hides the significance of the explanatory variables. Trescott found that the results consistently showed the strong influence of bank failures and negligible influence of deposit interest rates—which is consistent with earlier analyses. [Paul Trescott, "Bank Failures, Interest Rates, and the Great Currency Outflow in the United States, 1929–1933," *Research in Economic History* 11 (1988): 49–80.]

14. Friedman and Schwartz, *A Monetary History*, 394 and 399.
15. Friedman and Schwartz, *A Monetary History of the United States*, 411.
16. Jeffrey A. Miron, "Financial Panics, the Seasonality of the Nominal Interest Rate, and the Founding of the Fed," *American Economic Review* 76 (March 1986): 125–40.
17. Paul B. Trescott, "Federal Reserve Policy in the Great Contraction: A Counterfactual Assessment," *Explorations in Economic History* 19 (July 1982): 213 and 216–19.
18. Elmus Wicker, "Federal Reserve Monetary Policy, 1922–1933: A Reinterpretation," *Journal of Political Economy* 73 (August 1965): 325–43. See also Elmus Wicker, *Federal Reserve Monetary Policy, 1917–1933* (New York: Random House, 1966). Wicker had access to the minutes of the Open Market Investment Committee and Open Market Policy Conference from the 1922–1933 period, something that Friedman and Schwartz did not have.
19. Wicker, "Federal Reserve Monetary Policy," 336. In 1927 Strong had a meeting with the heads of the central banks in Great Britain, Germany, and France that was the "occasion for a bold experiment in central bank cooperation." They decided to reduce the interest rate differential between New York and London to reduce the gold inflow into the United States. In this way, there would not have to be a general rise in interest rates in Europe in the autumn of 1927.
20. Karl Brunner and Allen Meltzer, "What Did We Learn from the Monetary Experience of the United States in the Great Depression?" *Canadian Journal of Economics* 1 (May 1968): 334–48.
21. The Burgess-Riefler doctrine was named for two economists employed by the Federal Reserve System in the twenties who developed the concept.
22. Ibid., 342.
23. Ibid., 339.
24. David C. Wheelock, "The Strategy, Effectiveness, and Consistency of Federal Reserve Monetary Policy 1924–33," *Explorations in Economic History* 26 (October 1989): 453–76.
25. Mark Toma, "The Policy Effectiveness of Open Market Operations in the 1920s," *Explorations in Economic History* 26 (January 1989): 99–116.
26. Gary M. Anderson, William F. Shughart, II, and Robert D. Tollison, "A Public Choice Theory of the Great Depression," *Public Choice* 59 (October 1988): 3–23.
27. Ibid., 19. The Anderson-Shughart-Tollison thesis was vigorously attacked. See Douglas A. Huberman, "An Alternative to 'A Public Choice Theory of the Great Contraction,' " *Public Choice* 67 (December 1990): 257–68; and G. J. Santoni and T. Norman Van Cott, "The Ruthless Fed: A Critique of the AST Hypothesis," *Public Choice* 67 (December 1990): 269–75. Also see the reply to the critics, "Gary M. Anderson, William F. Shughart, II, and Robert D. Tollison, "A Public Choice Theory of the Great Contraction: Further Evidence," *Public Choice* 67 (December 1990): 277–83.
28. Gerald Epstein and Thomas Ferguson, "Monetary Policy, Loan Liquidation, and Industrial Conflict: The Federal Reserve and the Open Market Operations of 1932," *The Journal of Economic History* 44 (December 1984): 957–84. Epstein and Ferguson's study was criticized by Coelho and Santoni and they then replied to this criticism. See Philip R. P. Coelho and G. J. Santoni, "Regulatory Capture and the Monetary Contraction of 1932: A Comment on Epstein and Ferguson," *The Journal of Economic History* 51 (March 1991): 182–89; and Gerald Epstein and Thomas Ferguson, "Answers to Stock Questions: Fed Targets, Stock Prices, and the Gold Standard in the Great Depression," *The Journal of Economic History* 51 (March 1991): 190–200.
29. Epstein and Ferguson, "Monetary Policy, Loan Liquidation," 968–973.
30. Ibid., 973.

31. Ibid., 982–983.
32. Benjamin M. Anderson, *Economics and the Public Welfare: A Financial and Economic History of the United States, 1914–1946* (Indianapolis: Liberty Press, 1979 reprint of 1949 edition), 430–31.
33. Anderson, *Economics and the Public Welfare*, chapter 67.
34. Kenneth Roose, *The Economics of Recession and Revival* (New Haven: Yale University Press, 1954); E. Cary Brown, "Fiscal Policy in the Thirties: A Reappraisal," *American Economic Review* 46 (December 1956): 857–79, reprinted in Robert W. Fogel and Stanley L. Engerman, eds., *The Reinterpretation of American Economic History* (New York: Harper and Row, 1971); Larry Peppers, "Full-Employment Surplus Analysis and Structural Change: The 1930s," *Explorations in Economic History* 10 (Winter 1973): 197–210.
35. Friedman and Schwartz, *A Monetary History of the United States*, 543–45.
36. Michael Darby, "Three-and-a-Half Million Employees Have Been Mislaid: Or, An Explanation of Unemployment, 1934–1941," *Journal of Political Economy* 84 (February 1976): 1–16. See also Gene Smiley, "Some Austrian Perspectives on Keynesian Fiscal Policy and the Recovery in the Thirties," *Review of Austrian Economics* 1 (1987): 145–80.
37. Herbert Stein, *The Fiscal Revolution in America* (Chicago: University of Chicago Press, 1969), chapter 1.
38. Ibid., 10.
39. Ibid., 7.
40. James Gwartney and Richard Stroup, "The Tax Cuts of the 1920's," chapter 4 in *Tax Rates, Incentive Effects, and Economic Growth*, unpublished manuscript, 1981; John Mueller, "Lessons of the Tax-Cuts of Yesteryear," *The Wall Street Journal*, 5 March 1981. Gene Smiley, "Tax Rate Changes and Tax Avoidance, the 1915–1929 Era," unpublished manuscript, 1989.
41. Brown, "Fiscal Policy in the Thirties: A Reappraisal," 486.
42. Peppers, "Full-Employment Surplus Analysis and Structural Change,"
43. This is discussed some detail in Thomas Renaghan, "A New Look at Fiscal Policy in the 1930s," *Research in Economic History* 11 (1988): 172–175.
44. The weighted standardized surplus is defined as the change in tax receipts attributable to changes in the tax code weighted by the marginal propensity to consume less the change in government expenditures. Both the weighted change in tax receipts and the change in government expenditures are evaluated at the actual levels of GNP. The weighted full-employment surplus is the same except that the weighted change in tax receipts is evaluated at the estimated full-employment level of GNP.
45. Renaghan, "A New Look at Fiscal Policy in the 1930s."
46. Stein, *The Fiscal Revolution in America*, 24.
47. Stein, *The Fiscal Revolution in America*, 116.
48. Peppers, "Full-Employment Surplus Analysis," 204.
49. The increasing income inequality lowered the average propensity to consume and simultaneously raised the average propensity to save, making it difficult to generate the aggregate demand necessary to establish full-employment production. Seymour Harris, *Saving American Capitalism: A Liberal Economic Program* (New York: Alfred Knopf, 1948), and Paul M. Sweezy, *The Theory of Capitalist Development* (New York: Monthly Review Press, 1968).
50. Vladimir P. Timoshenko, *World Agriculture and the Depression*, Michigan Business Studies, vol. 5 (Ann Arbor: University of Michigan Press, 1933); W. Arthur Lewis, *Economic Survey, 1919–1939* (London: George Allen and Unwin Ltd., 1949); and Charles P. Kindleberger, *The World in Depression, 1929–1939* (Berkeley: University of California Press, 1973).

51. Gardiner C. Means, "Price Inflexibility and the Requirements of a Stabilizing Monetary Policy," *Journal of the American Statistical Association* 30 (June 1935): 401–13; and Gardiner C. Means and Adolf Berle, *The Modern Corporation and Private Property* (New York: Harcourt, Brace, and World, 1968).
52. Alvin H. Hansen, "Economic Progress and Declining Population Growth," *American Economic Review* 29 (March 1939): 1–15, and *Full Recovery or Stagnation?* (New York: Norton, 1941); Paul A. Baran and Paul M. Sweezy, *Monopoly Capital: An Essay on the American Economic and Social Order* (New York: Monthly Review Press, 1966); Michael Kalecki, *Studies in Economic Dynamics* (London: George Allen and Unwin, 1943), *Theory of Economic Dynamics: An Essay on Cyclical and Long-Run Changes in Capitalist Economy* (New York: Monthly Review Press, 1968), and *Studies in the Theory of Business Cycles, 1933–39* (New York: Augustus M. Kelly, 1969); David Weintraub, "Effects of Current and Prospective Technological Developments Upon Capital Formation," *American Economic Review* 29 (March 1939, supplement): 32; Josef Steindl, *Maturity and Stagnation in American Capitalism* (New York: Monthly Review Press, 1979).
53. Joseph A. Schumpeter, *Business Cycles: A Theoretical, Historical, and Statistical Analysis of the Capitalist Process*, 2 vols. (New York: McGraw-Hill Book Co., 1939). Simon Kuznets, "Long Swings in the Growth of Population and in Related Economic Variables," *Proceedings of the American Philosophical Society* 102 (February 1958): 25–52; Moses Abramovitz, "The Nature and Significance of Kuznets Cycles," *Economic Development and Cultural Change* 9 (April 1961): 225–48; Richard A. Easterlin, *Population, Labor Force, and Long Swings in Economic Growth: The American Experience* (New York: National Bureau of Economic Research, 1968).
54. Michael A. Bernstein, *The Great Depression: Delayed Recovery and Economic Change in America, 1929–1939* (New York: Cambridge University Press, 1987).
55. Robert E. Lucas, Jr. and Leonard A. Rapping, "Unemployment in the Great Depression: Is There a Full Explanation?" *Journal of Political Economy* 80 (January/February 1972): 186–91.
56. Darby, "Three-and-a-Half Million U.S. Employees," 9.
57. Darby also found that the wage data reported by the government showed a sharp rise in wage rates and a sharp decline in average hours worked in 1934, which is strange because a rise in average hours worked has generally been a reliable leading indicator of an expansion. Darby argues that the wage and hours data were spurious and attributable to the passage of the National Industrial Recovery Act. Average annual earnings per full-time employee showed no such highly unusual behavior in 1934, and he used this series.
58. Jonathan R. Kesselman and N. E. Savin, "Three-and-a-Half Million Workers Never Were Lost," *Economic Inquiry* 16 (April 1978): 205–25.
59. Darby's study was also criticized by Robert Gordon and James Wilcox. They found support for the anticipations-search model but concluded that the uncorrected unemployment rate series was superior. Robert J. Gordon and James A. Wilcox, "Monetarist Interpretations of the Great Depression: An Evaluation and Critique," in Karl Brunner, ed., *The Great Depression Revisited.* For a criticism of Gordon and Wilcox's analysis see, James R. Lothian, "Comments on 'Monetarist Interpretations of the Great Depression,' " in Karl Brunner, ed., *The Great Depression Revisited.*
60. Lester V. Chandler, *America's Greatest Depression, 1929–1941* (New York: Harper and Row, 1970), 133.
61. This is discussed in some detail in William E. Leuchtenberg, "The New Deal and the Analogue of War," in John Braeman et al., *Change and Continuity in Twentieth Century America* (New York: Harper and Row, 1967). It was also discussed by Jonathan Hughes. Hughes has pointed out that the historical roots of the National Recovery Administration

and the New Deal extend well into the nineteenth century. Jonathan Hughes, "Roots of Regulation: The New Deal," chapter 3 in Gary M. Walton, ed., *Regulatory Change in an Atmosphere of Crisis: Current Implications of the Roosevelt Years* (New York: Academic Press, 1979).

62. Arthur M. Schlesinger, Jr., *The Age of Roosevelt*, 3 vols. (Boston: Houghton Mifflin, 1964).
63. Paul Conkin, *The New Deal*, 2d ed. (Arlington Heights: AHM Publishing Company, 1975) 34.
64. Ibid., 35.
65. Ibid., 35.
66. Ibid., 36.
67. Lester Chandler and Peter Fearon have clear and thorough discussions of many aspects of the New Deal, and we will draw upon their work here. Chandler, *America's Greatest Depresssion*; and Peter Fearon, *War, Prosperity, & Depression: The U.S. Economy, 1917–45* (Lawrence, KS: University of Kansas Press, 1987).
68. This section draws upon Chandler, *America's Greatest Depression*, chapter 9; and Fearon, *War, Prosperity, & Depression*, chapter 13.
69. Fearon, *War, Prosperity & Depression, 236–37.*
70. Most of the discussion of this section is drawn from Chandler, *America's Greatest Depression*, chapter 12; and Fearon, *War, Prosperity & Depression*, chapter 11.
71. Ibid., 223.
72. Conkin, *The New Deal*, 71.
73. Ellis Hawley, *The New Deal and the Problem of Monopoly, 1933–1939* (Princeton: Princeton University Press, 1965), 286–87.
74. Wilson D. Miscamble, "Thurman Arnold Goes to Washington: A Look at Antitrust Policy in the Later New Deal," *Business History Review* 56 (Spring 1982): 295–304.
75. Don C. Reading, "New Deal Activity and the States, 1933 to 1939," *The Journal of Economic History* 33 (December 1973): 792–810.
76. Gavin Wright, "The Political Economy of New Deal Spending: An Econometric Analysis," *Review of Economics and Statistics* 56 (February 1974): 30–8.
77. Gary M. Anderson and Robert D. Tollison, "Congressional Influence and Patterns of New Deal Spending, 1933–1939," *The Journal of Law and Economics*, 34 (April 1991): 161–75.
78. Scheslinger, *The Age of Roosevelt.*
79. Joseph A. Schumpeter, *Business Cycles*, 2 vols. (New York: McGraw-Hill Book Co., 1939).
80. LeVerett S. Lyon, Paul T. Homan, Lewis L. Lorwin, George Terborgh, Charles L. Dearing, and Leon C. Marshall, *The National Recovery Administration: An Analysis and Appraisal* (Washington: The Brookings Institute, 1935).
81. Chandler, *America's Greatest Depression*, chapter 13.
82. Ibid., 239.
83. Hawley, *The New Deal*, chapter 7.
84. Conkin, *The New Deal*, 71.
85. Darby, "Three-and-a-Half Million Employees," 14.
86. John Joseph Wallis and Daniel K. Benjamin, "Public Relief and Private Employment in the Great Depression," *The Journal of Economic History* 41 (March 1981): 97–102.
87. Ibid., 102.
88. Weinstein, "Some Macroeconomic Impacts," and Recovery and Redistribution Under the NIRA.
89. Weinstein, "Some Macroeconomic Impacts," 269.

CHAPTER 7

What Caused the Great Depression?

The Great Depression of 1929–33 stands out as one of the watersheds in the history of the United States. In Chapter 2 we described the course of this great contraction and its effects on production, employment, and living standards. In Chapter 6 we examined the role of monetary and fiscal policies in counteracting the depression and spurring recovery, though, as we saw, there is considerable doubt as to whether the policies actually did this. What we will now do is try to understand why the Great Depression occurred, but it will become evident that this is no easy task. Though it has been extensively analyzed, there continues to be considerable disagreement on the explanation of the contraction.[1] A good place to begin is by briefly describing an economic contraction's general characteristics.

A Depression is a period of at least two consecutive quarters of declining real gross national product.[2] The last quarter prior to the beginning of the decline in real output is the peak of the expansion. The recovery begins when there are at least two consecutive quarters with a rising real gross national product. The previous quarter is then designated as the trough of the contraction. From peak to trough, real gross national product declines and is invariably accompanied by rising unemployment rates, declines in the average number of hours worked each week, and a declining utilization of industrial capital and of wholesale and retail distribution facilities and equipment. The Great Depression of 1929 to 1933 conforms to these definitions. The contraction began in the second quarter of 1929 and troughed in the first quarter of 1933. During this time real output and the overall level of prices both fell, though not always together or at the same rate over time. The unemployment rate rose until, for the entire year of 1933, it averaged 25 percent of the total labor force and nearly 38 percent of the nonfarm labor force. Manufacturing facilities all over the United States were idled, and storefronts were shuttered as businesses closed.

To understand an economic contraction, particularly of the magnitude of the Great Depression, it most be noted that the contraction is not initiated by a loss of knowledge or a noticeable loss of resources. Rather, a depression is a collapse in the volume of economic activity. During the Great Depression neither workers, plants, equipment, transportation facilities, nor raw materials disappeared—many just stood idle and unused because they were not demanded. People did not desire to go hungry, wear hand-me-down clothes, give up their phones, and stop purchasing "luxuries" like fresh fruit, new curtains, shoes, suits, and perfume. The loss of much or all of their income, due to reduced employment, forced them to reduce their demands for these and other goods.

A market system uses prices to coordinate economic activities. Consumers use market prices, given their individual preferences, to decide how to allocate their incomes among the possible goods and services they could purchase. Those consumer decisions lead individual producers to demand resources, given the prices and productivity of the resources, to produce the goods and services that consumers are demanding. The prices of the resources and the amount of resources that consumers supply determine their incomes. And these incomes become the basis of the consumers' effective demands.

The task of coordinating demands and supplies for this multitude of goods and resources falls primarily to the money prices of those resources and goods. If some markets have an excess supply while others have an excess demand, then relative money prices will change to induce resources to move toward markets with excess demands and induce consumers to shift their demands toward markets with excess supplies. Money prices provide low-cost information, facilitating specialization through the division of labor and coordinating the use of individuals' differing knowledge of the particular circumstances of time and place. Costly information and costly movement through space make perfect economic coordination unachievable.[3] However, generally the coordination process works rather well and is able to adjust to changes in the parameters underlying individual demand and supply functions in the various markets.[4]

A depression occurs when something disrupts this coordination process, and it is here that the disagreements begin. Most of the sources of such disruptions can be conveniently classified under the headings of the Keynesian explanation, the Monetarist explanation, or the Austrian explanation, though such classifications are rather arbitrary and do not do justice to their complexity.[5]

The Keynesian explanation generally assumes that demands for products and services in one or more private sectors decline, and this initially disrupts market coordination. Some contend that in time adjustments will again coordinate markets, but this period of time is so long that the government must intervene to guide the economy back to coordinated full employment. Others argue that, in fact, the market process is fundamentally flawed and government must continually guide the economy toward full employment to avert continuous depressions.

The Monetarist explanation generally assumes that markets work well to coordinate economic activities. Proponents of this view see the problem in money. Because of its crucial role as a medium of exchange, measure of value, and way to hold wealth, disruptions in the stock of money or in its acceptance for goods, services, or resources disrupt market coordination. Most Monetarists believe that the supply of money is too important to be left to the private sector and must become a government monopoly. The problem then becomes the wise or appropriate use of monetary policy; they argue that depressions, when government controls the stock of money, can be traced to failures of monetary policy.

Those who favor the Austrian explanation also argue that market processes work well to coordinate economic activity. However, they maintain that the knowledge problem makes it impossible for government to direct the economy. The individuals in the government who must actually make the decisions can never have the knowledge that is available to all of the market participants, particularly the knowledge of time, place, and circumstances available to individual market transactors. "Austrians" also argue that money is too important to be monopolized or controlled by government authorities because they can never have the knowledge necessary to wield monetary policy wisely, and there is too much temptation to let political agendas determine it. In general Austrians argue that depressions occur because governments disrupt market processes through such things as grants of monopoly, tariffs and trade barriers, and wage and price controls or through policies that alter the stock of money in ways that discoordinate economic activities.

THE AUSTRIAN EXPLANATION OF THE GREAT DEPRESSION

The Austrian explanation of a depression or "business cycle" was developed by Ludwig von Mises and Friedrich A. Hayek in the twenties and early thirties prior to the development of either the Keynesian or Monetarist explanations.[6] Overshadowed by the Keynesian approach since the publication of the *General Theory* in 1936, in the 1970s interest in the Austrian approach to economic analysis began to revive.[7] The Austrian explanation of the Great Depression can be summarized as follows.

In the twenties the Federal Reserve System engineered increases in the money stock beyond what was justified by the increases in the gold stock.[8] The Fed, concerned with speculation in the securities markets and enormous increases in securities prices, stopped increasing the monetary base (the nonbanking public's currency holdings and the banks' reserves) for most of 1928 and most of 1929. As long as the Federal Reserve System was increasing the monetary base, the banks had been able to make more business and consumer loans and purchase more financial securities, thereby expanding the stock of money. In doing this, interest rates were driven lower than they otherwise would have been. The lower interest rates induced individuals and firms to increase their borrowing and investment. As the interest rates declined, the market values of assets, particularly capital goods, increased, and the longer the life of an asset, the greater the rise in its market value. Entrepreneurs were also led by the lower interest rates to shift resources to productive uses farther removed from final consumption uses. These changes in the values of capital goods induced businesses to alter production techniques to use more capital goods with longer lives, because these processes had became more profitable. Businesses also altered the ways in which they financed their investments to take advantage of those relative price changes and, as a result, relied more on equity financing and the issuance of longer term debt. The result was to alter the pattern of production and financing.

Given the prices resulting from the expansion of the stock of money through the banking system, industrialists were making what appeared to be correct decisions. The investment boom induced them to divert resources from the production of consumer goods (whose prices had not changed as much because they have relatively short lives) toward investment goods (whose prices had risen more because they tend to have longer lives) and toward stages of production farther removed from final consumption. However, consumer preferences between current and future consumption had not altered in such a manner, and as the additional money was spent by the initial borrowers and began to circulate in the economy, consumer spending on currently produced goods rose, and consumer saving was insufficient to sustain the lower rates of interest. These demand changes and the rise in interest rates (with the resulting relative price changes) were postponed as the monetary authorities continued to expand the stock of money. However, once the monetary authorities stopped increasing the money stock in 1928, the restoration of consumers' preferences between spending and saving caused interest rates to rise and the market value of capital assets and the prices of raw materials to fall. The same investments and resources whose market values had risen the most with the lower interest rates experienced the largest price declines. Business firms found that they had undertaken unprofitable investments, and some partially completed investment projects could not be profitably completed. During the monetary expansion markets had became "discoordinated" because relative prices had been altered and had sent signals to industrialists to take actions that were actually inconsistent with consumer preferences. When prices adjusted with the end of the monetary expansion, the discovery of the malinvestments led to a drop in investment demand and in the demand for raw materials used in the production processes—particularly in stages of production farther removed from final consumption uses.

According to Austrian economists, this is how the downturn in the middle of 1929 originated. A "depression" of economic activity of some length was inevitable because it takes time to correct the previous malinvestments. However, a secondary depression created by further government intervention and a severe contraction of the stock of money associated with several banking crises transformed this into the protracted and extraordinarily severe Great Depression. At the end of 1929, President Hoover called several well-publicized conferences of leaders of major firms, asking them to maintain money wages because "labor was not a commodity to be liquidated." Hoover insisted that the first shock of the depression had to fall on profits and not upon wages. On November 18 the presidents of the major railroads were summoned, on November 21 the great industrial leaders were called in, on November 22 the leading representatives of the building and construction industries came, and on November 27 the leading public utility executives appeared. On December 4 a larger group of industrial leaders were called to Washington, D.C., where they agreed to Hoover's program, particularly the maintenance of money wage rates. The press and the labor unions hailed these "historic" new agreements.

Through the first half of 1930, nominal wage rates in major industries remained virtually constant. During this period product prices were falling so that real wages and real firm labor costs were rising. Firms began reducing production and employment as business profits were precipitously declining. By the end of 1930 and the beginning of 1931, firms could no longer resist the pressures and began cutting wage rates. However, real wage rates in many industries continued to rise through 1931. The constancy of money wages increased involuntary unemployment and stopped equilibrating price adjustments.[9] Lowell Gallaway and Richard Vedder point out that the failure to adjust wage rates in 1930 had serious second-round effects that made the decline more severe in 1931 and 1932. As prices and productivity fell while businesses held wages constant, profits were squeezed. By mid-1930, before the first banking crisis occurred, this severe profit squeeze was being noticed by the financial community, leading to a decline in the demand for corporate equities and debt. Corporate savings declined from $2.8 billion in 1929 to −$2.6 billion in 1930 and −$4.9 billion in 1931. The decreasing market value of business loans made by banks wiped out much of the net worth of many financial institutions and may have been a major factor in the banking crisis.[10]

This was not the only action taken during this period. In December of 1928, the Hawley-Smoot tariff, proposed to provide some protection for American farmers, received Hoover's blessing. During 1929 Congress worked on the tariff, and numerous special interests succeeded in gaining new or additional protection for all types of domestically produced commodities. Economists from across the United States denounced the tariff, and well before Hoover signed the tariff bill in June of 1930, other nations were threatening retaliatory actions. With the signing of the tariff, many other nations attempted to counteract it by new or altered quotas on U.S. exports and/or by sharply rising tariffs on commodities exported out of the United States. The Smoot-Hawley tariff and retaliatory tariffs by other nations sharply altered the supplies and demands for many products, necessitating a complex and extensive set of price and resource adjustments. The export-producing sectors in most countries are the most dynamic and innovative in the economy, so the trade war initiated by the Smoot-Hawley tariff was particularly harmful to the pace of development.[11]

Beginning in 1931 the initiation of a sharp decline in the stock of money and the intermittent banking panics, both of which ended in March of 1933, required further relative and absolute price adjustments, including interest rates on bank loans and yields on securities that were higher than they otherwise would have been, leading to greater decreases in the prices of long-term assets.

In the Austrian view, then, the Great Depression was the inevitable result of the boom of the twenties that was led by the Fed's creation of new money. The depression commenced when the mistakes made during the boom—the malinvestments—were discovered, and industrialists began to make adjustments. The shocks to the economic system during the depression—the tariff, banking panics, and declines in the stock of money—and the initial failure of wage rates to fall created a secondary depression that prolonged and deepened what already was a serious contraction.

Criticisms of the Austrian Explanation

The Austrian explanation of the Great Depression has been criticized on a number of points, not all of which can be presented here.[12] One criticism involves the extent of the investment maladjustments that would have arisen due to the inflation of the stock of money in the 1924–28 period. The general contention is that with relatively constant consumer and wholesale prices in the decade, it is difficult to believe that very large maladjustments in the structure of production and consumption could have occurred—certainly not ones large enough to have required massive resource reallocations capable of explaining the exceptional depth and length of the Great Depression. Austrians reply that rising prices are not necessary; all that is required is that the creation of money through bank lending drive the market rate of interest below that rate consistent with consumer preferences. In addition, Austrians also admit that the secondary depression, as Hayek termed it, was much more severe and responsible for the extraordinary length and severity of the depression as a whole, but, they argue, this should not blind us to the fact that the primary depression, which started the process, was caused by malinvestments due to the monetary expansion.

A second major point has been the importance of the constancy of money wage rates in 1930 and the resulting rise in real wage rates. Some have asserted that the economic structure changed after the 1920–21 depression, and real price and wage flexibility were lost.[13] Others argue that there was nothing unusual about the wage stickiness, and it was not a major factor in the length or severity of the depression.[14] However, then and now many have considered wages a major factor in the depression.[15]

Some have argued that declining wage rates would not have promoted recovery because the declining wage rates would have reduced consumer incomes and thus spending. Austrian responses to this involve two points. First it is wage *rates* that decline and not necessarily total wages paid. As wage rates decline, businesses will tend to hire more workers. Thus, even at lower wages the relatively greater employment may lead to nearly the same, or perhaps even greater, total wages paid. The second point is that Austrians do not argue that all wage rates have to fall equally or even that all wage rates have to fall. What is necessary is that a pattern of wage rates consistent with other prices and with consumer preferences be established. In the boom preceding a contraction, wage rates in the production of capital goods further removed from final consumption uses and in the production of raw materials for industrial uses will tend to rise more. In the contraction, as the malinvestments are liquidated, capital values reduced, and the pattern of production shortened, wage rates, particularly in the capital-goods producing industries, have to decline.

The Austrian explanation for the Great Depression received a considerable acceptance in the early 1930s, much of which was due to Hayek's arguments in the late 1920s that, given the Austrian theory of the business cycle, the boom, particularly in the United States, was not sustainable and a depression was coming. However, the Austrian policy proposals of letting the depression run its course to correct malinvestments and restructure wages and prices was considered by many to be an overly harsh solution. When Keynes proposed his theory in 1936, many quickly accepted it, some for its theoretical apparatus that seemed to them to better explain the Great Depression, and others for its policy implications that government could step in and replace private investment as a means to get depressed economies moving toward full employment. This eager acceptance cast the Austrian explanation aside and led to the dominance of the Keynesian explanation through the 1950s.

THE KEYNESIAN EXPLANATION

The Keynesian, or "spending," explanation asserts that the Great Depression began with a fall in one or more autonomous components of aggregate expenditures. The fall in spending led to a fall in incomes, and this brought on a further fall in induced investment spending, creating a general contraction of income and employment.[16] Early Keynesian economists who examined the Great Depression assumed that the only way that it could have been stopped prior to its natural ending would have been to directly stimulate commodities spending. They were convinced that in the thirties the American economy was operating in the "liquidity trap," making monetary policy ineffective.

In the Keynesian framework the key to analyzing and understanding the Great Depression is to find the component or components of planned autonomous expenditures that declined and set off the cyclical contraction. Several types of spending have been suggested as the culprits. The earliest explanations centered on declining housing construction and declining investment in the automobile industry at the end of the twenties. The most recent candidate is an autonomous fall in consumption expenditures during 1930.[17]

Excess Capacity and Saturation in the Automobile Market

The automobile industry had grown rapidly during the twenties. Though the number of firms fell, the surviving firms, especially Ford, General Motors, and Chrysler (after its creation in 1924) had expanded as the production of cars rose from 1,518,000 in 1921 to 4,587,400 in 1929. This expanded production required a substantial investment by the surviving producers, an investment that Keynesians contend began declining at the end of the twenties.

There were two interrelated aspects of the automobile industry's decline in investment spending. First, it was suggested that by the end of the twenties investment in the automobile industry had created excess capacity. Second, the market for automobiles was also supposed to be "saturated" so that at the existing incomes of families and the distribution of that income and given the preferences of families for automobiles compared to other commodities and services, the rate of sales of automobiles per period (or the rate of growth of the sales per period) was at a maximum. Thus, even if there were no current excess capacity, this would still have led to a fall in investment spending compared to what had been occurring, reducing aggregate demand and leading into the Great Depression.

In 1934 Edwin Nourse examined the extent of excess capacity in the automobile industry in the late twenties and found that it was substantial. However, Nourse's analysis was based on engineering and not economic concepts.[18] In a recent reexamination Lloyd J. Mercer and W. Douglas Morgan point out that "economic capacity" is given by the minimum point on the U-shaped short-run average cost curve, not by the maximum physical output the plant should be able to produce.[19] To evaluate the excess capacity argument, they estimated the capacity output where costs were minimized.[20] The utilization of the capital stock in the automobile industry during each period was then found by comparing the actual output in any year with the capacity output. When the ratio of actual to capacity output exceeded one it meant that unit costs were higher, providing an incentive for investment to lower the unit costs of production. When the ratio was less than one, it meant that the firms had excess capacity, leading to falling investment.

Figure 7.1 represents Mercer and Morgan's estimates of current capacity utilization rates in the American automobile industry quarterly from 1921 through 1940 and indicates that by the late twenties there was some excess capacity in the automobile industry. However, the amount of excess capacity is much less than the 1934 estimate of Edwin Nourse and appears to be much smaller than that described by many historians. In addition, the quarterly utilization rates suggest that there was some basis for increased expenditures on investment through the second quarter of 1929. It does not appear that "excess capacity" in the American automobile industry, and a resulting

Fig. 7.1 Estimated Quarterly Capacity Utilization in the American Automobile Industry

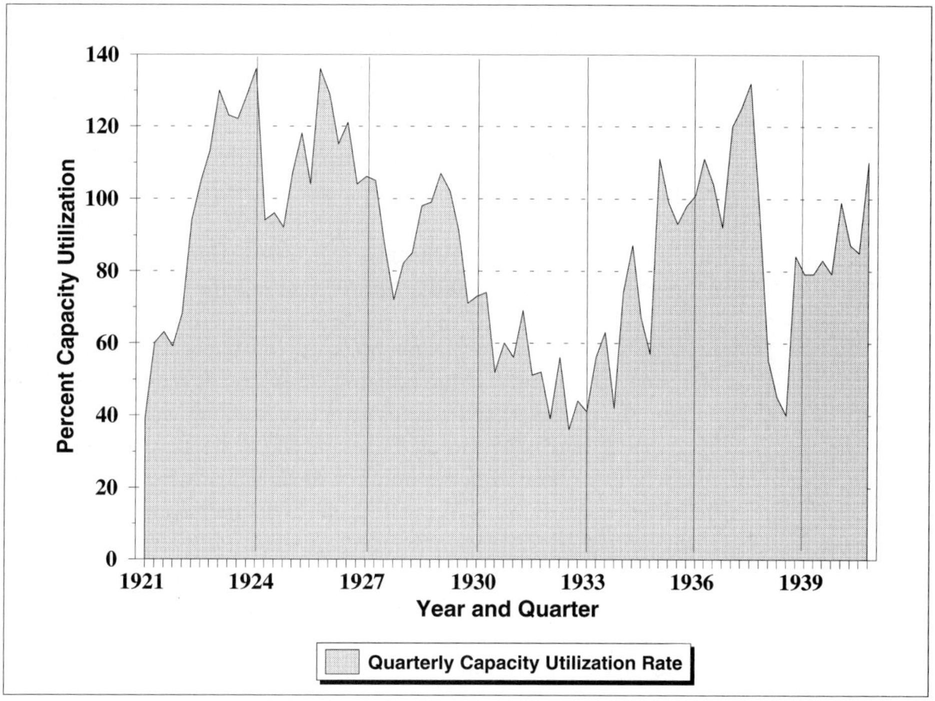

Source: L. J. Mercer and W. D. Morgan, "The Automobile Industry: Investment Demand, Capacity, and Capacity Utilization, 1921–1940," *Journal of Political Economy* 80 (November/December 1972): 1214–31.

decline in investment, would do more than account for some downturn in economic activity in 1929.

Regardless of whether there was excess capacity in the late twenties, investment in capital to produce automobiles might have declined if the automobile industry saw, or suspected, that the market for automobiles was "saturated" by the late twenties. Mercer and Morgan also evaluate this proposition.[21] They find that saturation in the level of the stock of automobiles did not exist prior to 1930. However, in dynamic terms using either total cars or cars per capita, saturation in the *growth* of the demand for automobiles existed from 1924 on (except for the single year of 1928) confirming the *tendency* toward saturation in the automobile market. However, these results have been questioned by two Canadian economists, P. J. George and E. H. Oksanen, who argue that Mercer and Morgan use an inappropriate income variable and fail to consider the possibility of a structural change around 1929.[22] Making these two corrections, George and Oksanen reexamine the saturation of the American automobile market in the late twenties and find that there were important shifts in the demand for automobiles after the start of the depression in 1929. When this is considered, there is then little evidence that the market for automobiles was saturated in the late twenties.

Housing Overinvestment in the Twenties

Many economists have suggested that the declining investment demand caused by falling housing construction was a more important factor in initiating the Great Depression, and that a "housing surplus" in the late twenties was a strong factor causing the decline in housing construction. In 1960 Bert Hickman and Richard Muth separately published studies that reached opposite conclusions on the existence of a housing surplus in the late twenties.[23] In 1971 Ben Bolch, Rendig Fels, and Marshall McMahon produced a study that reexamines the concept of a housing surplus, and in 1973 Bolch and John Pilgrim undertook a more extensive analysis of the effects of housing investment in the twenties on the Great Depression.[24] In the 1960 studies, Hickman had found that the housing stock was "excessive" by the late twenties, whereas Muth had found that the actual stock of housing was below the desired stock in 1929, 1931, 1932, and 1935. Bolch, Fels, and McMahon say that Hickman was discussing too many housing units for the number of families, whereas Muth was discussing underbuilding in the sense of too little real investment per individual house, and their own study attempted to see which effect was more important.

Real gross housing expenditures on new units can be separated into two multiplicative components; housing starts and the real average investment per unit.[25] After estimating the determinants of each, Bolch, Fels, and McMahon examined the building hypothesis by simulating what would have been the case in each situation if a "normal" situation had occurred.[26] The result was overbuilding in the number of housing units from 1922 through 1929. They also found "overinvestment" per individual housing unit from 1921 to 1928 and conclude that excessive housing starts relative to family formation led to the sharp decline in housing construction at the end of the twenties. In their view the demographic changes in the twenties were the proximate causes of this. In a 1978 study Clarence Barber was even more emphatic on the importance of demographic changes, suggesting that these were the ultimate explanation of the Great Depression.[27] Basing his explanation on a Harrod-Domar growth model, Barber argues that the rapid decline in the population's growth rate disturbed that equilibrium, and this rapid fall in the natural growth rate initiated the depression. The importance of the falling housing investment in relation to the Great Depression was further stressed in Bolch and Pilgrim's 1973 study. Using their econometric model of the American economy from 1919 to 1938, they conclude that the basic cycle of the interwar period was traceable to the residential construction cycle in the twenties, and this cycle was largely explained by demographic changes, specifically the declining birth rate of the domestic population and the sharp decline in immigration due to the passage of immigration laws.

Lloyd J. Mercer and W. Douglas Morgan argue that when Bolch, Fels, and McMahon undertook their estimates, they incorrectly omitted the separate effect of the stock of houses on housing starts, and this led to their finding of excessive gross construction expenditures on housing.[28] Mercer and Morgan find overbuilding of houses for 1921 through 1925 but a deficiency of housing starts, or underbuilding, for 1926 through 1933. Using the alternative static and dynamic saturation framework that they had developed, they find that dynamic saturation of the housing market began in 1926 and lasted until 1934.

Peter Temin holds that their conclusion as to the importance of the residential construction cycle (and by direct association, population growth) followed from the structure of the model they used.[29] He argues that ultimately the rate of family formation was the primary variable determining income movements in the model. However, if the rate of family formation also depended on income, then the decline in housing construction and the onset of the contraction could not be traced directly to population growth through the rate of family formation. A 1973 study by Bert Hickman found that the depression reduced housing construction by slowing the rate of family formation.[30] Barber argues that Temin did not interpret Hickman's model and results correctly.[31]

However, this raises questions about the causal relationship between housing construction and the onset of the Great Depression. In addition, given the earlier declines in housing construction, it is not clear why this did not initiate a contraction prior to the late spring of 1929.

An "Unexplained" Decline in Consumption Spending

The most recent candidate for the cause of the spending decline that initiated the Great Depression is an "unexplained" decline in consumption spending in 1930 that Peter Temin has discovered.[32] He finds that the decline in consumption spending from 1929 to 1930 was much larger than declines in the similar contractions of 1920–21 and 1937–38. Because he could find no satisfactory reason for the bulk of the decline in consumption spending from 1929 to 1930, Temin was forced to conclude that the Great Depression was started by an unexplained decline in consumption spending.

Frederick S. Mishkin's 1978 study provides a potential explanation for the large decline in consumption spending in 1930.[33] His "liquidity hypothesis" stresses the importance of the composition of the household balance sheet. During financial distress, households will prefer to have more financial assets compared to tangible assets. Rapid sales of tangible assets generally result in wealth losses. The likelihood that a household will suffer financial distress increases in direct proportion to the degree of the indebtedness and the relative percentage of holdings of tangible assets compared to financial assets. Consumers built up an unusually large indebtedness prior to the stock market crash. With the crash and falling prices during the contraction, the real value of household asset holdings fell and continued to fall through 1932. As a result, household balance sheets deteriorated noticeably. Mishkin suggests that much of the drop in consumer spending on housing and other tangible assets can be explained by the changes in household balance sheets.

Temin and Mishkin's theory of a consumption spending decline as the cause of the Great Depression may explain too much. Thomas Mayer argues that Temin should have compared 1930 with all of the interwar years rather than just 1921 and 1938 and should also have examined the residuals from the estimated consumption function for each year during the period.[34] In addition, Mayer suggests that Temin's consumption function was badly specified. Making these adjustments Mayer reestimates Temin's consumption function and finds that the results strongly reject Temin's contention of an unusually large unexplained fall in consumption spending in 1930. Mayer also estimates two better specified consumption functions for the 1921–41 period. Estimates from these provided little support for Temin's hypothesis. Mayer concludes that "the results can be best described as mixed, so that, as a whole, the evidence fails to establish Temin's hypothesis."

The Magnitude of the Initial Decline

Over the last several decades, an increasing number of economists and economic historians have expressed doubt as to the validity of the Keynesian explanation of the Great Depression. Recently Peter Temin has considered some aspects of this, and we can follow his examination.[35] Temin compares the percentage changes in real GNP and its major components during the initial stages of each of the three interwar contractions.[36] Table 7.1 contains Temin's data as well as, in parentheses, the more recent interwar GNP estimates of Joseph Swanson and Samuel Williamson.[37]

In the 1920–21, 1929–30, and 1937–38 comparisons, several features stand out. First, real GNP and consumption fell more in 1929–30 than in the other two contractions, while investment spending fell less. Because consumption spending depends largely on income and investment spending is less dependent upon income, changes in investment spending are usually taken to be the prime determinant of changes in eco-

Table 7.1 Percentage Changes in Real Macroeconomic Variables

	1920–21		1929–30		1937–38	
GNP	−2.4	(−0.4)	−8.9	(−11.1)	−5.4	(−5.2)
CONSUMPTION	+6.4	+(10.8)	−5.4	(−8.1)	−1.6	(−2.6)
INVESTMENT	−41.7	(−62.4)	−35.6	(−42.7)	−53.1	(−58.6)
EXPORTS	−14.2	(−32.5*)	−19.1	(−8.4*)	+1.7	(+147.2*)
	1919–21		**1928–30**		**1936–38**	
GNP	−3.5	(−2.0)	−3.4	(−4.9)	+2.3	(−0.1)
CONSUMPTION	+11.6	(+14.5)	−0.2	(−2.8)	+2.1	(+0.4)
INVESTMENT	−30.7	(−41.0)	−27.8	(−28.4)	−26.4	(−29.8)
EXPORTS	−19.7)	(−78.0*)	−15.7	(−26.3*)	+29.8	(+234.7*)

Source: Peter Temin, Did Monetary Forces Cause the Great Depression? (New York: W. W. Norton, 1976), table 6, p. 64; and Joseph Swanson and Samuel Williamson, "Estimates of National Income and Product for the United States Economy, 1919–1941," Explorations in Economic History 10 (Fall 1972). The data not in parentheses are from Temin. The data in parentheses are from Swanson and Williamson, with their current price data deflated by the implicit GNP price deflator. Investment and Exports refer to gross private domestic investment and merchandise exports, except for * which indicates that the figure is for percentage changes in the net exports of goods and services.

Table 7.2 Proportion of the Change in Investment in Various Components

	1920–21	1929–30	1937–38
CONSTRUCTION	0.06	0.42	0.10
EQUIPMENT	0.19	0.22	0.28
INVENTORIES	0.75	0.36	0.62
	1919–21	**1928–30**	**1936–38**
CONSTRUCTION	−0.09	0.82	−0.33
EQUIPMENT	0.20	0.18	0.28
INVENTORIES	0.89	0.00	1.06

Source: Peter Temin, Did Monetary Forces Cause the Great Depression? (New York: W. W. Norton, 1976), table 7, p. 65.

nomic activity. By this measure, either 1920–21 or 1937–38 should have been more severe contractions than 1929–30. However, these comparisons tend to overstate the 1929–30 changes. To partially, though not completely, adjust for this, the bottom portion of Table 7.1 compares percentage changes for the yearly values for the year prior to the peak to yearly values the year after the peak. John Kendrick's data that Temin uses show the 1919–21 contraction to be slightly more severe, while the Swanson and Williamson data show the 1928–30 downturn to be more severe. Investment spending still declined less in 1928–30 than in 1919–21. If investment spending is the key to the contractions, then this suggests that the 1920–21 contraction should have been more severe than that of 1929–30.

There is one more comparison Temin makes that can also be examined. Table 7.2 uses Swanson and Williamson's data to examine the proportion of the total investment change due to changes in categories of investment for these periods. In both the 1920–21 and 1937–38 (or 1919–21 and 1936–38) contractions, the bulk of the investment decline was in inventory investment, and the smallest was in construction; in 1929–30 (or 1928–30), the bulk of the decline was in construction.[38]

Temin suggests that the decline in construction activity from 1929 to 1930 might have "depressed expectations of investment in 1931 more than an equivalent fall" in inventory or equipment investment. But he admits that it is difficult to know how large this effect would have been if it actually existed. Temin's reasoning is that construction tends to be more stable than inventory investment. If it is low in one year, then individuals will generally expect it to be low in the next year. Thus, the relatively large decline in construction may have more sharply depressed expectations.

Beyond this, the Keynesian model does not suggest that income will decline more (or less) from a decline in construction as compared to an equivalent decline in inventory or equipment investment. It is the magnitude of the autonomous spending decline that is relevant to explain the income decline. Investment spending is generally considered to be the key category because it is relatively less dependent upon income and tends to be more volatile. However, as Temin points out, the fall in investment spending at the end of twenties does not appear to have been large enough to bring about such a major depression, and the fall in 1930 was not unusual for the size of the income decline that occurred in 1930.

The Absence of Equilibrating Adjustments

Declining housing construction in the late twenties due to overbuilding and declining investment in the automobile and related industries due to market saturation and excess capacity in the late twenties are the usual Keynesian explanations for the autonomous spending decline that set off the contraction; however, the studies cited above raise some doubts as to the importance of these explanations.

Certain other aspects of this should also be considered. If the overbuilding of housing was reducing the demands for housing at the same time as the costs of constructing housing were rising, this indicates that those resources were more valuable in alternative uses. If the automobile market was saturated, then there must have been other desirable goods that the consumers were turning toward. The role of the price system is to communicate this information to the individual transactors so as to promote these equilibrating adjustments in resources and the production of goods and services. It has often been pointed out that the Keynesian model tends to ignore this by proposing that if a component of aggregate demand declines, such as investment, this will cause, via the income multipler, an associated decline in most other components of aggregate demand. In this scenario the equilibrating role of the price system is not mentioned.

There is evidence, however, of wide variations in the behavior of various prices during the depression. Wheat prices could not cover the costs of harvesting some of the wheat crop; sheep prices were less than the costs of shipping sheep to market; cotton prices could not purchase enough food to keep pickers in the fields. The evidence indicates that there were massive disruptions in the price system and that prices failed to adjust rapidly enough to simultaneously clear the individual markets. One reason that such a disruption could occur is that there were large negative shocks (large sharp decreases) in the stock of money. It is this Monetarist explanation of the Great Depression to which we now turn.

THE MONETARIST EXPLANATION

The Monetarist explanation of the Great Depression is mainly concerned with explaining why a "normal," albeit relatively severe, contraction was transformed into the catastrophic depression and deflation from the end of 1930 through the first quarter of 1933. In this explanation a series of panics and banking failures initiated a sharp and continuing reduction in the stock of money. As individuals and firms attempted to restore the desired money balances, the decrease in spending caused production, employment, incomes, and prices to begin to fall. As long as the contraction of the stock of money continued, the real and nominal levels of economic activity also had to contract. Once the stock of money stopped falling at the end of the first quarter of 1933, the contraction of economic activity also ceased.

Ben Bernanke has extended this explanation by examining nonmonetary effects of the financial crisis.[39] Bernanke argues that the financial crises during the 1929–33 period reduced the ability of financial institutions to function as credit intermediaries and raised the costs of credit intermediation. This was particularly damaging to smaller borrowers as loans were recalled, and new loans often became unavailable. Larger firms, which might have borrowed, were reluctant to do so. Because of the rise in the costs of borrowing relative to the "safe" rate on savings, Bernanke asserts that this unambiguously reduced the demands for current-period goods and services. He believes that these nonmonetary financial effects are important in explaining the length and depth of the Great Depression.

The Onset of the Depression in 1929

Peter Temin and Anna Schwartz have recently suggested that the Fed's restrictive monetary policy in 1928 and 1929, adopted to dampen the stock market boom, initiated the contraction.[40] Alexander Field has found that the growth of the stock market from the mid-twenties to 1929 significantly increased the transactions demand to hold money balances by brokers and their customers.[41] Because Fed authorities failed to recognize this, they engaged in policies designed to dampen or break the boom in the stock market. As the amount of money balances demanded increased, along with the prices of stocks and the volume of stocks exchanged, the resulting liquidity crunch caused sharp increases in interest rates, as can be seen in Figure 7.2. These interest rate increases were an important factor in causing a further decline in housing construction in 1928 and, after April of 1929, a decline in sales of automobiles. He suggests that the Federal Reserve System might not have persisted in its antispeculative monetary policy if it had recognized the greater demand for money balances.[42] As it was, the policy was continued until the crash at the end of October of 1929.

The Effects of Panics and Bank Failures

By fall of 1930, the contraction was already noted as being quite severe. However, according to the Monetarists the contraction's character changed in November and December of 1930. The reason for this can be seen in Figure 7.3, which presents Friedman and Schwartz's monthly deposit-to-reserve ratios, deposit-to-currency ratios, and high-powered money stock for the period of 1928 through 1934.[43] After being roughly constant through 1928, 1929, and most of 1930, the deposit-to-reserve and deposit-to-currency ratios begin to fall in late 1930. The deposit-to-reserve ratio fell through 1935, though at a somewhat slower rate in 1934 and 1935. The deposit-to-currency ratio fell sharply in 1931, much more slowly in 1932, and then began to rise in early 1933. As individuals and firms held more currency relative to deposits by converting their deposit balances into currency, this depleted banks' reserves and caused a reduction in the total stock of money. As banks increased their reserve ratios, they decreased lending and deposit creation to build up the reserves causing a further fall in the stock of money. Therefore, the onset of falling deposit-to-reserve and deposit-to-currency ratios in late 1930 initiated huge declines in the stock of money. Though the

Fig. 7.2 Four Short-Term Interest Rate Series

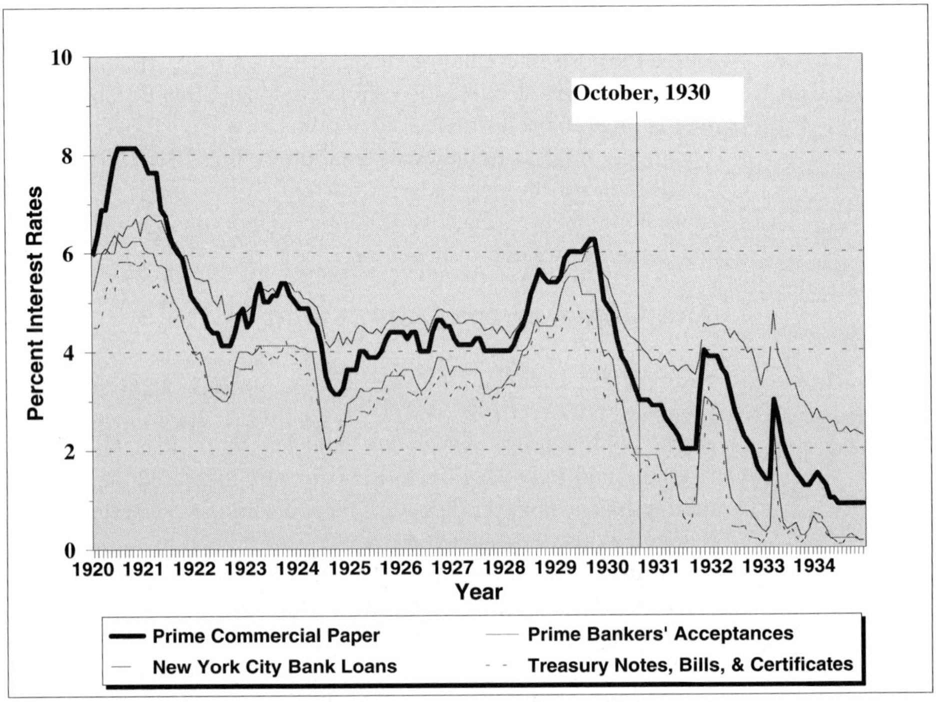

Source: *Banking and Monetary Statistics* (Washington: National Capital Press, 1943). Based upon Peter Temin, *Did Monetary Forces Cause the Great Depression?* (New York: W.W. Norton, 1976), figures 4 and 5, pp. 124–25.

Federal Reserve System began to increase the high-powered money, the increases were far too small to stop the money stock from falling.

The Monetarists contend that the rising bank reserve ratios and the public's increased holdings of currency relative to deposits indicated a general "liquidity scramble" initiated by the onset of banking panics and failures. The first panic in November of 1930 is crucial because it set off the liquidity scramble by the banks and the public and established the Federal Reserve System's failure to act to stop the liquidity scramble then and later in the contraction. As the stock of money fell due to the liquidity scramble and with a stable demand for money balances, this caused individuals and firms to reduce spending to restore the desired money balances.[44] The spending reductions, initiated by the fall in the stock of money beginning at the end of 1930, explain the extraordinary length and severity of the contraction. In addition, the recurring panics and bank failures brought into question the stability and soundness of the entire economic system, further depressing economic activity.

In general, the Monetarists contend that this was the result of inappropriate monetary policy by the Federal Reserve System. If the Fed had vigorously pursued an

Fig. 7.3 High Powered Money and the Deposit to Reserve and Deposit to Currency Ratios, 1928–34

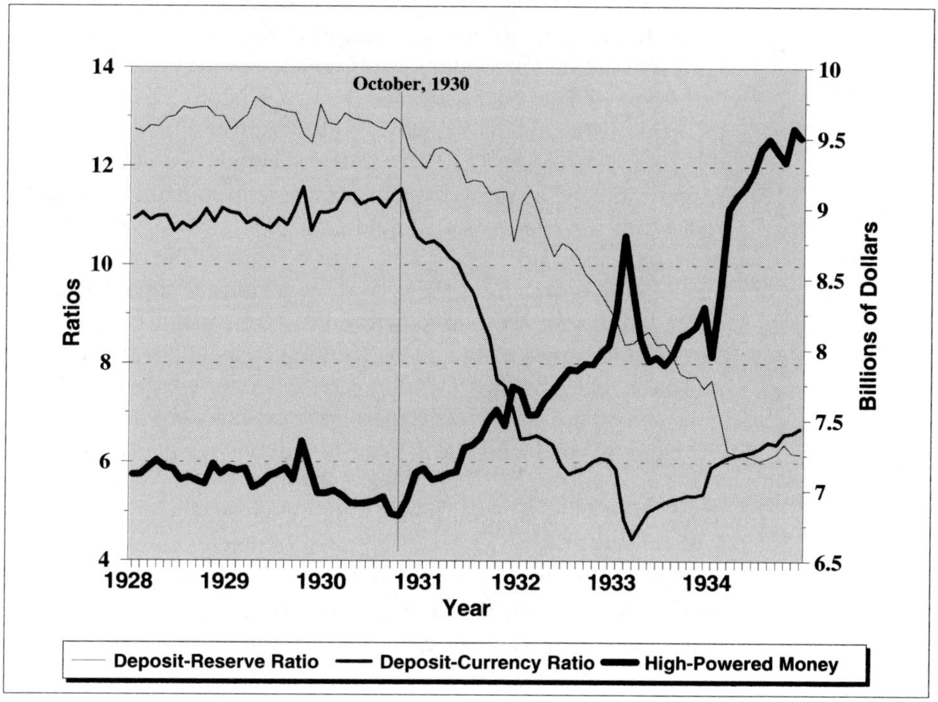

Source: Milton Friedman and Anna J. Schwartz, *A Monetary History of the United States, 1867–1960* (Princeton: Princeton University Press for the National Bureau of Economic Research, 1963).

expansionary monetary policy, then the stock of money need not have fallen with the liquidity scramble by the banks and public. Furthermore, if the money stock had been expanded sufficiently to meet the increased liquidity demands when the initial panics and rash of bank failures began occurring in late November of 1930, then the banks and the public would never have engaged in such a massive liquidity scramble, and the increase in the high-powered money which would have been necessary to stop the stock of money from falling would not have been as large. In this sense then, considering the period from the end of 1930 through the second quarter of 1933 as the Great Depression, the Monetarists contend that this was due to inept monetary policy by the governors of the Federal Reserve System.

Could the Fed Have "Put Out the Fire" in Late 1930?

According to the monetarists the first banking crisis in November and December of 1930 ignited the liquidity scramble and the decline of the money supply and set off the spiraling contraction of economic activity. This was due to the failure of the Fed to stop the banking crises, particularly that of 1930, which reduced the likelihood that they would act to stem later financial crises. Brunner and Meltzer imply that if the Fed had not allowed the money stock to decline during 1930, then the first banking crisis would not have occurred or would have been less severe.[45]

For the Fed to have stemmed the first liquidity crisis, it would have had to provide the banks experiencing the panic with whatever currency was necessary to satisfy the depositors' demands. The Fed had two methods to do this; rediscounting or open market operations. The rules of member bank rediscounting at that time required that banks rediscount short-term, "self-liquidating" commercial paper. Industrial bonds, government securities, stocks, and longer term assets of the member banks were not eligible. Rediscounting was used for very short periods of time, and nonmember banks could not rediscount except indirectly through a correspondent bank that was a member of the Fed. The localized nature of the banking crisis in November of 1930 (as shown later) and these rediscounting restrictions raise doubts as to whether the Fed would have been able to stem the late November banking crisis by providing the additional liquidity for the banks experiencing the deposit-to-currency conversions.

Open market operations were handled by the New York City Federal Reserve Bank. Purchases of securities on the open market did not immediately increase the money stock. More importantly, for open market purchases to have stemmed the first banking crisis, the purchases would have had to have been made with Federal Reserve System currency and directed only to those banks in the southeastern part of the United States where the banking crisis was occurring. It is doubtful if this could have been accomplished.

Recent research also suggests that a more expansionary monetary policy in 1930 prior to the banking crisis would not have prevented the crisis. An examination of the banks in the southeast that failed found that poor loans and investments in the twenties were a principal factor contributing to the banks that closed in the first banking crisis.[46] Another examination of the national banks that failed in 1930 found that most were small and in agricultural areas.[47] An examination of the balance sheets of these national banks found that through 1930 most of the failures could be predicted a year in advance, because failing banks usually had large amounts of poorly performing loans, many from the teens and twenties.[48] The economic contraction in 1929 and 1930 led to sharp declines in the prices of agricultural crops, and farmers and local merchants were often unable to repay their loans.

Elmus Wicker also found that the 120 banking failures the southeast in the last two weeks of November and the renewed failures in December were all linked to the failure of the large Nashville investment banking house, Caldwell and Company, and this "pinpoints the 'contagion of fear' that spread among depositors."[49] Caldwell and Company controlled the largest chain of banks in the south, with assets of over $200 million; the largest insurance group in the region, with assets totaling $230 million; and had controlling interests in other banks, insurance companies, industrial enterprises, investment trusts, and newspapers. From the middle of 1929 on, the Caldwell enterprises were in financial difficulty. In June 1930 they merged with a Kentucky bank-holding chain, Banco Kentucky, which also had financial problems. Apparently each thought the other would be its rescuer.

The failure of Caldwell and Company set off the crisis. In Arkansas, 54 of the suspended banks belonged to the A. B. Banks chain, whose stock was owned by the Caldwell-owned Home Insurance Co. The American Exchange Trust, the key chain bank, had lent the parent company $100,000 in the summer of 1930. When Caldwell and Company failed in November, a run began on the American Exchange Trust, and in four days it lost $4 million of deposits out of $15 million total. The bank closed, and within days the other 54 banks in the chain followed suit.[50] In Kentucky, the 15 or more banks that closed were affiliated with Banco Kentucky. In Tennessee, 10 of the bank failures were tied to Caldwell and Company, and the 15 bank failures around Asheville, North Carolina, had business arrangements with Rogers Caldwell and his Bank of Tennesee.[51] Therefore, it is doubtful that a more expansive monetary policy in 1930 prior to the panic—or quick action by the Fed during the panic—could have stopped the bank failures in the last half of November of 1930.[52]

Friedman and Schwartz also place considerable emphasis on the December, 1930, failure of the Brooklyn-based Bank of the United States.[53] They contend that this failure unduly diminished confidence in the banking system because of the bank's official sounding name and that authorities allowed an essentially sound bank to fail. Temin takes issue with this and in his examination finds evidence that it was not a basically sound bank.[54] White's statistical analysis finds that the failure of the Bank of the United States did not "appear to have been unique or unexpected."[55] And in a 1985 study Joseph L. Lucia has found that at the time of its failure, the Bank of the United States was both insolvent and illiquid.[56]

Wicker's 1980 study casts more doubt on the significance of the failure of the Bank of the United States.[57] If this failure was so destructive of confidence in the banking system, then the immediately following failures should have been in the region around New York City or at least geographically dispersed across the United States. Instead, the failures were concentrated in those areas where the November bank suspensions had occurred, the southeast. Wicker proposes that these failures were secondary effects from the November failure of Caldwell and Company.[58] This suggests that the failure of Brooklyn's Bank of the United States did not significantly accelerate the liquidity scramble.

Criticisms of the Monetarists' Explanation

In 1976 Peter Temin led the way in a major reevaluation of the Monetarists' explanation of the Great Depression. They contend that the turning point was November of 1930; the first banking panic and the failure of the Bank of the United States set off the liquidity scramble by the banks and the public. As the liquidity crisis accelerated, the second flurry of bank suspensions occurred between March and June of 1931. The falling deposit-to-currency and deposit-to-reserve ratios reduced the money supply and, through a stable money demand function, the stock of money. The falling stock of money led to faster price deflation and an accelerated decline in real output and employment.

A reduction in the supply of money relative to the demand for money will initially cause interest rates to rise and the prices of financial and real assets to fall, though given more time for adjustments to occur, interest rates will also fall. Temin wondered what assets the public will attempt to sell to restore money balances after the decline in the supply of money and found an answer in Friedman and Schwartz's work.[59] The effect of the reduction in the supply of money relative to the demand for money balances should be seen first in the interest rates or yields on those assets most like money, and they should rise soonest and farthest.

Figure 7.2 presents some of the interest rates that Temin gathered to examine this. As can be seen, Temin found no evidence of rising interest rates in late 1930 or early 1931, the period directly following the initial banking panic. In 1919–20, 1928–29, the fall of 1931, and the first quarter of 1933 because of Fed monetary policy, the supply of money fell relative to the demand for money balances, and interest rates rose as predicted. Temin concludes that in late 1930 and early 1931, the demand for money balances fell more than the supply of money fell and that this effect led to the decline in the stock of money. The Monetarists' explanation was, therefore, wrong.

Temin's study was quickly answered by a flood of additional studies and criticisms, some supporting and some rejecting his contentions. Thomas Mayer was one of the first to examine Temin's analysis.[60] Though he criticizes a number of Temin's points, he indicates that Temin has pointed out a particularly crucial problem emphasizing the failure of interest rates to rise as predicted. Anna Schwartz criticizes Temin's analysis, suggesting that in 1930 and 1931 the supply of commercial paper was reduced as much or more than the demand for it.[61] This explained the failure of commercial paper prices to fall and rates to rise. In addition, the reduction in the federal debt through December of 1930 increased the supply of loanable funds and reduced market clearing interest rates.

Temin and Peter Lindert both question Schwartz's analysis.[62] Schwartz asserts that commercial paper rates did not rise because banks used commercial paper to borrow currency from the Fed to meet the depositors' currency demands, but Temin notes that the failure of rates to rise meant that "Any deficiencies in money balances were not communicated to the investing and consuming public and therefore could not affect spending plans."[63] Brunner and Meltzer had earlier noted that rates had not risen and suggested that this was due to an inflow of gold.[64] A similar criticism applies because if the gold inflow stopped rates from rising, it must have supplied money to those banks, individuals, and nonfinancial firms who were attempting to build up reserves and restore money balances. Thus, the supply of money did not contract, and the Monetarists' explanation of the cause of the Great Depression, a falling supply of money in late 1930 and early 1931, is contradicted.[65]

It should be noted that few economists and economic historians disagree with the suggestion that the sharply falling stock of money beginning in the late spring of 1931 and the sharply restrictive Federal Reserve System monetary policy initiated in the fall of 1931 explain the contraction from 1931 through mid-1932. The disagreement revolves around the reasons for the onset of the sharply declining stock of money at the end of 1930. If the decline in the money supply relative to the demand for money was so pronounced following the late November and December 1930 banking crises, why did interest rates not rise as they clearly did when the money supply was reduced in 1919–20, 1928–29, the fall of 1931, and the first quarter of 1933? This is the major point of critics who suggest that for the late 1930-early 1931 period the Monetarists have placed too much emphasis on the decline in the supply of money and inadequate emphasis on the decline in the demand for money.

The Monetarist explanation, like the Keynesian and Austrian explanations, is essentially domestic in nature. All three assume that the contraction began in the United States and through international trade and monetary flows spread to other nations. Yet there is a long tradition that the worldwide depression began in a number of countries simultaneously rather than solely in the United States. We now turn to the international explanations of the Great Depression.

DISRUPTIONS IN THE INTERNATIONAL SECTOR

The view that the worldwide depression of the thirties was transmitted through changes in international trade and international lending has a long history, and no one would argue with the idea that this, in fact, did occur. The question is whether the depression began in the United States and was then transmitted to other nations or whether the depression began simultaneously in a number of countries and was then transmitted to the rest of the world through, say, the gold exchange standard, changes in international lending, or in the mechanisms for reparations and loan payments that arose out of the First World War. President Hoover, at the end of his term, blamed international forces and did not believe that the depression began in the United States. H. W. Arndt was one of thc earlier advocates of the idea that international disruptions transmitted the depression around the world.[66] More recently J. R. Hicks and Charles P. Kindleberger have restated this view.[67]

To Kindleberger the international economic system in the twenties was unstable because there was no dominant nation to consciously take responsibility for stabilizing the international economic system. The depression affected so many countries and was so long and severe because Great Britain could not and the United States would not provide stability by "(a) maintaining a relatively open market for distress goods; (b) providing counter-cyclical long-term lending; and, (c) discounting in crisis."[68]

The United States became the world's leading capital exporter in the twenties. Unlike Great Britain in the nineteenth century, U.S. overseas investment was positively related to the level of domestic economic activity. As economic activity expanded in the U.S., our overseas lending increased, stimulating economic activity in the recipient countries, and, through increased American exports, economic activity in the United States. When the American economy declined, as it did in 1929, overseas investment fell, foreign countries' economies began to decline, and American exporting fell. Therefore, according to Kindleberger, this procyclical pattern of American long-term overseas lending spread the economic contraction that began in the United States and European countries in 1929 and accelerated the decline in economic activity.[69]

Neither the United States nor Great Britain took responsibility among leading countries to maintain open markets for "distress goods."[70] In fact, the United States closed markets by passing the Smoot-Hawley tariff, which brought forth retaliation leading into a contractionary spiral of world trade. With an independent world depression in agriculture in the twenties, this accelerated the declines in aggregate demand. Kindleberger maintains that if Great Britain and particularly the United States had led the way in maintaining relatively open markets for distressed goods, especially agricultural products, the decline in world trade would have been smaller and the depression shorter and less severe in all of the affected countries.

Finally, the U.S. and British governments failed to discount during the banking crisis in Europe in 1931.[71] The onset of a run at Austria's Kreditanstalt on May 11, 1931, elicited loans from various central banks. However, Kindleberger argues that delays in putting the loans together and the "niggardliness" of the sums doomed the bank and caused the banking crisis to spread across Europe. Great Britain's withdrawal from lending and the United States' failure to do so ultimately drove Great Britain off the gold standard, causing the collapse of the gold exchange standard, another huge negative shock to international trade. Therefore, according to Kindleberger, at the end of the twenties and the beginning of the thirties, these economic conditions and failures in world economic leadership by Great Britain and the United States combined to bring about the worldwide Great Depression.[72]

Many scholars disagree with Kindleberger's contentions. Heywood Fleisig agrees that the world depression began with a decline in U.S. long-term international lending in 1928 and 1929 that was aggravated by a decline in American imports in 1930 and 1931.[73] However, he argues that both were domestic in origin. The decline in international lending was the result of the booming stock market and the restrictive monetary policies adopted by the Federal Reserve System. Christian Saint-Etienne comes to a similar conclusion.[74] Through its sheer size, the American economy transmitted its business cycles to the world through international markets, and he notes that this had happened in the 1920–21 depression. The cause of the initial downturn in 1929 was tight monetary policy, and the Hawley-Smoot tariff was the main factor in the change from a normal business cycle to an extraordinarily severe one.[75]

The importance of the Smoot-Hawley tariff is one point upon which many Keynesians, Monetarists, and Austrians agree. The imposition of this wedge between international transactions set off a spiraling contraction of world trade and economic activity. However, recently Charles Kindleberger and Barry Eichengreen have objected to this assessment, pointing out that the influence of the tariff has never been carefully assessed.[76] As Figure 7.4 shows, the tariff rates rose more sharply with the 1922 Fordney-McCumber tariff, and the percent of imports that were duty-free dropped as sharply. But there was no depression after this tariff. What made the 1930 Smoot-Hawley tariff seem so much worse after its passage was that dropping prices combined with specific tariff rates to make *ad valorem* rates rise dramatically and contributed to a sharp decline in the value of imports. (See Figure 7.5.) But these declines in prices and quantities may simply reflect the effect of the worldwide depression on international trade rather than the effect of the tariff in causing the worldwide depression.

Fig. 7.4 Import Duties in the United States, 1896–1932

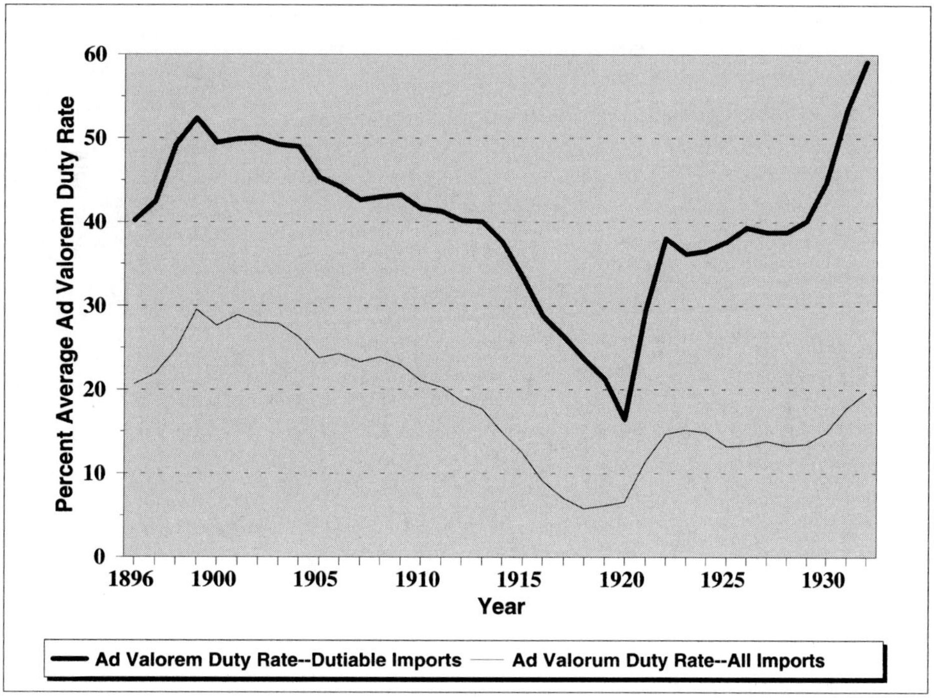

Source: Barry Eichengreen, "The Political Economy of the Smoot-Hawley Tariff," *Research in Economic History* 12 (1989): 1–43.

The tariff increased the domestic demand for domestic production, and this should have expanded production. The reduction in imports should have caused the prices of imports to decline somewhat.[77] Under fixed exchange rates and the gold standard, the reduction in dollars earned by foreign producers will not necessarily cause a quick reduction in American exports because foreign buyers can simply buy American exports with gold rather than the dollars received from American importers.[78] Therefore, the tariff may have expanded aggregate demand in the United States.

As Eichengreen notes, there are two offsets to this. First, the tariff marginally substitutes less efficient domestic production for more efficient foreign production, and this will be contractionary, though Eichengreen doubts that it was quantitatively important. The most important effect is tariff and quota retaliation by foreign nations, a point many economists have stressed. Though there was some explicit retaliation, such as the Wais Tariff of Spain, Eichengreen argues that this has been overstated. Between 1925 and 1929, 26 European countries revised their tariffs 33 times, and Latin American nations revised their tariffs 17 times. He points out that "In 1927 and 1928 Australia, Canada, and New Zealand all instituted broad upward revisions in tariff rates."[79] Italy's increase

Fig. 7.5 United States Imports, 1896–1932

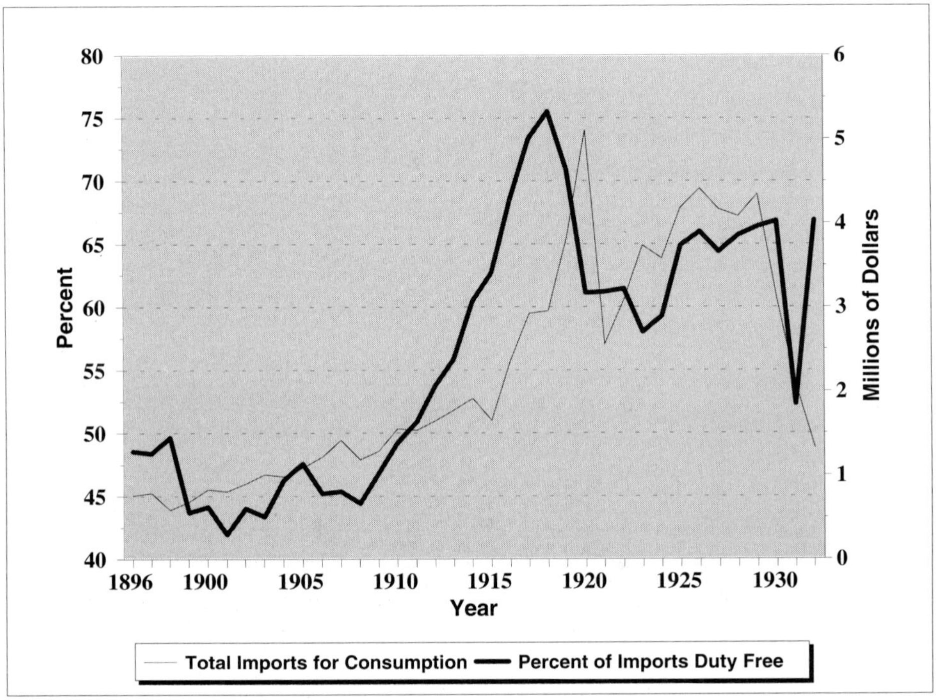

Source: Barry Eichengreen, "The Political Economy of the Smoot-Hawley Tariff," *Research in Economic History* 12 (1989): 1–43.

in tariffs on American automobiles was started several years earlier in order to aid Fiat, whose sales had slid 30 percent in three years. In the case of the Eastern European nations' tariff increases and Britain's 1932 general tariff revision, retaliation is never mentioned as the reason. Eichengreen argues that there is no clear evidence that Smoot-Hawley was a major factor in creating and spreading the worldwide contraction.

There is another process by which the tariffs effect economic activity. Rather than looking at aggregate effects, consider the individual markets. The tariff changes the demands for and supplies of the goods protected and exported, and this requires reallocations of resources and changes in numerous relative prices. For example, consider the automobile industry. The United States exported over 670,000 cars in 1929. With the new protectionist tariffs on American autos in Italy, Eastern Europe, and other countries, automobile exports quickly fell, exacerbating the production declines due to the contraction. Because resources cannot instantaneously and costlessly be reallocated and prices don't instantaneously adjust, this disruption to the price system transitionally reduced economic activity and magnified the contraction already underway. Thus, Smoot-Hawley's effects were not only aggregate ones.

Eichengreen believes the most important effect of Smoot-Hawley was to redistribute "gold from countries with weak reserve positions to a country whose position was strong, thereby undermining the system's resistance to exceptional destabilizing events."[80] And this is part of the contention that the worldwide depression can be traced to the gold standard and the First World War, an old position that has gained new followers in recent years.[81]

The gold standard was suspended, not abandoned, during the First World War. In none of the developed countries was there ever any serious thought given to not returning to the gold standard after the war, but the reconstitution of the gold standard in the twenties was far from easy. The United States had held 26.5 percent of the world's gold stocks in 1913, a figure that rose to 40 percent in 1918 and 44 percent in 1923.[82] By the end of the twenties, France and the United States held 60 percent of the world's gold stocks.[83]

Because there was a flood of paper money issues in all of the belligerent countries, price levels everywhere were much higher after the war than before. Returning to the gold standard imparted a deflationary bias everywhere except in the United States, which had excess gold reserves. The resumption of the gold standard in Britain in 1925, at the prewar price of gold, immediately ran into economic difficulties. Peter Temin observes that "The British economy was plunged into social conflict, symbolized by the General Strike of 1926, over the allocation of the burden of a high pound."[84] The Bank of England had to maintain higher discount rates to keep interest rates higher and attract capital to offset the British trade deficit, and this had adverse effects on production, investment, and unemployment. In December of 1926, France effectively returned to a gold standard and formally did so in June of 1928, but prior to that time the franc had been reduced to one-fifth of its prewar value, causing it to be undervalued. All countries adopted contractionary policies to stay on the gold standard. One means of doing so was to withdraw all gold coins from circulation to be used as bullion for central banks' monetary reserves. Only the United States continued to allow gold coins to circulate. As a result the international market for gold was dominated by central banks.

Germany, worried about stock market speculation and the maintenance of the gold standard, took steps to halt capital inflows in 1926. Between 1919 and 1931 gross capital inflows were over 5 percent of German national income, and net capital inflows were 2 percent of national income. The tax exemption status of foreign holders of German bonds was withdrawn, and the Reichsbank adopted the deflationary policy of reducing discounting by correspondent banks and inducing those banks to reduce their discounting for customers. The German stock market crashed in 1927, and by 1928 the German economy was sliding into a depression.[85]

In the last half of the twenties, to assure the financial community of their commitments to the gold standard, many countries raised their legal gold reserve requirements. This increased the demand for gold and had a deflationary effect across the globe.[86]

In 1927 the Fed lowered interest rates to reverse the gold flow from Britain to the United States and ease British difficulties in maintaining the gold standard. However, most of the gold actually went to France, not Great Britain. As gold left the United States from May 1927 to June 1928, the Fed became worried and changed policies to raise rates and reverse the gold flow. This caused the credit crunch of late 1928 and 1929 and helped bring on the contraction and American stock market crash.

As the contraction in the United States, Great Britain, France, Germany, and other countries worsened, the governments adopted deflationary policies because that was what the rules of the gold standard required. They desired to see prices and wages fall, and they built up gold reserves. Between 1928 and 1932 the gold reserves of 24 central banks increased by $2.4 billion, $2 billion for the Bank of France alone.[87] Governments were hamstrung by their commitment to the gold standard and could take no fiscal or monetary policy actions that were contrary to the deflationary rules implicit in the gold standard. Temin describes the situation this way.

> The Atlantic economy, in other words, was in the grip of deflationary policies at the end of the 1920s. Each national story differs, but they were all reflections of an underlying theme. The gold standard had been revived, but the conditions that had sustained it before the war no longer existed. The pound was overvalued; the franc, undervalued. Both the Americans and the Germans were trying to stamp out "speculation." The result was that government policies everywhere were set to discourage economic activity.[88]

It was the attempt to preserve the gold standard that produced the Great Depression. Great Britain left the gold standard in September of 1931, and its depression ended. France, with its huge reserves of gold, continued on the standard until 1936. The United States effectively began to back off from it with Roosevelt's new policies and, for all practical purposes, left the gold standard as it had been constituted when the dollar was devalued from $20.67 to $35 an ounce of gold in January of 1934 and private U.S. ownership of gold was prohibited.

THE GREAT DEPRESSION: AN ASSESSMENT

We have traveled a long and difficult path through a dense thicket of explanations for Great Depression of 1929–33, a path laden with theory and critical points and distinctions. And we have concluded with an explanation contending that the fundamental force or impulse bringing on the Great Depression was the gold standard and changes wrought by the First World War. Because we concluded with this explanation, does it mean that it is the correct one? Not necessarily. The explanation still leaves considerable room for an important role for other institutional changes and longer term growth dynamics. It is not likely that those economists who contend that the Great Depression was started in the United States and spread to the rest of the world, and there are many, will be convinced. Was the gold standard at fault, or was it the manner in which countries adopted the reconstituted gold standard, the gold exchange standard, that was at fault? In other words, how much was due to the institution of the gold standard, and how much was due to the policies nations chose when adopting the gold standard?

Finally, why is it that we cannot determine the primary reason for the Great Depression? Facts alone tell us nothing without some theory to guide their organization and selection. In the case of the Great Depression, facts alone cannot discriminate among alternative explanations. Theories allow us to select among the overwhelming mountains of available evidence, but not all theories select the same facts, and the explanation for the same fact often differs between theories. Perhaps one day we will have a better theory of aggregate economic activity that will allow us to come up with a comprehensive theory that weighs the importance of these factors in the Great Depression, but that day has yet to arrive.

SELECTED REFERENCES

Arndt, H. W. *Economic Lessons of the Nineteen Thirties*. London: F. W. Cass and Co., 1944.

Barber, Clarence L. "On the Origins of the Great Depression." *Southern Economic Journal* 44 (January 1978): 432–56.

Bernanke, Ben. "Nonmonetary Effects of the Financial Crisis in the Propagation of the Great Depression." *American Economic Review* 73 (June 1983): 257–76.

Bolch, Ben, Rendig Fels, and Marshall McMahon. "Housing Surplus in the 1920s?" *Explorations in Economic History* 8 (Spring 1971): 259–84.

Bolch, Ben, and John Pilgrim. "A Reappraisal of Some Factors Associated with Fluctuations in the United States in the Interwar Period." *Southern Economic Journal* 39 (January 1973): 327–44.

Bordo, Michael. "Austrian Influence on Business Cycle Theory." *Cato Journal* 6 (Fall 1986): 455–59.

Brunner, Karl, and Allen Meltzer. "What Did We Learn From the Monetary Experience of the United States in the Great Depression?" *Canadian Journal of Economics* 1 (May 1968): 334–48.

Eichengreen, Barry. "The Political Economy of the Smoot-Hawley Tariff." *Research in Economic History*. 12 (1989): 1–43.

__________. *Golden Fetters: The Gold Standard and the Great Depression, 1919–1939*. New York: Oxford University Press, 1992.

Fearon, Peter. *War, Prosperity & Depression: The U.S. Economy, 1917–1945*. Lawrence, KS: The University of Kansas Press, 1987.

Field, Alexander J. "Asset Exchanges and the Transactions Demand for Money, 1919–29." *American Economic Review*. 74 (March 1984): 43–59.

__________. "A New Interpretation of the Onset of the Great Depression." *The Journal of Economic History*. 44 (June 1984): 489–98.

Fleisig, Heywood. *Long-Term Capital Flows and the Great Depression: The Role of the United States, 1927–33*. New York: Arno Press, 1975.

__________. "War Related Debts and the Great Depression." *American Economic Review*. 66 (May 1976): 52–8.

Fremling, Gertrud M. "Did the United States Transmit the Great Depression to the Rest of the World?" *American Economic Review*. 75 (December 1985): 1181–85.

Friedman, Milton, and Anna J. Schwartz. *A Monetary History of the United Stats, 1867–1960*. Princeton: Princeton University Press for the National Bureau of Economic Research, 1963.

__________. "Money and Business Cycles." *Review of Economics and Statistics* 45 (February 1963): 32–78.

__________. "The Failure of the Bank of the United States: A Reappraisal: A Reply." *Explorations in Economic History* 23 (April 1986): 199–204.

Gallaway, Lowell and Richard Vedder. "Wages, Prices, and Employment: Von Mises and the Progressives." *The Review of Austrian Economics* 1 (1987): 33–80.

Gandolfi, Arthur E. "Stability of the Demand for Money During the Great Contraction—1929–1933." *Journal of Political Economy* 82 (September/October 1974): 969–84.

Gandolfi, Arthur E. and James R. Lothian. "The Demand for Money From the Great Depression to the Present." *American Economic Review* 66 (May 1976): 46–51.

Garrison, Roger. "Hayekian Trade Cycle Theory: A Reappraisal." *Cato Journal* 6 (Fall 1986): 437–59.

Garrison, Roger. "The Austrian Theory of the Business Cycle in the Light of Modern Macroeconomics." *The Review of Austrian Economics* 3 (1987): 3–30.

George, P. J. and Oksanen, E. H. "Saturation in the Automobile Market in the Late Twenties: Some Further Results." *Explorations in Economic History* 11 (Fall 1973): 73–86.

Glasner, David. *Free Banking and Monetary Reform*. New York: Cambridge University Press, 1989.

Gordon, Robert A. "Business Cycles in the Interwar Period: The Quantitative-Historical Approach." *American Economic Review* 39 (May 1949): 47–63.

__________. "Cyclical Experience in the Interwar Period: The Investment Boom of the Twenties." *Conference on Business Cycles*. New York: National Bureau of Economic Research, 1951.

__________. "Investment Behavior and Business Cycles." *Review of Economics and Statistics* 37 (February 1955): 23–34.

__________. "Population Growth and the Capital Coefficient." *American Economic Review* 46 (June 1956): 307–22.

__________. *Economic Instability and Growth: The American Record*. New York: Harper and Row, 1974.

Haberler, Gottfried. *The World Economy, Money, and the Great Depression, 1919–1939*. Washington: American Enterprise Institute Foreign Affairs Study 30, 1976.

__________. "Reflections on Hayek's Business Cycle Theory." *Cato Journal* 6 (Fall 1986): 421–35.

Hawtrey, Ralph G. *The Art of Central Banking*. London: Longmans Green, 1932.

__________. *The Gold Standard in Theory and Practice*, 5th ed. Longmans Green, 1947.

Hayek, Friedrich A. *Prices and Production*. New York: Augustus M. Kelly reprint of 1931 edition.

__________. *Monetary Theory and the Trade Cycle*. London: Jonathan Cape, 1933.

__________. *Individualism and Economic Order*. Chicago: University of Chicago Press, 1948.

Hickman, Bert G. *Growth and Stability of the Postwar Economy*. Washington: The Brookings Institution, 1960.

__________. "What Became of the Building Cycle?" *Nations and Households in Economic Growth: Essays in Honor of Moses Abramovitz*. Edited by Paul David and Melvin Reder. New York: Academic Press, 1973.

Hicks, John R. "Real and Monetary Forces in Economic Fluctuations." *Scottish Journal of Political Economy* (November 1974): 205–14.

Keynes, John Maynard. *Treatise on Money*, 2 vols. New York: Harcourt Brace, 1930.

__________. *The General Theory of Employment, Interest, and Money*. New York Harcourt Brace, 1936.

Kindleberger, Charles P. *The World in Depression, 1929–1939*. Berkeley: The University of California Press, 1973.

__________. *Manias, Panics, and Crashes: A History of Financial Crises*. New York: Basic Books, 1978.

__________. "The International Causes and Consequences of the Great Crash." *The Journal of Portfolio Management* 6 (Fall 1979): 11–14.

__________. *A Financial History of Western Europe*. London: George Allen and Unwin, 1984.

King, Wilford I. *The Causes of Economic Fluctuations*. New York: 1938.

Leijonhufuvud, Axel. "Real and Monetary Factors in Business Fluctuations." *Cato Journal* 6 (Fall 1986): 409–20.

Lucia, Joseph L. "The Failure of the Bank of the United States: A Reappraisal." *Explorations in Economic History* 22 (October 1985): 402–16.

Mayer, Thomas. "Consumption in the Great Depression." *Journal of Political Economy* 86 (February 1978): 139–46.

__________. "Money and the Great Depression: A Critique of Professor Temin's Thesis." *Explorations in Economic History* 15 (April 1978): 127–45.

McCulloch, J. Huston. "Misintermediation and Macroeconomic Fluctuations." *Journal of Monetary Economics* 8 (July 1981): 103–15.

Meltzer, Allen. "Money and Other Explanations of the Start of the Great Depression." *Journal of Monetary Economics* 2 (October 1976): 455–71.

Mercer, Lloyd J., and W. Douglas Morgan. "The American Automobile Industry, Investment Demand, Capacity, and Capacity Utilization, 1921–1940." *Journal of Political Economy* 80 (November/December 1972): 1214–31.

__________. "Alternative Interpretations of Market Saturation: Evaluation for the Automobile Market in the Late Twenties." *Explorations in Economic History* 9 (Spring 1972): 269–90.

__________. "Internal Funds and Automobile Industry Investment: An Evaluation of the Seltzer Hypothesis." *The Journal of Economic History* 32 (September 1972): 683–90.

__________. "Housing Surplus in the 1920's? Another Evaluation." *Explorations in Economic History* 10 (Spring 1973): 295–304.

Mises, Ludwig von. *The Theory of Money and Credit*. Indianapolis: Liberty Press, 1980; reprint of 1912 edition.

__________. *Human Action*, 3rd revised edition. Chicago: Henry Regnery and Co., 1953.

Mishkin, Frederic S. "The Household Balance Sheet and the Great Depression." *The Journal of Economic History* 38 (December 1978): 918–37.

Muth, Richard F. "The Demand for Non-Farm Housing." *The Demand for Durable Goods*. Edited by A. C. Harberger. Chicago: University of Chicago Press, 1960.

Nourse, Edwin et al. *America's Capacity to Produce*. Washington: The Brookings Institute, 1934.

O'Driscoll, Gerald P., Jr. *Economics as a Coordination Problem: The Contributions of Friedrich A. Hayek*. Kansas City: Sheed, Andrews, and McMeel, 1977.

Palyi, Melchoir. *The Twilight of Gold*. Chicago: Henry Regnery, 1972.

Reekie, W. Duncan. *Markets, Entrepreneurs and Liberty: An Austrian View of Capitalism*. New York: St. Martin's Press, 1984.

Robbins, Lionel. *The Great Depression*. New York: Macmillan, 1934.

__________. *Autobiography of an Economist*. London: Macmillan, 1971.

Rothbard, Murray N. *America's Great Depression*. Kansas City: Sheed and Ward, 1963.

__________. *Man, Economy and State: A Treatise on Economic Principles*. 2 vols. Los Angeles: Nash Publishing, 1970; reprint of 1962 edition.

__________. "Economic Depressions: Their Cause and Cure." *The Austrian Theory of the Trade Cycle and Other Essays* Edited by Richard M. Ebeling. Occasional Papers Series 8. New York: The Center for Libertarian Studies, 1978.

__________. "The Federal Reserve as a Cartelization Device: The Early Years, 1913–1930." *Money in Crisis: The Federal Reserve, the Economy, and Monetary Reform.* Edited by Barry N. Siegel. Cambridge, MA: Ballinger for the Pacific Institute for Public Policy Research, 1984.

Saint-Etienne, Christian. *The Great Depression, 1929–1938: Lessons for the 1980s.* Stanford, CA: Hoover Institution Press, 1984.

Schumpeter, Joseph A. *Business Cycles.* 2 vols. New York: McGraw-Hill, 1939.

Schwartz, Anna J. "Understanding 1929–1933." *The Great Depression Revisisted.* Edited by Karl Brunner. Boston: Martinus Nijhoff Publishing, 1981.

Skousen, Mark. "Saving the Depression: A New Look at World War II." *The Review of Austrian Economics.* 2 (1988): 211–28.

Skousen, Mark. "Why the U.S. Economy is Not Depression-Proof." *The Review of Austrian Economics* 3 (1989): 75–94.

Smiley, Gene. "Some Austrian Perspectives on Keynesian Fiscal Policy and the Recovery in the Thirties." *The Review of Austrian Economics* 1 (1987): 145–80.

Smiley, Gene. "Can Keynesianism Explain the 1930s? Reply to Cowen." *Critical Review* 5 (Winter 1991): 81–114.

Soule, George. *Prosperity Decade: From War to Depression, 1917–1929.* New York: Rinehart and Co., 1947.

Swanson, Joseph, and Samuel Williamson. "Estimates of National Product and Income for the United States Economy, 1919–1941." *Explorations in Economic History* 10 (Fall 1972): 53–74.

Temin, Peter. *Did Monetary Forces Cause the Great Depression?* New York: W. W. Norton, 1976.

__________. "Notes on the Causes of the Great Depression." *The Great Depression Revisited.* Edited by Karl Brunner. Boston: Martinus Nijhoff Publishing, 1981.

__________. *Lessons from the Great Depression.* Cambridge: The M.I.T. Press, 1989.

__________, and Barrie A. Wigmore. "The End of One Big Deflation." *Explorations in Economic History* 27 (October 1990): 483–502.

Tullock, Gordon. "Why the Austrians are Wrong About Depressions." *The Review of Austrian Economics* 2 (1988): 73–78.

Viner, Jacob. *Balanced Deflation, Inflation, or More Depression.* Minneapolis: University of Minnesota Press, 1933.

Wainhouse, Charles E. "Empirical Evidence for Hayek's Theory of Economic Fluctuations." *Money in Crisis: The Federal Reserve, the Economy, and Monetary Reform.* Edited by Barry N. Siegel. Cambridge, MA: Ballinger for the Pacific Institute for Public Policy Research, 1984.

White, Eugene Nelson. "A Reinterpretation of the Banking Crisis of 1930." *The Journal of Economic History* 44 (March 1984): 119–38.

Wicker, Elmus. "A Reconsideration of the Causes of the Banking Panic of 1930." *The Journal of Economic History* 40 (September 1980): 571–83.

__________. "Interest Rate and Expenditure Effects of the Banking Panic of 1930." *Explorations in Economic History* 19 (October 1982): 435–45.

Yeager, Leland. "The Significance of Monetary Disequilibrium." *Cato Journal* 6 (Fall 1986): 369–400.

NOTES

1. The extent of this disagreement can be easily seen in the papers by Paul A. Samuelson, Charles P. Kindleberger, and Milton and Rose D. Friedman in *The Journal of Portfolio Management* 6 (Fall 1979): 7–21.
2. There is no agreed upon standard to distinguish between a depression and a recession. Prior to the Second World War, economic contractions were generally called depressions. Perhaps to distinguish postwar contractions from these earlier ones, they were called recessions rather than depressions, and depression was reserved for a much more serious downturn. By the standards of contractions in the interwar period, the recession of 1981–1982 would have been called a depression.
3. This is indicated by the existence of frictional unemployment.
4. This discussion draws upon the writings of Friedrich A. Hayek. In particular, see the essays in *Individualism and Economic Order* (Chicago: University of Chicago Press, 1948). A more recent presentation of this can be found in Gerald P. O'Driscoll, Jr., *Economics as a Coordination Problem: The Contributions of Friedrich A. Hayek* (Kansas City: Sheed, Andrews, and McMeel, Inc., 1977).
5. These, of course, do not exhaust the explanations of the Great Depression, but they are the ones that have for a long time been given reasonable consideration. Many early explanations are no longer fashionable. For example, "underconsumption" explanations argued that the growing inequality in the distribution of income during the 1920s meant that consumers had less and less income to buy the increasing amount of goods and services produced, and these decreasing sales brought on a decline in production and investment. The Roosevelt administration attempted to deal with this by changes in the tax laws aimed at redistributing income from those with more to those with less. Another explanation fashionable in the mid-1930s argued that increasing monopoly power allowed firms to "administer" prices. These administered prices did not fall when there were demand decreases; rather, employment declines occurred, leading to falling incomes and further decreasing demand. The Roosevelt administration first attempted to deal with this by cartelizing, under government supervision, American firms and stores with the National Industrial Recovery Act. When this failed it moved toward a much more active antitrust policy to break up big businesses and reestablish competition and price flexibility. Both of these explanations have long since been discarded.
6. The Austrian school of economics is named after the area where the theoretical approach was developed. It began with Carl Menger (one of three discoverers of diminishing marginal utility) in the 1870s, and the theory was developed through suceeding students and disciples. Through the 1930s the proponents of Austrian analysis were primarily (but not solely) located in and around Austria.
7. The Austrian theory began when Ludwig von Mises combined elements of Knut Wicksel's work on the relationship between money and interest and Bohm-Bawerk's capital theory. [Ludwig von Mises, *The Theory of Money and Credit*, (Indianapolis: Liberty Press, 1980; reprint of 1912 edition), and *Human Action*, 3d revised ed. (Chicago: Henry Regnery and Co., 1953).] The first formal statement of the ideas and the first extensions of von Mises ideas were presented by Friedrich A. Hayek. [Friedrich A. Hayek, *Prices and Production* (New York: Augustus M. Kelly 1967; reprint of 1931 edition), and *Monetary Theory and the Trade Cycle* (London: Jonathan Cape, 1933).] The principle applications of the theory to the Great Depression can be found in studies by Lionel Robbins and Murray Rothbard. [Lionel Robbins, *The Great Depression* (New York: The Macmillan Co., 1934).] However,

it should be noted that by 1971 Robbins had come to believe that his opposition in this book to deficit spending as an anti-deflation device was wrong. [Lionel Robbins, *Autobiography of an Economist* (London: Macmillan, 1971).] Murray Rothbard's studies are more recent statements of the Austrian explanation. [Murray N. Rothbard, *America's Great Depression* (Kansas City: Sheed and Ward, 1963), *Man, Economy and State: A Treatise on Economic Principles*. 2 (Los Angeles: Nash Publishing, 1970; reprint of 1962 edition), "Economic Depressions: Their Cause and Cure," in Richard M. Ebeling, ed., *The Austrian Theory of the Trade Cycle and Other Essays*, Occasional Papers Series 8 (New York: The Center for Libertarian Studies, 1978), "The Federal Reserve as a Cartelization Device: The Early Years, 1913–1930," in Barry N. Siegel, ed., *Money in Crisis: The Federal Reserve, the Economy, and Monetary Reform* (Cambridge, MA: Ballinger for the Pacific Institute for Public Policy Research, 1984).] Recent expositions of the Austrian theory of the business cycle can be found in W. Duncan Reekie, *Markets, Entrepreneurs and Liberty: An Austrian View of Capitalism* (New York: St. Martin's Press, 1984); and O'Driscoll, *Economics as a Coordination Problem*. More recent extensions or additions to the Austrian explanation of the Great Depression can be found in the following studies: Roger Garrison, "Hayekian Trade Cycle Theory: A Reappraisal," *Cato Journal* 6 (Fall 1986): 437–59, and "The Austrian Theory of the Business Cycle in the Light of Modern Macroeconomics," *The Review of Austrian Economics* 3 (1987): 3–30; Charles E. Wainhouse, "Empirical Evidence for Hayek's Theory of Economic Fluctuations," in Barry N. Siegel, ed., *Money in Crisis: The Federal Reserve, the Economy, and Monetary Reform* (Cambridge, MA: Ballinger for the Pacific Institute for Public Policy Research, 1984); J. Huston McCulloch, "Misintermediation and Macroeconomic Fluctuations," *Journal of Monetary Economics* 8 (July 1981): 103–15; Lowell Gallaway and Richard K. Vedder, "Wages, Prices, and Employment: Von Mises and the Progressives," *The Review of Austrian Economics* 1 (1987): 33–80; Gene Smiley, "Some Austrian Perspectives on Keynesian Fiscal Policy and the Recovery in the Thirties," *The Review of Austrian Economics* 1 (1987): 145–80, and "Can Keynesianism Explain the 1930s? Reply to Cowen," *Critical Review* 5 (Winter 1991): 81–114.; Mark Skousen, "Saving the Depression: A New Look at World War II," *The Review of Austrian Economics* 2 (1988): 211–28, and "Why the U.S. Economy is Not Depression-Proof," *The Review of Austrian Economics* 3 (1989): 75–94.

8. Austrians term this an inflationary increase, however, they define inflation as an increase in the fiat money not backed by commodity money (gold or silver). The common meaning of inflation is a falling value of money relative to commodities or services, or, usually the same thing, a rising money price of commodities and services.
9. Rothbard, *The Great Depression*, 43–53 and 187–90.
10. Gallaway and Vedder, "Wage, Prices, and Employment," 45–52.
11. Christian Saint-Etienne, *The Great Depression, 1929–1938: Lessons for the 1980s* (Stanford, CA: Hoover Institution Press, 1984), 28.
12. These criticisms involve both the specific theoretical model the Austrians have developed as well as its application to the Great Depression. See the following papers: Gottfried Haberler, *The World Economy, Money, and the Great Depression, 1919–1939* (Washington: American Enterprise Institute Foreign Affairs Study 30, 1976), and, "Reflections on Hayek's Business Cycle Theory," *Cato Journal* 6 (Fall 1986): 421–35; Michael D. Bordo, "Austrian Influence on Business Cycle Theory," *Cato Journal* 6 (Fall 1986): 455–59; Axel Leijonhufuvud, "Real and Monetary Factors in Business Fluctuations," *Cato Journal* 6 (Fall 1986): 409–20; Leland B. Yeager, "The Significance of Monetary Disequilibrium," *Cato Journal* 6 (Fall 1986): 369–400; Gordon Tullock, "Why

the Austrians are Wrong About Depressions," *The Review of Austrian Economics* 2 (1988): 73–78. The primary responses to these criticisms can be found in Roger Garrison, "Hayekian Trade Cycle Theory: A Reappraisal," and "The Austrian Theory of Business Cycles in the Light of Modern Macroeconomics."

13. Charles P. Kindleberger, *The World in Depression* (Berkeley: The University of California Press, 1973), 32–3.
14. Peter Temin, *Did Monetary Forces Cause the Great Depression?* (New York: W. W. Norton, 1976), 138–41.
15. Robbins, *The Great Depression*; Jacob Viner, *Balanced Deflation, Inflation, or More Depression*. (Minneapolis: University of Minnesota Press, 1933); Wilford I. King, *The Causes of Economic Fluctuations* (New York, 1938); Gallaway and Vedder, "Wages, Prices, and Employment"; Gene Smiley, "Can Keynesianism Explain the 1930s?"
16. The interaction of the spending multiplier, from the consumption function, and the investment accelerator, from the investment function, leads to cyclical expansion and contractions of economic activity. It is generally called the *multipler-acclerator mechanism.*
17. The following studies have argued strongly for the importance of declining investment, particularly declining housing investment, in the automobile industry: Robert A. Gordon, "Business cycles in the Interwar Period: The Quantitative-Historical Approach," *American Economic Review* 39 (May 1949): 47–63, "Cyclical Experience in the Interwar Period: The Investment Boom of the Twenties," in *Conference on Business Cycles* (New York: National Bureau of Economic Research, 1951), "Investment Behavior and Business Cycles," *Review of Economics and Statistics* 37 (February 1955): 23–34, "Population Growth and the Capital Coefficient," *American Economic Review* 46 (June 1956): 307–22, and *Economic Instability and Growth: The American Record* (New York: Harper and Row, 1974); Joseph Schumpeter, *Business Cycles*, 2 vols. (New York: McGraw-Hill Book Co., 1939); George Soule, *Prosperity Decade: From War to Depression, 1917–1929*, (New York: Rinehart and Co., 1947), chapter 13.
18. Edwin Nourse et al., *America's Capacity to Produce* (Washington: The Brookings Institute, 1934).
19. Lloyd J. Mercer and Douglas W. Morgan, "The American Automobile Industry, Investment Demand, Capacity, and Capacity Utilization, 1921–1940," *Journal of Political Economy* 80 (November/December 1972): 1214–31, "Alternative Interpretations of Market Saturation: Evaluation for the Automobile Market in the Late Twenties," *Explorations in Economic History* 9 (Spring 1972): 269–90, and "Internal Funds and Automobile Industry Investment: An Evaluation of the Seltzer Hypothesis," *The Journal of Economic History* 32 (September 1972): 683–90.
20. To do this, they formulated and estimated an investment demand function based upon a partial adjustment of the actual stock of capital toward the desired stock of capital. From this they could then estimate, given the capital, the capacity output.
21. They formulated a definition of *market saturation* and they chose to examine the desired and actual stock of automobiles. *State saturation* exists when the desired stock of automobiles in a year is less than or equal to the stock in the previous year. *Dynamic saturation* exists when the rate of growth of the desired stock of automobiles this year is less than or equal to the rate of growth of the actual stock of automobiles in the previous year. Mercer and Morgan believe that the desired versus actual stock of automobiles was the preferred way to measure saturation. The desired stock of automobiles was considered to be a function of the relative price of automobiles, real disposable income, and a time trend to capture other effects not explicitly included such as the growing availability of credit (installment

financing), growing stock of household wealth, improved roads and service facilities, and so forth. Mercer and Morgan, "Alternative Interpretations of Market Saturation."

22. P. J. George and E. H. Oksanen, "Saturation in the Automobile Market in the Late Twenties: Some Further Results," *Explorations in Economic History* 11 (Fall 1973): 73–86. They argued that the appropriate income variable in "stock adjustment models" is not current real income but the expected real income, because durable goods yield their services over a period of time. Second, George and Oksanen suggested that Mercer and Morgan should have examined the possibility of a structural break around 1929.
23. Bert G. Hickman, *Growth and Stability of the Postwar Economy* (Washington: The Brookings Institution, 1960); Richard F. Muth, "The Demand for Non-Farm Housing," in A. C. Harberger, ed., *The Demand for Durable Goods* (Chicago: University of Chicago Press, 1960).
24. Ben Bolch, Rendig Fels, and Marshall McMahon, "Housing Surplus in the 1920's?" *Explorations in Economic History* 8 (Spring 1971): 259–84. Ben Bolch and John Pilgrim, "A Reappraisal of Some Factors Associated with Fluctuations in the United States in the Interwar Period," *Southern Economic Journal* 39 (January 1973): 327–44.
25. The real average investment per unit was assumed to depend upon rents relative to construction costs, permanent real income per family, and the interest rate. Housing starts were assumed to be determined by the relative shortage or abundance of housing as indicated by the ratio of total nonfarm families to total available housing units and by real construction costs.
26. For overbuilding in terms of too many housing units they let the ratio of nonfarm families to housing units available take its mean value for the 1920s and allowed the real price of housing to vary as it actually had.
27. Clarence L. Barber, "On the Origins of the Great Depression," *Southern Economic Journal* 44 (January 1978): 432–56.
28. Lloyd J. Mercer and W. Douglas Morgan, "Housing Surplus in the 1920's? Another Evaluation," *Explorations in Economic History* 10 (Spring 1973): 295–304. Housing starts were a function of the ratio of nonfarm families to available housing and the real cost of new housing. When they held the ratio of nonfarm families to available housing constant in their simulation, the variation in housing starts could only arise from variation in the real cost of housing. Because this did not vary to any large extent, their simulation produced largely constant gross expenditures on housing during the twenties.
29. Temin, *Did Monetary Forces Cause the Great Depression?*, 45–7.
30. Bert G. Hickman, "What Became of the Building Cycle?" in Paul David and Melvin Reder, eds., *Nations and Households in Economic Growth: Essays in Honor of Moses Abramovitz* (New York: Academic Press, 1973).
31. Barber, "On the Origins of the Great Depression," 443.
32. Temin, *Did Monetary Forces Cause the Great Depression?*, 69–83.
33. Frederic S. Mishkin, "The Household Balance Sheet and the Great Depression," *The Journal of Economic History* 38 (December 1978): 918–37.
34. Thomas Mayer, "Consumption in the Great Depression," *Journal of Political Economy* 86 (February 1978): 139–46.
35. Temin, *Did Monetary Forces Cause the Great Depression?* 62–8.
36. These comparisons can only be suggestive because they are not accurate measures of the changes. The 1920–21 contraction began quite early in 1920 and sharply led to the trough in the first quarter of 1921, after which a relatively strong expansion began. The average values for all of 1920 understate the peak values reached, and the average values for all of

1921 overstate the values at the trough of the contraction. In 1929 there was an unusually strong expansion of real economic activity in the first half of the year. The contraction in the last half of 1929 does not seem to be as severe as the contraction after the peak in 1920. The contraction continued all through 1930, whereas the earlier contraction troughed early in 1921. Because there are more months of strong expansion in 1929 than 1920, the average values for 1929 will be relatively larger. And because the contraction continued all through 1930 whereas the 1920–21 contraction troughed early in 1921, the 1930 values will be relatively smaller than the 1921 values. Similar problems exist for the comparisons to the 1937–38 percentage changes. For these reasons Temin also examined percentage changes from 1919–1921, 1928–1930, and 1936–38. These temper, but certainly do not eliminate, the data problems.

37. Joseph A. Swanson and Samuel Williamson, "Estimates of National Product and Income for the United States Economy, 1919–1941," *Explorations in Economic History* 10 (Fall 1972): 53–74.

38. This should not be too surprising. The rapid inflation of 1918–19 induced firms to speculate and build up large inventories of raw materials and intermediate and finished products to gain from the rising prices. The Federal Reserve System's rapid turn to a very restrictive monetary policy at the end of 1919 and beginning of 1920 set off the contraction and a rapid price deflation causing firms to undertake a massive liquidation of those accumulated inventories. In 1935–37 the pace of economic recovery quickened after the Supreme Court ruled the NIRA unconstitutional. Wholesale prices, which had fallen 9.2 percent per year from 1929 to 1933, rose 9.7 percent per year from 1933 to 1935, largely because of the NIRA. They rose 1 percent from 1935 to 1936 and 6.6 percent from 1936 to 1937. Firms were rebuilding inventories dramatically depleted by the depression, and the rising prices probably led to more inventory accumulation than otherwise would have occurred. When the Fed doubled member bank reserve requirements between August of 1936 and May of 1937, this initiated the 1937–38 contraction. Wholesale prices fell 9.3 percent from 1937 to 1938. The contraction and change from rising to falling prices led to sharp inventory liquidations. Wholesale prices were falling in the late twenties, and with falling prices firms generally had an incentive to minimize inventory investment. When the contraction began in the middle of 1929, firms did not have excessive inventories to be liquidated. Consequently, less of the declining investment in 1929–30 was in inventories as compared to the 1920–21 and 1937–38 contractions.

39. Ben Bernanke, "Nonmonetary Effects of the Financial Crisis in the Propagation of the Great Depression," *American Economic Review* 73 (June 1983): 257–76.

40. Temin, *Did Monetary Forces Cause the Great Depression?*, 1, 123, 137, and 170; Anna J. Schwartz, "Understanding 1929–1933," in Karl Brunner, ed., *The Great Depression Revisited* (Boston: Martinus Nijhoff Publishing, 1981), 25–6. Temin suggested that John Maynard Keynes believed that the Fed's action could effect the entire economy. [Temin, *Did Monetary Forces Cause the Great Depression?* 123. See John Maynard Keynes, *Treatise on Money*, 2 vols. (New York: Harcourt Brace, 1930). 2: 196.]

41. Alexander J. Field, "Asset Exchanges and the Transactions Demand for Money, 1919–29," *American Economic Review* 74 (March 1984): 43–59.

42. Alexander J. Field, "A New Interpretation of the Onset of the Great Depression," *The Journal of Economic History* 44 (June 1984): 489–98.

43. Friedman and Schwartz, *A Monetary History of the United States*.

44. Arthur E. Gandolfi, "Stability of the Demand for Money During the Great Contraction—1929–1933," *Journal of Political Economy* 82 (September/October 1974): 969–84; Arthur

E. Gandolfi and James R. Lothian, "The Demand for Money From the Great Depression to the Present," *American Economic Review* 66 (May 1976): 46–51.
45. Karl Brunner and Allen Meltzer, "What Did We Learn From the Monetary Experience of the United States in the Great Depression?" *Canadian Journal of Economics* 1 (May 1968): 334–48; and Allen H. Meltzer, "Money and Other Explanations of the Start of the Great Depression," *Journal of Monetary Economics* 2 (October 1976): 455–71.
46. Elmus Wicker, "A Reconsideration of the Causes of the Banking Panic of 1930," *The Journal of Economic History* 40 (September 1980): 571–83.
47. Eugene Nelson White, "A Reinterpretation of the Banking Crisis of 1930," *The Journal of Economic History* 44 (March 1984): 119–38.
48. White was limited to an examination of national banks that were members of the Federal Reserve System, whereas the majority of the small rural banks which failed were state banks. However, he argued that the small rural national banks that failed were good indicators of the problems besetting the state banks.
49. Wicker, "Causes of the Banking Panic of 1930," 572.
50. The key city bank in chain banking held much of the reserves for the smaller banks in the chain.
51. Wicker, "Causes of the Banking Panic of 1930," 573–74.
52. Ibid., 577, 579–80.
53. Friedman and Schwartz, *A Monetary History of the United States*, chapter 7.
54. Temin, *Did Monetary Forces Cause the Great Depression?* 90–5.
55. White, "A Reinterpretation of the Banking Crisis of 1930," 135.
56. Joseph L. Lucia, "The Failure of the Bank of the United States: A Reappraisal," *Explorations in Economic History* 22 (October 1985): 402–16. But also see the sharp reply to other assertions of Lucia in Milton Friedman and Anna J. Schwartz, "The Failure of the Bank of the United States: A Reappraisal. A Reply," *Explorations in Economic History* 23 (April 1986): 199–204.
57. Wicker, "A Reconsideration of the Causes of the Banking Panic of 1930," 580–83.
58. Ibid., 582. There were a number of closings in Mississippi and North Carolina. Forty percent of the Mississippi closings were within a 30–mile radius in the northeast corner of the state. The bulk of the North Carolina closings were again concentrated in western North Carolina, where the November failures were. The 12 banks in Arkansas that suspended did so "when the public learned that a director of the closed American Exchange Bank of Little Rock had an interest in eleven of the banks!"
59. Temin, *Did Monetary Forces Cause the Great Depression?* 97–8. See also Milton Friedman and Anna J. Schwartz, "Money and Business Cycles," *Review of Economics and Statistics* 45 (February 1963): 32–78. This scenario, which Temin called the "pebble in the pond" theory, indicates that those individuals who experience reduced money balances will sell financial assets— securities—which are closest to money in liquidity. As the prices of those assets fall, asset holders will begin turning to less liquid financial assets and, as these prices begin falling, to other financial assets, then nonfinancial assets, and finally begin reducing the purchases of current services.
60. Thomas Mayer, "Money and the Great Depression: A Critique of Professor Temin's Thesis," *Explorations in Economic History* 15 (April 1978): 127–45.
61. Anna J. Schwartz, "Understanding 1929–1933."
62. Peter Temin, "Notes on the Causes of the Great Depression," in Karl Brunner, ed., *The Great Depression Revisited*; Peter Lindert, "Comments on 'Understanding 1929–1933'," in Karl Brunner, ed., *The Great Depression Revisited.*

63. Temin, "Notes on the Causes of the Great Depression," 121.
64. Brunner and Meltzer, "What Did We Learn From the Monetary Experience of the Great Depression?"
65. Elmus Wicker in a study extending his previous one of 1980, found that in the southeast, where the late November and December 1930 banking crisis occurred, the evidence does not suggest that this initiated a sharp change in depositor and banker behavior that would have led into a decline in the supply of money. Elmus Wicker, "Interest Rate and Expenditure Effects of the Banking Panic of 1930," *Explorations in Economic History* 19 (October 1982): 435–45.
66. H. W. Arndt, *Economic Lessons of the Nineteen Thirties* (London: F. W. Cass and Co., 1944).
67. John R. Hicks, "Real and Monetary Forces in Economic Fluctuations," *Scottish Journal of Political Economy* (November 1974): 205–14; Charles P. Kindleberger, *The World in Depression, 1929–1933* (Berkeley: University of California Press, 1973). See also Charles P. Kindleberger, *Manias, Panics, and Crashes: A History of Financial Crises* (New York: Basic Books, Inc., 1978); and Charles P. Kindleberger, "The International Causes and Consequences of the Great Crash," *The Journal of Portfolio Management* 6 (Fall 1979): 11–14. Heywood Fleisig emphasized the role of capital flows in spreading the depression across the developed world. See Heywood Fleisig, *Long-Term Capital Flows and the Great Depression: The Role of the United States, 1927–33* (New York: Arno Press, 1975); and Heywood Fleisig, "War Related Debts and the Great Depression," *American Economic Review* 66 (May 1976): 52–8.
68. Kindleberger, *The World in Depression, 1929–1939*, 291–92.
69. Ibid., 292–93.
70. Ibid., 292–94.
71. Ibid., 148–52.
72. Ibid., chapter 14.
73. Fleisig, "War Related Debts and the Great Depression," 55–56.
74. Christian Saint-Etienne, *The Great Depression, 1929–1938: Lessons for the 1980s* (Stanford, CA: Hoover Institution Press, 1984).
75. Ibid., 18–20, 48, and 55.
76. Charles P. Kindleberger, *A Financial History of Western Europe* (London: George Allen and Unwin, 1984). [See especially the discussion on pp. 366–367.] Barry Eichengreen, "The Political Economy of the Smoot-Hawley Tariff," *Research in Economic History* 12 (1989): 1–43. The following discussion draws primarily on Eichengreen.
77. In other words, the United States was too large in international trade for the small country assumption. A decrease in the American demand for imports would significantly effect the foreign producers' demand curves and cause prices to fall because of the demand reduction.
78. If the terms of the gold standard were adhered to, as these countries lost gold to the United States to purchase American exports the money stock would have fallen, causing prices to fall, reducing the demand for American exports. But this does not happen quickly. So temporarily, *without retaliation*, the demand for American exports should have been little affected.
79. Eichengreen, "The Political Economy of the Smoot-Hawley Tariff," 32.
80. Ibid., 30.
81. David Glasner attributes the first development of this explanation to Ralph Hawtrey in 1932 and says that the Swedish economist Gustav Cassell had developed a similar explanation by 1936 (but Glasner provides no citation to a work by Cassell expounding this). See the fol-

lowing studies: Ralph Hawtrey, *The Art of Central Banking* (London: Longmans Green, 1932), and *The Gold Standard in Theory and Practice*, 5th ed. (London: Longmans Green, 1947); Barry Eichengreen, *Golden Fetters: The Gold Standard and the Great Depression* (New York: Oxford University Press, 1992); Gertrude M. Fremling, "Did the United States Transmit the Great Depression to the Rest of the World?" *American Economic Review* 75 (December 1985): 1181–85; David Glasner, *Free Banking and Monetary Reform* (New York: Cambridge University Press, 1989), chapter 6; Peter Temin, *Lessons from the Great Depression* (Cambridge: The M.I.T. Press, 1989). The following discussion draws primarily on Glasner's and Temin's studies.

82. Glasner, *Free Banking*, 113.
83. Temin *Lessons*, 22–23.
84. Ibid., 19.
85. Ibid., 23–25.
86. Glasner, *Free Banking*, 115.
87. Ibid., 127.
88. Temin, *Lessons*, 25.

CHAPTER 8

The American Economy During the 1940s

Throughout the interwar period the United States had been staunchly isolationist in foreign policy.[1] With Hitler's invasion of Poland in September of 1939, this sentiment began to change. The United States began to expand its military production and by late 1941 the United States was clearly preparing for war. In May of 1940, the National Defense Advisory Council was established to advise the government on its military preparedness. In September of 1940, Congress passed the Selective Service Act, establishing the first peacetime draft in the history of the United States, and the military was actively drafting men by 1941. In an economy with idle resources, it was easy to expand military and civilian production and still increase the size of the armed forces.

THE SECOND WORLD WAR

With the Japanese attack on Pearl Harbor on December 7, 1941, the United States shifted into a full-fledged war economy, and factories were quickly transformed to build military equipment. To facilitate this transformation, controls were imposed on the allocation of resources and the types of products produced. The reduction in the production of civilian products was soon accompanied by price controls and rationing.

Real incomes rose, and unemployment virtually disappeared. (See Figure 8.1.) Prices rose little but this does not mean that there was little inflation because inflation is a fall in the value of money, and with price controls inflation is registered by people's inability to purchase goods even though they have the money to do so. Price indexes are of doubtful relevance in the presence of price controls and rationing. (See Figure 8.2.)

On July 16, 1942, the War Labor Board handed down its "Little Steel" ruling directing that wage increases for union employees of the little steel firms be held to 15 percent because that was how much the consumer price index (CPI) had increased. This made the CPI a "cost of living" index, something that the Bureau of Labor Statistics had previously asserted it was not. The War Labor Board then began to tie wage increases to increases in the CPI. The AFL (American Federation of Labor) and CIO (Congress of Industrial Organizations) began a series of vigorous attacks on the CPI, arguing that it was biased and understated rates of price inflation.[2]

Because of the priorities of war production, business investment and home construction dropped sharply during the war; in fact, residential construction nearly ceased. Real per capita consumption was no larger in 1944 than in 1941 and was even less in 1942 and 1943. The decline was concentrated in durable goods consumption.

Administrative Changes During the War

Because it is easy to become lost among the "alphabet agencies" created to administer and control war and civilian production, we will concentrate on the most important of these agencies and administrative changes.[3] In May of 1940, an Office for Emergency Management (OEM) was created; in January of 1941, the Office of Production

Fig. 8.1 Real GNP Per Capita and the Rate of Unemployment 1940–1950

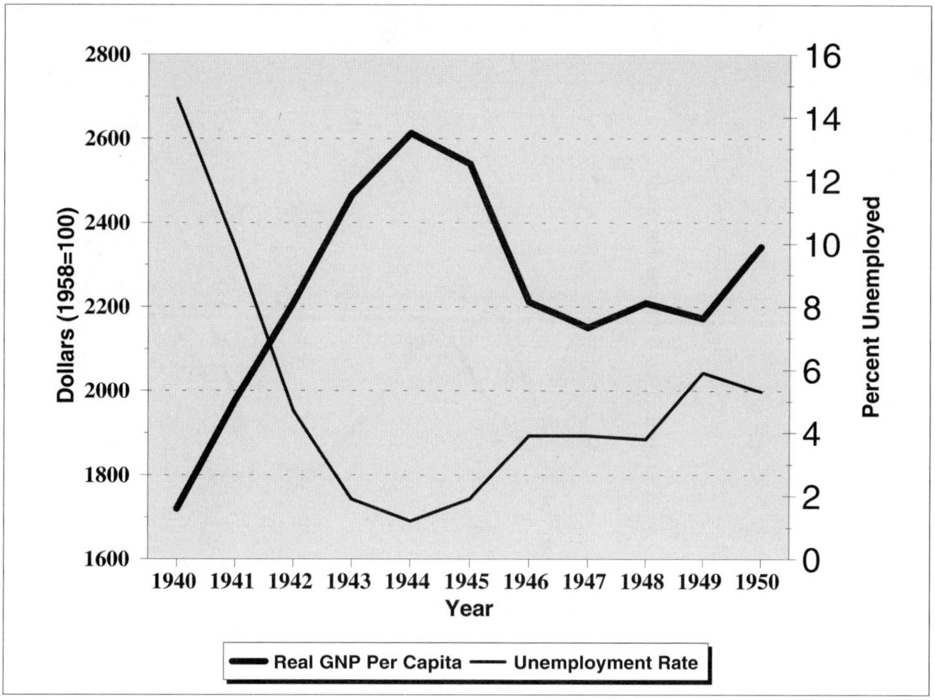

Source: *Historical Statistics of the United States: Colonial Times to 1970* (Washington, D.C.: U.S. Government Printing Office, 1976).

Management (OPM) took over establishing production and procurement priorities. The Office of Price Administration and Civilian Supply—set up in August of 1941—had the task of providing price guidelines to reduce inflation and guidelines to the OPM concerning essential and nonessential civilian goods. Prior to December of 1941, these two agencies were not very successful. They had limited powers and were "ungainly, lumbering, tortuously fashioned administrative structure[s]."[4]

With the entrance into the war after the attack on Pearl Harbor, changes were made in the administrative machinery. The War Production Board (WPB) replaced several prewar agencies and concentrated its efforts in the allocation of raw and semifinished materials among producers. The Office of Price Administration (OPA) was made a separate agency. The War Labor Board (WLB) worked with the Employment Service and the National Labor Relations Board to stabilize wages and ensure smooth labor-management relations. To make sure that it was able to stabilize wages, the WLB was given the power to seize plants and firms that violated wage guidelines. It could cancel

Fig. 8.2 Rates of Change in the Consumer Price Index and the Wholesale Price Index and the Level of the Stock of Money

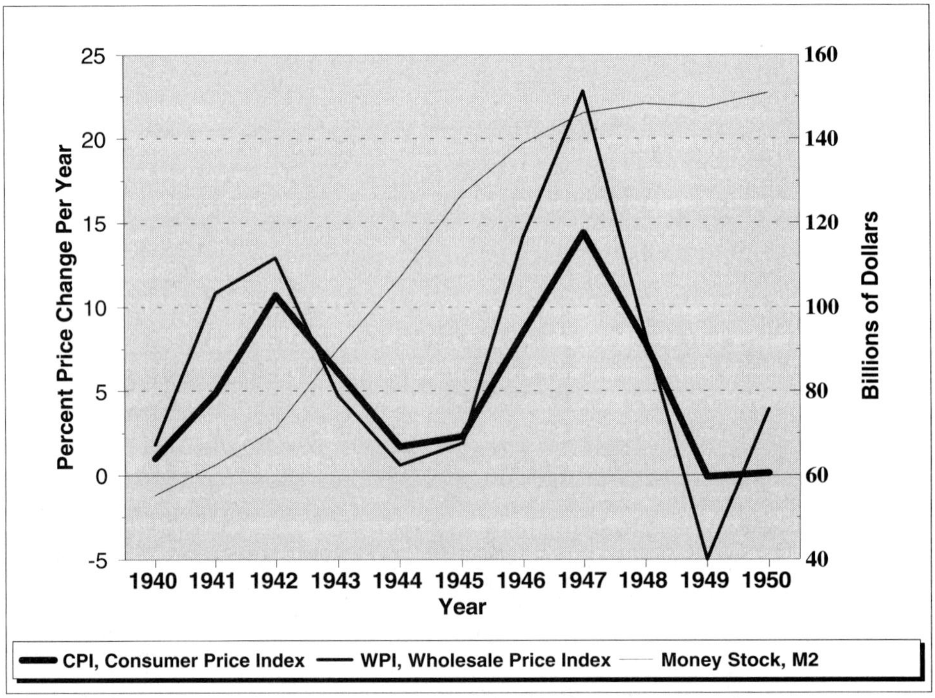

Source: *Historical Statistics of the United States: Colonial Times to 1970* (Washington, D.C.: U.S. Government Printing Office, 1976).

contracts, request that the WPB deny a firm's priority in resource allocation, and refer firms to the Bureau of Internal Revenue for the disallowance of tax deductions on wages paid in excess of the WLB's directives.[5] In order to develop more unified programs and policies, the Office of War Mobilization (OWM) was created in 1943 and given a status equal to that of the OEM and the WPB. By the end of the war, 165 agencies had been created. This proliferation of agencies, many of which were independent of the others led to conflicting directives, edicts, and bans in the attempt to mobilize and direct resources for war production.[6]

In spite of the administrative problems the U.S. economy produced a massive amount of war materials. Prior to the Second World War, the United States had produced less than 1,200 combat planes and less than 1,200 tanks.[7] During the five years of the war, the United States built nearly 300,000 planes, over 72,000 naval ships, nearly 5,000 merchant ships, 17,000 tanks, and 17.4 million rifles, carbines, and side arms.[8] By 1944 the United States was producing 40 percent of the world's armaments, and its production supported the entire Allied war effort.[9] So prodigious was the American production of war goods that by the summer of 1944 the WPB actually cut back on military production.

Mobilizing the Population

The entry of the United States into the war led to explosive increases in military personnel. From less than 500,000 men and women on active duty in 1940, the number increased to over twelve million in 1945. However, even with an increase of more than 11.5 million military personnel, the civilian labor force declined only 1.78 million during the war. (See Figure 8.3.) There were a number of sources for this additional labor. Unemployment effectively disappeared, and the overall participation rate also increased. In 1940 less than 28 percent of the women of working age were in the labor force, compared to over 36 percent by 1944. Even so, by the beginning of 1943, there was a labor shortage. Firms began pirating and hoarding labor and, in spite of controls, nominal and real wage rates rose, as did the average work week in manufacturing.

Mobilizing all of this labor produced many problems. War production tended to be concentrated in the industrial midwest and coastal states, particularly in the west. This required a substantial migration as blacks and farm labor moved from Southern and rural areas to industrial locations. Laborers just entering or reentering the labor force and workers moving to new jobs in war plants often had no skills or skills that were not

Fig. 8.3 The Civilian Labor Force, the Number Unemployed, and the Number of Active Duty Military Personnel

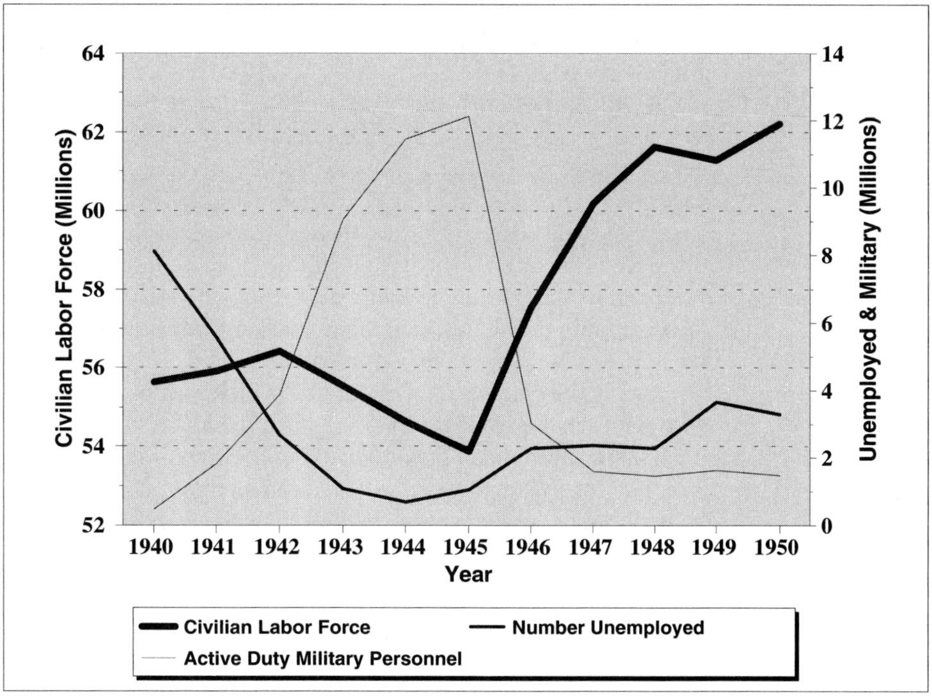

Source: *Historical Statistics of the United States: Colonial Times to 1970* (Washington, D.C.: U.S. Government Printing Office, 1976).

adaptable to the production of war materials. Worker placement then included refresher courses, vocational training, and accelerated in-plant apprenticeship programs to overcome labor shortages.

In midwestern and coastal cities where new war plants were located, the influx of new workers resulted in shortages of housing and other services. Temporary housing construction was accelerated in an attempt to relieve the congestion. As more women entered the labor force, child care services had to be provided, though these virtually ceased at the end of the war. The migration of blacks to cities with concentrations of war production and the entry of women into the labor force brought a rising tide of discrimination complaints. To reduce discrimination in 1941 President Roosevelt ordered the establishment of a Fair Employment Practices Committee.[10]

Unions. Both the AFL and the CIO increased their membership by about two thirds during the war. By 1945 union members were 35.8 percent of the nonagricultural labor force, and they remained at about one third well into the 1950s. Increasing union membership was due to the effectiveness of the National Labor Relations Act and the scarcity of labor during the war. In addition, the War Labor Board agreed to a "maintenance of membership" feature. New hires in a unionized plant automatically became union members unless they contracted out of this within 15 days of their employment.

Other agreements between unions and wartime administrators did not work as smoothly. A no-strike agreement was widely violated by wildcat strikes, though most were less than five days long.[11] Twice Roosevelt seized the coal mines because of strikes. Late in 1943 the railroads were seized for three weeks due to a strike threat. In fact, 63 government seizures were recorded during the war.[12] Most of the strikes concerned wage rates because the War Labor Board attempted to keep wage rate increases below the cost of living increases to reduce inflationary pressures and refused to grant wage rate increases to reflect rising productivity. In 1943 the War Manpower Commission decided to freeze selected workers in their current employment if their jobs were in essential lines of production. This also incurred the wrath of labor because it stopped workers from moving to higher paying jobs.

As Figure 8.4 shows, real manufacturing wage rates did rise, and combined with the increases in the average hours worked each week, real weekly and annual incomes rose during the war. The WLB did allow increases in fringe benefits because this did not directly increase wages and was construed as less inflationary. Workers received more vacations, holiday pay, higher overtime pay, work-shift premiums, health insurance, and other fringe benefits. The strike activity in 1943 led to the Smith-Connally Antistrike Act. On the whole, by the end of the war unions were in the strongest position they had ever held in the American economy.

Expanding Production

The expansion of agricultural and industrial production during the war, with fewer workers, was a dramatic accomplishment. Transportation, which had been a serious bottleneck in the First World War, did not cause problems in the Second World War.

Fig. 8.4 Current and Real Average Hourly Earnings and the Average Weekly Hours Worked in Manufacturing

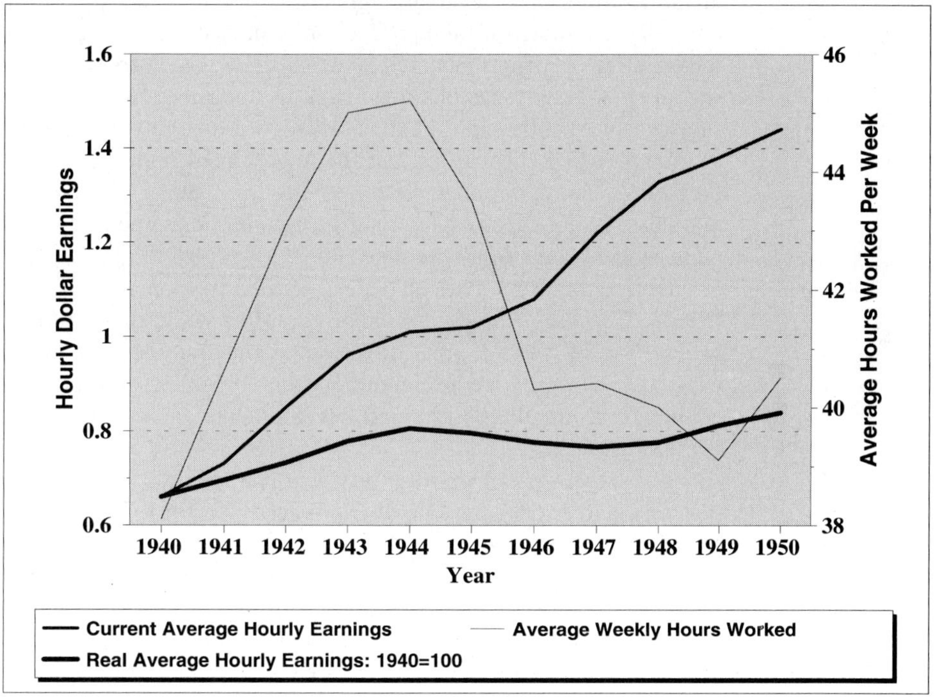

Source: *Historical Statistics of the United States: Colonial Times to 1970* (Washington, D.C.: U.S. Government Printing Office, 1976).

Agriculture. By the time the United States entered the war, agricultural exports had eliminated the large stored surpluses of the 1930s.[13] Farm production expanded by 17 percent during the war, while farm employment and population fell. The average size of farms rose 11 percent during the war. The transformation to tractor-based farming continued while farm productivity rose sharply. A large share of all farm production was exported to Allied nations and used to feed the armed forces.

This increased production was accomplished by the use of more tractors and other implements that released additional land for the production of crops for human consumption; by the greater use of wives and teenage children of farm families; by mechanical and scientific advances; and by the continued extension of electrical service to farmers. Continued genetic research and new insecticides and herbicides such as DDT and 2,4-D also raised farm productivity. Farm prices increased. The rising productivity and prices raised farm incomes, allowing farmers to reduce their mortgage indebtedness by 28 percent. Unlike during the First World War, few farmers went deeply into debt to expand.

Industry. Manufacturing production expanded rapidly, while the growth of mining and utilities was much more modest and consistent throughout the 1940s. In manufacturing most of the growth came from the need for durable goods for the war effort. To facilitate this, the production of most consumer durable goods, such as cars, refrigerators, sewing machines, and bicycles, was suspended for the duration of the war. By 1942 shortages of some materials appeared. New plants solved the aluminum shortages. Gasoline and fuel oil shortages were largely confined to the East Coast due to transportation difficulties, but the government built pipelines that alleviated these problems. Though rubber shortages occurred when the Japanese invasion cut off Southeast Asian supplies, the rapid expansion of synthetic neoprene and, particularly, buna rubber production eliminated all shortages by 1944.[14]

During the war American technological developments far surpassed those of Great Britain, Germany, Japan, and other countries while the production of war materials generally resulted in a great diffusion of existing and new technical knowledge and expertise.[15] There were no lightning technological breakthroughs. Instead, there was a continued accumulation of small developments and steady improvements due to the learning process.

The expansion of military production by American industry proved to be a task that was neither easy nor quickly embraced.[16] Prior to December, 1941, business was reluctant to accept the new defense contracts because of worries about the possibility of substantial excess capacity if new plants were built, limitations on returns on investment or excess-profits taxes, and if government financed the new capacity, the possibility that it might move to competitively restructure the industry. Finally, most businesses were again producing for a newly robust civilian market and were not anxious to forgo this for much more risky defense production. The result was what some business critics called the "strike of capital" in the summer of 1940.[17]

Several solutions to the problem of obtaining business cooperation were adopted. Advertised competitive bidding was for the most part discarded. In its place cost-plus-fixed-fee contracts were negotiated with businesses able to satisfy the military requirements. The fixed fee was usually limited to 7 percent of the *estimated* costs. However, as production geared up, the learning curve allowed most producers to lower costs, and fixed fees as a percent of costs then rose substantially. The effect of cost-plus-fixed-fee contracts was to guarantee businesses a profit.

Advance payments and progress payments provided working capital, reducing business borrowing. Tax laws were changed. Corporate profits taxes were increased and excess-profits taxes imposed. However, Congress allowed an accelerated depreciation of facilities built for war production, and loss carry-back provisions on corporate income taxes provided a form of income averaging, further reducing the likelihood of businesses paying excess-profits taxes.

To overcome business inertia in the construction of facilities, Congress allowed the army and navy to directly construct plants, which were then leased to private operating companies.[18] As a result most of the risks were again borne by the government. From July 1940 through June 1945, one third of all corporate plant construction was financed by the federal government, while over 70 percent was government-financed in the basic metals, metal fabricating, and chemicals industries.[19] By June of 1945, some estimates found that the federal government's Defense Plant Corporation owned between 10 and 12 percent of American industrial capacity. At the end of the war, 90 percent of the facilities to produce synthetic rubber, aircraft, magnesium, and ships; 70 percent of the facilities to produce aluminum; and 50 percent of the facilities to produce machine tools were DPC owned.[20] The corporate lessees had great freedom in operating these plants and generally expected to be able to purchase the plant after the war at a "fair" price.

One of the enduring criticisms of the process was that most contracts and production went to the large corporate firms.[21] In July, 1941, six large firms held nearly one third of all military contracts, and by the middle of 1944, 26 large corporations leased 50 percent of all Defense Plant Corporation facilities. In response to complaints that small firms were unable to obtain contracts, Congress authorized the creation of the Smaller War Plants Corporation (SWPC) but on the whole it was not very successful. Smaller firms did better at becoming subcontractors, and estimates suggest that 30 percent of war production was subcontracted to the smaller firms. The issue of the treatment of smaller firms surfaced again during reconversion and the disposal of surplus war facilities.

Transportation. There was concern about the performance of the transportation system as the war began, but the fears turned out to be unwarranted. The Second World War marked the last great period of prosperity for the railroads. During the war the movement of freight and passengers by motor vehicles was reduced through gasoline rationing to reduce rubber tire consumption. Inland waterway traffic also dropped because the military production bound for the coasts generally could not move this way. The share for oil pipelines rose because of government construction of oil pipelines. Railroads' share of freight traffic rose by over 9 percent from 1940 to 1943 and then slipped slightly through 1946. Railroad passenger traffic showed an even greater rise as wartime gasoline rationing led travelers to switch to the trains. With the end of the war, railroad passenger traffic commenced on a sharp decline that would continue into the 1970s.

Financing the War

To finance the war, the federal government drew on its experience in raising funds during the First World War, maintaining the income tax system during the interwar period, and selling debt during the 1930s.[22] Taxes were raised almost everywhere possible; however, taxes provided only about 46 percent of the federal expenditures during the war. The bulk of the increased tax receipts came from increased personal and corporate income taxes. Figure 8.5 shows how individual federal income taxes collected changed during the war.

Though personal income taxes had increased during the 1930s, they continued to focus on the upper income families and individuals. As war preparations were made the personal exemptions declined, the rates rose, and the level of income at which taxes were first paid dropped. (See Table 8.1.) With the onset of the war in 1942, rates were raised dramatically. By 1945 individual income tax receipts were 20 times larger than in 1940.[23] In June of 1943, Congress approved the Current Tax Payment Act. Drawing upon experience with the pay-as-you-go Social Security taxes, federal income taxes were now to be withheld by the employer as incomes were received. This move reduced borrowing problems for the government, reduced collection costs, and made it more difficult for individuals to avoid paying personal income taxes.

Though other taxes were also increased, personal and corporate income taxes provided the bulk of the tax revenues. The Second World War transformed the federal income tax into a nearly universal tax, something that was almost inevitable given the revenue demands generated by the war. At the end of the war, few families and individuals escaped paying some federal income taxes. The withholding feature was adopted by the states as more and more of them imposed income taxes.

The portion of federal expenditures financed by tax receipts during the Second World War was smaller than the portion financed by tax receipts during the First World War. Part of the difference is explained by the much more costly nature of the Second

Fig. 8.5 Federal Government Receipts and Its Components

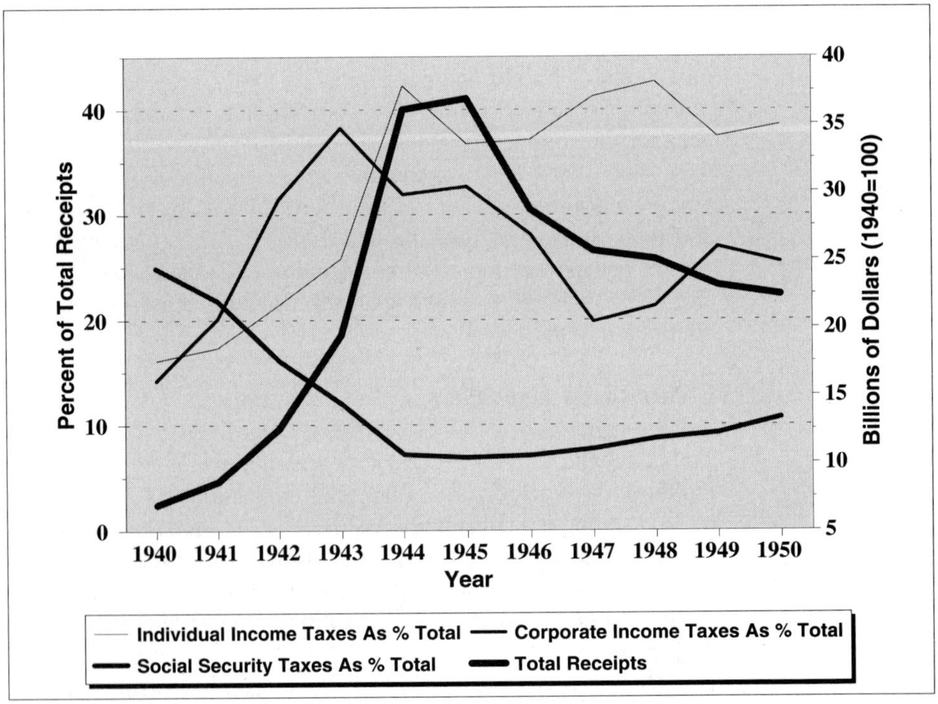

Source: *Historical Statistics of the United States: Colonial Times to 1970* (Washington, D.C.: U.S. Government Printing Office, 1976).

TABLE 8.1 Individual Income Tax Brackets

Year	Personal Exemptions		First Bracket		Top Bracket	
	Single	Married, 2 Dependents	Rate	Income	Rate	Income
1936-39	1,000	3,300	4.0	6,000	79.0	5,000,000
1940	800	2,800	4.4	4,000	81.1	5,000,000
1941	750	2,300	10.0	2,000	81.0	5,000,000
1942-43	500	1,900	19.0	2,000	88.0	200,000
1944-45	500	2,000	23.0	2,000	94.0	200,000
1946-47	500	2,000	19.0	2,000	86.45	200,000
1948-49	600	2,400	16.6	2,000	82.13	200,000
1950	600	2,400	17.4	2,000	84.36	200,000

Source: Department of Commerce, *Historical Statistics of the United States: Colonial Times to 1970* (Washington, D.C.: U.S. Government Printing Office, 1976).

World War compared to the First World War. Congress also had to consider the disincentives to work and produce that might have arisen if taxes had been made even higher for most families and individuals. By the end of the war, there were signs that patriotism was becoming less effective in eliciting the participation of the civilian population in the war effort.

The other method of financing the war was through direct borrowing. Figure 8.6 shows both the level of the federal debt and the federal debt as a percent of Gross National Product from 1940 through 1950. As can be seen, there was a huge increase in the federal debt because about 54 percent of the expenditures during the war were financed by federal borrowing. The debt as a percent of GNP rose from 50.6 percent in 1940 to 130.5 percent in 1945, the largest relative debt in the history of the United States, and then began to decline.

There were seven War Loan drives and a final Victory Loan drive between November 1942 and December 1945. These were aimed at institutional and individual investors believing that sale of these bonds would reduce their cash and thus reduce inflationary pressures. Banks were allowed to create War Loan deposit accounts whereby funds were loaned to individuals to purchase federal securities. These accounts carried no reserve requirements.

Because the stock of money expanded rapidly during the war and taxes did not rise enough to soak up all of the excess real and nominal income, one would have expected a rapid price inflation. Though prices rose more rapidly in 1941 and 1942, they rose much more slowly until the end of the war in 1945. This was due to the extensive array of wage and price controls and rationing imposed on the civilian economy. Controlling prices and rationing goods and services left civilians with considerable income that they could invest in government bonds directly or indirectly by placing the funds in banks, which then invested in government bonds. The controls therefore became an additional way to force consumers to save and thus transfer real resources to the federal government.

Fig. 8.6 The Federal Debt

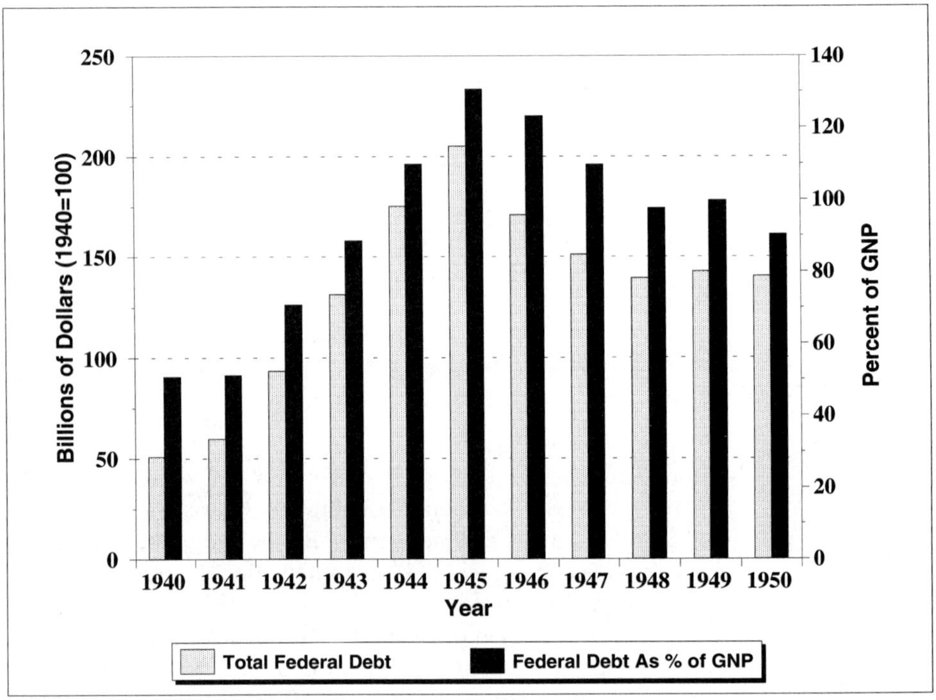

Source: *Historical Statistics of the United States: Colonial Times to 1970* (Washington, D.C.: U.S. Government Printing Office, 1976).

Wage and Price Controls

Roosevelt's first moves toward wage and price controls came when he established a Price Stabilization Division of the National Defense Advisory Council on May 29, 1940, but it had little effect because compliance was voluntary.[24] On April 11, 1941, the Office of Price Administration (OPA) was established. After Pearl Harbor this office was given the power to require that its price guidelines be adhered to. On April 28, 1942, the Office of Price Administration issued the General Maximum Price Regulation (GMPR) which froze prices at the highest level reached in March of 1942. In April, 1943, President Roosevelt issued the famous "Hold the Line" Order to stop further price increases. A full-fledged set of wage and price controls combined with rationing were imposed and held in place until VJ Day when Japan surrendered. From VJ Day to June 1946, there was a diminishing influence of these controls. In June of 1946, wage and price controls were removed, but complaints about rising prices led to their selective reimposition in July of 1946. They were removed for good in October of that year.

The Rationing of Consumer Goods. According to Hugh Rockoff, the *siege motive* was the initial rationale behind the rationing programs as the government sought to more fairly ration goods and ensure that shortsighted consumers spread out their consumption. Another rationale that soon appeared was to *aid in the enforcement of price controls*. By assuring each consumer of a small share of a commodity, rationing inhibited the scramble for supplies that produces black markets and other forms of evasion. Food rationing, in particular, was undertaken to aid in the enforcement of price controls.[25] Tires were the first commodity to be rationed, because the war cut off natural rubber supplies from Southeast Asia. To reduce the wear of existing tires on automobiles, gasoline was rationed to reduce driving. Durable goods were also soon rationed as manufacturers switched to the production of munitions.

Rationing Techniques. The government used two primary rationing techniques: the *unit system* and the *point system*. Under the unit system a ration ticket permitted the consumer to purchase a specified quantity of the rationed good at the fixed monetary price. This was used for most products other than processed foods, meats, and fats. The share for each consumer could be made equal or, as for gasoline, relatively complex to tailor the consumer's ration to his or her "needs."

The point system was used to ration processed foods [the "blue" point system] and meats and fats [the "red" point system]. Under point rationing the consumer was given a certain number of points that could be used to purchase a specified range of rationed commodities that sold at varying point prices. The consumer had to pay the controlled money prices for the food products. According to Rockoff, this allowed consumers some choice while still receiving a fair share of the controlled commodity. "The system also gave the rationing authorities some flexibility: they could alter point prices to correct imbalances between supply and demand of particular commodities."[26]

Problems with Price Controls and Rationing. The ration tickets were like currency and were frequently referred to as ration currency. Consequently there was *counterfeiting* of ration coupons and sometimes *currency overissue*, which lead to *point inflation*, or bare shelves, an issue which became critical in late 1944 when the OPA invalidated all small-change tokens to ensure that they could not be accumulated and then used to empty store shelves.[27]

A third problem with rationing was *market efficiency*. Because prices could not adjust between commodities and regional variation of prices for a single commodity could not occur, prices could not reallocate supplies, and locational shortages developed. Shortages of fluid milk in various southern and western cities arose in 1942 and 1943.[28] The gasoline market in the northeast was plagued by shortages,[29] and shortages of clothing, particularly in the west and in rural areas, periodically appeared.

A fourth problem was with *evasion* of the rationing controls, which became widespread toward the end of the war. To suppress evasion, the OPA had to seek more and more control over the market place. There were four sanctions: injunctions, license suspension, treble damage suits, and criminal proceedings. The treble damage suit was the most used sanction. The bulk of the OPA sanctions occurred in a few areas: for example, in 1944, 68.6 percent of the sanctions were in meat and dairy, groceries, agricultural commodities, gasoline rationing and rent.[30]

Food. Overcharging of food prices and tie-in sales were frequent events. Wholesalers complained that meat packers forced them to take a variety of unwanted products along with more desirable cuts. Quality deterioration, or "adulteration," became a serious problem. Fat was added to hamburger. The butterfat content of milk was reduced. Cornstarch was added to spices. Coffee was stretched with fillers. Upgrading, where lower quality merchandise was sold as if it were higher quality, and shortweighting were common. A famous case was the "shrinking candy bar." Between 1939 and 1943, 19 of 20 candy bars had shrunk in size, hiding a price increase of 23 percent. Candy makers also substituted inferior ingredients. The worst black market was in meat, particularly beef and poultry.

Clothing. This was a most difficult area for OPA because it was a highly diversified commodity and seasonal changes made it hard to specify prices. In addition to this, much cotton was used, and the cotton industry had powerful "friends" in Congress. Evasion took two forms: quality deterioration and forced uptrading. One official testified that quality deterioration took forms such as men's shorts made of cheesecloth with enough added sizing to give it form until washed once, women's slips made of coarse, heavily sized muslin; "water-resistant" baby pants that allowed a third of a glass of water to drain through after being washed once; and cotton sweaters that were so loosely knit they could not hold their shape.[31] More important toward the end of the period was "forced uptrading" because profit margins were typically larger on higher priced lines.[32]

Firms were often concerned with the long-range impact of the controls, because some regulators saw the programs as a way to eliminate brands and trademarks to make markets, in their opinions, more "competitive." For example, Coopers Incorporated, now Jockey International, did not engage in forced uptrading because it had no low-priced lines and did not object to the price controls. Rather, the firm objected to concentration and standardization programs that would have destroyed the value of the Jockey brand, which it had spent several decades creating.[33]

Shelter. Despite apparently widespread support for rent controls, evasion was widespread. Owner-occupied housing was not controlled. Rental owners could evict the current tenants and then sell the property to them, or anyone who would buy it, at the market price. This could be varied by allowing the purchaser to pay in monthly installments in which the accumulation of equity was extremely slow; that is, the tenant was simply paying rent above the legal maximum. Other forms of evasion included bribes and cash on the side. In Portland, Oregon, in June of 1946, rents ranged from \$38 to \$60 for five unfurnished rooms. Black market bribes ranged from \$5 to \$500 to get an apartment with monthly side payments of \$10 to \$15. In Chicago a six-room apartment could be rented for the OPA ceiling of \$75 per month; however, the tenant also had to buy the furniture for $1,500. Maintenance expenditures were often reduced.[34]

Fuel. Often stations would sell gasoline without receiving ration coupons, and the counterfeiting of these coupons was common. Early in 1944 Chester Bowles estimated that 5 percent of all gasoline was purchased without coupons or with counterfeited or stolen coupons. By January of 1945, it was estimated that 1 of every 16 gasoline stations had sanctions imposed. Without price adjustments spot shortages arose, and quality deterioration was common.[35] Quality deterioration, upgrading, shortweighting, tie-in sales, and cash on the side were also common problems in coal.

Rationing and Price Controls: Conclusions. Rockoff argues that the controls did reduce inflation and "protect vulnerable incomes" as long as they were applied across the board and backed up by committed enforcement and rationing. When controls were removed at the end of the war, prices surged. In his opinion the bureaucracy necessary to administer the controls during the Second World War was not really a "large" one. However, there was evidence of an extensive black market, which could have been controlled only by an "extension of governmental power that would have been unacceptable to most Americans in a peacetime economy."[36]

Rockoff concludes that the state is able to control prices, but this necessitates a vast regimentation of economic life. Such a regimentation may be appropriate in times of war so as to protect the incomes of "vulnerable groups" and to reduce inflationary expectations. But the community has to be willing to accept this, and during the Second World War it was. As soon as the war ended, however, this was no longer the case; the costs of wage and price controls and rationing swung against the benefits, and they were ended.[37] Rockoff argues that it is the ultimate inevitability of the government regimentation of economic activity that "makes permanent controls on the the Second World War model an unacceptable alternative."[38]

The Second World War and the Recovery from the Thirties

It has long been an article of faith that the Second World War brought an end to the long depression of the thirties. The rapid rise of government spending associated with the war was the missing Keynesian aggregate demand stimulus, and this brought about the move to full employment. This demonstration of the Keynesian model was probably the most important force in bringing about the quick acceptance of Keynesian theory in the postwar period.

But there have long been questions not only about what caused the recovery but also about how much recovery there was prior to 1946. For example, monetary policy changed dramatically as the Fed engineered a rapid expansion of the stock of money by expanding the high-powered money.[39] (See Figure 8.2.) Given such a monetary policy, one could hardly ascribe the expansion solely, or perhaps even primarily, to fiscal policy.

It has also been noted that there was a shift in demand toward the capital goods sectors, the sectors that had contracted the most during the thirties and then were hit with large relative wage increases from unionization at the end of the thirties. Thus, the nature of the war demands may have provided some coordinating price adjustments that otherwise would have been slower to occur and brought about a more rapid recovery.[40] In addition, the extra saving, voluntary and quasi-voluntary, allowed the rapid expansion of the production of war materials.[41]

However, since the early work of Simon Kuznets on the national income and product accounts, there have been questions about how much recovery actually occurred during the war. As Figure 8.7 shows, the official Department of Commerce data point to an enormous rise in real GNP during the war and an equally sharp drop after the war. Real consumption, outlined in Figure 8.8, shows a decline from 1941 to 1942 and a slower recovery until the end of the war. In real per capital terms, consumption declines and does not exceed its postwar value until 1946. Even this consumption series should be viewed with considerable skepticism because consumers were often forced into long-distance relocation for jobs and placed in crowded housing. Transportation became increasingly difficult as there were no new cars produced, used car prices rose sharply, and gasoline was rationed and increasingly unavailable. Many goods simply disappeared. "People were . . . working harder, longer, more inconveniently, and at greater physical risk in order to get the available goods."[42] This is hardly evidence of a pronounced recovery.

Robert Higgs has pointed out that by 1944 the armed forces had pulled in more people than the total number of unemployed workers in 1940.[43] Between 1940 and 1943 the number of unemployed workers fell by 7.05 million, while the number in the armed forces rose by 8.4 million.[44] No macroeconomic model is required to understand why unemployment—one of the measures of the contraction—disappeared.

The sharp increases in GNP are also problematical. Simon Kuznets (a leader in developing national income accounting and primary creator of the United States' national income accounts) had criticized the figures because they inadequately corrected for inflation during the war and "did not satisfactorily deal with the decline in the relative prices of munitions during the war." Though the Commerce Department admitted that Kuznets' criticisms were correct, they would not make any corrections.[45] In 1952 Kuznets produced revised estimates of national product during the war years that showed no fall in real GNP after the war.[46] Kuznets also argued for a "peacetime" concept of GNP when examining long-term growth and to this end developed another GNP estimate, Variant III, which excluded military spending other than for military capital stock.[47] These estimates show a decline in real GNP during the war.

Finally, the figures themselves cannot be taken to mean what they would seem to mean. During the war there were extensive price controls and rationing of commodities and services. Credit was controlled, and the government created a command economy to direct the allocation of scarce resources according to government priorities. But the national income statistics presuppose a free market system with uncontrolled prices. These figures simply cannot be compared to years when markets directed economic

Fig. 8.7 Indexes of Real Gross National Product, 1939–1949

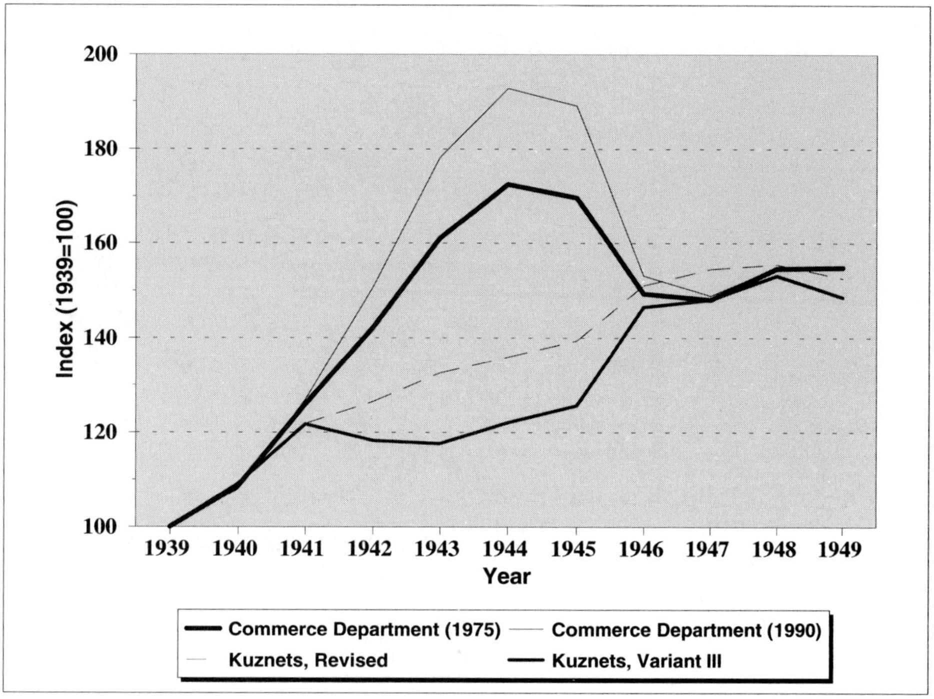

Source: Robert Higgs, "Wartime Prosperity? A Reassessment of the U.S. Economy in the 1940s," *The Journal of Economic History* 52 (March 1992): 41–60.

activity. The national income data showing such amazing prosperity during the war is simply not believable. As Higgs says, "As the war ended, real prosperity returned."[48]

THE POSTWAR BOOM

Economists using the new Keynesian analysis said that when the war ended, the decline in government spending acting through the consumption multiplier would lead to a severe depression, and suggested that government spending remain at high levels to avoid this. The actual results were quite different. American consumers had been unable to purchase durable goods for four years; with the end of the war and the reconversion from military to civilian production, they went on a spending spree, buying houses, cars, refrigerators, furniture, and other durable consumer goods that had not been produced since the war began.

Fig. 8.8 Indexes of Real Consumption and Real Consumption Per Capita

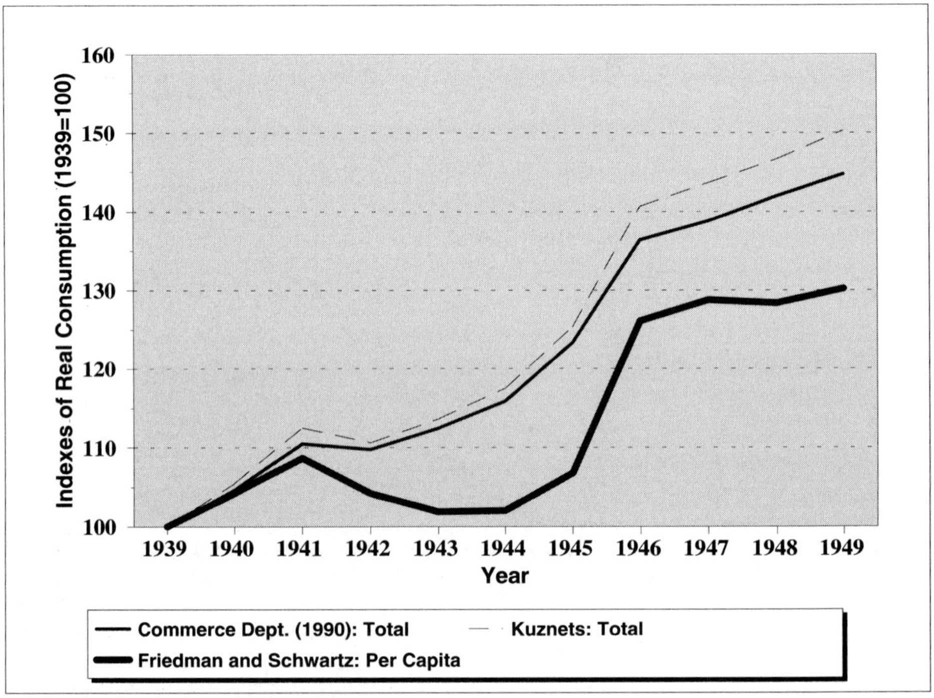

Source: Robert Higgs, "Wartime Prosperity? A Reassessment of the U.S. Economy in the 1940s," *The Journal of Economic History* 52 (March 1992): 41–60.

Demobilization and Reconversion

As early as 1943, demobilization planning began. In 1944 Congress created the Office of War Mobilization and Reconversion (OWMR) to avoid the chaos that had reined at the end of the First World War, but the advance preparation had little influence at the end of the war.[49] Termination of war production contracts had actually began as early as 1943, and by 1944 some contracts were terminated with as little as three days notice.[50] In June of 1944, the War Production Board issued Priorities Regulation 25 directing the regional offices of the WPB to allow civilian production in plants where war contracts were fulfilled or terminated. The regional WPB offices could then allocate supplies to those plants. The issuance of PR 25 set off a bitter struggle; by the fall of 1944, there was little implementation of it. Barton Bernstein argued that in order to prevent smaller firms, whose contracts would have been terminated, from gaining a competitive advantage, particularly in the scramble for resources, big businesses effectively stopped the process.[51]

When the war ended with VJ Day on August 14, 1945 a battle ensued between the two most important agencies, the WPB under Julius Krug and the OPA under Chester

Bowles.[52] With the end of the war, Krug began a policy of deregulation, arguing that the free markets would rapidly employ the returning soldiers and modify any price increases. Bowles argued that price controls and resource allocations had to be gradually removed to modify unacceptable inflation, reduce big businesses' unfair advantage in obtaining scarce resources, and stop a likely shift toward the production of less essential, higher priced luxury items. Though President Truman issued a directive which apparently overrode Krug's decontrol program, he quickly began removing controls and by November 3, 1945 only 55 of 650 wartime control orders remained. The OPA more gradually removed price controls, and not until June of 1946 were all removed, only to have some briefly reimposed in July of 1946.

The majority of the government's capital investments were in separate facilities, but the rest were "scrambled" facilities, where government-constructed plants and equipment were intermingled with privately constructed and owned plants and equipment. In the case of scrambled facilities (about twenty-two hundred plants) the operators of the plants were clearly in a favorable position to purchase the facilities once the war ended; in fact, there probably was no other feasible alternative. The lessees of the separate plants usually had options allowing them to purchase the plants and equipment once the government's needs ceased at the end of the war.

On October 3, 1944, Congress passed the Surplus Property Act to ensure that the disposal of the facilities constructed by the DPC were consistent with their social goals, primarily strengthening small businesses, reducing monopolistic tendencies, and obtaining a "fair," or high, value for the properties.[53] The act's goals were not always consistent. For example, attempting to receive a high price for a facility often required selling it to a large or dominant firm rather than a smaller firm because the plants were designed for large scale production.

In only a few industries was concentration clearly affected by the disposal of surplus property. Dow Chemical was the only feasible purchaser of the magnesium plants. The synthetic rubber plants were largely sold to the dominant rubber firms. Concentration in the synthetic ammonia industry was reduced because government plants were sold to three new entrants, reducing the market shares of Allied Chemical and Du Pont.[54] The most famous case was aluminum. In 1945 the Aluminum Company of America, Alcoa, had been found guilty of monopolization. The War Assets Administration decided that with the antitrust decision it would be inappropriate to sell the surplus aluminum plants to Alcoa and finally elicited bids from the Kaiser and Reynolds Corporations after obtaining Alcoa's agreement that it would share its patents and essentially guaranteeing that the two new firms would not incur losses in aluminum production.[55]

Some Other Postwar Changes

The combined impact of the new prosperity and the end of the war led American families to begin having more children. In spite of the war the population growth rate rose from 0.7 percent per year in the 1930s to 1.13 percent per year from 1940 to 1946. With the end of the war, the baby boom raised the rate of population growth to an average of 1.77 percent a year. This baby boom continued into the early 1960s when it quickly ended.

Automobiles. The automobile industry had seen a dramatic decline in the number of producing firms in the interwar period, and no new firm had entered since the twenties. The great postwar demand for cars led to the entry of new companies. Crosley, Tucker, and Playboy all tried to enter but only Crosley succeeded in producing a car for a few years. The Kaiser-Fraser company did begin production in 1946. However, they were insufficiently capitalized and by 1957 had withdrawn from automobile production—though they continued to produce Jeep utility vehicles at Toledo, Ohio. Kaiser-Fraser and the independents, had paid premium prices for labor and capital to get into production and develop a market share and this led to serious financial difficulties in the early 1950s.[56]

The Taft-Hartley Act. The 1935 Wagner Act, or National Labor Relations Act, had marked a significant change in government's role in labor markets by giving labor new bargaining powers. In the postwar period Congress passed the Taft-Hartley Act, or Labor-Management Act, the first major amendment to the Wagner Act. Union membership had grown during the war, attaining greater economic and political power. During 1944 to 1946 there was a wave of strikes as unions sought higher wages and more benefits, which had they had been unable to obtain during the war.

The Taft-Hartley Act, in many ways a reaction to this, established a number of definitions of unfair labor practices more or less paralleling the Wagner Act's definitions of unfair management practices. Closed shops, secondary boycotts, jurisdictional strikes, featherbedding, union discrimination against nonunion employees, and the requirement that unions had to engage in collective bargaining were part of the act. The postwar anxiety about communism was also seen in the requirement that the services of the NLRB would only be available to unions whose officers signed affidavits that they were not communists. Finally, the act allowed the president to call a "cooling-off" period in strikes so that collective bargaining could resume, a feature that has been used a number of times since 1947.

Veterans' Benefits. In 1944 Congress, worried about the unemployment of the returning veterans, passed the Servicemen's Readjustment Bill, more commonly known as the G.I. Bill. The bill provided for veterans to receive one year of unemployment allowances of $20 a week, and about a million veterans received this during 1946 and 1947.[57] It also provided for subsidies to veterans to purchase farms and homes and for payments to veterans who enrolled in on-the-job or apprenticeship vocational training or in colleges.[58] Roughly a million veterans enrolled in colleges from 1946 through 1948, nearly 850,000 in 1949 and almost 600,000 in 1950. From 1946 to 1948, veterans made up from 40 to 50 percent of the total college enrollment. The act opened the way for similar acts for Korean and Vietnam war veterans.[59] In many ways the G.I. Bill and the inundation of veterans onto college campuses changed the nature and face of higher education.

The Full-Employment Act. In 1946 the federal government passed the Full-Employment Act, which redefined some of the roles of the federal government. This was "proposed in embryo form as early as 1943 by the National Resources Planning Board," and sections of the Surplus Property Act of 1944 also foreshadowed it.[60] Richard Gardner has argued that the bill represents the United States' response to British demands during the Second World War that the United States stabilize its economy if the dollar were to become the reserve currency of a new international financial order.[61] This law marked a fundamental shift in the concept of government responsibility because it directed the government to adopt policies to maintain employment, maximize economic growth, and maintain stable prices. Jonathan Hughes argues that unlike the New Deal changes in the role of the federal government, this one can be termed "revolutionary" in its redefinition of the roles and responsibilities of the individual and the state.[62] However, Robert Higgs has argued that the "ratchet effect" has led government to expand its role in the economy after every crisis since the turn of the century.[63]

Postwar International Developments

The international economy had been in disarray throughout most of the interwar period and early in the war the United States began a call for a reduction in trade barriers.[64] The world's stock of monetary gold increasingly came to be concentrated in the United States during the war, and at the war's end the United States held about two thirds of the world's monetary gold stock.

Bretton Woods. In July of 1944, the United Nations sponsored a conference at Bretton Woods, New Hampshire to consider the question of how to reconstitute the international economy. The representatives agreed to institute fixed exchange rates backed up by a stabilization fund to temporarily assist nations that were experiencing payments problems. The International Monetary Fund (IMF) was created as the stabilization loan fund envisioned by the United States with its monetary resources coming from the contributions of the member nations. The International Bank for Reconstruction and Development (IBRD) was created to facilitate the flow of long-term development capital, primarily to less developed countries, but it was always undercapitalized. The International Trade Organization (ITO) intended to promote freer trade through tariff and quota reductions, was stillborn. Some of the powers and goals of the ITO were resurrected in the General Agreement on Trade and Tariffs, or GATT, which arose in 1947 and was ratified in 1948.

The Marshall Plan. On June 5, 1947, in a commencement address at Harvard University, Secretary of State George Marshall proposed a program to bring about European recovery to relieve "hunger, poverty, desperation, and chaos."[65] The program, which France and Great Britain developed, treated Europe as a whole rather than as separate countries.[66] The Organization of European Economic Cooperation (OEEC) became the forerunner of the Schuman Plan of 1950, the European Coal and Steel

Community of 1951, and finally of the European Common Market in 1957. As soon as a structure had been established in Europe and requests made, Congress passed an act directing that $13 billion of aid be transmitted to Europe over a four year period.

Though Marshall's speech stressed humanitarian motives, the aid was also expected to stop the advances of communism in Europe. In addition, the economic recovery of Europe was expected to boost international trade and this would benefit American businesses. The Marshall Plan did stop the further encroachment of communism in Europe and accelerated the economic recovery of the war-torn European economies. Large amounts of raw materials and foodstuffs were shipped to Europe and allocated by the OEEC under the plan. However, it appears that the main reason the aid plan seemed to work so well was that the European nations already had skilled labor and the requisite technical knowledge. As the United States was to learn, aid sent to nations where these skills and knowledge did not exist did not produce the same results.

Was It a Postwar Boom or "The Great Depression of 1946"?

Although contemporary observers and later analysts have always called the immediate postwar years a boom period, someone examining a recent *Economic Report of the President*, say for 1990, would find that those figures show something else. The fall in real GNP from 1945 to 1946 was 19 percent, the largest single-year decline recorded for the United States, and the decline from 1944 to 1947 was nearly 23 percent, with nearly a 25 percent decline in real GNP per capita. Real GNP per capita did not regain its 1944 level until 1964, an astounding 20-year depression.[67] And this occurred with the rate of unemployment never rising as high as four percent between 1945 and 1948. In fact, as one traces through the annual *Economic Reports of the President* since 1960, this "depression," though mild at first, grows longer and deeper in each of the following *Reports*.

As was pointed out above, there is good reason to believe that the Commerce Department's real GNP figures for the war years are unrealistically high, and it is likely that real GNP, like real consumption, rose when the war ended. As Richard Vedder and Lowell Gallaway have shown, the unusual and, over time, increasingly severe contraction in the immediate postwar years is a statistical artifact.[68] The price index used to compute real GNP uses current period weights, which change every year. These changing weights combined with a faster rate of increase in the price of government goods and services have combined over time to make the postwar downturn become greater. Their estimates show no such significant decline. There was, in fact, an economic boom in the postwar years.

This boom occurred in the midst of an enormous decline in federal spending and a change from a budget deficit to a budget surplus. In 1944 and 1945 Keynesians were arguing that the expected decline in federal spending would lead to a severe depression at the end of the war. When the depression did not occur, it was explained by the opening of the pent-up demand for consumer goods. Vedder and Gallaway have argued that this interpretation is in error. From the second quarter of 1945 through the first quarter

Fig. 8.9 Employee Compensation as a Percent of GNP and as a Percent of Personal Income

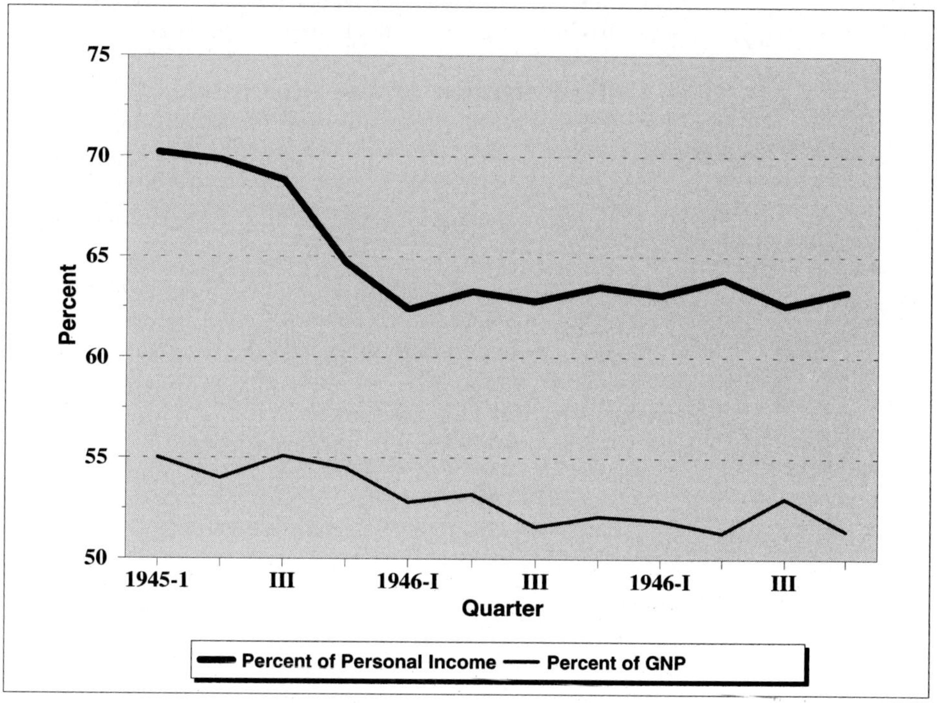

Source: Lowell Gallaway and Richard Vedder, "The Great Depression of 1946," *The Review of Austrian Economics* 5 (1991): 3–32.

of 1946, the increase in consumption spending was only 20 percent of the decline in federal spending, and the increase in consumption and investment spending together were still $20 billion short of the decline in government spending. Consumption spending did not rise above predicted levels until 1947.[69]

What does explain the boom and the employment of the 10.5 million men released from the armed forces? Vedder and Gallaway argue that real wage rates declined and made it worthwhile for firms to employ the returning veterans. Using different estimates of the wage rate and price index, they found that almost all show declines in real wages—a median decline of 2.35 percent in 1946 and a median decline from 1945 of 7.15 percent in 1947.[70] A more accurate measure is the change in employee compensation as a percent of GNP or of personal income. These two measures are shown in Figure 8.9 and show the effect of falling real wages.

In addition to money wages not rising as fast as prices, part of the decline was due to the elimination of overtime work, because New Deal legislation had mandated time-and-a-half pay for overtime work, and part may have been due to some decline in union power in the immediate postwar years. The falling real wages spurred employment, increased corporate profits, and helped spur business investment demand, "the only truly robust component of aggregate demand" from the end of the war to 1947.[71] Thus, Vedder and Gallaway argue that neglected real wage adjustments in the labor markets were the driving force behind the immediate postwar boom.

The United States at the End of the 1940s

The United States emerged from the Second World War with a strong economy. The dreary depression and war years were over, and its citizens could return to the business of producing and consuming goods. As the "arsenal of democracy," it began providing a flow of consumer and military goods to other nations. But there were other important changes. With the end of the war, the United States, under the direction of the Federal Reserve System, embarked on a course of inflation from which no end is in sight. The war provided the opportunity to expand the personal income tax base to nearly the entire population and to raise the rates. And, at the conclusion of the war, the federal government stated its direct responsibility for guiding and controlling aggregate economic activity, and this was a momentous change.

SELECTED REFERENCES

Bernstein, Barton J. "The Removal of War Production Board Controls on Business, 1944–1946." *Business History Review* 39 (Summer 1965): 243–60.

__________. "The Debate on Industrial Reconversion: The Protection of Oligopoly and Military Control of the Economy." *The American Journal of Economics and Sociology* 26 (April 1967): 159–72.

Cain, Louis, and George Neumann. "Planning for Peace: The Surplus Property Act of 1944." *The Journal of Economic History* 41 (March 1981): 129–35.

Fearon, Peter. *War, Prosperity & Depression: The U.S. Economy, 1917–1945*. Lawrence, KS: University of Kansas Press, 1987.

Heath, Jim. "American War Mobilization and the Use of Small Manufacturers, 1939–1943." *Business History Review* 46 (Autumn 1972): 295–319.

Higgs, Robert. *Crisis and Leviathan: Critical Episodes in Growth of American Government.* New York: Oxford University Press, 1987.

__________. "Wartime Prosperity? A Reassessment of the U.S. Economy in the 1940s." *The Journal of Economic History* 52 (March 1992): 41–60.

Historical Statistics of the United States: Colonial Times to 1970. Washington, D.C.: U.S. Government Printing Office, 1976.

Hughes, Jonathan. *The Governmental Habit: Economic Controls from Colonial Times to the Present*. New York: Basic Books, 1977.

Keehn, Richard H., and Gene Smiley. "Small Business Reaction to World War II Government Controls." *Essays in Economic and Business History* 8 (1990): 303–16.

Kuznets, Simon. *National Product in Wartime*. New York: National Bureau of Economic Research, 1945.

__________. "Government Product and National Income." *Income and Wealth*. Edited by Erik Lundberg. Cambridge: Cambridge University Press, 1951.

__________. "Long-Term Changes in the National Income of the United States of America Since 1870." *Income and Wealth of the United States: Trends and Structure*, ed. by Simon Kuznets. Cambridge: Cambridge University Press, 1952.

Milward, Alan S. *War, Economy and Society, 1939–1945*. Berkeley: University of California Press, 1979.

Myers, Margaret G. *A Financial History of the United States*. New York: Columbia University Press, 1970.

Rae, John B. *The American Automobile Industry*. Boston: Twayne Publishers, 1984.

Rockoff, Hugh. *Drastic Measures: A History of Wage and Price Controls in the United States.* New York: Cambridge University Press, 1984.

Schlebecker, John T. *Whereby We Thrive: A History of American Farming, 1607–1972*. Ames, IA: The Iowa State University Press, 1975.

Skousen, Mark. "Saving the Depression: A New Look at World War II." *The Review of Austrian Economics* 2 (1988): 211–26.

Smiley, Gene. "Some Austrian Perspectives on Keynesian Fiscal Policy and the Recovery in the Thirties." *The Review of Austrian Economics* 1 (1987): 145–80.

Stein, Harold, ed. *Public Administration and Policy Development: A Case Book.* New York: Harcourt, Brace and Company, 1952.

Vatter, Harold G. *The U.S. Economy in World War II.* New York: Columbia University Press, 1985.

Vedder, Richard K., and Lowell Gallaway. "The Great Depression of 1946." *The Review of Austrian Economics* 5 (1991): 3–31.

NOTES

1. Most of the discussion in this chapter is drawn from Harold G. Vatter, *The U.S. Economy in World War II* (New York: Columbia University Press, 1985). Another source of information is Alan S. Milward, *War, Economy and Society, 1939–1945* (Berkeley: University of California Press, 1979).
2. See Kathryn Smul Arnow, "The Attack on the Cost of Living Index," in Harold Stein, ed., *Public Administration and Policy Development: A Case Book* (New York: Harcourt, Brace and Company, 1952).
3. Most of this section draws upon Vatter, *The U.S. Economy in the Second World War*, chapters 2 and 4. Also see Otis Graham, Jr., *Toward a Planned Society: From Roosevelt to Nixon* (New York: Oxford University Press, 1976); as cited in Jonathan Hughes, *American Economic History*, 3d ed. (Glenview, IL: Scott, Foresman and Company, 1987), 494.
4. Vatter, *The U.S. Economy in World War II*, 37, 39.
5. The War Labor Board incurred the wrath of labor by carrying out the provisions of the 1943 Smith-Connally Antistrike Act. But it also received bitter denunciations from business for violating the wage guidelines by allowing great increases in fringe benefits, directing that women receive equal wages for equal work, requiring the removal of intraplant inequities and implementation of uniform wage structures, and protecting several union interests. Vatter, *The U.S. Economy in the Second World War*, 79.
6. Ibid., 70–71.
7. Harry N. Scheiber, Harold G. Vatter, and Harold Underwood Faulkner, *American Economic History* (New York: Harper and Row, 1976), 408.
8. Ibid., p. 408; and, Vatter, *The U.S. Economy in the Second World War*, 23.

9. Alan S. Milward, *War, Economy and Society: 1939–1945*, 67.
10. One of the most serious cases of discrimination is still a controversial topic. In March 1942, 110,000 Japanese were harshly forced to leave their West Coast homes and businesses and "relocate" to ten internment camps. Most of those interned were *Nisei*, or American citizens. The relocation destroyed the agricultural base the Japanese had developed in truck farming, and one estimate suggests that they lost $200 million worth of property. The government later paid $38 million in recompense. In the late 1980s Congress voted to award $20,000 to each survivor of the relocation camps. However, citing the continuing federal deficits, Congress refused to appropriate the funds to make the payments, and no payments had been made by 1990. Alan S. Milward, *War, Economy and Society: 1939–1945*, 135. See also Dillon S. Meyer, *Uprooted Americans* (Tucson: University of Arizona Press, 1971), 248, 254–255; as cited in Vatter, *The U.S. Economy in the Second World War*, 135.
11. Scheiber, Vatter, and Faulkner, *American Economic History*, 412.
12. John L. Blackman, Jr., *Presidential Seizure in Labor Disputes* (Cambridge: Harvard University Press, 1967), 261–75; as cited in Vatter, *The U.S. Economy in the Second World War*, 124.
13. The two primary sources for most of the information in this section are Walter W. Wilcox, *The Farm in the Second World War* (Ames, IA: The Iowa State College Press, 1947); and, John T. Schlebecker, *Whereby We Thrive: A History of American Farming, 1607–1972* (Ames, IA: The Iowa State University Press, 1975). Information was also drawn from Vatter, *The U.S. Economy in the Second World War*, chapter 3; and Peter Fearon, *War, Prosperity & Depression: The U.S. Economy, 1917–1945* (Lawrence, KS: University of Kansas Press, 1987), chapter 16.
14. Milward, *War Economy and Society, 1939–1945*, 179.
15. Ibid., 173. Chapter 6 in general covers war and technology.
16. Most of the following discussion is drawn from an unpublished paper by Robert Higgs, "Private Profit, Public Risk: Institutional Antecedents of the Modern Military Procurement System in the Rearmament Program of 1940–1941."
17. One such critic was I. F. Stone, *Business As Usual: The First Year of Defense* (New York: Modern Age Books, 1941), 159, 163; as cited in Higgs, "Private Profit, Public Risk."
18. The Reconstruction Finance Corporation created a subsidiary called the Defense Plant Corporation which then financed the construction and leased the plants to corporate businesses. The problems in the development and approval of the Defense Plant Corporation are discussed in Clifford J. Durr, "The Defense Plant Corporation," in Stein, ed., *Public Administration and Policy Development.*
19. Calculated from table 3 in Higgs, "Private Profit, Public Risk." Higgs' source was Smaller War Plants Corporation, *Economic Concentration and the Second World War* (Washington: U.S. Government Printing Office, 1946), 38.
20. Scheiber, Vatter, Faulkner, *American Economic History*, 407–8.
21. Once small firms failed to land defense contracts, the priority allocations of resources then virtually assured that they would not be able to obtain them. Jim Heath, "American War Mobilization and the Use of Small Manufacturers, 1939–1943," *Business History Review* 46 (Autumn 1972): 295–319; and Vatter, *The U.S. Economy in the Second World War*, chapter 3.
22. This section primarily draws upon Margaret G. Myers, *A Financial History of the United States* (New York: Columbia University Press, 1970), chapter 15; and Vatter, *The U.S. Economy in the Second World War*, chapter 6.
23. Myers, *A Financial History of the United States*, 346.

24. This discussion is primarily based on Hugh Rockoff, *Drastic Measures: A History of Wage and Price Controls in the United States* (New York: Cambridge University Press, 1984). See also Vatter, *The U.S. Economy in World War II*, chapter 5.
25. Rockoff, *Drastic Measures*, 127–28.
26. Ibid., 132.
27. The OPA had issued tokens that could be used as change and could be stored and used to make purchases at a later date. By late 1944 surveys showed that consumers had built up a large stock of tokens. The OPA feared that a change in expectations or attitudes could lead consumers to run on stores and empty the shelves; i.e., "bankrupt" the rationing programs. The problem was that if used the tokens defeated the coupon rationing. If the tokens were invalidated they broke a promise to the consumers. Chester Bowles of the OPA decided to invalidate all token currency issued before recent dates to make certain that they could not be used.
28. In some cases local governments relaxed standards to allow milk sales that in other times would not have been allowed. The sale of heavy cream was prohibited so as to increase the supply of whole milk. The OPA granted reductions in butterfat content without reducing the price of milk, in effect granting price increases.
29. German submarine warfare prevented tankers from providing normal supplies. Ocean tanker firms, afraid of losing postwar markets, prevented the OPA from directing that more oil be moved by railroad tank car to the northeast.
30. Ibid., table 5.5, p. 145.
31. Ibid., 151.
32. Manufacturers often added cheap trim to low-priced lines to transform them into high-priced lines. At one point, to attempt to control this, the OPA issued dollar-and-cents ceilings at the wholesale and manufacturing levels for a variety of garments and specified the construction of the garments entitled to those prices in great detail—all the way down to the diameter of the buttons.
33. Richard H. Keehn and Gene Smiley, "Small Business Reaction to World War II Government Controls," *Essays in Economic and Business History*, 8 (1990): 303–16.
34. Rockoff, *Drastic Measures,* 154–58.
35. A substance called "Lubrigas" was added to regular gasoline, and the product was then sold as "premium" gasoline. Rockoff, *Drastic Measures*, 159.
36. Rockoff, *Drastic Measures*, 174–175.
37. Ibid., 176.
38. Ibid., 140.
39. Gene Smiley, "Some Austrian Perspectives on Keynesian Fiscal Policy and the Recovery in the Thirties," *The Review of Austrian Economics* 1 (1987): 167.
40. The increased demands in the capital goods sectors, where unionization had been concentrated, allowed for a more rapid recovery in those sectors that had experienced larger cost and price increases and in response had decreased output and employment more.
41. Mark Skousen, "Saving the Depression: A New Look at World War II," *The Review of Austrian Economics* 2 (1988): 211–26.
42. Robert Higgs, "Wartime Prosperity? A Reassessment of the U.S. Economy in the 1940s," *The Journal of Economic History* 52 (March 1992): 49–53.
43. Ibid., 43.
44. Calculated from the *Historical Statistics of the United States: Colonial Times to 1970* (Washington, D.C.: U.S. Government Printing Office, 1976).
45. Higgs, "Wartime Prosperity?," 45–46. See note 13 on p. 46.

46. Simon Kuznets, "Long-Term Changes in the National Income of the United States of America Since 1870," in Simon Kuznets, ed., *Income & Wealth of the United States: Trends and Structure* (Cambridge: Cambridge University Press, 1952), 39–40, as cited in Higgs, "Wartime Prosperity?" 46.
47. Kuznets's justification was that "even though military durables and construction are used for military purposes, they represent capital that could be employed for nonmilitary purposes—a justification that seems far-fetched with regard to many forms of military capital." Higgs, "Wartime Prosperity?" 46.
48. Ibid., 58.
49. Vatter, *The U.S. Economy in World War II*, 85.
50. Ibid., 62–63.
51. Barton J. Bernstein, "The Debate on Industrial Reconversion: The Protection of Oligopoly and Military Control of the Economy," *The American Journal of Economics and Sociology* 26 (April 1967): 159–72.
52. This discussion draws upon Barton J. Bernstein, "The Removal of War Production Board Controls on Business, 1944–1946," *Business History Review* 39 (Summer 1965): 243–60. See also Vatter, *The U.S. Economy in World War II*, 83–88.
53. The following is based upon Louis Cain and George Neumann, "Planning for Peace: The Surplus Property Act of 1944," *The Journal of Economic History* 41 (March 1981): 129–35; and, Harold Stein, "The Disposal of the Aluminum Plants," in Stein, ed., *Public Administration and Policy Development*.
54. Ibid., 132.
55. Stein, "The Disposal of the Aluminum Plants."
56. This information is drawn from John B. Rae, *The American Automobile Industry* (Boston: Twayne Publishers, 1984), chapter 9.
57. Vatter, *The U.S. Economy in World War II*, 136.
58. As cited in Vatter; see Keith W. Olson, *The G.I. Bill, the Veterans, and the Colleges* (Lexington, KY: University of Kentucky Press, 1974); and Davis R. B. Ross, *Preparing for Ulysses* (New York: Columbia University Press, 1969).
59. Olson, *The G.I. Bill*, table 1, p. 44; as cited in Vatter, *The U.S. Economy in World War II*, 137.
60. Vatter, *The U.S. Economy in World War II*, 150, and Cain and Neumann, "Planning for Peace," 130.
61. Richard Gardner, *Sterling-Dollar Diplomacy* (New York: Oxford University Press, 1956), as cited in Hughes, *American Economic History*, p. 505. See also Milward, *War, Economy and Society*, 337–45.
62. Jonathan R. T. Hughes, *The Governmental Habit: Economic Controls from Colonial Times to the Present* (New York: Basic Books, 1977), 148 and 197–98.
63. Robert Higgs, *Crisis and Leviathan: Critical Episodes in the Growth of Government* (New York: Oxford University Press, 1987).
64. Most of this discussion of the international economy and the Bretton Woods agreements draws upon Milward, *War, Economy and Society*, chapter 10; and, Vatter, *The U.S. Economy in World War II*, chapter 8.
65. The discussion of the Marshall Plan is based upon the following studies: Richard Mayne, *The Recovery of Europe* (New York: Harper and Row, 1970); Harry B. Price, *The Marshall Plan and Its Meaning* (New York: Cornell University Press, 1955); and Immanuel Wexler, *The Marshall Plan Revisited* (Westport, CT: Greenwood Press, 1983). The quotation is from Price, *The Marshall Plan and Its Meaning*, 25.

66. The Soviet Union denounced this and pulled out of the conference, and no other communist country joined the conferences.
67. This discussion draws upon Richard Vedder and Lowell Gallaway, "The Great Depression of 1946," *The Review of Austrian Economics* 5 (1991): 3–31.
68. Ibid., 11–13.
69. Ibid., 20–21.
70. Ibid., 25.
71. Ibid., 28.

CHAPTER 9

American Economic Growth and Development, Population Changes, and Labor Force Developments, 1950 to the Present

POSTWAR ECONOMIC GROWTH

In the immediate post-Second World War era, many economists were confident that the tools to eliminate the business cycle and ensure a more rapid rate of real economic growth had been found. Though the dramatic boom and bust of the twenties and thirties did not reappear, Americans soon discovered that government monetary and fiscal policies were not effective in stopping economic contractions and were unable to accelerate or raise the rate of real economic growth.

For the entire 40-year period since 1950, real GNP has grown at the rate of 3.1 percent per year, while real GNP per capita, a better measure of growth in average income and welfare, grew 1.83 percent per year. (See Figure 9.1.) The average over the 40-year period hides considerable variation in this growth. When calculated over decades, the 1950s show the slowest rate of growth of real GNP per capita, while the 1960s show the most rapid rate, however, the lowest average annual unemployment rate was during the 1950s, not the 1960s. The rate of inflation was also considerably lower in the 1950s than in other decades. (See Figures 9.2 and 9.3.)

The higher rate of economic growth in the 1960s led to expectations that the federal government would be able to manage the economy well enough to maintain higher

Fig. 9.1 Real GNP and Real GNP Per Capita

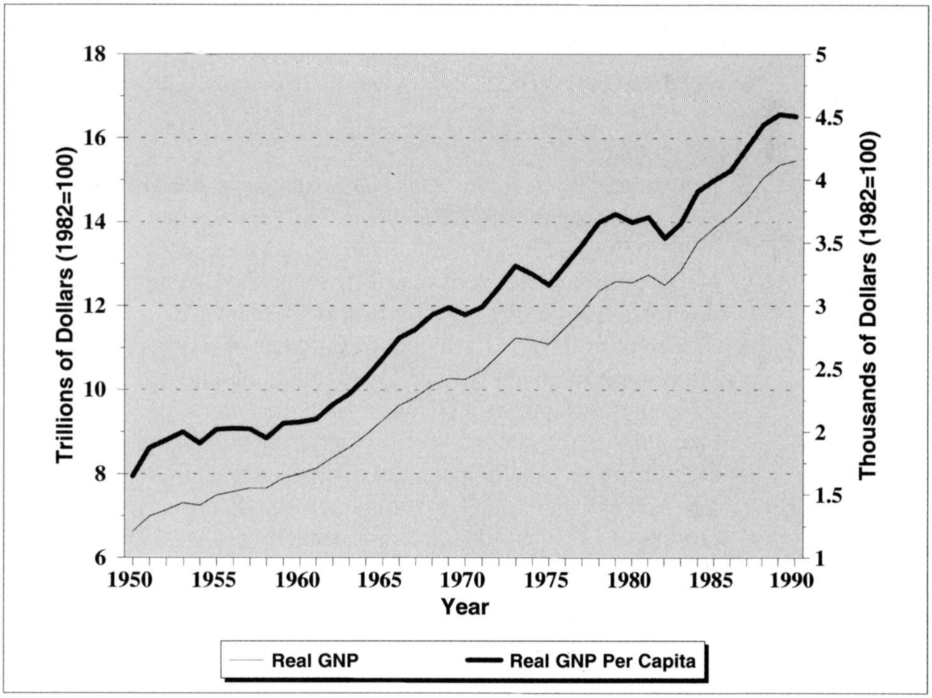

Source: *Economic Report of the President* (Washington, D.C.: U.S. Government Printing Office, 1991).

Fig. 9.2 The Rate of Unemployment

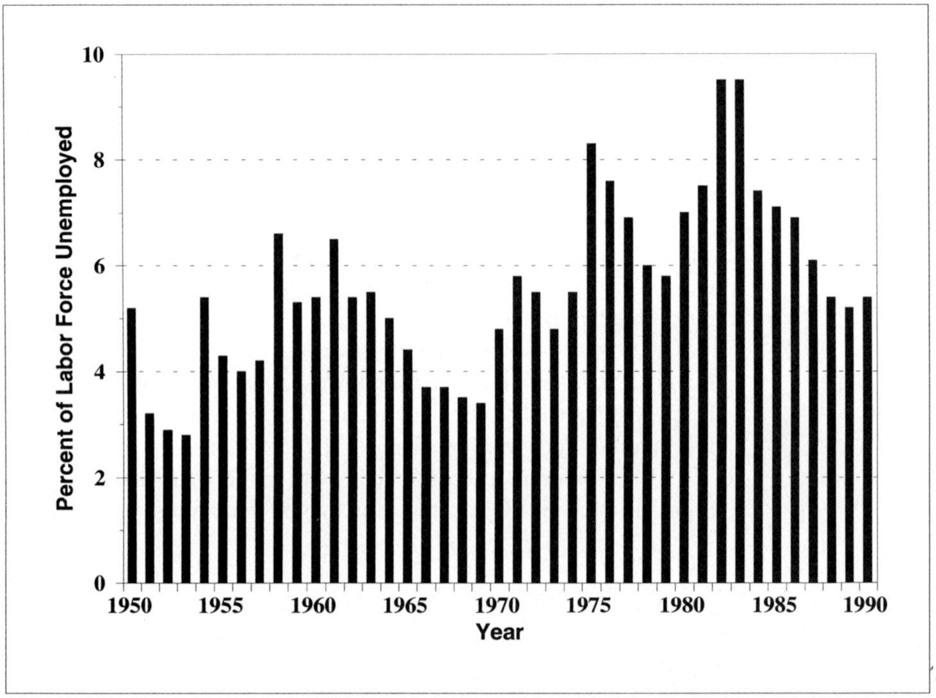

Source: Source: *Economic Report of the President* (Washington, D.C.: U.S. Government Printing Office, 1991).

growth rates in the future. This was not the case, because the rate of growth of real GNP per capita dropped after the 1960s, while the average annual unemployment rate rose in the 1970s and in the 1980s. The rate of inflation rose slightly in the 1960s compared to the 1950s and then rose sharply in the 1970s. Though declining in the 1980s, the rate of inflation was still high by historical standards. In fact, in the years prior to the Second World War, excluding years when the United States was engaged in a war, prices were more likely to be found falling in any year than rising.

Another significant change was in the federal government's budget deficit or surplus. Prior to the Second World War during nondepressed peacetime periods the federal government usually had a surplus, which was used to reduce the federal debt. In the post-war era the federal government ran a deficit in almost every year and, as a percentage of GNP, this deficit was much larger in the 1970s and 1980s. (See Figure 9.4.)

AN OVERVIEW OF THE 1950–1990 PERIOD

By 1950 most of the excess demands for durable consumer goods which had been unavailable during the Second World War had been satisfied. The Korean War began

Fig. 9.3 Annual Rates of Change for the Consumer Price Index and the M2 Stock of Money

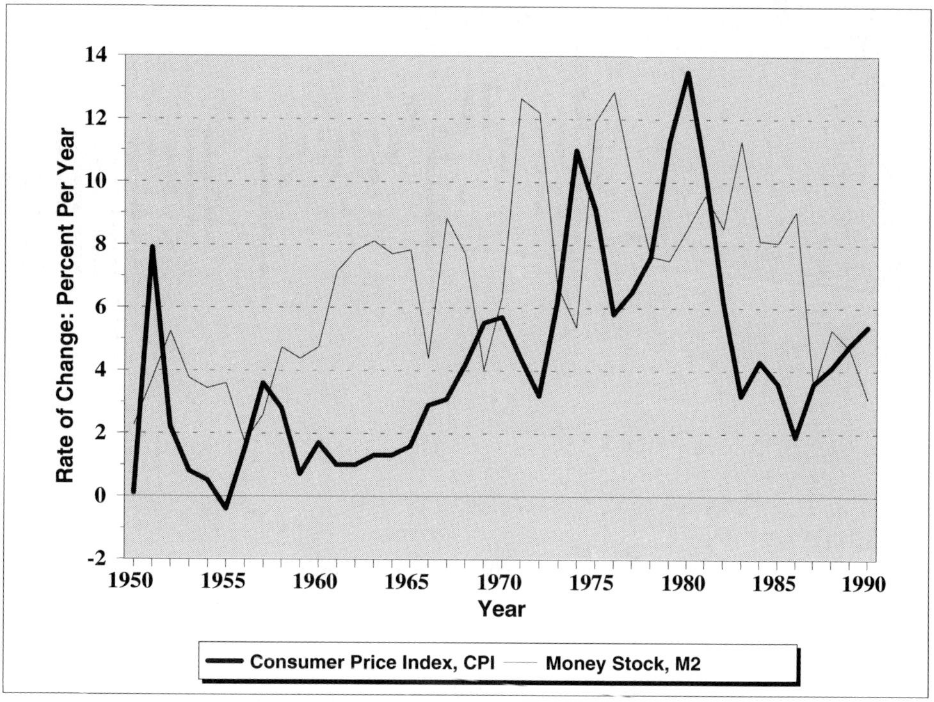

Source: *Economic Report of the President* (Washington, D.C.: U.S. Government Printing Office, 1991).

in June 1950. Though some price controls were imposed, they had little effect.[1] Following the Korean War, the tendency for prices to rise at what were historically high rates of price inflation was quite unsettling. In addition, the unemployment rate kept inching higher after the recessions of 1949, 1954, and 1958. Combined with the decline in economic growth toward the end of the 1950s, this made the economy a prime target of political controversy.

The postwar baby boom was reaching its height at the end of the 1950s, setting off a wave of investment in educational facilities that would roll on through the colleges in the 1970s. A growing array of household durable goods and convenience foods provided opportunities for more and more women to enter the labor force at the same time that growing incomes led to greater growth in the demands for services. Technological change reduced farm population at an increasing rate, while the price-support programs spawned by the New Deal led to a crisis in the growing surpluses of agricultural commodities. The militarization of the economy to fight the communist threat led to peacetime conscription, a growing military budget, and increased production of military hardware. At the end of his term as President in 1960, Dwight D. Eisenhower warned of the threat that was inherent in the growing "military-industrial complex," thus introducing a new term into the American vocabulary.

Fig. 9.4 The Federal Surplus or Deficit as a Percent of GNP

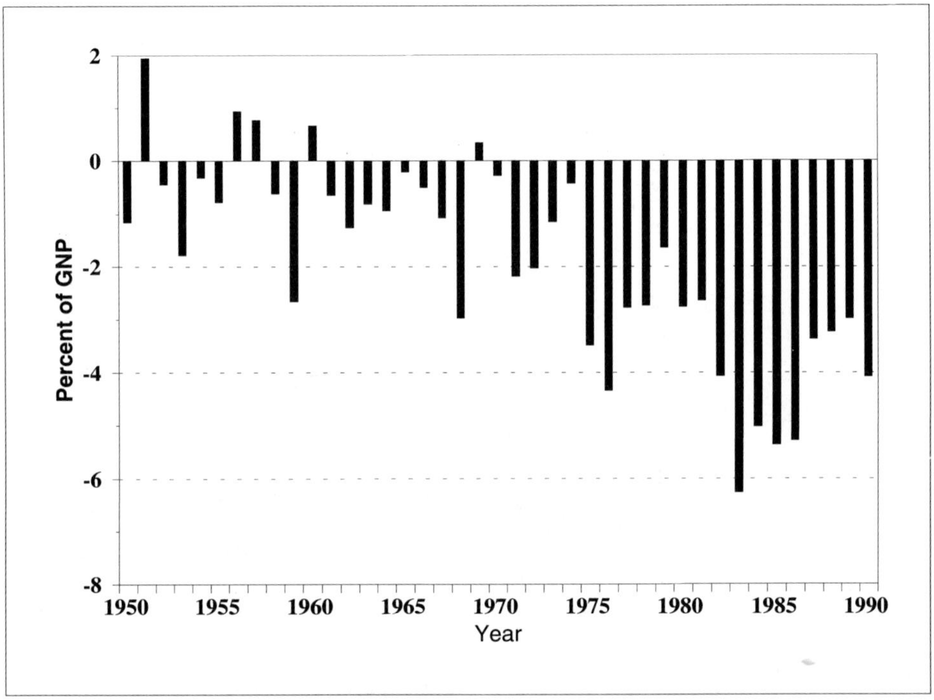

Source: *Economic Report of the President* (Washington, D.C.: U.S. Government Printing Office, 1991).

The 1960s

The controversial presidential campaign of 1960 gave John F. Kennedy a narrow victory and ushered a more activist federal government. One of the ideas of the time was that "cost-push" inflation was the result of large firms with monopoly power setting higher prices as powerful unions demanded higher wages, thus requiring federal government intervention. Kennedy had a direct confrontation with Roger Blough of U.S. Steel in April, 1961, as he attempted to stop the large integrated steel producers from raising prices on basic steel products. A sharp break in stock market prices at the time was often blamed on Kennedy's face-off with the steel industry.

Kennedy administration economists, particularly Walter Heller, also pushed for the first explicit use of Keynesian fiscal policy. Arguing that the economy was growing slower than it should, Kennedy proposed that tax rates be reduced to stimulate economic activity even though the federal government was already running a deficit. Kennedy's assassination thrust Lyndon Baines Johnson into the presidency, and he finished getting Kennedy's tax cut passed, dropping marginal personal income tax rates. These tax rate reductions were intended to increase the long-run rate of economic growth rather than counteract a short-run cyclical fluctuation in economic activity. At the same time that the tax rate cuts took effect, the Federal Reserve System began to expand the stock of money at a faster rate. These two policy actions were given credit for spurring a reduction in the rate of unemployment and an acceleration in the rate of real economic growth and helped spur the "go-go" stock market that developed in the 1960s. they also accelerated a minor merger wave that had started in the mid-1950s.

Johnson's presidency was complicated by the rising costs of military involvement in South Viewnam after congress passed the Gulf of Tonkin resolution in 1964, and by his "War on Poverty" that led to new government programs and consequently increases in government spending. Because of the inflation and economic growth, tax revenues did grow, but not sufficiently to cover the increasing spending. A 1968 income tax surcharge was supposed to "cool down" the "overheated" economy, though it had little initial effect.

The 1970s

In 1968 President Johnson, seeing growing dissatisfaction with his pursuit of the war in Vietnam, chose not to run for reelection. Richard M. Nixon defeated Hubert Humphrey in the election and within three years pulled most of the U.S. forces out of Vietnam. Though espousing the traditional Republican commitment to free markets, on August 15, 1971, Nixon, in a surprise move, imposed peacetime price controls on the American economy. In various phases parts of these price controls lasted into 1974. At the same time he devalued the dollar and limited the convertibility of dollars to gold to foreign central banks. In February of 1973, the United States officially abandoned the fixed exchange rate gold standard and went to a floating exchange rate against other currencies.

These events were the ominous introduction to the economic dislocations of the 1970s. The next major disruption came in agriculture. A combination of factors led to an explosion of meat and grain prices in late 1972 and early 1973. Though the meat price increases slowed down, so did the supply of beef. Consumers began organizing beef and supermarket boycotts, blaming, as usual, the "middlemen," that is, the packing houses and supermarkets, for the rise in prices. Beef virtually disappeared from supermarket shelves for some weeks.

The federal government's price controls continued during 1973. In the fall of 1973, a new Israeli-Arab war broke out. The Arab members of the Organization of Petroleum Exporting Countries (OPEC) decided to impose an embargo on petroleum shipped and sold to the United States and other major allies of Israel to bring pressure on Israel, and also began raising crude oil prices. Within a year crude petroleum prices had quadrupled, initiating a series of sharp price increases for gasoline and other petroleum products. When the price controls were combined with the government's attempt to allocate gasoline supplies among regions, the result was periodic shortages of gasoline through the winter of 1973–74.

Real crude petroleum prices began to fall by 1976 as consumers in the United States and around the world continued to adjust their consumption of crude oil derivatives. In the United States the dependence on imported crude petroleum rose as price controls reduced the production and exploration for domestic crude oil. In 1979 the outbreak of the Iraq-Iran war again reduced the production and shipment of crude petroleum. Gasoline prices in the United States rose sharply, and price controls and federal government distribution of gasoline again created spot shortages.

The rising real prices of gasoline reduced the demand for larger automobiles, which the Big Three American producers primarily supplied, and increased the demand for smaller cars. The Japanese producers were better situated to respond to this, and sales of imported cars rose sharply after 1975 and again after 1979. The domestic firms' profits were severely reduced, and Chrysler Corporation came perilously close to declaring bankruptcy.

The disruptions ushered in with the explosion of petroleum prices in 1973–74 brought on a recession. Aided by the Federal Reserve System's increase in the stock of money of 24.8 percent between 1974 and 1976, consumer prices rose 11 percent from 1974 to 1975 and 9.1 percent from 1975 to 1976. The Fed continued with a rapid growth of the stock of money for the next several years and this, combined with a rising income velocity of money, led to an acceleration in the rate of inflation. Consumer prices rose 13.5 percent from 1979 to 1980. In the fall of 1979, the Fed announced to the world that monetary policy was being changed and henceforth would be based largely on controlling the growth of the stock of money. Once the Fed stopped trying to control interest rates, rates rose sharply and during 1980 financial institutions struggled through one of the worst bond market crashes in history.

There was a growing reaction against some of the older economic regulation beginning in the mid-1970s, and the Ford administration began several studies to consider the impacts of regulation and deregulation. It was commonly charged by economists that economic regulation often acted to protect the regulated firms against the interests of the consuming public. When Jimmy Carter defeated Gerald Ford for the presidency in 1976, his administration initiated deregulation in interstate airlines, trucking, and communications.

The 1980s

Ronald Reagan was elected president on a "supply-side" platform of cutting taxes and reducing spending. Some supply-side economists argued that a sharp cut in tax rates could so increase incentives to produce that the resulting rise in economic activity could actually generate as much or more tax revenue on much lower tax rates. One of Reagan's first acts was to end all price controls on crude petroleum production and end the federal government's allocation of the differentially priced imported and domestic crude petroleum among American refiners. He then asked Congress to approve a sharp cut in income tax rates. Though expenditures were supposed to be reduced, there was merely a minor reduction in some social expenditures and increases in military expenditures so that federal expenditures actually increased, creating much larger federal budget deficits.

A combination of enormous increases in interest rates and a falling rate of inflation brought on the severe recession of 1981–82. The economic recovery that began in December of 1982 combined with lower inflation rates and higher real rates of interest to create an increasing foreign demand for American securities. The strengthening of the dollar decreased American exports and increased foreign imports into the United States to generate the dollars to invest in American financial and real assets.

One of the sectors hit by falling foreign demand due to the stronger dollar was the farm sector. Rising costs and falling revenues forced many farmers into bankruptcy, and many small-town banks failed along with the farmers. The agricultural depression pulled down many other farm-related businesses. By early 1988 most of the adjustments had been made, and the recovery in the farm sector had begun.

In real terms, stock prices had fallen throughout most of the 1970s. Spurred by the tax cuts of 1982 and 1986, the stock market boomed in a manner comparable to the 1920s. In August of 1987, stock prices peaked and began an uneven decline, and on Monday, October 19, 1987, the stock market crashed. The Dow-Jones Index fell 508 points for the greatest one-day loss (in both nominal and real terms) in the history of the New York Stock Exchange. Prompt action by the Federal Reserve System apparently stopped a further panic-stricken decline, and within a few months stock prices slowly began to recover, though it took nearly two years to reach the precrash levels. Unlike 1929, the 1987 crash was not associated with an economic depression. As in the past the bull market was accompanied by a merger wave, many of which were engineered using higher default risk "junk bonds," which were often purchased by financial institutions.

And financial institutions had their own difficulties in the 1980s. Bank and thrift failures reached alarming levels, and the first depositor runs since the early 1930s occurred. Caught between inflation, rising interest rates, regulated ceilings on deposit rates, and many older, long-term, low-interest rate mortgage loans, the thrifts began to suffer losses and created new types of higher rate deposit instruments to counter the exodus of funds. Banks began to drop national charters for state charters and to leave the Federal Reserve System to lower costs and improve profits. The Fed argued that this weakened its ability to conduct monetary policy.

In 1980 Congress passed the Depository Deregulation and Monetary Control Act, which brought all banks and thrifts under Fed control and gradually removed all regulations on deposit rates. Thrifts were allowed to purchase other types of assets, and the distinction between commercial banks and thrifts largely disappeared. By the late 1980s, a depression in the oil-producing states and falling real estate values had produced a crisis in the thrift industry. Thrifts as a whole suffered losses, and hundreds were closed down by the regulators. Congress had to bail out the deposit insurance fund which had been exhausted in covering the losses in the banking and thrift industry.

In the following chapters we will examine in more detail these themes and events, such as monetary and fiscal policies, deregulation, the gasoline crises, the agricultural depression, and the financial sector's gyrations. Now, however, we need to survey postwar changes in the American population and labor force.

THE POSTWAR AMERICAN POPULATION

From 1930 through 1945, Americans delayed marriage and had smaller families. As a result the birth rate and the growth of the native population plummeted. As Richard A. Easterlin has noted, "Before World War II it was confidently assumed that American population growth was grinding to a halt."[2] With the end of the war, the prosperity led Americans to begin having larger families, thus setting off a population boom. Writing in 1960, Bert G. Hickman argued that this quite possibly was "the most unexpected and remarkable feature" of the era.[3] Population growth accelerated in the late 1940s and reached a one-year peak in 1950 of 2.05 percent. Population growth declined sharply during the 1960s. Since 1970 the rate of population growth has averaged about 1.0 percent per year.

The population growth sent a wave of children into the school systems, leading to construction programs and the hiring of many more teachers. As the population growth subsided, school enrollments began falling, buildings were closed and sold, and teachers were released. Firms producing products for infants found a demand that grew raidly in the 1950s and 1960s and fell just as rapidly in the 1970s.The great rise and fall of population growth brought dramatic shifts in the age distribution of the population. The rising share of the 65-and-over age group has been termed the "graying of the population." When the Social Security System was set up in the late 1930s, there were about six to seven Americans working for every retired American. By the 1980s there were about three persons working for every person drawing Social Security payments, a ratio projected to fall as low as two to one around the turn of the century. Because of its pay-as-you-go nature, this required increases in Social Security tax rates and the level of income subject to Social Security taxes. The graying of the population led to a much more rapidly rising demand for medical services than would have been predicted just by the rate of total population growth, and this was one of the factors leading to the "inflation" in health care costs of the period.

Mortality

The graying of the population is due to falling death rates as well as falling birth rates. Figure 9.5 presents the components of population change expressed in rates per thousand people. From the late 1940s through the beginning of the 1970s, the crude death rate remained relatively constant, declined in the early 1970s, and since 1975 has been relatively stable, resulting in longer life expectancies. An age-adjusted mortality rate reported by Richard Easterlin is free of distortions caused by age shifts in the population and is, therefore, a better measure of mortality improvements.[4] From the mid-1930s through about 1954, there was a downward trend in age-adjusted mortality, which Easterlin suggests was largely "due to the diffusion of a succession of newly

Fig. 9.5 Percentage Population Shares by Age Groups

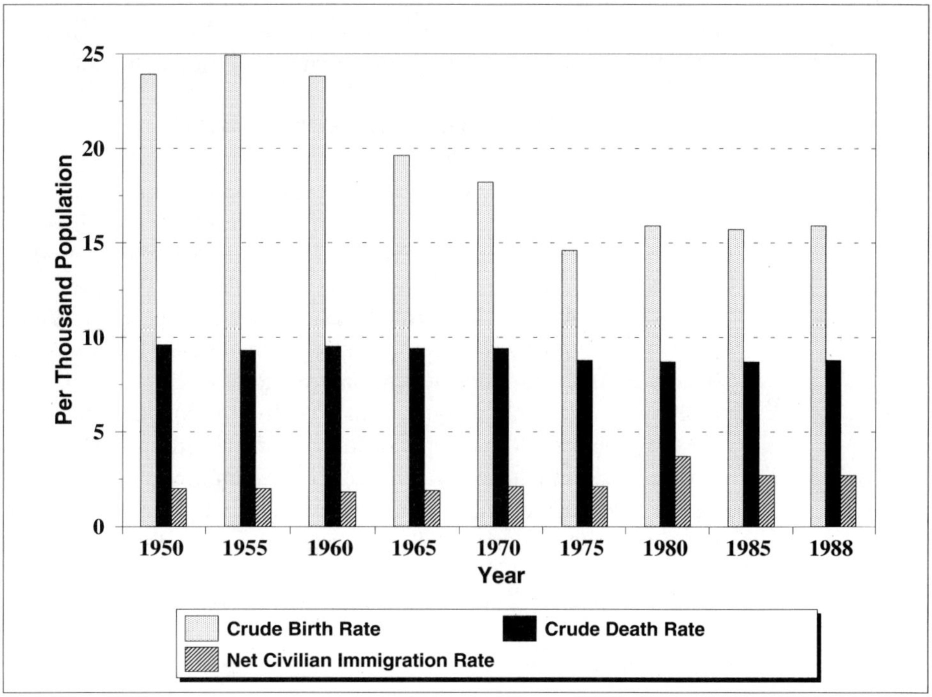

Source: *Economic Report of the President* (Washington, D.C.: U.S. Government Printing Office, 1991).

discovered antibiotic 'wonder drugs,' first introduced in the 1930s."[5] From 1954 through 1968, the age-adjusted mortality rate stopped declining, and it was widely thought that no further decreases could be expected. However, after 1968 mortality again began declining at a faster rate than in the 1930-to-1954 period.

Easterlin suggests that the post 1968-decline in mortality appears to be related to declines in cardiovascular diseases, particularly among the older population, and to a lesser extent to declines in mortality from infectious diseases. The reduction in cardiovascular diseases seems to be related both to identification and treatment of higher risk cases and to lifestyle changes such as the "reduction of smoking, improved diet, and greater exercise."[6]

Fertility

Though the crude birth rate shows a striking decline from 1965 through 1975, a better measure is the total fertility rate. This rate indicates the number of births that 1,000 women would have during their lifetimes. A total fertility rate of 2,110 represents the rate necessary to replace the population, given the current mortality rate and assuming no net immigration to the United States. Since the early 1970s the fertility rate has remained well below the replacement rate. In the 1980s, if the total fertility rate and mortality rates were to continue, the American population would eventually begin declining by about 0.5 percent per year (assuming no net immigration).

Causes of the Baby Boom and Bust

Richard Easterlin has surveyed the proposed causes of the postwar baby boom and bust. One explanation centers on advances in birth control technology in the 1960s.[7] However, Easterlin argues against such explanations because the 1930s show that Americans could effectively use other methods of birth control when they desired to do so.[8] Another explanation, which Easterlin terms the "New Woman" hypothesis, proposes "that a drastic shift has occurred in an antinatal, prowork direction."[9] As women have become better educated and more career oriented, work outside of the home has replaced work in the home, and a side consequence has been falling fertility.[10] Easterlin points out that some of these premises are incorrect because women actually enjoyed a slight education advantage over men in the 1950s and 1960s, whereas in the last two decades men have enjoyed a slight educational advantage, and surveys have not shown any fundamental shift in attitudes.[11] A third explanation proposes that an increasing demand for female labor has led to a decline in women's fertility.[12] However, Easterlin argues that into the 1980s the growth in the demand for female labor was largely "dependent on the growth of a limited number of occupations in the professional, clerical, sales, and service fields," and these did not grow more rapidly after 1960 than before.

A fourth explanation is one which Easterlin has developed; he calls it the "relative income hypothesis." A couple judges their prospects for achieving a desired lifestyle by the ratio between their potential earning power and their material aspirations. Either exceptionally high expectations of earnings or relatively lower material aspirations can lead to reduced pressures on a young woman to work outside of the home during childbearing and childrearing years. Easterlin argues that the experience of the first few years in the labor market in terms of the ease of acquiring a job, wages, and advancement is probably most important in determining the earnings outlook. Material aspirations are probably primarily determined by the family of origin. Easterlin says, "The expectations of young adults about how they ought to live are largely the unconscious product of the material environment that they experienced during their upbringing."[13] And, of course, this environment is largely determined by the income of the family of origin. Easterlin's empirical examination of the relative income hypothesis suggests it is a plausible explanation of the postwar baby boom and bust.

Immigration

Immigration has continued to be a less important force in population growth, though the origination of immigrants has changed. In the aftermath of the Vietnam war, immigration from Southeast Asia grew markedly. The other primary source of immigration has been Mexico, the Caribbean countries, and Central America. In fact, it was generally argued that the official statistics seriously undercounted the legal and illegal immigrants from Mexico and Central America. Easterlin estimates that in the 1970s, if illegal immigration had been properly counted, immigration might have accounted for one third of American population growth, compared to one tenth in the 1950s.[14] Illegal immigration has been a prominent concern because it is widely believed that illegal immigrants represent a drain on the American taxpayers through welfare, health, and other benefits. However, as Easterlin notes, and according to other studies, "Illegal aliens are more likely to pay taxes than they are to receive the benefits of government-sponsored facilities and services."[15]

THE POSTWAR AMERICAN LABOR FORCE

Because of rising rates of participation in the civilian labor force, it has grown faster than the population. The most common measuring method is to calculate participation rates based on the relevant civilian population potentially in the labor force. These ratios are shown in Figure 9.6. The total participation rate rose sharply between 1950 and 1990. This was composed of two offsetting trends. Male participation in the labor force fell, while female participation rates rose dramatically.

Most of the decline in the overall male labor force participation rate is explained by a fall in the participation rates for the 55–64 and 65-and-over age groups, though there were declines for all age groups.[16] Several factors are responsible for this, the most important of which is expanded Social Security coverage.[17] Other determinants include the spread of private pension plans, changes in laws regarding the vesting of pensions, and strong incentives to retire including mandatory retirement.

For females, participation rates for all age groups rose except the over-65 group. The largest increases in female labor force participation rates are in the 25-to-44-year-old groups, the prime child-rearing years. One element that helps to explain this is the change in household technology, which has reduced the time necessary to devote to household chores. The growth in the provision of child care services also increasingly allowed women to move into the labor force and to leave it for shorter periods after bearing children. Finally, during this period there was a clear change in social attitudes as it became "more socially acceptable for women to devote themselves to careers as opposed to marriage and family,"[18] though it is not clear which causes which.

Occupations

Just as participation in the labor force was changing, so was the occupational status of American workers. Agricultural employment declined steadily from 1950 through 1970. White-collar employment has risen sharply, while blue-collar and farm-related employment has fallen. Within the category of white-collar employment, most of the gains have been in clerical, professional, and technical workers. Within blue-collar employment, the decline has been concentrated in operatives. Paralleling this the share

Fig. 9.6 Civilian Labor Force Participation Rates

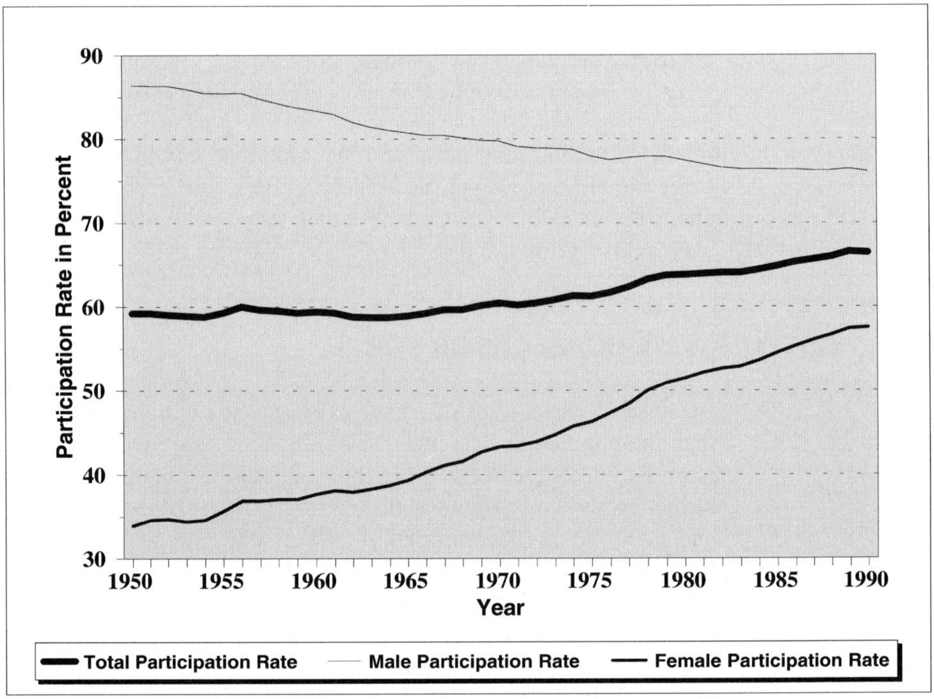

Source: *Economic Report of the President* (Washington, D.C.: U.S. Government Printing Office, 1991).

of employment in manufacturing, transportation, and public utilities have fallen sharply, whereas employment in retail trade and services have grown the most.

Unemployment

Figures 9.7 through 9.10 summarize the unemployment experience of American workers since 1950. The aggregate unemployment rates released at frequent intervals hide great variations in unemployment rates for different groups. For example, from the early 1960 to the early 1980s, female unemployment rates were generally higher than male unemployment rates but since then have been essentially the same. Unemployment rates for teenages, nonwhites, and women who maintain families have also been much higher. The unemployment rates for nonwhites have generally been much higher. Experienced wage and salary workers have generally had unemployment rates around the national average, while married men, whose spouses are present, have had unemployment rates well below the national average.

The unemployment rate depends upon two characteristics: the frequency with which individuals become unemployed and the average length of time that individuals are unemployed. As can be seen when the unemployment rate has increased, the length

Fig. 9.7 Civilian Unemployment Rates for Male and Female Workers

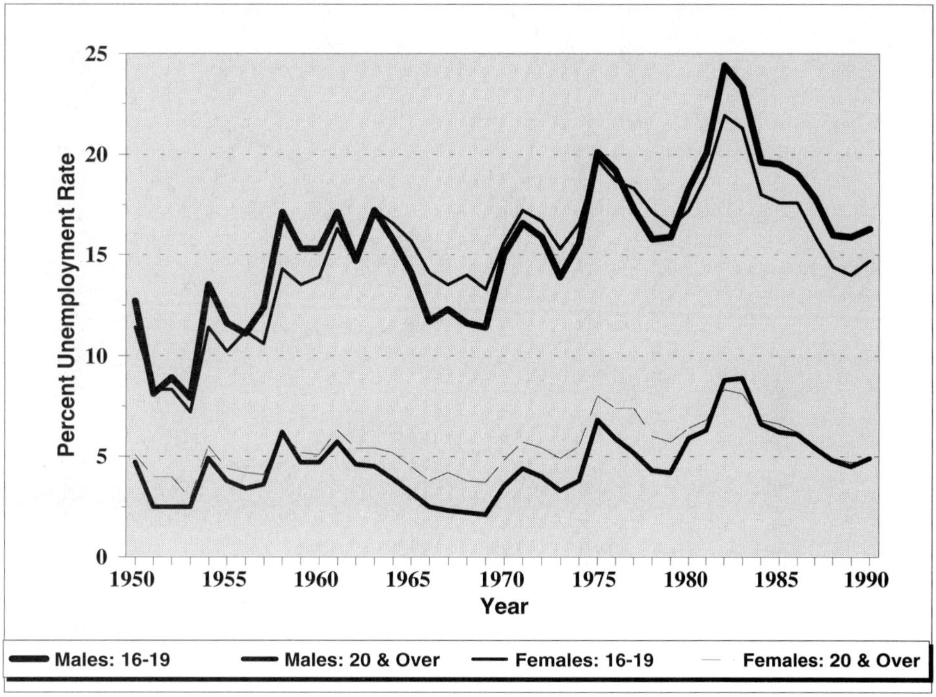

Source: *Economic Report of the President* (Washington, D.C.: U.S. Government Printing Office, 1991).

of time that unemployed individuals search for a job also increased sharply. The two most severe recessions since the Second World War were in 1974–75 and 1981–82. In the 1974–75 recession the percent unemployed for less than 5 weeks declined from 51.0 to 37.1 percent, and those unemployed for 27 weeks or more rose from 7.9 to 18.2 percent. The average duration of unemployment rose from 10 weeks to 15.8. Similar—but more pronounced—types of changes occurred in 1981–82.

There are four reasons why a person becomes unemployed—losing a job, leaving a job voluntarily, entering the labor force for the first time, or reentering the labor force. Contrary to common perception, job losers are generally less than half of the individuals unemployed at any time, with reentrants to the labor force making up the next largest group. When recessions occur, the proportion of those unemployed who have lost their jobs rises, and the proportion who leave their jobs falls, as can be seen in the recessions in 1974–75 and 1981–82.

Productivity and Wages

Richard B. Freeman has said, "Perhaps the most disturbing post-World War II trend in the American labor market has been the notable retardation in the growth of real wages

Fig. 9.8 Percentage of the Unemployed for Selected Periods

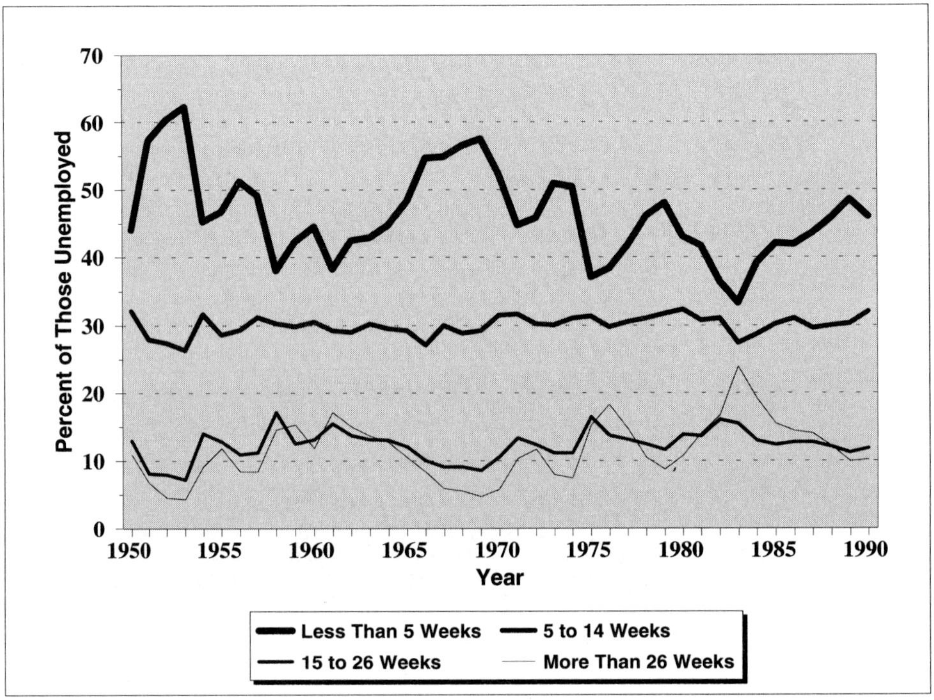

Source: *Economic Report of the President* (Washington, D.C.: U.S. Government Printing Office, 1991).

and output per labor hour that began in the late 1960s."[19] It is productivity growth, or the growth in the output per labor hour, that propels the growth in real wages and earnings. Writing in 1980, Freeman found that labor productivity growth had averaged 3.30 percent a year from 1947 to 1966 and only 1.83 percent a year from 1966 to 1978. Figure 9.11 presents the real average hourly wage for all private nonagricultural industries from 1950 through 1990. Real hourly earnings increased from less than $5.50 an hour in 1950 to $8.55 in 1973 but have since declined to $7.54, about the same as in 1965. Real average weekly earnings show a similar pattern. The greater decline in weekly earnings than hourly earnings represents the effect of the falling workweek.

The sources of the decline in productivity growth have been very hard to locate. A small share of the decline in the overall industry productivity growth is due to sectoral shifts in the economy, such as out of agriculture and into services. Freeman reports that about 22 percent of the slowdown in productivity growth in the 1970s can be attributed to sectoral shifts. However, because productivity declines have occurred in most sectors, sectoral shifts cannot be a major factor.[20] The sluggish growth of the national economy is also not the explanation, because the slow productivity growth explains the slow growth in national economy. Other factors in the productivity slowdown include

Fig. 9.9 Duration of Unemployment

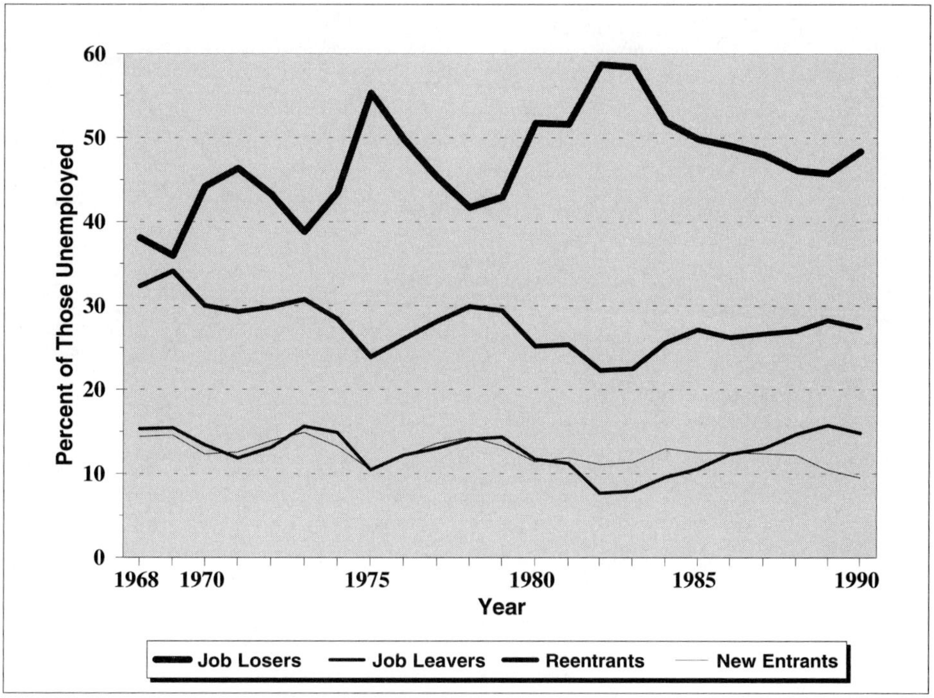

Source: *Economic Report of the President* (Washington, D.C.: U.S. Government Printing Office, 1991).

the reduction in hours worked and the changing age-sex composition of the labor force. These are balanced by the increasing education of the labor force. Growing governmental regulations are generally agreed to have reduced measured productivity, but it has been difficult to develop measures of this effect. As has generally been the case, most of the changes in productivity are attributed to advances in knowledge and other miscellaneous determinants, a catch-all category for those factors that we cannot specify.

As indicated above, the reason for the concern with productivity growth is that this is the primary determinant of growth in real wage rates and earnings. These figures are, however, somewhat misleading. Figure 9.11 presents the gross dollar earnings received by the workers and excludes all fringe benefits such as medical and dental insurance, employer contributions to unemployment insurance and social security, and employer contributions to private retirement plans. We know that the tax exempt status of health insurance and employer contributions to private retirement plans has led to the more rapid growth of this type of compensation in the 1970s and 1980s. Thus the figures understate the growth in earnings in the 1970s and overstate the decline in the 1980s. How much error is involved is not known. There also are flaws in the consumer price indexes, which have created an inflationary bias leading to an understatement of real earnings gains.[21]

Fig. 9.10 Reasons for Unemployment

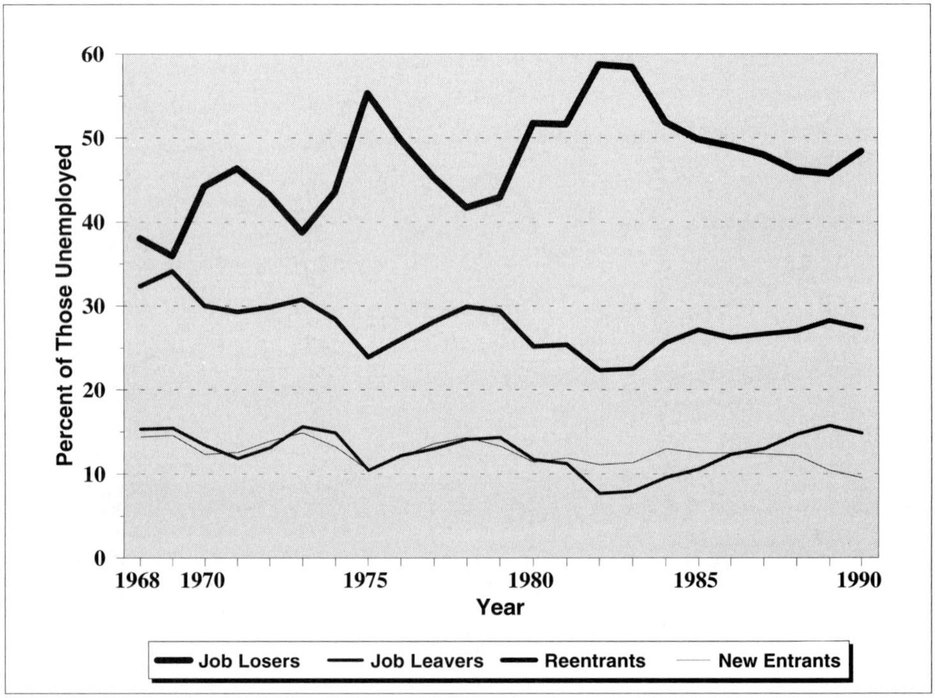

Source: *Economic Report of the President* (Washington, D.C.: U.S. Government Printing Office, 1991).

Robert J. Myers, who was the chief actuary of the Social Security Administration from 1947 until 1970, argues that the wage-indexing series developed by the Social Security Administration (SSA) is superior to the Bureau of Labor Statistics' (BLS) series in chronicling wage movements.[22] The SSA series is somewhat lower than the BLS series in the 1950s and 1960s, quite similar during the 1970s, but diverges after 1979. The SSA's real earnings are 2.4 percent higher than the BLS's in 1980 and 17.6 percent higher than the BLS real earnings in 1989. According to the SSA series, real wages in 1989 exceeded the 1972 real earnings by 3.4 percent. Myers argues that a method to check which series is right is to match them against a third, independent series, for example, the average weekly wages in employment covered by state unemployment programs. He reports that the relationship between the SSA series and the unemployment insurance series has been constant, whereas the relationship between the BLS series and the unemployment insurance series has not been. Thus Myers concludes that the BLS series is biased and therefore that real wages did rise during the 1980s.

The declining productivity figures have been criticized by John W. Kendrick—an authority in productivity analysis—who had predicted that demographic changes, the

Fig. 9.11 Average Real Hourly and Weekly Earnings in Private Nonagricultural Industries

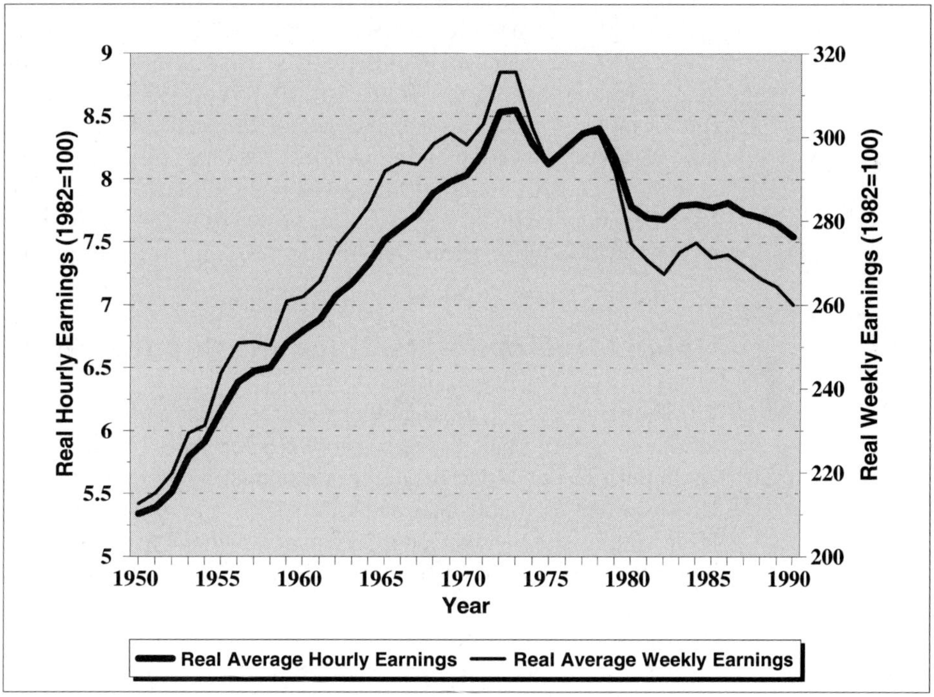

Source: *Economic Report of the President* (Washington, D.C.: U.S. Government Printing Office, 1991).

ending of the aftereffects of the oil price shocks of the 1970s, and a reduced rate of price inflation would accelerate productivity growth during the 1980s.[23] However, the official estimates failed to show the growth he had expected. He argues that the government's estimates of real gross national product significantly understate the real rate of economic growth and artificially depress official productivity statistics. There are three sources of this bias. First, some sectors use estimates of labor inputs rather than output which (contrary to independent studies) necessarily assumes no increase in labor productivity; second, the price deflators are inappropriate; third, the official estimates make inadequate allowances for improvements in the quality of goods and services. When Kendrick added these sources of bias together, he estimated that these conservative expedients adopted by the BEA have led to an underestimate of the growth rate of real GNP and of real business product per hour of about 20 percent.

The criticisms of Myers, Kendrick, and others suggest that real wages and labor productivity may well have risen in the 1980s rather than declined. However, unless the biases in the data have increased in the last 15 to 20 years, which Kendrick considers a possibility, the rates of growth of real wages and labor productivity have been reduced.

POSTWAR AMERICAN LABOR UNIONS

Since the late 1950s union membership as a share of the labor force has been falling, and its influence has diminished.[24] Figure 9.12 presents data on union membership since 1950. As Michael Goldfield has discussed, unions' political influence has declined since the 1960s.[25] In the late 1930s and 1940s unions generally won 80 percent or more of certification elections, but this percentage declined after 1945, and by the 1980s unions were winning well less than half of the certification elections.[26] The number of decertification elections has risen in the 1970s and 1980s and unions have been winning one quarter or less of these.[27] The defensive posture of unions at the end of the 1980s is far different than the aggressive, confident picture they presented just after World War II.

Union Developments Since the Second World War

The Taft-Hartley Act, among other features, required that officers sign anticommunist affidavits or forgo the utilization of NLRB services. The CIO then moved to purge the communist leadership or expel the communist-led unions. Between 1948 and 1950 the CIO expelled 11 unions that had consistently adopted pro-Soviet positions. With new leadership in 1952 and a Congress less sympathetic to union causes, the CIO and AFL began the process of reunification. In December of 1955 the reunification was formally completed.[28]

In the late 1950s the McClellan hearings produced sensational charges of criminal elements in unions and of the abridgement of the basic democratic rights of union members. The 1959 Labor Management Reporting and Disclosure Act, better known as the Landrum-Griffin Act, required disclosure of labor unions' internal functioning, electoral reforms, and guaranteed normal democratic freedoms to union members.[29] Throughout the 1960s there was criticism that the AFL-CIO was unnecessarily slow in cleaning up its discriminatory practices, and in some cases black workers used Title VII of the 1964 Civil Rights Act to sue unions and employers with de facto discrimination.[30]

Unions made a number of gains in collective bargaining during the 1950s and 1960s. These included the Cost of Living Adjustment (COLA), Annual Improvement Factor (AIF) to compensate workers for rising productivity, Supplementary Unemployment Benefits, and fringe benefits, such as pensions, health care provisions, group insurance, and vacations with pay. Some unions administered their own pension and health plans. The Teamsters' huge pension funds led to corruption and strengthened the ties of its leadership to organized crime.

Since 1960 there has been an unrelenting diminution of union effectiveness. In the 1970s and 1980s most bills for which unions lobbied hard were defeated. Absolute union membership grew slowly and since the late 1970s has declined. Troubles in the steel industry since the late 1960s and in the automobile industry since the 1970s have devastated the United Automobile Workers' and United Steelworkers' memberships. The UAW's membership fell from 1,468,000 in 1964 to 917,000 in 1989. The United Steelworkers' membership declined from 1,400,000 to only 481,000 in 1989.

Fig. 9.12 Union Membership for Selected Years

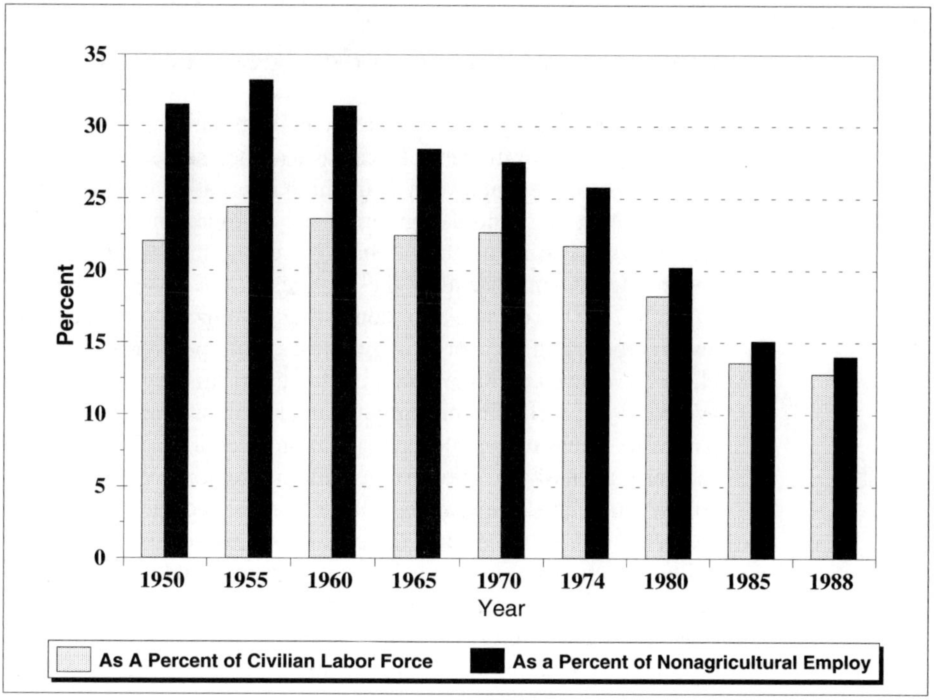

Source: *Economic Report of the President* (Washington, D.C.: U.S. Government Printing Office, 1991).

Membership in the International Brotherhood of Electrical Workers fell from 1,041,000 in 1980 to 744,000 in 1989, while the International Association of Machinists declined from 917,000 in 1976 to 517,000 in 1989.

Public Sector Unionism

The data presented in Figure 9.11 understate the decline in unionism in the private sector because the totals and percentages include public sector unions, whose membership has grown rapidly. In 1955 there were about 400,000 members of public sector unions, but there were 5,411,000 by 1983. The percentage of public sector workers who were members of a union was higher than for the private sector.[31]

Strikes by public employees have became much more common since the late 1960s. Strikes by public employees are generally illegal, so strikes by policemen and firemen are usually called the "blue flu" because they call in sick en masse. State and local governments have increasingly resorted to mediation, fact-finding, and binding arbitration. In the summer of 1970, the postal workers and letter carriers went on strike, and the National Guard temporarily delivered the mail.[32] In August 1981 the Professional Air Traffic Controllers Organization (PATCO) went on strike. Because the strike was illegal, President Reagan gave them 48 hours to return to work and after the deadline fired those continuing to strike. PATCO was later decertified.[33]

Causes of Declining Union Membership

Absolute union membership has fallen since the mid-1970s, whereas union membership as a percent of the labor force has declined since the mid-1950s. Explanations that rely upon recent events, such as the high international price of the dollar, higher quality imported goods, and deregulation, are unimportant because the decline began earlier. Analysts also argue that a changing economic struture is unimportant.[34] There is general agreement that after the changes in the labor laws in 1947 and 1959, firms began to take the offensive in contesting unionization, and unions themselves became less aggressive in their organizing drives, with perhaps one third of the decline attributable to reduced union organizing effort.[35] Firms began to adopt multiple strategies to avoid unions, including hiring labor-management consultants who specialized in campaigns to defeat unions in representations elections. Benefits of unions were offered, such as higher wages, good fringe benefits, seniority protection, and so on, without the costs of membership in unions. Illegal tactics, such as identifying and firing pro-union workers, were used because the penalties were relatively light and such actions often chilled union representation elections. Freeman and Medoff suggest that a quarter to a half of the decline in union membership can be attributed to the increasing effectiveness of firms in contesting union representation elections.[36] Perhaps a third of the representation elections won by unions never resulted in union contracts as the firms were able to continue with nonunion workers. Unionized stores were closed and reopened as nonunionized stores. When unions went on strike, firms were quicker to announce an impasse and begin hiring permanent replacement workers.

Freeman and Medoff point out that if the trend were to continue, union membership would virtually disappear: however, they believe that union strength will return. The reason is that "unions have rarely grown at a moderate steady pace. Instead they have advanced in fits and starts."[37] The most recent spurt came in the U.S. public sector, but they do not foresee which group of workers will bring on the next spurt in union membership.

SELECTED REFERENCES

Easterlin, Richard A. "American Population Since 1940." Chapter 4 in *The American Economy in Transition*. Edited by Martin Feldstein. Chicago: The University of Chicago Press for the National Bureau of Economic Research, 1980.

Easterlin, Richard A. *Birth and Fortune: The Impact of Numbers of Personal Welfare*. New York: Basic Books, 1980.

Freeman, Richard B. "The Evolution of the American Labor Market, 1948–80." Chapter 5 in *The American Economy in Transition* Edited by Martin Feldstein. Chicago: The University of Chicago Press for the National Bureau of Economic Research, 1980.

Freeman, Richard B., and James L. Medoff. *What Do Unions Do?* New York: Basic Books, Inc., 1984.

Goldfield, Michael. *The Decline of Organized Labor in the United States*. Chicago: The University of Chicago Press, 1987.

Hickman, Bert G. *Growth and Stability in the Postwar Economy*. Washington: The Brookings Instition, 1960.

Kendrick, John W. "The Economy's Even Better Than It Looks." *The Wall Street Journal*, 24 October, 1989.

Myers, Robert J. "Real Wages Went Up in the 1980s." *The Wall Street Journal*, 21 August, 1990.

Rees, Albert. *The Economics of Trade Unions*, 3d ed. Chicago: The University of Chicago Press, 1989.

Rockoff, Hugh. *Drastic Measures: A History of Wage & Price Controls in the United States*. New York: Cambridge University Press, 1984.

Westoff, Charles F., and Norman B. Ryder. *The Contraceptive Revolution.* Princeton: Princeton University Press, 1977.

Westoff, Charles F. "Some Speculation on the Future of Marriage and Fertility." *Family Planning Perspectives* 10 (March/April, 1978).

Zeiger, Robert H. *American Workers, American Unions, 1920–1985*. Baltimore: The Johns Hopkins University Press, 1986.

NOTES

1. See Hugh Rockoff, *Drastic Measures: A History of Wage & Price Controls in the United States* (New York: Cambridge University Press, 1984), chapter 6.
2. Richard A. Easterlin, "American Population Since 1940." Chapter 4 in Martin Feldstein, ed., *The American Economy in Transition* (Chicago: The University of Chicago Press for the National Bureau of Economic Research, 1980), 275. Much of this section will draw upon this excellent survey study. Easterlin has discussed many of these topics in more depth in Richard A. Easterlin, *Birth and Fortune: The Impact of Numbers on Personal Welfare* (New York: Basic Books, 1980).
3. Bert G. Hickman, *Growth and Stability in the Postwar Economy* (Washington: The Brookings Institution, 1960), 161–62.
4. Easterlin, "The American Population," 297. Most of the following discussion is drawn from Easterlin, 297–301.
5. Ibid., 297.
6. Ibid. 300.
7. See Charles F. Westoff and Norman B. Ryder, *The Contraceptive Revolution* (Princeton: Princeton University Press, 1977).
8. Easterlin, "The American Population," 277.
9. Ibid., 278.
10. Charles F. Westoff, "Some Speculation on the Future of Marriage and Fertility," *Family Planning Perspectives* 10 (March/April, 1978): 81.
11. Easterlin, "The American Population," 278–80.
12. Ibid., 280–81.
13. Ibid., 283.
14. Ibid., 304.

15. Ibid., 304.
16. Richard B. Freeman, "The Evolution of the American Labor Market, 1948–80." Chapter 5 in Martin Feldstein, ed., *The American Economy in Transition* (Chicago: The University of Chicago Press for the National Bureau of Economic Research, 1980), 359.
17. Ibid., 361.
18. Ibid., 361.
19. Ibid., 351.
20. Ibid., 352–53.
21. We know that the fixed weights based on budget studies prior to the sharp rise in petroleum prices in 1973–74 overstated the rate of inflation in the 1970s. Similarly the BLS's method of measuring the consumer cost of housing in the index, a factor contributing nearly a quarter of the weight in the CPI, was severely flawed. Though improved in the 1980s the housing component still has its problems. The bias toward inflation means that in a period of more rapid price increases, such as in the mid- and late 1970s and early 1980s, using the consumer price index will increasingly understate real earnings.
22. Robert J. Myers, "Real Wages Went Up in the 1980s," *The Wall Street Journal*, 21 August, 1990. Most analyses arguing that there was no boom for wage-earners during the 1980s rely upon a data series developed by the BLS. Myers argues that the BLS data do not reflect annual earnings but are calculated as the average weekly earnings times 52. Because it ignores unemployment it tends to overstate earnings. By sampling only production and nonsupervisory wage earners on nonagricultural payrolls, Myers argues that the series then tends to understate earnings. Finally, Myers argues that the BLS's survey sampling techniques introduce further errors. In contrast the SSA's series is based upon a complete count of the total earnings in the first quarter of each year, which is then annualized.
23. John W. Kendrick, "The Economy's Even Better Than It Looks," *The Wall Street Journal*, 24 October, 1989.
24. This section draws heavily upon the following studies: Freeman, "The American Labor Market," 367–76; Robert H. Zeiger, *American Workers, American Unions, 1920–1985* (Baltimore: The Johns Hopkins University Press, 1986); Michael Goldfield, *The Decline of Organized Labor in the United States* (Chicago: The University of Chicago Press, 1987).
25. Goldfield, *The Decline of Organized Labor*, chapter 2.
26. Ibid., 22–25.
27. Ibid., 51–52.
28. Zieger, *American Workers*, 161.
29. Goldfield, *The Decline of Organized Labor*, 85.
30. Zieger, *American Workers*, 177.
31. Albert Rees, *The Economics of Trade Unions*, 3d ed. (Chicago: The University of Chicago Press, 1989), 181.
32. Zieger, *American Workers*, 165–66.
33. Rees, *The Economics of Trade Unions*, 183–84.
34. Rees, *The Economics of Trade Unions*, chapter 13; Goldfield, *The Decline of Organized Labor*, chapter 10.; Richard B. Freeman and James L. Medoff, *What Do Unions Do?* (New York: Basic Books, Inc., 1984), chapter 15.
35. Freeman-Medoff, *What Do Unions Do?* 229–30.
36. Ibid., 237.
37. Ibid., 244.

CHAPTER 10

Developments in Agriculture, 1950 to the Present

AN OVERVIEW OF POST-WORLD WAR II AGRICULTURE

Since the Second World War, American agriculture has been a sector of dramatic contrasts. Though it is generally presented as the textbook competitive market, it is one of the most heavily government-subsidized sectors in the economy. Productivity increases in agriculture have consistently been faster than in almost every other sector of the American economy, but it has been a continually declining sector with low incomes, a shrinking population, and a decreasing number of farms.

The contours of the postwar decline in the agricultural sector can be seen in Figure 10.1. The percentage declines in farm employment and population and in the share of GNP originating in farming between 1950 and 1988 are similar and pronounced. The number and average size of farm families plunged; this reduced the number of farms, which led to a 112.7 percent increase in average farm size from 1950 to 1988. The number of farms of 500 acres or larger has grown more rapidly than the number of smaller farms. Although they comprised less than 18 percent of all farms in 1987, larg-

Fig. 10.1 Farm Population and Employment and the Percent of GNP Originating in Farming

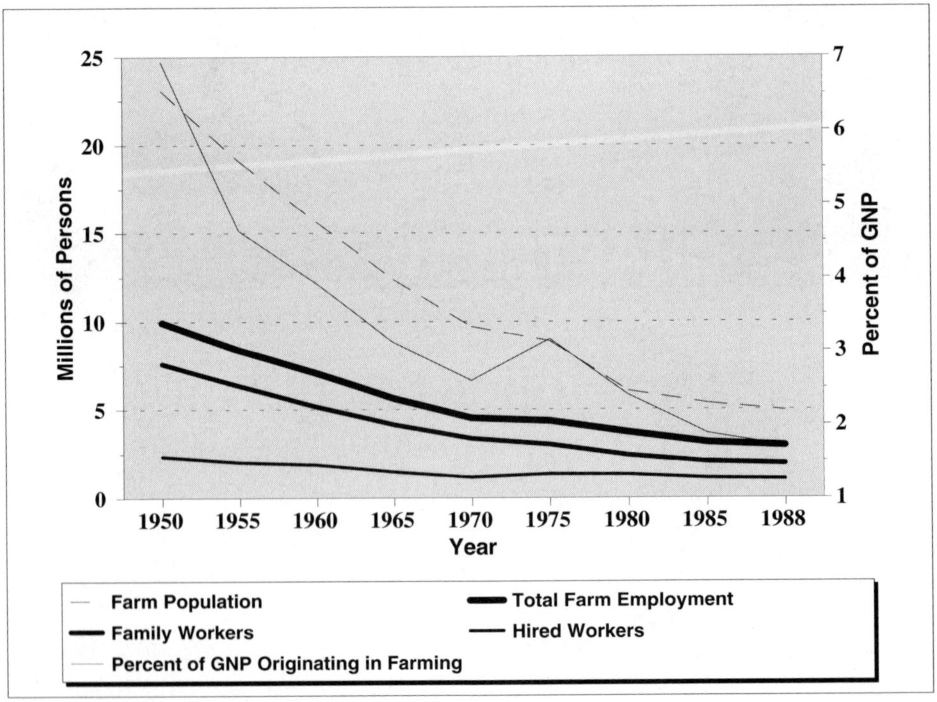

Source: *Statistical Abstract of the United States* (Washington, D.C.: U.S. Government Printing Office, various years). *Historical Statistics of the United States: Colonial Times to 1970* (Washington, D.C.: U.S. Government Printing Office, 1976). *Agricultural Statistics* (Washington, D.C.: U.S. Government Printing Office, various years).

er farms accounted for nearly 67 percent of the harvested cropland as compared to 13.4 percent of the farms and 51.3 percent of the harvested cropland in 1969.

The regional differences in farm sizes are also distinct. The West North Central, West South Central, and, particularly, Mountain regions with their larger cattle raising and breeding ranches and wheat ranches, have continued to have the largest farms. Farms in the East North Central states tend to dominate the production of corn, sorghum, soybeans, and the feedlot finishing of beef cattle. Farms in the New England and Middle Atlantic regions, where there is relatively more dairy, hay, and truck farming, have not grown as rapidly. The South Atlantic and East South Central regions are the primary producers of tobacco and cotton. As the mechanization of planting and harvesting of these crops—especially cotton—increased, the smaller farms were combined into more efficient sizes. The Pacific states—especially California—have became the nation's primary producers of vegetables and fruits.

Though the absolute increase in the number of farm implements, such as tractors, grain combines, and corn pickers, ended in the 1960s, the declining number of farms meant that the number of implements per farm rose. The real average value per acre of farmland and buildings rose until 1980, rising at a more rapid rate in the late 1970s. Then, in a manner reminiscent of the twenties, farmers watched with dismay as the real value of their property (and their real wealth) diminished. (See Figure 10.2.) The 1980s decline more than wiped out all of the gains of the 1970s.

The distress of farmers in the 1980s can also be seen in Figures 10.3 and 10.4. The farm parity ratio shows a steady deterioration in farmers' terms of trade compared to the 1910–14 period. The real average net income per farm rose from 1955 to 1975 and then plunged; by 1988 it had not recovered the 1975 level. Farm real estate debt rose to 1980 and has since fallen, but the falling value of farmland and buildings in the 1980s caused the farm debt to asset ratio to rise sharply from 1980 to 1985. It is still higher than in any year prior to 1980.

The agricultural distress of the 1980s was associated, among other things, with the decline in agricultural exports. Since the Second World War, the federal government's agricultural programs have attempted (unsuccessfully) to isolate American market prices from world market prices to reduce price fluctuations and maintain higher prices. Not surprisingly, agricultural exports were lower in the 1950s, but these markets have since became more important for American farmers. Since 1965 the majority of the wheat produced on American farms has been exported, including almost 80 percent of the 1988 American wheat harvest. The exports of corn, soybeans, and cotton have also been large.

In response to the growing demand, particularly overseas demand, agricultural production expanded throughout the postwar era. Corn, rice, hay, and peanut production have grown most rapidly, while tobacco production has declined, primarily since 1975. Cotton production plummeted between 1965 and 1975 but has since recovered. Milk and egg production have grown slowly, while among livestock only beef production grew. Poultry production has expanded dramatically because consumers have been substituting poultry for red meat in their diets.

Fig. 10.2 The Real Value per Acre of Farmland and Buildings

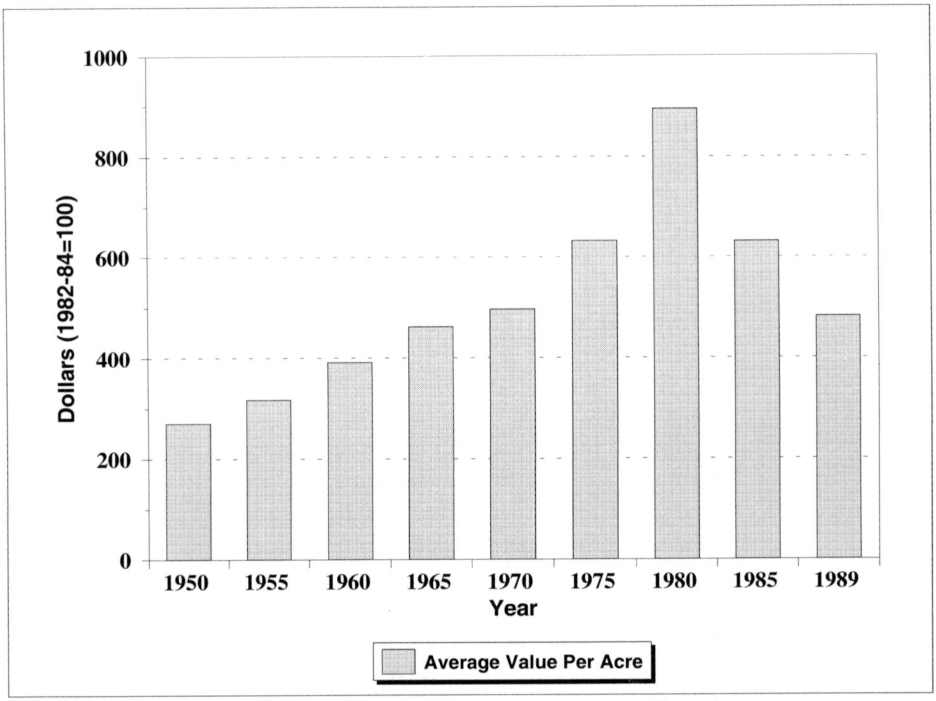

Source: *Statistical Abstract of the United States* (Washington, D.C.: U.S. Government Printing Office, various years). *Historical Statistics of the United States: Colonial Times to 1970* (Washington, D.C.: U.S. Government Printing Office, 1976). *Agricultural Statistics* (Washington, D.C.: U.S. Government Printing Office, various years).

This increased production has occurred in spite of a dramatic decline in farm labor inputs. The employment of machinery did not increase until the prosperous 1970s and then declined sharply between 1980 and 1985. The primary growth input was agricultural chemicals, a change indicative of the productivity revolution in agriculture since the end of the Second World War.

TECHNOLOGICAL CHANGE IN AGRICULTURE

The decline in the hours required to produce a unit of corn, sorghum, wheat, soybeans, tobacco, hay, potatoes, sugarbeets, and cotton averaged 84 percent from the late 1940's to the mid-1980s and ranged from −96.6 percent for cotton to −74.4 percent for tobacco. Two changes brought this about—decreases in the hours required per acre and increases in the per unit yields. The average decline in the hours required per acre was −66.7 percent and ranged from −52.6 percent for tobacco to −94 percent for cotton.

Fig. 10.3 The Farm Parity Ratio and the Real Average Net Income per Farm

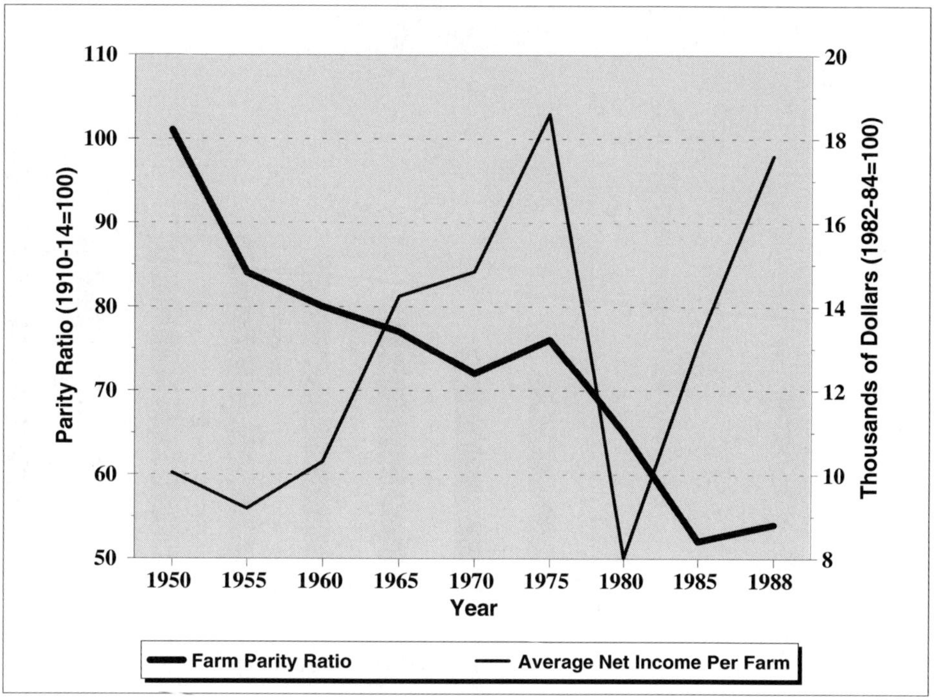

Source: *Statistical Abstract of the United States* (Washington, D.C.: U.S. Government Printing Office, various years). *Historical Statistics of the United States: Colonial Times to 1970* (Washington, D.C.: U.S. Government Printing Office, 1976). *Agricultural Statistics* (Washington, D.C.: U.S. Government Printing Office, various years).

The mean rise in yields per acre was 120.2 percent, and this ranged from 50 percent for sugarbeets to 240.5 percent for sorghum.

In dairying, the pounds of milk per cow rose 155.1 percent, while the labor-hours required per cow fell 81.4 percent to yield a 92.3 percent decline in the hours per hundredweight of milk. Similar changes occurred in egg production, when the labor-hours per 100 eggs produced declined 81.7 percent over this period. The labor-hours required per hundredweight of beef and pork produced fell 77.5 and 90 percent, respectively. The most dramatic changes occurred in broiler and turkey production where the labor-hours required per hundredweight fell by 98.2 and 98.5 percent, respectively.

These productivity increases are the result of the application of science to farm machinery, fertilizers and herbicides, and the life processes of animals and plants, that began in the late 1930s. This research and development has come from the seed, chemical, and machinery producers; from the Department of Agriculture, particularly the Office of Experiment Stations; and from government-subsidized laboratories of state universities.[1] To provide more detail on these productivity-enhancing developments,

Fig. 10.4 Farm Real Estate Debt and the Debt to Asset Ratio of Farmers

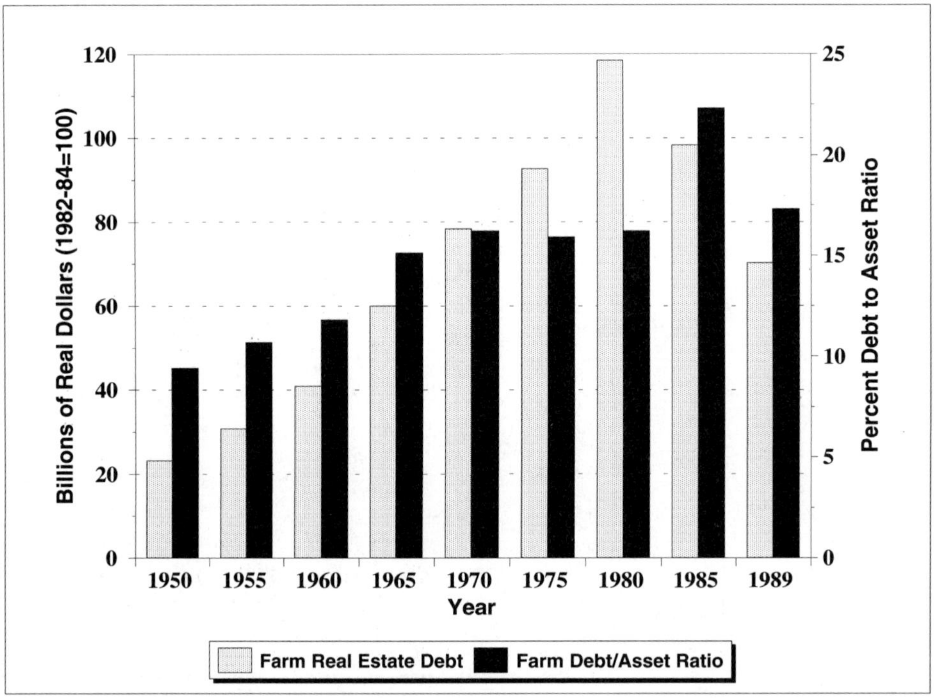

Source: *Statistical Abstract of the United States* (Washington, D.C.: U.S. Government Printing Office, various years). *Historical Statistics of the United States: Colonial Times to 1970* (Washington, D.C.: U.S. Government Printing Office, 1976). *Agricultural Statistics* (Washington, D.C.: U.S. Government Printing Office, various years).

we can look at changes in farm machinery, fertilizers, herbicides and insecticides, and genetics and modern breeding.

Machinery

Changes in the types of farm machinery allowed one person to effectively farm increasingly larger amounts of land and tend larger quantities of livestock and poultry. By the 1970s large four-wheel drive and steering tractors were replacing the smaller two-wheel drive, front-steered row-crop tractor developed in the 1920s. These new tractors often had enclosed, air-conditioned cabs and complex, sensitive electronic equipment to monitor performance. The increasing size and power of these tractors allowed farmers to increase the size of plows so that plowing an acre of land took much less time. By the 1980s computer-guided laser equipment could adjust the depth of plowing and movement of plows instantaneously to compensate for changes in terrain. As the speed of plowing increased, this led to pressure to speed up the seeding operations. Improved seed drills could plant more rows and the capability for "precision planting produced better stands of crops—stronger and more uniform. The use of drills reduced seed and fertilizer costs."[2]

Similar changes occurred in harvesting machinery. Through the 1940s and 1950s most cornpickers were separate units either mounted on the row-crop tractor or pulled behind the it. Once picked, the corn was allowed to dry before being shelled. The portable corn dryer was first developed in 1949, and this began to allow shelling to take place in the field at the same time the corn was picked. The picker-shellers soon gave way to combines. By 1960, 20 percent of the combines produced were larger self-propelled combines. Automatic transmissions and automatic leveling of the separator units, regardless of the pitch of the ground and the rest of the machine, quickly appeared. In a short time the self-propelled combines could be adapted to pick and shell corn as well as harvest grains. By 1965 the combine corn picker-sheller was the most common machinery used for corn harvesting.[3]

The postwar development of the mechanical cotton picker allowed small sharecropping farms to be combined into the larger units required to use cotton-picking machinery.[4] Other mechanical improvements increased the use of silage and improved haying operations. By the 1950s the twine field baler had displaced the use of haystacks in the field. By the 1970s new balers created huge round bales that could be left in the field until required and then carried by tractor to the feedlot, which resulted in a dramatic reduction in labor requirements in haying operations.

Fertilizers, Herbicides, and Insecticides

Farmers had always faced the problem of maintaining soil fertility, and crop rotation was the time-honored method of doing so. The development of commercial fertilizers eliminated the need to rotate crops. Farmers could reduce the variety of crops grown and concentrate production on those that had better markets. Dry and unpressurized liquid fertilizers began to be applied at the same time as plowing and/or seeding took place, and it became possible to meter the fertilizer operations to spread fertilizers uniformly on uneven ground or at varying ground speeds. Anhydrous ammonia gained popularity as a means to provide nitrogen to the soil.[5]

Weed and insect control have always been problems for farmers. Weeds compete for soil nutrients and crowd out crop growth. The herbicide 2,4-D first came to the market in 1945 and rapidly gained acceptance by farmers. Other herbicides, such as 2,4,5-T followed. Insecticides to control insect pests dated to the development of DDT prior to the Second World War. By 1946 the harmful effects of DDT had been discovered. Its use was curtailed, but other insecticides came onto the market.[6] Other methods of pest control were also developed. In 1955 the Department of Agriculture developed a method to eliminate screwworms.[7] Species of flies that attacked fruit began to be controlled by trapping and destroying the males or by large-scale spraying. In 1947 scientists discovered metallic arsenate poisons that could kill parasites such as tapeworms and stomach worms, and in the 1950s and 1960s a host of such poisons were developed for large-scale application.[8]

Genetics and Modern Breeding

Twentieth century advances in genetics have brought about radical changes. The development of knowledge dealing with the fundamental biological processes of life and growth has made it possible to create new seed strains and livestock breeds that possess desired characteristics. One major thrust has been to redesign plants—such as cotton, rice, tomatoes, and corn—for mechanized agriculture.[9]

With improved biological knowledge in the postwar years, new beef cattle breeds were developed. Artificial insemination, begun by dairy farms, spread to beef cattle herds; this helped disseminate the new breeds and made possible the selection of more desirable breeding stock. New feeds incorporated such additives to accelerate growth. Antibiotics stimulated growth and increased survival rates. Dairy herds began to be composed of purebred cattle, and milk production per cow increased.

Poultry production presents another interesting example of the changes which occurred. Through the 1940s chicken and turkey were expensive and rare meats, consumed only on special occasions. They were raised on farms where they were allowed to run in the yards or fenced lots.[10] Around 1950 a revolution began in poultry production when assembly-line techniques were adopted. Chickens were raised in indoor individual cages, thus reducing losses from disease and accidents, requiring much less labor, and allowing greater control of feed and greater selection in birds for breeding purposes. Prices plummeted and by 1987 Americans consumed more chicken than beef, ending 30 years of beef's dominating American meat consumption.[11]

The effect of the changes described here was to make agriculture in the postwar period the sector with the fastest rates of productivity increase in the American economy.

THE MEAT CRISIS OF 1973

"The year 1973 was a watershed in American farm experience. Until then farm prices were generally depressed, and price supports . . . determined farm price levels."[12] (See Figures 10.5 to 10.8.) For three years after that, prices were generally above support levels, but they fell 24 percent by the end of 1977, reducing farm incomes and leading to strikes by farmers and pressure for higher farm prices. As a result of the explosion of beef and other meat prices in the spring of 1973, consumers, blaming "middlemen" for the price increases, organized boycotts, and price controls were reimposed. Farmers, responding to the jumps in price, increased production to the detriment of crop and livestock prices several years later.

These events began in the summer of 1972, when it was discovered that the Soviet Union had used a number of private grain brokers and purchased, in the aggregate, about 25 percent of the forthcoming 1972 wheat crop initiating a phenomenal 177 percent rise in wheat prices in a matter of months. Prices would not have been driven so high if the Soviet Union had contracted in the summer of 1972 to purchase wheat from the 1973 crop because more wheat could have been planted and harvested. Since most

Fig. 10.5 Selected Real Crop Prices, 1970–1988

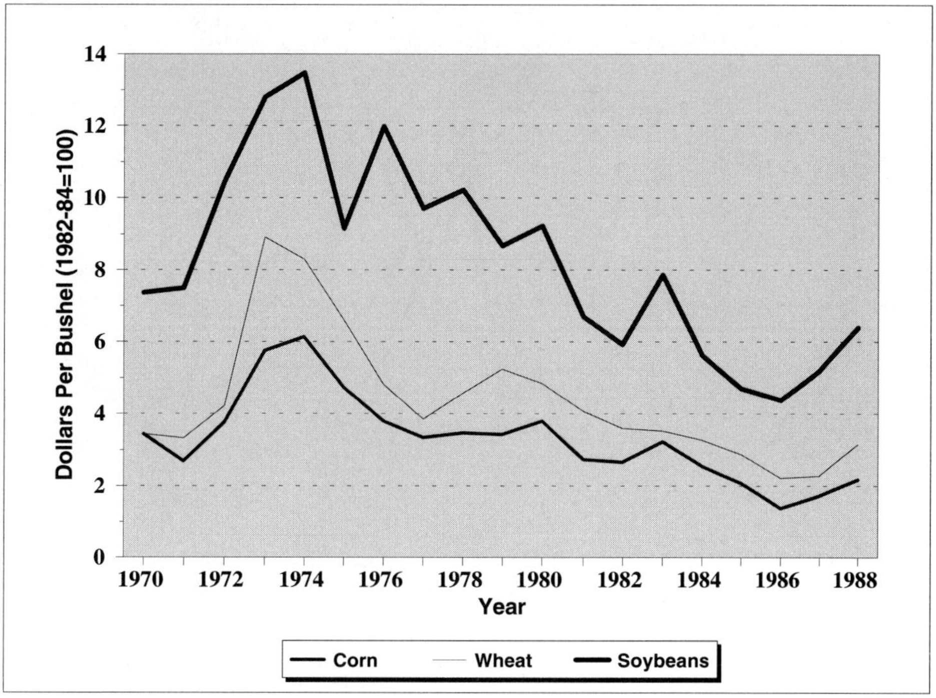

Source: *Statistical Abstract of the United States* (Washington, D.C.: U.S. Government Printing Office, various years). *Historical Statistics of the United States: Colonial Times to 1970* (Washington, D.C.: U.S. Government Printing Office, 1976). *Agricultural Statistics* (Washington, D.C.: U.S. Government Printing Office, various years).

grains are good substitutes for each other, the rising wheat prices induced an increase in the demand for soybeans, corn, oats, and rye; all of these prices also rose rapidly.

Further complications appeared in 1972. The Humboldt current, off the west coast of South America, is one of the main sources for anchovies. In 1972 the current shifted, carrying much of the anchovy crop with it. The catches dropped alarmingly, and the Peruvian government put a ban on anchovy fishing so as not to permanently damage the breeding grounds. Anchovy prices soared. The main use of anchovies is as animal feed, and rising anchovy prices led to the use of feed grains, particularly soybeans, as a substitute.

The rising cost of cattle feed began to affect the supply of beef. Farmers began cutting back on beef production as it became less profitable. However, to decrease the longer run supply of beef requires an initial increase in supply as the cattle breeding stock is reduced. In July of 1972, real Omaha beef prices were $89.72 per 100 pounds. By September of 1972, Omaha beef prices had dropped to $78.95 and then began to rise.

Fig. 10.6 Selected Real Crop Prices, 1970–1988

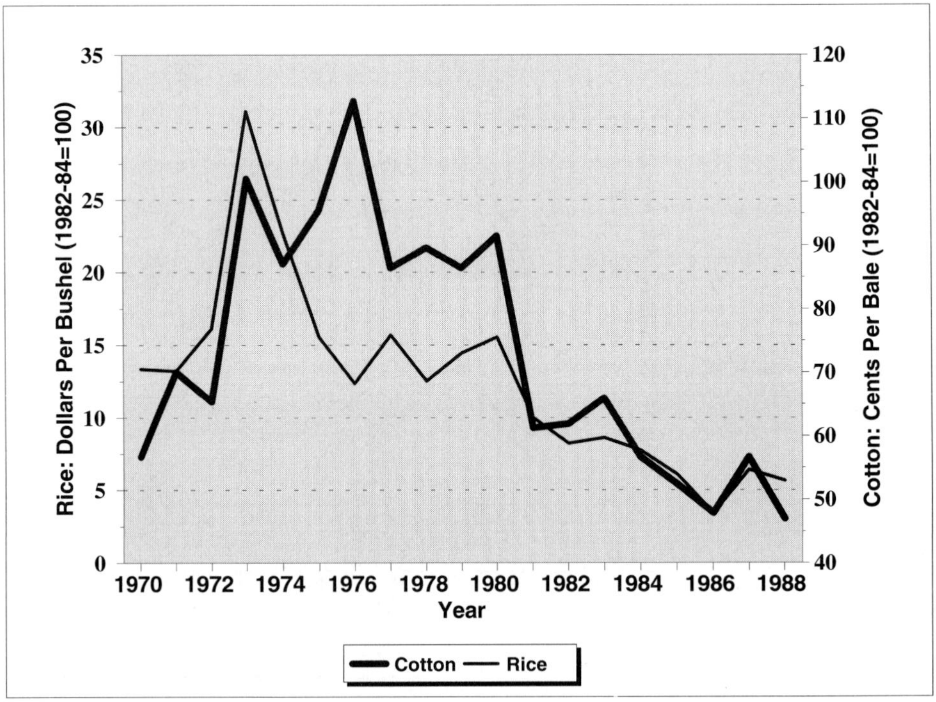

Source: *Statistical Abstract of the United States* (Washington, D.C.: U.S. Government Printing Office, various years). *Historical Statistics of the United States: Colonial Times to 1970* (Washington, D.C.: U.S. Government Printing Office, 1976). *Agricultural Statistics* (Washington, D.C.: U.S. Government Printing Office, various years).

As the culminating factor, the second devaluation of the U.S. dollar took place in February, 1973. The devaluation caused all U.S. products to be cheaper in terms of foreign currencies and all imports into the U.S. of foreign products to be more expensive in U.S. dollars. This had two effects. First, the price of U.S. soybean animal feed immediately became less expensive overseas increasing the total demand for U.S. soybeans, and thereby generating further increases in soybean prices. Second, the devaluation increased the domestic demand for domestically produced beef as consumers and businesses substituted away from suddenly higher priced imported beef.

Thus, the two sets of events combined to cause an explosion of beef prices in the spring of 1973. The increased cost of producing beef, due to soaring grain and soybean prices, caused a decrease in the supply of beef, and the exchange rate devaluation, which increased the domestic price of imported beef, caused an increase in demand for domestically produced beef. As the price of beef rose, the demand for substitutes, such as chicken, pork, lamb, and fish, also rose, and their prices also began rising. These events culminated in nearly empty meat shelves in supermarkets, a reimposition of

Fig. 10.7 Selected Real Livestock Prices, 1970–1988

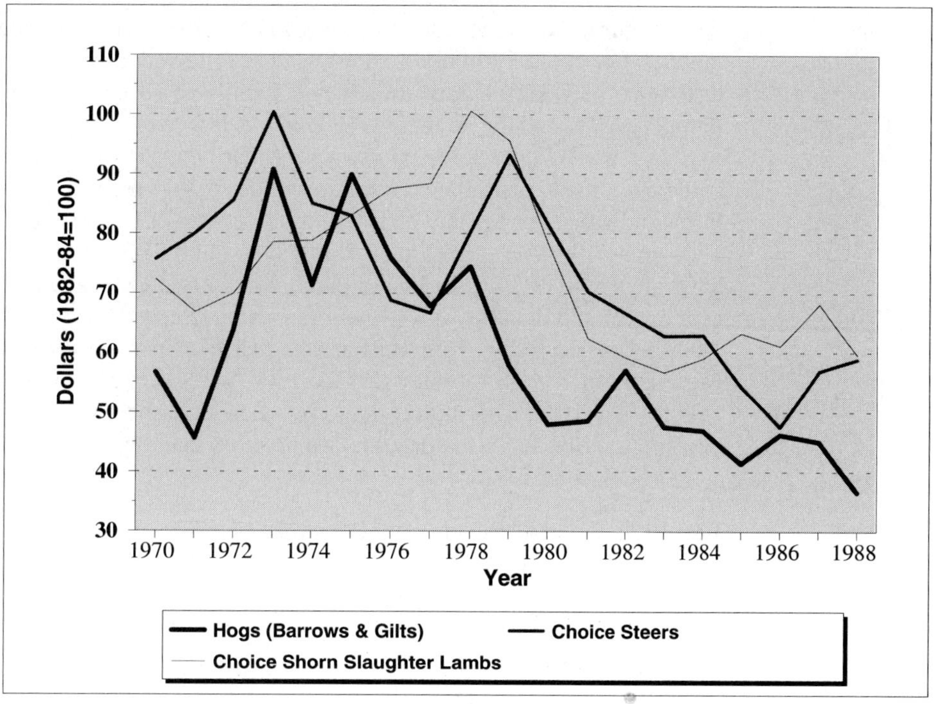

Source: *Statistical Abstract of the United States* (Washington, D.C.: U.S. Government Printing Office, various years). *Historical Statistics of the United States: Colonial Times to 1970* (Washington, D.C.: U.S. Government Printing Office, 1976). *Agricultural Statistics* (Washington, D.C.: U.S. Government Printing Office, various years).

price controls, and consumer boycotts. Farmers may have contributed to the shortages to some extent by withholding beef cattle from the market in anticipation that the removal of price controls would result in higher prices.

Though declining, crop and livestock prices remained relatively high through the 1970s. Average net income per farm dropped sharply after the 1973 peak, while both farm equity and farm debt began growing. (See Figures 10.9 and 10.10.) Though wheat exports declined after the 1972–73 peak, exports of other crops, particularly corn, rose. These changes set the stage for the farm debt crisis of the 1980s.

THE FARM DEBT CRISIS OF THE 1980s

Conditions for farmers had deteriorated in the late 1970s and became much worse in the 1980s. Large numbers of farmers had their mortgages foreclosed. The farm debt crisis of the 1980s reminded many of the depressed state of farming in the 1920s though there were significant differences. As Table 10.1 shows, the debt crisis peaked in 1985 and 1986. Farm real estate debt increased during the 1970s and, with the rise in interest rates, did so most sharply from 1979 to 1980. The debt began to decline more rapidly after 1983. Farm non-real estate debt followed a similar path. Farm equity, the difference between all farm assets and liabilities, rose sharply until 1980 and then dropped just as rapidly so that by 1985 it was less than in 1970.

The rise and fall in farm equity was primarily due to rising and collapsing farmland values. For the United States, farmland values fell 41 percent between 1982 and 1987. Farmland values in Iowa, which was in the center of the farm debt crisis, were about $400 an acre in 1970, $834 an acre in 1974, and $2,150 an acre in 1981. They fell to $800 an acre in 1986, a decline of 63 percent in five years and recovered to $1,050 an acre by 1988.[13] Because of declining farmland values, the farm debt/asset ratio rose to 1985 before declining. Neil Harl argues that a 40 percent debt/asset ratio is critical, because farmers with a debt/asset ratio of 40 percent of higher are particularly vulnerable to changes in agricultural markets, whereas farmers with a debt/asset ratio of 70 percent or more can be expected to last no more than two years.[14] Young farmers, who

Fig. 10.8 Selected Real Poultry Prices, 1970–1988

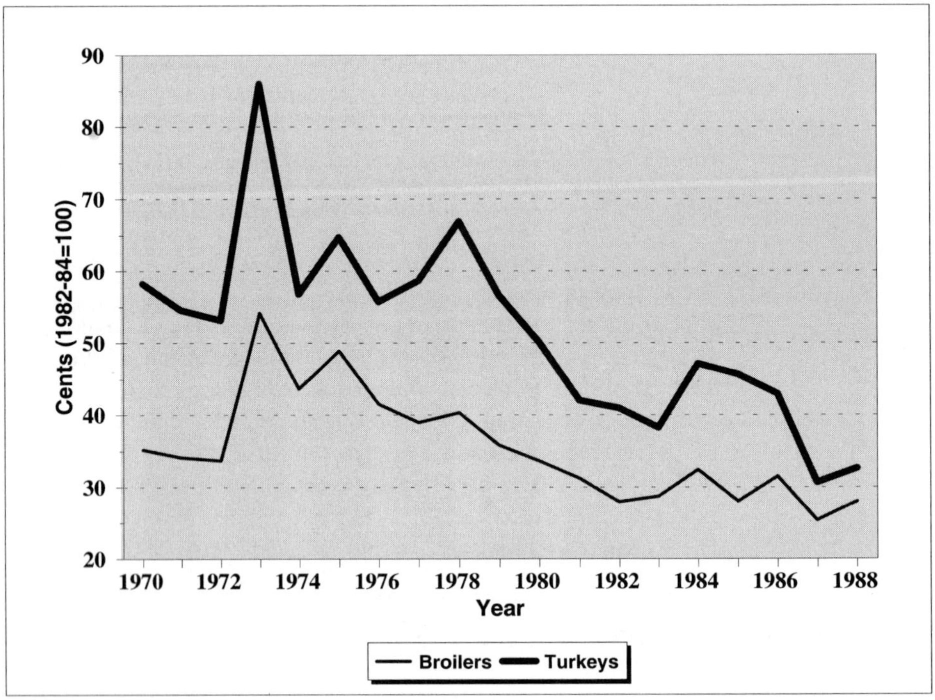

Source: *Statistical Abstract of the United States* (Washington, D.C.: U.S. Government Printing Office, various years). *Historical Statistics of the United States: Colonial Times to 1970* (Washington, D.C.: U.S. Government Printing Office, 1976). *Agricultural Statistics* (Washington, D.C.: U.S. Government Printing Office, various years).

Fig. 10.9 Selected Farm Statistics, 1970–1988

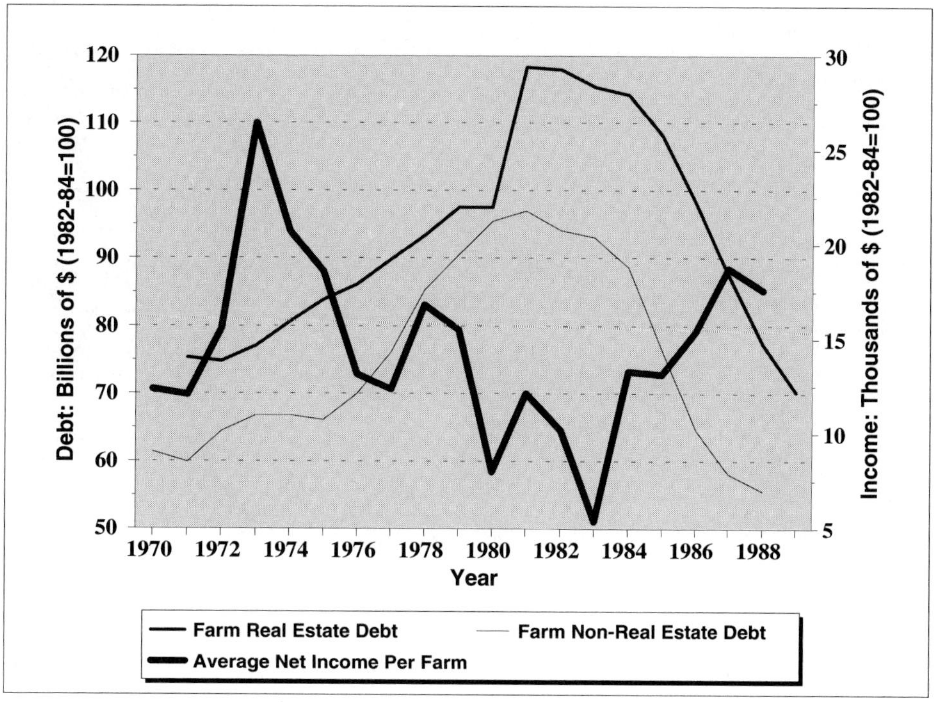

Source: *Statistical Abstract of the United States* (Washington, D.C.: U.S. Government Printing Office, various years). *Historical Statistics of the United States: Colonial Times to 1970* (Washington, D.C.: U.S. Government Printing Office, 1976). *Agricultural Statistics* (Washington, D.C.: U.S. Government Printing Office, various years).

Table 10.1 Indicators of Financial Stress in Agriculture in the 1980s (In Percent)

Financial Stress Indicator	1980	1985	1986	1987	1988
Average Delinquency Rate[1]	—	5.3	6.0	2.7	1.6
Farm Borrowers Who Had Bank Financing Discontinued	4.5	4.5	5.6	3.3	1.7
Farm Borrowers Loaned-Up to Practical Limit[2]	27.0	37.0	39.0	29.0	23.0
Farmers in Bank Lending Area Who Went Out of Business	2.1	4.8	6.2	4.6	2.8
Farmers in Bank Lending Area Who Went Through Bankruptcy	—	3.8	4.2	3.3	2.2

[1]Percentage of dollar farm loan volume 30 days or more delinquent.
[2]Farm customers who have reached their maximum debt load.

Source: *Statistical Abstract of the United States* (Washington, D.C.: U.S. Government Printing Office, 1990).

Fig. 10.10 Selected Farm Statistics, 1970–1988

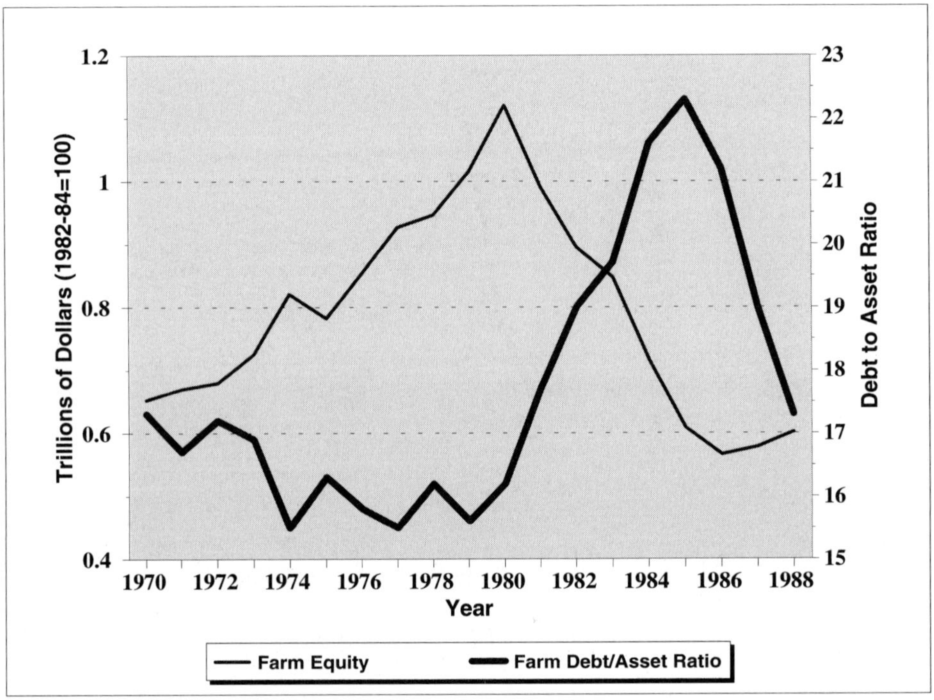

Source: *Statistical Abstract of the United States* (Washington, D.C.: U.S. Government Printing Office, various years). *Historical Statistics of the United States: Colonial Times to 1970* (Washington, D.C.: U.S. Government Printing Office, 1976). *Agricultural Statistics* (Washington, D.C.: U.S. Government Printing Office, various years).

generally had more debt and less equity, were more vulnerable. The real average net income per farm from farming, which had reached $26,000 dollars in 1973, fell to extraordinarily low levels by the mid-1980s. Real crop and livestock prices fell during the 1980s and reached unusually low levels in the late 1980s.

The farm crisis of the 1980s had its roots both in the nature of farming and in a set of external events associated with actions by the federal government. As a competitive industry, economic profits tend to be short run. When extranormal returns persist, they become rents received by the factor or factors that are least elastic in supply. In farming that factor is land, so extranormal earnings, such as in 1973 and 1974, resulted in a bidding up of land prices. Any farmer who wishes to gain from the expansion of demand and higher agricultural prices in agriculture has to own land, which has always represented most of a farmer's wealth. Farmers were bitter and frustrated in the 1980s as they watched their wealth decline with the value of their farmland.

In the 1970s, after the explosion of grain prices, farmers began to buy additional farmland. Lenders, both private banks and federal agencies such as the Farm Credit System banks, were eager to lend on such good assets. The 1978 extension of the investment tax credit to single-purpose agricultural and horticultural structures encouraged a number of farmers to invest in additional facilities, particularly those geared toward hog production, further increasing their debtload. As long as farmland prices rose at least as fast as the rate of price inflation, and crop, livestock, and poultry prices tended to rise about as much as prices did, the situation was manageable.

These conditions did not continue. There were droughts in 1980 and 1983, and the southeast suffered a protracted drought in the late 1970s. Cattle producers had incurred losses in the late 1970s, and hog producers generally suffered losses from 1980 through 1985. In 1979 the Federal Reserve System decided to change its policies to better combat the inflation raging through the economy. The policy changes announced on October 6, 1979, resulted in an immediate increase in nominal interest rates. Real interest rates shot up dramatically, and farmers who had taken out loans with adjustable interest rates found their interest costs rising as a result. The growing budget deficits of the 1980s further increased real interest rates.

The higher real interest rates resulting from the larger budget deficits and tighter monetary policy affected farmers in several ways.[15] First, higher real interest rates increased the direct cost of production credit for farmers. Second, farmers with variable rate mortgages found increasing interest costs for the land they owned. Third, higher interest rates in the United States attracted foreign investment funds, strengthened the dollar and raised the foreign prices of American exports, which reduced the quantitites demanded. Fourth, higher real interest rates raised the production costs and prices of inputs that farmers purchased. Finally, higher real interest rates increased the costs of carrying farm products in inventory whether by the farmer or by intermediaries who purchased farm products.

Thus, the effects of higher real interest rates reduced domestic demand and foreign demand and caused incomes to fall. As incomes fell, so did farmland prices. Often the amount of supposedly safe equity of farmland backing up loans became less than the outstanding loan amount, and farmers were increasingly unable to meet their debt obligations. By 1985 farm exports had plunged to a seven-year low.[16] To make matters worse, by the mid-1980s some crop harvests were huge. The 1985 and 1986 corn harvests were called "the crop that won't quit."[17] The conventional storage areas were quickly used up, and corn was stored on town streets, in former silica sand mines, in converted bulk liquid containers at a former oil tank farm, and on barges floating in the Mississippi River.

As crop prices fell, more and more acres of crops were placed under federal crop price supports, and the federal government was again forced by default to purchase larger and larger amounts of crops. The Commodity Credit Corporation (CCC) purchased over 0.5 billion bushels of corn in 1985 and 1.3 billion bushels of corn in 1986. Between 1982 and 1986 the CCC purchased 1.1 billion bushels of wheat in order to support wheat prices. In 1984 and 1985, 452 million bushels of soybeans were purchased. The federal expenditures to support crop prices were growing at an alarming rate. By 1986 federal crop subsidies were approaching $30 billion.[18]

The Farm Credit System's troubles mounted during the early and mid-1980s. The FCS held more than a third of all agricultural debt in the mid-1980s. To raise funds to make loans, the system sells bonds to the general public. The loans made to farmers were secured by the farm real estate and by the value of the crop production. During good times, the FCS banks had encouraged farmers to borrow to expand. With the deteriorating conditions of the 1980s, farmers began to be unable to repay loans as scheduled, and an increasing number of loans became delinquent. The FCS banks began to refuse to renew loans and finally began to foreclose on farmers who were severely delinquent. Because of accounting gimmicks that might well have been illegal in the private sector, the seriousness of the losses in the FCS were hidden for a time.[19] The Farm Credit System had losses of $2.7 billion in 1985 and $1.9 billion in 1986. By the middle of 1987, the Farmers Home Administration held 1.6 million acres of foreclosed farmland, and the Farm Credit System held 2.7 million acres of foreclosed farmland.[20] By the end of 1985, the FCS "held some $6 billion in loans of which the face amount exceeded the value of the collateral."[21] 1986 congressional legislation authorized the FCS to use "creative accounting to avoid tapping the U.S. Treasury for assistance and permitted the losses to be spread over as many as twenty years."[22] In 1987 congress, seeing that earlier acts had not provided remedies, enacted additional legislation.

Many small-town private banks that had made loans to farmers secured by the farm's real estate went out of business during the 1980s. As farm incomes fell, farmers reduced their spending to try to continue to make loan payments. Retail businesses in the smaller towns in agricultural areas were devastated. Farm equipment sales plummeted and farm implement dealers and manufacturers went out of business. In short, the farm debt crisis of the 1980s devastated farmers and rural communities.

FEDERAL FARM PROGRAMS

Federal agricultural policies and programs in the postwar era are an extension of programs initiated during the New Deal of the 1930s, and they have worked no better in the postwar period than they worked before. As James Bovard has stated, "For sixty years, the U.S. government has devotedly repeated the same agricultural policy mistakes."[23]

The first important changes in federal farm programs after the Second World War came with the Agricultural Acts of 1948 and 1949, that gave the CCC permanent status and borrowing authorization and maintained support prices at 90 percent of parity.[24] After the Korean War, the CCC inventories began accumulating at an alarming rate. The Agricultural Act of 1954 simply made the provisions of the 1949 act effective. Five of the six basic commodities were given flexible supports at 82.5 to 90 percent of parity, and the act further postponed changing to a modern parity formula.[25] Some of the CCC stocks could be set aside for donation or sale for enumerated worthy causes.

Officials in the Department of Agriculture and members of Congress had underestimated the rapidity with which huge surpluses would accumulate due to the relatively high price supports. The school lunch programs and the food stamp program were already in place to use some of the surpluses, but these fell far short of using up all of the excess. In 1954 Congress passed Public Law 480, an export program whereby less developed countries could purchase surplus government foodstuffs in the country's own currency and the funds could not, in general, be taken out of that country. It incurred the wrath of other agricultural exporting countries.

The surpluses continued to mount. Beginning in 1956 Congress enacted soil bank programs in hopes of achieving a 10 to 17 percent reduction in plowland as farmers took cropland out of production by "banking" or "renting" it to the government. Even farmers who did not directly participate in the soil bank program would benefit because, it was believed, the reduced output would raise crop prices.

Twenty-eight million acres were taken out of production, but the surpluses continued to mount because too few farmers participated and those that did kept the best land in production and placed the least fertile land into the soil bank, increased the nonland inputs, and produced as much if not more output. Because the output did not decline to any significant extent, the market price did not rise, and the only farmers who benefited were the participating farmers.

By 1960, the CCC wheat inventory was equal to the entire 1960 crop or to two years domestic wheat consumption. The corn stocks were five times what they had been in 1952, and wheat stocks were eight times what they had been in 1952. In desperation, Congress passed the Emergency Feed Grain Bill of 1961. It offered much higher payments for cropland diversion, and by 1963, 18 percent of the 1959–60 acreage was diverted, and feed grain carryover actually dropped. However, the program turned out to be extraordinarily expensive for the federal government. Congress finally extended the program to wheat in 1965; it was enormously expensive, costing five to six billion dollars a year, with the bulk of the payments going to the larger and wealthier wheat farmers.

There was general unhappiness with the farm programs as they existed in the late 1960s, and a new agricultural act was passed in 1970. This required a mandatory acreage set aside and attempted to limit the subisidies to any one farmer, but it was not very effective and continued to use outdated parity prices based on the 1910–14 period. The Agriculture and Consumer Protection Act of 1973 ended the use of parity prices by establishing support prices and target prices, which were desired prices generally above the market clearing level. The target prices could be set higher than support prices, and support prices could be set somewhere around the world market-clearing prices or lower. If prices dropped below support price levels, the CCC stepped in and made purchases through its loan program to move prices toward the support level. So long as prices were above the support price level, they were left free to find their own market-clearing level, facilitating international trade and exports of farm commodities. If market prices were above the support price levels but below the target price levels, the U.S. government made deficiency payments to the farmers in the amount of the difference between the target and market prices multiplied by the farmer's allotment. Each farmer's allotment represented his or her share of the national acreage required to meet domestic and export needs as defined by the secretary of agriculture. A limit of $20,000 in annual deficiency payments to each farmer under the wheat, cotton, and feed grain programs was established, but again this was not effective.

In 1977 Congress passed the Food and Agriculture Act, which continued and extended features of the 1973 act. Target prices were now to be based on the average cost of production, and support prices were made somewhat flexible so as to interfere as little as possible with the marketing of the farm products. The secretary of agriculture was authorized to require farmers to set aside part of the cropland to be eligible for the deficiency payments. The 1977 act set the target price on the basis of the farmers' costs of production. However, as D. Gale Johnson points out, a large part of the cost of production is the cost of land, and land prices are merely the discounted present value of the product that the land can produce.[26] Thus, the value of the land actually depended upon the target prices that the government set. Therefore, within a broad range, government officials could set the target prices anywhere they chose and ultimately the land prices (and therefore costs of production) would increase up to that target price.

Between 1975 and 1982 Presidents Ford, Carter, and Reagan and the various Congresses continued to raise support prices even though target and support prices were generally above world prices.[27] In January of 1980, President Carter embargoed U.S. grain sales to the Soviet Union in order to punish it for its invasion of Afghanistan—an act that primarily harmed American grain farmers rather than the Soviet Union. In 1981 Congress passed farm legislation that called for crop target and loan prices to increase by 4 to 5 percent annually. By 1982, program costs were much higher, exports were declining, and government-owned surpluses were growing. Still, federal support prices for corn and wheat were raised.

In December of 1982, President Reagan proposed a new program called Payment-In-Kind, or PIK, which went into effect in 1983. Farmers who idled farmland were given surplus commodities from the CCC's holdings. Farmers responded by idling 77 million acres, or one third of all eligible farmland.[28] It was by all standards a generous program because the participating farmers received the equivalent of the crop output without incurring any of the production expenses, and the USDA then gave the farmers $391 million to store their crops so that they could wait and sell the PIK receipts at the most profitable time. Unfortunately, other producers were harmed. Egg, cattle, and pork producers faced higher prices for their feed and saw the profits from their farming operations drop. The program drove fertilizer, farm equipment, and seed dealers out of business across the United States.[29] A 1983 drought, combined with much greater participation in PIK than forecast, used up the government's stored surpluses, and the USDA actually had to go to the open market to purchase grain for some farmers participating in PIK.[30] PIK was a costly failure and was discontinued at the end of 1983.

The 1985 Food Security Act, which included attempts to save the Farm Credit System, again made minor adjustments to the continuing programs. Farmers were paid up to $200 an acre to divert land from the production of subsidized crops but were allowed to grow any unsubsidized crops on the same acreage. The shift from subsidized crops in surplus to unsubsidized ones simply developed surpluses in crop markets that previously were balanced, such as potatoes, edible beans, and popcorn. James Bovard has called this the "1986 massacre of unsubsidized farmers."[31] The price support programs have resulted in other distortions. The 1985 bill raised the support price for barley so that it was 96 cents a bushel higher than for oats; consequently, farmers planted much more barley and less oats. The resulting drop in oats production caused severe supply problems for producers that used oats in their products.[32] A sharply higher support price for sugarbeets, compared to wheat, allowed sugarbeet producers in western Minnesota to outbid wheat producers who had been renting the land for years creating great bitterness among the farmers.[33] The farm bill passed by Congress in October of 1990 essentially continued all of these programs.[34]

Milk prices are supported under a convoluted set of rules that takes up three volumes.[35] The supported price of milk rises with the distance from Eau Claire, Wisconsin. This discourages the shipment of milk from areas better suited to specialize in milk production and encourages more inefficient production, for example, in much hotter areas such as Florida where dairy cows produce less milk. To maintain the minimum price, the CCC buys "surplus" dairy products. Consumers then end up paying taxes to purchase and store the surplus and paying higher retail prices for dairy products. Several times in the 1980s, the Department of Agriculture freely distributed surplus cheese to low-income and elderly citizens to keep it from being lost through spoilage. High domestic cheese prices led to greater imports, requiring quotas to limit cheese imports. In 1981 the CCC was purchasing nonfat dry milk at 94 cents a pound to support its price and then reselling it at 55 cents a pound to farmers to supplement their hog feed. In 1983, 1986, and 1987 the USDA launched "one-time" buyout programs to pay farmers to slaughter dairy cattle, thus reducing the dairy herds and surpluses. Farmers sent their least productive cows to the slaughter houses, raising the per cow milk production. The more generous 1986 program resulted in so many dairy cows being sent to slaughter that it devastated beef markets and bankrupted some beef cattle producers.

Sugar producers have also been heavily subsidized.[36] Extensive quotas and price supports ensure that little sugar is imported and sugar prices remain high. In the mid-1970s world sugar prices rose sharply. Sugar was then pushed into the free market by removing the price supports and import limitations, but as prices then began to decline, demands from sugar producers led to a restoration of price supports and full statutory protection in 1981. The high prices for sugar from sugarbeets and sugarcane led to an increase in the use of corn sweeteners.

The peanut quota system was established in 1941. Similar to those for tobacco, the quotas amount to a government license allowing a farmer to sell peanuts and therefore are a way to limit or reduce output and keep prices higher.[37] These quotas allot production each year farm by farm, county by county, and state by state throughout the peanut belt. Prices are kept high by restricting production and imports and by the USDA guaranteeing minimum support prices (based on production costs) for quota holders. Peanut growers without a government quota can only sell their peanuts in the lower priced export market and for domestic production as peanut oil and meal. In 1990 the price for that excess production was $149.75 a ton, while the support price for quota peanuts was $631.47 a ton. The USDA employs "peanut police" to ensure that lower priced nonquota peanuts are not diverted from export and sold as more expensive quota peanuts.

Federal marketing orders for various fruits and nuts also date to the New Deal of the 1930s. Such marketing orders have included lemons, oranges, raisins, filberts, almonds, hops, nectarines, plums, cherries, spearmint, grapefruit, and prunes. Federal marketing orders are quotas assigned to individual growers. Production in excess of a quota requires that the excess be destroyed. Giving the excess away is even illegal.[38] The marketing orders, or quotas, are determined by committees sanctioned by the USDA. Not surprisingly, such committees are dominated by the larger growers, and commonly there are charges of bias toward the larger growers in the assignments of marketing orders.[39]

The conclusion that postwar federal agricultural programs have seriously harmed many American farmers and the American public is inescapable. The cost of these programs climbed dramatically during the 1980s. At the beginning of the 1980s, federal spending on farm programs was less than $3 billion but by 1986 and 1987 approached $30 billion. These figures do not include the indirect costs of higher prices for food and dairy products—higher prices that impinge most harshly on the poorest segments of the American population.

Resource migration out of the agricultural sector was not stopped, but merely slowed down. In fact, it is not clear that this was ever an aim of the programs. No funds were ever authorized to ease the transfer out of farming by providing retraining programs for farmers, no funds were made available to lower the costs of moving from farm to nonfarm work and living environments, and the government never provided information about nonfarm alternatives. Throughout the postwar period, nearly every study and survey has shown that most of the benefits were funneled to the wealthiest farmers; very little went to the poorest farmers, who had the greatest need for assistance.

Though it has long been argued that the farm programs were necessary to raise the average incomes of farmers up toward the average incomes of nonfarmers, now even this is of doubtful validity. In a 1987 U.S. Department of Agriculture publication, Lloyd D. Teigen concluded that in every year since 1964, the average income of farm families exceeded the median income of all families.[40] From 1964 to 1970 the ratio was 106.8; from 1971 to 1980 it was 121.3; and from 1981 to 1987 it was 124.2.[41]

If the aim of the federal agricultural programs begun in the New Deal of the 1930s was to raise the incomes of farmers up to those of nonfarmers, that aim was achieved 25 years ago, and those programs have now outlived their usefulness.

SELECTED REFERENCES

Bovard, James. *The Farm Fiasco*. San Francisco: The ICS Press, 1989.

Harl, Neil. *The Farm Debt Crisis of the 1980s*. Ames, IA: The Iowa State University Press, 1990.

Goodman, John C., and Edwin G. Dolan. "Farm Policy : Welfare for the Rich?" Chapter 8 in *Economics of Public Policy*, 3d ed. St. Paul: West Publishing Co., 1985.

Johnson, D. Gale. "The Food and Agriculture Act of 1977: Implications for Farmers, Consumers, and Taxpayers." *Contemporary Economic Problems, 1978*. Edited by William Fellner. Washington: American Enterprise Institute, 1978.

Parker, William N. "Agriculture." Chapter 11 in *American Economic Growth: An Economist's History of the United States*. L. E. Davis, R. A. Easterlin, W. N. Parker et al. New York: Harper and Row, 1972.

Rosenberg, Nathan. *Technology and American Economic Growth*. New York: Harper and Row, 1972.

Schlebecker, John T. *Whereby We Thrive: A History of American Farming, 1607–1972*. Ames, IA: The Iowa State University Press, 1975.

Suits, Daniel. "Agriculture." Chapter 1 in *The Structure of American Industry*. 5th ed. Edited by Walter Adams. New York: Macmillan Publishing Co., 1977.

Teigen, Lloyd D. *Agricultural Parity: Historical Review and Alternative Calculations*. Washington, D.C.: U.S. Department of Agriculture, 1987.

Weiss, Leonard W. "Pure Competition and Agriculture." Chapter 2 in *Case Studies in American Industry*. 3d ed. New York: John Wiley and Sons, 1980.

NOTES

1. This discussion of technological change in farming draws primarily upon the following sources: John T. Schlebecker, *Whereby We Thrive: A History of American Farming, 1607–1972* (Ames, IA: The Iowa State University Press, 1975); Daniel Suits, "Agriculture," Chapter 1 in Walter Adams, *The Structure of American Industry*, 5th ed. (New York: Macmillan Publishing Co., 1977); Nathan Rosenberg, *Technology and American Economic Growth* (New York: Harper and Row, 1972); William N. Parker, , "Agriculture," chapter 11 in L. E. Davis, R. A. Easterlin, W. N. Parker et al., *American Economic Growth: An Economist's History of the United States* (New York: Harper and Row, 1972), 397.
2. Schlebecker, *Whereby We Thrive*, 295.
3. Ibid., 297.
4. Ibid., 298.
5. Ibid., 301.
6. Ibid., 310.
7. Ibid., 311.
8. Ibid., 312.
9. Rosenberg, *Technology and American Economic Growth*, 134.
10. Suits, "Agriculture," 27.
11. Timothy K. Smith, "Changing Tastes: By End of this Year, Poultry Will Surpass Beef in the U.S. Diet," *The Wall Street Journal*, 17 September, 1987. Prior to the late 1950s, Americans consumed more pork than beef.
12. Leonard W. Weiss, "Pure Competition and Agriculture," chapter 2 in Leonard W. Weiss, *Case Studies in American Industry*, 3d ed. (New York: John Wiley & Sons, 1980), 68.
13. Neil E. Harl, *The Farm Debt Crisis of the 1980s* (Ames, IA: The Iowa State University Press, 1990), 38–39. Much of the following discussion relies on Harl's book.
14. Ibid., 30–37.
15. Ibid., 12.
16. "Farm Exports Plunge to 7-Year Low," *The Milwaukee Journal*, 7 November, 1985.
17. Dennis McCann, "Bountiful Harvest, Costly Problems: The Crop That Won't Quit," *The Milwaukee Journal*, 21 September, 1986.

18. Dennis McCann, "Too High a Price?" *The Milwaukee Journal*, 23 September, 1986.
19. For example, in some cases FCS books showed accrued interest payments on loans for which no payments had been received for three or four years. Charles F. McCoy and Jeff Bailey, "Blighted Ledgers: Farm Credit System Relies on Accounting That Hides Bad Loans," *The Wall Street Journal*, 7 October, 1985. Jeff Bailey and Charles F. McCoy, "Tricky Ledgers: To Hide Huge Losses, Financial Officials Use Accounting Gimmicks: Farm Credit System Plans Two Sets of Books; Insolvent S & L's Stay Open," *The Wall Street Journal*, 12 January, 1987.
20. Jean Marie Brown, "Farm Optimism Rises, but Woes Persist: Federal Outlays Stay High, Land Values Fall," *The Wall Street Journal*, 11 May, 1987.
21. Harl, *The Farm Debt Crisis of the 1980s*, 137.
22. Ibid., 142.
23. James Bovard, *The Farm Fiasco* (San Francisco: The ICS Press, The Institute for Contemporary Studies, 1989), 1.
24. The 1949 act defined three groups of commodities: (1) six "basics" of wheat, corn, cotton, tobacco, rice, and peanuts; (2) five "designated nonbasics" of wool and mohair, tung nuts, honey, Irish potatoes, and milk and milk products; and, (3) "other nonbasics," or the rest of some 170 U.S. farm commodities.
25. The parity formula compares the ratio of a current commodity price to a current index of farm input prices with a ratio of a commodity price in 1910–14 to the 1910–14 index of farm input prices. The assumption is that if the parity ratio is 100, farmers are relatively as well off today as in 1910–14 (the "golden era of farming"). The use of this parity ratio assumes that farmers were as productive in 1910–14 as they are today. However, everyone recognizes that the productivity of farm labor, capital, and land has increased dramatically since the 1910–14 era. By the 1950s most saw the need to revise the parity formulas to account for this, however, the use of the parity formula based on 1910–14 prices and productivity benefited farmers and there was great resistance to modernizing the parity formula.
26. D. Gale Johnson, "The Food and Agriculture Act of 1977: Implications for Farmers, Consumers, and Taxpayers," in William Fellner, ed., *Contemporary Economic Problems, 1978* (Washington, D.C.: American Enterprise Institute, 1978).
27. Bovard, *The Farm Fiasco*, 37.
28. The farmland idled was equivalent to all of Ohio and Indiana and half of Illinois.
29. Ibid., 88.
30. John C. Goodman and Edwin G. Dolan, "Farm Policy: Welfare for the Rich?" chapter 8 in Goodman and Dolan, *Economics of Public Policy*, 3d ed. (St. Paul: West Publishing Co., 1985), 96–98.
31. Bovard, *The Farm Fiasco*, 95.
32. Bruce Ingersoll, "Random Harvest: Why Is Oats Output Down, Demand Up? Blame 1985 Farm Law: Its Mix of Subsidies and Curbs Dims Sunflowers, Bolsters An Abundance of Barley," *The Wall Street Journal*, 10 June, 1988.
33. Honey prices have been supported since 1950. The 1985 bill supported the 1,600 full-time beekeepers at a price of 66 cents per pound for honey, a price 15 cents above the wholesale price. The costs for the honey program rose from $4 million in 1980 to $88 million in 1985 and resulted in the CCC acquiring 115 million pounds of honey. Wool producers were subsidized at a price of $1.73 per pound for wool when the market price was around 75 cents a pound. James J. Kilpatrick reported in 1985 that 65 producers received support checks for over $100,000 and one producer received a price support check for $560,000.
34. For one example see Thomas M. Burton, "Cash Crop: Many Farmers Harvest Government Subsidies in Violation of Law: The Conner Family 'Split Up' Its Big Holdings to Get A

Larger Federal Payment," *The Wall Street Journal*, 8 May, 1990; and, Charles McCoy, "Slaking a Thirst: Big Farmers in West Get Subsidized Water Despite Drought Crisis: Many Divide Their Holdings to Elude Federal Rules That Limit Allotments," *The Wall Street Journal*, 30 May, 1991. Also see Bovard, *The Farm Fiasco*, chapter 3.

35. This section is based on the following: Bovard, "Redistribution via Cows," chapter 6 in *The Farm Fiasco*; and Scott Kilman, "Market Maze: Why the Price of Milk Depends on Distance from Eau Claire, Wisconsin: Convoluted U.S. Price Rules Dismay Many Economists, Some Dairy People Too," *The Wall Street Journal*, 20 May, 1991.
36. See Lindley H. Clark, Jr., "How Protectionism Soured the Sugar Market," *The Wall Street Journal*, 5 November, 1987, and Bovard, *The Farm Fiasco*, 62–66.
37. Bruce Ingersoll, "Shell Game: Peanut Quota System Comes Under Attack for Distorting Market: Limits on Output and Imports Raise Ire of Processors; Congress Weighs Changes," *The Wall Street Journal*, 1 May, 1990.
38. Bovard, *The Farm Fiasco*, 180. Bovard's chapter 9, "Trampling Individual Rights," discusses marketing orders in some detail.
39. In 1980 the USDA threatened to sue Carl Pescosolido for giving his surplus oranges to San Francisco churches. Co-op and independent almond packers in California are required to spend 2.5 cents on specific advertising for each pound of almonds they sell. The almond marketing board is dominated by the California Almond Growers Exchange (CAGE) which markets the Blue Diamond brand of almonds. They easily spend the 2.5 cents per pound of almonds advertising the Blue Diamond brand, whereas the small growers, which export or sell wholesale their almonds, have no specific brands to advertise. Therefore they are forced to forfeit the 2.5 cents per pound to the almond marketing board.
40. Lloyd D. Teigen, *Agricultural Parity: Historical Review and Alternative Calculations*, prepared for the U.S. Department of Agriculture, 1987, cited in Bovard, *The Farm Fiasco*, 48.
41. Calculated from Bovard, *The Farm Fiasco*, table 3–2, p. 49.

CHAPTER 11

Developments in Manufacturing, 1950 to the Present

It is common to use "industrialization" as the touchstone of economic development and to exhort other nations to "industrialize" and therefore spur economic development. If those countries concentrate on the production and exportation of primary products and raw materials, it is often taken as a sure sign of failure to promote economic development. However, this fails to recognize that economic development is a much broader process than simply "industrialization." At the same time that a manufacturing sector was emerging in most of the now advanced countries, agricultural and transportation developments were allowing fewer farmers to support a growing number of "nonfarmers," thus allowing a continued shift of labor from agricultural to manufacturing and service activities.

Industrialization, therefore, is only a part of the much broader economic development of a society. The manufacturing sector is important because of its sheer size in relation to the rest of the economy and because of the size of the individual firms in the sector. The phrase "big business" was first used in the late nineteenth century to describe the large manufacturing firms that came into being at that time and is used in the same sense today. Manufacturing still dominates the American economy in many ways. It accounts for a major portion of the corporate profits received, and the largest and most visible manufacturing concerns continue to have great economic and political influence.

MANUFACTURING'S IMPORTANCE: SIZE, GROWTH, AND LOCATION

We begin our examination of manufacturing in the postwar American economy by considering its size. Figure 11.1 presents data on the share of GNP that originates in all manufacturing as well as in the components of durable and nondurable goods manufacturing. Similar data are shown for the share of total employment in manufacturing. The share of GNP originating in all manufacturing declined by 1.1 percentage points per year between 1950 and 1988, while durable goods share declined by 1 percentage point a year and nondurable manufacturing's share declined by 1.1 percentage points a year. As can be seen, employment shares behaved in a similar manner.

Figure 11.2 presents the yearly employment share divided by the GNP share. Changes in this ratio over time can be thought of as crude measures of changes in labor productivity in manufacturing compared to the other sectors of the economy. If labor productivity in manufacturing is rising faster than in the other sectors of the economy, then even though manufacturing's share of GNP is falling, its share of employment will be falling faster, and the ratio of the employment share to the GNP share will decline. However, if labor's productivity is rising more slowly than in the other sectors of the economy, then manufacturing labor will not be released as fast, and the ratio of the employment share to the GNP share will rise. As can be seen, the employment to GNP shares fell over the 1950 to 1988 period, indicating that labor productivity in manufacturing was rising more rapidly than in most other sectors of the economy. The most rapid declines came between 1974 and 1977 and between 1982 and 1988. Both were periods of difficulty for many manufacturing firms as rising energy prices and increas-

Fig. 11.1 Manufacturing's Share of GNP and Manufacturing's Share of Employment

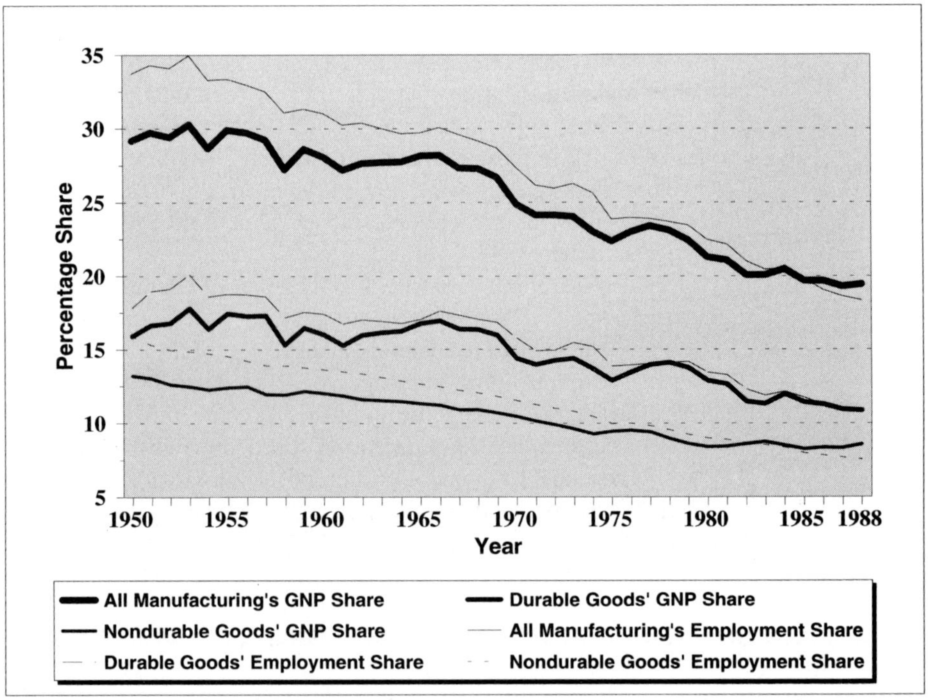

Source: *Economic Report of the President* (Washington, D.C.: U.S. Government Printing Office, 1991).

ing competition from imported products forced manufacturers to strive to improve productivity and lower production costs.

Manufacturing activity is not evenly dispersed around the United States. Historically, the New England states were the first to develop an industrial sector, and these were followed by the Middle Atlantic states and then the states in the East North Central region. In the twentieth century manufacturing activity has become more evenly dispersed. In the postwar period the the south and west coast areas have been the largest gainers. The primary gains in shares of manufacturing employment have been in six states, North Carolina, Georgia, and Florida in the South Atlantic region; Tennessee in the East South Central region; Texas in the West South Central region; and California in the Pacific Coast region. California's gain in the share of national manufacturing employment overwhelms all of the other states' gains.

The New England, Middle Atlantic, and East North Central regions have had the highest real wage rates. As firms matured and plants and machinery began to be replaced, they began to migrate toward lower labor cost areas, particularly the southern "sunbelt" areas. By no means, however, can all of the shift be attributed to the actual migration of firms out of the northeastern "snowbelt." Part of the shift is due to the

Fig. 11.3 The Manufacturing's Employment Share Divided by Manufacturing's GNP Share

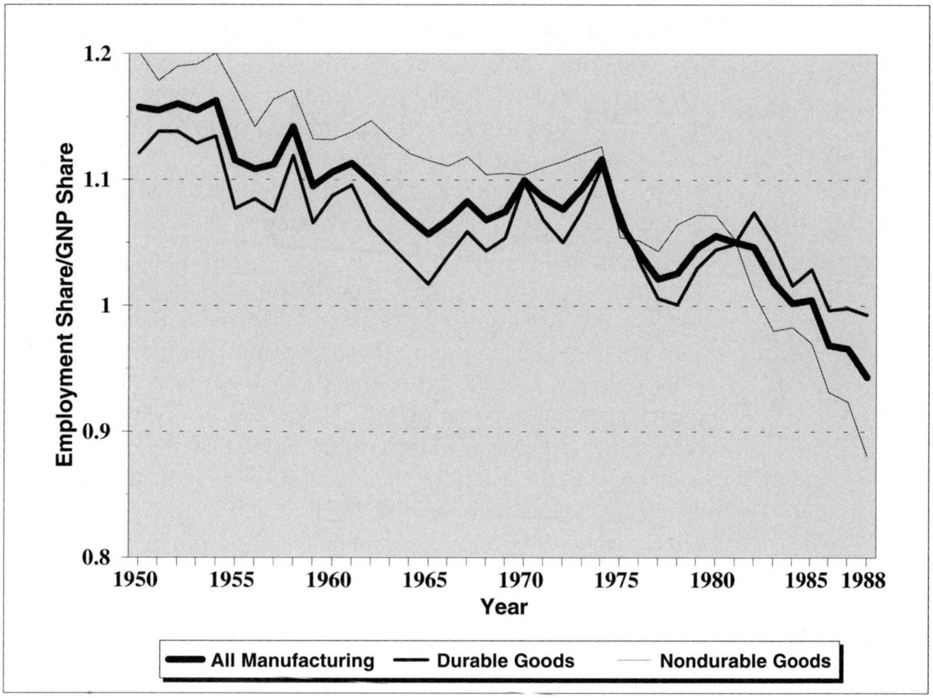

Source: *Economic Report of the President* (Washington, D.C.: U.S. Government Printing Office, 1991).

location in the sunbelt and Pacific Coast regions of newer industries and firms. The national capital market leads firms, all else the same, to choose a location where wage rates are somewhat lower, such as the south. The advent of air conditioning has particularly aided industrial development in the southern states by making them much more attractive to firms and workers. Improved, lower cost communications systems allowed firms to disperse more of their manufacturing activity while still being able to adequately monitor, coordinate, and control activity among widely scattered manufacturing plants. The result has been a dispersion of manufacturing activity among regions such that differences in their industrial-agricultural orientation have became far less pronounced.

American industries have also grown at different rates. In the postwar era the output of nondurable goods has grown slightly faster than the output of durable goods; although there is great variation within each category. Among the durable goods industries, electrical machinery and instruments were the fastest growing, while primary metals production was the slowest and, in fact, primary metals production declined between 1970 and 1988. Excluding the primary metals industry, in the most recent period the fastest growing durable goods industries grew twice as fast as the slowest growing industries.

Similarly, among the nondurable goods industries the rubber and miscellaneous plastics products and chemicals and allied products industries grew much faster than other industries, while leather and leather products declined. Increasingly leather products, especially shoes, have been imported, and many domestic producers have either gone out of business or moved their production to foreign plants. Other than the leather industry, in the most recent period the fastest growing nondurable goods industries grew from 2.3 to 8.4 times as fast as the slowest growing ones.

Table 11.1 ranks industries according to their real value added in 1987.[1] Transportation equipment and food and kindred products have been the largest industries throughout the postwar period. The instruments and related products and rubber and miscellaneous plastics products grew much faster than other industries, whereas the primary metals, apparel and related products, textile mill products, and leather and leather products industies grew the slowest—in fact, the leather and leather products industry declined over the period. There also is a considerable disparity in size. The largest 5 industries have a larger value added than the next 15 industries.

In general, the declining or slower growing industries were those producing basic consumer products such as food, textiles, and leather products, while the faster growing ones tended to produce complex scientific products such as chemicals, scientific

Table 11.1 Manufacturing Value Added: Selected Industries and Years (Billions of 1982–1984 Dollars)

Industry	1947	1958	1967	1977	1987
Transportation Equipment	22.401	52.889	84.353	106.091	119.527
Food and Kindred Products	34.447	61.194	79.704	92.512	107.459
Chemicals and Allied Products	20.477	42.467	70.509	93.599	106.727
Machinery Excluding Electrical	29.817	42.882	83.341	110.929	104.942
Electric and Electronic Equipment	14.863	35.969	73.314	83.112	84.470
Printing and Publishing	16.294	27.471	42.979	52.772	78.528
Fabricated Metal Products	18.782	32.606	54.021	75.102	66.464
Instruments and Related Products	4.122	10.055	19.216	30.960	62.929
Paper and Allied Products	10.973	19.747	29.210	36.586	43.773
Primary Metal Industries	22.004	40.384	59.814	61.993	40.990
Rubber and Misc. Plastics Products	4.973	11.339	20.359	32.574	38.990
Apparel and Related Products	16.958	20.799	30.132	32.460	29.323
Stone, Clay, and Glass Products	8.802	19.152	24.949	31.568	29.116
Lumber and Wood Products	9.531	11.014	14.889	26.771	25.168
Textile Mill Products	20.385	16.809	24.410	26.576	22.900
Furniture and Fixtures	5.260	8.145	12.485	14.723	17.816
Petroleum and Coal Products	7.691	8.713	16.246	27.026	16.196
Miscellaneous Manufacturing	7.977	16.453	30.506	16.982	15.345
Tobacco Products	2.447	4.889	6.089	7.167	12.554
Leather and Leather Products	5.851	6.567	7.865	6.137	3.763

Sources: *Statistical Abstract of the United States* (Washington, D.C.: U.S. Government Printing Office, Various Years).

instruments and related products, synthetic rubber and plastics, and producers' goods such as machinery. Although risky when discussing such broad industrial categories, a few tentative generalizations can be made. The income elasticity for food products and many other consumer nondurable commodities tends to be lower than for consumer durable goods and services, which contributes to the slower growth of the food and kindred products, textile mill products, apparels, and leather industries. The proliferation of consumer durable goods since the Second World War helps explain the more rapid growth of producers' durable goods industries because these products can be used to produce many types of consumer durables.

Contrary to what seems to be the popular opinion, it is not easy for the largest firms to remain dominant. Changes in technologies, consumer tastes, and the availability of natural resources require continuous adjustments by firms. Not all firms respond to the same extent. As a result there seems to have been considerable mobility among the largest industrial firms. Richard C. Edwards notes that there is a general consensus that "of the top one hundred firms in the opening decades of the century, roughly thirty to forty-five would appear on the list fifty years later."[2]

Edwards has recently examined this while correcting for entrants and exits resulting from mergers and court-ordered dissolutions. Using several measures he finds greater corporate stability in the post-1920 period than in the 1890 to 1920 period. "In the earlier period, on the average two to four firms every year dropped below the minimum (constant dollar) assets of the smallest firm in the top one hundred in the base year. In the later period, it took approximately five years for one firm to drop out of the group."[3] His conclusion is that the industrial system emerging from the pre-1919 consolidations was a system of "monopoly capitalism—a system in which the industrial center of the economy is dominated by large, oligopolistic, 'eternal-life' corporations."[4]

Other economists have also noticed that once a firm attains a larger size, it tends to remain relatively larger, suggesting greater corporate stability in the latter part of the twentieth century. Herman Krooss suggests that rather than indicating the development of monopoly capitalism, "this argues more for the stability of the American economy and the astuteness of management than it does for anything else."[5] With the increasingly sophisticated techniques available to evaluate markets and the demand for potential (and existing) products, one would expect to find that the firm failure rate is lower today than in the past. With today's diversified firms the failure of a single product no longer means the firm's failure. Thus, the lower failure rate may well indicate an improved ability to allocate resources in the present economy.

PRODUCTIVITY DEVELOPMENTS

It has been common during the past two decades to blame manufacturing for most of the decline in productivity growth in the American economy. Agriculture's share is too small too have much influence, and the service industries have historically had lower levels of labor productivity growth. We know that some part of the well accepted decline in productivity growth since the late 1960s is due to the shift of resources, particularly labor, from manufacturing to services, but most of the decline is blamed on a declining rate of productivity growth in manufacturing.

An examination of average annual growth rates of output per labor-hour for all manufacturing and selected manufacturing industries shows no such decline—in fact, the decade of the 1980s was one of the fastest growing periods. Growth rates did vary sharply between industries. Growth in output per labor-hour in bakery products was, on average, slower than for bottled and canned soft drinks. Growth for petroleum refining was relatively rapid through 1975, but in the 1975–85 decade, with higher real prices and relatively higher profits, output per labor-hour growth fell sharply. Since 1985, with much lower petroleum prices and profits, output per labor-hour growth has risen sharply. Output per labor-hour in footwear manufacturing has been extremely slow and actually declined from 1975–80 and 1985–87, helping to explain why production moved overseas where relatively lower real wage rates prevailed.

Two industries that have tended to epitomize the problems in American manufacturing in the last two decades are motor vehicles and steel. Motor vehicle output per labor-hour growth has varied sharply from little growth in the late 1960s and late 1970s to much more rapid growth in the early 1970s and early 1980s. In the early 1970s production and sales were growing rapidly as domestic production of passenger cars was 8.6 million in 1971, 8.8 million in 1972, and 9.7 million in 1973. Though sales were high in the late 1970s, growing competition from imports and the necessity to redesign and retool toward smaller cars in response to the rapid escalation of fuel prices reduced productivity gains. In the early 1980s, the severe contraction and growing imports led Chrysler to retrench and cut the number of plants and employment nearly in half. GM and Ford both began revising production techniques to raise labor productivity.

Output per labor-hour in the steel industry grew a respectable 4.36 percent per year between 1960 and 1965. After 1965 the slowness to adopt the newer, lower cost technologies such as the Basic Oxygen Furnace and relatively high wages led to a much slower growth in labor productivity. A reduced growth in the demand for steel—due to competition from imported European and Japanese steel, and from other materials such as structural concrete, plastics, and new types of ceramics—led to declining plant utilization further reducing labor productivity. In the 1980s as the integrated steel producers such as United States Steel (now USX) and Bethlehem closed or modernized a few plants and reduced employment, and as the newer, smaller mini-mills expanded production, output per labor-hour grew more rapidly.[6]

Research and Development

The most important source of productivity growth is technological change either through new machinery, new inputs, new processes or managerial innovations in directing and coordinating production processes. The expenditures on research and development (R&D) represent one measure of the attempts to bring about technological change but not the success of those efforts. Figures 11.3 and 11.4 provide data on R&D expenditures from 1955 to 1988. R&D funds as a percent of GNP peaked in

Fig. 11.3 Research and Development Expenditures as a Percent of GNP

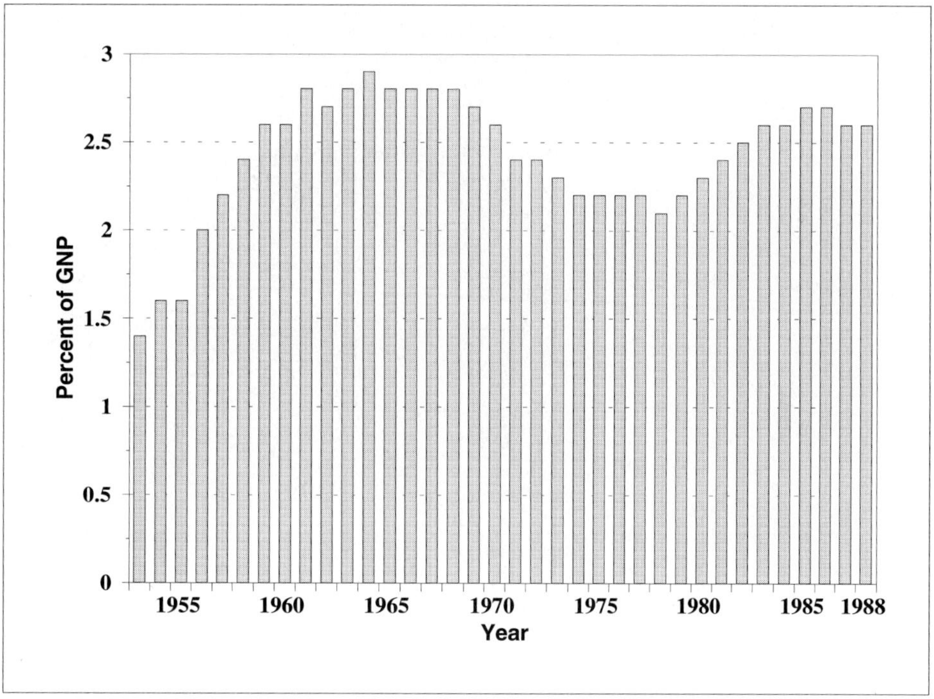

Source: *Statistical Abstract of the United States* (Washington, D.C.: U.S. Government Printing Office, Various Years).

1964, fell through 1978, and rose into the 1980s. The share of the funds that came from the federal government exceeded 60 percent during most of the 1960s but then began falling and was less than 50 percent in the 1980s.

The share of R&D expenditures devoted to defense has declined since the early 1960s, while space research peaked in the late 1960s. Generally two thirds of all research and development has been devoted to development. In private industry, basic research has comprised about 7 percent of R&D expenditures, applied research 25 percent, and development about 70 percent.[7]

Edwin Mansfield reports that, "results obtained during the 1960s provide reasonably persuasive evidence that R&D has had a significant effect on the rate of productivity increase in the industries [chemicals, petroleum, and agriculture] that have been studied."[8] There has been a direct relationship between R&D spending and productivity growth, with the private rate of return on R&D spending averaging 17 percent though "higher in chemicals and petroleum, lower in aircraft and electrical equipment."[9] Another study found a considerably higher rate of return of 30 percent.[10] The evidence also suggests that industrial R&D raised productivity in other industries,

Fig. 11.4 The Percent of Research and Development Funded by the Federal Government

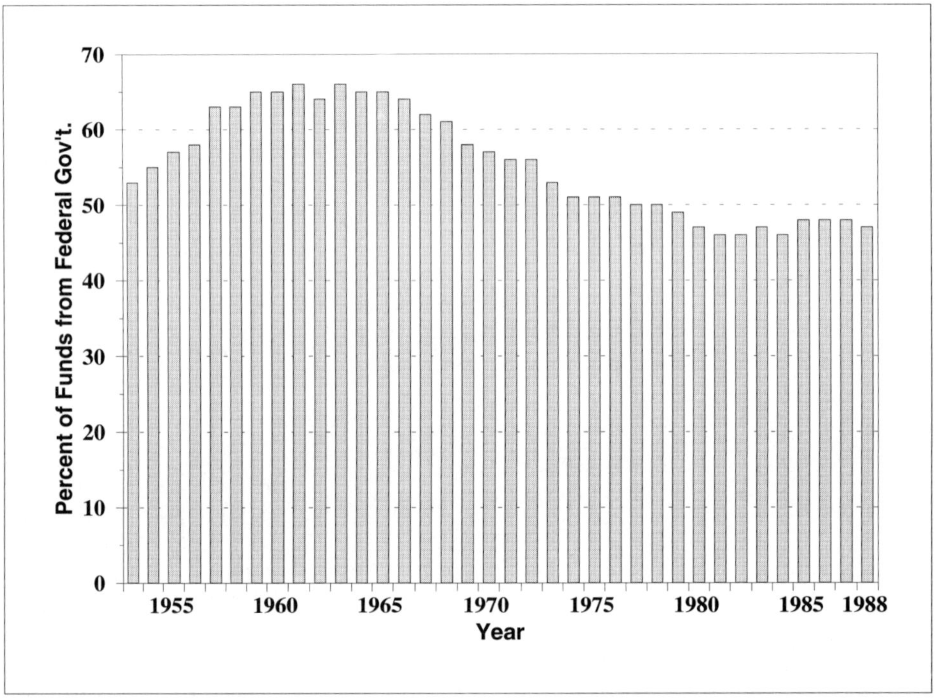

Source: *Statistical Abstract of the United States* (Washington, D.C.: U.S. Government Printing Office, Various Years).

because many durable goods industries produce machines and other inputs used in other manufacturing processes.

Patents

Another indicator of technological change is patent activity, a measure often used to indicate the rate of invention in various industries. However, as Mansfield reports, there are some disadvantages in using patents in this manner. The relative importance of patents to an industry may vary considerably over time and place, and "the proportion of the total inventions that are patented may vary significantly."[11] Most patents have been for inventions, and this activity has become increasingly dominated by corporations in the postwar era with a few industries dominating the receipt of patent grants.

There are some who argue that the patent system needs to be changed. Patents, though generally short lived, create legal, monopolistic property rights that bar entry and reduce the quantity of resources devoted to utilizing the knowledge covered by the patent. However, patents yield positive benefits because the creation of property rights in new knowledge provides the financial incentive to induce greater efforts in advancing knowledge. Nathan Rosenberg points out that most research is now undertaken by collective enterprises, a process he has described as "the increasing socialization of knowledge production," a change that calls into question the "privatized, individualistic conception" that is the basis of the patent system. An appropriate patent system would be one in which the marginal benefits due to the patent laws would equal or just exceed the marginal costs of monopoly restrictions on the use of the knowledge. The continued retention of the American patent system presupposes that the incremental benefits exceed the incremental costs but "this presupposition is, under present circumstances, certainly far from obvious."[12]

The Materials Revolution

Nathan Rosenberg has been one of the leaders in examining technological change in the nineteenth- and twentieth-century American economy.[13] According to Rosenberg, in the twentieth century "an increasing proportion of technological changes have been dependent upon prior advances in systematized knowledge, a knowledge which has brought with it a much more deeply-rooted understanding of the forces of nature and the physical universe."[14] Technical advances in the twentieth century are much less dependent upon casual empiricism, practical knowledge, and mechanical ingenuity and much more dependent upon applications of knowledge from such scientific disciplines as chemistry and physics. The development of increasingly sophisticated instruments brought together data and knowledge from several scientific areas.

This growing knowledge of materials led to the developments such as the use of chromium and tungsten in steel alloys and new uses for materials such as titanium and magnesium. Entirely new industries devoted to producing artificial organic polymers have developed. New products include the whole range of plastics, synthetic fibers, packaging materials, synthetic rubber, lightweight thermal insulation, water-repellent coating, and high-strength adhesives—all coming from the petrochemical industry. These twentieth-century developments have worked to reduce our dependence upon specific natural resource inputs, especially unprocessed natural resources.[15] Finally, by increasing the number of good substitutes for industrial products, new dimensions to the competitive process have been created.

Managerial Developments

Another source of productivity improvements is innovations or changes in the way in which manufacturing firms are managed. There is considerable historical evidence of the importance of the management and organization of firms. Alfred D. Chandler, Jr.'s work on the historical development of the multidivisional, decentralized firm is among the best expositions of this.[16]

Martin N. Baily and Alok K. Chakrabarti have recently suggested that part of the recent productivity lag in the United States may be due to a frequent failure of management to take advantage of productivity-enhancing technology.[17] They contend that American companies have not developed any system for exploiting new ideas. Eric von Hippel suggests that the way to overcome this is to organize the process of innovation and that firms need to pinpoint the sources of innovation in their industries and develop networks to communicate that information as well as incentives to develop and use such innovations.[18] In addition to technical staffs in companies, innovations are frequently developed by the product users. An important part of the process is then to develop links, say among the field-service representatives and the sales force, to bring information on innovative developments back to the firm. Baily and Chakrabarti believe that in recent decades the performance of managers in promoting a continuing flow of new ideas and applying those new ideas has been less than satisfactory.

Manufacturing Productivity Changes in the Postwar Period

The brief survey has not answered the question of why there is a productivity lag in American manufacturing. When we look at the growth of output per labor-hour we see that it varies significantly across industries but was not systematically lower in the 1980s—in fact, it was often higher. Research and development expenditures as a percent of GNP declined during the 1970s but rose in the 1980s as private sector funding increasingly replaced federal funding. Neither do patents show any decline reflecting reduced inventive activity. The productivity lag in American manufacturing compared to other countries may simply be due to weaknesses in management, something that is not as easily quantified. However, there is considerable anecdotal evidence to support this.

In 1991 a small firm in Danville, Illinois, was producing lightweight pickup truck bumpers for Japanese automobile manufacturers.[19] To increase productivity at the firm and raise the quality of the output, Toyota sent a team of manufacturing experts to conduct a crash course in the Toyota Production System. As a result, productivity at the firm rose by 60 percent and the number of defects dropped by 80 percent.

An Orrville, Ohio foundry was losing $125,000 a month when the Condec Corporation decided to close it down. The former general manager bought the foundry, cleaned it up, purchased some new and salvaged machinery, and found lower priced sources for raw materials. His new company saw sales increase from $2 million to almost $9 million, and the foundry generated pretax profits of nearly $500,000 in 1990. Labor productivity improved fourfold, and the improved quality attracted many new customers.[20]

Throughout much of the 1970s the Chrysler Corporation experienced losses and by the end of the decade was on the verge of collapse. In the United States in the 1970s, two of Chrysler Corporation's domestic models, the Dodge Aspen and the Plymouth Volare, earned unenviable reputations for poor-quality construction and components. However, the Chrysler subsidiary in Mexico was producing the *same* cars, under the old names of Dart and Valiant, and it experienced much more rapid growth than other Mexican automobile producers because of their cars' reputation for high quality.

In 1974 Matsushita Electrical Company, which markets Panasonic products, bought the Motorola Corporation and took over Motorola's TV manufacturing plant in Franklin Park, Illinois. The plant had been operating at a loss with a high rejection rate on its television sets. Matsushita brought in a new management team, cut some existing managerial staff, and reorganized production. By 1978 productivity at the plant had risen 25 percent, and the rejection rate on TV sets had dropped from 20 percent in 1974 to 2 percent in 1978.

During the late 1970s and the 1980s the American automobile producers struggled under a severe cost disadvantage compared to Japanese automobile producers. In the last half of the 1980s, GM, Ford, and Chrysler began programs to reorganize the design and development and production of their cars. By the early 1990s Chrysler and Ford had reduced the cost disadvantages to less than $150 per vehicle. Chrysler had reduced its product development teams from 2,000 to 740 people and engineered cars in 39 months compared to 54 months in the early 1980s.[21] General Motors, unable to restructure effectively, suffered a $795 cost disadvantage compared to Ford and Chrysler and continued to incur huge losses. Of the three companies, it was General Motors that had invested most heavily in new plants and technology, particularly robots, but this did not offset the weaknesses of its internal structure and management.

Though difficult to quantify and neatly categorize, it is clear that the management of a firm can play an important role in raising productivity. These examples suggest that a part of the productivity lag in American manufacturing may be traced to American management.

COMPETITION, MONOPOLY, AND THE GOVERNMENT

Monopolization in American industry has long been a concern of many politicians and economists. In the 1970s several congressional bills to break up large firms were introduced. Other recent proposals included government-mandated divestiture for the huge oil companies. Contrary to such proposals, however, it is not clear that there is increasing monopolization in American industry nor that excessive monopoly power already exists. Neither is it clear that merely the absolute size of a firm is an indication of its monopoly powers. This section briefly examines the structure of the manufacturing industry since the Second World War. Historically, mergers have been an important means of increasing market power, so we consider this before we examine the development of and changes in antitrust policy by the federal government. We conclude with some brief evaluations of industry performance.

Mergers

Most of the mergers since the 1950s have been termed *conglomerate mergers*. Under FTC classifications, conglomerate mergers are classified as *product line extensions*, *market extensions*, or *pure conglomerates*. Scherer and Ross illustrate a product line extension merger by Procter and Gamble's attempted purchase of Chlorox, where a leading detergent maker attempted to acquire a leading bleach producer. A market extension merger can be illustrated by Safeway's acquisition of supermarkets so as to move into geographic markets that the chain had not previously served. Pure conglomerate mergers are those lacking such complementarities, for example, Beatrice Food's diversification into luggage manufacturing and the production of auto parts.

As Figure 11.5 shows, there was a cluster of mergers in the late 1960s—due primarily to a sharp increase in pure conglomerate mergers. After declining during the 1970s, merger activity increased sharply in the 1980s. Several features differentiated the 1980s merger wave from previous ones. When it started, there was no boom in the stock market. In fact, stock prices were not uncommonly below the book value of the physical assets of a firm so that it was often less costly to expand by purchasing an existing firm than by constructing new plants and equipment. As Scherer and Ross describe it, "Bargain seeking merger activity soared."[22] With the onset of a stock market boom in 1983, more traditional merger activity occurred, and firms rushed in to buy other firms before stock prices rose more. When stock prices collapsed in October of 1987, merger activity did not follow a similar path. Rather, as Scherer and Ross report, foreign firms, lured by a weak dollar and relatively low stock prices in the United States, began purchasing American firms.

The Reagan administration adopted a more lenient antitrust policy, and an increasing number of mergers in the 1980s were horizontal mergers. The Federal Trade Commission approved nine huge mergers that were the largest in American history: Socal and Gulf, Texaco and Getty Oil, Du Pont and Conoco, United States Steel and Marathon Oil, Mobil and Superior Oil, the Southern Pacific and Santa Fe railroads, the Connecticut General and INA insurance companies, Texas Gulf and ELF Aquitaine, and Cities Service and Occidental Oil. It also approved a joint venture between General Motors and Toyota, the first- and third-largest automobile manufacturers in the world.[23]

Another difference in the 1980s was the dramatic growth of hostile takeovers using new financial devices, especially junk bonds. In some cases friendly takeovers were engineered to deflect hostile takeovers. In other cases managements created "poison pills" to increase the costs of hostile takeovers in an attempt to deflect such activity. These new devices allowed raiders to take over some giant firms such as Gulf Oil, Getty Oil, RCA, Burlington Industries, Trans-World Airlines, and Federated Stores, among others.

Assessing the results of mergers is, at best, difficult. The two standard methods are to analyze stock prices using the logic of the Capital Asset Pricing Theory or to examine other indices of firm performance such as profitability, sales, and market shares. In general, the studies of stock prices have found that prior to the merger the shareholders of the firm to be acquired gained while the shareholders of the acquiring firm usually neither gained nor lost. However, studies of performance after the mergers found that stock prices generally declined.[24] The other evaluation methods provide somewhat different results. Most studies of mergers in the 1950s, 1960s, and 1970s have found that

Fig. 11.5 Merger Activity: Thousands of Firms Acquired

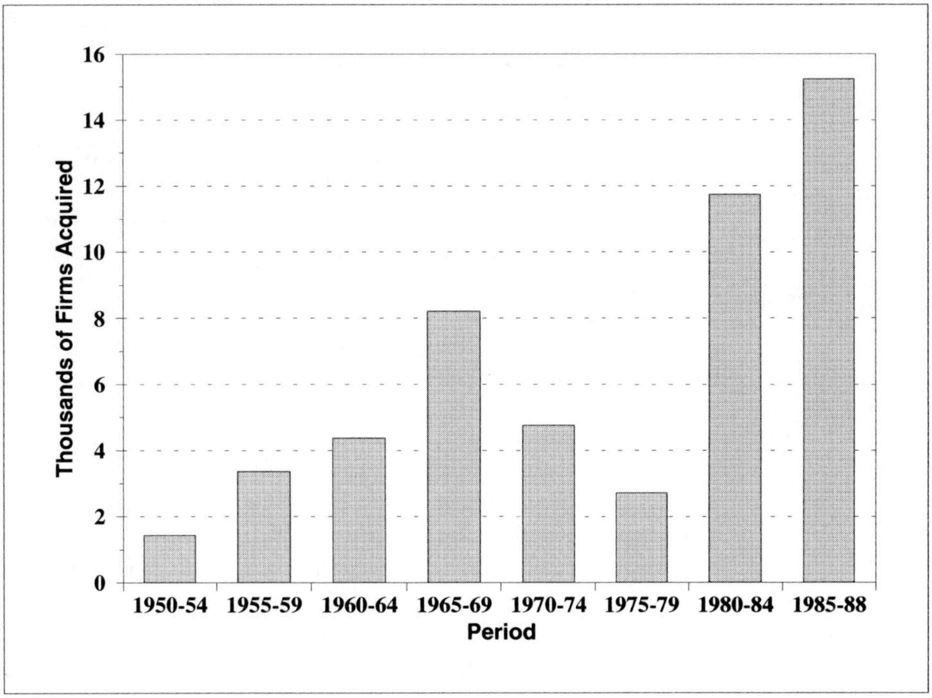

Source: *Statistical Abstract of the United States* (Washington, D.C.: U.S. Government Printing Office, Various Years).

prior to the merger the target firms were considerably more profitable than the acquiring firms, and this was particularly so the smaller the firm to be acquired. There was evidence that the premerger growth in profitability of the target firms had slowed, leading to stock market price declines because profits growth trigger changes in stock prices. In the case of tender offers, it appeared that the target firms were often in industries that were experiencing difficulties, rather than the individual firms experiencing the difficulty themselves.

When the postmerger performance of merged firms is assessed, a pessimistic picture emerges, one that Scherer and Ross describe as "widespread failure, considerable mediocrity, and occasional successes."[25] Frequently, lines of the acquired firms were sold, profits declined, and market shares eroded. The erosion in market shares was much larger for conglomerate mergers than for horizontal mergers. Scherer and Ross conclude that although arguments for mergers are generally made in terms of greater profitability and efficiency, the statistical evidence generally does not support this. It appears, in fact, that efficiency is reduced, particularly when smaller firms are merged into "bureaucratic" enterprises. Of course, counterexamples of increased efficiency can be found, but "the overall record is far from reassuring."[26]

Postwar Antitrust Policy

Essentially the entire edifice of United States federal antitrust laws rests upon the Sherman Act of 1890 and the Clayton and Federal Trade Commission Acts of 1914, but over the years the interpretation of those laws has changed. Though initiated in 1937, the *Alcoa* case was not ruled upon until 1945, when Judge Learned Hand presented his decision that overturned the "rule of reason" and made sheer size illegal per se. The *United Shoe Machinery* decision reinforced this.[27] In 1949 A&P was found guilty of conspiring to monopolize but not of actually monopolizing because its nationwide share of retail grocery sales was less than 10 percent. In general, by the 1950s a large firm dominating its market had became illegal simply because of its size under the changed interpretation of the antitrust laws. It made no difference how the size was attained or maintained.

Section 7 of the Clayton Act deals with corporate mergers by condemning those that substantially lessen competition or tend to create a monopoly. The Celler-Kefauver amendment in 1950 closed what was considered a loophole by also prohibiting asset acquisitions. The *du Pont-General Motors* case, decided in 1957, marked two changes in application. First, Section 7 was extended to apply to vertical mergers; second, it dictated that a merger's legality was to be decided on the facts existing at the time the case was brought to trial—the conditions existing at the time of the merger were not relevant to the lawsuit. The courts ruled that du Pont's purchase of 23 percent of GM stock in 1917–19, when General Motors did not dominate the automobile market, foreclosed much of the market for automotive finishes and materials to competing companies in the 1950s.

The revised section 7 and the concept of *incipiency* began to take their toll with the *Brown Shoe* decision of 1962. The concept of incipiency holds that it is possible to ascertain practices that potentially limit competition and to stop those practices before they reduce competition. The *Brown Shoe* decision ruled that the purchase of the G. R. Kinney Company, mainly a retailer, by the Brown Shoe Company, mainly a shoe producer, threatened to substantially lessen competition at both the manufacturing and retailing levels. It did not matter than the shoe industry was close to the classroom model of pure competition and characterized by extreme ease of entry.[28] The *Continental Can* and *Alcoa* cases of 1964, and the 1966 *Von's Grocery* and *Pabst* decisions continued this type of reasoning. Ernest Gellhorn suggests that the *Pabst* decision indicated that the government only had to show that a merger would have a substantial effect somewhere in the country without requiring the market to be defined.[29]

With horizontal and vertical mergers severely diminished, more attention was given to conglomerate mergers. In 1967 the Supreme Court presented the *Procter and Gamble* decision, whereby Procter and Gamble's acquisition of the Chlorox Company was found illegal because, among other rationales, Procter and Gamble was the leading potential candidate for entry into the bleach market, so the merger was anticompetitive because it diminished actual and future competition.[30] In addition to the potential competitor theory, the FTC also developed a "toehold" theory and applied it in 1971 rulings against the Bendix Corporation's acquisition of Fram and Kennecott Copper's acquisition of Peabody Coal. Each should have purchased a much smaller firm to gain a "toehold" in the industry and therefore "improve" competition in the auto filter and coal markets.

In 1973 the FTC charged that Xerox had monopolized the copier industry by using leasing and patent tactics similar to those used by United Shoe Machinery 25 years earlier. In the middle of 1975, a consent decree was signed whereby Xerox agreed to license its patents (including up to three patents royalty-free on each copier product) and to supply its know-how to all competitors except IBM. Xerox's market share subsequently declined, though other factors were also responsible.[31]

Other cases initiated in the 1970s have turned out differently. In 1972 the FTC launched an attack on the four major breakfast cereal manufacturers under a "shared monopoly" concept. The FTC did not contend that the four firms conspired or colluded; instead it charged that through advertising and brand proliferation they shared monopoly prices and barred entry by "little guys" who could not afford the necessary advertising outlay. In September of 1981, the complaint was dismissed as the FTC apparently abandoned its shared monopoly concept.[32]

The Justice Department's case against IBM, which began in 1969, was settled in 1982. IBM had been charged with using tactics that monopolized the computer industry, but it vigorously fought the charges, and the case stretched out for a decade. By 1982 conditions in the computer industry had changed. New mainframe computers, minicomputers pioneered and produced by other firms such as Digital Equipment Corporation, and the microcomputer revolution led by Apple Computer were creating pervasive new competition for IBM. Scherer and Ross comment that "the case had become a historical relic, and the government had good reasons for withdrawing."[33]

Beginning in 1974 the Supreme Court took a more lenient attitude toward horizontal mergers. In the *General Dynamics* case, the Supreme Court reversed lower court rulings and found that the coal companies that General Dynamics' subsidiary had acquired to become the nation's fifth-largest coal producer did not reduce competition in two states. In 1979 Pillsbury's acquisition of Fox Deluxe Foods, was allowed to stand even though both of them produced frozen pizzas. New merger guidelines, written in 1982, recognized this position. Though the Reagan administration allowed some large horizontal mergers, especially among petroleum companies, others, such as the proposed merger between Republic Steel and Jones and Laughlin Steel and the proposed merger between the brewers Schlitz and Heileman, were opposed.[34]

By the 1970s there was a growing criticism of antitrust policies. In 1978 Robert Bork argued that the tendency to view productive efficiency "as pernicious by calling it a 'barrier to entry' or a 'competitive advantage' . . . is probably the major reason for the deformation of antitrust's doctrines."[35] Yale Brozen argued that "open entry is sufficient to enforce competitive behavior in most, if not all, circumstances," but the Antitrust Division had found barriers to entry that were not barriers at all and, in the process, may have became an entry barrier in its own right.[36] Antitrust policy has always had political and social dimensions as well as an economic one. Criticisms such as these led to an elevation of the economic dimension and a recognition that many past antitrust decisions and policies had, in fact, worsened the economic impact while achieving social and political goals.[37] This was an important force leading to the dominance of the economic dimension of antitrust policy. Marc Allen Eisner has pointed out that current antitrust enforcement focuses on price-fixing and related forms of white-collar crime, while vertical restraint and mergers have received less attention; this, he argues, is consistent with the focus on antitrust as economic policy.[38]

This change can be seen in monopolization cases where there was an increased emphasis on the "rule of reason criteria" and a retreat from the strong structuralist position represented by the *Alcoa* decision. Merger policy also began to allow horizontal mergers that a few years earlier would likely have been challenged. When Ronald Reagan assumed the presidency, his administration further altered antitrust policy. "Key antitrust agency positions were staffed with more conservative individuals, and a stream of new appointments accelerated the federal judiciary's drift toward greater skepticism of government intervention into markets, whether its purpose was ostensibly to stimulate or (through regulation) restrict competition."[39]

The announced goal of the Reagan administration was to reduce the intrusive role of government into everyday affairs and, in the process, revitalize market mechanisms, "thus reestablishing the foundations of a strong, vital economy."[40] A reformation of antitrust policy was a part of the Reagan revolution, and the policy revolution was executed through administrative means by appointing "Chicago school lawyers and economists to leadership positions in the antitrust agencies."[41] Though this is a common explanation, it is also incomplete. The redefinition of policy had been taking place throughout the 1970s as part of an evolutionary change. "Despite their rhetorical elegance and analytic rigor, the Reagan appointees were preaching to the converted. Indeed, it is questionable whether any enforcement agenda other than that supported by the administration could have been possible."[42] In many ways, these changes resulted from a convergence of law and economics in antitrust policy. The rebuilding of the FTC in the 1970s had brought in academic economists with Ph.D.s, and their influence had grown. The appointment by Reagan of William T. Baxter as assistant attorney general for antitrust furthered this process because, "Baxter's desire to redefine policy in the terms suggested by the Chicago School was as striking as his faith in economic analysis."[43]

In a kind of cyclical process, policy changes since the 1970s seem to have moved back toward the rule-of-reason policies prevalent in the interwar period and away from the structure-conduct-performance paradigm prominent in the two and a half decades after the Second World War.

Industrial Concentration and Economic Performance

The structure-conduct-performance paradigm asserts that the greater the dominance of a few firms in an industry, the more they should be able to conduct their businesses in a manner yielding the supranormal profits indicative of economic inefficiency. In the postwar era considerable efforts were devoted to measuring and assessing the relationships between industry concentration and industry profits. If established, these relationships, could then guide public policies designed to reduce industrial concentration and improve economic performance in the American economy.

Empirical studies of the relationship between industry concentration and profitability faced a number of daunting measurement problems.[44] How were supranormal (or higher than normal) profits to be measured, and how was the concentration of firms in an industry to be measured? Several measures of supranormal profits have been proposed and used. One early attempt was the Lerner index for the difference between price and marginal cost. However, marginal cost can rarely be observed for a single product, let alone a multiproduct firm. In addition, the index depends upon the price elasticity of demand and is neither very sensitive nor useful. Other surrogates, such as the accounting rate of return on the stockholder's equity or on capital; Tobin's *q*, which measures the divergence between the market value of a firm and the replacement value of its assets; the Census Bureau's plant-specific price-cost-margin; and the Profit Impact of Market Strategy (PIMS) data set were used at various times. The data used often presented problems due to differences in accounting techniques because it is common for firms to use different accounting methods for the IRS as compared to financial reporting.

Other measurement problems in empirical studies included the problem of how to allocate common costs such as for the central office, joint sales forces, and basic research facilities, the arbitrariness of internal firm transfer prices; the sometimes extraordinarily high salaries for the managers of owner-managed firms, and the capitalization of monopoly returns through mergers. Other empirical questions focused on how to measure concentration, for example, with a four-firm concentration ratio or the Hirfindahl-Hirschman Index (the measure now generally favored), how to define the industry; the functional form for estimation; and the difficulties associated with measuring entry barriers.

The studies that followed Joe Bain's pioneering efforts attempted to overcome these problems.[45] Most of these cross-sectional studies found, in varying degrees, evidence of a positive relationship between concentration and profitability.[46] The results began lending support to calls for changes in public policies to reduce industrial concentration and thereby increase economic efficiency. However, there were a number of economists who raised questions about such studies and urged restraint in any policy changes.[47]

In the 1970s these economists proposed that the higher industry profits in more concentrated industries were explained by the larger shares of the dominant firms that earned the higher profit rates because of their superiority. Harold Demsetz has shown that rates of return did not rise for all of the firms in concentrated industries, and, in fact, there was a negative correlation between concentration and profit rates of smaller firms in either a time-series or cross-sectional examination.[48]

Until the early 1980s these arguments were viewed skeptically by industrial organization economists accepting the structure-conduct-performance paradigm. At that time studies using better data began consistently showing that "price-cost margins were positively associated with lines' market shares . . . but if anything, *negatively* associated with seller concentration."[49] It is now conceded that for most studies up to the early 1980s where positive relationships between seller concentration and industry profitability were found, the associations were spurious, "a construct of aggregating from the line of business to the industry level."[50] Time-series studies in the 1980s have offered some evidence supporting an association between concentration and profitability, but weaknesses with statistical techniques and data continue to leave open the empirical question of such an association.

How significant are monopoly distortions in the American economy? After reviewing other estimates of the deadweight welfare loss due to monopolistic resource misallocation, Scherer and Ross estimate that it "lies somewhere between 0.5 and 2 percent of gross national product."[51] This is not far from Arnold Harberger's much-criticized 1954 estimate that the deadweight welfare loss in the 1924–28 period was slightly less than 0.1 percent of GNP.[52] However, this quantitatively insignificant figure may still understate the costs. For example, costs may be higher due to a monopoly firm's lax efforts to control costs and to wasteful expenditures in "rent seeking" (or expenditures undertaken in the attempt to obtain monopoly profits). Considering this, Scherer and Ross still conclude "that the social costs directly ascribable to monopoly power are modest."[53] They explain this by providing the following reasons, listed in descending order of importance.

Probably half or more of the American economy is composed of industries with enough sellers to maintain workable, though not perfect, competition—as long as government does not intrude to encourage and/or condone anticompetitive behavior. Second, many oligopolistic industries do not possess the power to hold prices above costs for any extended period because of the ease of entry of new firms, the expansion of existing firms, and/or the entry of additional imports. Third, high long-run elasticities of demand due to potential product substitution discourage firms from trying to exploit short-run monopoly power. Fourth, countervailing power from large buyers may offset the power of large sellers. Finally, public policy has played a role in constraining monopoly power.[54]

It seems fair to say that American manufacturing in the postwar era has been reasonably competitive.

SELECTED REFERENCES

Armentano, Dominick T. *The Myths of Antitrust*. New Rochelle, NY: Basic Books, 1978.

Bain, Joe S. "Relation of Profit Rate to Industry Concentration: American Manufacturing, 1936–1940." *Quarterly Journal of Economics* 65 (August 1951): 392–24.

__________. *Barriers to New Competition*. Cambridge, MA: Harvard University Press, 1956.

Barnett, Donald F., and Louis Schorsch. *Steel: Upheaval in a Basic Industry*. Cambridge, MA: Ballinger Publishing Co., 1983.

__________. *Up from the Ashes: The Rise of the Steel Minimill in the United States*. Washington, D.C.: The Brookings Institution, 1986.

Bork, Robert. *The Antitrust Paradox: A Policy at War with Itself*. New York: Basic Books, 1978.

Brozen, Yale. "Competition, Efficiency, and Antitrust." *Journal of World Trade Law* 3 (1969). Reprinted in *The Competitive Economy: Selected Readings* Edited by Yale Brozen. Morristown, NJ: General Learning Press, 1975.

__________. "Concentration and Structural and Market Disequilbria." *Antitrust Bulletin* 16 (Summer 1971): 244–48.

Caves, Richard E. "International Trade and Industrial Organization: Problems, Solved and Unsolved." *European Economic Review* 28 (August 1985): 377–95.

Chandler, Alfred D., Jr. *Strategy and Structure: Chapters in the History of American Industrial Enterprise*. Cambridge, MA: The M.I.T. Press, 1962.

__________. *The Visible Hand: The Managerial Revolution in American Business*. Cambridge, MA: Harvard University Press, 1977.

Demsetz, Harold. "Industry Structure, Market Rivalry, and Public Policy." *The Journal of Law and Economics* 16 (April 1973) 1–9.

__________. *The Market Concentration Doctrine*. Washington: The American Enterprise Institute, 1973.

__________. "Two Systems of Belief About Monopoly." *Industrial Concentration: The New Learning*. Edited by Harvey J. Goldschmid et al. Boston: Little Brown, 1974.

Edwards, Richard C. "Stages of Corporate Stability and the Risks of Corporate Failure." *The Journal of Economic History* 35 (June 1975): 428–57.

Eisner, Marc Allen. *Antitrust and the Triumph of Economics: Institutions, Expertise & Policy Change*. Chapel Hill, NC: University of North Carolina Press, 1991.

Gellhorn, Ernest. *Antitrust Law and Economics*. St. Paul: West Publishing Co., 1976.

Geroski, Paul A. "Pursuit of Monopoly Power: Recent Quantitative Work in Industrial Economics." *Journal of Applied Econometrics* 3 (April 1988): 107–23.

Harberger, Arnold C. "Monopoly and Resource Allocation." *American Economic Review* 44 (1954): 77–87.

Hippel, Eric von. *The Sources of Innovation*. New York: Oxford University Press, 1988.

Krooss, Herman. *American Economic Development*, third edition. Englewood Cliffs, NJ: Prentice-Hall, 1974.

Mancke, Richard B. "Causes of Interfirm Profitability Differences: A New Interpretation of the Evidence." *Quarterly Journal of Economics* 88 (May 1974): 181–93.

Mansfield, Edwin. "Technology and Productivity in the United States." *The American Economy in Transition*. Edited by Martin Feldstein. Chicago: University of Chicago Press for the National Bureau of Economic Research, 1980.

Markham, Jesse. "Survey of the Evidence and Findings on Mergers." *Business Concentration and Price Policy*. New York: National Bureau of Economic Research, 1955.

Nelson, Ralph L. *Merger Movements in American Industry, 1895–1956*. Princeton: Princeton University Press, 1959.

Peterman, John L. "The Brown Shoe Case." *The Journal of Law and Economics* 13 (April 1975): 81–146.

Porter, Glenn. *The Rise of Big Business, 1860–1910*. New York: Thomas Y. Crowell Co., 1973.

Reid, Samuel Richardson. *Mergers, Managers, and the Economy*. New York: McGraw-Hill Book Co., 1968.

Rosenberg, Nathan. *Technology and American Economic Growth*. New York: Harper and Row, 1972.

__________. *Perspectives on Technology*. New York: Cambridge University Press, 1976.

Scherer, Frederick M. and Ross, David. *Industrial Market Structure and Economic Performance*, 3d ed. Boston: Houghton Mifflin Co., 1990.

__________. "Antitrust: Ideology or Economics?" *Critical Review* 5 (Fall 1991): 497–511.

Schmalensee, Richard L. "Inter-Industry Studies of Structure and Performance." *Handbook of Industrial Organization* Edited by Richard L. Schmalensee and Robert D. Willig. Amsterdam: North-Holland, 1989.

Terleckyj, Nestor E. "What Do R & D Numbers Tell Us About Technological Change?" *American Economic Review* 70 (May 1980): 55–61.

Waldman, Don E. *The Economics of Antitrust: Cases and Analysis*. Boston: Little Brown and Co., 1986.

Weiss, Leonard W. "Quantitative Studies of Industrial Organization." *Frontiers of Quantitative Economics*. Edited by Michael D. Intriligator. Amsterdam: North-Holland, 1971.

__________. "The Concentration-Profits Relationship and Antitrust." *Industrial Concentration: The New Learning* Edited by Harvey J. Goldschmid et al. Boston: Little Brown, 1974.

NOTES

1. Industries can also be ranked by the number of employees. Though there are differences, the rankings are roughly consistent.
2. Richard C. Edwards, "Stages of Corporate Stability and the Risks of Corporate Failure," *The Journal of Economic History* 35 (June 1975): 430.
3. Ibid., 438.
4. Ibid., 442–43.
5. Herman Krooss, *American Economic Development*, 3d ed. (Englewood Cliffs, NJ: Prentice-Hall, 1974), 205.
6. Donald F. Barnett and Louis Schorsch, *Steel: Upheaval in a Basic Industry* (Cambridge, MA: Ballinger Publishing Co., 1983); and *Up from the Ashes: The Rise of the Steel Minimill in the United States* (Washington, D.C.: The Brookings Institution, 1986).
7. Nathan Rosenberg, *Technology and American Economic Growth* (New York: Harper and Row, 1972), 182.
8. Edwin Mansfield, "Technology and Productivity in the United States," in Martin Feldstein, ed., *The American Economy in Transition* (Chicago: University of Chicago Press for the National Bureau of Economic Research, 1980), 569.
9. Ibid., 569.
10. Nestor E. Terleckyj, *Effects of R & D on the Productivity Growth of Industries: An Exploratory Study* (Washington, D.C.: National Planning Association, 1974), cited in Mansfield, "Technology and Productivity," 569. See also Nestor E. Terleckyj, "What Do R & D Numbers Tell Us About Technological Change?" *American Economic Review* 70 (May 1980): 55–61.
11. Mansfield, "Technology and Productivity," 575.
12. Rosenberg, *Technology and American Economic Growth*, 187–89.
13. Rosenberg, *Technology and American Economic Growth*, and *Perspectives on Technology* (New York: Cambridge University Press, 1976).
14. Rosenberg, *Technology and American Economic Growth*, 117.
15. Ibid., 145.
16. Alfred D. Chandler, Jr., Strategy and Structure: Chapters in the History of the American Industrial Enterprise (Cambridge, MA: The M.I.T. Press, 1962), and The Visible Hand: The Managerial Revolution in American Business (Cambridge, MA: Harvard University Press, 1977).

17. Martin N. Baily and Alok K. Chakrabarti, "Innovation and the Productivity Crisis," The Brookings Institution, cited and discussed in Lindley H. Clark, Jr., "Speaking of Business: Productivity Lag May Be Management's Fault," *The Wall Street Journal*, 11 January, 1989.
18. Eric von Hippel, *The Sources of Innovation* (New York: Oxford University Press, 1988), cited in Lindley H. Clark, Jr., "Speaking of Business: Productivity Lag May Be Management's Fault," *The Wall Street Journal*, 11 January, 1989.
19. Joseph B. White, "Foreign Aid: Japanese Auto Makers Help U.S. Suppliers Become More Efficient: Toyota Drills an Illinois Firm in Fine Points of Building Bumpers Faster, Cheaper," *The Wall Street Journal*, 9 September, 1991.
20. Joel Kotkin, "The American Way," *Inc.: The Magazine for Growing Companies*, 13 (September 1991), 98.
21. Paul Ingrassia and Joseph B. White, "Major Overhaul: Determined to Change, General Motors is Said to Pick New Chairman: It's Expected to Give Smale Stempel's Job and Speed Pace of its Downsizing." *The Wall Street Journal*, 23 October, 1992.
22. Ibid., 158.
23. Marc Allen Eisner, *Antitrust and the Triumph of Economics: Institutions, Expertise & Policy Change* (Chapel Hill, NC: University of North Carolina Press, 1991), 221.
24. Ibid., 170.
25. Ibid., 173.
26. Ibid., 174.
27. In many respects the case against United Shoe Machinery was no different from the monopolization case against the firm 35 years earlier when it was found not guilty of monopolization.
28. John L. Peterman has charged that the government's evidence was extraordinarily weak and at times bordered on fiction. [John L. Peterman, "The Brown Shoe Case," *The Journal of Law and Economics* 13 (April 1975): 143.] Robert Bork has said that the *Brown Shoe* decision has considerable claim to the distinction of being "the worst antitrust essay every written" and that the decision transformed Section 7 of the Clayton Act into a "virulently anticompetitive regulation." [Robert Bork, *The Antitrust Paradox* (New York: Basic Books, 1978), 198 and 210.]
29. Ernest Gellhorn, *Antitrust Law and Economics* (St. Paul: West Publishing Co., 1976), 333.
30. Dominick T. Armentano, *The Myths of Antitrust* (New Rochelle, NY: Basic Books, 1978), 263.
31. Don E. Waldman, *The Economics of Antitrust: Cases and Analysis* (Boston: Little Brown and Co., 1986), 71–72.
32. Ibid., 75. See also Scherer and Ross, *Industrial Market Structure and Performance*, 466. At the same time that the FTC attacked advertising as an anticompetitive device creating a "shared monopoly" for the cereal companies, it also adopted regulations outlawing bans on advertising for eyeglasses and examinations because advertising is a competitive device. It is not clear how the FTC could conclude that advertising was simultaneously a monopoly barrier and a creator of competitive conditions.
33. Scherer and Ross, *Industrial Market Structure and Performance*, 462.
34. Ibid., 97–101.
35. Bork, *The Antitrust Paradox*, 405.
36. Yale Brozen, "Competition, Efficiency, and Antitrust," *Journal of World Trade Law* 3 (1969), reprinted in Yale Brozen, ed., *The Competitive Economy: Selected Readings* (Morristown, NJ: General Learning Press, 1975), 8.
37. F. M Scherer, "Antitrust: Ideology or Economics?" *Critical Review* 5 (Fall 1991): 502–503.

38. Eisner, *Antitrust and the Triumph of Economics*, 235.
39. Scherer and Ross, *Industrial Market Structure and Performance*, 190–191.
40. Eisner, *Antitrust and the Triumph of Economicse*, 184.
41. Ibid., 185.
42. Ibid., 185.
43. Ibid., 188.
44. These measurement problems are discussed in detail in Scherer and Ross, *Industrial Market Structure and Performance*, 411–426.
45. Joe S. Bain, "Relation of Profit Rate to Industry Concentration: American Manufacturing, 1936–1940," *Quarterly Journal of Economics* 65 (August 1951): 293–324, and *Barriers to New Competition* (Cambridge, MA: Harvard University Press, 1956).
46. Scherer and Ross, *Industrial Market Structure and Performance*, 412, suggest examining the following surveys: Leonard W. Weiss, "Quantitative Studies of Industrial Organization," in Michael D. Intriligator, ed., *Frontiers of Quantitative Economics* (Amsterdam: North-Holland, 1971), 362–411; Leonard Weiss, "The Concentration-Profits Relationship and Antitrust," in Harvey J. Goldschmid et al., *Industrial Concentration: The New Learning* (Boston: Little Brown, 1974), 201–220; Richard E. Caves, "International Trade and Industrial Organization: Problems, Solved and Unsolved," *European Economic Review* 28 (August 1985): 377–95; Paul A. Geroski, "Pursuit of Monopoly Power: Recent Quantitative Work in Industrial Economics," *Journal of Applied Econometrics* 3 (April 1988),: 107–23. Richard L. Schmalensee, "Inter-Industry Studies of Structure and Performance," in Richard L. Schmalensee and Robert D. Willig, eds., *Handbook of Industrial Organization* (Amsterdam: North-Holland, 1989).
47. For example see the following: Yale Brozen, "Concentration and Structural and Market disequilibria," *Antitrust Bulletin* 16 (Summer 1971): 244–48. Harold Demsetz, "Industry Structure, Market Rivalry, and Public Policy," *Journal of Law and Economics* 16 (April 1973): 1–9, *The Market Concentration Doctrine* (Washington, D.C.: The American Enterprise Institute, 1973), "Two Systems of Belief About Monopoly," in Goldschmid, ed., *Industrial Concentration*, 175–181; Richard B. Mancke, "Causes of Interfirm Profitability Differences: A New Interpretation of the Evidence," *Quarterly Journal of Economics* 88 (May 1974): 181–93.
48. Demsetz, "Industry Structure, Market Rivalry, and Public Policy;" and *The Market Concentration Doctrine*.
49. Scherer and Ross, *Industrial Market Structure and Performance*, 429.
50. Ibid., 430.
51. Ibid., 667.
52. Arnold C. Harberger, "Monopoly and Resource Allocation," *American Economic Review* 44 (1954): 77–87.
53. Scherer and Ross, Industrial Market Structure and Economic Performance, 678.
54. Ibid., 678–679.

CHAPTER 12

Developments in Energy and Transportation, 1950 to the Present

It would be incorrect to suggest that a few sectors or events have been more significant than any other in the postwar economic history of the United States. If pressed, however, most economists would surely agree that events in the energy sector were among the more important. The energy sector was in the forefront of environmental concerns, and changes in the availability and prices of types of energy played a major role in the economic roller coaster of the 1970s and early 1980s and initiated significant industrial shifts in the American economy.

The transportation sector was among the sectors most directly affected by the energy changes. Riding the wave of declining real gasoline and diesel fuel prices from the Second World War to the early 1970s and the expanding network of high-speed expressways, trucking, automobile, and airline use grew at the expense of urban mass transit, railroad freight and passenger traffic, and intercity buslines. Fueled by the low costs of energy and transportation, cities and their suburbs expanded, and central business districts declined as multiple retail shopping districts arose in the suburbs.

We begin our examination of these changes with a survey of developments in the postwar American energy industries.

ENERGY

The energy markets have had a tumultuous history since the Second World War. New energy sources, primarily nuclear power, arose to provide competition for the established sources. Environmental worries added to concerns over energy self-sufficiency in the United States, leading to more and more political control over energy markets.

As Figure 12.1 shows, total energy production grew rapidly from 1950 through 1970 but much more slowly after that. Coal was our primary energy source in 1950, but it rapidly lost markets to petroleum and natural gas through 1970. Since then coal has regained some of its former market share. Petroleum's peak share was in 1955, and it has declined to the present time. The share of energy production from natural gas rose rapidly from 1950 to 1970, but with rising real prices and a relatively unreliable supply, its share has fallen.

Petroleum

The petroleum industry involves four different levels of operation: production of crude oil, refining, marketing, and transportation.[1] The most important derivative of crude oil is gasoline, which has accounted for an average of 46.5 percent of all refined petroleum products in the postwar period. The share of distillate fuel oil, used primarily for heating, has since fallen slightly since 1960. Residual fuel oil has declined in importance, while jet fuel and petrochemical feedstocks have both become more important.

Crude Oil. As Figure 12.2 shows, domestic crude oil production peaked in 1970 at 3.5 billion barrels. Importation of crude oil rose rapidly in the 1970s and peaked in 1977. Domestic consumption of crude oil peaked in 1978 at 5.5 billion barrels. The real

Fig. 12.1 Energy Production, 1950–1988

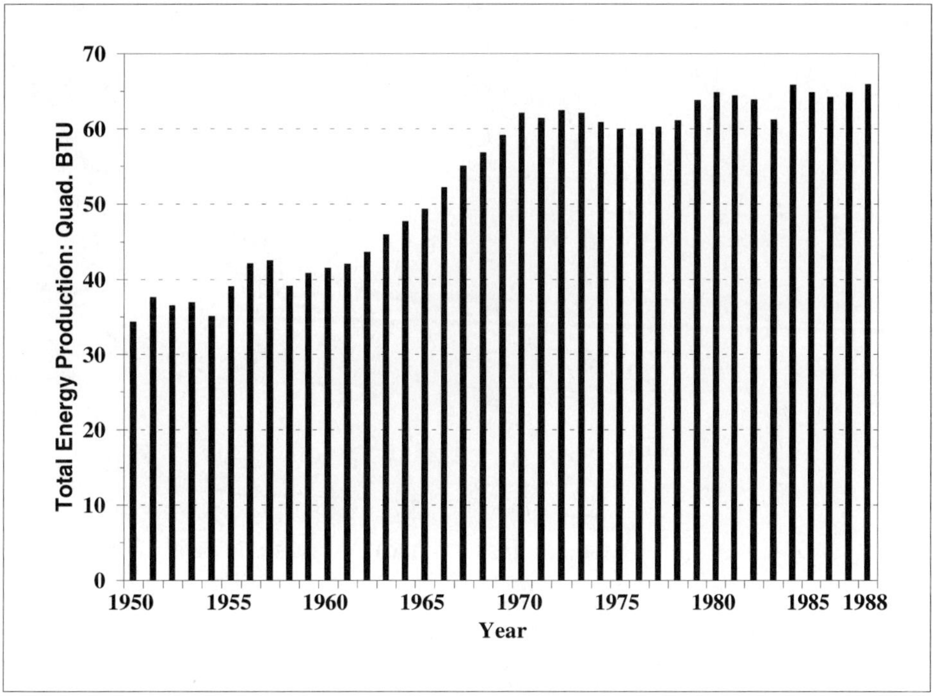

Source: *Statistical Abstract of the United States* (Washington, D.C.: U.S. Government Printing Office, various years).

average price per barrel of crude oil fell from 1950 through 1972, but under the umbrella of OPEC-led price increases it rose to $14.26 per barrel in 1975 and $26.20 in 1980. (See Figure 12.3.) Since then the real price of petroleum has fallen almost as much and as rapidly as it rose.

Though crude oil markets in the United States had initially been quite competitive, the Texas Railroad Commission exercised demand prorationing from the mid-1930s to the late 1940s to prevent excessively rapid extraction of crude oil from commonly held reserves.[2] Most of the other oil-producing states established similar commissions. Such commissions could limit output from wells transforming demand prorationing into a mechanism to reduce output and raise prices. Because of its dominant position in United States production and before the emergence of the Persian Gulf and Venezuela as major oil suppliers, the Texas Railroad Commission was able to "effectively determine domestic crude oil prices . . . [and] in effect operated on behalf of Texas oil producers as the first international cartel."[3] The expansion of Persian Gulf crude oil production pushed world prices below domestic prices, and by 1948 the United States had switched from being a net exporter of crude oil to a net importer.

Fig. 12.2 Domestically Produced and Imported Crude Oil

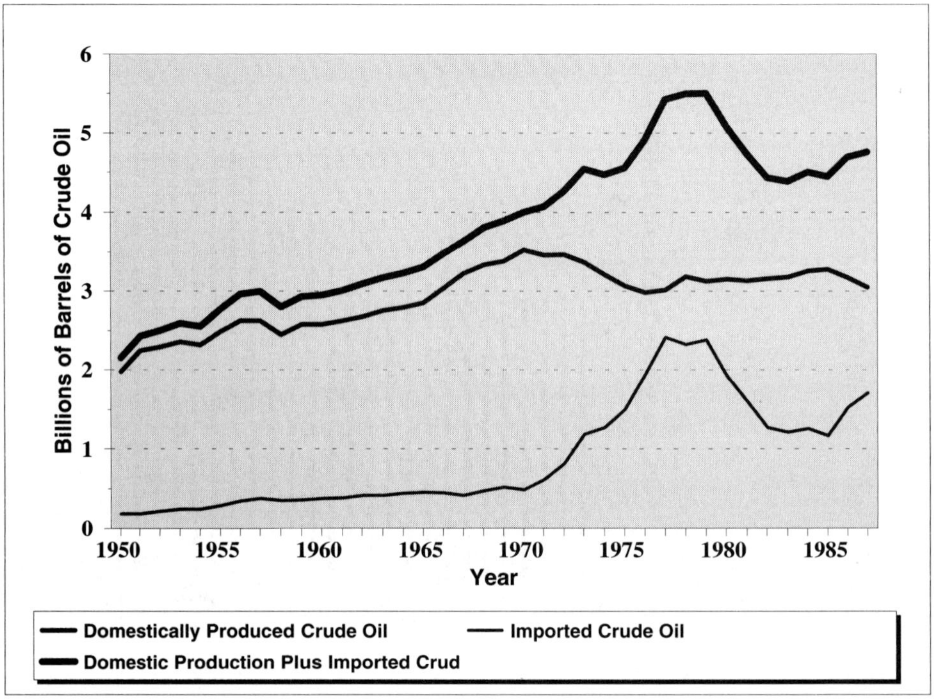

Source: *Statistical Abstract of the United States* (Washington, D.C.: U.S. Government Printing Office, various years).

Though the major international oil companies initially dominated Persian Gulf crude oil markets and attempted to limit production to keep prices higher, this strategy failed. Starting with the 1954 Iranian consortium, the entry of independent producers and the demand for additional tax revenues by the Persian Gulf countries and Libya boosted production. When combined with increasing production from Venezuela and the Soviet Union, production grew faster than a rapidly expanding demand, and world and domestic crude oil transaction prices began falling, although the posted prices did not. Because the producing countries collected taxes on the posted prices for crude oil, in 1960 Exxon reduced its posted crude oil prices to reflect the extensive declines in transactions prices. Angered by this, in September of 1960 Saudi Arabia, Iraq, Iran, Kuwait, and Venezuela met and agreed to establish OPEC, the Organization of Petroleum Exporting Countries.[4]

With the world price of crude oil below the domestic price and imports growing, the domestic price began falling, and by 1954 domestic oil producers began to call for limits on crude oil imports. Under the pretext that limiting crude oil imports was vital to national security, in 1955 and 1957 voluntary guidelines were established but these failed to stem the growth of imported crude oil.[5] In 1959 a Mandatory Oil Import

Fig. 12.3 Real Average Price Per Barrel of Crude Oil (1982–84=100)

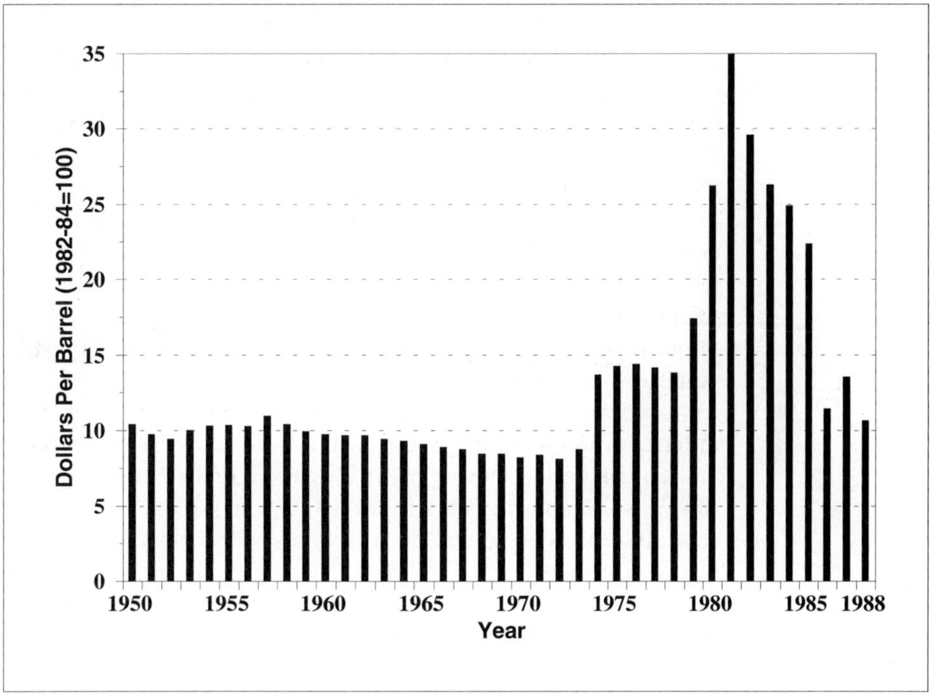

Source: *Statistical Abstract of the United States* (Washington, D.C.: U.S. Government Printing Office, various years).

Program was instituted with the objective of not allowing imports to exceed 9 percent of domestic demand, a goal that was never achieved.[6]

This program established quotas and required that importers of crude oil and refined products obtain import quota tickets from the Treasury. Controversy erupted over the allocation of the tickets; finally "a so-called sliding scale awarded proportionately more import quotas to small refiners than to larger ones."[7] Many of the smaller refineries were located inland, requiring expensive transportation of the oil. The program allowed refiners to exchange import tickets for oil. Smaller inland refiners generally exchanged their imported oil at coastal receiving ports for domestic crude oil produced near their refineries, thus saving most of the transportation costs. Because imported crude oil had a lower price than domestic crude oil, this amounted to a subsidy to small refiners of about a $1.25 per barrel, or 38 percent of the domestic price, during most of the 1960s.[8]

Political competition for import quota tickets during the 1960s was intense, and an increasing number of tickets were issued, forcing the real price of domestic crude oil to decline. The oil producers' unhappiness with this led President Nixon to establish a task force to examine the Mandatory Oil Import Program. They recommended that a simple tariff replace the program; however, because this would no longer benefit the smaller producers that were subsidized under the program, the recommendation was rejected, and nothing was changed.

Beginning with the Libyan revolution of September, 1969, Middle East nations began demanding concessions to raise crude oil prices and taxes and finally a number began nationalizing oil operations within their borders.[9] World crude oil prices began rising and by early 1973 surpassed domestic prices. The United States froze domestic oil prices in June, 1973. The Cost of Living Council then created an artificial distinction between "old" and "new" oil; old oil came from domestic wells producing prior to 1973; new oil was oil from existing wells in excess of that produced in the corresponding month in 1972 as well as oil from newly drilled wells. Old oil had to be sold at lower, frozen prices, while new oil could be sold at market prices. The restrictions on competition caused growing chaos in petroleum markets, and oil firms increasingly resorted to political competition to gain advantages.[10] The Arab oil embargo dramatically increased world oil prices from $3.01 to $5.11 a barrel in October, 1973, and to $11.65 in January, 1974, creating greater gains from access to "old" domestic crude oil.[11]

To handle the intense political pressures, the Federal Energy Office created the Buy-Sell Program in February of 1974, which required refiners with above average capacity utilization to sell oil to refiners with below average capacity utilization, at below market prices.[12] However, the program discouraged imports of crude oil and actually resulted in sales from small refiners to major oil companies—the reverse of congressional objectives—and it was revised in May, 1974, so that only the 15 largest refiners would be sellers. The Buy-Sell Program was replaced by the Entitlements Program. Refiners were then required to have a Federal Energy Office entitlement for each barrel of old oil refined, and entitlements were distributed to refineries in proportion to the total amount of oil refined. Like the Mandatory Oil Import Program, it effectively subsidized small refiners.[13]

The Emergency Petroleum Allocation Act, which allowed the federal government to control petroleum prices, was extended to the end of 1975 and then replaced by the Emergency Petroleum Conservation Act, under which the petroleum markets were to be decontrolled on September 30, 1981. Real petroleum prices fell slowly from 1975 to the end of 1978. In January, 1979, a revolution brought down the Shah of Iran and led to a reduction in Iranian crude oil exports. The "aftermath of instability and violence so unsettled world markets that the price of crude oil rose almost continuously from January 1979 to March 1980."[14] In June of 1979, as President Carter began the gradual decontrol of petroleum prices and allocations, he requested and congress approved a Windfall Profits Tax on oil producers, which was simply an additional excise tax on oil production rather than a capture of non-existent windfall profits from decontrol.

Soon after his inauguration in 1980, President Reagan ordered the immediate decontrol of all petroleum and gasoline markets. Although there were loud protests that decontrol would result in a dramatic increase in crude oil and gasoline prices before they stabilized at a much higher real level, within a short time prices began to fall and continued to do so throughout the 1980s. By 1987 real crude oil prices were only 52 percent of what they had been in 1980.

Gasoline. As crude oil prices fell through the 1950s and 1960s, so did gasoline prices. President Nixon's August 15, 1971, freeze of wages and prices applied price controls to the gasoline market. Gasoline and heating oil prices vary during the year, reflecting seasonal demands. Because of relatively high heating oil stocks and mild temperatures, no serious problems were encountered in the winter of 1971–72. However, the freeze did not allow heating oil and gasoline prices their usual seasonal variation. Gasoline prices were high relative to heating oil prices throughout 1972, and heating oil inventories were not built up as they normally would have been.

When controls ended on January 10, 1973, heating oil prices quickly began to rise relative to gasoline prices. This brought bitter protests from distillate fuel oil users. The Cost of Living Council then issued Special Rule Number One to recontrol heating oil prices for the 23 largest firms in the industry, which effectively reduced crude oil imports and wreaked havoc in product markets.[15] During 1973 prices of crude oil and refined products rose rapidly, while spot shortages of gasoline, heating oil, and propane gas appeared. The Cost of Living Council tried several tactics to reduce the rate of price increases before finally allowing changes in ceiling prices only once a month.

In October, 1973, the Arab countries embargoed crude oil to the United States and Netherlands and sharply raised posted crude oil prices. Within a short time shortages of gasoline became widespread in the United States because the price controls, particularly the once-a-month rule, made it difficult to pass the bulk of the additional costs of crude oil on to the gasoline purchasers. "Facing rapidly rising costs and an excess demand for gasoline, dealers had a powerful incentive to sell supplies early in the month and build up stocks later in the month in anticipation of an imminent price increase."[16] As shortages spread panic buying commenced, and drivers began to top off their gasoline tanks to keep them full, effectively increasing the demand for inventories of gasoline.

The gasoline crisis led the federal government to further intervene in the market. Fearing another shortage of heating oil in the winter of 1973–1974, the Federal Energy Office allowed heating oil prices to rise more than gasoline prices between September, 1973 and June, 1974, provided that the refiners increased the production and inventories of heating oil. Because this came at the expense of gasoline, it further exacerbated the gasoline crisis. In addition to controlling prices, the Federal Energy Office began to direct the allocation of gasoline supplies to various users and to regions based on historical consumption patterns. This resulted in more severe shortages in some regions. "To avoid being cut off from supplies far from home, motorists curtailed long-distance driving. This meant that gasoline became plentiful in most rural and resort areas, while shortages became increasingly concentrated in urban areas."[17]

By April of 1974, gasoline price ceilings had been increased sufficiently to eliminate most of the gasoline shortages. From the summer of 1974 through the end of 1978, the real price of crude oil and gasoline fell slowly as consumption demands began to adjust to the higher real prices of gasoline. The 1979 revolution in Iran disrupted markets, and gasoline prices again began rising. Although prices were still controlled, refiners drew upon "banked costs" to raise gasoline prices and initially shortages were limited.[18] By May serious shortages were occurring, particularly in California; from there they spread to other parts of the United States and continued through July of 1979.

When President Reagan finished the decontrol of petroleum markets shortly after he assumed office in 1981, there were dire predictions of gasoline prices reaching $2.00 a gallon or higher within a few years. Gasoline prices on December 30, 1980, averaged $1.234 for regular gasoline; rose to $1.387 a gallon in March 1981; and then began to fall reaching, $1.224 per gallon in May 1982.[19] Gasoline prices continued to fall throughout the 1980s. In 1990, in spite of a 59 percent increase in the consumer price index during the 1980s, prices were lower in nominal terms than in 1980.[20] The inescapable conclusion is that the 1970s gasoline crises stemmed from the creation of federal government price and allocation controls.

Natural Gas

At the end of the 1980s there were some 5,000 producers connected to 1,443 local utilities through a two-million-mile network of pipelines operated by 45 independent companies. Natural gas use expanded rapidly from 1950 to 1970, but fell from 1970 through 1985.[21] Prices, which had fallen from 1963 to 1972, rose sharply. (See Figure 12.4.) Industry has been the largest consumer of natural gas, and its use grew rapidly to 1970 but has since fallen 28 percent. Residential consumption peaked in 1975 and has fallen 10.2 percent since then, and, though at a lower level, commercial consumption has a similar pattern.

Federal regulation in the natural gas market began with the Natural Gas Act of 1938.[22] An attempt to eliminate the Federal Power Commission's (FPC) regulation of producers was vetoed by President Truman in 1949. In 1954 the Supreme Court ruled that producers of natural gas were to be regulated under the 1938 act. Another bill to eliminate the FPC's regulation of producers was vetoed by President Eisenhower in 1956.[23] In 1959 the Supreme Court required that the FPC review the prices in all new contracts to be sure they were in line with existing prices under similar conditions. This effectively froze prices in new contracts because it simply could not handle such a load of price evaluations; by 1960 only 10 of 2,900 submitted applications for increased rates had been acted upon.[24] To get out of the logjam, the FPC decided to determine prices by area and divided the United States into five producing areas, however, by the early 1970s price ceilings had been determined for only two areas, so the prices were effectively frozen at the 1959–60 levels.

Natural gas prices in new contracts apparently remained below FPC ceiling levels during the early 1960s.[25] One indication was that prices for new contracts for natural gas sold only in intrastate markets, which the FPC did not regulate, first rose above the interstate price in 1966. Following that the price gap between intrastate and interstate natural gas prices grew to 6 cents per million cubic feet in 1969, 18 cents in 1971, and 83 cents in 1975.[26]

Natural gas contracts with most industrial users and utilities were written to be interruptible in case of shortages. In the winter of 1972–73, natural gas deliveries even to noninterruptible customers were at times curtailed. The Federal Power Commission

Fig. 12.4 Real Average Value of Natural Gas at the Wellhead. (cents per 1,000 cubic feet. 1982–84=100)

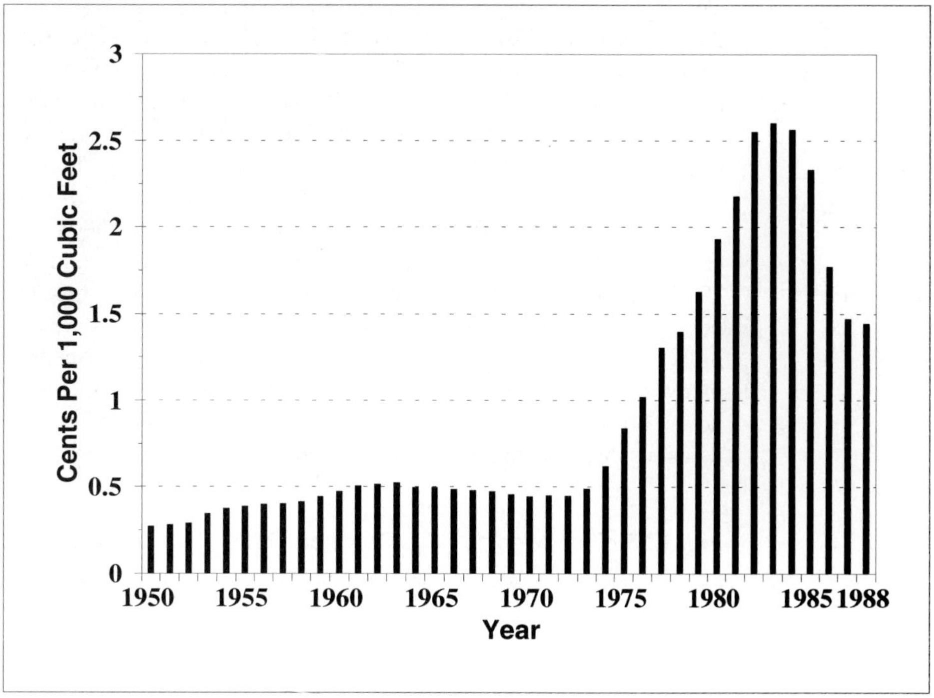

Source: *Statistical Abstract of the United States* (Washington, D.C.: U.S. Government Printing Office, various years).

then began to raise ceiling prices at a more rapid rate, but the gap between intrastate and interstate prices for natural gas continued to grow, and each winter through 1978–79 there were widespread shortages and service interruptions. In the severe winter of 1977, interruptions were widespread, and in areas of the midwest, especially Ohio, schools and businesses had to be closed down due to the temporary loss of natural gas deliveries.

Congress responded by passing the Natural Gas Policy Act of 1978. The FPC's regulatory power was extended to the intrastate markets, however, prices were increased, and the legislation provided for the gradual decontrol of prices between 1978 and January 1, 1985 or 1987, depending on the category of natural gas. By 1985 natural gas prices had been largely decontrolled, and, in fact, prices peaked in 1983. Natural gas consumption declined in the 1980s reflecting both the rapid increase in prices between 1975 and 1983 and the remembrance of the severe shortages and cut-offs, particularly to industrial and institutional users, in the winter of 1977. As recently as 1991, natural gas sellers found it difficult to sell natural gas to industrial and institutional consumers.[27]

Coal

Coal's contribution to total energy production declined from 50.0 percent in 1945 to 23.5 percent in 1970. Since then its use has risen and it provided 31.8 percent of all energy production in 1988.[28] The production of anthracite (hard) coal fell nearly 90.7 percent between 1950 and 1987, while the production of bituminous coal rose 85.9 percent over the same period. The price of coal fell until 1968 and then began to rise, especially from 1973 to 1975. By 1988 the real price of coal had fallen to about its level in 1973. (See Figure 12.5.)

These changes reflect the interaction of changes in the demand for and supply of coal. The demand for coal declined from the end of the Second World War to the early 1970s. At the end of the war, coal was a common heating source in residences and businesses. Most railroads used coal-fired steam locomotives. Steel, rolling, and cement mills as well as other manufacturing industries used significant amounts of coal, and many electric generating plants were coal powered. With the exception of electric power utilities—which now consume nearly 75 percent of all coal production—these demands declined in the postwar period and virtually disappeared in some instances.

Fig. 12.5 Real Average Price Per Short Ton of Bituminous Coal (1982–84=100)

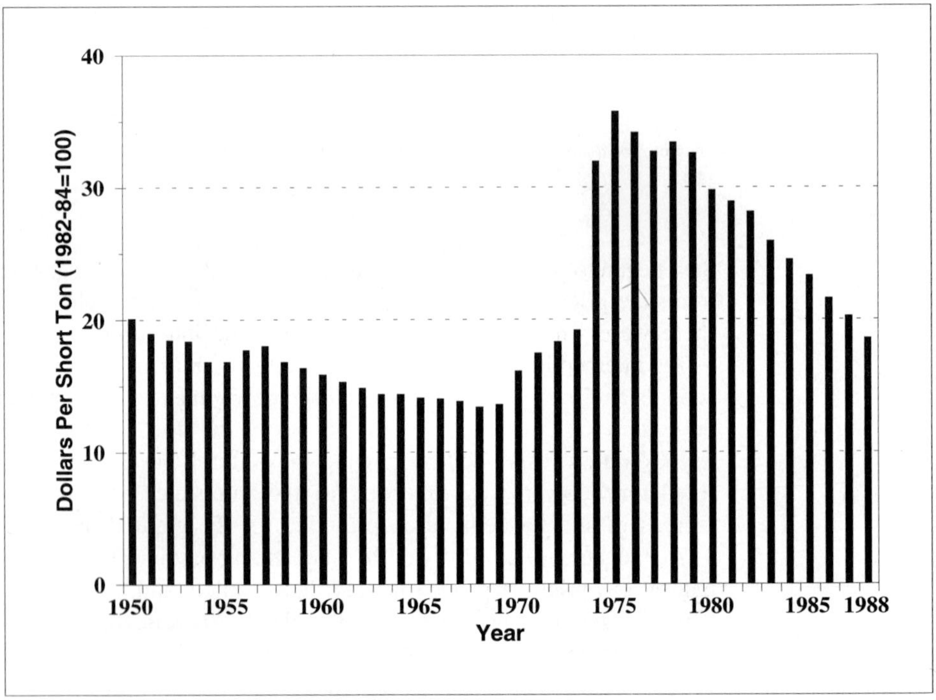

Source: *Statistical Abstract of the United States* (Washington, D.C.: U.S. Government Printing Office, various years).

As production shifted from the east and midwest to the west, where large surface mines could produce coal at a much lower cost the supply of coal increased. Older, less efficient underground mines in the east were closed down and labor productivity in coal mining rose overall. The dramatic rise in petroleum prices associated with the Arab oil embargo caused a substitution toward other energy sources such as coal, and the increased demand caused coal prices to rise 62 percent between 1973 and 1975. Older, less efficient mines were reopened. The 65 percent fall in real coal prices between 1975 and 1988 caused the closing of those older, less efficient underground mines and the continued shift to surface mines.[29]

The transportation of coal has always been a major factor because these costs were often almost as large as the price of coal at the mines. The percentage of coal being shipped by rail has been rising over the postwar period as it became feasible to use unit trains (trains dedicated only to coal shipments) to run directly from mines to electric utilities.[30] This lowered transportation costs and particularly helped western coal.

Electricity

In addition to the energy sources discussed previously, electricity, as a means of distributing power, can be generated by waterpower and by nuclear energy. Coal has always been the most important of these generating sources. Hydroelectric power has steadily declined, while residual fuel oil and natural gas's shares have dropped since the early 1970s. Nuclear power's share of electric energy production was negligible until the late 1960s and rose from 1.4 percent in 1970 to 19.5 percent in 1988.

A declining rate of growth in the production and consumption of electricity is partly explained by the changes in real rates for electricity. From 1950 to 1970, real rates per kilowatt hour fell. (See Figure 12.6.) After that the rise in the prices of energy sources, led by increases in crude oil prices in the early 1970s, caused real rates to rise into the early 1980s, though they have since begun falling.

The rapid growth of electricity production and consumption during the 1950s and 1960s reflects the combination of rapidly expanding generating capacity and technological advances. The management of the utilities adopted what has been called a "grow and build strategy," a strategy that had been developed early in the century.[31] The utilities also counted on steady advances in the technology of generating electricity to continue to lower costs. Technological advances led to huge increases in the maximum capacity of the largest steam-turbine generator units between 1950 and 1970, which sparked extensive campaigns by utilities to promote the use of electricity.[32] Residential use grew rapidly as new electrical appliances became much more common.[33]

By the 1950s a new source of energy, nuclear power, to drive the steam turbines of generating plants had been developed, but utilities were concerned that the possibility of an accident presented such a huge liability problem that no insurers would consider coverage for a nuclear generating plant. In 1957 Congress passed the Price-Anderson Act, which limited the liabilities of utilities in case of a nuclear accident.[34] With limits to their liability in place, the utilities began to develop nuclear plants. From then through 1974, there was a rapid expansion in the demand for nuclear plants.

Fig. 12.6 Real Electricity Rates (cents per kilowatt-hour. 1982–84=100)

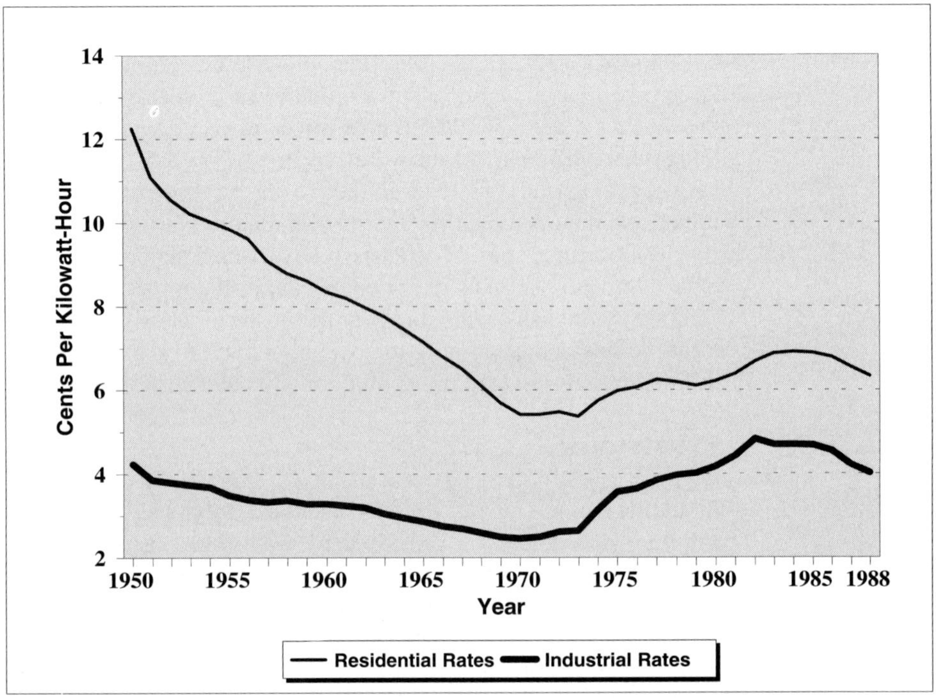

Source: *Statistical Abstract of the United States* (Washington, D.C.: U.S. Government Printing Office, various years).

In November, 1965, there was an extensive electrical blackout in the northeast. Richard F. Hirsch reports that, "the blackout led to the creation of regional power pool arrangements through the new North American Electric Reliability Council."[35] A total of nine regional pools were created, and this integrated smaller utilities into the larger systems. The increased size of the customer base in the regional pools meant that utilities could invest in larger generating units, because a common rule of thumb limited the size of new generating units to 7 to 10 percent of capacity. The pools, therefore, led to demands for considerably larger generating units, particularly nuclear plants, even at small utilities.

The 1970s were something of a shock to the managers of the nation's electric utilities. By the late 1960s an apparent limit seemed to have been reached in thermal-efficiency improvements. In 1947 power plants transformed only 21.8 percent of a fuel's energy content into electricity, but by 1965 this had increased to 32.9 percent and then stopped. "Fluctuating within a narrow range after the mid-1960s, the average efficiency for all plants in 1980 registered only 32.5%, a figure slightly lower than the 1965 rate."[36] The growth in size of individual power units also ceased. The average size of nuclear units in 1975 was about 1,000 megawatts, but by 1980 the average size was only 1,100 megawatts.[37] The technological progress that had allowed greater growth and lower costs appeared to have ended.

The onset of more rapidly rising real fuel prices, varying rates of inflation, and a slowing in the growth of the demand for electricity made calculations and forecasts increasingly difficult. By the mid-1970s environmental concerns had led various groups to oppose both additional nuclear and steam-powered generating plants. The last order for a new nuclear plant was placed in 1974, though given the long construction time, they continued to be built well into the 1980s. The public's concern about the safety of nuclear generating plants was sharply increased after an accident at the Three Mile Island nuclear generating plant in Pennsylvania in March of 1979.[38]

By 1980 electric utility companies across the United States were pushing conservation in order to avoid the costs and difficulties of constructing new generating plants.[39] Many argued against the construction of new coal-fired plants because of environmental problems, especially acid rain; the real costs of reducing emissions were also rising rapidly as increasingly tougher standards were imposed. By the end of the 1980s, no permanent depository for spent nuclear fuel had yet been designated, and storage was becoming an increasingly serious problem.

Energy in the Postwar American Economy

Energy sources are, within limits, substitutes. This means that to understand changes in one market, we also have to consider changes in other markets due to these interdependencies. For example, at the end of the Second World War, coal was an important source of energy for heating homes and businesses. However, as the prices of electricity, fuel oil, and natural and liquified petroleum gas (LP) fell over the next 25 years, businesses and homeowners began switching from coal heat to cleaner, more convenient alternative fuels.

The disruptions in crude oil imports and rising prices of imported crude oil induced substitutions toward domestic crude oil, coal, and natural gas, and all of these prices also rose sharply. The federal government's attempts to control the prices of natural gas and crude oil (and its derivatives, gasoline and fuel oil) and to direct the allocation of crude oil and its derivatives exacerbated the problems. The rising prices of these energy sources brought on increases in the prices of electricity. In the 1980s, when government controls on prices and allocations were relaxed or removed, energy prices fell.

The turbulence in the energy markets in the 1970s and early 1980s also affected other sectors. The competition that American automobile manufacturers faced from imported small cars made in Japan and western Europe was magnified by the sharp increases in fuel prices. These increases also made it difficult for the regulatory authorities to modify rates in a timely and appropriate fashion for trucking, railroads, and air transportation. This helped propel changes in American passenger and freight transportation—a topic we now turn to.

TRANSPORTATION

With the exception of Amtrak, the federally owned national passenger train service, passenger and freight transportation are privately provided in the United States. However, much of the transportation infrastructure has been publicly provided. Private automobiles, trucks, and buses use the publicly provided roads. Barges use the inland waterways, which are maintained by the Army Corps of Engineers. The federal government has maintained the electronic highways in the air, which commercial aviation has used, as well as provided a considerable portion of the funds to construct airports.

At the end of the Second World War congress appropriated funds to rebuild the existing surfaced roads and establish a system of federal highways not to exceed 40,000 miles in length. The rising volume of traffic led to increasing congestion and traffic jams, and a National Highway Users Conference was created to lobby for more and better roads.[40] In 1956 Congress authorized the National Defense Highway System, or, as more commonly known, the Interstate Highway System. It was initially designed to provide about 41,000 miles of highway and was to be completed in 1969; by 1971, however, over 10,000 additional miles had been scheduled, and the completion date had been moved back to 1977.

The investment in the inland waterways has been undertaken by the Army Corps of Engineers as they have dredged rivers to provide shipping channels, built and operated dams and locks to control water levels, and generally undertaken most harbor investment.[41] Since water shippers generally pay neither user fees nor license fees, they have been heavily subsidized.

The capital investment for the airways has also received varying amounts of federal government subsidy. Through the FAA the federal government has undertaken to provide the capital to create the electronic highways in the sky, extensive weather reporting, and, for safety purposes, control of traffic in the air and traffic landing and takeoffs at major airports. Though obviously benefiting the users of the airways, no attempts were made to impose user costs for these services. After 1960 government subsidies for airport construction began to decrease, and as traffic increased, user fees began to cover operating costs and finally, at larger airports, the capital costs.

Freight Traffic

There has been a pronounced shift in freight traffic from railroads to trucks and oil pipelines in the postwar period. A major factor in this decline has been the rate-setting policies of the ICC. When the ICC was given control over interstate trucking in 1935, similar rate structures were imposed on trucks and railroads to "maintain competition." With similar tariffs for long distance shipment of the same goods—rather than incremental cost-pricing—it is usually more desirable to ship compact, higher valued goods by truck than by rail. As a result, in the postwar period trucks increasingly took over these shipments, even though studies continued to indicate that at longer distances railroads are more efficient carriers than trucks. Trucks' advantages lie in shorter distance hauls because of their lower fixed costs relative to higher variable costs. The ICC's reluctance to allow lines to abandon very low use branch and spur lines required that profits from trunk line traffic be used to cover losses on branch and spur line service, further harming railroads.[42]

The competitive position of the railroads was worsened by railway labor unions that resisted the installation of most labor saving devices and insisted upon work rules relevant to the technology of 50 to 100 years earlier.[43] For example, firemen were required on diesel locomotives where there were no coal cars nor steam engines, and a one-hundred-mile trip was a "day's work."

The railroad industry also argued that trucks received an implicit subsidy from the federal and state governments in the form of the highways, while railroads had to maintain and pay property taxes on their own roadbeds. The argument has not been particularly persuasive. Highways were largely constructed on a pay-as-you-go basis, using revenues from fuel taxes and license fees. There also is evidence that, though trucks do not pay the full cost of the roadbed, they have pretty much paid their share as fuel taxes and license fees roughly correspond to incremental costs.[44] Because the roadway is used both by commercial trucks and by private automobiles, efficiency requires that the user costs are shared between the two according to the incremental costs of the type of vehicle.

In 1976 Congress initiated regulatory reform to provide more freedom for railroads. By 1978, in response to increasing criticism, the ICC changed its policy to encourage more consolidations to preserve "essential services" rather than trying to preserve intact the entire system of financially weak lines. In early 1980, partly under pressure from the general movement for deregulation, the ICC began to give railroads more freedom to set their own rates for "demand sensitive" commodities,[45] and on October 14, 1980, the Staggers Rail Act was signed.[46] The act reversed existing policies by its premise that the railroad industry was no longer a monopoly. The goal was to assist the railroad industry in its rehabilitation under private ownership and to reform federal regulatory policy to achieve a more efficient and stable system while balancing the needs of carriers, shippers, and the public. To do this, the act proposed that unprofitable services be eliminated, and that railroads be free to set rates according to market conditions as well as entering into contracts with individual carriers.

By 1980 the move for transportation deregulation had spread to trucking, and the ICC took steps toward de facto deregulation. Deregulation was more difficult in this area because of the size and political power of the opponents of trucking deregulation—the large common carrier trucking firms and the powerful Teamsters Union—even though nearly all studies suggest that there are no economies of scale in trucking and that industry entry and exit would be very easy in the absence of regulation.[47]

The share of intercity ton-miles of truck freight carried by ICC-regulated carriers, common and contract, dropped from the early 1960s through the beginning of the 1980s. ICC regulations on common carriers also effectively stopped the entry of new firms unless they purchased ICC certificates of operating authority from existing firms.[48] Rates and entry were controlled so as to protect the profits of the existing carriers, and, as a result, the certificates of operating authority were very valuable, generally 15 to 20 percent of the gross revenue earned on an operating route in a year. The rates were set by associations of common carriers called "rate bureaus" and sanctioned by the ICC. In this way the regulated common carriers operated as a cartel, with no price competition allowed.

ICC regulations contributed to inefficiency and higher trucking costs. As more trucking shifted to private carriers, "deadheading," or empty backhauls, increased. The ICC regularly disallowed route changes that might have provided for fuel and time savings if there was any potential to harm the competitive position of another carrier. Circuitous routes resulting from the arbitrary travel restrictions imposed by the ICC added to shipping times, requiring firms to carry more inventory and provide more warehouse and storage space. Shipper dissatisfaction with the existing carriers was generally dismissed as a reason to allow new competitors to enter. In the "yak fat" case, a trucking firm facetiously requested a rate for a nonmarketed product, yak fat, and found that the existing firms, through the rate bureaus, immediately protested this rate without knowing or finding out what it was for. The ICC subsequently disallowed the yak fat rate.

Congress finally passed the Motor Carrier Act of 1980, designed to deregulate interstate trucking. Like the airline deregulation bill, deregulation of trucking was to be phased in gradually. Entry and route restrictions were eased, and rules on private carriers were relaxed.[49] As an indication of the effectiveness of the deregulation, the aggregate value of the certificates of operating authority, which were valued at an average of $5.1 billion in the years prior to 1979, quickly fell.[50] However, the markets did not completely disappear, and the values did not fall to zero because deregulation under the Motor Carrier Act of 1980 was considerably less complete than for, say, the Staggers Rail Act of 1980.[51]

Competition quickly appeared in the trucking industry. During the expansion from 1983–85 20 percent of the largest 100 carriers from the pre-1980 era failed. By 1985 nearly 15,000 new carriers had entered, the majority of which were small truckload operators. With excess capacity from the new competition, truckload rates fell, and this spilled over into the less-than-truckload (LTL) carrier market.[52] The LTL carriers did not face the same entry but found themselves facing new competitors as routes were opened, reorganized, and rationalized, and these rates also dropped and became simply the starting point for negotiated discounts.[53] By the middle of the 1980s, concentration among the LTL carriers had increased. The share of the largest 4 LTL carriers had risen from 20 to 35 percent between 1978 and 1985, while the share of the largest 20 LTL carriers had risen from 43 to 67 percent during that same period, though it is not clear that this had lessened the intense competition among the carriers.[54]

Passenger Traffic

After the Second World War passenger traffic was quickly diverted to automobiles (and later to airlines) from trains and buslines. There appears to be nothing that could have altered this shift. The advantages of passenger travel by private automobile and plane are such that it seems likely that the direct costs and prices of car and air travel would have to be several times higher than the current direct costs and prices of train or bus travel to divert significant numbers of passengers back to trains and buses.

By the mid-1950s two of the three national intercity buslines—Trailways and Continental—had merged into Continental Trailways to survive. Greyhound remained the dominant carrier in a declining market, and in the 1980s Continental Trailways went out of business. In 1990 Greyhound's precarious financial position led it to demand wage cuts and other concessions from its drivers, and it declared bankruptcy to protect its assets while giving it time to reorganize. Smaller regional intercity buslines continued to do business in some areas of the United States. However, by 1988 all intercity buslines carried only 1.2 percent of passenger traffic.

Passenger rail traffic fell from 382 million passenger miles in 1949 to 108 million in 1969.[55] Losses from passenger service absorbed about 25 percent of the freight-generated profits.[56] The ICC slowed down reductions in passenger service and in 1970 to maintain some rail passenger service, the federal government created a quasi-national agency, the National Railroad Passenger Corporation, or Amtrak, to take over rail passenger service. In 1981, after continuous government subsidies to keep Amtrak going, it was made a fully government-owned corporation.[57]

Airline traffic grew as rail and bus passenger traffic declined. Interstate airlines were regulated by the Civil Aeronautics Board (CAB) the counterpart of the ICC. In the 1950s the CAB regularized the process of setting airfares to achieve rates of return of 10.5 percent for large airlines and 12.0 percent for small airlines. To maintain the local service and regional airlines, the CAB provided subsidies to them from 1940 to 1978. Subsidies to the trunk airlines generally ended in 1959. Doing all of this and ensuring safety taxed the CAB, and in 1958 the Civil Aeronautics Act of 1938 was amended to create the Federal Aviation Administration to regulate safety by setting standards for aircraft, taking over air traffic control, and investigating accidents. The CAB was then freed to concentrate on economic regulation.[58]

Passenger traffic on the airlines was spurred by the introduction in 1954 of the Boeing 707, the first successful commercial jet. It was much faster and quieter than propeller planes and was commonly said to have shrunk the world in half due to its faster speed.[59] Another shot in the arm for air passenger traffic came in the late 1960s with the introduction of the Boeing 747 and other jumbo jets.

From its creation until deregulation in the late 1970s, the CAB did not allow any new trunk, or national, airlines. Local and regional lines' routes were kept limited, to reduce competition for the trunk carriers. The CAB, acting as a cartel manager, allocated routes, especially new routes, so as to limit competition. It rarely approved fare decreases and required that all airlines flying the same route have the same rates. From 1969 to 1973, the average airline fare increased 52 percent, well in excess of the general rise in prices, but these fare increases did not increase the rates of return earned by airlines. Airlines continued to compete in terms of such amenities as in-flight meals, drinks, movies, and other personal services, and in terms of the number of flights originating at airports, particularly the largest ones. The increased costs arising from quality competition dissipated the monopoly rents. Costs were high because the prices, or fares set by the CAB, were high, not the reverse.[60]

As the merits and demerits of deregulation were being discussed in 1977, the CAB, under Alfred Kahn's direction, began moving toward a policy of freer rate changes and easier entry into new routes. In 1978 Congress passed the Airline Deregulation Act, which provided that by January 1, 1982, CAB route restrictions would end and by January 1, 1983, all regulation of passenger fares would end. With an elastic demand for discretionary air travel, as fares dropped profits rose and in 1978 the airlines generated a 24.8 percent return on equity, while their five-year average had only been 10.5 percent.

As routes were quickly opened up, new strategies were developed, and new airlines, offering no-frills, discount-priced service between limited routes, appeared. Service to the smaller communities was maintained through the development of commuter airlines using small propeller-driven aircraft rather than jets. There was a rapid move of some airlines into international markets. Other airlines expanded rapidly—but not always successfully. Some lines quickly initiated mergers to grow more rapidly and thereby gain a competitive advantage.

To handle complex route expansions, airlines developed the hub-and-spoke strategy, whereby a few airports served as hubs. Originating flights would then go to the hub airports to transfer passengers to other flights to continue on to their final destinations. This allowed airlines to serve more cities, but tight schedules meant that delays in one or two flights could lead to often lengthy delays for most of the flights out of a hub and throw off schedules for most of a day. Pricing strategies began to change quickly, especially under the pressure of the new discount airlines. Discounts were available for advanced booking and for booking with no refunds, and bonus mileage programs (frequent flyer programs) encouraged flyers to use only one airline. Price discrimination became common as late-booking business flyers paid substantially higher fares than the discretionary flyer traveling for personal reasons. Fares became much more demand- sensitive rather than based on costs.[61]

In the 1979–82 period, severe problems affected the entire industry. Rapidly rising fuel costs in 1979–80 forced fare increases and reduced profits. The rising fares combined with the severe economic contraction in 1981–82 to sharply reduce passenger travel. The labor unions (pilots, attendants, maintenance personnel, and so on) had shared in the monopoly rents created under CAB regulation. The new carriers entering after deregulation used nonunion personnel, and wages were lower. As fares began to drop and monopoly rents began to decline, the existing airlines came under great pressure to reduce the wages of the unionized personnel.

It has been estimated that by the mid-1980s ticket prices were about 30 percent lower than they otherwise would have been. Airline load factors, the percentage of available seats filled with fare paying passengers, rose from 56 percent in 1977 to 62 percent in the mid-1980s.[62] However, most assessments argue that service deteriorated as the hub and spoke arrangement began to lead to frequent and lengthy delays. The quality of the meals and the number of flight attendants per passenger declined, and seating became more crowded. Entry was not as open as many had envisioned. The bottleneck of boarding gates and time slots at major airports increased and limited competitive entry.

Transportation in the Postwar American Economy

At the beginning of the postwar period, the transportation sector was one of the most heavily regulated sectors in the American economy. For over two and a half decades these regulations slowed down but did not stop improvements in transportation. In the late 1970s Congress began experimenting with deregulating some sectors of the economy, and the first wave of deregulation took place in transportation. As price controls and entry barriers were removed, real prices fell, new firms entered, and existing firms found themselves free to choose routes, schedules, and rates. The smaller and leaner railroads generally became profitable again. Monopoly rents for trucking and airline carriers fell. Deregulation in the United States contributed to the breakup of the transatlantic airline cartel, the International Air Transport Association, in 1978.[63]

There were some costs to the deregulation. Without the protection of regulation, some airlines—such as Eastern and Pan American—failed. Others—such as Braniff and Continental—expanded unwisely and also failed. With a broad range of volatile prices, consumers found that they had to undertake more extensive searches when purchasing tickets. There were frequent complaints of delayed flights, more crowded planes, and poorer service in general. There were a few calls for some reregulation to improve service. However, overall it appeared that deregulation in the transportation sector was a success.

SELECTED REFERENCES

Adelman, Morris. *The World Petroleum Market.* Baltimore: The Johns Hopkins University Press, 1972.

Allvine, Fred C., and James C. Patterson. *Highway Robbery: An Analysis of the Gasoline Crisis.* Bloomington, IN: University of Indiana Press, 1974.

Bina, Cyrus. *The Economics of the Oil Crisis: Theories of Oil Crisis, Oil Rent, and Internationalization of Capital in the Oil Industry.* New York: St. Martin's Presss, 1985.

Breen, Dennis A. "The Monopoly Value of Household-Goods Carrier Operating Certificates." *The Journal of Law and Economics* 20 (April 1977): 153–86.

Douglas, George W., and James C. Miller, III. "Quality Competition, Industry Equilibrium, and Efficiency in the Price-Constrained Airline Market." *American Economic Review* 64 (September 1974): 657–69.

Felton, John Richard, and Dale G. Anderson, eds. *Regulation and Deregulation of the Motor Carrier Industry.* Ames, IA: The Iowa State University Press, 1989.

Glaskowsky, Nicholas A. *Effects of Deregulation on Motor Carriers.* Westport, CT: Eno Foundation for Transportation, Inc., 1986.

Glasner, David. *Politics, Prices, and Petroleum: The Political Economy of Energy.* Cambridge, MA: Ballinger Publishing Co., 1985.

Gordon, Richard L. *Coal in the U.S. Energy Market: History and Prospects.* Lexington, MA: Lexington Books, 1978.

Harris, Richard A. *Coal Firms Under the New Social Regulation*. Durham, NC: Duke University Press, 1985.

Hirsh, Richard F. *Technology and Transformation in the American Electric Utility Industry*. New York: Cambridge University Press, 1989.

Joskow, Paul L., and Richard Schmalensee. *Markets for Power: An Analysis of Electric Utility Deregulation*. Cambridge, MA: The M.I.T. Press, 1983.

Keeler, Theodore E. *Railroads, Freight, and Public Policy*. Washington: The Brookings Institution, 1983.

Kitch, Edmund W. "Regulation of the Field Market for Natural Gas by the Federal Power Commission." *The Journal of Law and Economics* 11 (October 1968): 243–80.

Lansing, John B. *Transportation and Public Policy*. New York: The Free Press, 1966.

MacAvoy, Paul W., and John W. Snow, eds. *Regulation of Passenger Fares and Competition among the Airlines*. Washington, D.C.: American Enterprise Institute, 1977.

Martin, Stephen. "The Petroleum Industry." Chapter 2 in *The Structure of American Industry*, 8th ed. Edited by Walter Adams. New York: Macmillan Publishing Co., 1990.

Meyer, John R., and Clinton V. Oster, eds. *Airline Deregulation: The Early Experience*. Boston: Auburn House Publishing Co., 1981.

Rose, Mark H. "PAR—Project Adequate Roads: Traffic Jams, Business, and Government, 1945–56." *Business and Economic History*. 2d series, 4 (1975): 120–36.

__________. *Interstate Express Highway Politics, 1941–1956*. Lawrence, KA: The Regents Press of Kansas, 1979.

Saunders, Richard. *The Railroad Mergers and the Coming of Conrail*. Westport, CT: Greenwood Press, 1978.

Schurr, Sam H., Calvin C. Burwell, Warren D. Devine, Jr., and Sidney Sonenblum. *Electricity in the American Economy: Agent of Technological Progress*. Westport, CT: Greenwood Press, 1990.

Shepherd, William G. "The Airline Industry." *The Structure of American Industry*, 8th ed. Edited by Walter Adams. New York: Macmillan Publishing Co., 1990.

Weaver, R. Kent. *The Politics of Industrial Change: Railway Policy in North America*. Washington: The Brookings Institution, 1985.

NOTES

1. This section primarily draws upon David Glasner, *Politics, Prices, and Petroleum: The Political Economy of Energy* (Cambridge, MA: Ballinger Publishing Co., 1985), chapters 4–7. Other sources include Morris Adelman, *The World Petroleum Market* (Baltimore, MD: Johns Hopkins University Press, 1972); Fred C. Allvine and James C. Patterson, *Highway Robbery: An Analysis of the Gasoline Crisis* (Bloomington, IN: University of Indiana Press, 1974); Yoram Barzel and Christopher D. Hall, *The Political Economy of the Oil Import Quota* (Stanford CA: Hoover Institution Press, 1977); Stephen Martin, "The Petroleum Industry," chapter 2 in Walter Adams, ed., *The Structure of American Industry*, 8th ed., (New York: Macmillan Publishing Company, 1990).
2. Under demand prorationing, the state commission would develop demand projections for the next month and compare this to the state's oil producing capacity. To avoid "overproduction" and keep the price higher each producing well was allowed to produce an amount of crude oil equal to its productive capacity times the "market-demand factor" which was the ratio of the projected demand to the state's productive capacity. As Glasner says, "Thus

each well had a prorata share, based on the well's productive capacity, of the state's total demand." For a more complete explanation of this see, Glasner, *Politics, Prices, and Petroleum*, pp. 143–144.

3. Ibid., 144.
4. Martin, "The Petroleum Industry," 42–46.
5. Glasner, *Politics, Prices, and Petroleum*, 144–145. Four presidents, Eisenhower, Kennedy, Johnson, and Nixon, all used this rationale. Glasner reports that it was said that the mere mention of the national security argument for limiting oil imports "would elicit uproarious laughter at the Petroleum Club."
6. This discussion follows Glasner, chapter 7.
7. Glasner, *Prices, Politics, and Petroleum*, 151.
8. Ibid., 152. During much of the 1960s domestic crude oil was priced around $3.25 a barrel, while imported crude oil carried a price of about $2.00 a barrel so that the subsidy amounted to $1.25 a barrel of crude oil.
9. Martin, "The Petroleum Industry," 46–47.
10. Glasner, *Politics, Prices, and Petroleum*, 156.
11. The crude oil prices are those for Saudi Arabian Light Crude Oil. Cyrus Bina, *The Economics of the Oil Crisis: Theories of Oil Crisis, Oil Rent, and Internationalization of Capital in the Oil Industry* (New York: St. Martin's Press, 1985), 15.
12. Glasner, Politics, Prices, and Petroleum, 157–58.
13. Ibid., 159.
14. Ibid., 130.
15. Ibid., 98.
16. Ibid., 104.
17. Ibid., 108.
18. When refiners did not increase product prices, say gasoline and heating oil prices, as much as their costs had increased, primarily the cost of crude oil, they were allowed to "bank" the costs that they had not passed on to consumers and use these later on if they so chose. Refiners were not, of course, being socially responsible. Using a market analogy, the increased costs shift the marginal cost curves upward, so the market supply curve decreases (or moves upward). Because there was no demand shift, consumers were not willing to purchase as much refined petroleum products when the prices increased and moved up their demand curves. Refiners, therefore, were able to only pass along a portion of their increased costs due to the increased prices of crude oil, and the government allowed the portion of the costs not passed on to the consumers to be "banked." The analysis is similar to the analysis of the effects of an excise tax in competitive markets.
19. Glasner, *Prices, Politics, and Petroleum,* 180–81 and 189.
20. As an illustration, taking the December, 1980, price as $1.234 per gallon and the average price in 1990 as $1.00 per gallon and deflating by the all-items consumer price index (1982–84 = 100), the real price in 1980 was $1.49 per gallon, while the real price in 1990 was $0.77 per gallon.
21. This section draws primarily upon Glasner, *Politics, Prices, and Petroleum*, chapter 9, pp. 193–248; and Edmund W. Kitch, "Regulation of the Field Market for Natural Gas by the Federal Power Commission," *Journal of Law and Economics* 11 (October 1968): 243–80.
22. Kitch, "Regulation of the Field Market for Natural Gas," 254.
23. Ibid., 256.
24. Glasner, *Politics, Prices, and Petroleum,* 224.
25. Ibid., 229.

26. Ibid., 231.
27. Robert Johnson, "Pipe Dream: Glut and a Poor Image Dash the Grand Hopes Held for Natural Gas: Its Price Has Been Dropping, But Many Customers Say Deliveries are Unreliable," *The Wall Street Journal,* 1 August, 1991.
28. Richard L. Gordon, *Coal in the U.S. Energy Market: History and Prospects* (Lexington, MA: Lexington Books, 1978), table 2–1, p. 22.
29. Gordon, *Coal in the U.S. Energy Market, 5.* For an extensive discussion of this act see Harris, Coal Firms Under the New Social Regulation.
30. Gordon, *Coal in the U.S. Energy Market,* 95.
31. Richard F. *Hirsh, Technology and Transformation in the American Utility Industry* (New York: Cambridge University Press, 1989), 47.
32. Ibid., figure 2, p. 5. In general, see chapters 4–6.
33. Ibid., 50. The role of electricity as an agent of technological progress in the American economy in manufacturing, commercial, agricultural, and residential uses is discussed in considerable detail in, Sam H. Schurr, Calvin C. Burwell, Warren D. Devine, Jr., and Sidney Sonenblum, *Electricity in the American Economy: Agent of Technological Progress* (Westport, CT: Greenwood Press, 1990).
34. Hirsh, *Technology and Transformation in the American Electric Utility Industry,* 116.
35. Ibid., 57.
36. Ibid., 90.
37. Ibid., 94–95.
38. For example, see the following: David L. Sills, C. P. Wolf, and Vivien B. Shelanski, eds., *Accident at Three Mile Island: The Human Dimensions* (Boulder, CO: Westview Press, 1982); Edward J. Walsh, *Democracy in the Shadows: Citizen Mobilization in the Wake of the Accident at Three Mile Island* (New York: Greenwood Press, 1988).
39. Bill Paul, "Current Trend: Big Electric Utilities and Consumers Push Conservation Strategy: Producers Gladly Avoid Costs of Constructing Plants, and Users Get Innovative," *The Wall Street Journal*, 8 December, 1987.
40. Mark H. Rose, "PAR—Project Adequate Roads: Traffic Jams, Business, and Government, 1945–56," *Business and Economic History*, 2d series, 4 (1975): 120–36. See also Mark H. Rose, *Interstate Express Highway Politics, 1941–1956* (Lawrence, KA: The Regents Press of Kansas, 1979).
41. The Army Corps of Engineers had also undertaken some investment on the Great Lakes in improving connecting channels and on the coasts for harbor work and deep-water channels, but the bulk of all of their work has been in river systems and the intracoastal canals of the Atlantic Coast and Gulf Coast areas.
42. Theodore E. Keeler, *Railroads, Freight, and Public Policy* (Washington, D.C.: The Brookings Institution, 1983), 38–39.
43. Ibid., 40–41.
44. John B. Lansing, *Transportation and Public Policy* (New York: The Free Press, 1966). The largest trucks failed to pay their incremental costs largely because of the relatively greater fuel efficiency of the diesel engines over gasoline engines.
45. "ICC Proposes More Freedom for Roads to Set Some Rates," *The Wall Street Journal*, 20 February, 1980.
46. Keeler, *Railroads, Freight, and Public Policy*, 98–103.
47. See Dennis A. Breen, "The Monopoly Value of Household-Goods Carrier Operating Certificates." *The Journal of Law and Economics* 20 (April 1977): 153–86.
48. The Motor Carrier Act of 1935 and trucking regulation between 1935 and 1980 are dis-

cussed in some detail in John Richard Felton and Dale G. Anderson, eds., *Regulation and Deregulation of the Motor Carrier Industry* (Ames, IA: The Iowa State University Press, 1989). The certificates of operating authority held by the existing firms either came originally from a firm grandfathered in 1935 or the firm was one of the firms grandfathered in 1935.

49. John Richard Felton, "Motor Carrier Act of 1980: An Assessment," chapter 11 in Felton and Anderson, *Regulation and Deregulation of the Motor Carrier Industry*, 145.
50. Ibid., 158.
51. Ibid., 161.
52. Nicholas A. Glaskowsky, *Effects of Deregulation on Motor Carriers* (Westport, CT: Eno Foundation for Transportation, Inc., 1986), 8.
53. Ibid., 10.
54. Ibid., 26.
55. The following discussion of Amtrak is drawn from Weaver, *The Politics of Industrial Change*, 88–97.
56. Ibid., 89.
57. Ibid., 97.
58. Ivor P. Morgan, "Government and the Industry's Early Development," chapter 2 in John R. Meyer and Clinton V. Oster, Jr., eds., *Airline Deregulation: The Early Experience* (Boston, MA: Auburn House Publishing Company, 1981), 19.
59. Rick Wartzman, "Boeing Deep-Sixes the 707, a Pioneer of Passenger Jets: Chapter in Aerospace History Inspired by British Rivalry Ends with a British Order," *The Wall Street Journal*, 3 September, 1991.
60. George W. Douglas and James C. Miller III, "Quality Competition, Industry Equilibrium, and Efficiency in the Price-Constrained Airline Market," *American Economic Review* 64 (September 1974): 657–69. These and other characteristics of the airline industry are also discussed in William G. Shepherd, "The Airline Industry," chapter 8 in Walter Adams, ed., *The Structure of American Industry*, 8th ed. (New York: Macmillan Publishing Company, 1990).
61. Fare for flights to and from cities with little competition from other airlines began to rise, while fares for flights to and from cities with more competing airlines fell.
62. Shepherd, "The Airline Industry," 234.
63. "British Air Says It Will Leave IATA Unless Low Fares Set," *The Wall Street Journal*, 9 June, 1978. "IATA Moves to Loosen Membership Rules by Paring Its Power Over Airline Rates," *The Wall Street Journal*, 5 July, 1978.

CHAPTER 13

Developments in Communications and Finance, 1950 to the Present

COMMUNICATIONS

The communications industry underwent profound changes in the postwar era. The development of microwave communications reduced the costs of long distance communications while opening it up to competition. Computers allowed the quick transfer of huge amounts of information, allowing firms to more closely monitor and direct decentralized production. The growth of FM radio and television brought national news and entertainment into nearly every living room and altered the leisure habits of Americans.

Mass Communications

Newspapers. Mass communications media—of which newspapers are the oldest form—are directed at the population in general and, for the most part, provide news and entertainment. The decline in the number of newspapers, which began before the First World War, continued after the Second World War. Daily and Sunday newspaper circulation has grown but not as fast as population grew. The number of cities with competing daily newspapers has declined.[1] Big-city afternoon daily newspapers, in particular, continue to vanish—victims of the changing economy. Manufacturing employees go to work earlier and get home earlier than urban office and other service workers. The typical office worker is more likely to read a paper in the morning before leaving for work. In the afternoon, TV news and new suburban, community-oriented newspapers compete with the big-city afternoon daily. Early deadlines and the higher cost of trucking papers for delivery during the afternoon rush hours has also hurt the afternoon daily.[2] The Newspaper Preservation Act of 1970 authorized joint operating arrangements to allow weak newspapers to combine with stronger ones to reduce printing and business office expenses but this did not always cure the financial problems.[3] Another trend in the postwar period was the strong growth of newspaper groups or chains. By 1977 the five largest groups controlled 25 percent of the nation's newspapers.[4]

Newspapers, generally seeing no growth in circulation, faced increasing cost pressures as real newsprint and labor costs continued to rise. Computerization allowed newspapers to abandon the labor-intensive setting of hot type for news and ads in favor of swift and easy computer technologies. Critics commonly claimed that newspapers failed to raise their advertising rates—from which they receive the bulk of their revenues—enough to cover rising production costs.[5] However, this complaint relies upon the common fallacy that costs determine prices. Rather, it is demand that determines prices. With the rise in competing advertising mediums, such as television, FM radio, the Yellow Pages, and suburban and shopper newspapers, the daily and Sunday newspapers were constrained in raising advertising rates because of the possibility of increased substitution to competing advertising mediums. Figures 13.1 through 13.2 provide some statistics on advertising expenditures. Newspapers' share of national advertising dropped from 16.4 percent to 5.5 percent as television's share grew, while their share of local advertising has been reduced by over 10 percentage points.

Fig. 13.1 Estimated Shares of National Advertising

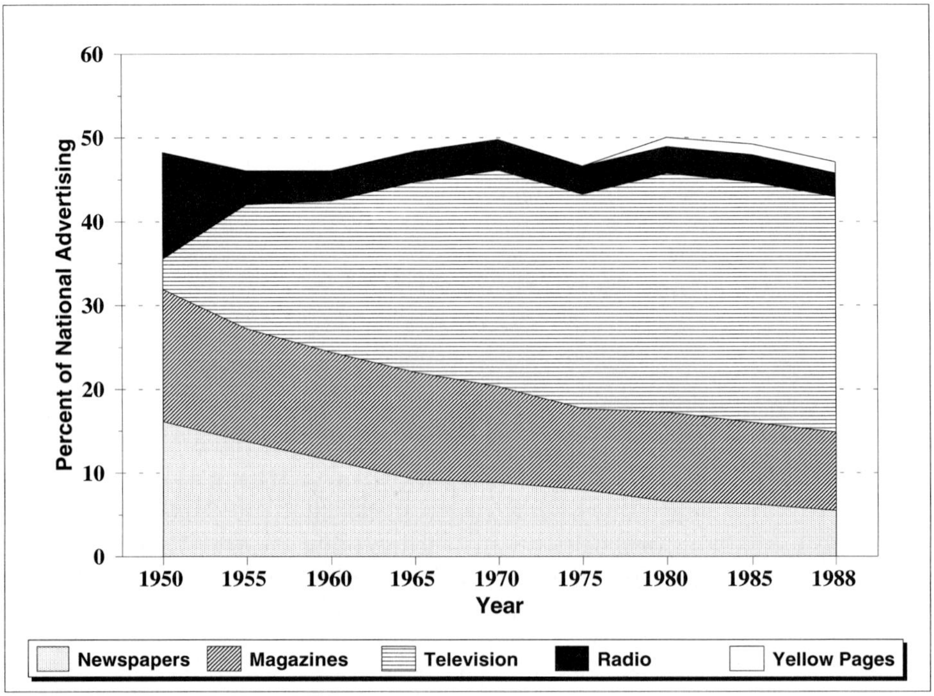

(Yellow Pages not separately reported prior to 1980). Shares do not add to one due to the omission of other mediums—farm publications, direct mail, business papers, outdoors, and other miscellaneous mediums. Sources: *Historical Statistics of the United States: Colonial Times to 1970* (Washington, D.C.: U.S. Government Printing Office, 1976); *Statistical Abstract of the United States* (Washington, D.C.: U.S. Government Printing Office, various years).

AM Radio. Although both FM radio and television were developed prior to the Second World War, disputes about frequency allocations and the war itself delayed their appearance allowing AM radio to remain the principal broadcast medium into the late 1940s. Immediately after the war national networks dominated broadcasting time on AM radio, contributing 40 percent or more of advertising time sales.[6] With the introduction of television network broadcasting in 1947, national advertisers began to move to television. Radio network advertising time sales declined rapidly after 1951. AM radio stations had been so dependent on the networks that many felt that the future of AM radio was threatened. However, AM radio underwent a remarkable transformation, and the number of AM radio stations continued to grow. Though radio's share of local advertising declined between 1950 and 1955, it then rose to 1975, where it has remained.

To adjust to the reduction in revenues from network broadcasts, AM radio stations cut costs. Live programs gave way to recorded ones using magnetic tape, the new long-playing 33 and 45 rpm records, and the older 78 rpm records. New, more reliable

Fig. 13.2 Estimated Shares of Local Advertising

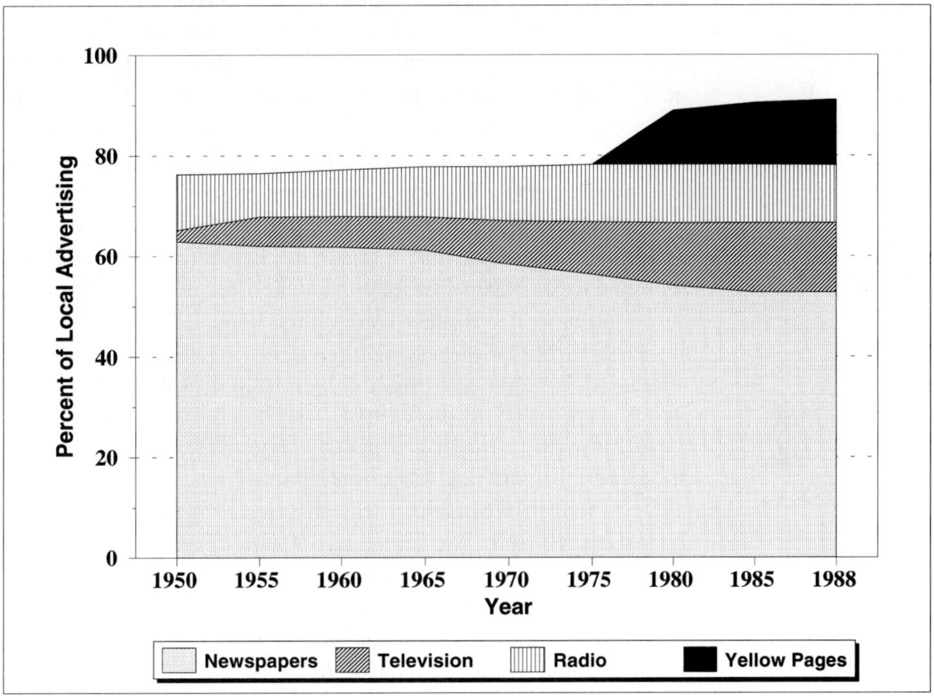

(Yellow Pages not separately reported prior to 1980). Shares do not add to one due to the omission of other mediums—farm publications, direct mail, business papers, outdoors, and other miscellaneous mediums. Sources: *Historical Statistics of the United States: Colonial Times to 1970* (Washington, D.C.: U.S. Government Printing Office, 1976); *Statistical Abstract of the United States* (Washington, D.C.: U.S. Government Printing Office, various years).

equipment allowed announcers to play recordings, put announcements on the air, and adjust signal levels, which obviated the need for large, highly paid staffs. With the virtual cessation of live programs, the large broadcast halls were no longer needed, and stations moved into smaller broadcasting facilities. Stations also began to specialize in programming such as country, classical, or rock music, agricultural and weather news, and so on. FCC reports showed that the average annual operating costs of an AM radio station dropped from $1,230,769 (in 1982–84 dollars) in 1946 to $533,088 in 1956.[7]

FM Radio. Immediately prior to the Second World War, FM radio had appeared to have a bright future. FM radio transmissions could eliminate static, had a broader frequency range for higher fidelity sound, and could have higher quality reception at greater distances from the transmitter.[8] Initially the FCC gave FM 35 wide-band channels in the 43-to-58 MHz range, enough for about 1,500 to 2,000 stations in the United States. By 1941, 58 stations were on the air, and 400,000 sets had been produced.[9]

However, work during the war had led the FCC to calculate that there would be too much cochannel interference in the 43-to-58 MHz FM band, and with the war's end they moved quickly on June 27, 1945, before commercial receiver production was to resume, to shift the FM band to 88 to 108 MHz.[10] This occurred despite opposition from "FM equipment and FM station owners . . . from the Commission's own panel of industry experts . . . and RCA."[11] Vincent Mosco believes that the spectrum shift may have been motivated by a desire to protect AM radio stations and that it did harm FM radio's development. The FCC intended FM to be supplementary to AM and in 1945 also reduced the maximum station power and lowered antenna heights, thus reducing the effective coverage from a radius of 150 miles to 45 miles.[12] AM stations were encouraged to take over FM stations and duplicate programming.

The number of FM stations declined from 1951 to 1957. By the beginning of the 1950s there were few receivers sold and few listeners. Part of this was due to technical problems. Multipath distortion in hilly terrain distorted the signal. Until 1957 FM radio receivers were likely to drift slowly off the chosen station. Although FM signals had less distortion and a wider frequency range than AM signals, FM receivers were generally no better than their AM counterparts. Thus, the sound of FM was not noticeably superior to that of AM. Radio was still tied to network programming, which was too expensive for FM stations, and network signals were of low quality with a limited frequency range and therefore unable to use FM's superior features. Finally, few autos had FM radios.

After 1957 a number of changes came together to cause FM to begin growing again. The near disappearance of network radio, improved equipment, cost-cutting changes, and the moves toward music programming began to boost FM. The development of Automatic Frequency Control (AFC) eliminated FM drift, and the rise of high-fidelity components and rock music, which generally required truer reproduction, also increased its popularity. Stereo broadcasting was authorized in 1961, which gave a strong impetus to further FM development. As a group, FM-only stations first became profitable in 1976 and have become increasingly profitable in the following years.[13]

Television. After the war the National Television System Committee's standards were instated, and 13 VHF channels were assigned to television. Channel 1 was later reallocated to FM broadcasting leaving, 12 VHF channels for television. Initial license applications were slow to arrive due to the much larger costs of beginning broadcasting; one television camera cost as much as all of the equipment for a small radio station. In 1949 operating costs for a television station were roughly six times as much as for a radio station. Television required new and unfamiliar programming and production techniques. Finally, given the small number of television sets in existence, there was uncertainty over the commercial future of television.

Development was also slowed by CBS's support of a color television system, which was not compatible with the RCA monochrome broadcasting system that had been adopted.[14] When CBS's petition for its color system on UHF channels was denied in 1947, new applications for VHF licenses poured in faster than the FCC could handle them, and it soon became evident that there were insufficient channels in the larger markets. Complaints of cochannel interference also began rising.[15] Having been criticized for channel assignments that allowed cochannel interference in AM radio, the FCC was not eager to be subjected to this again. Its response was to impose a "freeze" on all station assignments on September 24, 1948, and at the end of the freeze in April, 1952, only 108 stations were broadcasting.[16]

The FCC severely limited the number of VHF channels in each city to ensure that no VHF cochannel interference arose, and reserved one VHF channel in every city for educational or public broadcasting.[17] Channels 14 to 83 were assigned to the UHF spectrum of 470 to 890 MHz, but UHF broadcast signals were inferior to VHF signals, and until 1964 few television sets included UHF receivers. The FCC refused to adopt the principle of deintermixture—that is, "the assignment of VHF-only or UHF-only channels to each city."[18] If this had been adopted, competition between VHF and UHF would have been avoided, and UHF would have found much more ready acceptance. The FCC virtually ensured that VHF would dominate UHF, created longstanding monopoly rents for VHF licensees, and, as we shall see, effectively limited the number of national television networks.[19]

In February, 1948, when AT&T was authorized to begin providing network television transmissions, seven companies—NBC, CBS, ABC, Mutual, DuMont, Philco, and Paramount—were ready or planning to enter into network television broadcasting.[20] Because the FCC limited the networks to outright ownership of five television stations, they had to develop by affiliation with existing television stations. NBC and CBS's already well developed networks of affiliated radio stations gave them an advantage in this. Early in 1948 both Mutual and Philco dropped their television network plans. Paramount did little more than operate two television stations, leaving four national television networks: NBC, CBS, ABC, and DuMont.

The freeze placed ABC and DuMont at a disadvantage compared to NBC and CBS because they did not have affiliates in all of the major cities. In 1949 DuMont formally proposed to the FCC that it institute a policy of deintermixture so that each network could get an affiliate in each major city.[21] The FCC refused and, with the lifting of the freeze and severe reduction of VHF channels in most cities, virtually guaranteed that ABC and/or DuMont would fail.[22]

AT&T's interconnection charges also placed ABC and DuMont at a disadvantage. Networks that contracted for service eight hours a day, seven days a week—NBC and CBS—were charged $39.50 per month per mile. Occasional-use networks—ABC and DuMont—were charged $69 per month per mile for two hours each day in a month. The FCC turned a deaf ear to ABC's and DuMont's protests.[23] The competitive disadvantages retarded ABC and DuMont's development and after DuMont gave up in 1955, ABC picked up many of its former affiliates and "was able finally to begin a rise toward parity with CBS and NBC in the television broadcasting industry."[24]

Television turned out to be a financial bonanza for VHF license holders; the industry became profitable in 1951 and saw its revenues grow on average 15 percent per year from 1950 to 1980.[25] Television became the dominant national advertising medium as early as 1960, with an 18 percent share. By 1970, 25.8 percent of national advertising was directed to television, a share that has not grown much since. Television's share of local advertising grew steadily to the late 1980s, though remaining a distant second to newspapers. In contrast, UHF stations struggled even after the 1963 amendment to the

1934 Communications Act required televisions to receive both VHF and UHF signals. As a group, they became profitable in 1976.[26]

Due to rising competition from cable television systems, the profits of local stations and national networks stopped growing in the mid-1980s. Cable television began in 1948 as subscriber systems to bring in signals to areas that normally could not pick them up.[27] The rise of satellite program distribution opened the market to the development of "superstations" and cable networks; subscribers had to pay for some, and other were included as part of the basic cable subscription.[28] UHF stations were given new life by the development of cable, which made access to their signal as easy as for the local VHF network stations. In the late 1980s a new national network, Fox Broadcasting, began by affiliating with local UHF stations, most of which could easily reach the viewing audience via cable systems.

In the early 1980s a wave of cable construction swept across the United States. By 1984 it was felt that policies covering cable systems were necessary, and the 1934 Communications Act was amended to provide for cable systems. The act covered franchising and franchise fees; requirements for channels with public access and public, governmental, and educational use; copyright fees; and duplicate programming of locally broadcast programs. It also required that all rates were to be deregulated by 1987 in communities that the FCC judged to have effective competition.

Court tests of the monopoly franchises of local cable companies yielded contradictory decisions. Meanwhile, when local control of subscription fees was removed in 1987, cable companies began exercising their monopoly power as rates quickly rose. By 1989 charges of excessive rate increases were commonplace, and critics were proposing congressional action to reregulate cable TV rates.[29] Late in 1991, preliminary approval was given to telephone companies to develop proposals to install fiber-optic cables that could carry not only telephone signals but also all of the programs currently transmitted through cable lines. If allowed, this would likely provide effective competition for the local cable TV monopolies.

Interpersonal and Business Communications

Postal Services. In contrast to mass communications, interpersonal and business communications are between individuals and/or firms, and there is a charge for each communication. The U.S. Postal Service is the oldest such communications medium, and it is an enormous organization.[30] It is the largest single user of floor space in the United States, and is exceeded only by the military as a purchaser of transport equipment. Overall it handles about half of the world's mail. If we assume that the Postal Service's contribution to GNP can be measured by its expenditures, then on average from 1950 through 1988, it has contributed 0.75 percent of GNP. The Postal Service is extremely labor-intensive, with 80 to 85 percent of its budget in payroll.[31]

The Post Office had never been known as a model of efficiency. In 1966 the 13 story Chicago Post Office essentially ground to a halt stopping mail movement through it and slowing mail delivery across large areas of the United States. By the 1960s the patronage system of appointing postmasters and rural letter carriers was drawing criticism.[32] President Johnson directed that the Kappel Commission undertake a study of postal affairs. The commission's report recommended that the U.S. Post Office be reorganized into the U.S. Postal Service, a quasi-independent body which was approved in 1970, and began operations on July 1, 1971. The patronage system was replaced with civil service career employees to make the Postal Service more professional, and the new organization was supposed to make the Postal Service more efficient and reduce the government subsidies. The federal government's appropriations as a percent of revenues have fallen since 1970.

The arguments supporting the legal monopoly of first-class letter delivery services have generally involved economies of scale and "cream-skimming." However, few studies have found the economies of scale that would justify a legal monopoly, and, of course, the Postal Service does not have a monopoly on other classes of mail. "Cream skimming" is the practice of delivering higher profit mail, such as letters within a city, and not delivering lower profit mail, say, letters between states. Such a practice can only occur when the Postal Service practices price discrimination, which is what a uniform rate per ounce of first-class mail amounts to.[33] Because of the legal monopoly on first-class mail delivery, first-class mail also effectively subsidizes other types of mail handled by the Postal Service. In fact, the U.S. Postal Service has a clear advantage over private mail and parcel post delivery services because of its legal monopoly on first-class letters; complete exemptions from all corporate, property, and business taxes; and the subsidies from Congress. The Postal Service has vigorously defended its monopoly by prosecuting firms that have attempted to move into the delivery of first-class mail.

Even with these advantages the Postal Service's performance has been dismal. Lacking incentives to be efficient, it has been extremely slow to adopt labor-saving machinery and has allowed wage rates to rise well above market levels.[34] To cover the growing inefficiency, real first-class letter rates rose substantially between 1950 and 1975, though they have declined somewhat since then because of competition from falling long distance telephone rates, the growing use of FAX technology, and electronic mail through computers (E-mail). (See Figure 13.3.) The Postal Service's share of the courier/overnight mail business has plummeted to 12 percent since the early 1980s, as private firms such as Federal Express now handle most of this business. The Postal Service's share of the fourth-class parcel business is now down to 6 to 8 percent as United Parcel Service, a private company, now handles the bulk of this business.

Rather than improving, Postal Service delivery has been growing worse. By 1991 it took 22 percent longer on average for a first-class letter to reach its destination than in 1969.[35] This deteriorating performance led to a number of calls to either privatize the U.S. Postal Service or eliminate its legal monopoly to open up the delivery of first-class mail to competing firms. As of 1991 no move had been made in this direction.

Telecommunications Services. The demand for telephone service continued to rise after the Second World War and telephone use grew rapidly, especially toll calls as long distance rates fell.[36] (See Figure 13.4.) Until the 1970s AT&T provided the only long distance connection between the local exchanges. Eighty percent of the population

Fig. 13.3 Pieces of Mail Handled and Real First-Class Letter Rates (1982–84=100)

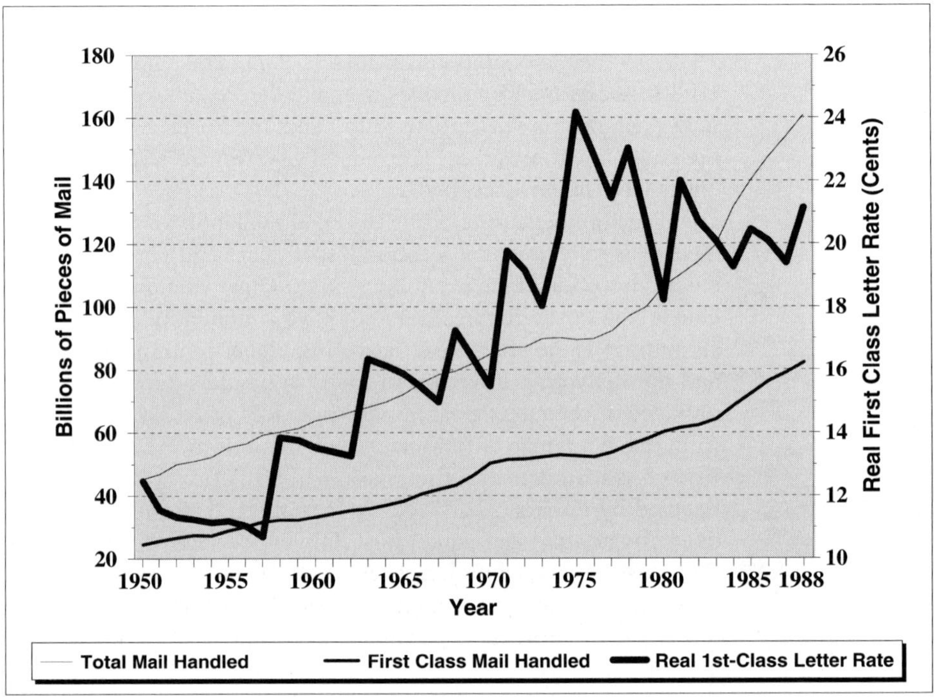

Sources: *Historical Statistics of the United States: Colonial Times to 1970* (Washington, D.C.: U.S. Government Printing Office, 1976); *Statistical Abstract of the United States* (Washington, D.C.: U.S. Government Printing Office, various years).

received their local phone service from an AT&T local company. Long distance service was regulated by the FCC whereas the local exchanges were regulated by various state public utility commissions. AT&T supplied end-to-end service, including the ownership of all equipment—it leased phones to customers.[37]

The postwar period saw a number of developments. As AT&T began to switch from systems with a central operator to direct dial automatic connection, the share of customers on private lines rather than party lines rose from 25 percent in 1950 to 73 percent in 1965.[38] By 1960, 97 percent of Bell customers had local-direct dial service, and by 1963, 80 percent of Bell customers had long distance direct dialing.[39]

By the late 1960s AT&T was failing to keep up with the growing use of the telephone. In New York City overloaded circuits began resulting in waits of two to three minutes for a dial tone, false busy signals, dead lines, crosstalk, false rings, and incorrect phone bills. On July 8, 1969 there was a near total failure of a key New York City exchange, incapacitating phones for several days. Outages struck other parts of the city later in 1969 and 1970. In 1970 Boston had telephone snarls that were even worse than

Fig. 13.4 Real Telephone Toll Rates from New York City to Selected Cities (1982–84=100)

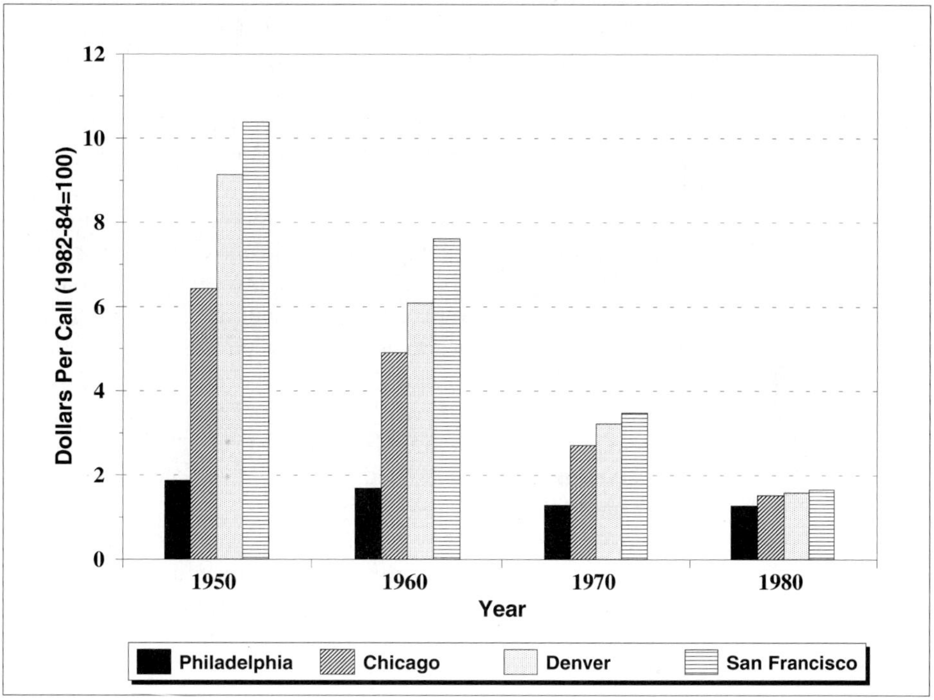

Sources: *Historical Statistics of the United States: Colonial Times to 1970* (Washington, D.C.: U.S. Government Printing Office, 1976); *Statistical Abstract of the United States* (Washington, D.C.: U.S. Government Printing Office, various years).

those in New York City. Denver and Houston also experienced telephone problems that year.[40]

In the 1970s, under new leadership, AT&T recovered.[41] By the beginning of the 1980s, AT&T was the largest corporation in the United States.[42] However, legal and competitive pressures that had been building for two and a half decades came to a head on January 8, 1982, when AT&T signed a consent decree to restructure itself. On January 1, 1984, AT&T divested itself of all of its local operating companies and emerged as a much smaller corporation facing a competitive long distance telephone market.

The roots of these changes lie in FCC decisions initially made during the Second World War. As long distance calls increased and the Long Lines Division's profits rose early in the war, the FCC directed AT&T to replace its board-to-board accounting with station-to-station accounting.[43] This shifted costs from the local operating companies to the Long Lines Division and required that revenues be transferred from the Long Lines Division to the local operating companies. These shifts allowed the FCC and state regulators to lower local rates and move closer to universal local service, a goal the FCC and state regulators desired.

Because this separation of costs and revenues was arbitrary, it could be changed. In 1947 about 2.5 percent of the local exchange plant was allocated to interstate service, but by 1980 about 25 percent was so allocated. These local charges against long distance revenues—access charges—were 35 percent ($7 billion) of total interstate revenues in 1981.[44] As a result, even though technological developments lowered the costs of providing long distance service, long distance rates did not fall commensurately.[45]

In the mid-1950s AT&T began developing a microwave transmission network to thwart the television networks that were proposing building their own microwave networks.[46] In 1959 the *Above 890* decision allowed private microwave networks above 890 MHz. In 1963 Microwave Communications, Inc.—MCI—requested permission to provide private-line network service between Chicago and St. Louis, and in 1969 this was granted. With the competitive door opened, by the middle of 1970 the FCC was inundated by 2,000 applications to provide private line service. The FCC's *Specialized Common Carriers* decision of 1971 developed general rules for such carriers. As the competitive invasion accelerated, AT&T introduced its "Hi-Lo" tariff in 1974 which lowered rates for its private-line circuits.[47]

In November of 1974, the Justice Department filed an antitrust suit against AT&T. Meanwhile the competitive invasion continued. In 1976 firms were allowed to create value-added networks by simply leasing private-line circuits to add some functions and then reselling them to the general public.[48] The competitive invasion that the FCC had created now went beyond its control when MCI began offering its own ordinary long-distance telephone service in 1974—the Circuit Court of Appeals approved this in 1977.[49]

The whole problem, of course, had been created by the FCC's insistence on long distance rates reflecting station-to-station costs and the growing gulf between station-to-station and board-to-board costs. If MCI's long distance telephone service was allowed to subscribe to local telephone service at ordinary business rates, it would have been subsidized by AT&T's Long Lines through the separations charges, and the result would have been one-third lower capital costs for the same long distance facilities.[50] Decisions in 1978 and 1980 required all Bell Telephone companies and independent local telephone companies to interconnect with other long distance services.[51] AT&T proposed an interconnection tariff for other long distance carriers equal to that assigned to the Long Lines Division, but the tariff was vigorously opposed, and the other carriers received large discounts on their connections.[52]

AT&T was unsuccessful in its attempt to get legislation passed that would have forestalled the Justice Department's antitrust suit. By 1981 statements by the judge hearing the Justice Department's case forecast a decision against AT&T, and juries had found for Litton and MCI in their private antitrust suits against AT&T. AT&T began to negotiate a settlement with Assistant Attorney General William F. Baxter.

The consent decree, announced on January 8, 1982, was to take effect on January 1, 1984. AT&T was dismembered. The operating companies were divided into seven regional companies with at least $15 to 20 billion in assets. The new regional companies were not allowed to manufacture or sell terminal equipment, but they retained control of the highly profitable Yellow Pages publishing. The new AT&T was freed to compete in any field it chose, retained both Western Electric and Bell Laboratories, and was allowed to compete on price with the new long distance companies. On January 1, 1984, "when each of AT&T's 3 million stockholder accounts became eight accounts, they comprised close to half of the stockholder accounts in the United States."[53]

Competing long distance companies were given equal access to local exchanges via "dial one" service.[54] The initial estimate of $7 per customer to replace AT&T's lost separations charges and maintain the lower local service rates, were reduced to access charges of $2 a month for residential service and $4 a month for business service. This aroused the anger of customers, while other long distance carriers were angry because their cost advantages largely disappeared.[55]

Real long distance rates, as shown in Figure 13.5, fell, while real local rates rose.[56] Between 1983 and 1987 AT&T's share of the long distance market fell from 90 to 72 percent, while its competitor, Sprint, became the leader in installing the new long distance fiber-optic networks.[57]

Fig. 13.5 Indexes of Real Telephone Rates, 1977–1986

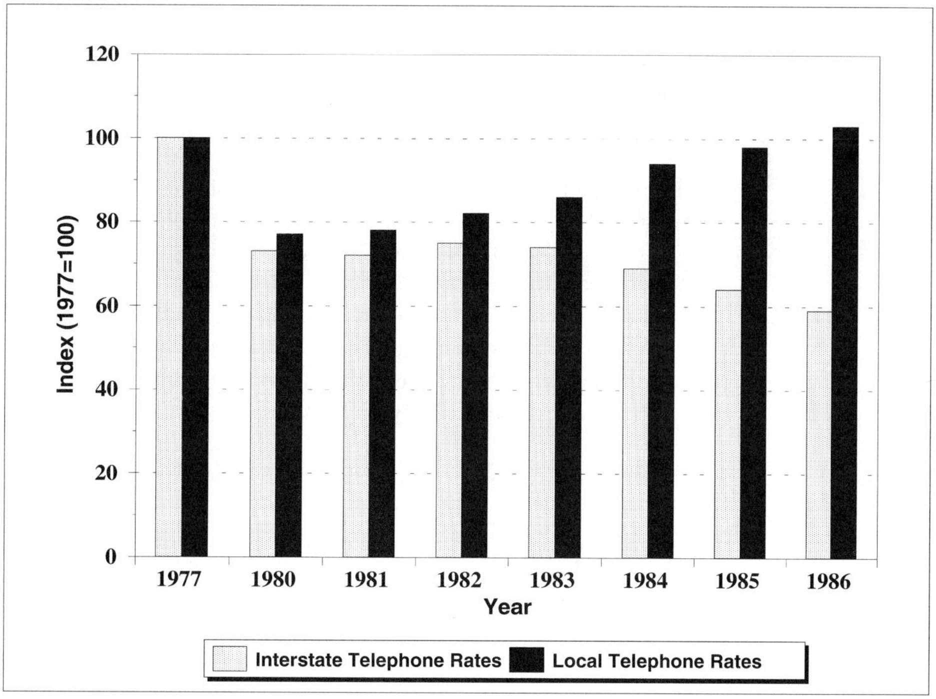

Source: Robert W. Crandall, "Local Phone Rates Catch Up With Costs," *The Wall Street Journal*, 27 February, 1987.

Communications Changes in the Postwar American Economy

For better or for worse, postwar developments in mass communications changed America's entertainment and leisure activities. Television has undeniably allowed many millions to see types of entertainment they would otherwise not have seen. Though it has been criticized as a "vast wasteland," it has also provided nearly instantaneous, visual news and information and lessened regional and rural differences and isolation. Declines in attendance at live theater productions and motion pictures and in newspaper readership and other leisure activities have offset some of the benefits from the rise of television. However, radio—both AM and FM—adapted well to the rapid rise of television.

Developments in interpersonal and business communications have accelerated in recent decades. The completion of microwave transmission networks allowed easy and virtually instantaneous communication across long distances. The rise of competition lowered the costs of long distance communications, and the expansion of computer transmissions allowed firms to monitor and coordinate internal activities much more closely. These were crucial to such developments as "just-in-time" production, which lowered inventory costs, and, for many firms, a decentralization and dispersion of production facilities. These cost-decreasing changes have contributed to the increases in America's real incomes.

FINANCIAL MARKETS

There were numerous changes in the financial sector. Competitive developments in banking began to erase the distinction between deposit and nondeposit banking, and banks moved into nonbank financial and nonfinancial activities. The 1980s saw a steep rise in bank and thrift failures. Credit cards arose as a new payment mechanism, and electronic banking altered the nature of banking. The securities markets saw two booms, one in the late 1960s and the other in the mid-1980s. In the following brief survey of postwar financial markets, we shall examine the most important financial markets: commercial banking, thrifts, and credit unions; credit cards; insurance; and the securities markets, particularly the New York Stock Exchange.

Banking

After the Second World War, commercial banks provided financial services to commercial and industrial customers and were the only financial institutions allowed to offer third-party demand deposits, which were then used primarily by businesses, not households—as late as 1946 only 34 percent of households had a checking account.[58] Household savings deposits and consumer loans were largely handled by savings banks, savings and loan associations, and credit unions.

In the postwar period commercial banks had far more assets but their assets grew slower than those of thrifts and credit unions. Commercial banks faced an erosion of their traditional markets; their largest corporate customers often turned to the commercial paper market, and smaller ones frequently sought out commercial finance companies. Because of the prohibition on interest payments on demand deposits, corporate treasurers began placing liquid funds in higher yielding assets, such as commercial paper and Treasury Bills.[59]

Counterbalancing the erosion of the corporate markets, commercial banks found that consumer deposits and loans were much more important. Consumer deposits provided a lower cost source of funds and commercial banks aggressively pursued both the consumer deposit and credit markets. The shift from noninterest-bearing demand deposits to interest-bearing savings and time deposits raised banks' costs of obtaining funds, even though passbook rates were controlled under Regulation Q. As the ceiling rates were raised, the difference between passbook rates at thrifts and banks narrowed, so in 1966 Congress mandated a 0.5 percent higher ceiling rate (reduced to 0.25 percent in 1975) for thrifts.[60]

The 1970s ushered in new competition for banks and thrifts. The thrift institutions began to behave much more like banks by edging into banks' traditional market for demand deposits. Money market mutual funds developed to provide consumers with income-earning deposits that also included limited check-writing capabilities. This lured funds away from commercial banks and from thrifts. "Nondeposit financial conglomerates—ranging from insurance, credit card, and brokerage companies to manufacturers and retail chain stores—elected to aggressively challenge banks for both their conventional credit and deposit accounts and for new service lines, especially in insurance agency, real estate and security brokerage, and loan-servicing activities."[61]

As the rate of inflation increased, nominal interest rates also increased. Thrift institutions do well as long as there is an upward-sloping yield curve and relative rate stability, but when rates begin rising, they encounter difficulty. With their portfolio of long-term assets and short-term deposits, the cost of obtaining funds can rise toward and even surpass the yields of their assets, and this happened in the 1970s. Savings and time deposit rates were capped to try and keep thrifts profitable. Disintermediation led to an outflow of deposits from both thrifts and commercial banks.

Thrifts began offering both variable rate mortgages and new, higher yielding savings certificates requiring larger minimum deposits with penalties for early withdrawal. In 1972 a Massachusetts savings banks introduced a Negotiable Order of Withdrawal (NOW) account—essentially a checking deposit that paid interest. Other thrifts in the northeast followed suit and credit unions began offering Share Drafts. By the end of the 1970s, these were spreading to other regions. Commercial banks responded by creating automatic funds transfer services (ATS), which transferred money from savings accounts to checking accounts to allow depositors to earn interest on some of their deposits. Money market mutual funds, also introduced in 1972, grew during the 1970s.[62] The number of money market mutual funds began to grow rapidly in 1978 as open-market interest rates rose. "By year-end 1979, money-fund assets totaled $45 billion and then spiraled upward to exceed $200 billion in 1982."[63] Other types of specialized funds were created in their wake.

Commercial banks complained that rulings allowing thrifts to offer interest-paying checking accounts (NOWs) and higher interest rates on savings accounts had left them at a disadvantage. Thrifts complained that they were not allowed to develop an adequately diversified asset portfolio. State-chartered banks that were members of the Federal Reserve System had been dropping their memberships, and an increasing number of national banks began converting to less restrictive state charters and dropping Federal Reserve membership. The Fed became increasingly concerned that its ability to exercise monetary policy was being undermined by these trends. In response, in 1980 Congress passed the Depository Institutions Deregulation and Monetary Control Act (DIDMCA) and, in 1982, the Garn-St. Germain Depository Institutions Act.[64]

DICMCA required *all* depository institutions to have the same reserve requirements, as set by the Fed, and granted all depository institutions access to the Fed's discount window. Commercial banks were allowed to offer NOW accounts as well as automatic transfer services, and in the middle of 1983 the Depository Institutions Deregulation Committee recommended that Congress repeal the prohibitions on interest payments on demand deposits.[65] Interest rate ceilings on time and savings deposits for thrifts and commercial banks were to be equalized by 1984 and phased out by 1986. Thrifts were allowed to offer consumer and commercial loans, credit cards, and trust services. The maximum size of FDIC- and FSLIC-insured individual deposits was raised to $100,000 from the $40,000 limit set in 1978.

The Garn-St. Germain Depository Act was passed in October of 1982 in response to the plight of the banks and thrifts in the 1980–82 period. They were given expanded lending and investment powers and allowed to offer new deposits. It also gave "the Bank Board the authority to arrange mergers of failing thrifts with other thrifts, commercial banks, savings and loan holding companies, bank holding companies, and nondepository companies."[66] A program was established to provide capital assistance for thrifts with seriously low net worths. The act authorized banks and savings and loans to offer Money Market Deposit Accounts (MMDAs) to compete with the Money Market Mutual Funds' share accounts. These new accounts were extraordinarily successful and "by May 1983, approximately six months after their inauguration, MMDA volume exceeded $300 billion—roughly half the size of the nation's narrowly defined (M1) money supply."[67]

The financial crisis that had brought about the Garn-St. Germain Act extended back into the early 1970s. The rising inflation rates and severe recession of 1974–75 had increased the number of failing and problem banks. From 1970 through 1981, there were an average of 262 problem banks each year. With the onset of new, more severe recessions in 1980 and 1981, bank failures increased, especially among banks that had become involved in energy loans. The banking crisis grew worse in the 1980s. As Figure 13.6 shows, the number of banks closed or assisted grew throughout the 1980s.

The 1980s were even worse for the thrifts; they experienced two crisis periods, 1979 to 1982 and 1987 to 1992. The rising interest rates on deposits, combined with lower yields on their mortgage portfolios, had progressively squeezed the thrifts' earn-

Fig. 13.6 Banks Closed or Assisted

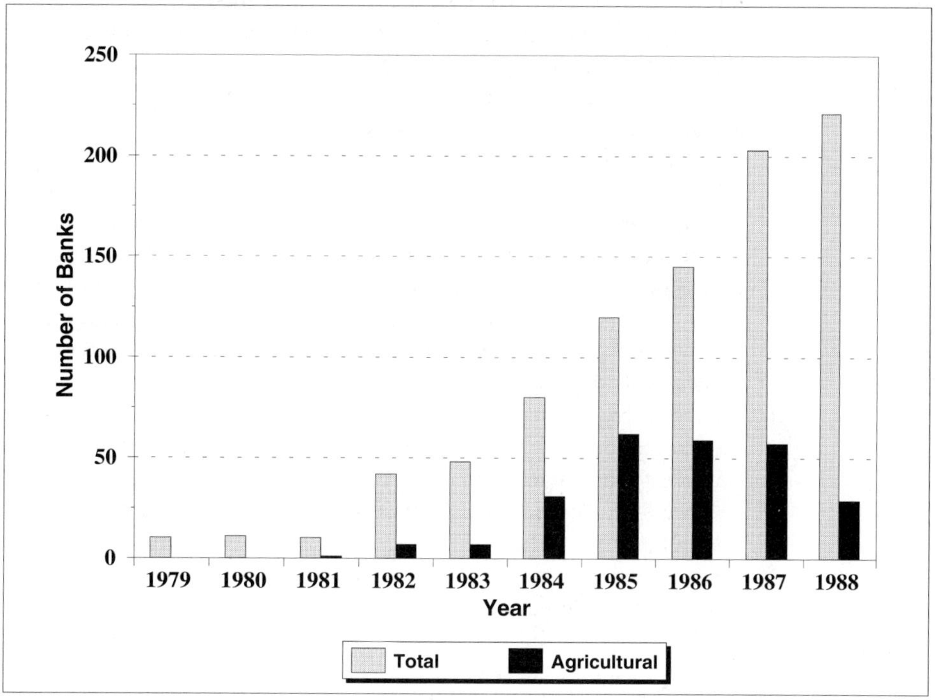

(Agricultural banks are banks with at least 25 percent of their portfolio devoted to farm loans.)
Sources: *Statistical Abstract of the United States* (Washington, D.C.: U.S. Government Printing Office, various years).

ings during the 1970s, and the thrifts were in a weakened condition by 1979. There were rapid increases in interest rates from 1979 through 1981, and in 1981 and 1982 FSLIC-insured thrift institutions as a group had net losses of 14.3 and 15 percent of the previous year's regulatory net worth.[68] The regulatory net worth of these institutions declined by 24.5 percent from 1980 to 1983, and in 1982, 252 FSLIC-insured institutions, or 7.5 percent of their total number, failed. The largest number of insured thrifts to fail in a single year prior to that was 13 in 1941. Between 1980 and 1986, 664 thrifts failed.[69] Voluntary and supervised thrift mergers rose sharply. As interest rates declined in 1982, thrifts returned to profitability, but the initial damage had been done.

Although the number of failures declined, the number of insolvent thrifts continued to rise due to the erosion of their net worths. Because of the FSLIC's reduced reserves (necessary to close insolvent thrifts) the Federal Home Loan Bank Board changed its accounting practices to allow thrifts to spread their losses on asset sales over the remaining life of the assets sold.[70] They reduced the minimum net worth requirements from 5 percent in 1979 to 3 percent in 1982 and, until March of 1985, allowed the use of "five-year averaging" and "twenty-year phase-in" to further reduce the regulatory net worth of the thrifts.[71] Although this reduced the number of technically insolvent thrifts requiring FSLIC merger or liquidation, it did nothing to alleviate the actual financial problems.

Between 1982 and 1987 several disturbing trends developed. Thrifts began to make greater use of Jumbo deposits (large CD's over $100,000) and brokered deposits of $100,000, the maximum individual amount insured by the FSLIC. These carried higher interest rates, particularly after full interest rate deregulation in 1986, and this "hot money" was subject to much more sudden withdrawal. This, combined with reduced net worth requirements, accounting techniques created to maximize short-run income and regulatory net worth, and failure to close the growing number of effectively insolvent institutions, induced institutional gambling and brought on a new crisis.

Individual deposits were FSLIC guaranteed up to $100,000, and the FSLIC insurance costs did not differentiate between "safe" and "risky" thrift institutions. The only hope to regain solvency was to grow in order to gain the additional assets that could generate the income to become solvent. To grow, the thrifts had to pay above-market interest rates to get Jumbo and brokered CDs, then invest in riskier assets that could, if successful, generate the income to again become solvent.[72] The process of adverse selection meant that the fastest growing thrifts were the riskiest insolvent thrifts, and this accelerated the potential future cost to the FSLIC.[73] The decline in the rate of inflation and the depression in energy-related activities in the southwest caused real estate prices to begin falling. By 1987 there was evidence of serious excess construction of commercial and apartment property in the southeast and southwest, especially Texas and Oklahoma. In early 1987 the General Accounting Office (GAO) declared FSLIC insolvent.[74]

By 1986 it was clear that conditions were worsening rather than improving in the thrift industry, and the Federal Home Loan Bank Board and U.S. Treasury developed a plan to raise funds through the Federal Home Loan Bank to provide capital for the FSLIC to close insolvent institutions and dispose of their assets. The initial legislation of 1987—the Financial Institutions Competitive Equality Act—was authorized, raising only $10.8 billion.[75] By late 1987 official estimates of the amounts required to bail out the thrift industry had risen to $15 billion. The Federal Home Loan Bank's "Southwest Plan" provided large tax breaks and subsidies to entice private investors to take over insolvent thrifts in Oklahoma and Texas.

As more information became available, the size of the bailout began growing, reaching $40–$50 billion by the middle of 1989. On August 9, 1989, a $50 billion savings and loan bailout bill was signed. A new agency, the Resolution Trust Corporation (RTC) was created to sell $30 billion in 30-year bonds to help cover the costs of closing or selling insolvent thrifts. The Treasury was to contribute $18.8 billion and the FHLB $1.2 billion. The RTC took possession of all thrifts insolvent as of January 1, 1989, and all thrifts declared insolvent after that date to dispose of their assets. Thrift industry insurance premiums were increased, and a new Savings Association Insurance Fund (SAIF) and a new Bank Insurance Fund (BIF) were established to replace the FSLIC; both were controlled by the FDIC. Tougher capital requirements were imposed, and new uniform capital accounting standards were to be developed to enforce them. Thrifts were also no longer allowed to make huge, unsecured loans to a single borrower.

The estimated size of the S&L bailout continued to mount as insolvency grew, and the RTC was slow to dispose of the assets of the seized thrifts. In November of 1990, the cost of bailing out the S&L industry, *excluding* any interest costs on the money borrowed, was estimated at $178 to $200 billion.[76] By August 1991, the estimate of the cost had risen to $230 billion.[77] Charges of incompetence and capricious regulation by the RTC were common.[78]

Credit Cards

Credit cards date to just prior to the First World War and began as an extension of the traditional consumer credit that had always been provided by American merchants.[79] In 1914 some large retail stores began issuing cards to their wealthiest customers and in 1928 began issuing "charge-plates," which were embossed metal address plates to identify charging customers and facilitate mailing bills and keeping records. By the late 1920s gasoline companies began issuing courtesy cards for purchases at their stations. Between 1928 and 1958 retailers developed a number of innovations in credit cards such as minimum monthly payments on the unpaid balance, initially set at one sixth thereof; finance charges on the unpaid balance each month; and the thirty-day grace period on finance charges.

The first universal card—the Diners Club Card—began in 1949. For the first time a company acted as an intermediary between the merchant and the consumer and charged each a fee for the service. These credit cards came to be called Travel and Entertainment (T&E) cards. American Express, worried about competition to its profitable travelers' cheque business, established its T&E card in 1958, the same year that the Hilton Hotel Corporation launched its Carte Blanche card, and the nation's two largest banks, Bank of America and Chase Manhattan, started their own credit card operations.

The primary obstacle to the acceptance and use of universal credit cards was the lack of a national network. To solve this problem, Bank of America licensed its BankAmericard across the United States in 1966. Sensing the competition, several other large banks joined together to counter BankAmericard by creating the Interbank Card Association. In 1976 BankAmericard changed its name to Visa; somewhat earlier, Interbank Card had become Master Charge, and in 1980 it switched names again to become MasterCard. Unsolicited mass mailings of the cards and marketing blitzes in the late 1960s increased the installed cardholder bases.[80] In 1973 retail cards were over half of all credit cards, however, the use of bank credit cards grew rapidly during the 1970s. During the 1980s major retailers began to accept the bank credit cards in addition to their own retail credit cards, and by 1986, 55 percent of all families had at least one bank credit card.

Through the 1970s bank credit cards were only marginally profitable, and much less so than the T&E credit cards. Interest rates on unpaid balances on credit card accounts rose along with other interest rates at the end of the 1970s and in the early 1980s. As interest rates fell after 1982, credit card interest rates fell less swiftly. Banks and other card issuers realized that the easy access to an unsecured line of credit, combined with the generally small unpaid balances, made the demand for the cards' credit relatively interest inelastic. Bank credit cards became an increasingly profitable business in the 1980s and, by the end of the decade, an important source of banks' earnings.

By the end of the 1980s, electronic funds transfers (EFTs) were taking away some of the credit cards' business. The debit cards could obtain cash from automated teller machines and be used at participating merchants to make the payment directly from checking accounts. However, due to the easy access to credit, it was not expected that credit cards would disappear.

Insurance

The private insurance industry in the United States is a vast enterprise affecting nearly every person in our society. It is composed of companies providing life, property, casualty, health, and other types of insurance, with many companies providing more than one type of insurance coverage. Our primary interest is in life insurance because of its role in the financial markets. Whole life insurance policies and many term policies have provided investment vehicles for the individuals insured and given life insurance companies funds to invest.

In the depressed thirties and during the Second World War, life insurance companies had became major investors in federal government securities, and nearly 25 percent of their assets were still invested in government securities in 1950. They continued to be an important source of corporate funds as they generally held from 36 to 41 percent of their assets in corporate bonds, and their corporate stock holdings rose from 3.3 to 9 percent. The other important asset owned by life insurance companies is mortgages. This share of their assets rose through 1965 and has since declined from 37.8 percent to 20 percent as new competitors for mortgages—especially mortgage pools and trusts—arose. (See Figure 13.7.) Despite this decline, life insurance companies continue to be important sources of funds for mortgage and corporate lending.

Securities Markets

The securities markets raise new capital through the sale of bonds and stocks and handle the transfer of ownership of existing bonds and shares of stock. In the postwar period the New York Stock Exchange has continued to dominate all other organized securities exchanges.[81] Figure 13.8 shows the real and current price Standard and Poor's common stock index for the New York Stock Exchange.[82] The nominal stock price indexes show a tremendous growth over the entire period, but this is not so for the real price index, which fell 66.4 percent from 1965 to 1980 and rose 44.6 percent from 1980 to 1988.

The volume of trading on the NYSE grew dramatically during the 1980s. (See Figure 13.9.) The trading volume had remained low from the depressed 1930s through

Fig. 13.7 Shares of Mortgage Debt Outstanding by Type of Holder

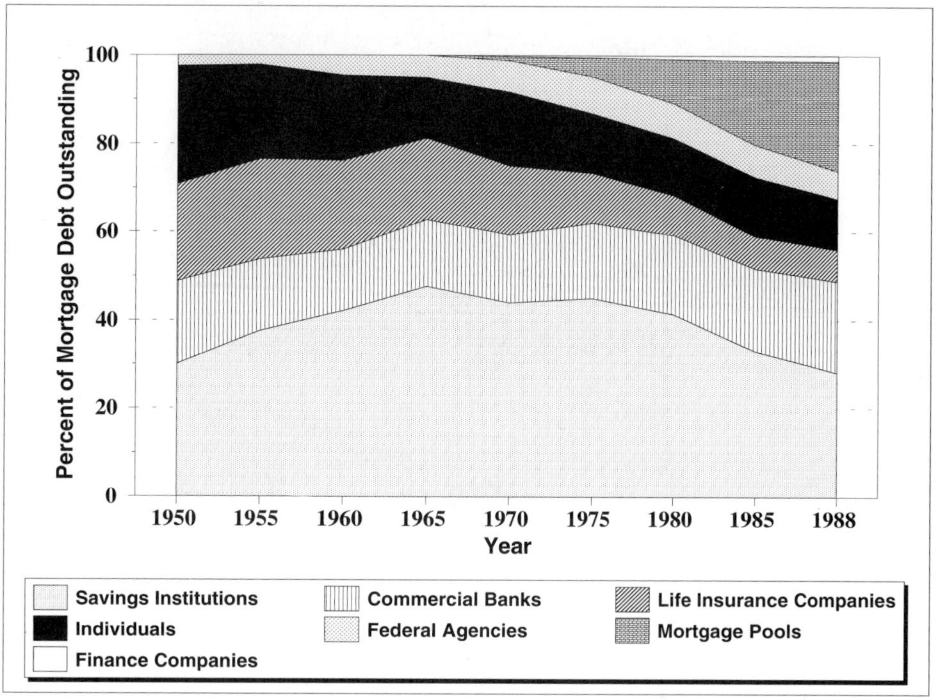

(Savings institutions include savings and loan associations, credit unions, and mutual savings banks.)
Sources: *Historical Statistics of the United States: Colonial Times to 1970* (Washington, D.C.: U.S. Government Printing Office, 1976); *Statistical Abstract of the United States* (Washington, D.C.: U.S. Government Printing Office, various years).

the first half of the 1960s but began to pick up in the late 1960s when the record for the monthly trading volume set in October 1929 was surpassed by the 45 million shares exchanged in October 1965.[83]

Aiding this increase in volume was a change in the nature of trading. Prior to the Second World War the bulk of all trading had been undertaken by individual traders. After the war institutional investors—mutual funds, trusts, pension funds, insurance portfolios, and foundations—began playing a more important role. In the 1950s "institutional holdings of all stocks had risen from 12.5 per cent of all equities to almost 20 percent."[84] By 1969 institutional investors engaged in 60 percent of the dollar volume of public transactions. Their influence continued to grow into the 1980s, when computer-programmed trades would buy and sell thousands of shares at a time when predetermined prices were reached.

Stock prices and trading activity remained low from the end of the Second World War to the beginning of the Eisenhower bull market in September of 1953. In December of that year the Dow Jones Index finally exceeded the level reached in

Fig. 13.8 Standard and Poor's Common Stock Price Index

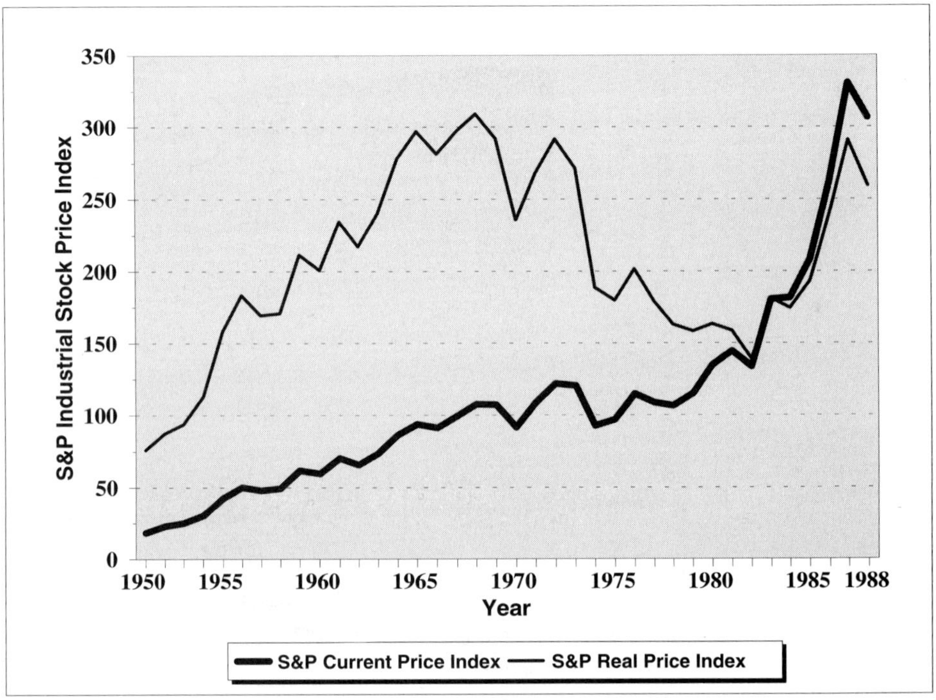

(Real Index is the current price index deflated by the all-items CPI, 1982–84=100.)
Sources: *Historical Statistics of the United States: Colonial Times to 1970* (Washington, D.C.: U.S. Government Printing Office, 1976); *Statistical Abstract of the United States* (Washington, D.C.: U.S. Government Printing Office, various years).

September of 1929 and continued rising to peak at 760 in September of 1961. By December of 1963, stock prices were again rising and continued to rise until a new peak of 1,001 was reached on February 9, 1966. The "go-go" market of 1967 to 1969 did not quite bring prices back to the 1,000 level. The dominant characteristic of this bull market was a sharp rise in the volume of trading, particularly in 1968.[85] There are various reasons suggested for the go-go market of the late 1960s. The economy was growing and in the midst of a long continuing expansion. In 1964 there were substantial cuts in federal income tax rates, and the Federal Reserve System began to increase the stock of money at a faster rate. Generally the end of the boom was attributed to President Johnson's 1968 surtax and the FRS switch to a tighter monetary policy in late 1968, actions that foretold the end of the 1960s expansion.

Prices dropped and activity declined in 1969 and 1970, and prices rose little in nominal terms during the rest of the 1970s. In the early 1970s fixed common broker fees were eliminated to allow transactions fees to be competitively set, and the price of a seat on the NYSE declined sharply, at one point becoming less expensive than the

Fig. 13.9 Shares Traded on the New York Stock Exchange

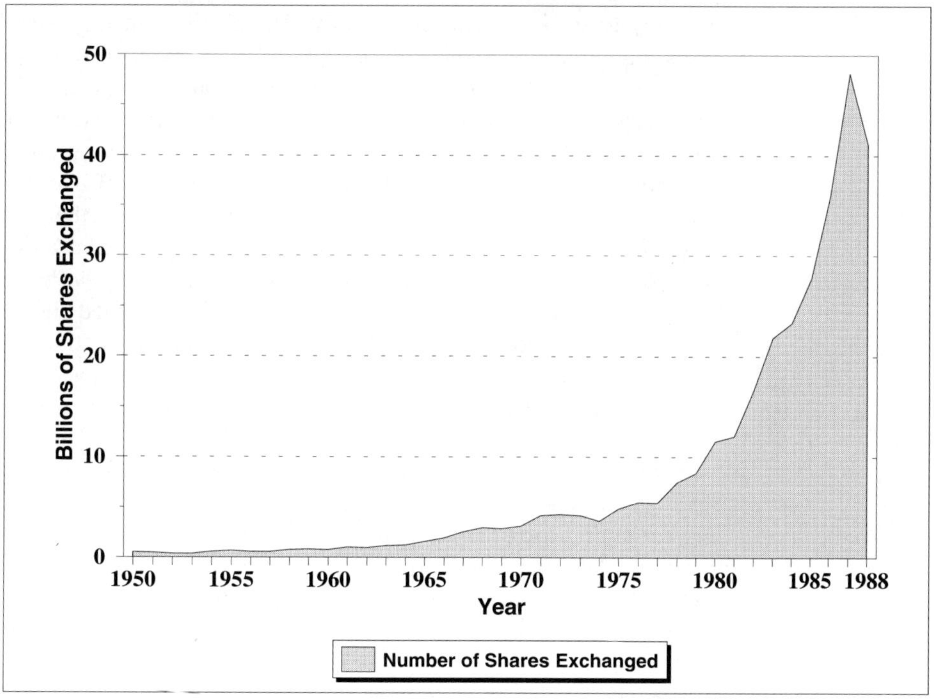

Sources: *Historical Statistics of the United States: Colonial Times to 1970* (Washington, D.C.: U.S. Government Printing Office, 1976); *Statistical Abstract of the United States* (Washington, D.C.: U.S. Government Printing Office, various years).

purchase of a New York City taxicab medallion. There is no satisfactory explanation for the failure of stock prices to rise during the 1970s.

Late in 1982 a new bull market developed. Between August 12, 1982, and August 25, 1987, the Dow Jones Index rose from 777 to 2,722. By 1987, 200-million-share days were common. The most commonly offered reasons for the five-year boom were the long expansion, which in fact continued until 1990; the sharp declines in the rate of price inflation; and the tax cuts of 1981 and 1986.

From the August 25 peak, prices began to decline, and by the end of Thursday, October 15, the DJI stood at 2,355. On Friday, October 16, the index fell 108 points on a volume of 338.48 million shares. On Monday, October 19, 1987, the full force of the hurricane of selling was felt as the DJI fell 508 points on a volume of 604.33 million shares. The percentage decline was larger than either Black Thursday or Tragic Tuesday during the October, 1929, crash. From the opening on Monday, October 12, to the close on Monday, October 19, the DJI fell 743 points, wiping out all of the 1987 gains.

The Federal Reserve System moved quickly to pump liquidity into the system, and the federal funds rate, a key barometer of monetary conditions fell from 7.5 percent on Monday to 6.75 percent on Tuesday. The Fed's monetary ease helped stabilize the stock market and enabled banks to provide liquidity to customers.

The New York Stock Exchange moved quickly to curb computer-programmed trading, which many blamed for the severity of the crash. Three smaller securities firms closed, and a fourth one had to be taken over in the aftermath of the crash. Thousands of employees at Wall Street financial firms were laid off over the next several years. Firms that had been planning on equity offerings canceled their plans, and a number of large firms announced plans to begin buying equity back because of the low prices on their stocks. Some drew remarkable and eerie parallels with the bull market of the 1920s and crash of the market in 1929 and publicly worried about a depression such as had occurred in the early 1930s. However, real economic activity was remarkably unaffected, and stock prices began to recover, but at a slower pace. In 1989 the Dow Jones Index surpassed the August 25, 1987, peak and in 1991 surpassed the 3,000 level.

Many reasons were proposed for the decline. One commonly accepted explanation was that the House Ways and Means Committee had just agreed to a bill to control leveraged buyouts and stop company takeovers, an activity that had boosted the stock market during the boom.[86] Other factors supposedly included disappointing news on the twin deficits (federal budget and international trade) and the Federal Reserve System's tightening of the money supply between March and September of 1987 to raise interest rates and attempt to stop the fall of the dollar in foreign exchange markets.[87]

Whatever the exact reasons that initiated the stock sell-off, most attributed the severity of the decline and the astonishingly large volume to programmed trades, which resulted in huge sell (or buy) orders once the predetermined prices were reached. The NYSE and the SEC set up rules to eliminate the resulting huge volatility.

Changes in Financial Markets in the Postwar American Economy

In the wake of the financial disasters of the Great Depression, government authorities attempted to segregate types of financial institutions and control interest rates in order to reduce competition between financial intermediaries and bring stability to the financial structure. In the postwar period these changes disintegrated.

Generally these changes in the financial markets increased consumer welfare by bringing about the payment of interest on their demand deposits and removing interest rate ceilings on other consumer deposits. Though increasing competition for consumer loans tended to lower loan rates, rising costs of funds reduced the supply of consumer loans, providing an offsetting force on consumer loan rates. The rapidly rising use of credit and debit cards lowered the costs of making transactions and facilitated record keeping, generally enhancing consumer welfare, though some experienced difficulty because of the easy access to an unsecured line of credit.

These postwar changes also benefited business firms. The ability to generate income on cash balances and access to lower cost borrowed funds reduced firms' costs. The boom in the securities markets in the 1960s and again in the 1980s provided corporations with lower cost funds for expansion. In particular, in the 1980s the sale of lower grade bonds provided funds for expansion and both friendly and unfriendly acquisitions, fueling the great merger wave of the 1980s.[88] The great stock market crash of 1987 reduced this activity, but there was no depression as the expansion, which had begun in 1982, continued, and the Federal Reserve System quickly and vigorously acted to provide liquidity in the aftermath of the crash. By 1990 the securities markets had fully recovered from the 1987 stock market crash.

SELECTED REFERENCES

Adie, Douglas K. *An Evaluation of Postal Service Wage Rates*. Washington, D.C.: American Enterprise Institute for Public Policy Research, 1977.

Baldwin, Thomas F., and D. Stevens McVoy. *Cable Communication*, 2d ed. Englewood Cliffs, NJ: Prentice-Hall, 1988.

Benjaminson, Peter. *Death in the Afternoon: America's Newspaper Giants Struggle for Survival*. Kansas City: Andrews, McMeel & Parker, 1984.

Brooks, John. *Telephone: The First Hundred Years*. New York: Harper and Row, 1976.

__________, *The Go-Go Years*. New York: Weybright and Tally, 1972.

Brumbaugh, R. Dan, Jr. *Thrifts Under Seige: Restoring Order to American Banking*. Cambridge, MA: Ballinger Publishing Co., 1988.

Emery, Edwin, and Michael Emery. *The Press and America*, 4th ed. Englewood Cliffs, NJ: Prentice-Hall, 1978.

Inglis, Andrew F. *Behind the Tube: A History of Broadcasting Technology and Business*. Boston: Focal Press, 1990.

Irwin, Manley R. "The Telecommunications Industry." *The Structure of American Industry*, 8th ed. Edited by Walter Adams. New York: Macmillan Publishing Co., 1990.

Kane, Edward J. *The S & L Insurance Mess: How Did It Happen?* Washington, D.C.: The Urban Institute Press, 1989.

Klebaner, Benjamin J. *American Commercial Banking: A History*. Boston: Twayne Publishers, 1990.

Long, Stewart L. "Television Network Development: The Early Years." *Business and Economic History: Papers Presented at the Twenty-Third Annual Meeting of the Business History Conference*. 2d series, 6 (1977): 69–83.

Mandell, Lewis. *The Credit Card Industry: A History*. Boston: Twayne Publishers, 1990.

Mitchell, Mark. "Triggering the 1987 Stock Market Crash." *Journal of Financial Economics* 24 (September 1989): 37–68.

Mosco, Vincent. *Broadcasting in the United States: Innovative Challenge and Organizational Control*. Norwood, NJ: Ablex Publishing Co., 1979.

Rose, Peter S. *The Changing Structure of American Banking*. New York: Columbia University Press, 1987.

Shooshan, Harry M., III. ed. *Disconnecting Bell: The Impact of the AT&T Divestiture*. New York: Pergamon Press, 1984.

Sobel, Robert. *The Big Board: A History of the New York Stock Exchange*. New York: The Free Press, 1965.

Temin, Peter. *The Fall of the Bell System*. New York: Cambridge University Press, 1987.

NOTES

1. Edwin Emery and Michael Emery, *The Press and America*, 4th ed. (Englewood Cliffs, NJ: Prentice-Hall, 1978), 436.
2. Peter Benjaminson, *Death in the Afternoon: America's Newspaper Giants Struggle for Survival* (Kansas City: Andrews, McMeel & Parker, 1984), viii-x.
3. Krystal Miller, "Red Ink: Detroit's Dailies Upset Idea that Profits Flow When Papers Link Up: Rate Rises, Delivery Snafus Send Many Advertisers, Readers to Suburban Press," *The Wall Street Journal*, 14 November, 1991. JOAs did not save afternoon papers in Shreveport, Louisiana and in Miami.
4. Ibid., 440.
5. Ibid., 437.
6. Andrew F. Inglis, *Behind the Tube: A History of Broadcasting Technology and Business* (Boston: Focal Press, 1990), 59. Most of the discussion of AM radio is drawn from chapter 2 of this source, especially, pp. 59–60.
7. Ibid., 60. In current dollars the figures were $240,000 in 1946 and $145,000 in 1956.
8. Vincent Mosco, *Broadcasting in the United States: Innovative Challenge and Organizational Control* (Norwood, NJ: Ablex Publishing Co. 1979), 52.
9. Inglis, *Behind the Tube*, 128–29.
10. *Cochannel interference* means that the signals from two stations operating on the same frequency overlap or interfere with each other. For example, suppose that an FM station in Milwaukee, Wisconsin, and one in Madison, Wisconsin, each operated at 98.3 MHz. Unless station power is properly limited, listeners between the two cities would not be able to pick up either station due to cochannel (or signal) interence. An FCC engineer, Kenneth Norton, was the driving force behind the frequency shift.
11. Mosco, *Broadcasting in the United States*, 56.
12. Ibid., 61.
13. Inglis, *Behind the Tube*, 145.
14. Ibid., 190–93 and 237–72.
15. Ibid., 193.
16. Ibid., 194.
17. "For example, in Chicago commercial channels were reduced from 7 to 4, in San Francisco from 7 to 4, in Boston from 5 to 3, in Cleveland from 5 to 3, in Dallas/Fort Worth from 6 to 4, in Houston from 4 to 2, in San Diego from 4 to 2, and in Scranton/Wilkes-Barre from 4 to 0." Inglis, *Behind the Tube*, 200.
18. Ibid., 201.
19. Mosco, *Broadcasting in the United States*, 70–84.
20. Much of the following discussion draws upon Stewart L. Long, "Television Network Development: The Early Years," *Business and Economic History: Papers Presented at the Twenty-Third Annual Meeting of the Business History Conference*, 2d series, 6 (1977): 69–83.
21. With deintermixture, cities would have gained only VHF or UHF signal allocations. This would have allowed more VHF channels in each city that had only VHF channels. UHF

channels were not so limited.

22. Inglis, *Behind the Tube*, 200. See also Long, "Television Network Development," 79–81.
23. Long, "Television Network Development," 81. As a final insult, AT&T required DuMont to purchase the same audio facilities as NBC, CBS, and ABC did for their radio networks, even though DuMont had no radio network.
24. Ibid., 81.
25. Inglis, *Behind the Tube*, 209.
26. Ibid., 207.
27. The following discussion of cable television draws principally upon the following sources: Inglis, *Behind the Tube*, 360–391; Thomas F. Baldwin and D. Stevens McVoy, *Cable Communication*, 2d ed. (Englewood Cliffs, NJ: Prentice-Hall, 1988), 2–7 and 174–91; Vernone Sparkes, "Cable Television in the United States: A Story of Continuing Growth and Change," in Realph M. Negrine, ed., *Cable Television and the Future of Broadcasting* (New York: St. Martin's Press, 1985).
28. "Superstations" were local stations that broadcast all over the United States by means of microwave cable transmission. The primary superstations were WWOR of New York, WGN of Chicago, and WTBS of Atlanta. The leader in the creation of cable networks was Time Inc.'s Home Box Office (HBO), which first aired on September 20, 1975.
29. See the following articles: Laura Landro, "Airing Grievances: As Cable-TV Industry Keeps Growing, Rivals Demand Reregulation: Broadcasters and Others Call The Competition Unfair, And Utilities Want Shares," *The Wall Street Journal*, 17 September, 1987; John R. Emshwiller, "Prying Open the Cable-TV Monopolies: Prices, Lawsuits Place Pressure On the Industry," *The Wall Street Journal*, 10 August, 1989; Mary Lu Carnevale, "Danforth Proposes Bill to Re-Regulate Cable-TV Rates," *The Wall Street Journal*, 16 November, 1989; Thomas W. Hazlett, "Who's Behind the Cable Scam," *The Wall Street Journal*, 30 March, 1990; Laura Landro, "Despite a Robust Basic Business, Picture is Flawed for Cable TV," *The Wall Street Journal*, 21 March, 1991.
30. The Continental Congress legislated a federal post office and this monopoly legislation was carried forward into the Constitution.
31. Douglas K. Adie, *An Evaluation of Postal Service Wage Rates* (Washington, D.C.: American Enterprise Institute for Public Policy Research, 1977), 1.
32. Ibid., 30–32. See also John Haldi, *Postal Monopoly* (Washington, D.C.: American Enterprise Institute for Public Policy, 1974); and Morton S. Baratz, *The Economics of the Postal Service* (Washington, D.C.: Public Affairs Press, 1962).
33. A letter mailed in, say, Milwaukee, to another address in Milwaukee does not cost as much to deliver as a letter mailed in Milwaukee to be delivered to an address in, say, San Francisco. Because the price is the same, this amounts to price discrimination where the intracity sender is subsidizing the interstate sender.
34. Adie, *An Evaluation of Postal Service Wage Rates*, 91. James Bovard reported that nominal wages and benefits for Postal Service workers in December of 1989 averaged $43,000 and a Postal Inspection Service study found that for mail clerks, Postal Service employees were paid 84 percent more than their state government counterparts. (James Bovard, "Mail Monopoly Says Happy New Year," *The Wall Street Journal*, 29 December, 1989.)
35. James Bovard, "'On-Time Delivery:' The Great Mail Fraud," *The Wall Street Journal*, 30 January, 1991. The following data are taken from this article.
36. Peter Temin, *The Fall of the Bell System* (New York: Cambridge University Press, 1987), 20.
37. In 1947 three scientists at Bell Laboratories, William Shockley, John Bardeen, and Walter

H. Brattan, developed the transistor for which they were awarded the Nobel Prize in 1956. (John Brooks, *Telephone: The First Hundred Years* (New York: Harper and Row, 1976), 222–23.)

38. Ibid., 267.
39. Ibid., 266.
40. Ibid., 292.
41. Temin, *The Fall of the Bell System*, 4–5.
42. Harry M. Shooshan III, "The Bell Breakup: Putting It In Perspective," in Harry M. Shooshan III, ed., *Disconnecting Bell: The Impact of the AT&T Divestiture* (New York: Pergamon Press, 1984), 8.
43. The distinctions between board-to-board and station-to-station accounting, which were crucial to this, can be explained as follows. The local exchange in, say, Milwaukee has a switch that connects it to the long distance lines. The switch is called a "board." Under the board-to-board accounting of costs, if a party in Milwaukee calls a party in Omaha, the toll call is the board-to-board call between the switches in the two cities and only the costs associated with the board-to-board service are relevant to the toll charge. The Milwaukee party's call to the Milwaukee board is a local call, just as the call received in Omaha from the Omaha board to the Omaha party is a local call. However, under the station-to-station concept the long distance toll call is the entire call from the home of the Milwaukee caller to the home of the Omaha party. The costs of the toll call therefore include some of the costs associated with providing local service. The problem was to separate those costs that were local from those that were long distance when using the station-to-station cost accounting approach. There was no such problem with the board-to-board approach. Complicating this was the fact that a significant portion of the local companies' costs were fixed (or possession), costs which did not vary with use. Any allocation of possession costs between local and long distance service was completely arbitrary. By 1947 the Bell system had developed a *Separations Manual* to direct the process of separating these costs. (Temin, *The Fall of the Bell System*, 23.)
44. Ibid., 26 and 306.
45. Ibid., 24.
46. Richard E. Wiley, "The End of Monopoly: Regulatory Change and the Promotion of Competition," in Shooshan, ed., *Disconnecting Bell: The Impact of the AT&T* Divestiture, 31.
47. Ibid., 33. The FCC declared the Hi-Lo tariff null and void in 1976.
48. Wiley, "The End of Monopoly," 35–36.
49. Ibid., 36.
50. Temin, *The Fall of the Bell System*, 137.
51. Wiley, "The End of Monopoly," 36–37.
52. Temin, *The Fall of the Bell System*, 138–39 and 315.
53. Ibid., 332.
54. Previously only AT&T had this. AT&T long distance users only had to dial 1, the area code, and the phone number to reach their party. Users of other long distance carriers had first to dial a local phone number for the long distance carrier, then dial the area code and phone number of the party being called.
55. Ibid., 311.
56. For example, see the following articles: Robert W. Crandall, "Local Phone Rates Catch Up With Costs," *The Wall Street Journal*, 27 February, 1987; Bill Richards, "Country Blues: Deregulation Raises Prices, Cuts Services In Many Rural Areas: Phone Bill of Mrs.

McGinnis Is Up 300% in Nebraska; A Sick Man Misses the Bus," *The Wall Street Journal*, 5 October, 1987.

57. Manley R. Irwin, "The Telecommunications Industry," in Walter Adams, ed., *The Structure of American Industry*, 8th ed. (New York: Macmillan Publishing Co., 1990), 250–51.
58. Benjamin J. Klebaner, *American Commercial Banking: A History* (Boston: Twayne Publishers, 1990), 214.
59. Peter S. Rose, *The Changing Structure of American Banking* (New York: Columbia University Press, 1987), 6–7.
60. Klebaner, *American Commercial Banking*, 217.
61. Rose, *The Changing Structure of American Banking,* 26.
62. R. Dan Brumbaugh, Jr., *Thrifts Under Siege: Restoring Order to American Banking* (Cambridge, MA: Ballinger Publishing Company, 1988), 15.
63. Rose, *The Changing Structure of American Banking*, 313.
64. Ibid., chapter 12, especially pp. 364–70.
65. Ibid., 364.
66. Brumbaugh, *Thrifts Under Siege,* 151; see also pp. 15–20, 47–48, 76, 151–52, and 156–58 for related information.
67. Rose, *The Changing Structure of American Banking*, 368.
68. Brumbaugh, *Thrifts Under Siege,* 38. Most of the following information and data are drawn from chapters 2 and 3 of this book.
69. Ibid., 39.
70. Ibid., 43–44.
71. See Ibid., 47 for a discussion of these techniques.
72. Edward J. Kane, *The S & L Insurance Mess: How Did It Happen?* (Washington, D.C.: The Urban Institute Press, 1989), 4. Such riskier assets included construction, acquisition, and development loans as compared to mortgage loans.
73. An early indication of the results of regulatory gambling came in Ohio and Maryland in 1985. (Kane, *The S & L Insurance Mess,* chapter 5 discusses this in some detail.)
74. Brumbaugh, *Thrifts Under Siege*, 51.
75. Ibid., 80.
76. Paulette Thomas and Thomas E. Ricks, "Tracing the Billions: Just What Happened To All That Money Savings & Loans Lost?: Most Went, Not to Crooks, But to Investors, Builders, Savers—and Homeowners," *The Wall Street Journal,* 5 November, 1990.
77. Charles McCoy, "Bad Bets: Many Big S&L Losses Turn Out to Be Due To a Financial Gamble: 'Risk-Controlled Arbitrage' Was Sold by Wall Street And Backed by Regulators," *The Wall Street Journal,* 9 August, 1991.
78. For example, see, "At Franklin Savings: Capricious Regulation," The Wall Street Journal, 19 September, 1990. Also see the August 19, 1991 episode of the PBS television show, *Frontline,* "The Savings and Loan Mess."
79. The information and data in this section are drawn from Lewis Mandell, *The Credit Card Industry: A History* (Boston: Twayne Publishers, 1990).
80. In 1970 the FTC banned such unsolicited credit card mailings. In 1972 the Fair Credit Billing Act provided protective legislation for cardholders and directed the Fed to regulate the credit card companies. The 1973 Federal Privacy Act protected cardholders from unauthorized use of their credit records, and the 1977 Equal Credit Opportunity Act prohibited discriminatory practices in issuing or denying credit.
81. This section draws upon the following sources: Robert Sobel, *The Big Board: A History of the New York Stock Market* (New York: The Free Press, 1965), and *Amex: A History of the*

American Stock Exchange, 1921–1971 (New York: Weybright and Talley, 1972); John Brooks, *The Go-Go Years* (New York: Weybright and Talley, 1972); and newspaper articles from *The Wall Street Journal.*

82. The Standard and Poor's common stock price index covers a broad selection of 500 stocks.
83. Brooks, *The Go-Go Years*, 100.
84. Sobel, *The Big Board*, 331.
85. Brooks, *The Go-Go Years*, 195.
86. Robert L. Bartley, "1929 and All That," *The Wall Street Journal*, 24 November, 1987. See also Susan Lee, "Efficient Market Theory Lives!" *The Wall Street Journal*, 6 May, 1988. A more detailed presentation of this explanation is found in Mark Mitchell, "Triggering the 1987 Stock Market Crash," *Journal of Financial Economics*, 24 (September 1989): 37–68. Black Monday was reviewed five years later in articles in the "Money and Investing" section of the 16 October, 1992 edition of *The Wall Street Journal.* The 1987 crash was also examined in a symposium on the "Brady Commission Report on the October 1987 Stock Market Crash," *The Journal of Economic Perspectives* 2 (Summer 1988): 3–50.
87. For example see the following: David Schwartzman, *Economic Policy: An Agenda for the Nineties* (New York: Praeger, 1989); Charles Kindleberger, "The 1930's and 1980's: Parallels and Differences," *Banca-Nazionale-del-Lavoro-Quarterly-Review* (June 1988): 134–45. Other analyses are included in the book *Black Monday and the Future of Financial Markets*, Mid-America Institute for Public Policy Research (Homewood, IL: Dow Jones-Irwin, 1989).
88. Lower grade bonds are often called "junk" bonds as compared to "investment" grade bonds, which are assigned lower risks of default.

CHAPTER 14

Developments in Domestic and International Trade, 1950 to the Present

DOMESTIC TRADE

During the meat crisis in the spring of 1973 and the explosion of coffee prices in 1975, consumers and press articles frequently blamed "middlemen" for the rising prices. In fact, highly visible intermediaries have frequently been convenient scapegoats. Yet today, just as they have for centuries, intermediaries in domestic trade raise real incomes by reducing the transactions costs that accompany market exchanges.

In the postwar period the trade and service sectors grew relative to agriculture and industry. As Figure 14.1 shows, retail trade employment as a percent of total nonagricultural employment rose from 14.92 percent to 17.94 percent between 1950 and 1990, while service employment—excluding employment in finance, insurance, real estate, and all governments—rose from 11.85 percent to 25.57 percent. If we include employment in finance, insurance, and real estate, the percent of the total labor force rose from 26.7 percent to 49.0 percent between 1950 and 1990. Finally, including all government employees raises the percentages to 36.4 percent in 1950 and 63.7 percent in 1990.

Fig. 14.1 Employment in Wholesale Trade, Retail Trade, and Private Sector Services as a Percent of Total Nonagricultural Employment

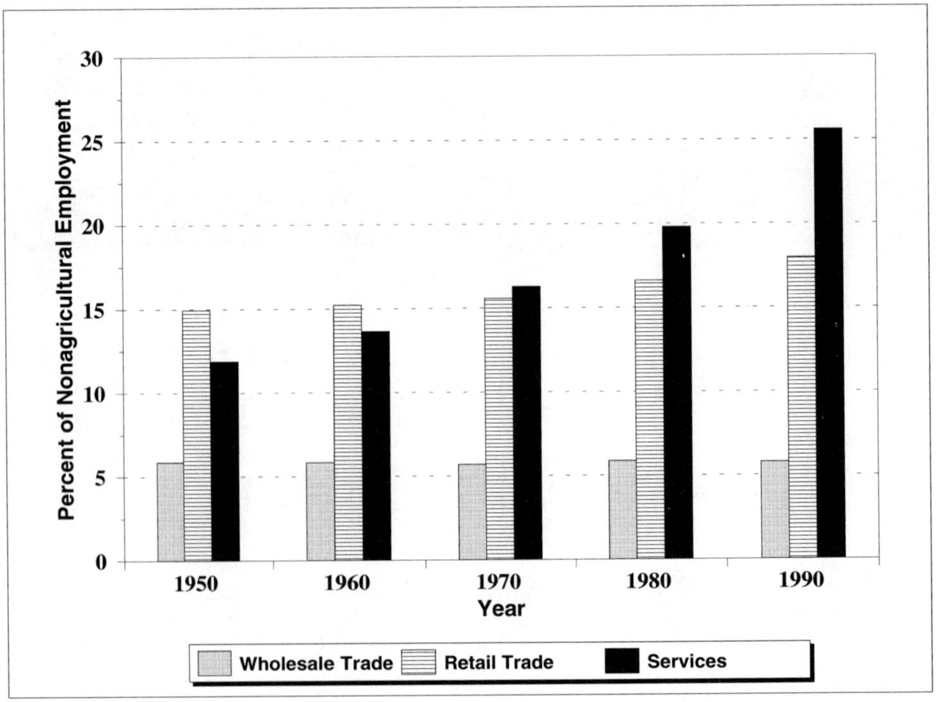

(Private sector service employment excludes all employment in finance, insurance, real estate, and governments.)
Source: *Economic Report of the President* (Washington, D.C.: U.S. Government Printing Office, 1990).

The share of GNP originating in the wholesale and retail trade sectors declined from 17.9 to 16.0 percent, while the proportion of GNP originating in the service sector rose from 8.4 to 17.9 percent between 1950 and 1988. "By the end of the 1980s McDonald's employed more people than the United States Steel Corporation."[1] During the 1970s and 1980s about 70 percent of all new jobs created were involved the distribution, marketing, and maintenance of consumer products and providing consumer services.

Shopping Centers

One of the dominant trends since the end of the Second World War has been the rise of shopping centers as retail business migrated from the central business districts (CBDs) toward the suburban areas of the cities in pursuit of the population which was moving there. In 1950 there were only about 100 shopping centers, but that number swelled to around 20,000 by 1980 and over 32,000 by 1988.[2] By the 1980s it was not uncommon for a single large regional shopping center to handle more retail sales in a year than all retail stores in that region's CBD.

Through the 1950s most of the shopping centers followed the model of Kansas City's Country Club Plaza. Stores were laid out along or around a central plaza with abundant free parking surrounding the shopping center, and the center was anchored by several large department stores.[3] These typically paid little or no rent but were expected to engage in continuous, extensive advertising, which drew customers to the malls. The smaller specialty stores benefited from the foot traffic and paid rents to the owner(s) of the shopping center.

The early malls were generally unenclosed, but by the late 1960s the malls being built were generally enclosed and climate controlled. In the 1970s and 1980s most of the older, unenclosed malls undertook extensive remodeling to better compete with the newer, enclosed ones, while super regional shopping malls of 2,000,000 or more square feet were constructed. As the American landscape was "malled," competition between shopping centers, as well as changes in design began to lead to the revitalization of existing shopping centers.[4]

In the 1980s, in an attempt to revive the CBD of some large cities, downtown enclosed malls with attached parking were constructed.[5] By the late 1980s strip malls were redirecting some retail business away from the shopping mall complexes. These were generally built as a line of stores along a major street with parking in front of the stores. The investment was less, and rents were lower, allowing the stores to price their merchandise lower than comparable stores in the shopping malls. The development of outlet malls in the 1980s provided additional competition for the regional shopping centers.

Supermarkets

The supermarkets were well placed to dominate the retail food industry in the postwar period. They had 10 percent of the food business in 1940, 30 percent in 1949, and 70 percent by 1959.[6] The size of the stores increased from an average of 10,000 square feet at the end of the 1930s to 15,000 square feet by the beginning of the 1950s, and 33,000 square feet by 1980. In the mid-1950s some supermarkets began offering trading stamps to gain a competitive advantage, and their use spread until it was nearly universal, eliminating the competitive advantages. The use of trading stamps peaked in 1965 and fell off rapidly and by 1970 had nearly disappeared.

New equipment raised the efficiency of the stores. For example, new open display shelf, self-defrosting freezer cases were more convenient for shoppers and easier to maintain and clean. Self-service meat departments with precut and wrapped meats lowered labor costs. Rollers and mechanical conveyors to move merchandise from the trucks to the store and within store areas also were more efficient and lowered operating costs.[7]

On May 2, 1972, the Universal Product Code (UPC) was finalized and published for industry-wide use.[8] The UPC could be read by digital scanners at the checkout counters when totaling shoppers' bills. The standard machine-readable code for the source, or producer, marking of merchandise allowed for better inventory control, closer control of financial transactions, more current information, and opportunities to assess more quickly and accurately changes in promotional and pricing strategies. When adopted, no longer did the unit price have to be marked on each food item, further reducing labor costs. Supermarkets began introducing electronic scanners to read the UPC at checkout in the mid-1970s.[9] By the mid-1980s electronic scanners were in nearly universal use in supermarkets and were widely used by many other retail businesses.

Another development in food retailing was the chain convenience store.[10] These were generally only 5 to 10 percent as large as supermarkets, carried fewer items and product lines usually did not carry fresh meat or produce, and sold at premium prices, sometimes as much as 15 percent higher than at supermarkets. They were located in residential areas, and many customers were willing to pay higher prices for their close convenience and quick checkout.

Department, Specialty, and Chain Stores

By 1950 most large city department stores were in department store groups. These relied on a structure built around one very large flagship department store in the center of the city, where, it was generally felt, the department store had a competitive advantage.[11] The increasing shift of retail business to suburban areas and, particularly, suburban shopping centers forced the old-line department stores to rethink their reliance on this concept.

Malcolm McNair and Eleanor May report that into the 1950s generally accepted marketing concepts argued that merchandise in department stores consisted of "shopping goods." These more expensive durable goods were purchased by consumers who compared the varieties and values among stores carrying a wide selection of stock. Suburban locations were for "convenience goods" which were less expensive with a more rapid turnover. "Only in centrally located downtown stores was it possible to draw on a sufficiently large market to justify the necessary large inventories."[12]

However, the management of the department stores found that it was possible to carry a relatively complete line of products in stores about one third to one quarter the size of the flagship downtown stores. Over time the relative size of the suburban stores also grew so that the discrepancy in size between them and the flagship store diminished.

Perhaps more difficult was the change in management that a true chain of department stores required. The original department stores were organized vertically, with the managers of the different departments responsible for both the purchasing of the department's lines as well as retail sales. However, true chains were managed differently. Purchasing and selling were separated. To take advantage of scale economies and maintain consistency between the different stores, purchasing was centralized by the management of the chain "with highly integrated merchandise distribution systems operating between offices, warehouses, and individual stores."[13] The department managers in each of the stores in the chain were responsible only for the selling of the lines in the department.

Competitive forces pushed the department stores to adopt these changes to survive.[14] Over time the percentage of sales made by the downtown flagship stores fell, and in many cases the downtown flagship stores were closed. Catalog sales divisions also declined.[15] In the late 1940s several chains were commonly referred to as "junior department stores."[16] These chains generally had more limited lines and concentrated on soft goods rather than hardware, however, they and the full-line department stores faced similar changes.

Throughout this period chain stores, and the closely related franchise stores, came to dominate retailing, especially in department, variety, grocery, clothing, shoe, and drug stores. Franchising proved to be a popular method of expansion. In a chain, each store is owned by the corporation, and the managers of each store are salaried employees of the corporate chain. In a franchise, the store is owned by individual entrepreneurs who are often from the area where the franchised store is located. By contracting with the national corporation, the franchise store is allowed to use its products, name, and corporate image, providing instant recognition to consumers. The franchisee agrees to "sell only the specified products, pay an initial fee for the franchise, and return the franchiser a percentage of the sales."[17] For the small entrepreneur franchising reduces the risks and start-up costs of establishing an identity for the firm. In the postwar period, franchises became common in many retail lines such as casual restaurants, electronics, bookstores, handicrafts, toys, and many other product lines and services.[18]

Discount Stores

Beginning in the 1950s, there was an explosive growth of discount stores. The two roots of this were the demise of the so-called fair trade laws and the retailing developments pioneered by the supermarkets. The 1937 Miller-Tydings Act had allowed states to pass fair trade and minimum markup laws. Typically a retailer would sign a contract with a manufacturer, agreeing to sell at the manufacturer's suggested retail price. The fair trade laws made such contracts legal and frequently included a "nonsigners' clause requiring even retail firms which did not sign the contract to abide by the manufacturer's suggested retail price.

"Allegedly, such tactics confused consumers as to the real value of the brand and destroyed the interest of other retailers to carry and promote it, causing the manufacturer the loss of the goodwill that he had obtained at the cost of much effort."[19] As a practical matter, the most vocal lobbyists for the bill were the small retailers and their associations, which believed that such a law would destroy the large chains' ability to sell at lower prices and therefore protect the small retailers.

The enforcement of such laws was generally left to the manufacturers. In large cities it was difficult to monitor all sales, so although 45 states had such laws by 1941 some discounting began to appear and after the war this increased as exclusive membership stores sold at discount prices. Becoming bolder, the discounters opened stores to the general public and began advertising their reduced prices.[20] In 1951 the Supreme Court ruled that the nonsigner provision was unconstitutional because the Miller-Tydings Act did not explicitly provide for it. Though Congress tried to patch up the legislation, the door had been opened, and with the onset of a flood of discounters states began rescinding the legislation. By 1970 only 17 states still had such legislation.[21]

The discount stores were unabashedly self-service in nature, with open displays, low prices, shopping carts, and a line of checkout counters at the front of the store. All of these concepts had already been developed by the supermarkets. In the 1970s, when the supermarkets pioneered the use of the Universal Product Code and automated checkout, it was the discount stores that were among the first to follow their lead and adopt the use of scanners. The discount stores generally followed a common pattern. Located in suburban areas on major thoroughfares, they opened up as independent stores, not as a part of a regional shopping center, and provided large amounts of free parking.

In the 1980s a new development occurred with the opening of factory outlet discount malls, in which the stores were operated directly by the manufacturers. These malls were generally opened in fringe areas to reduce competition with the retail stores carrying merchandise from the same manufacturers.[22] Commonly prices were presented as 40 percent below regular retail prices, though some argued that discounts were often closer to 25 percent.

Developments in Domestic Trade in the Postwar American Economy

Developments in domestic trade have continued to lower the costs of distributing goods to consumers. Retail stores have followed consumers to the suburbs to facilitate shopping access. Led by supermarkets and discounters, new techniques were developed to reduce the resources used in retail distribution and lower transactions costs. Competitive pressures induced retail firms to adopt cost-reducing techniques.

Earlier we examined productivity in American manufacturing during the postwar period and found that its productivity had grown faster than in other sectors because manufacturing's share of nonagricultural employment declined faster than its share of GNP. We can similarly examine productivity changes for domestic trade and private sector services, and this is shown in Figure 14.2. Though we have discussed a number of productivity enhancing changes in retail trade, it is clear that labor productivity in

Fig. 14.2 The Nonagricultural Employment Share Divided by the GNP Share for Wholesale and Retail Trade and for Private Sector Services

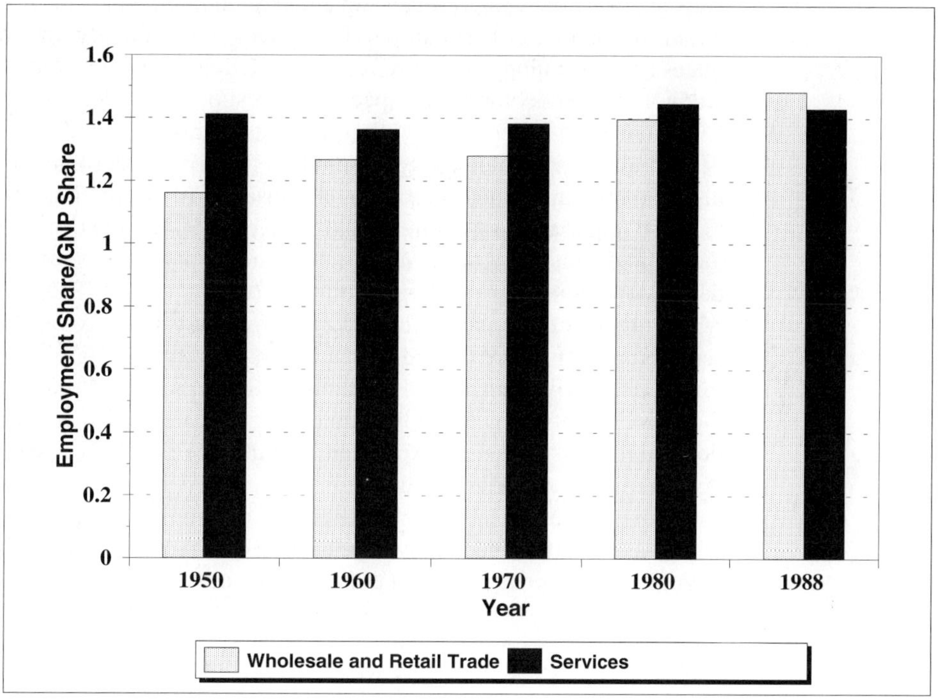

(Private sector service employment excludes all employment in finance, insurance, and real estate.)
Source: *Economic Report of the President* (Washington, D.C.: U.S. Government Printing Office, 1990).

this sector did not rise as fast as in manufacturing or even in private sector services (excluding finance, insurance, and real estate). The employment share relative to the GNP share rose from 1950 through 1988. In contrast, though private sector services expanded rapidly in the postwar period, productivity rose almost as fast because the ratio of the employment share to GNP rose only slightly between 1950 and 1988. These measures are extremely crude and do no more than suggest trends, but they do imply that the much-maligned service sector has seen more productivity gains than is commonly presumed and that retail and wholesale trade continues to lag behind the other sectors in productivity-enhancing developments.

INTERNATIONAL TRADE

There are several distinct episodes in the postwar international trade experience of the United States. From 1945 to the late 1950s, there was a dollar shortage as other countries demanded more dollars than were available to them. From the late 1950s to 1971, there was a growing glut of dollars worldwide, and other countries began exchanging some of their dollars for the gold that the United States held to back up its currency. In August, 1971, the United States devalued the dollar and by early 1973 had moved the world to floating, rather than fixed, exchange rates. Finally, in the 1980s, the United States began running huge current account deficits and quickly moved from being a net creditor to a net debtor with respect to the rest of the world.

From 1945 to 1971, the U.S. dollar was firmly anchored in a fixed exchange rate of 35 dollars for an ounce of gold and was the primary currency in which noncommunist countries undertook international transactions. A growing volume of world trade required larger and larger foreign balances of U.S. dollars. During most of this period, the United States exported more merchandise and services than it imported; thus, demanding rather than supplying dollars to other countries. There were two methods by which this was offset. First, the U.S. government undertook various aid programs that sent dollars out of the United States to those countries eligible for official aid. More importantly, private firms and financial institutions in the United States undertook foreign investments, which supplied dollars to the foreign owners of assets purchased by domestic firms. These net exports of capital were primarily responsible for supplying dollars to the rest of the world.

Government aid largely went to the developing countries, determined primarily by what was considered tactically necessary to combat communist influences. Private foreign investment primarily went to the already developed countries, particularly those in Western Europe. By the 1960s some European countries, especially France, were worried about the growing U.S. investment and began to complain about the Americanization of their countries. As the accumulation of dollars in the foreign reserves of European countries increased, some of the American dollars were exchanged for gold. The outflow of gold, along with the large foreign holdings of American dollars, began to weaken confidence in the American dollar and raise questions about whether the United States would be able to continue to support the dollar at its current fixed exchange rate.

In August, 1971, President Nixon devalued the dollar and began the process that a little more than a year and a half later would place the United States dollar on a floating exchange rate, ending the Bretton Woods fixed exchange rate system. At about the same time, the declining surpluses in the current account balances began to turn to deficits as imports climbed, particularly imports of crude petroleum. Through the 1970s these deficits remained relatively small. In the 1980s the deficits in the current account balance rose dramatically. Because there has to be offsetting monetary flows to bring about a balance in the overall international payments, capital began to be exported out of the United States. As can be seen in Figure 14.3 in 1982 the U.S. net creditor position was $141.8 billion, but this had virtually disappeared by 1984 and moved to a net debtor position of $109.9 billion in 1985, from which it has continued to grow.[23]

There was a wide range of foreign investment in the United States. Japanese automobile companies built manufacturing facilities in the United States and became joint partners in other ventures with domestic automobile firms. Existing manufacturing facilities to produce such disparate products as television sets, ball bearings, and soy

Fig. 14.3 The Net International Investment Position of the United States

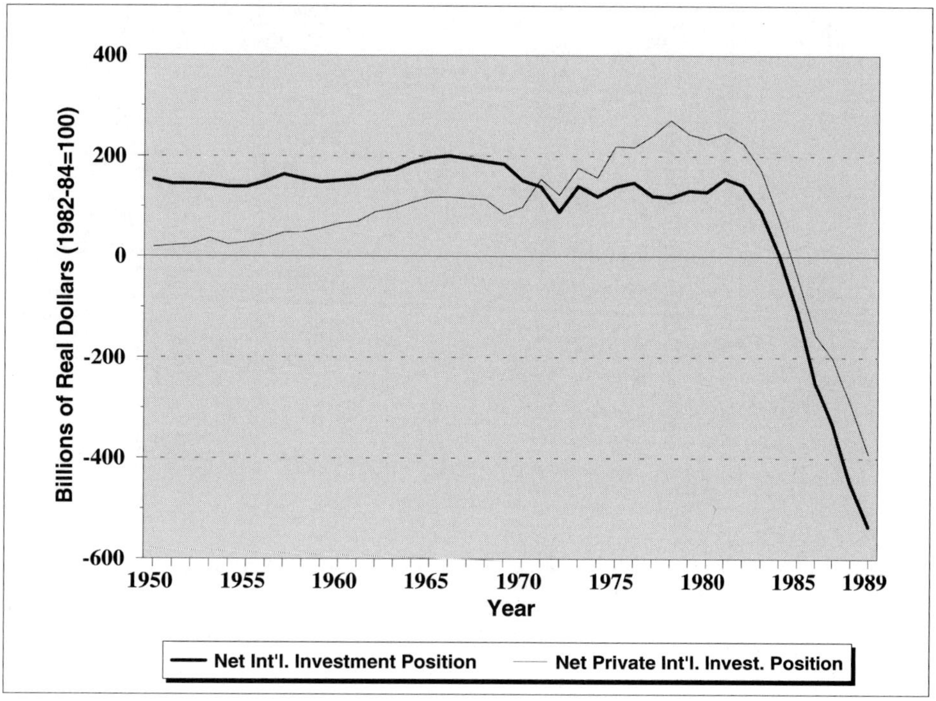

(Net private international investment position excludes U.S. official reserve and other government assets held abroad and foreign government official assets held in the United States.)
Source: *Economic Report of the President* (Washington, D.C.: U.S. Government Printing Office, various years) and *Historical Statistics of the United States* (Washington, D.C.: U.S. Government Printing Office, 1976).

sauce were purchased by foreign firms. Golf courses and farmland were also favored purchases by foreign firms and individuals. In addition, the United States exported a large volume of federal government debt and private sector stocks and bonds.

In the face of the huge current account deficits and increasing foreign ownership of assets in the United States, protectionist fervor rose, and the U.S. government began repeatedly threatening to raise its protectionist barriers if other countries, particularly Japan, did not lower their trade barriers.

Merchandise and Service Trade

Public discussion of the United States' trade surpluses or deficits almost always focuses on the current account balance. (See Figure 14.4.) Though the current account is dominated by the exports and imports of merchandise, there are a several other categories in this account. Investment income reports the income earned on foreign real and financial investments by domestic firms and the domestic income exported to the foreign owners of real and financial assets in the United States. In the 1950s investment income receipts

Fig. 14.4 The United States' Real Current Account Balance

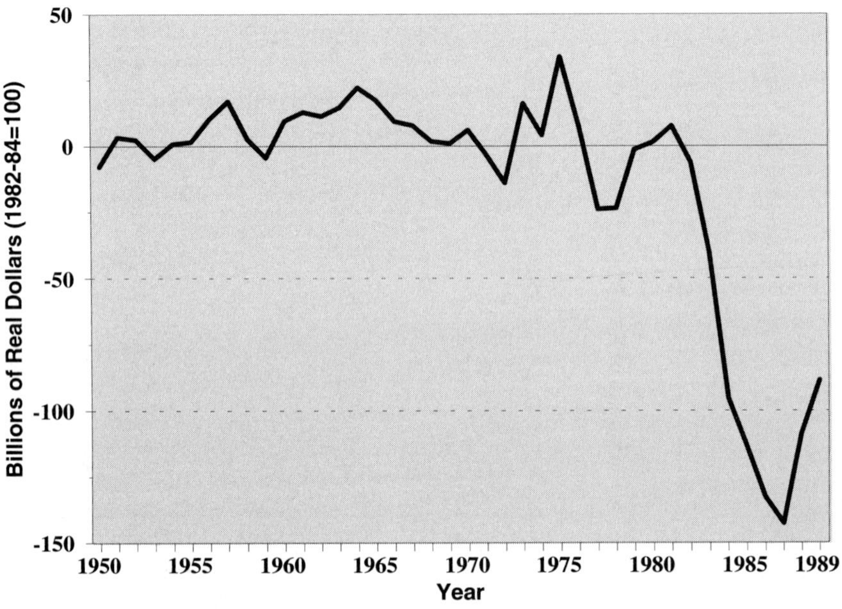

Source: *Economic Report of the President* (Washington, D.C.: U.S. Government Printing Office, 1990).

averaged only 22 percent of merchandise exports, while investment income payments averaged only 5.93 percent of merchandise imports. In the 1980s investment income receipts averaged 36.84 percent of merchandise exports, while investment income payments averaged 21.62 percent of merchandise imports. Thus, investment income has been playing a more important role in current account transactions. (See Figure 14.5.)

Though generally positive, the real balance on the current account was small until 1982. By 1987 the real deficit was $142.88 billion from which it shrank to $88.73 billion by 1989. From 1976 through 1989, merchandise imports consistently exceeded merchandise exports, but the difference grew sharply after 1982. Through 1982 the surplus of investment income receipts over investment income payments helped keep the current account balance generally positive, but the growing merchandise deficit and diminishing investment income differential caused the current account deficit to balloon after 1982.

Unlike many other developed and developing countries during the 1950s and 1960s, international trade in goods, services, and assets was a relatively small proportion of economic activity in the United States. (See Figure 14.6.) In the 1970s and 1980s these activities became much more important in overall economic activity. By 1980 merchandise imports exceeded 9 percent of GNP, while merchandise exports

Fig. 14.5 Selected United States Real Current Account International Transactions

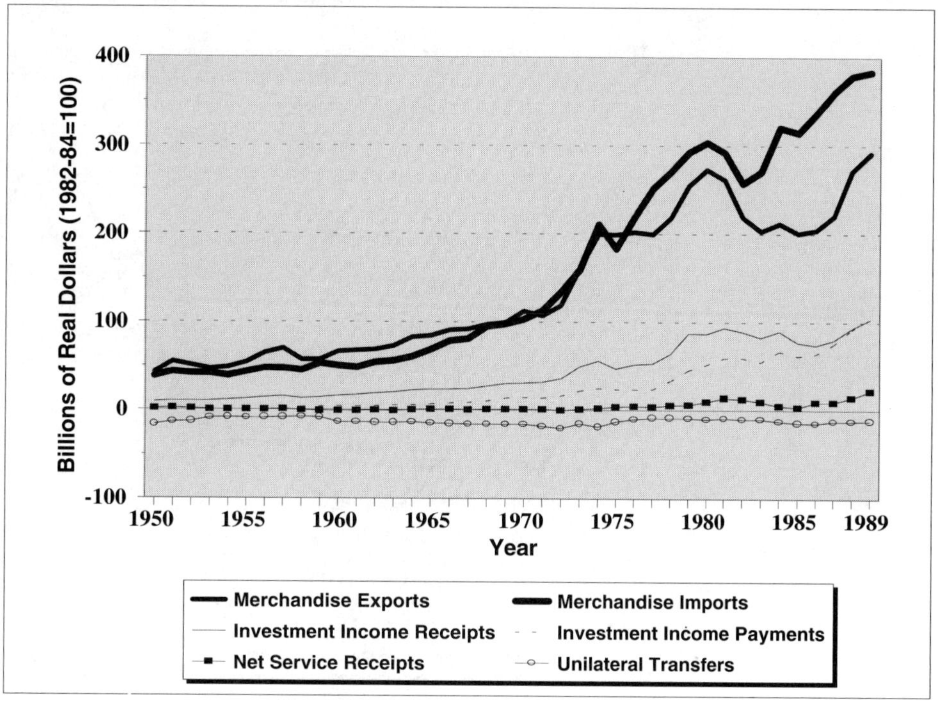

Source: *Economic Report of the President* (Washington, D.C.: U.S. Government Printing Office, 1990).

exceeded 8 percent of GNP. The deficit in merchandise trade grew in the 1980s as exports fell.

Our international trade in the postwar period has been dominated by Canada. This should hardly be surprising, given that Canada shares a lengthy border, language, and level of development with the United States. Exports from the United States to other Western Hemisphere nations have declined over the period. The share of American exports to Europe remained above 33 percent from 1955 through 1970, but then dropped to around 28 percent in the 1980s. Our exports to Japan and other Asian countries rose from 4.1 to 11.8 percent for Japan and from 10.9 to 19.4 percent for other Asian nations. There was a sharp jump in exports to other Asian nations in the early 1970s coincident with the sharp rise in world petroleum prices and the increase in U.S. imports of crude petroleum.

The share of our imports coming from Western Hemisphere countries other than Canada dropped from 35.1 percent in 1950 to 11.6 percent in 1988, whereas the share originating in Europe rose from 1950 to 1970 and has since declined. The most dramatic increase has been in imports from Japan and other Asian nations. For other Asian nations, this relative rise in exports to the United States is dominated by the rising value

Fig. 14.6 Exports and Imports as a Percent of GNP

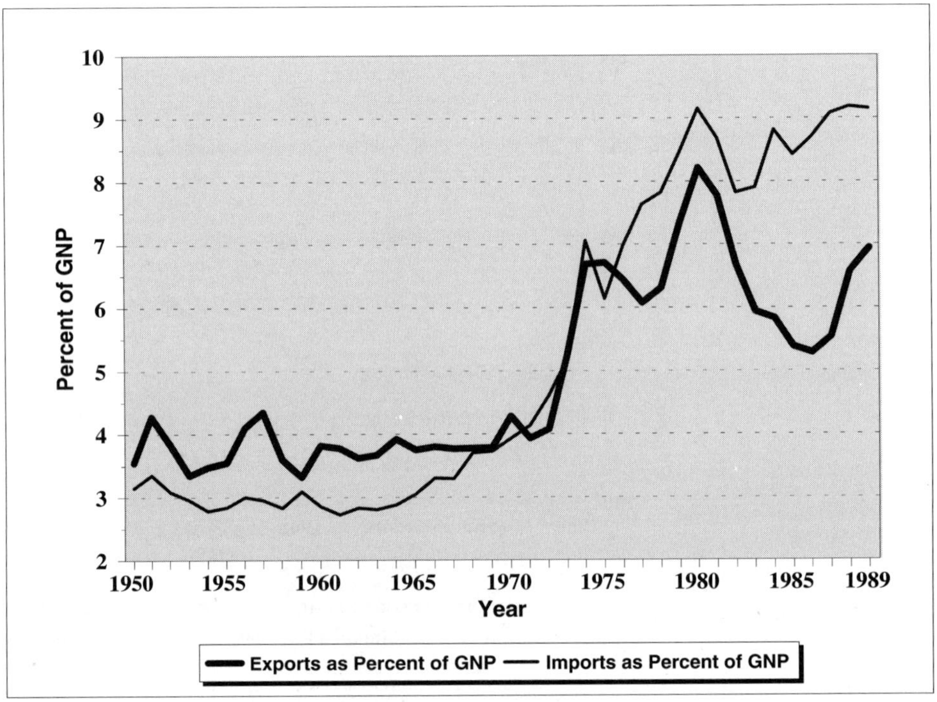

Source: *Economic Report of the President* (Washington, D.C.: U.S. Government Printing Office, 1990).

and quantity of crude petroleum after 1970; the Japanese increase covers a broad array of merchandise and capital goods.

Exchange Rates

The international monetary arrangements fashioned at Bretton Woods, New Hampshire, in 1944 were the clear statement of the belief that national governments could control and direct overall economic activity, including prices, employment, and economic growth. The arrangements mandated fixed exchange rates to facilitate international trade and investment but tied these to the U.S. dollar, the strongest currency in the world at the time. The U.S. dollar was fixed in terms of gold; all other currencies were fixed in their exchange rates with the dollar. The United States was to stand ready to redeem its dollars for gold as demanded by other central banks. Because other countries did not tie their currencies to gold, they were free to develop their domestic economies as they saw fit, subject to maintaining balance-of-payments discipline through the fixed currency relationships. Robert Roosa has argued that, contrary to common caricatures, the architects of the Bretton Woods system recognized that there would be variations in the real growth of the countries.[24] However, they expected that only moderate changes in the fixed exchange rates would be necessary. Changes in foreign exchange reserves would signal the need to modify "domestic policies affecting the prices, interest rates, production, employment, and short-term capital flows of each country."[25] Therefore, alterations in exchange rates would be neither frequent nor large.

In practice, such was not the case. Countries with strong currencies that were gaining international reserves were reluctant to appreciate their currencies and threaten export-led booms, and the Bretton Woods system had little leverage to induce them to do this. Between 1946 and 1971, there were only four parity increases. However, countries with weak currencies that were losing reserves depreciated their currencies over 100 times during this period.[26] Countries also were reluctant to undertake domestic policy changes that presumably would have lessened the problems if these were expected to have adverse domestic economic or political consequences. Most importantly, the linchpin of the Bretton Woods system, the fixed dollar price of gold and redeemability of dollars for gold, also weakened and ultimately failed.

Through 1957 the Bretton Woods system seemed to work relatively well. Though the United States supplied dollars to the rest of the world, other countries were content to retain these dollars, and the stock of gold in the United States was as large in 1957 as it was in 1950. Following 1957, American private overseas investment boomed rising from 15 percent of merchandise exports to 25 percent—an amount significantly larger than the current account surplus.[27] With the development of a dollar glut overseas countries began to exchange dollars for gold. Between 1957 and 1970 the United States' gold stock fell from $22.9 billion to $11.1 billion, and in 1970 alone the gold stock fell almost 7 percent. In 1971 the gold stock fell below $10 billion, and there were serious questions as to the ability of the United States to honor its commitment to redeem its dollars held by foreigners for gold at $35 an ounce.

In August of 1971, President Richard Nixon, in a surprise move, temporarily halted the redemption of dollars held by foreign central banks for gold, and allowed the dollar to depreciate. To further aid the current account balance, a temporary 10 percent surcharge on imports was levied. In December of 1971, the dollar was repegged at $38 an ounce. However, the deficit on the current account balance did not improve, and in February of 1973, the dollar was further devalued to $42.22 an ounce. Finally in March of 1973, the United States moved to a floating exchange rate by ceasing to exchange gold for dollars held by foreign central banks. This effectively ended the Bretton Woods system.

Robert Roosa has argued that the Bretton Woods system of fixed exchange rates would have been unsustainable even if the United States had moved more quickly and aggressively to adjust its gold price. First, there was too wide a variation in countries' economic growth, given the Bretton Woods system's methods of adjusting to these variations. Second, with the development of the process whereby dollars could be created offshore through the Eurodollar market, it became impossible for the United States to provide the rest of the world with a controlled supply of reserve currency. Third, "capital flows among nations, and among national currencies in the newly emerging extraterritorial markets, became at times so large as to overwhelm the influence of goods and services transactions upon the market exchange rates of the major countries."[28]

The floating exchange rates that were created were not left completely to free market forces. At times the central banks of various nations, including the United States, have intervened by buying or selling currencies to ease the depreciation or appreciation of particular currencies. However, these attempts have been sporadic and not particularly successful for more than short periods of time due to the power of the international flows of commodities and capital.

The broadest indicator of the exchange rate is the index of the multilateral trade-weighted value of the U.S. dollar, shown in Figure 14.7.[29] Because the United States officially adopted floating exchange rates in 1973, the index has been calculated in real as well as nominal terms. Between 1969 and 1973 the dollar depreciated by a sharp 21.1 percent. In real terms it continued to depreciate or weaken during the 1970s, falling by 15.3 percent from 1973 to 1980. Between 1980 and 1985 the dollar underwent a remarkable appreciation or strengthening of 44.2 percent and then fell almost as rapidly from 1985 to 1990.

Fig. 14.7 The Multilateral Trade-Weighted Value of the United States Dollar

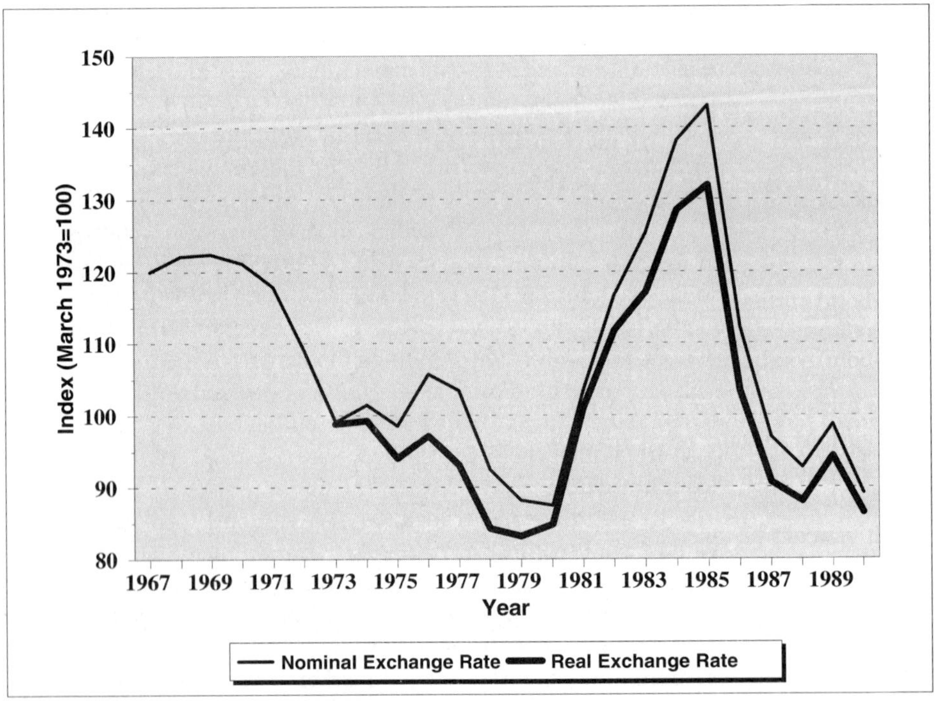

Source: *Economic Report of the President* (Washington, D.C.: U.S. Government Printing Office, 1990).

The great variability in exchange rates in the 1980s is usually conceded to have been a disruptive influence, and proposals have been made to modify the procedures determining exchange rates to provide greater rate stability. Generally these involve requiring more active intervention by central banks to keep rates within some specific range, often one determined by purchasing power parity between currencies.[30] However, many argue that floating exchange rates have not been excessively volatile but have simply reflected the underlying volatility of the real forces determining the rates. For the United States in the 1980s, it appears that capital movements were the force that primarily determined exchange rate movements, even though capital movements were smaller than commodity and service exports or imports.[31]

Beginning in 1981 the federal government's budget deficits grew dramatically and real *ex post* interest rates rose sharply as government borrowing expanded. The American economy embarked on a long expansion after the end of the 1981–82 recession. These forces also initiated a great boom in the securities market from 1982 through 1987. The strength of the American economy, as well as falling rates of price inflation and rising real interest rates, made investment in real and financial assets in the United States very desirable. To obtain the U.S. dollars necessary for the purchase of American assets, foreign firms and individuals bid up the price of the dollar in terms of their currencies. The rising foreign exchange value of the dollar made U.S. exports more expensive in foreign countries and imports into the U.S. less expensive in U.S. dollars, resulting in a sharply increased deficit in the current account balance and a growing amount of U.S. dollars that foreigners could use to purchase U.S. real and financial assets. Because of lags due to contractual arrangements, the largest current account deficit occurred two years after the peak in the appreciation of the dollar. Since 1987 the current account deficit has declined, while the dollar has continued to depreciate.

Trade Policies

The postwar period has seen a general trend in U.S. trade policies toward freer trade or, as it is often called, liberalization of trade. Tariff rates have been successfully reduced during a series of 30 bilateral agreements and 8 multilateral negotiations engineered by GATT, the General Agreement on Tariffs and Trade.[32] Prior to 1947, tariff reductions were bilateral agreements on an item-by-item approach. GATT was created in 1947 as a mechanism to bring about multilateral bargaining and faster tariff reductions.

The first GATT conference was held in Geneva, Switzerland, in 1947 and resulted in an average cut in import duties of 21.1 percent. The next four GATT conferences—Annecy, France, in 1949; Torquay, England, in 1951; Geneva in 1956; and Geneva in 1962—are generally judged not to have been as successful.[33] The sixth (or Kennedy) round, held in Geneva from 1964 to 1967, resulted in average cuts of 36 percent and is considered to have been much more successful, though it had little success at reducing the barrier to trade in agricultural products.[34]

The Tokyo Round from 1974 to 1979 was relatively successful and reduced import duties on average by 29.6 percent, though the U.S. cuts were much smaller. The act provided for easier and more generous treatment of claims for relief by firms suffering from import competition, and for import restrictions if it was felt that imports threatened to impair the national security, came from countries that unreasonably or unjustifiably discriminated against U.S. exports, were subsidized by foreign governments, or were dumped. The most recent round, which began in Uruguay in 1986, had an ambitious agenda but has had little success.[35]

Much of the protectionist pressure of the last several decades has came from three basic import competing industries, textiles, steel, and autos, while our agricultural policies have complicated negotiations to further reduce trade barriers.

Agriculture. Agricultural policies have became one of the stumbling blocks in moves toward freer trade. Beginning in the mid-1930s, the United States developed agricultural policies to support many produce prices. Such policies raised domestic prices above world prices and required barriers to the importation of agricultural produce that would compete with domestic price-supported produce. In addition, the U.S. government developed policies to subsidize, when necessary, U.S. farm exports to sell some of the surplus domestic production. In the postwar period the countries in the European Common Market (EEC), Japan, and some other countries have developed similar agricultural policies.

The U.S. has subsidized exports of grain to foreign countries through programs such as Public Law 480, Commodity Credit Corporation subsidized sales, or government subsidized credit, though the percentage of agricultural exports subsidized fell through the early 1980s.[36] The Export Enhancement Program created in the 1980s was designed to combat the subsidized commodities exported from EEC countries. Under this program, exporters could receive CCC grain stocks to compensate them for export sales at prices lower than domestic support prices.[37] These export subsidies, as well as barriers to the imports of other agricultural products such as sugar and cheese, have been a stumbling block in reducing trade barriers.

DRAM Computer Chips. The first miniaturized computer memory chips were created in the United States in 1971, and into the late 1970s U.S. producers dominated the market. In the early 1980s Japanese producers of DRAMs (Dynamic Random Access Memory computer chips) expanded production. By 1985, there was a worldwide glut of DRAM chips, and prices fell dramatically. U.S. producers brought charges of dumping by Japanese producers of DRAM chips, alleging that they were selling at prices less than production costs. Facing the threat of punitive duties, the Japanese government and U.S. trade representatives negotiated a deal in July of 1986. Production controls were imposed, price floors established, and 20 percent of the Japanese market for computer chips was reserved for U.S. and other producers. By 1988 there was a worldwide shortage of DRAM chips, and prices rose dramatically. Japanese DRAM producers and the few U.S. producers left received windfall profits, and computer manufacturers and computer purchasers ended up paying much higher prices. The governments liked this arrangement so much that in 1991, in altered form, the agreement was continued another five years.

Textiles and Apparel. The textile and apparel industry has a long history of non-tariff trade barriers.[38] In the postwar period Japanese exports of cotton textiles and apparel to the U.S. grew.[39] Japan joined GATT in 1955, and to compensate for reduced U.S. tariffs, in 1957 a new Voluntary Export Restraint (VER) agreement was negotiated. With Japanese exports to the U.S. reduced, producers in other countries stepped up their exports, and by 1960 a new arrangement covering other countries was required. Between 1961 and 1973 there were arrangements on cotton textile trade which departed from GATT rules by allowing the United States to unilaterally and selectively impose import restrctions.[40]

Once again substitutes eroded the agreement. This time the limitations on imports of cotton textiles and apparel led producers in foreign countries to expand the production of textiles and apparel using synthetic fibers.[41] In response, as a part of GATT negotiations, a Multifiber Agreement which restricted the growth of textile and apparel exports to the United States, was reached with some 50 governments in December of 1973. These agreements depressed textile and apparel imports into the U.S. by 28 percent in 1981. An estimated 150,000 jobs in textile production and 390,000 jobs in apparel production were saved in that same year, but the cost to domestic consumers of textiles and apparel was around $37,000 per job.[42] The agreement was extended into the 1980s, when new quotas were bilaterally negotiated. In 1986 congressional pressure led to sharp reductions in the quotas on the growth of imported textiles and apparel.

Steel. Through the 1950s the American steel industry faced little competition from imported steel.[43] By the beginning of the 1960s, the rebuilt and technologically advanced steel industries in Europe and Japan were able to begin exporting steel. The U.S. steel industries, facing little foreign competition in the 1950s and escalating union wage demands, had been raising wages and passing these on as higher prices.[44] As profit rates in steel began declining, there were increasing calls for protection from imported steel, and in 1968 the government negotiated Voluntary Restraint Agreements (VRAs) to reduce steel imports.[45] In 1974 and 1975 the steel industry intensified its lobbying for protection and used a new tactic; charges of dumping by foreign steel firms.[46]

A flurry of dumping suits from the steel industry threatened to overwhelm the U.S. government and create a trade conflict with the EEC. The government had to calculate complex constructed values of the steel in each case to determine whether the prices were below costs.[47] The Carter administration responded by proposing a Trigger Price Mechanism (TPM), whereby if prices for a country's imported steel dropped below the benchmark price of Japanese steel, protective duties would automatically be triggered.[48] In 1977 the Carter administration agreed to implement this as long as the steel firms did not file dumping lawsuits. But, in 1980 it fell apart when the U.S. Steel Corporation filed a dumping suit. This "brought concessions in the area of foreign trade—a more restrictive TPM—but also promises of relief, as well as some action, in such unrelated areas as taxation and environmental standards."[49] The Trigger Price Mechanism was not fully satisfactory, and in 1982 it collapsed. Since then, Voluntary

Restraint Agreements have again been the primary method of limiting steel imports to protect the American steel industry. By 1985 the number of VRAs had increased to 15, covering 80 percent of the U.S. market. As a consequence, U.S. prices consistently remained above foreign export prices by about 15 to 20 percent in the 1970s and about 40 percent by the mid-1980s.[50]

Autos. From the late 1950s through 1970, small car imports continued to rise. By 1970 sales of imports reached 15 percent of all new car sales in the U.S. GM, Ford, and Chrysler and the United Auto Workers union began to increase the frequency of their complaints. On May 1, 1981, the Reagan administration announced a Voluntary Export Restraint agreement with the Japanese government to reduce the exports of Japanese automobiles to the United States for three years. The Japanese agreed because it was clear that if no "voluntary" agreement was reached, quotas and/or tariffs would be imposed. In 1985 the Japanese government refused to renew the VER, but the Japanese automobile manufacturers continued to voluntarily hold down their exports to the United States. A Voluntary Export Restraint was employed due to previous experience with this in textiles and steel and because "voluntary" agreements did not violate GATT rules.

Like the steel firms a decade earlier, the automobile companies argued that the import relief would give them breathing room to produce competitive new models. They also used the reduction in imports to sharply raise the prices of domestic cars. Japanese producers initially increased the exports of vans and light trucks, but this loophole was soon closed. Facing absolute limits on the number of automobiles that could be exported to the U.S., Japanese companies began to export only the larger, better-equipped, and more expensive automobiles and to design larger cars to compete directly in the important mid-size market that American companies dominated. By the end of the 1980s, Japanese companies were producing a full range of car lines. Seeing future trade barriers to cars imported from Japanese factories, the Japanese companies began the process of developing manufacturing and assembling plants in the United States. By the end of the 1980s, half of Japanese nameplate cars (and all of some models) were manufactured in the United States.

The price increases associated with the introduction of the VER were dramatic. Robert C. Feenstra estimates that between 1980 and 1981 the average price of Japanese imports rose nearly 20 percent, of which two thirds was due to the importation of higher quality cars while one third was a pure price increase due to excess demand. Domestic large car prices rose 16.8 percent, whereas domestic small car prices rose 11.4 percent.[51] Barry Eichengreen suggests that this understates the price effects as other studies found that prices were generally 25 percent higher. In 1979–80, prior to the VER, American consumers paid about $500 more than Japanese consumers for the same vehicle, but in 1985 the difference was $3000. Adjusting for transportation and preparation, this suggests a rise of $2,500 in price due to the VER.[52] Clearly American consumers paid dearly to raise the profits of the American automobile companies and preserve UAW employment.

Developments in International Trade in the Postwar American Economy

As previously discussed, the postwar changes in the United States' international trade have been pronounced. The United States gradually moved from being a net exporter to a net importer of merchandise and from being a net purchaser to a net seller of capital assets. The net flow of dollars out of the United States eroded confidence in the dollar, forcing the Bretton Woods system of fixed exchange rates based on the dollar to give way to floating exchange rates. The energy crises of the 1970s contributed to rising imports and exports as foreign trade became much more important to the American economy. The increasing competition from foreign firms in the 1970s and 1980s was difficult for domestic producers, though many became more efficient and the quality of American manufactures increased. The rising competition and, in the 1980s, growing deficit in the current account led to increasing calls for greater protection of domestic producers. Though tariffs generally were not raised, quotas were sometimes used, and threats of increased U.S. trade barriers led foreign governments to impose "voluntary" quotas (or export restraints) on their exporting firms. By the beginning of the 1990s protectionist pressures were increasing.[53]

SELECTED REFERENCES

Appleyard, Dennis R., and Alfred J. Field Jr. *International Economics*. Homewood, IL: R. D. Irwin, Inc., 1992.

Baldwin, Robert E., and Anne O. Krueger, eds. *The Structure and Evolution of Recent U.S. Trade Policy*. Chicago: The University of Chicago Press for the National Bureau of Economic Research, 1984.

Bryant, Keith L., and Henry C. Dethloff. *A History of American Business*, 2d ed. Englewood Cliffs, NJ: Prentice-Hall, 1990.

Bucklin, Louis P. *Competition and Evolution in the Distributive Trades*. Englewood Cliffs, NJ: Prentice-Hall, 1972.

Dawson, John A., and J. Dennis Lord, eds. *Shopping Centre Development: Policies and Prospects*. New York: Nichols Publishing Co., 1985.

Feldstein, Martin, ed. *The United States in the World Economy*. Chicago: University of Chicago Press for the National Bureau of Economic Research, 1988.

Finger, J. Michael, and Thomas D. Willett, eds. *The Internationalization of the American Economy. The Annals of the American Academy of Political and Social Science*, 46 (March, 1982).

Gardner, Richard. *Sterling-Dollar Diplomacy*. New York: Oxford University Press, 1956.

Hughes, Jonathan. *American Economic History*, 3d ed. Glenview, IL: Scott, Foresman, and Co., 1990.

Krugman, Paul R., and Maurice Obstfeld. *International Economics: Theory and Policy*, 2d ed. New York: Harper Collins, 1991.

Lusch, Robert F., and Paul H. Zinzer, eds. *Contemporary Issues in Marketing Channels*. Norman, OK: The University of Oklahoma, 1979.

McNair, Malcolm P., and Eleanor G. May. *The Evolution of Retail Institutions in the United States*. Cambridge, MA: The Marketing Science Institute, 1976.

Nevett, Terence, and Ronald A. Fullerton, eds. *Historical Perspectives in Marketing*. Lexington, MA: Lexington Books, 1988.

Peak, Hugh S., and Ellen F. Peak. *Supermarket Merchandising and Management*. Englewood Cliffs, NJ: Prentice-Hall, 1977).

Sternlieb, George, and James W. Hughes. *Shopping Centers: U.S.A.* Piscataway, NJ: Center for Urban Policy Research, Rutgers, the State University of New Jersey, 1981.

The International Monetary System: Forty Years After Bretton Woods. Proceedings of a conference held at Bretton Woods, New Hampshire. Boston: Federal Reserve Bank of Boston, May 1984.

NOTES

1. Keith L. Bryant, Jr. and Henry C. Dethloff, *A History of American Business*, 2d ed. (Englewood Cliffs, NJ: Prentice-Hall, 1990), 321.
2. J. Dennis Lord, "The Malling of the American Landscape," in John A. Dawson and J. Dennis Lord, eds., *Shopping Centre Development: Policies and Prospects* (New York: Nichols Publishing Company, 1985), 209; and *Statistical Abstract of the United States* (Washington, D.C.: U.S. Government Printing Office, 1990).
3. Bryant and Dethloff, *A History of American Business*, 328.
4. J. Dennis Lord, "Revitalization of Shopping Centers," in Dawson and Lord, eds., *Shopping Centre Development: Policies and Prospects* (New York: Nichols Publishing Company, 1985), 209.
5. For a discussion of this see, "Section III: Appraising the Central City Option," in George Sternlieb and James W. Hughes, eds., *Shopping Centers: U.S.A.* (Piscataway, NJ: Center for Urban Policy Research, Rutgers, the State University of New Jersey, 1981).
6. Hugh S. Peak and Ellen F. Peak, *Supermarket Merchandising and Management* (Englewood Cliffs, NJ: Prentice-Hall, 1977), 23–24.
7. Ibid., 22.
8. Ibid., 43.
9. Richard K. Robinson and Frederick W. Langrehr, "Supermarket Scanner Checkouts: A View from the Consumer Side of the Counter," in Robert F. Lusch and Paul H. Zinszer, eds., *Contemporary Issues in Marketing Channels* (Norman OK: The University of Oklahoma, 1979), 141.
10. Philip Kotler, "The Convenience Store: Past Developments and Future Prospects," in Terence Nevett and Ronald A. Fullerton, eds., *Historical Perspectives in Marketing* (Lexington, MA: Lexington Books, 1988).
11. Most of the discussion in this section is drawn from this source and from Louis P. Bucklin, *Competition and Evolution in the Distributive Trades* (Englewood Cliffs, NJ: Prentice-Hall, 1972).
12. Malcolm P. McNair and Eleanor G. May, *The Evolution of Retail Institutions in the United States* (Cambridge, MA: The Marketing Science Institute, 1976), 41.
13. Ibid., 42.
14. Ibid., 20. Some of these chains in 1948 were financial chains. The figures also include Sears and Wards, which makes the percentages much higher.
15. Ralph Shaffer, "A Catalog That Can Be Remade to Order," *The Wall Street Journal*, 16

September, 1991.

16. These included the W. T. Grant, Belk Brothers, and J. C. Penney store chains.
17. Keith L. Bryant, Jr., and Henry C. Dethloff, *A History of American Business*, 2d ed. (Englewood Cliffs, NJ: Prentice-Hall, 1990), 335.
18. Ibid.
19. Bucklin, *Competition and Evolution in the Distributive Trades*, 151.
20. Ibid., 88.
21. Ibid., 155.
22. Kay Murphy Nolan, "Outlet Malls: Driving a Hard Bargain: Consumers Will Travel Miles for Brand Names, Outlet Prices," *Waukesha County Freeman*, 2 November, 1991.
23. The net international investment position includes U.S. official reserve assets and other U.S. government assets held abroad and foreign official government assets held in the United States. The net private international investment position excludes all U.S. and foreign government assets to include only U.S. and foreign private assets.
24. Robert V. Roosa, "Exchange Rate Arrangements in the Eighties," *The International Monetary System: Forty Years After Bretton Woods*, proceedings of a conference held at Bretton Woods, New Hampshire (Boston: Federal Reserve Bank of Boston, May 1984), 105.
25. Ibid., 105.
26. Ibid., 106.
27. Edward M. Bernstein, "Reflections on Bretton Woods," *The International Monetary System: Forty Years After Bretton Woods*, 19.
28. Roosa, "Exchange Rate Arrangements in the Eighties," 106.
29. The multilateral trade-weighted indexes are measures of the nominal and real value of the U.S. dollar in terms of a basket of 15 industrial country currencies. The currencies are weighted by their share of trade with the United States. An increase is a dollar appreciation; a decrease a dollar depreciation.
30. For example, see Roosa, "Exchange Rate Arrangements in the Eighties." The theory of purchasing power parity states that the exchange rate between two countries' currencies will equal the ratio of the two countries' price levels. For a discussion of this, see an intermediate level International Economics textbook, for example, Paul R. Krugman and Maurice Obstfeld, *International Economics: Theory and Policy*, 2d ed. (New York: Harper Collins, 1991), 380–83.
31. Henry C. Wallich, "Capital Movements—The Tail That Wags the Dog," *The International Monetary System: Forty Years After Bretton Woods*, 179.
32. Robert E. Baldwin, "The Changing Nature of U.S. Trade Policy Since the Second World War," in Robert E. Baldwin and Anne O. Krueger, eds., *The Structure and Evolution of Recent U.S. Trade Policy* (Chicago: The University of Chicago Press for the National Bureau of Economic Research, 1984), 5.
33. The average duty cuts were 1.9, 3.0, 3.5, and 2.4 percent, respectively. Dennis R. Appleyard and Alfred J. Field, Jr., *International Economics* (Homewood, IL: R. D. Irwin, Inc., 1992), 418–23.
34. Ibid., 419.
35. Ibid., 422.
36. Bruce L. Gardner, "International Competition in Agriculture and U.S. Farm Policy," in Martin Feldstein, ed., *The United States in the World Economy* (Chicago: University of Chicago Press for the NBER, 1988), table 7.8, p. 452.
37. Ibid., 448–49.
38. This section draws upon three studies: Barry Eichengreen, "International Competition in the

Products of U.S. Basic Industries," in Feldstein, ed., *The United States in the World Economy*, 320–322; Joseph Pelzman, "The Textile Industry," in J. Michael Finger and Thomas D. Willett, eds., *The Internationalization of the American Economy*, *The Annals of the American Academy of Political and Social Science*, 460 (March, 1982): 92–100, and "The Multifiber Arrangement and Its Effect on the Profit Performance of the U.S. Textile Industry," in Baldwin and Krueger, eds., *The Structure and Evolution of Recent U.S. Trade Policy*, 111–141.

39. Joseph Pelzman, "The Textile Industry," 93.
40. Barry Eichengreen, "International Competition in the Products of U.S. Basic Industries," 320.
41. Joseph Pelzman, "The Textile Industry," 95.
42. Barry Eichengreen, "International Competition in the Products of U.S. Basic Industries," 322.
43. This section is based on the following studies. Hans G. Mueller, "The Steel Industry," in Finger and Willett, eds., *The Internationalization of the American Economy*, 73–82; Barry Eichengreen and Hans van der Ven, "U.S. Antidumping Policies: The Case of Steel," in Baldwin and Krueger, eds., *The Structure and Evolution of Recent U.S. Trade Policy*, 67–103; Barry Eichengreen, "International Competition in the Products of U.S. Basic Industries," 322–25.
44. Steel prices rose twice as fast as wholesale prices from 1945 to 1960. Hans G. Mueller, "The Steel Industry," 74.
45. Ibid., 75.
46. Ibid., 76. Originally *dumping* had been defined as price discrimination between the markets in the exporting foreign country and the United States.
47. Eichengreen and van der Ven, "U.S. Antidumping Policies: The Case of Steel," 70.
48. Japan was judged to have the most efficient steel industry in the world, and therefore its constructed value was to be calculated and used as the benchmark. This eliminated the necessity to construct values for steel from all of the other exporting countries. If the prices of imported steel products dropped below the constructed value trigger price of Japanese steel products adjusted for extras and transport charges, an investigation would commence that could result in countervailing duties.
49. Hans G. Mueller, "The Steel Industry," 76.
50. Barry Eichengreen, "International Competition in the Products of U.S. Basic Industries," 324–25.
51. Feenstra, "Voluntary Export Restrain in U.S. Autos, 1980–81: Quality, Employment, and Welfare Effects," in Baldwin and Krueger, eds., *The Structure and Evolution of Recent U.S. Trade Policy*, table 2.2, pp. 45 and 56–57. See also Norman S. Fieleke, "The Automobile Industry," in Finger and Willett, eds., *The Internationalization of the American Economy*.
52. Eichengreen, "International Competition in the Products of U.S. Basic Industries," 327.
53. In 1992 the United States threatened to impose prohibitive duties on European white wine unless France reduced its barriers to the importation of U.S. soybean oil and other agricultural exports. A North American Free Trade Agreement between Canada, the United States, and Mexico was negotiated, but growing opposition to the agreement raised serious questions as to whether Congress would approve the agreement. For example, see Bob Davis, "Fighting 'Nafta': Free-Trade Pact Spurs A Diverse Coalition of Grass-Roots Foes: They Link Forces to Protect Jobs, Clean Air, Dolphins, Mexican Quality of Life," *The Wall Street Journal*, 23 December, 1992.

CHAPTER 15

Government and the Postwar American Economy

Government in the postwar American economy has continued to grow as both expenditures and taxes have grown faster than economic activity in general, a trend that, of course, stretches well back into the nineteenth century. Robert Higgs argues that in the twentieth century, and especially since the 1930s, government has grown not just in its scale of operations, which he calls *big* government, but, most importantly, has grown in its intrusiveness and control of private market activities, becoming the Leviathan or *BIG* government.[1] The result has been a deluge of laws to control and reshape economic activity in ways deemed appropriate by governmental bodies.

By the 1950s there were three relatively distinct government functions. For all governments, one function was the traditional *night watchman's* role of providing the foundation for a private market system through the definition and enforcement of private property rights, adjudication of disputes over private property rights, and provision of those goods and services that private markets would fail to provide or not provide in optimal amounts. A second function was to reshape private behavior in ways deemed socially responsible and to redistribute income in ways considered politically acceptable. Finally, in the Full Employment Act of 1946, the federal government adopted the objective of stabilizing aggregate economic activity and prices and promoting the maximum rate of economic growth. The pursuit of these objectives has led to a burgeoning government in the postwar period.

THE GROWTH OF GOVERNMENT

The growth of government can be examined by looking at government employment, taxes and other receipts, or expenditures. Figure 15.1 presents government employment as a percent of nonagricultural employment for each year from 1950 through 1990. Employment by all governments grew steadily to 1975 and then declined, although the 1990 employment share is still higher than for any year before 1966. The federal government's employment share has, for the most part, declined since the early 1950s. As can be seen, the bulk of all government employment resides at the state and local level.

Another measure that can be used is to examine the growth of government receipts, largely composed of tax collections. Figure 15.2 presents government receipts as a percent of GNP. For all governments, taxes collected have grown faster than GNP throughout the period. Different patterns are seen in the growth of federal taxes compared to state and local taxes. Generally federal receipts as a percent of GNP tended to slowly decline until the mid-1970s, however, the pattern is anything but smooth. Increases in federal tax collections in the early 1950s and late 1960s were associated with financing the Korean and Vietnam wars. Following 1975 federal receipts relative to GNP began to rise, and excluding the severe contraction of 1981–82 rose to 18 percent of GNP in 1989 and 1990.

State and local government receipts as a percent of GNP exhibit a different pattern. These tax receipts relatively increased until 1977, declined slightly through 1981 and have since been just less than the peak share in 1977. Thus, the trend of rising govern-

Fig. 15.1 Government Employment as a Percent of Nonagricultural Employment

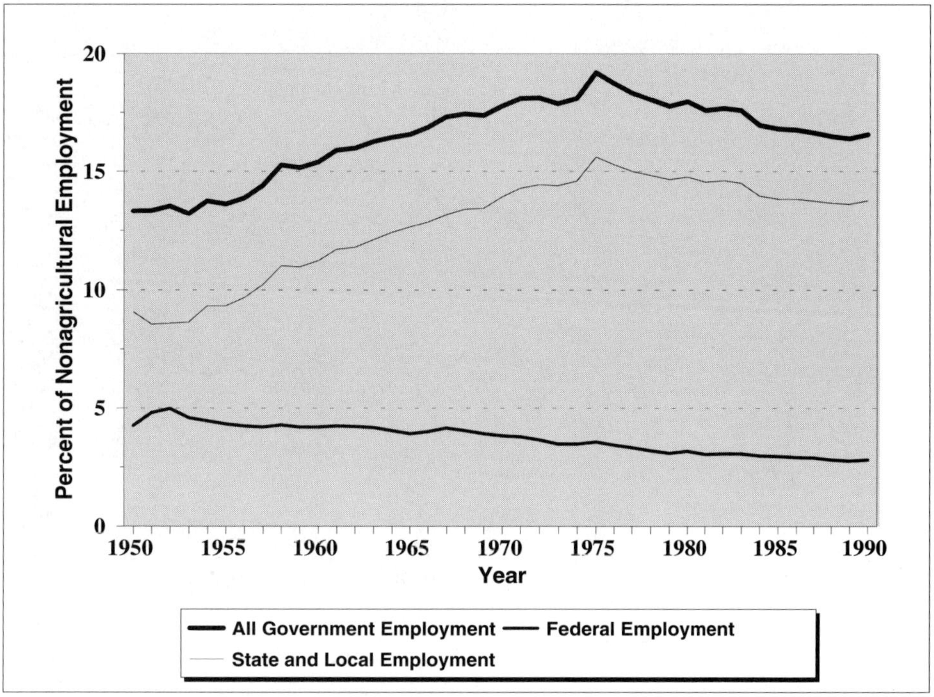

Sources: *Historical Statistics of the United States: Colonial Times to 1970* (Washington, D.C.: U.S. Government Printing Office, 1976); *Statistical Abstract of the United States* (Washington, D.C.: U.S. Government Printing Office, various years); and *Economic Report of the President* (Washington, D.C.: U.S. Government Printing Office, various years).

ment tax receipts over the entire 1950–90 period is due to rising state and local government receipts from 1950 through the mid-1970s and rising federal receipts from the mid-1970s to the present.

Because the federal government can, and has, operated with budget deficits over long periods of time, government expenditures have grown faster than government receipts. Government expenditures as a percent of GNP are shown in Figure 15.3. Relative federal expenditures rose sharply during the Korean and Vietnam Wars. They also were relatively larger in the more severe recessions of 1974–75 and 1981–82. Adjusting for the war and recessionary increases, federal expenditures as a percent of GNP tended to rise little through the 1970s. In the early 1980s, federal expenditures rose sharply to 22 percent of GNP and, though declining somewhat in the late 1980s, remained above 20 percent of GNP and well above the relative level of federal government spending in the decades prior to 1980.

State and local government expenditures rose smoothly until 1975, then declined to 1984 and have since risen somewhat. The overall trend of rising government expenditures is thus due primarily to an increase in state and local government spending from

Fig. 15.2 Government Receipts as a Percent of GNP

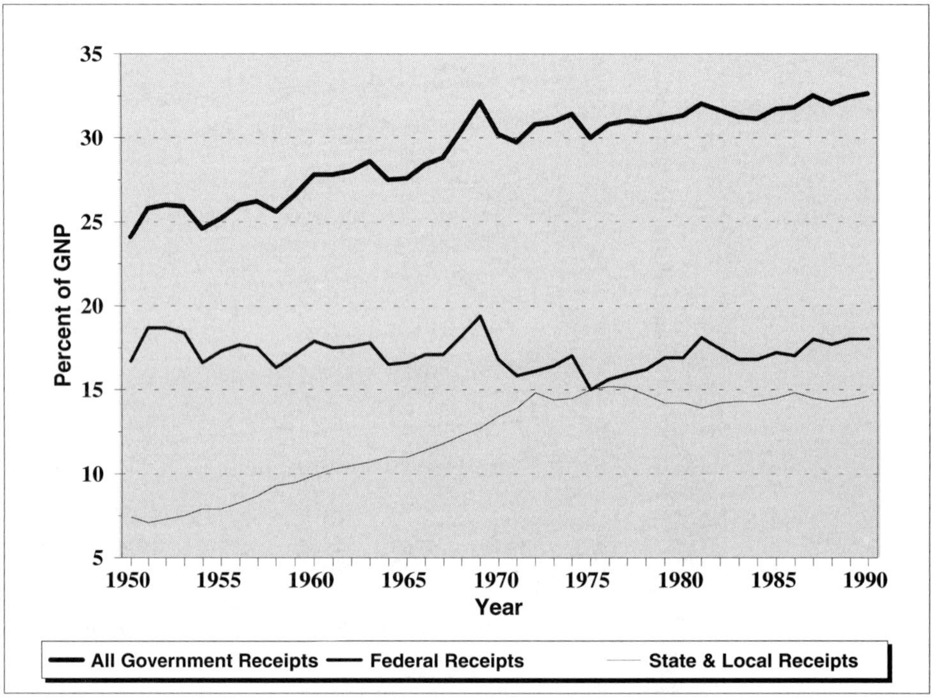

Sources: *Historical Statistics of the United States: Colonial Times to 1970* (Washington, D.C.: U.S. Government Printing Office, 1976); *Statistical Abstract of the United States* (Washington, D.C.: U.S. Government Printing Office, various years); and *Economic Report of the President* (Washington, D.C.: U.S. Government Printing Office, various years).

1950 through 1974, rising federal spending in the early 1980s, and rising state and local government spending in the late 1980s.

It is also useful to examine government spending in another way. Federal, state, and local government spending can be classified into two broad categories. First, there is spending on labor services and resources necessary to produce the goods and services that are distributed by nonmarket criteria to the population. Second, all levels of governments undertake transfers of income to selected recipients. Though some scarce resources are used to administer the income transfers, the income transfers do not use scarce resources. They do have affects in changing the demands for goods and services from what would have been the situation without the transfers and, to some disputed extent, alter the incentives to engage in productive and taxable activities.

Figure 15.4 presents government expenditures excluding transfers to persons.[2] Though showing considerable variation, all government expenditures (less transfers) as a percent of GNP shows no consistent trend to increase or decrease over the postwar period. Federal spending declined from the Korean War to 1980. By the late 1970s federal transfers to persons averaged 8.53 percent of GNP, or about 50 percent of all fed-

Fig. 15.3 Government Expenditures as a Percent of GNP

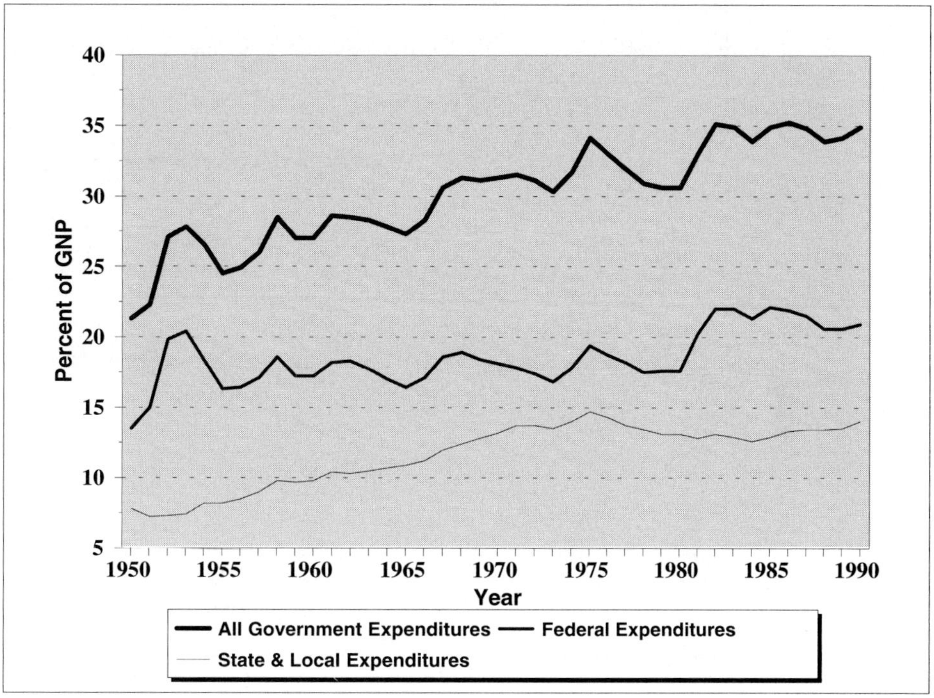

Sources: *Historical Statistics of the United States: Colonial Times to 1970* (Washington, D.C.: U.S. Government Printing Office, 1976); *Statistical Abstract of the United States* (Washington, D.C.: U.S. Government Printing Office, various years); and *Economic Report of the President* (Washington, D.C.: U.S. Government Printing Office, various years).

eral spending. State and local transfers to persons averaged only 2.35 percent of GNP, or about 17 percent of all state and local government spending. Through 1965 the rising state and local spending (less transfers) roughly offset the falling federal spending (less transfers), to hold the total government spending relative to GNP roughly constant. From 1965–79 declines in federal and (after 1975) state and local spending (less transfers) caused total government spending (less transfers) as a share of GNP to decline. A sharp increase in federal spending in the early 1980s combined with slightly rising state and local spending after 1984, caused all government spending (less transfers to persons) as a percent of GNP to be higher in the 1980s.

Figure 15.5 shows the sources of federal receipts as shares of total federal receipts. Throughout the postwar period the federal government has primarily relied on personal income taxes as a source of revenue. Corporate income taxes as a share of total receipts have fallen over most of the period. Historically, excise taxes have been a major source of federal revenue, but they also fell almost continuously in the postwar era. Estate and gift taxes have generally been less than 2 percent of federal revenues, and customs duties and fees have been less than 2 percent over the whole period. The

Fig. 15.4 Government Expenditures Less Transfers to Persons as a Percent of GNP

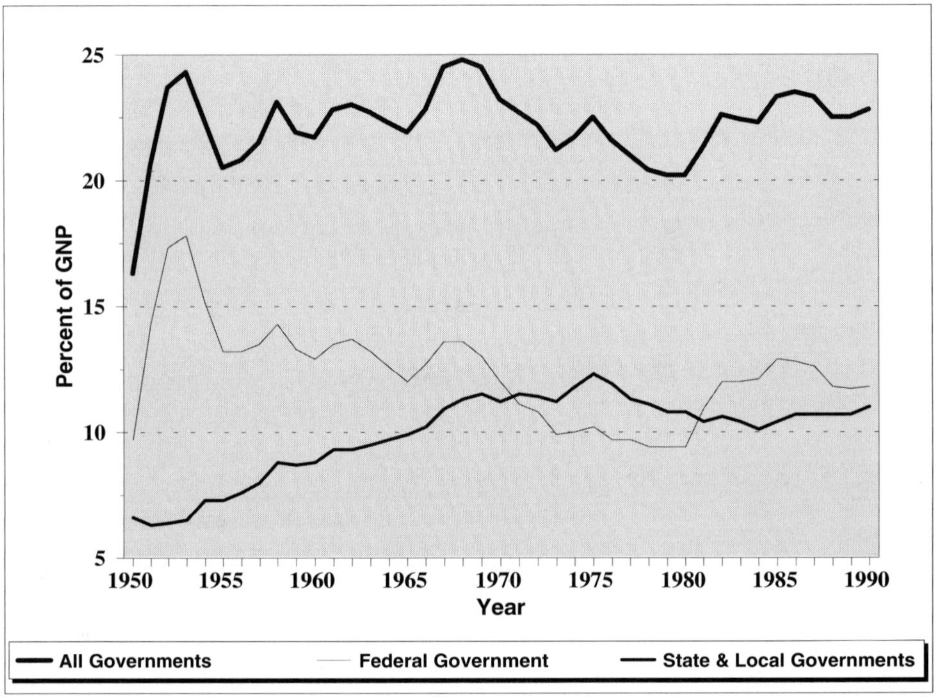

Sources: *Historical Statistics of the United States: Colonial Times to 1970* (Washington, D.C.: U.S. Government Printing Office, 1976); *Statistical Abstract of the United States* (Washington, D.C.: U.S. Government Printing Office, various years); and *Economic Report of the President* (Washington, D.C.: U.S. Government Printing Office, various years).

primary growth in federal revenues came from social insurance taxes and contributions; the counterpart to the growth of federal transfers to persons.

Figure 15.6 shows selected categories of federal outlays as a percent of total federal outlays, and as can be seen, these have changed dramatically over the postwar period. National defense as a share of total federal outlays declined sharply from the Korean War to 1981. The Reagan administration's military buildup increased defense spending but its share had dropped back to the 1981 level by 1990. Net interest on the federal debt as a share of expenditures was roughly constant from the early 1950s to the late 1970s, but increased sharply from just over 7 percent in 1975 to 10 percent in 1981 to nearly 15 percent by 1990. Agricultural outlays have steadily declined and were less than 1 percent of expenditures by 1990, while commerce and transportation have consumed about 3 to 6 percent of federal outlays with no noticeable trend of growth or decline. Veterans benefits and services have almost disappeared.

The two categories that have grown sharply are income security and education, labor, and health. Income security includes Social Security outlays, unemployment

Fig. 15.5 Selected Federal Receipts as a Percent of Total Federal Receipts

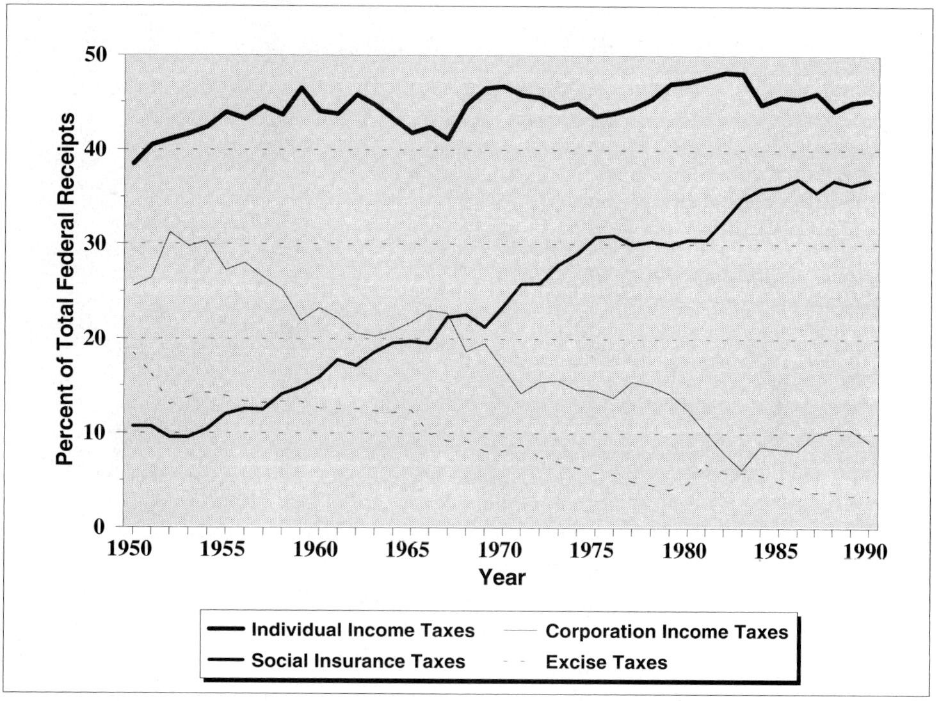

Sources: *Historical Statistics of the United States: Colonial Times to 1970* (Washington, D.C.: U.S. Government Printing Office, 1976); *Statistical Abstract of the United States* (Washington, D.C.: U.S. Government Printing Office, various years); and *Economic Report of the President* (Washington, D.C.: U.S. Government Printing Office, various years).

supplements to state governments, pension outlays for miners and railroad workers, the food stamp programs, grants to states for Aid to Families with Dependent Children, and other income transfer programs. (Prior to 1975 Social Security was not reported separately from these other programs.) These programs, particularly Social Security transfers, grew rapidly from 1952 through 1961 and from 1969 through 1976. Since 1975, Social Security outlays as a percent of total federal outlays have remained essentially constant at about 20 to 21 percent, while other income security outlays have declined from 16.68 percent to 11.77 percent of all federal outlays.

In a similar fashion, Medicare was not reported separately from education, labor, and health outlays until 1975. Programs to improve training, health, and, later, education grew rapidly after the mid-1960s, growing from less than 3 percent of all federal outlays in the early 1960s to nearly 13 percent by the mid-1970s. Medicare has continued to grow since 1975, from less than 4 percent of federal outlays to 7.84 percent in 1990. Other education, labor, and health outlays reached over 10 percent by 1979, declined to less than 7 percent by 1987 and have since risen to 7.69 percent in 1990.

Fig. 15.6 Selected Federal Outlays as a Percent of Total Federal Outlays

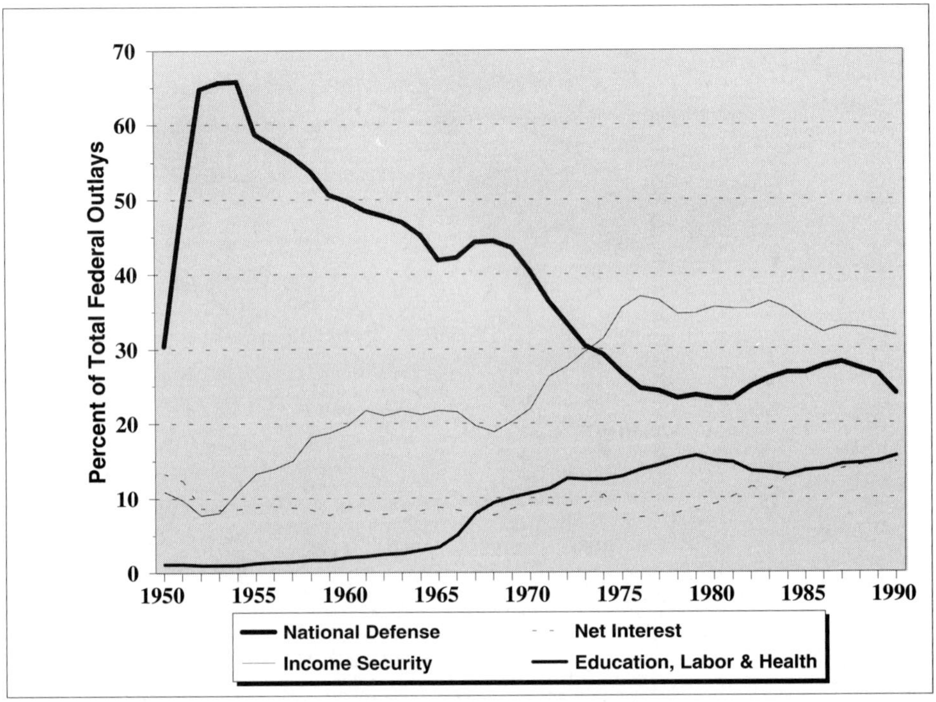

Sources: *Historical Statistics of the United States: Colonial Times to 1970* (Washington, D.C.: U.S. Government Printing Office, 1976); *Statistical Abstract of the United States* (Washington, D.C.: U.S. Government Printing Office, various years); and *Economic Report of the President* (Washington, D.C.: U.S. Government Printing Office, various years).

Figure 15.7 shows selected state and local government revenues as a percent of total state and local government revenues. In the early 1950s over 34 percent of these revenues came from property taxes, however, growing revenue demands and property owner resistance decreased the importance of this revenue source. The other longtime cornerstone of state and local government revenues is sales and gross receipts taxes, and this share declined gradually over the period. Corporation net income taxes changed little in the postwar era. The growth in state and local government revenue stems primarily from the growth in individual income tax collections and revenue sharing from the federal government. Individual income taxes rose from less than 4 percent of all revenues to over 12 percent. Federal revenue sharing had grown from 10 to over 21 percent by the end of the 1970s, but this share declined to 16 percent by 1989. State and local governments also collect many other fees and charges, such as drivers' license and license plate fees, and park use fees. These increased from over 23 percent of all revenues to 29 percent in the 1980s.

State and local government expenditures by broad categories are shown in Figure 15.8. Education has generally been the largest single expenditure item. The other two

Fig. 15.7 Selected State and Local Government Revenues as a Percent of Total Revenues

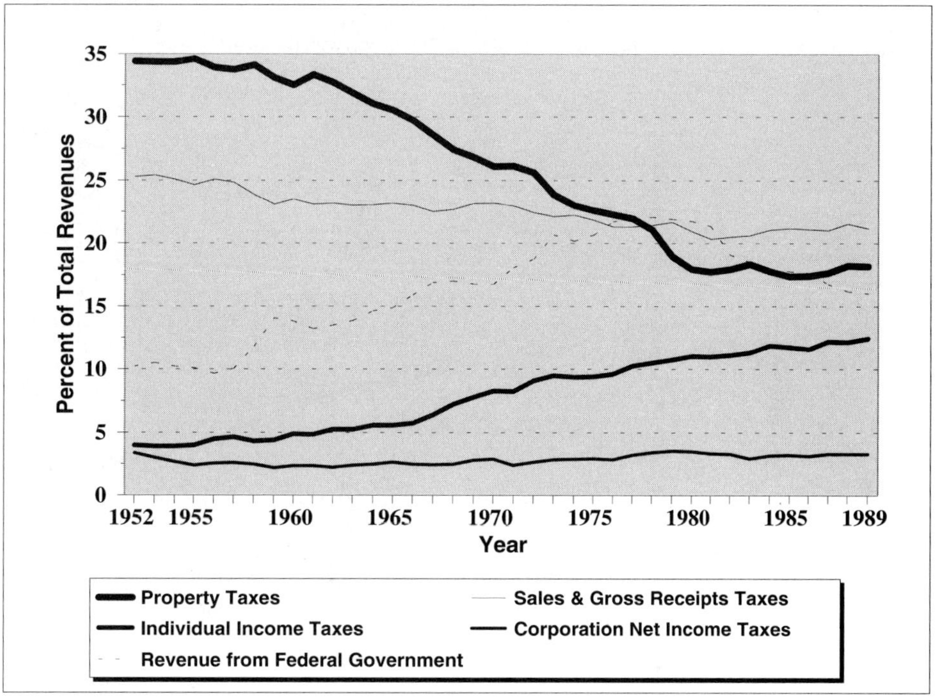

Sources: *Historical Statistics of the United States: Colonial Times to 1970* (Washington, D.C.: U.S. Government Printing Office, 1976); *Statistical Abstract of the United States* (Washington, D.C.: U.S. Government Printing Office, various years); and *Economic Report of the President* (Washington, D.C.: U.S. Government Printing Office, various years).

large categories are highways and public welfare. State and local highway construction as a share of all expenditures declined from the end of the 1950s to the early 1980s. Public welfare outlays as a share declined in the early 1950s, were roughly constant to 1966, and then rose sharply as President Johnson launched his war on poverty. The share has changed little since the early 1970s. The "all other" category includes such diverse expenditures as state and local police, fire protection, sanitation services, parks and recreation, and all of the rest of the varied state and local services. These expenditures have been rising since the late 1950s.

Only the federal government can run nearly continuous deficits and it has done this in the postwar era. This behavior, in fact, is a significant change. Deficits during wars and severe economic contractions built up debt that was reduced by surpluses generated in most other years. Several times in the nineteenth century the national debt nearly disappeared. In the postwar era federal budget surpluses have become a vanishing species. Figure 15.9 presents the federal surplus or deficit as a percent of GNP, and, as can be seen, the last federal budget surplus was in 1969.

Fig. 15.8 Selected State and Local Government Outlays as a Percent of Total Outlays

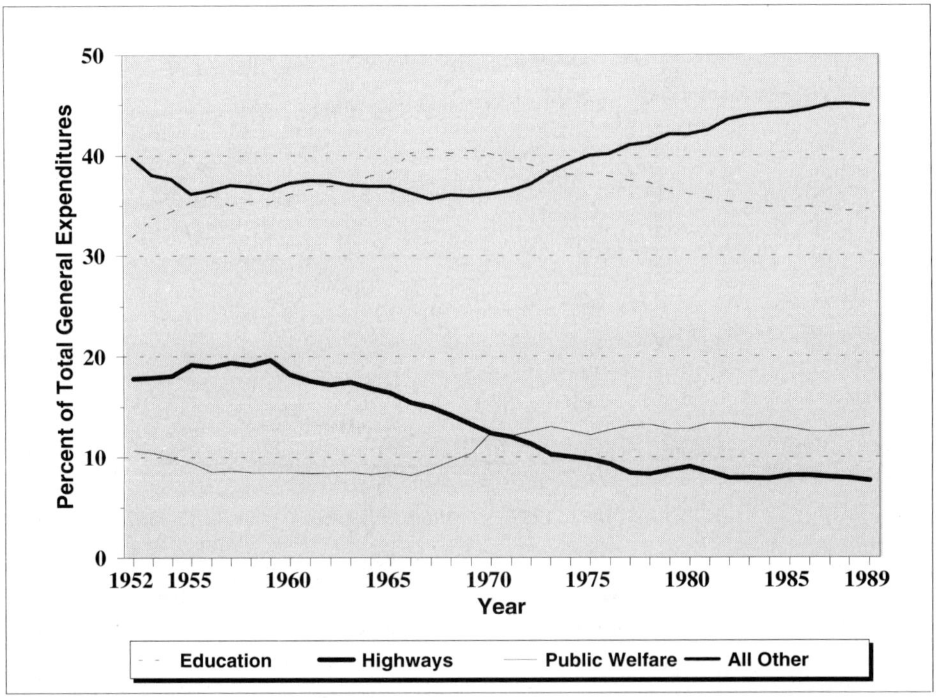

Sources: *Historical Statistics of the United States: Colonial Times to 1970* (Washington, D.C.: U.S. Government Printing Office, 1976); *Statistical Abstract of the United States* (Washington, D.C.: U.S. Government Printing Office, various years); and *Economic Report of the President* (Washington, D.C.: U.S. Government Printing Office, various years).

Continuing deficits mean increases in the federal debt. Figure 15.10 shows the federal debt as a percent of GNP and the shares of the debt held by major holders. The ratio of the federal debt to GNP fell sharply through the early 1970s and more gradually through the rest of the 1970s. This occurred for two reasons. First, GNP grew faster than the federal debt did, causing the ratio to fall. Second, once issued the outstanding debt remains fixed in nominal value, and so the continuing postwar inflation engineered by the Federal Reserve System began reducing the real value of the debt. The Reagan budget deficits of the 1980s led to an explosion of the debt. The real debt rose from $1,060.1 billion in 1980 to $2,439.2 billion in 1990. The federal debt as a percent of GNP reversed its long decline and rose from 34 percent in 1980 to 59.3 percent in 1990.

Who has held the debt during the postwar era has also varied. The largest share has been held by the public (a grouping which includes all foreign, corporate, and financial institution holdings). The public's share declined to 1974 and rose to the mid-1980s. The next largest holder of the federal debt is the federal government itself, primarily the Social Security Trust Fund, which, by law, must invest collections in excess of dis-

Fig. 15.9 Federal Government Surplus or Deficit as a Percent of GNP

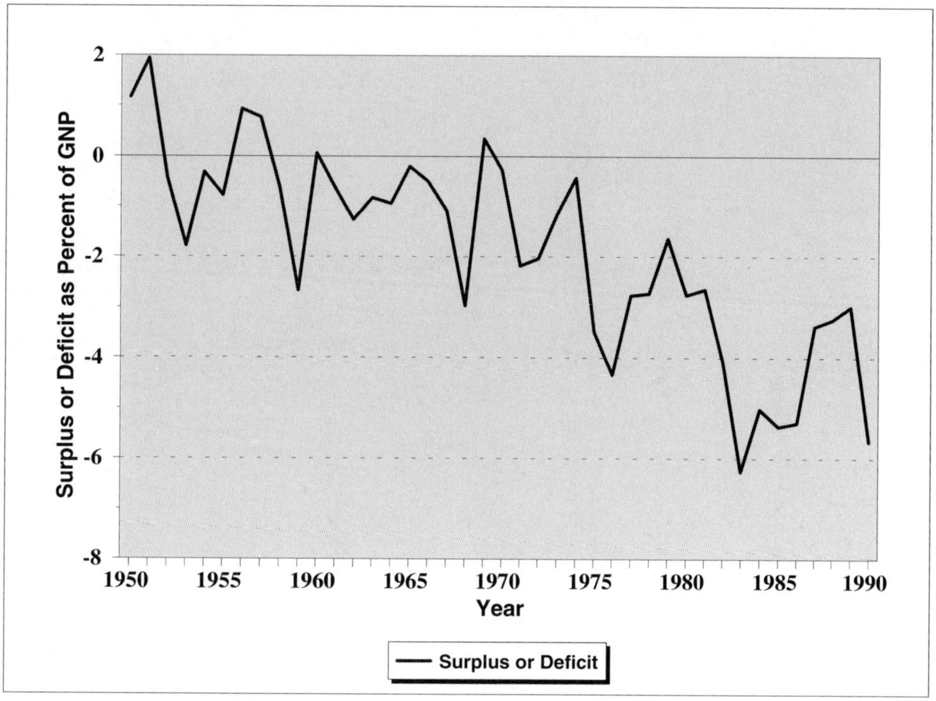

Sources: *Historical Statistics of the United States: Colonial Times to 1970* (Washington, D.C.: U.S. Government Printing Office, 1976); *Statistical Abstract of the United States* (Washington, D.C.: U.S. Government Printing Office, various years); and *Economic Report of the President* (Washington, D.C.: U.S. Government Printing Office, various years).

bursements in U.S. government securities.[3] The share of the federal government debt held by the Federal Reserve System was roughly constant through the 1950s and then began rising to a peak of 16.6 percent in 1974. Since then, the holdings of the Federal Reserve System have fallen to 7.3 percent in 1990. Heavily criticized for the higher rates of price inflation of the 1970s, the Federal Reserve System was unwilling to acquire more of the debt. To have done so would have meant a larger increase in the monetary base, the stock of money, and almost certainly the rate of price inflation. Such behavior would have resulted in a quite different monetary policy, a topic we now turn to.

STABILIZATION POLICIES

Policies to stabilize economic activity and achieve the goals of the Full Employment Act of 1946 are conducted by the Federal Reserve System and the federal government.[4]

Fig. 15.10 The Federal Debt as a Percent of GNP and Shares of the Debt Held by Major Holders

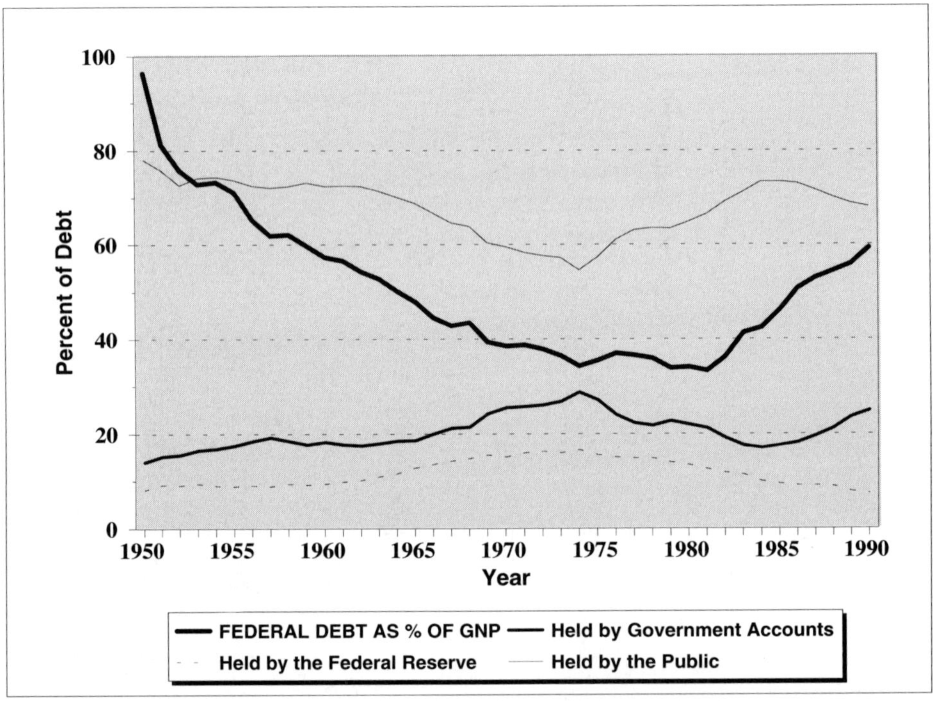

Sources: *Historical Statistics of the United States: Colonial Times to 1970* (Washington, D.C.: U.S. Government Printing Office, 1976); *Statistical Abstract of the United States* (Washington, D.C.: U.S. Government Printing Office, various years); and *Economic Report of the President* (Washington, D.C.: U.S. Government Printing Office, various years).

Though the Federal Reserve System was ostensibly created as a quasi-independent agency, in practice it has generally coordinated its policies with those of the federal government and not swayed too far from the wishes of Congress. It was quickly realized that there were problems with fiscal policy conducted by the federal government. Deciding what to do and then acting upon that decision was slow and difficult because of the necessity of getting agreement between the House of Representatives, the Senate, and the administration. The lags necessitated by this decision-making process, added to the lags in recognizing changes in economic activity, have been a problem for stabilization policies throughout the postwar period.

The Late 1940s and 1950s

During the war there were several proposals that the federal government should have a national policy aimed at achieving full-employment. In 1945 a bill was introduced to make full-employment a national goal by setting federal expenditures at whatever level was necessary to attain this.[5] The bill was an outgrowth of Keynesian ideas that government could control or moderate cyclical fluctuations such as had occurred in the interwar era,[6] and was also a response to the emerging role of the U.S. dollar as the new international legal reserve currency.[7]

What emerged in 1946 was considerably weaker than the first proposals. Instead of "full" employment the objective was to achieve "high" employment. The "right" of each person to work was eliminated, as were the requirements for a national budget that would forecast actual and full-employment demand for the president to take steps to initiate programs to close the gap if one existed. Republicans and business interests saw this as opening the door to national planning by the federal government as well as to the possibility of unlimited federal deficits.[8] The act did create a three-person Council of Economic Advisors and directed the president and the council to submit an economic report in January of each year. The Employment Act of 1946 was the first explicit statement of the federal government's responsibility to promote maximum employment, production, and purchasing power. Harry S. Truman was the first president to operate under the new act, but his "Fair Deal" undertook little in the way of stabilization policy. Truman vetoed bills to cut tax rates from the high wartime levels, and Congress found that much of the federal budget was uncontrollable.[9]

Herbert Stein argues that something of a consensus had developed in the interval between the end of the Second World War and the Korean War. The aim of fiscal policy was to be stabilization of economic activity, and the annual balancing of the federal budget was to be avoided if this interfered with stabilization.[10] Though fiscal policy was the primary stabilization tool, it had drawbacks. Forecasts were too unreliable, fiscal actions were too slow, and it could not be assumed that fiscal policy would be devoted exclusively to stabilization. Thus, the Fed's monetary policy, which had been relegated to a virtually nonexistent role after the early 1930s, was to become more flexible in its role of supporting fiscal policy.[11]

However, until 1951 monetary policy was constrained in attempting to implement any stabilization policies. After the war, the Fed continued its wartime policy of maintaining low interest rates and higher government bond prices.[12] The Treasury wanted to ease refinancing requirements as they arose and both the Fed and the treasury feared "disorderly" financial markets and problems for the financial institutions, which held large amounts of federal government securities, if interest rates rose and securities prices fell. However, differences between the Fed and the Treasury arose.[13] Though long-term rates were "pegged" at 2.5 percent, the Fed wanted to allow short-term rates to rise and made moves in this direction in 1947 and 1948. Throughout 1949 and 1950 discussions between the Fed and the Treasury continued on which rates to peg and at what level.

With the beginning of the Korean War on June 25, 1950, the struggle between the Fed and the Treasury intensified. Throughout the rest of 1950 and into early 1951, the Treasury, President Truman, Congress, and the Fed continued to discuss and disagree in public and in private as to what should be done. Finally, on March 3, 1951, a brief announcement was issued stating that the Treasury and the Fed had reached an accord. For the first time since prior to the Second World War, the Fed was freed to exercise discretionary monetary policy. The initial accord was limited to freeing the Fed on short-term rates, and the Fed did not stop supporting the prices of government securities. Not until 1953 "did the System explicitly forswear support of the prices of government securities as an aim of policy."[14]

There were three minor recessions during the Eisenhower years—1954–55, 1957–58, and 1960–61. The federal government relied upon the automatic stabilizers of the progressive income tax system and unemployment compensation payments rather than taking discretionary actions.[15] The Fed, under William McChesney Martin, Jr., relied upon open-market operations primarily through the purchase and sale of short-term bills for the monetary policy that it undertook.[16]

The 1960s

The focus of stabilization policies in the decade of the 1960s was on fiscal policy. For the first time an administration explicitly used Keynesian theory in attempting to direct activity within the economy. The expansion that began in February of 1961 continued until December of 1969 and became the longest on record. The new president, John F. Kennedy, brought in leading Keynesian economists as his advisors. As a group these economic advisors were more willing to consider market intervention to obtain their desired results; they were less concerned with inflation and more enamored of the idea of an inflation-unemployment trade-off, the so-called Phillips Curve. Kennedy's advisors were worried that the high tax rates and potential budget surpluses at full-employment would stop the economy from achieving full-employment. They believed that balance-of-payments deficits prohibited the use of monetary policy because lower interest rates would have exacerbated the deficits. This left only fiscal policy as the means to stimulate the economy, and they believed that this should be done through tax reductions, something Congress was generally sympathetic to. Because Kennedy had campaigned on a platform of balanced budgets and expanded spending, he had to be gradually converted to this Keynesian view.

The decision to cut taxes was not adopted until June 7, 1962, and Kennedy announced that he would propose an across-the-board reduction of individual and corporate income taxes to take effect January 1, 1963. First the House and then the Senate held up the bill, and it had not moved in the Senate on November 22, 1963, when Kennedy was assassinated. Lyndon Baines Johnson then took over the bill and agreed to hold down spending as requested by the Senate Finance Committee. After the budget appeared, the bill was reported out of the Senate Finance Committee on January 28, 1964. The Senate-House differences were ironed out by February 26, 1964, and Johnson signed the bill the same day.[17]

The act reduced taxes by about 20 percent on average with the first part of the reduction in 1964, and the final part in 1965. Withholding rates and corporate tax rates were also reduced. The result, in conjunction with a defense buildup and the onset of Johnson's War on Poverty, was to eliminate the full-employment budget surplus that the Keynesians had calculated. The Federal Reserve System contributed by increasing the rate of growth of the stock of money in 1964 and 1965.

This episode was really the first conscious use of Keynesian theory to formulate fiscal policy. In some ways, however, this was not a stabilization policy because the stated long-run purpose was to move the economy to a higher level of employment during the recovery and increase the rate of economic growth—not to promote recovery from a contraction. It also took a long time to obtain the tax cut. First proposed by administration economists in 1961, the bill was not signed until late February of 1964. Only about half the tax cuts took effect in 1964, with the rest effective in 1965. Therefore, it took nearly four years for the proposal to become a reality.

By 1966 the economy was at full employment, and prices were rising more rapidly. President Johnson resisted recommendations to raise taxes to reduce excess demand and lower inflationary pressures, but the Fed did increase the discount rate and reduce the growth of the monetary base in 1966, producing a credit crunch. In January, 1967, Johnson proposed a 6 percent surtax on corporate and personal income taxes, and Social Security tax rates were increased to provide for a congressionally mandated benefits increase. The Fed eased up on monetary policy. Congress finally passed a temporary surtax for the 1969 fiscal year. Savings, but not spending, declined, and the Fed adopted an easier monetary policy. As a result, the only significant change was the last federal budget surplus. Monetarist forecasts of economic activity were quite good during this period, providing support for their contentions on the power of monetary policy compared to fiscal policy.[18]

The 1970s

Robert Degen has suggested that "there is a certain morbid symmetry about our monetary experiences in the 1970s: the decade began and ended in an atmosphere of crisis, deflation, and reform of the Federal Reserve methods of operation."[19] Richard M. Nixon, a Republican president who supposedly abhorred comprehensive controls, went ahead and imposed them. The Bretton Woods international financial system created at the end of the Second World War collapsed and was replaced by a system of floating exchange rates.

With Richard Nixon's assumption of the presidency in 1969, something of a conservative trend in economics and politics took effect; monetary policy began to play a more important role. Keynesian-style fiscal policy appeared to be unable to constrain the rising price inflation and was being more seriously questioned both inside and outside of academia.[20] Arthur Burns, in his new role of chief architect of the nation's monetary policy, apparently felt constrained by the 1970 recession and a financial crisis initiated by the June, 1970, Penn Central collapse. Monetary policy had to be eased to handle these situations. However, this conflicted with the goal of gradually reducing the growth rate of the stock of money to lower inflation without bringing on a contraction. Prices continued to rise during the 1970 recession. During 1970 and 1971, Burns came to believe that wage-price guidelines could effectively supplement monetary policy in reducing the rate of inflation.[21] Congress was also pushing for guidelines and in early 1970 passed the Economic Stabilization Act, giving the president the authority to impose economic controls. Nixon initially disavowed their use, but by early 1971 several aspects of an incomes policy had been employed.[22]

Still, the sudden imposition of wage and price controls on August 15, 1971, was a nearly complete surprise. There were four phases to the wage and price controls. Phase I froze wages, prices, and rents for 90 days. At the same time, a 10 percent investment tax credit was passed, excise taxes on automobiles and trucks were eliminated, personal exemptions were increased, and some revenue sharing programs were canceled. On the international agenda, the dollar was devalued and convertibility suspended. The dollar was again devalued in February, 1973, and in March, 1973, the United States went to a floating exchange rate, effectively ending the Bretton Woods System.[23]

Phase II established a mandatory system of wage and price controls to allow for controlled adjustments. Phase II lasted through 1972, when Phase III began. Phase III moved toward voluntary controls and a greater reliance on market adjustments. However, prices rose rapidly under Phase III. The administration's response was to impose a 60-day freeze on many wages and prices in June of 1973. The public response was poor and many distortions appeared, particularly shortages of various food products. Phase IV was introduced in August 1973 and industries began to be decontrolled. Finally, on April 30, 1974, all wage and price controls were terminated.[24]

Most economists agree that the wage and price controls did not work. By creating supply uncertainties and resource misallocations, they reduced production, causing even higher prices. For the most part, profit margins of firms were reduced rather than holding back wages at the same rate as prices were restrained. This suggested that once the controls were removed, there would be a catch-up in price inflation, an event that did occur. Price increases during the period of controls from August 15, 1971, to April 30, 1974, cannot measure inflation because prices were controlled and not free to measure the inflation that was occurring. As Robert J. Gordon pointed out in 1973, the wage and price controls had no long-run effect on inflation.[25] In his survey and analysis of wage and price controls in the early 1970s, Rockoff found that "many professional economists have agreed that the Vietnam episode with controls was especially unsuccessful."[26]

The Federal Reserve System's basis for monetary policy was also changing throughout the early 1970s. Under Arthur Burns, the Federal Reserve System began to emphasize various monetary aggregates as well as money market conditions. The 1970s became a transition decade for the Federal Reserve System as its operating procedures evolved to combine "monetary aggregates as intermediate targets with reserves and interest rates as operating targets."[27] Congressional pressure to make the Fed more accountable to Congress led the board of governors to begin reporting money growth targets to the Senate in May of 1975, and legislation in 1977 and 1978 expanded this.

In the early 1970s, these changes were still in their infancy and, when combined with the varying phases of wage and price controls, led to erratic monetary policy. A series of economic "shocks," or rapid changes, in 1972 and 1973 helped usher in a recession. These were the devaluation and floating of the American dollar, sharply rising prices of many foodstuffs (such as wheat), reduced supplies and huge price increases for crude oil and gasoline, and the April, 1974 removal of all wage and price controls.[28] By November of 1973, these supply shocks and the distortions caused by wage and price controls had brought on a recession. With the lifting of wage and price controls, the long-repressed inflation quickly resulted in rapid price increases even though the recession was underway and continued until March of 1975. The rate of inflation, measured by the change in the CPI, peaked at 12.2 percent around the middle of 1974 and averaged 11 percent for the entire year. The rate of unemployment averaged 8.3 percent for all of 1975.

Gerald R. Ford, who became president when Richard M. Nixon resigned, was initially concerned with the double-digit inflation. His attention soon shifted to the recession as he proposed tax cuts and rebates in the Tax Reduction Act of 1975. Most economists believe that the 1975 tax cuts were, at best, ineffective. The recession ended before the rebates on 1974 taxes were in the hands of consumers.[29] The temporary nature of the tax cuts also suggested that consumers might save these rather than spend the extra disposable income. In addition, other economists suggested that crowding out reduced the effectiveness of the tax cuts.[30]

Following the 1974–75 recession, there was great variability in the rate of growth of the stock of money, and the rate of price inflation began to accelerate. The Carter administration proposed voluntary wage and price guidelines to reduce the rate of price inflation, but these were ineffective. Monetary policy under Arthur Burns and, after January of 1978, his replacement, G. William Miller, can best be described as erratic. As inflationary expectations increased, these became incorporated into nominal interest rates, causing interest rates to increase, and by the end of the 1970s nominal interest rates were historically very high. Higher interest rates led to growing losses at banks and thrifts. Further complicating the Fed's monetary policy was the growth of the income velocity of money at the end of the 1970s; a trend which forecast worsening inflation. (See Figure 15.11.)

When Paul Volcker replaced Miller in the middle of 1979, the financial sector was in a dreadful state.[31] The rate of inflation and the fall of the dollar in the foreign exchange markets both accelerated in the months prior to October of 1979. As turmoil enveloped the financial markets, Robert Degen reports that Paul Volcker abruptly left an International Monetary Fund meeting in Belgrade, Yugoslavia to return to the United States. "In an extraordinary meeting of the Federal Open Market Committee on Saturday night, October 6, 1979, quickly deemed 'historic' by financial writers, the Federal Reserve adopted a new policy stance."[32]

This new policy stance was apparently strongly influenced by the Monetarists. The Federal Reserve System announced that it would begin targeting the unborrowed reserves of the member banks rather than the federal funds rate. The announcement was hailed by Monetarists everywhere as a serious attempt to reduce the growth rate of the stock of money and begin reducing the rate of price inflation. To reinforce the policy change, the Fed sharply increased the discount rate to 12 percent and increased reserve requirements on selected accounts such as Eurodollar accounts. With the announcement, interest rates began to rise, and the dollar's foreign exchange value stabilized. These changes led the way into the macroeconomic policies of the 1980s.

Fig. 15.11 The Income Velocity of the Stock of Money

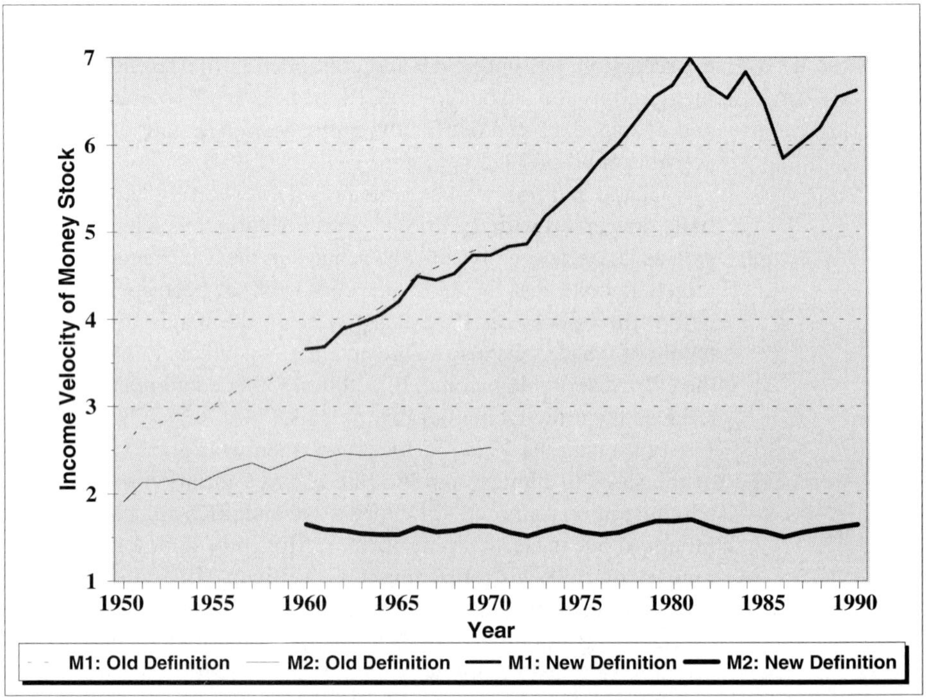

Sources: *Historical Statistics of the United States: Colonial Times to 1970* (Washington, D.C.: U.S. Government Printing Office, 1976); *Statistical Abstract of the United States* (Washington, D.C.: U.S. Government Printing Office, various years); and *Economic Report of the President* (Washington, D.C.: U.S. Government Printing Office, various years).

The 1980s

Large segments of the American population had become increasingly dissatisfied with government in the 1970s. Taxes and the sizes of government seemed to continually grow at a faster rate than the incomes of ordinary citizens.[33] In 1980 Ronald W. Reagan campaigned for the presidency on what was essentially an antigovernment platform, proposing that federal taxes be cut to stimulate the supply of savings and investment and boost productive economic activity. The size of the federal government was to be reduced along with federal regulations on businesses to allow firms to be more productive and enable free markets to more fully direct the allocation of the nation's scarce productive resources. With this anti-Washington theme Reagan won the election over the incumbent president, Jimmy Carter.

Reagan was proposing the adoption of what had come to be called supply-side economics, and the full set of his administration's economic programs, of which supply-side economics was an integral part, was frequently referred to as "Reaganomics."[34] Supply-side economics argued that increases beyond a certain tax rate led to decreases in tax revenues as productive taxable activity was choked off. The more extreme supply-side positions argued that in the late 1970s tax rates were so high that reductions in federal tax rates could actually increase federal tax revenues. Other less extreme positions argued that tax rate reductions combined with spending cuts could provide the economic stimulus to get the economy growing faster and end "stagflation." Supply-siders also argued that the historical record showed that sharp tax rate reductions actually increased the share of the tax burden borne by the higher income taxpayers who, because of progressive tax rates, would have greater absolute reductions in tax rates.

The program proposed by newly elected President Reagan combined these supply-side ideas with more traditional conservative concepts. The most important component was reductions in personal federal income tax rates amounting to an average of 25 percent over a three-year period. When fully phased in, the top marginal rate was to drop from 70 to 50 percent, and rates would be indexed against future price inflation. This was the most important of the tax cuts. Federal spending growth was to be reduced by cutting almost all nondefense spending, excluding Social Security, and regulations that raised business expenses unnecessarily or reduced competition were to be reduced or eliminated. Finally, the Federal Reserve System, under Paul Volcker, was asked to restrain the growth of the stock of money in a monetarist fashion to bring down the rate of price inflation.

These reductions were enacted in the Economic Recovery Tax Act, which President Reagan signed on August 13, 1981.[35] In 1985, after his reelection, President Reagan again requested cuts in personal income tax rates, which, beginning in 1986, were lowered to a maximum of 28 percent with a reduction in the number of rate brackets and elimination of many tax breaks.[36] In 1981 the Office of Management and Budget used highly optimistic estimates of inflation, interest rates, and economic growth to predict that the economic program would result in a balanced budget by 1984.

However, the Reagan administration's program got off to a much different start. The October, 1979, change in monetary policy allowed interest rates to begin rising sharply. As bond yields rose, bond prices fell, and 1980 became known as the year of the great bond market crash as banks, thrifts, and insurance companies saw the value of their bond portfolios decline dramatically. A short recession began in January of 1980 and ended in July of 1980. In the meantime, interest rates continued to rise. Short-term interest rates reached nearly 20 percent in 1981, while new mortgage yields were around 15 percent in 1981 and 1982. The rate of inflation averaged nearly 13 percent during 1981. A new recession began in July 1981 and did not end until December of 1982. This was the longest and most severe postwar contraction. In December of 1982, the unemployment rate hit 10.8 percent.

Many analyses argue that the length and severity of the contraction was due to the Federal Reserve System's policies to quickly lower the rate of price inflation. However, the accelerating inflation of the last half of the 1970s had generated severe price distortions and malinvestments that were exposed once the rate of price inflation dropped sharply. For example, firms that had expanded often chose debt instruments that were poorer choices in a disinflating environment. Farmers had been lured by rising land and crop support prices—which were significantly driven by the price inflation—and low real interest rates to expand and go into debt which could not be sustained in a low-inflation, higher real interest rate environment. With the disinflation and much higher real interest rates of the 1980s, these massive dislocations in the agricultural sector as well as dramatic adjustments for nonagricultural firms were unavoidable.

The Reagan administration had counted on a rapid supply-side-driven recovery from a mild contraction to meet its projections. The actual result was a rapid and dramatic rise in federal budget deficits. The peacetime federal deficits incurred under the Reagan administration during the 1980s had no precedent in the history of the United States. The deficits and public criticism of the federal government spurred Congress into action in late 1985, and it passed the Gramm-Rudman bill, an act supposed to automatically trigger across-the-board spending reductions if projections of the federal deficit exceeded legislated maximums. The bill had little effect.

Monetary policy in the 1980s also followed a rocky path. By 1982 the Monetarist-type policy of controlling the growth of unborrowed reserves of the banking system, announced with such fanfare in October of 1979, had been abandoned. The Monetarist proposals were formulated on the basis of a relatively stable income velocity of money. However, as Figure 15.11 shows, in the 1980s the M1 income velocity of money became quite variable.[37] Interest rate ceilings on time and savings deposits were gradually raised and eliminated in 1986. Checking accounts began to pay interest and the incentives to minimize balances in checking deposits to hold funds in interest bearing time or savings deposits were minimized. Confronted with new deposit accounts, which blurred the distinction between transactions balances and short-term investment funds, the Fed again began to redefine the monetary aggregates.[38]

In the third quarter of 1982, the Fed abandoned its Monetarist guidelines and adopted moving targets for the growth rates of M1 and M2, adjusting these as they felt necessary. The results were dramatic variations in the growth rate of monetary aggregates as the Fed "leaned against the wind," trying to adjust to changes in the income velocity of money and in economic activity. In spite of rapid increases in M1, M2, and the monetary base, the rate of inflation fell sharply because of the declining income velocity of money—from 13.5 percent in 1980 to 3.2 percent in 1983. From 1983 through 1989, the rate of price inflation averaged 3.6 percent.

The recovery that started at the beginning of 1983 continued to the second quarter of 1990. During that long recovery, the rate of unemployment slowly declined from 9.5 percent to 5.2 percent. Real GNP per capita rose 2.8 percent a year on average. Real federal spending rose only 2.68 percent per year, while under the Carter administration real federal spending had risen 4.44 percent per year and under the Nixon-Ford administrations had risen 3.24 percent per year. The recession, which began in 1990, continued until the second quarter of 1992. Under the administration of President George Bush, the federal budget deficit and the real rate of growth of federal spending both began rising. These events made for a somber transition into the 1990s.

SOCIAL POLICIES

American governments, like all other governments, have always developed and implemented social policies. During the New Deal of the 1930s, the federal government had expanded its policies designed to enhance the welfare and economic security of most individuals as well as more closely monitor business firms and industries. In the 1962–78 period, there was another tumultuous expansion of social policies that differed in scope and nature from previous ones. New laws to protect consumers and the environment were created along with new and expanded regulation of businesses, a phenomenon that Murray Weidenbaum has termed the "new regulation."[39] The "discovery" of poverty in the United States initiated a new range of social policies designed to eliminate it, including an expansion of the security nets for the aged, poor, and disabled. One of these social policies that expanded rapidly to dominate the federal budget and become a continuing source of difficulties was Social Security.

Social Security

The Social Security program began in 1935.[40] The Social Security Act created an Old-Age Insurance (OAI) program as well as the Unemployment Insurance program (UI), the Aid to Families with Dependent Children program (AFDC), and the Old-Age Assistance program (OAA). The initial act intended the program to provide basic income security but not a full income for the retired elderly.[41] And the OAI program was intended to be a fully funded trust fund. However, at the end of the 1930s, Congress wished to begin distributing benefits at an earlier date, so the law was changed to abandon this and implement pay-as-you-go financing.

Later amendments continued to alter the program. In 1950 the benefits of the program were extended to dependents of retired workers and the survivors of deceased workers. The program added a payroll tax for this. In 1965 Congress added disability benefits for workers under 65 and hospital benefits for those over 65. Payroll taxes for these benefits were included, and the program became the OASDHI (Old Age, Survivors, Disability, and Hospital Insurance) program. Though the hospital insurance was funded through the OASDHI program, a medical insurance program to cover physicians' and surgeons' services for those over 65 was separately funded, and the hospital and medical insurance programs together became known as Medicare. The Old-Age Assistance program which had been created in 1935, was instituted to provide income assistance for the needy elderly who otherwise did not qualify. It was initially much larger than OAI and exceeded OAI as late as 1950. In 1972 Congress replaced all of the state-federal OAA programs with a uniform federal Supplemental Security Income program (SSI), which continued to be financed from general revenues and not by the OASDHI taxes.

When Congress established the payroll taxes for the program, half of the tax was to be deducted from the employee's paycheck and the other half was to be paid directly by the employer. Of course, it is clear that the employer's portion of the tax is a labor cost just as wages and salaries are, and if the employer did not pay this portion of the OASDHI tax, it would be paid to the employee.[42] The initial rate was 2 percent—1 percent for the employee and 1 percent for the employer—and this rate continued through 1949. In 1950 the payroll tax rate rose to 3 percent and in 1990 reached 15.3 percent.[43] The maximum income subject to the OASDHI tax was $3,000 from 1937 to 1950 but was gradually raised to over $54,000 by 1990. The original coverage excluded workers in agriculture, domestic service, all governments and nonprofit institutions, railroads, and the self-employed. Coverage was extended until by the 1980s virtually everyone in the economy was covered. The OASDHI rate has remained slightly lower for self-employed workers.

The OASDHI program dominates the federal budget and has been the largest single expenditure since 1973. The revenues from OASDHI payroll taxes have been the most rapidly growing source of revenues for the federal government since the early 1950s and now rank second only to individual income taxes as a federal revenue source. Because of its sheer size and its beginning in the New Deal, the Social Security program has been "the showpiece of America's welfare state."[44] However, the program has some serious flaws and problems.

Though the Social Security program has always been characterized as an insurance program, it is, in fact, a combination of an insurance program and a welfare program.[45] In 1939 Congress began paying out benefits to retirees on a pay-as-you-go basis because it was felt that the early retirees needed the Social Security income even though they had contributed very little to the funds. Douglas Munro calculated that for males who retired in 1940, 97.7 percent of the Social Security benefits they received were a welfare transfer, a figure that had fallen to 66.4 percent by 1971.[46]

A second welfare aspect of Social Security is the progressive method of calculating benefits. A retired worker's benefits are calculated on their average monthly earnings (AME) over their lifetime. Until 1979 monthly benefits were 155.38 percent of the first $110 of the AME, but declined in increments to 21.3 percent of the AME in excess of $1,375. The 1977 changes indexed the AME, but kept the declining pattern. The result is that the "formula is heavily weighted so that those with low earning histories will receive relatively higher benefits for their past taxes than those with high earning histories."[47]

Other characteristics that make Social Security a welfare program include minimum benefits and "benefits for spouses and dependents of beneficiaries who qualify for benefits themselves."[48] Benefits are reduced for those who earn above certain income limits. Finally, a wife is required to forgo her own retirement benefits in order to receive the benefits she is allotted based on her husband's earning record. Widows under 60 years of age are also required to remain single to receive survivor's benefits.

Though the Social Security program is described as having trust funds, there are no true trust funds to generate the regular payments to the beneficiaries. By 1978 the trust funds constituted only 0.8 percent of the unfunded liability of the OASDI program. In fact, the trust funds were only 24 percent of the annual outlays of OASDI in 1980.[49] The 1977 changes were projected to increase the trust funds through 2010 after which they again begin falling to 2028 when they are exhausted. The fact that the Social Security program has always operated on essentially a pay-as-you-go system did not stop the Social Security Administration from describing the program as a true trust fund.[50]

Finally, some economists have argued that Social Security contributions reduce other private savings, and the overall rate of capital formation is thereby reduced. In several studies Martin Feldstein has argued that individuals consider their Social Security contributions to be equivalent to their savings into private pension plans, and the increase in Social Security contributions has led to a decline in private savings and capital formation, an effect called the *asset-substitution effect*.[51] Alicia H. Munnell, among others, has argued that there is a countervailing effect called the *retirement effect*, whereby Social Security induces individuals to retire earlier, leading to higher savings rates.[52] Robert Barro has argued that parents realize that Social Security represents a forced transfer from their children to them, thus reducing the ability of their children to accumulate assets. Parents then increase their savings to leave a larger bequest to their children at their death.[53] Differing estimates of the reduction in private saving arise due to econometric estimation difficulties and differing assumptions. At the present the question of the size of the reduction in private saving and capital formation is still open.[54]

Eliminating Poverty and Welfare

As Charles Murray describes it, through the 1950s there was a general consensus in the United States about the cause of poverty and the purpose of public welfare. "A civilized society does not let its people starve in the streets. It makes a 'decent provision'. . . for those who would otherwise be destitute."[55] However, there was a fundamental conflict because attempts to aid the "deserving poor"—the involuntarily unemployed and the helpless—would also aid the "undeserving poor"—vagrants and others who could provide for themselves if public welfare were unavailable. And most felt that the provision of public welfare would encourage more people to become part of this latter group. "It was seen as a truism that a welfare system was perpetually in danger of tilting the balance in favor of the easy way out."[56]

Roosevelt's changes to the welfare system in the New Deal were consistent with this attitude. Social Security was *insurance* and forced workers to provide for their old age themselves. Aid to Families with Dependent Children (AFDC) provided welfare payments to widows with children; if they remarried, or when the children became adults, public aid grants ceased. Workmen's Compensation was to assist workers injured during employment and left unable to work, while Unemployment Compensation was a temporary grant to workers who were involuntarily unemployed. "Nothing in the New Deal provided help just because a person was poor or hampered by social disadvantages."[57]

By the late 1950s conditions were developing that would disrupt this general consensus. Welfare seemed to become more permanent, and there was growing resentment at the continued support of what seemed to be healthy adults, particularly the growing AFDC program where most of the women enrolled were not widows as had been anticipated.[58] For many there was also a growing outrage at what were termed the "pervasive injustices" in the American system. In the South there was a growing civil rights movement aimed at bringing about equality of opportunity and treatment between blacks and whites.

By the beginning of the 1960s, there was a discernible change in many attitudes toward poverty and public welfare. An increasing number of people felt that the proper role for the federal government was to create policies that would allow the poor to rise out of poverty, rather than just taking care of them. In a small way this was the first shift toward the view that poverty was structural in nature—in other words, that poverty was caused by the structure of the economic and social system in the United States rather than by the poverty-stricken individual's own behavior. The slogan, "give a hand, not a handout," which became the rallying cry for the War on Poverty, proposed helping individuals escape from the dole. The premise was that most people would work if given an appropriate opportunity, and it was the continuing responsibility of the federal government to help Americans help themselves.[59]

Kennedy's initial programs—the Area Redevelopment Act of 1961 and the Manpower Development and Training Act of 1962—were quite small in size. Under Lyndon Johnson, the War on Poverty quickly expanded. His initial antipoverty bill in 1964, the Economic Opportunity Act, included funding for job training and opportunities through such programs as Jobs Corp, Operation Mainstream, New Careers, Job Opportunities, and the Neighborhood Youth Corps; community antipoverty projects; loans to low-income farmers and small businesses; and the creation of Vista, the domestic version of Kennedy's overseas Peace Corps. In all of the titles of the act, there was a clear "willingness of the federal government to bypass established structures, particularly state and local governments, in order to create the programs needed."[60]

Title VII of the Civil Rights Act of 1964 aided the War on Poverty by forbidding discrimination in hiring, promotion, firing, transfers, training, and pay. To monitor this, it created the Equal Employment Opportunity Commission (EEOC), though it was not given enforcement powers until 1972. From 1964 to 1967, new in-kind transfer programs were created in the form of Medicaid for low-income persons, Medicare for Social Security recipients, and food stamps for low-income persons, while the existing housing programs were expanded. All of these were means tested.[61] Rule liberalization and increasing real benefits were part of the expansions in the AFDC, unemployment insurance, and general welfare programs.

In general, the War on Poverty programs from 1964 to 1967 can be categorized as temporary community action programs and job training programs because it was assumed that as more and better jobs were created and those in poverty obtained better skills, most of the able-bodied poor would obtain jobs and permanently escape poverty. By 1967 it was becoming clear that the War on Poverty was not working. Late in 1967 Lyndon Johnson's principal aide, Joseph Califano, announced that government studies had found that only 1 percent of the persons on welfare were capable of gaining the skills and training necessary to achieve self-sufficiency. As Charles Murray states, "The repudiation of the dream—to end the dole once and for all—was complete."[62]

The structural poverty thesis took on a growing importance. Continued economic growth, it was claimed, would not further reduce poverty because of the way that the economic system distributed income.[63] Radical reforms of the system were required to eliminate or reduce some of the poverty. In other cases Americans would have to accept the long-term assistance of the working poor. Laws began to be passed to enforce equality of result, not just equality of opportunity. Quotas and reverse discrimination often became explicitly or implicitly required to correct past discrimination. And the size of the transfer programs began to grow.

The share of families receiving AFDC payments rose from 1.78 percent in 1960 to 6.57 percent in 1980.[64] The number of disability beneficiaries rose from 687,000 in 1960 to 4,352,000 in 1975.[65] In 1965, the food stamp program had 424,000 participants but 21.1 million in 1980, and by the early 1990s 1 in 11 families received food stamps. The work training programs enrolled 825,000 in 1967 and over 4 million at the peak at the end of the 1970s.[66] Total federal social welfare expenditures rose from 3.07 percent of GNP in 1953 to 5.37 percent in 1965, to 11.15 percent in 1976. If federal expenditures on social insurance and veterans' programs are excluded and only public aid, health and medical programs, education, housing, and other social welfare expenditures included, this rose from 0.82 percent of GNP in 1955 to 1.41 percent in 1965, to 3.33 percent of GNP in 1976.[67]

By 1967 those who pushed the structuralist explanation of poverty were arguing that some form of guaranteed annual income was a necessity if poverty was to be eradicated. Finally Congress approved the most ambitious controlled social science experiment in history, the Negative Income Tax (NIT) experiment.[68] The project began in 1968 and continued until 1978. "The proponents of the NIT in the Johnson administration were out to slay the folk beliefs that welfare makes people shiftless. The NIT, properly designed, would provide work incentives and get people off the welfare rolls."[69]

In each experiment a sample of low-income people was separated into experimental and control groups. Members of the experimental group were told that their incomes would not be allowed to drop below a minimum level (the poverty line) for a specific number of years (three in the first experiments). The control group received no benefits. The experiments began in New Jersey and Pennsylvania between 1968 and 1972, then moved to rural low-income families in Iowa and North Carolina from 1970 to 1972 and an AFDC group in Gary, Indiana from 1971 to 1974. "The largest, longest, and best-evaluated experiments were in Seattle and Denver from 1971 to 1978."[70]

The results tended to confirm the popular wisdom. In all the experiments there was a significant reduction of the work effort. In the Seattle-Denver experiments the NIT led husbands to reduce their work hours by 9 percent and wives by 20 percent. For husbands, the reduction primarily lay in men who opted out of work altogether. The reduction in the work effort by wives was disturbing, because it removed a major source of escape from poverty for many families.[71] There was also a dramatic 43 percent reduction in the work effort for young, single males. Periods of unemployment were significantly longer, and, in the Seattle-Denver experiments, there was a 36 percent increase in the dissolution of marriages.[72]

By almost all measures, poverty was declining from the end of the Second World War through the end of the 1950s. From 1960 to 1969, the number of persons in poverty in the United States fell sharply, then fell much more slowly to 1973, and has risen since 1973. The one group that should have benefited most from the antipoverty programs was people of working age, but in this group poverty declined from 1960 to 1969, remained relatively constant through the late 1970s, and then began rising. Latent poverty, or poverty before all government transfers, fell from 1950 to 1968 but has since been slowly rising.[73] In spite of a dramatic real growth in federal programs and transfers to reduce poverty in the late 1960s and 1970s, the reduction in poverty seems to have stopped the 1970s. Reducing or eliminating poverty in the United States has presented seemingly intractable problems.[74]

Businesses: The New Regulation

The development of programs to eliminate poverty between 1962 and 1978 had their counterparts in the "new regulation of business." Government's economic regulation of business in the United States can be traced back to the founding of the nation, but the regulatory agencies with which we associate most economic regulation began with the creation of the Interstate Commerce Commission (ICC) in 1887. Until 1960 most regulatory agencies were created following the ICC model.[75] These economic regulatory agencies typically focused their activities on the markets, rates, and the obligation to serve of the firms in the regulated industries. Under this model the health of the industry being regulated was a closely related, and frequently major, concern of the regulatory agency.[76]

This close relationship between the regulating agency and the regulated industry was conducive to the development of regulatory "capture" or "collusion," whereby the regulatory commission became a captive of the industry it was supposed to regulate. Murray Weidenbaum suggests that this widely held view had some basis in fact.[77] Concerns about this regulatory capture process and that consumers were worse off with some of this economic regulation contributed to demands for deregulation in the latter part of the 1970s.

Three reasons are generally presented to explain the regulation of businesses: monopolies, inadequate information, and externalities.[78] The new social regulation of businesses was based primarily on the rationales of inadequate information and the externalities created by businesses in providing goods and/or services.[79] There were four major areas of involvement: consumer products, employment conditions, environment, and energy.[80]

Since 1962 there has been a growing array of increasingly stringent regulations to protect consumers. After the Thalidomide scare, Congress amended the Food and Drug Act to require all drugs to be tested for safety and effectiveness before they were released to the public.[81] Growing concern about the effects of cigarette smoking on health led Congress in 1965 to require cigarette manufacturers to add labels to cigarette packages warning of the dangers of smoking. In 1966 Congress moved to ban the sale of hazardous children's toys and articles. In 1966 Congress passed the Traffic Safety Act, which "provides for a national safety program, including setting national safety standards for motor vehicles."[82] In 1967 Congress broadened a 1953 law prohibiting the manufacture, sale, or import of clothing so flammable as to be dangerous when worn by individuals. Consumer finance protection was provided in a series of acts, beginning with the 1968 Truth-in-Lending Act. In 1970 acts were passed to regulate credit bureaus, give customers access to their credit records, prohibit companies from issuing unsolicited credit cards, and protect the customers of securities brokers and dealers. In 1972 an act created the Consumer Products Safety Commission (CPSC) to establish and administer safety standards for all consumer products. In 1974 the

Magnuson-Moss Warranty Act established federal standards for written consumer product warranties. In 1977 Congress moved to require warning labels on all products containing the sugar substitute saccharin because some studies suggested that it might be a carcinogen.

Another area of new regulations concerned employee working conditions and terms of employment. In the 1960s laws were passed to provide equal employment opportunities to all applicants and to eliminate sex-based wage differentials. The Civil Rights Act of 1964 established the Equal Employment Opportunity Commission to investigate charges of discrimination in hiring, promotion, firing, transfers, training, and pay. The Age Discrimination in Employment Act of 1967 prohibited job discrimination against individuals aged 40 to 65, and a 1978 act raised the permissible mandatory retirement age from 65 to 70. Affirmative action for the handicapped was instituted in 1973.[83] The most wide-ranging employee regulation came in 1970, with the far reaching Occupational Safety and Health Act, which established the Occupational Safety and Health Administration (OSHA). OSHA was given extensive powers to develop and enforce safety and health standards in the employee workplace.

Environmental regulations have also extensively affected businesses. Following the Air Pollution Control Act of 1962, congress passed laws to control water pollution, require environmental impact statements on construction projects, and control the noise of manufactured products and transportation vehicles. "In more recent years the federal government has also enacted a series of laws emphasizing the development and conservation of energy resources."[84] These laws include the Emergency Petroleum Allocation Act of 1973 and the Federal Energy Administration Act of 1974. In 1977 Congress created the Department of Energy.

The jurisdiction of the economic regulators extended over the specific industry that they regulated, making them responsible for ensuring that their regulations were not so costly as to harm the firms in the industry.[85] The new social regulation of businesses extends over virtually the entire marketplace and they do not have to be concerned with the costs they impose on specific operations.[86] The new regulators become involved in detailed aspects of the firm's production processes often greatly restricting the firm's production choices.[87] Not infrequently, the regulations of different agencies conflict with each other. These characteristics also make it unlikely that any one industry would have an incentive to attempt to capture one of the new social regulatory agencies.

At its peak in the 1970s, the sheer volume of these new social regulations of business was overwhelming. Lilley and Miller report that in the year 1975 alone, 177 proposed new rules appeared, as did 2,865 proposed amendments to existing rules, 309 new final rules, and 7,305 final rule amendments for a total of 10,656 new and proposed rules and amendments, most of which applied to nearly all firms. Between 1970 and 1975, seven new major federal regulatory agencies were created.[88]

The paperwork burden of this regulation is enormous and creates an unintended side effect. The regulatory costs are less than proportional to the size of the firm, penalizing smaller institutions and rewarding bigger ones, potentially leading to more concentrated industries and larger unions.[89] By the 1970s there were rapidly growing complaints from all types of businesses about the escalating burden of paperwork. In 1977 a national commission on paperwork estimated that the burden of regulatory paperwork cost the nation over $100 billion annually—or nearly $500 per capita. Business organizations were filling out an estimated ten billion sheets of paper annually by the end of the 1970s.[90]

In addition to paperwork, the regulations imposed additional costs on firms. In 1976 the Council on Environmental Quality estimated that EPA regulations would cost the economy an extra $40 billion per year by 1984,[91] and in the same year an OSHA-commissioned study found that its own noise regulations under consideration would impose capital costs of $18.5 billion on firms, with billions of dollars more in annual operating costs.[92]

As Murray Weidenbaum says, "Only a Scrooge or misanthrope would quarrel with the intent of the new wave of federal regulation—safer working conditions, better products for the consumer, elimination of discrimination in employment, reduction of environmental pollution, and so forth."[93] The regulations have yielded benefits to consumers, employees, and firms and opened up new opportunities for some. These points are not disputed. What is at issue are the costs of these regulations relative to their benefits.

The critics argue that there is a tendency for the marginal costs of the new social regulation of businesses to exceed the marginal benefits for two reasons. First, because the new agencies do not regulate all of a firm's activities, it becomes harder to measure the benefits of regulation relative to the costs. Second, Lilley and Miller argue that the regulation costs much more than it should and offer the following reasons for this. First, many decisions are reached on the basis of grossly inadequate information. Second, even when information is available, "decisions do not necessarily reflect rational judgment concerning costs and benefits." Regulators may use extreme and unrealistic assumptions to conclude that a regulation's benefits cover its costs. And often little attempt is made to trade off costs and benefits. "Finally, in all too many cases there is strong resistance to considering alternative and sometimes truly innovative approaches."[94] They argue that much of the problem lies with the decision makers at the regulatory agencies because such agencies tend to attract personnel who "believe" in the regulation. "The risk-aversion and security-consciousness of government regulators cause them to try to avoid criticism, which in turn breeds rigidity and inflexibility."[95] Though Lilley and Miller first put forth this argument in 1977, there was little evidence of changes in this situation in the 1980s.

GOVERNMENT AND THE ECONOMY: A PERSONAL ASSESSMENT

This chapter began with a description of the three roles of government, the traditional night watchman's role, reshaping private behavior and redistributing income, and stabilizing economic activity. The first role, based as it is in the Constitution, remains strong in American society. Though there has been some erosion in private property rights, these still remain the firm basis of our free market system. No stronger evidence in support of the importance of private property rights and free markets can be found than the collapse of the centrally planned communist economies of Eastern Europe and the former Soviet Union. Whatever its other flaws, a private property, free-market economy can outproduce any alternative system. And those private property rights also support the democratic societies of the free world.[96]

Many government policies to eliminate poverty—most of which have not worked—require redistributive policies that often conflict with private property rights. The new social regulations on businesses have imposed enormous costs, and it is far from clear that the marginal benefits have exceeded these marginal costs. Many have argued that these new regulations have reduced and often even eliminated productivity growth in the affected industries and that this is a major reason for the slower growth of real incomes and the sharp reduction in the growth of real wages in the 1970s and 1980s.

The federal government's continuing deficits have to be financed by Federal Reserve System purchases or by borrowing through the private credit markets. To the extent that the Federal Reserve System monetizes some of the deficit, the money stock is increased faster, and there is a faster rate of price inflation. But, in the 1980s more of the debt was purchased by the private sector. Overall, this has to divert scarce savings away from productive investment and into federal government spending—spending that does not create additional productive capital. And this has to reduce the real rate of economic growth. Thus, a second reason for the slower rate of economic growth in the late 1970s and 1980s is a relative reduction in the rate of capital formation.

Greater variability in the rate of economic growth has also reappeared with the severe recessions of 1974–75 and 1981–82 and the long recession at the beginning of the 1990s. As a practical matter it has become clear that fiscal policies cannot be used in a discretionary manner to stabilize economic activity. The lags in the recognition of changes in economic activity and in the effective enactment of changes in discretionary spending and taxing policies worsen rather than ameliorate economic fluctuations. And a considerable number of economists doubt whether fiscal policy fundamentally can exert stabilizing influences. Monetary policy has generally been a destabilizing influence for most of the postwar period. In their attempts to lean against the wind in the 1970s, the Fed brought on greater rates of price inflation and destabilized economic activity, resulting in the severe 1981–82 recession. Both Monetarists and Austrians have long argued that because changes in the stock of money have such powerful effects that are unpredictable in their timing, the best policy is to maintain a low, constant rate of growth of the stock of money or, according to the Austrians, to hold the stock of money constant. In this scenario, government, in its fiscal and monetary policies, has been the major source of economic instability in the postwar period.

Few would argue that we do not need governments at the national, state, and local levels. The questions are how large those governments should be and in what activities they should be engaged. If we wish to maximize the welfare of all of our citizens, then clearly governments should only engage in activities for which the marginal benefits exceed the marginal costs. The real question, with which we are still grappling, is how to identify and measure those costs and benefits.

SELECTED REFERENCES

Anderson, Martin. Welfare: *The Political Economy of Welfare Reform in the United States.* Stanford, CA: Hoover Institution Press, 1978.

Asch, Peter. *Consumer Safety Regulation: Putting a Price on Life and Limb.* New York: Oxford University Press, 1988.

Barr, Nicholas. "Economic Theory and the Welfare State: A Survey and Interpretation." *Journal of Economic Literature* 30 (June 1992): 741–803.

Barro, Robert J. "Are Government Bonds Net Wealth?" *Journal of Political Economy* 82 (November/December 1974): 1095–1117.

__________. *The Impact of Social Security on Private Savings.* Washington, D.C.: American Enterprise Insitute, 1977.

Bartlett, Bruce T. *Reagonomics: Supply-Side Economics in Action.* Westport, CT: Arlington House, 1981.

Berger, Suzanne, ed. *The Utilisation of the Social Sciences in Policy-Making in the United States.* Paris: OECD, 1980.

Campagna, Anthony S. *U.S. National Economic Policy, 1917–1985.* Westport, CT: Praeger, 1987.

Cromartie, Michael. *Gaining Ground: New Approaches to Poverty and Dependency,* Ethics and Public Policy Essay no. 60. Washington, D.C.: Ethics and Public Policy Center, August 1985.

Degen, Robert A. *The American Monetary System: A Concise Survey of Its Evolution Since 1896.* Lexingon, MA: Lexington Books, 1987.

Feldstein, Martin. "Toward a Reform of Social Security." *The Public Interest,* Summer 1975.

__________. "Social Security, Induced Retirement, and Aggregate Capital Accumulation." *Journal of Political Economy* 82 (September/October 1974): 905–26.

Ferrara, Peter J. *Social Security: The Inherent Contradiction.* San Francisco: The Cato Institute, 1980.

Fink, Richard H., ed. *Supply-Side Economics: A Critical Appraisal.* Frederick, MD: Alethia Books, University Publications of America, 1982.

Friedman, Milton, and Anna Jacobson Schwartz. *A Monetary History of the United States, 1867–1960.* Princeton, NJ: Princeton University Press for the National Bureau of Economic Research, 1963.

Gordon, Robert J. "The Response of Wages and Prices to the First Two Years of Controls." *Brookings Papers on Economic Activity* 3 (1973): 777–78.

Harrington, Michael. *The Other America.* New York: Macmillan, 1962.

Higgs, Robert. *Crisis and Leviathan: Critical Episodes in the Growth of American Government.* New York: Oxford University Press, 1987.

Hughes, Jonathan. *American Economic History,* 3d ed. Glenview, IL: Scott Foresman/Little Brown Higher Education, 1990.

Kershaw, David, and Jerilyn Fair. *The New Jersey Income-Maintenance Experiment.* Institute for Research on Poverty Monograph Series. Vol. 1. New York: Academic Press, 1976.

Kimzey, Bruce W. *Reagonomics.* St. Paul, MN: West Publishing Co., 1983.

Laffer, Arthur B., and Jan P. Seymour, eds. *The Economics of the Tax Revolt.* New York: Harcourt Brace Jovanovich, 1979.

Lilley, William, III, and James C. Miller III. "The New 'Social Regulation.' " *The Public Interest* 47 (Spring 1977): 49–61.

Miringoff, Marc L., and Sandra Opdycke. *American Social Welfare Policy: Reassessment and*

Reform. Englewood Cliffs, NJ: Prentice-Hall, 1986.

Moffit, Robert A. "The Negative Income Tax: Would It Discourage Work?" *Monthly Labor Review* 104 (April 1981): 23–27.

Munnell, Alicia H. *The Future of Social Security.* Washington, D.C.: The Brookings Institution, 1977.

__________. "The Impact of Social Security on Personal Savings." *National Tax Journal* 27 (December 1974): 553–67.

__________. *The Economics of Private Pension Savings.* Washington, D.C.: The Brookings Institution, 1982.

Murray, Charles. *Losing Ground: American Social Policy, 1950–1980.* New York: Basic Books, 1984.

Rockoff, Hugh. *Drastic Measures: A History of Wage and Price Controls in the United States.* New York: Cambridge University Press, 1984.

Spulber, Nicolas. *Managing the American Economy from Roosevelt to Reagan.* Bloomington, IN: Indiana University Press, 1989.

Stein, Herbert. *The Fiscal Revolution in America.* Chicago: University of Chicago Press, 1969.

Weidenbaum, Murray L. *Business, Government, and the Public,* 2d ed. Englewood Cliffs, NJ: Prentice-Hall, 1981.

NOTES

1. Robert Higgs, *Crisis and Leviathan: Critical Episodes in the Growth of American Government* (New York: Oxford University Press, 1987).
2. At both the state and local and, particularly, the federal level, net interest payments to holders of government debt is included. Similarly, transfers to foreigners by the federal government, though small, are also included. Therefore, the government expenditures, excluding transfers to persons, includes more than the direct purchase of goods and services by governments.
3. It should be noted that purchases of government debt by government accounts is something of a shell game. Fundamentally all that is occurring is that rather than increasing federal personal and corporate income taxes, excise taxes, customs duties, and so forth to finance some of the growing federal expenditures, these are being financed by growing social insurance taxes, and the federal securities are substituted for this money in the trust accounts.
4. This discussion of stabilization policies is drawn primarily from the following sources: Anthony S. Campagna, *U.S. National Economic Policy, 1917–1985* (Westport, CT: Praeger, 1987); Robert A. Degen, *The American Monetary System: A Concise Survey of Its Evolution Since 1896* (Lexington, MA: Lexington Books, 1987); Milton Friedman and Anna Jacobson Schwartz, *A Monetary History of the United States, 1867–1960* (Princeton, NJ: Princeton University Press for the NBER, 1963); Nocolas Spulber, *Managing the American Economy from Roosevelt to Reagan* (Bloomington, IN: Indiana University Press, 1989); Herbert Stein, *The Fiscal Revolution in America* (Chicago: University of Chicago Press, 1969).
5. Campagna, *U.S. National Economic Policy*, 196.
6. Spulber, *Managing the American Economy,* 25. The terms Keynesian and Monetarist will be used frequently in the following discussion. Refer to Chapter 7 for an explanation of these terms.
7. Richard Gardner, *Sterling-Dollar Diplomacy* (New York: Oxford University Press, 1956),

as cited in Jonathan Hughes, *American Economic History*, 3d ed. (Glenview, IL: Scott, Foresman/Little Brown Higher Education, 1990), 524–25.

8. Campagna, *U.S. Economic Policy*, 196.
9. Ibid., 198, 210.
10. Stein, *The Fiscal Revolution in America*, chapter 9.
11. Ibid., 241.
12. Friedman and Schwartz, *A Monetary History of the United States*, 625.
13. See Stein *The Fiscal Revolution in America,* 241–80.
14. Friedman and Schwartz, *A Monetary History of the United States*, 625.
15. Stein, *The Fiscal Revolution in America*, 281.
16. Degen, *The American Monetary System*, 122. The comprehensive examination of monetary policy in the 1950s is Daniel S. Ahearn, *Federal Reserve Policy Reappraised, 1951–1959* (New York: Columbia University Press, 1963).
17. Stein, *The Fiscal Revolution in America*, 452–53.
18. Ibid., 137–38.
19. Ibid., 143.
20. Campagna, *U.S. Economic Policy*, 345.
21. Degen, *The American Monetary System*, 152–53.
22. Campagna, *U.S. National Economic Policy*, 362.
23. Ibid., 362.
24. Campagna, *U.S. Economic Policy*, 375–76; Hugh Rockoff, *Drastic Measures: A History of Wage and Price Controls in the United States* (New York: Cambridge University Press, 1984), 210–12.
25. Robert J. Gordon, "The Response of Wages and Prices to the First Two Years of Controls," *Brookings Papers on Economic Activity* 3 (1973): 777–78, as cited in Campagna, *U.S. Economic Policy,* 379–80.
26. Rockoff, *Drastic Measures,* 233.
27. Degen, *The American Monetary System,* 159.
28. Ibid., 160–61.
29. Alan Blinder estimates that most of the spending that arose from the rebates and tax reductions occurred in 1976, not 1975, so that there was no fiscal stimulus until the recovery was well underway. (Alan Blinder, *Economic Activity and the Great Stagflation* (New York: Academic Press, 1979), 164–65, as cited in Campagna, *U.S. National Economic Policy*, 401.)
30. Because the federal government had to enter the credit market to borrow the funds to reduce and rebate taxes to consumers, the stimulus arising from the additional spending due to the rebates would only offset the reduced spending due to the crowding out of borrowers in the credit markets as interest rates rose to reallocate funds from private market borrowers to the federal government.
31. Degen, *The American Monetary System*, 162.
32. Ibid., 163–64.
33. The Kemp-Roth tax cut bill of 1977 proposed substantial cuts in federal income tax rates. In 1978 the Steiger-Hansen tax bill sought to roll back capital gains taxes from the then 49.1 percent rate to the pre-1969 rate of 25 percent. In June of 1978, California voters approved Proposition 13, the Jarvis-Gann Initiative, to roll back California property taxes and limit future increases; within a few years Massachusetts voters approved a similar type of property tax initiative. For a discussion of these, see the papers in Sections 2, 4, and 5 in Arthur B. Laffer and Jan P. Seymour, eds., *The Economics of the Tax Revolt* (New York: Harcourt

Brace Jovanovich, 1979).

34. On "Reaganomics," see Bruce T. Bartlett, *Reagonomics: Supply-Side Economics in Action* (Westport, CT: Arlington House, 1981); and Bruce W. Kimzey, *Reaganomics* (St. Paul, MN: West Publishing Co., 1983).
35. In 1982 the Reagan administration retreated somewhat with the Tax Equity and Fiscal Responsibility Act.
36. Because personal exemptions were eliminated for higher income taxpayers, there was a range of taxable incomes where the marginal income tax rate was effectively 33 percent.
37. The Depository Institutions Deregulation and Monetary Control Act of 1980 and the Garn-St. Germain Depository Institutions Act of 1982.
38. Degen, *The American Monetary System*, 191–92.
39. Murray L. Weidenbaum, *Business, Government, and the Public*, 2d ed. (Englewood Cliffs, NJ: Prentice-Hall, 1981), chapter 2.
40. Most of the following discussion is drawn from Peter J. Ferrara, *Social Security: The Inherent Contradiction* (San Francisco: The Cato Institute, 1980). A shorter version can be found in Peter J. Ferrara, *Social Security: Averting the Crisis* (San Francisco: The Cato Institute Studies in Domestic Issues, 1982).
41. Ferrara discusses this in some detail in *Social Security*, 17–27.
42. The Social Security Administration has continued to confuse this by claiming that the employee pays only one half the tax while the employer pays the other, implying that the employee's contribution to the social security programs is only one half of the amount actually paid. This is, of course, nonsense. The worker bears directly and indirectly the entire OASDHI payroll tax.
43. In each of these cases, the direct employee payroll tax rate is one half of the total rate.
44. Ferrara, *Social Security: The Inherent Contradiction*, 3.
45. Ibid., 53–60.
46. Douglas Munro, "Welfare Component and Labor Supply Effects of OASDHI Retirement Benefits," (Ph.D. diss., Ohio State University, 1976), as cited in Ferrara, *Social Security: The Inherent Contradiction*, 55.
47. The 1977 amendments indexed average monthly earnings (AIME) and changed the primary insurance amount formula to 90 percent of the first $180 of the AIME, 32 percent of the next $905 of the AIME, and 15 percent of the rest. Ferrara, *Social Security: The Inherent Contradiction*, 55.
48. Ibid., 56.
49. Ibid., appendix tables 20–21.
50. The Social Security Administration has consistently used false and misleading statements to misrepresent the program to the public in an effort to gain general support. Prior to 1965 their publications stated that Americans contributed to special trust funds and benefits were paid *from* those segregated trust funds when the worker retired, died, or was disabled. This, of course, was an outright lie, and intense criticism caused the SSA to alter the statement so that this was implied but not actually stated. The Social Security Administration's misinformation campaign has, however, led many workers to believe that their OASDHI contributions are being accumulated in a trust fund that they can draw on at retirement or in the event of disability. In a 1960 Supreme Court decision that upheld the SSA's elimination of benefits to the wife of a deported communist who had long paid Social Security taxes, an outraged Justice Hugo Black railed at the SSA's misinformation campaign. (See *Your Social Security*, HEW Publication, N. (SSA) 76–10035, June, 1976, as cited in Ferrara, *Social Security: The Inherent Contradiction*, 66. The SSA's misleading assertions are dis-

cussed in detail in Ferrara, 66–74.)

51. See the following papers by Martin Feldstein: "Toward a Reform of Social Security," *The Public Interest* (Summer 1975), and "Social Security, Induced Retirement, and Aggregate Capital Accumulation," *Journal of Political Economy* 82 (September-October 1974): 905–26.
52. See the following studies by Alicia H. Munnell: *The Future of Social Security* (Washington, D.C.: Brookings Institution, 1977), "The Impact of Social Security on Personal Savings," *National Tax Journal* 27 (December 1974): 553–67, and *The Economics of Private Pensions* (Washington, D.C.: The Brookings Institution, 1982).
53. See Robert J. Barro, "Are Government Bonds Net Wealth?" *Journal of Political Economy* 82 (November/December 1974): 1095–1117, and *The Impact of Social Security on Private Savings* (Washington, D.C.: American Enterprise Institute, 1977).
54. For example, see Nicholas Barr, "Economic Theory and the Welfare State: A Survey and Interpretation," *Journal of Economic Literature* 30 (June 1992): 741–803.
55. Charles Murray, *Losing Ground: American Social Policy, 1950–1980* (New York: Basic Books, Inc., 1984), 16. Most of this section draws upon Murray's seminal study. Murray suggests that the roots of this can be traced to the Poor Laws of Elizabethan England.
56. Ibid., 16.
57. Ibid., 17.
58. Though the illegitimacy rate had risen from 4.5 percent to 5.3 percent, or by 17.8 percentage points, between 1955 and 1960, this was still far lower than it was later to become. (Ibid., pp. 18–19.) Murray discusses this in some detail, especially the largely unjustified focus on black families on AFDC.
59. The publication of Michael Harrington's *The Other America* in 1962 is often credited with igniting the War on Poverty and was widely read by members of the Kennedy and the Johnson administrations, though, of course, other forces were simultaneously at work. (Michael Harrington, *The Other America* (New York: Macmillan, 1962); other influential works were Richard Cloward and Lloyd Ohlin, *Delinquency and Opportunity* (Glencoe, IL: Free Press, 1960); and Dwight MacDonald, "Our Invisible Poor," *The New Yorker*, 19 January, 1963.]
60. Marc L. Miringoff and Sandara Opdycke, *American Social Welfare Policy: Reassessment and Reform* (Englewood Cliffs, NJ: Prentice-Hall, 1986), 62.
61. "Means tested" indicates that to be eligible, individuals or families had to fall below a threshold income (or sometimes asset) level.
62. Murray, *Losing Ground*, 40.
63. Women heading households with small children, the unskilled, and those discriminated against because of race, age, sex, or religion would not share in the fruits of economic growth.
64. Ibid., 244.
65. Ibid., 47.
66. Ibid., 48.
67. Ibid., 242–43.
68. With a negative income tax, if a person's income drops below a specified level (typically the poverty level) the government pays the person enough (i.e., *negative* taxes) to bring his/her income up to the specified level. Only when the person's income rises above the specified level does (s)he begin paying taxes into the government rather than receiving taxes.
69. Ibid., 150.

70. Ibid.
71. Ibid., 151.
72. These results certainly understate the magnitude of the effects. (Ibid., 153.) On the origins of the NIT see Hugh Heclo and Martin Rein, "Social Science and Negative Income Taxation," in Suzanne Berger, ed., *The Utilisation of the Social Sciences in Policy-Making in the United States* (Paris: OECD, 1980); and Martin Anderson, *Welfare: The Political Economy of Welfare Reform in the United States* (Stanford, CA: Hoover Institution Press, 1978). The fall 1980 issue of the *Journal of Human Resources* was devoted entirely to the NIT results. Also see: David Kershaw and Jerilyn Fair, *The New Jersey Income-Maintenance Experiment*, Institute for Research on Poverty Monograph Series, vol. 1 (New York: Academic Press, 1976); and Robert A. Moffit, "The Negative Income Tax: Would It Discourage Work?" *Monthly Labor Review* 104 (April 1981): 23–27.
73. These data are taken from Murray, *Losing Ground*, chapters 4–10.
74. There is a continuing debate about the reasons for this. In his seminal book, *Losing Ground*, Charles Murray attributed these distressing results to the unintended negative consequences of good intentions. He contended that federal policy makers of the 1960s and 1970s did not take into account three essentially correct premises of the popular wisdom: People do respond to incentives and disincentives (or, the carrot and the stick *do* work); people are not inherently hard working or moral; and people must be held responsible for their actions. (Murray, *Losing Ground*, p. 146.) His book provoked a vigorous response. See Robert Royal, "Charles Murray and his Critics," in Michael Cromartie, ed., *Gaining Ground: New Approaches to Poverty and Dependency*, Ethics and Public Policy Essay no. 60, (Washington, D.C.: Ethics and Public Policy Center, August 1985), 25.
75. Weidenbaum, *Business, Government and the Public*, 20.
76. Weidenbaum, *Business, Government, and the Public*, 16. This section draws upon Weidenbaum and the following two studies: William Lilley III and James C. Miller III, "The New 'Social' Regulation," *The Public Interest* 47 (Spring 1977): 49–61; Peter Asch, *Consumer Safety Regulation: Putting a Price on Life and Limb* (New York: Oxford University Press, 1988).
77. Weidenbaum, *Business, Government, and the Public*, 17.
78. Ibid., 12–14.
79. In *Consumer Safety Regulation*, chapter 3, Peter Asch extensively discusses the inadequate consumer information rationale for consumer safety regulation.
80. Forty-six major consumer safety and business regulation laws were passed between 1962 and 1978. These are listed in tables in the following two books. Murray L. Weidenbaum, *Business, Government, and the Public*, 2d ed. (Englewood Cliffs, NJ: Prentice-Hall, 1981), table 1–1, pp. 8–10; and, Peter Asch, *Consumer Safety Regulation: Putting a Price on Life and Limb* (New York: Oxford University Press, 1988), table 1.2, p. 6.
81. In the early 1960s a new sedative, Thalidomide, came on the market. It soon became clear that women who used Thalidomide while pregnant were likely to give birth to children with deformities, and the drug was withdrawn from the market. The belief that this would not have occurred if Thalidomide had been more extensively tested prior to marketing, brought about the amendments to the Food and Drug Act.
82. Weidenbaum, *Business, Government, and the Public*, 7.
83. The Americans with Disabilities Act, which went into effect in the middle of 1992, outlawed discrimination against the handicapped and also greatly expanded the definition of handicapped status.
84. Weidenbaum, *Business, Government, and the Public*, 10–11.

85. Ibid., 18.
86. Ibid., 19–20.
87. Lilley and Miller, "The New 'Social' Regulation," 53.
88. Lilley and Miller, "The New Social Regulation," 51.
89. Ibid.
90. Weidenbaum, Business, Government, and the Public, 198.
91. Council on Environmental Quality, *Environmental Quality: Seventh Annual Report* (Washington, D.C.: U.S. Government Printing Office, 1976), 145, as cited in Lilley and Miller, "The New 'Social' Regulation," 51.
92. Bolt, Beranek and Newman, Inc., *Economic Impact Analysis of Proposed Noise Control Regulations* (Washington, D.C.: OSHA, 1976), as cited in Lilley and Miller, "The New 'Social' Regulations," 51.
93. Weidenbaum, *Business, Government, and the Public*, 21.
94. Lilley and Miller, "The New 'Social' Regulation," 56.
95. Ibid., 59.
96. Some, in fact, argue that economic freedom and political freedom are essentially inseparable.

CHAPTER 16

The American Achievement

At the beginning of the 1990s, the communist economies of the Soviet Union and most of Eastern Europe collapsed. The Berlin Wall was torn down, and East and West Germany reunited. The Soviet Union and Czechoslovakia splintered into largely autonomous nation-states, while Poland, Hungary, and Rumania began a long march toward establishing market economies. Yugoslavia was torn apart by long submerged ethnic strife, and, on the other side of the world, China appeared to be taking a few tentative steps toward allowing some free markets to operate. Though dogmatic communist societies continued to exist, it appeared that the long experiment in establishing them was winding down.

The siren song of communism was always that it could establish a classless society—a society whose members produced up to and according to their ability while receiving what they needed independently of what they had produced. In practice, these societies were never able to divorce production and income, but they did eliminate private property in an attempt to equalize incomes. However, these changes required the creation of a police state and the reduction of individual freedom.

These societies failed because their citizens wanted more freedom and because they simply were not very good at producing consumer goods and services. Their output was low and grew slowly, and the quality of what was produced was, by any standard, shoddy. By Western standards many communist industrial areas were environmental disasters. Today there can be no question about the ability of a market-directed economy to outproduce other economic systems. By harnessing self-interest and initiative, market directed economies lead individuals and firms to produce more and better goods and services.

This continues to leave open the question of how market economies distribute income among their citizens. Did the United States, as a market-based economy, tend to create greater inequalities in the distribution of income? Another issue is the current economic status of the United States vis-à-vis other countries. Is the United States growing more slowly, and has it been surpassed in per capita incomes by other economically advanced countries, such as Japan and West Germany? These are the issues we will examine in this concluding chapter.

THE DISTRIBUTION OF INCOME

Stanley Lebergott has noted that the distribution of "power, prestige, and pelf" has been a constant concern in almost all societies.[1] In the past this could be measured in fairly simple terms by counting the number of acres (or slaves) one owned, the number of serfs controlled, or the size of flocks or herds of livestock. Technological changes have created geographic and social mobility in modern industrial societies making such measures inadequate to determine status. Today ones money income relative to others is the primary indicator of status, and changes in the size (or personal) distribution of income the primary aggregate measure of changing equality.

The distribution of income can also be measured by examining the shares of income received by productive resources—the functional distribution of income. The concern with status and equality focuses the analysis on the size distribution of income. However, the two are not independent. The highest income households usually receive a larger share of their income as property income, because labor income tends to be much more equally distributed. If the share of property income in total income tends to, say, rise, then often this suggests increasing inequality in the size distribution of income.

The Functional Distribution of Income

In broad terms the shares that are of interest are the share of income received as compensation for labor services and the share of income received as compensation for nonhuman, or property, services. These two categories are usually termed *employee compensation* and *property income*. However, when examining functional income shares for more than the corporate business sector, there is a third category for the income of unincorporated enterprises—*entrepreneurial* or *proprietors income*. This represents returns to both property and labor, but the share of each cannot be separated from the total.[2]

Figure 16.1 presents shares of all national income received by resource owners for overlapping decadal averages since the beginning of this century.[3] These data are available on an annual basis beginning in 1929 and are shown in Figure 16.2. There are similar long-term trends of a rising share of employee compensation and a declining share of proprietors' income. It is possible that these trends are influenced by the growing size of governments because they generate only employee compensation—no property income. To compensate, we can examine the functional shares for national income originating in the domestic business sector. This excludes the income originating in government, households, nonprofit institutions, and in the rest of the world. These are shown in Figure 16.3.

Though the levels of the shares change somewhat the general trends are the same. Property income's share has varied around 20 percent with no trend, while labor's share has generally risen or fallen inversely to the proprietors' share. Property income is composed of corporate profits, rental income of persons, and net interest. Corporate profits as a share of all national income declined from 14.3 percent in 1950 to 8 percent in 1980 and to 7.2 percent in 1990. In contrast, net interest rose from 1.7 percent of all national income in 1950 to 9.1 percent in 1980 and 11 percent in 1990. Rental income of persons was 3 percent or more from 1950 to 1965 and then began falling to become a −0.2 percent in 1989. Therefore, though property income's share was roughly constant, its components' shares were not. For employee compensation, wages and salaries declined slightly from 62.2 percent of all national income in 1950 to 61.4 percent in 1990, while supplements to wages and salaries rose from 3.3 percent in 1950 to 12.4 percent of all national income in 1990. Within proprietors' income, farm proprietors' share of all national income fell from 5.8 percent in 1950 to 1 percent in 1990, while

Fig. 16.1 Income Distribution by Functional Shares: All National Income (Overlapping Decadal Averages)

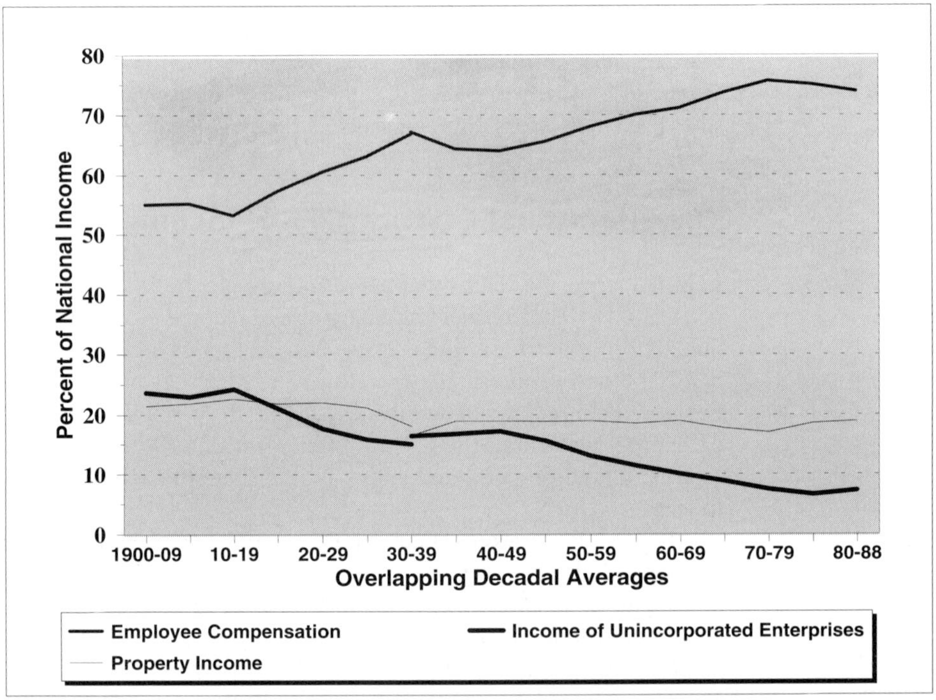

Sources: *Historical Statistics of the United States* (Washington, D.C.: U.S. Government Printing Office, 1976), and *Statistical Abstract of the United States* (Washington, D.C.: U.S. Government Printing Office, various years).

nonfarm proprietors' share fell somewhat less from 10.5 percent in 1950 to 7 percent in 1985 and then rose back to 7.4 percent in 1990. Unfortunately, proprietors' incomes (or the incomes of unincorporated enterprises) are actually composed of income going to property and to labor, and we have no idea how this was distributed between the two or if and how the distribution changed over time.

We can accurately say how the shares of income between labor and capital changed over time if we examine only the national income originating in the corporate business sector, and this is shown in Figure 16.4. During the Great Depression property income fell as low as zero, then rose sharply during the Second World War. After the war property income's share began to fall and generally fell through the mid-1970s. Since then property income's share has tended to rise. This increase to the mid-1970s in labor's share of national income originating in the corporate business sector suggests that, all else the same, there should have been some increase in the equality of the size distribution of income. The decline since the mid-1970s suggests that some increase in inequality in the size distribution of income should be seen.

Fig. 16.2 Income Distribution by Functional Shares: All National Income

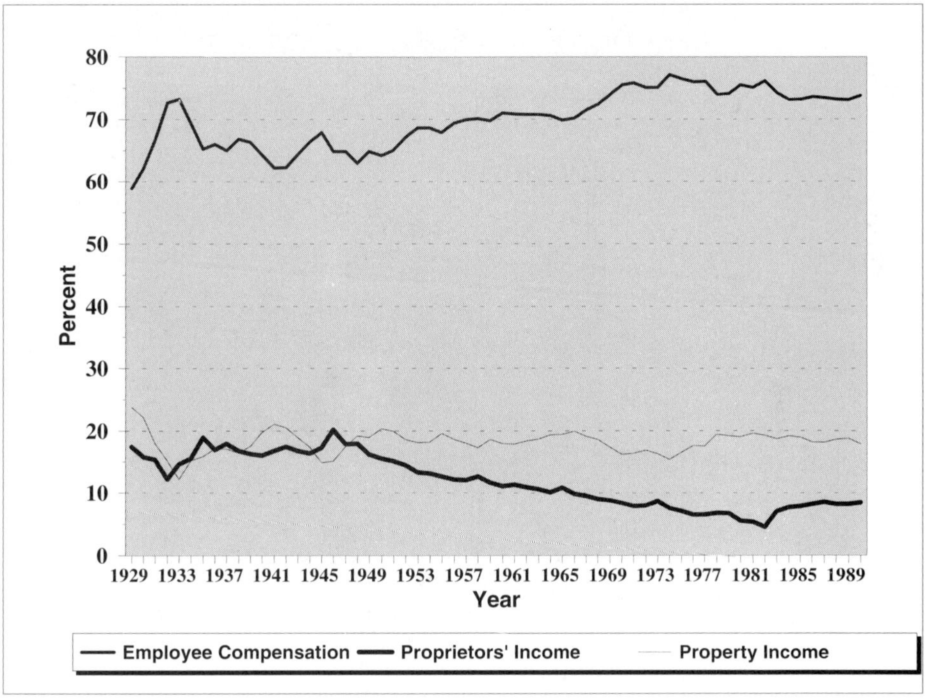

Sources: *Historical Statistics of the United States* (Washington, D.C.: U.S. Government Printing Office, 1976), and *Statistical Abstract of the United States* (Washington, D.C.: U.S. Government Printing Office, various years).

The Size (or Personal) Distribution of Income

The size distribution of income is often used as a welfare measure. Frequently, an increase in equality in the income distribution is considered desirable even though we cannot, in fact, conclude this without agreed-upon measures for interpersonal utility comparisons.[4] There are two usual methods to evaluate the size distribution of income. In the first, the federal government reports by quintiles the percentage share of money income received by families as well as the percentage of income received by the top 5 percent of the nation's families based on money income. If the data are less aggregated, another method can be used. A *Lorenz curve* shows the cumulative income share in summing over units from the lowest to the highest income units. The area between the Lorenz curve and the curve of perfect equality indicates the amount of inequality and can be used to assess changes in inequality in the personal income distribution. Because this is a visual measure, it is less precise and can yield ambiguous results. The *Gini coefficient* is a numerical, and more precise, measure of the area between a Lorenz curve and the curve of perfect equality. If one income unit receives all of the income in the society, the value of the Gini coefficient is 1. If all n income units in the society

Fig. 16.3 Income Distribution by Functional Shares: National Income Originating in the Domestic Business Sector

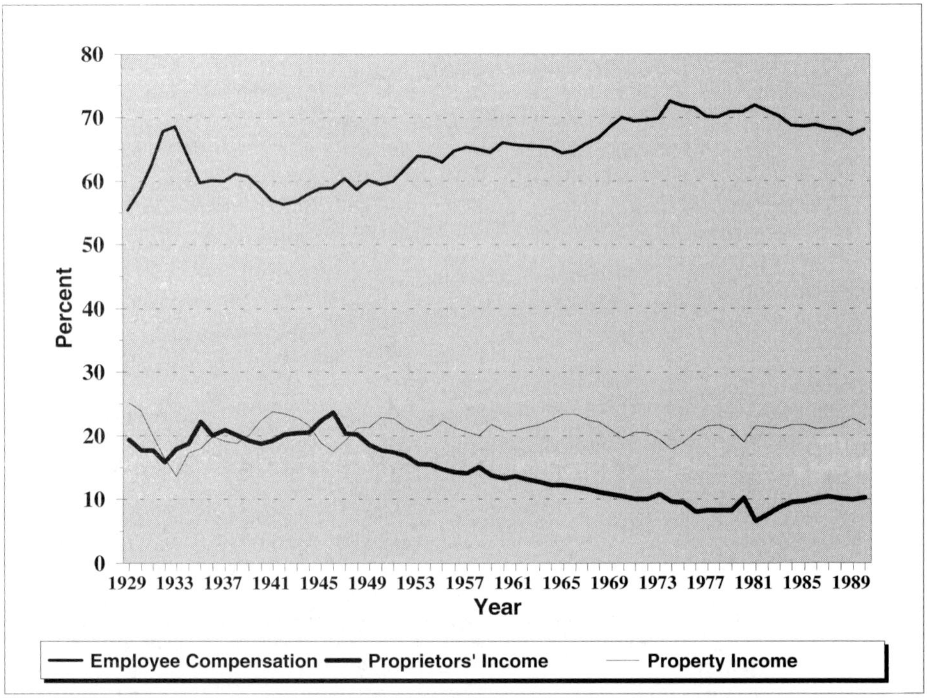

Sources: *Historical Statistics of the United States* (Washington, D.C.: U.S. Government Printing Office, 1976), and *Statistical Abstract of the United States* (Washington, D.C.: U.S. Government Printing Office, various years).

receive exactly *1/n* share of the total income, or equal shares, then the Lorenz curve and the diagonal line of perfect equality match, and the Gini coefficient takes a value of zero. As the Gini coefficient increases toward 1 the inequality in the size distribution of income increases.

The Interwar Period. Unfortunately the interwar data with which we can examine the size distribution of income are woefully weak. Most have concluded that there was growing inequality in the distribution of income in the twenties and growing equality during the thirties, but how much is still a debatable topic. The reported data on federal income taxes provide evidence on how income was distributed among the families and individuals who paid income taxes, but only a small percentage (7 to 15 percent) of families and individuals generally had incomes large enough to be subject to the federal income tax in this period. Thus, the evidence relates to only a small segment in the upper end of the income distribution.

There are two ways to use this data. First, the data can be used to construct *inverse Pareto coefficients*. These measure how the incomes varied among those who paid

Fig. 16.4 Income Distribution by Functional Shares: National Income Originating in the Corporate Business Sector

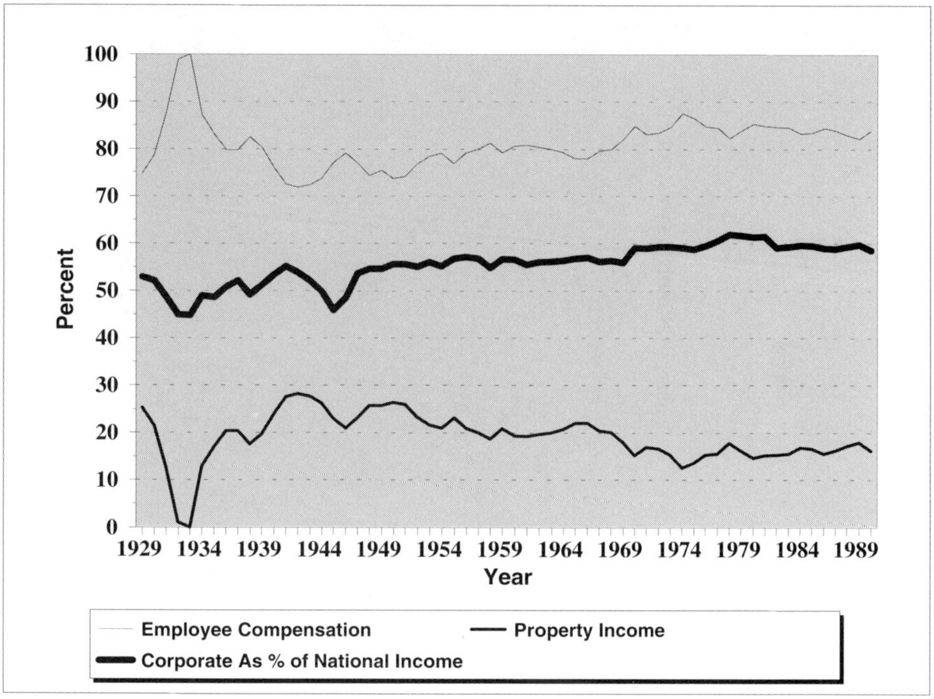

Sources: *Historical Statistics of the United States* (Washington, D.C.: U.S. Government Printing Office, 1976), and *Statistical Abstract of the United States* (Washington, D.C.: U.S. Government Printing Office, various years).

taxes. Lee Soltow has estimated these coefficients, and they are shown in Figure 16.5.[5] These show that inequality *among the highest income recipients* declined from the 1913–19 to the 1920–24 period, rose in the late twenties, and fell through the 1930s. A similarly constructed measure for 1965 shows continued decline.

A second indicator of the interwar income distribution was constructed by Simon Kuznets.[6] He constructed estimates of the shares of disposable income received by various nonfarm percentiles at the upper end of the income distribution and the share received by the lower 93 percent of the nonfarm population. These are shown in Figure 16.6. Kuznets' measure showed a surge in inequality during the prosperous twenties and a rising equality during the depressed thirties.[7]

Charles Holt used the percentile shares developed by Kuznets to construct estimates of nominal and real per capita income during the twenties for the percentiles.[8] Holt found that these shares showed much greater inequality trends in the twenties because the nominal and real per capita incomes of the lower 93 percent of the population declined from 1923 to 1929. These results suggested that rather than just *more* of the increases in income going to the higher income recipients, the higher income recip-

Fig. 16.5 Evidence on U.S. Income Inequality: Inverse Pareto Coefficients.

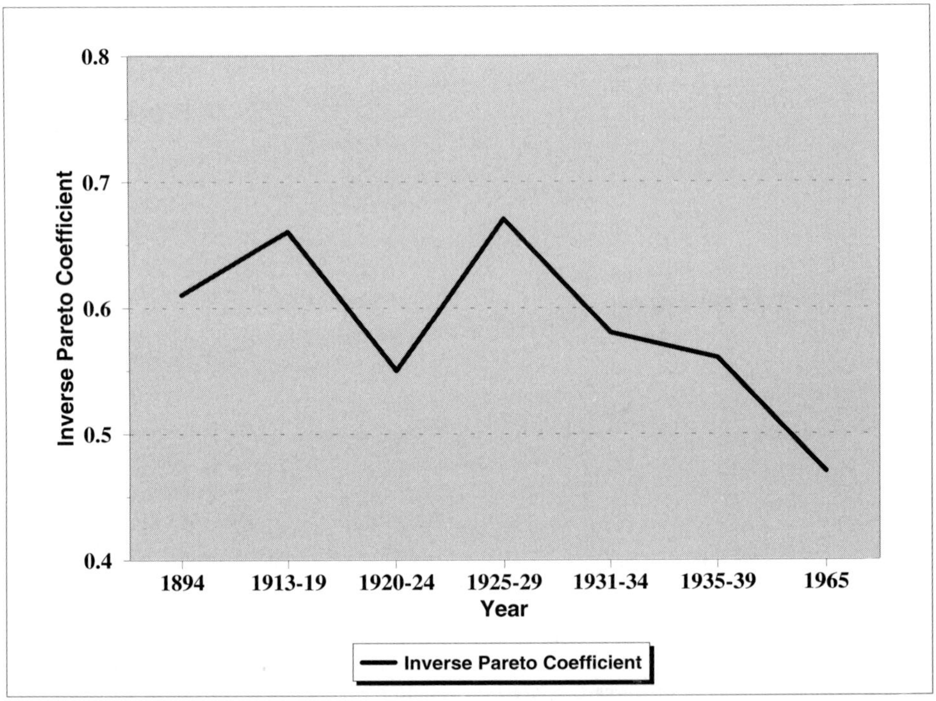

Source: Lee Soltow, "Evidence of Income Inequality in the United States, 1866–1965," *Journal of Economic History* 29 (June 1969): table 2, p. 282.

ients had received *all* of the income gains plus some of the income formerly received by the lower income households. However, as pointed out by Gene Smiley, these estimates are suspect because neither Soltow nor Kuznets corrected for tax avoidance behavior in response to huge variations in income tax rates between 1913 and 1925. As tax rates skyrocketed from 1913 through 1918, higher income individuals sheltered their income from taxes, and as tax rates fell from 1921 through 1925, higher income individuals moved income back into taxable assets. Thus the increase in income reported by higher income taxpayers on their federal taxes overstates the actual increases.[9]

During the First World War there were temporary declines in the share of income going to owners of capital and temporary increases in the share of income going to labor. This would have resulted in more equality in the size distribution of income.[10] The move back to more normal conditions in the twenties would certainly have led to an increase in inequality compared to the 1916–19 period. Although it is likely that there were increases in inequality in the size distribution of income during the twenties, the Soltow and Kuznets measures overstate the decline in inequality from 1913 through the beginning of the twenties and the rise in inequality during the twenties.

Fig. 16.6 Percentage Shares of Kuznets' Disposable Income

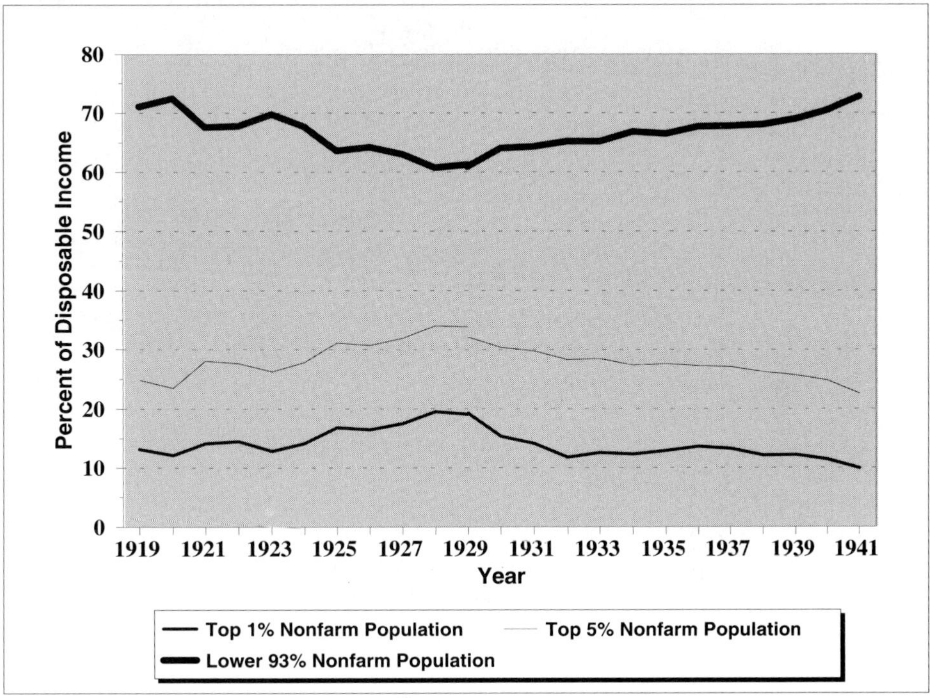

Source: Simon Kuznets, *Shares of Upper Income Groups in Income and Savings* (New York: National Bureau of Economic Research, 1953).

After the apparent rise in personal income inequality in the twenties, most studies agree that the depression of the thirties brought on a trend toward greater equality. Mark Schmitz and Price Fishback have applied Kuznets' procedure to state income estimates for 1929, 1933, and 1939 and found a similar, though much more variable, fall in the income share of the higher income recipients.[11] However, as Louis Cain has pointed out, these equality trends are most likely overstated because they do not correct for the tax avoidance that almost certainly accompanied tax rate increases in the thirties.[12]

The dramatic increase in federal personal income tax rates in 1932 and the increase in the progressiveness of the income tax in 1936 were not major factors in redistributing income in a more equal fashion. Thomas Renaghan has found that the income distribution before and after taxes in 1933 were much the same, just as he has found for 1929.[13] The "soak the rich" tax changes of Roosevelt in 1934, 1935, and 1936 tended to promote more equality in the after-tax income distribution compared to the pre-tax distribution. In 1938 congress repealed the undistributed corporate profits tax and lowered the capital gains tax, and Renaghan has found that the difference between the pre- and post-tax distribution of income was sharply reduced. He also argued that an increased regressivity in the taxes of the lower income classes largely offset the increased progressivity of the taxes on the higher income groups.

Income Distribution during the Forties. Most analyses agree that the trend toward increasing equality in the size distribution of income continued in the forties.[14] Figure 16.7 presents shares of family income by quintiles from 1935–36 to 1950. As can be seen, the share for the highest fifth fell from 1935–36 to 1944 and then was roughly constant, while the shares for lower fifths—especially the second and third fifths—rose. There was little apparent change from 1944 to 1950. In the thirties the equality trend was due to the decline in property incomes—the primary source of income for the highest income recipients. The forties were extremely prosperous rather than depressed, however, due to price controls and increased business taxes, property incomes probably did not rise as much as labor incomes. The high employment and scarcity of labor due to the massive conscription of men of prime working ages meant most jobs were full-time. Wage rate increases were greater for the lowest paying jobs so that incomes rose more for those in the lowest income brackets, where employment

Fig. 16.7 Shares of Family Personal Income Received by Each Fifth of Families and Unattached Individuals

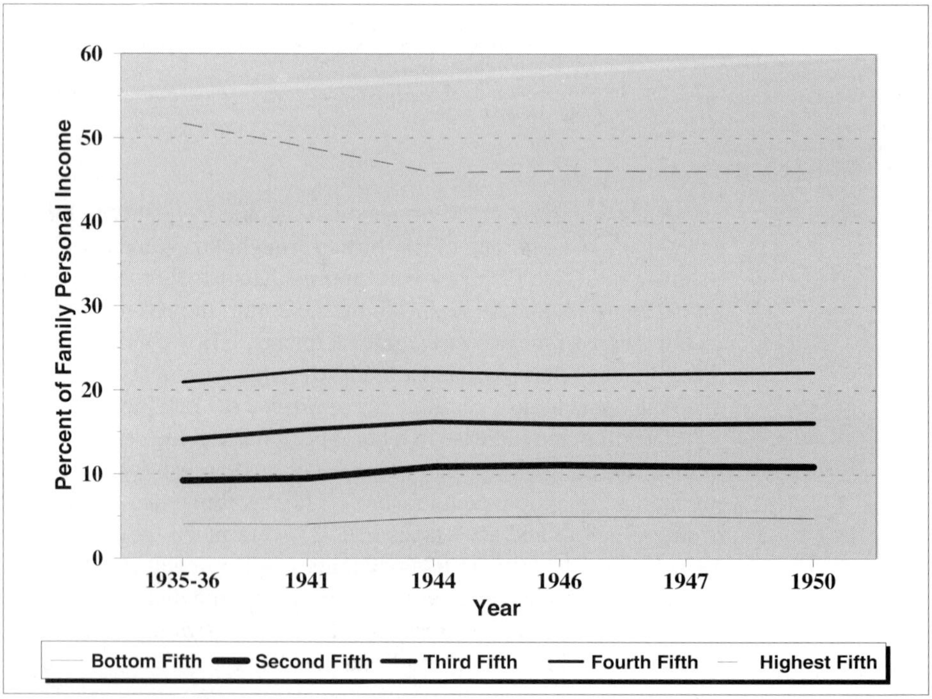

Source: *Historical Statistics of the United States* (Washington, D.C.: U.S. Government Printing Office, 1976).

and income was much more uncertain during the thirties. Finally, during the war farmers enjoyed much higher real incomes than during the twenties and thirties. Because farmers typically have low cash incomes, this relative growth in their incomes during the war years also contributed to declining income inequality.

Income Distribution in the Postwar Period. The trend of increasing equality in the size distribution of income did not continue throughout the postwar period. The quintile shares in Figure 16.8 show little change until the late 1970s, when it appears that inequality began increasing. The Gini coefficients in Figure 16.9 are much more accurate measures of these changes. From 1947 through the end of the 1960s, there is a mild trend of increasing equality, though with considerable variation. From the end of the 1960s through the end of the 1980s, there is a stronger trend of increasing inequality. By the late 1980s, the Gini coefficients show more inequality than existed in 1950.

Poverty measures generally reflect these trends. Poverty was declining during the late 1940s and 1950s.[15] Since 1959, the government has kept measures of poverty in the United States, which are shown in Figures 16.10 through 16.13. The percentage of

Fig. 16.8 Shares of Money Income for Families (data for 1953 through 1962 are for families and unrelated individuals; data for 1963 through 1990 are for families only)

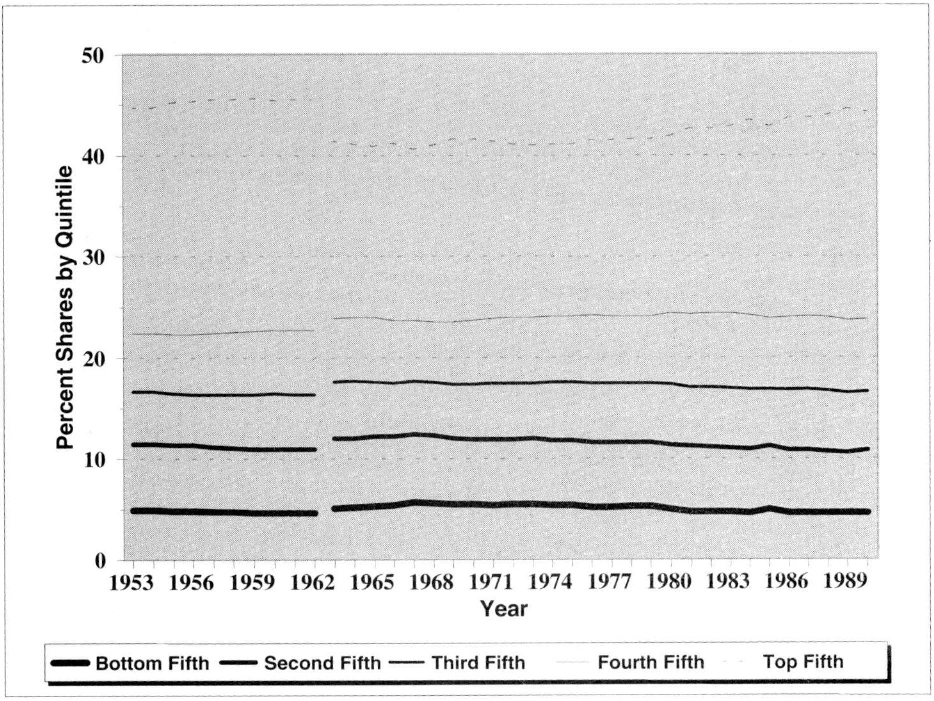

Sources: *Historical Statistics of the United States* (Washington, D.C.: U.S. Government Printing Office, 1976), and *Statistical Abstract of the United States* (Washington D.C.: U.S. Government Printing Office, various years).

Fig. 16.9 Lorenz Gini Coefficients

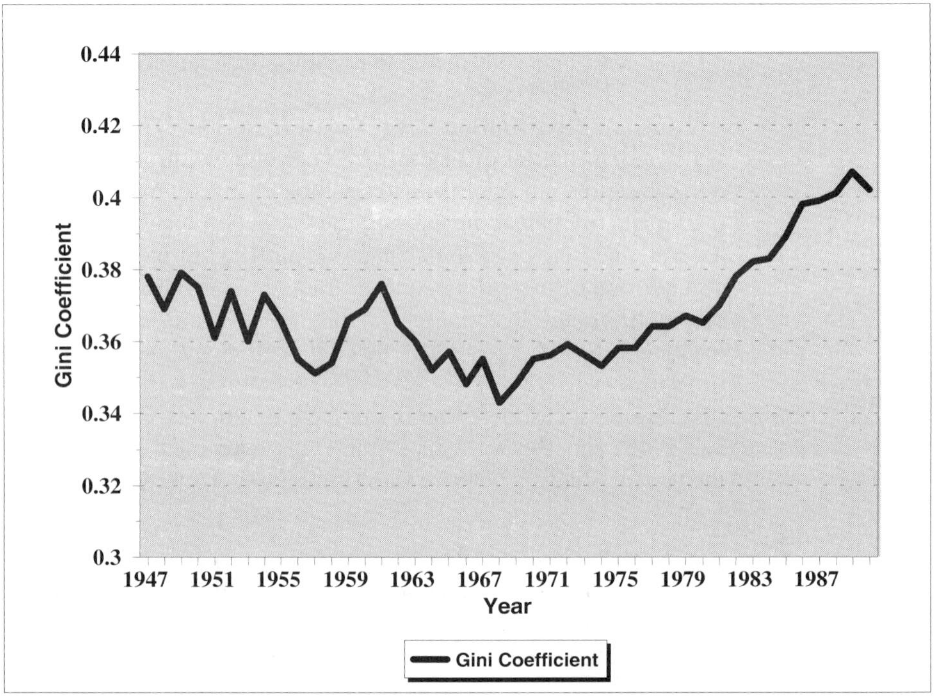

(Lorenz Gini coefficients for 1973 through 1990 are adjusted to be consistent with the Lorenz Gini coefficients for 1947 through 1972)
Sources: Morton Paglin, "The Measurement and Trend of Inequality: A Basic Revision," *American Economic Review* 65 (September 1975): 598–609; and Current Population Reports, *Consumer Income: Studies in the Distribution of Income* (Washington, D.C.: U.S. Government Printing Office, October 1972).

all individuals in poverty declined sharply from 1959 through the end of the 1960s, declined little during the 1970s, rose from 1979 through 1983—the period of the sharpest postwar recession—and has since declined, though in 1990 the percentage of individuals in poverty was higher than in the 1970s. The trends for white, black, and Hispanic individuals were similar, although the percentages of individuals in poverty were higher for blacks than for Hispanics and whites. The trends for families, shown in Figures 16.12 and 16.13, are similar to that for individuals.

Several explanations of this trend have been proposed. Nan Maxwell argues that the increases in economic inequality since the 1970s have several sources.[16] She found that the income distribution has become more "polarized" since the early 1970s. The decrease in higher paying manufacturing employment, the rising proportion of households headed by females, and, to a smaller extent, increased population dependency arising from the baby boom contributed to growing inequality. Offsetting the forces

Fig. 16.10 Number and Percentage of All Individuals in Poverty

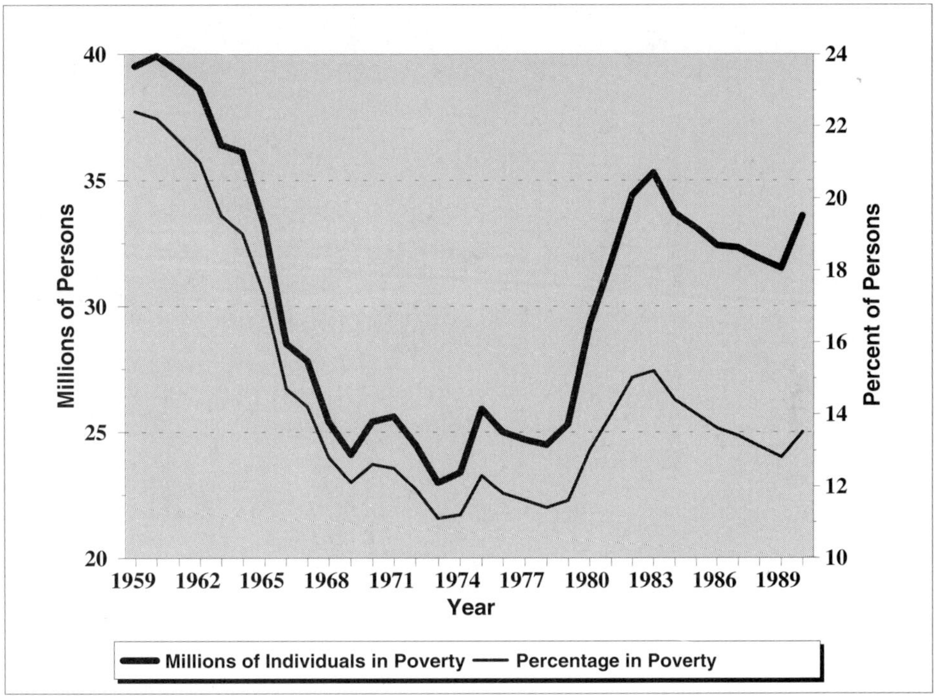

Source: *Statistical Abstract of the United States* (Washington, D.C.: U.S. Government Printing Office, various years).

promoting inequality were the increased female labor force participation and, although weaker, the increased social-insurance expenditures. Maxwell argued that "the equalizing impact from female labor force participation weakened after 1980."[17] Not unexpectedly, the "feminization of poverty" as well as differential employment and demographic impacts associated with race increased inequality.

Frank Levy has found that the most important determinant of these trends was overall productivity growth. Productivity increases during the 1945–73 period allowed real income to grow and slowly equalized the size distribution of money income. Over the 1974–82 period, Levy notes that productivity grew much more slowly, about 0.8 percent annually compared to 3.3 percent per year during 1945–83. The oil supply shocks of the early 1970s and the rapid entrance of baby boomers and women of all ages into the labor force in this period effectively lowered the amount of capital per worker, thus reducing productivity. Government regulations diverted business research efforts toward increasing safety and reducing pollution. Other factors were also listed, such as the slower growth of overseas markets after 1973 and increasing competition in the domestic markets from foreign producers.[18] Levy argues that the shift away from manufacturing is not important because this shift has been occurring for a long time

Fig. 16.11 Percentage of All Individuals in Poverty by Groups

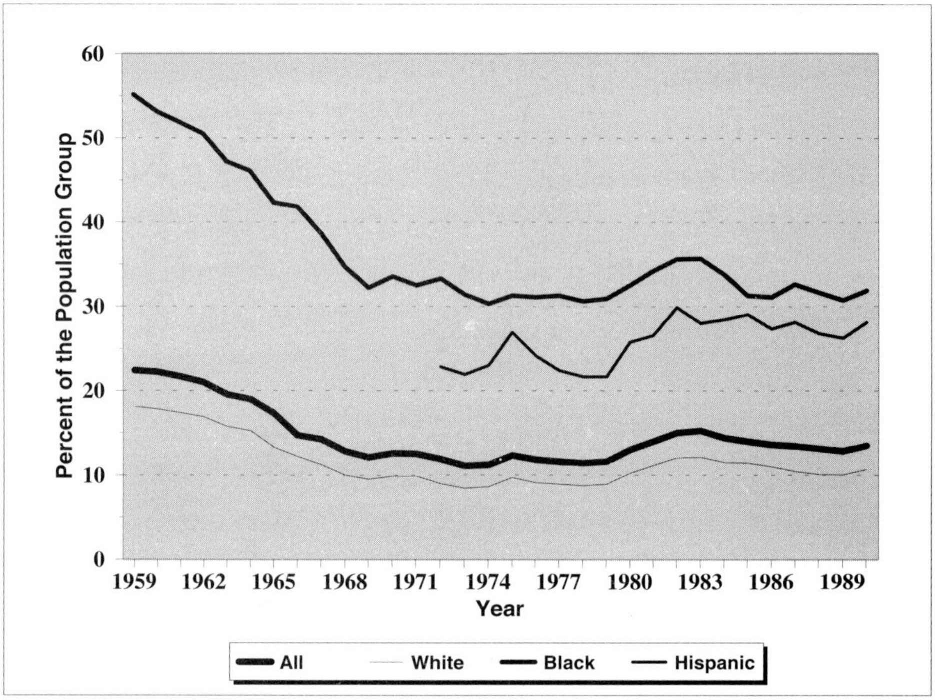

Source: *Statistical Abstract of the United States* (Washington, D.C.: U.S. Government Printing Office, various years).

and did not accelerate around 1973, when an abrupt, and worldwide, reduction in productivity growth began.[19] The majority of the sources of the decline in productivity growth have not been determined.

Limitations on Analyzing the Size Distribution of Income. Simon Kuznets has presented five specifications that should be adhered to when measuring the size distribution of income.[20] First, Kuznets argues, incomes should be recorded and grouped for family expenditure units rather than for individuals with the family expenditure units properly adjusted for the number of persons in each. Second, the measures of the distribution of incomes should cover all of the family expenditure units in a country rather than just a segment at either the upper or lower end of the distribution. Third, when possible, the units whose main income earners are in the learning or retired stages of their life cycles should not be considered in such analyses to avoid complicating the picture by including incomes not associated with full-time, full-fledged participation in economic activity. Fourth, Kuznets proposes that income should be defined in the same manner in which national income in the United States currently is. It should be the income received by individuals, including income in kind, before and after direct taxes

Fig. 16.12 Number and Percentage of All Families in Poverty

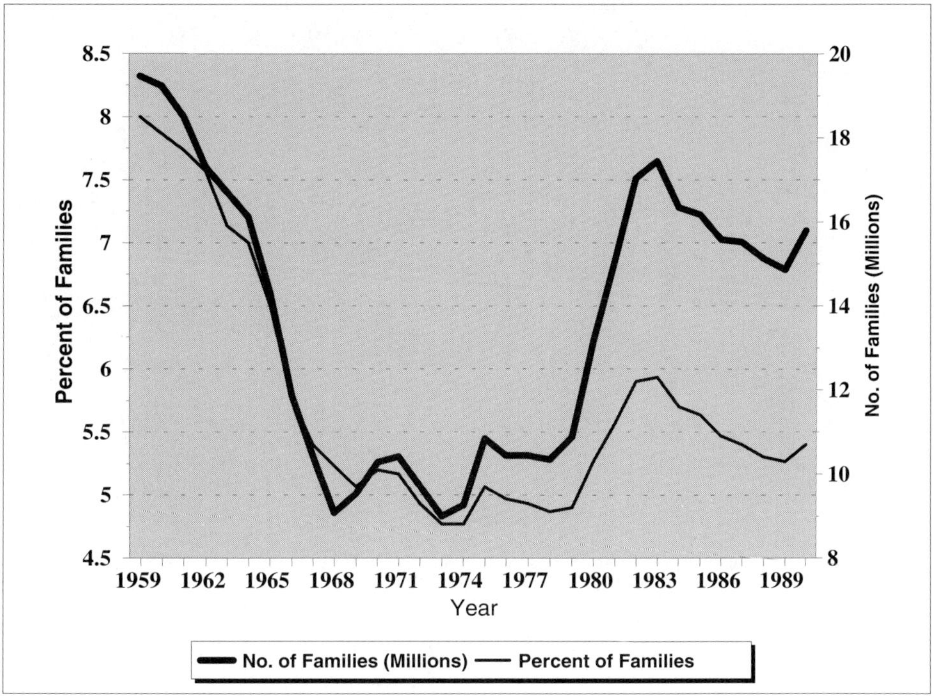

Source: *Statistical Abstract of the United States* (Washington, D.C.: U.S. Government Printing Office, various years).

and excluding capital gains. Fifth, the family expenditure units should be grouped by secular levels of income, free of cyclical and other transient disturbances. These mature family expenditure units should be arrayed in fixed ordinal groups, for example deciles or quintiles, and classified by average income levels for a long enough period, say, 25 years, so as to form "income-status groups." In this way each group will only contain "residents" and not some "migrants" who temporarily have higher or lower incomes. Kuznets argues that "without such a long period of reference and the resulting separation between 'resident' and 'migrant' units at different relative income levels, the very distinction between 'low' and 'high' income classes loses its meaning, particularly in a study of long-term changes in shares and in inequalities in the distribution."[21] We can only say that the lower income classes lost (or gained) in their share of income over, say, the last 5, 10, or 20 years if the family expenditure units in those lower income classes have been members of that class throughout those years. According to Kuzents, for family expenditure units that might have moved into or out of the lower classes during that time period, such a statement has no significance.

The lack of data that meet these requirements limits the assessments of changes in the size distribution of income. Stanley Lebergott has noted other practical problems

Fig. 16.13 Percentage of Families in Poverty by Groups

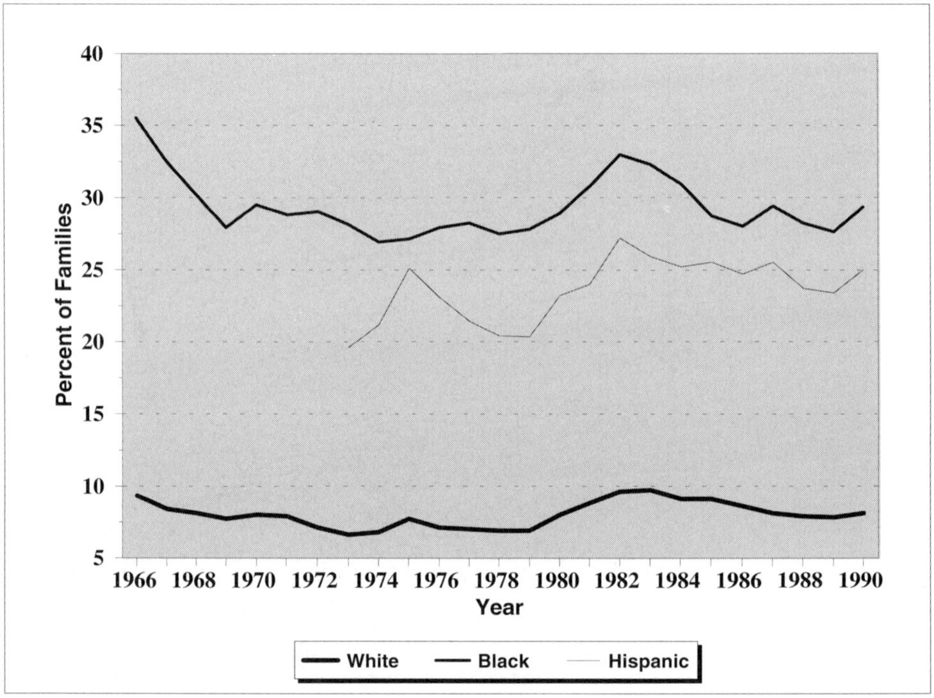

Source: *Statistical Abstract of the United States* (Washington, D.C.: U.S. Government Printing Office, various years).

with this data.[22] First, incomes measured before taxes will be substantially more skewed or unequal than incomes measured on an after-tax basis. Second, expenditures by governments, whether local, state, and/or federal, will not benefit all families equally. Third, even if the incomes are equal, this does not necessarily translate into an equal command over goods and services because of discrimination and differing transportation costs of going to market. Finally, governments have been providing more goods and services without direct user charges so that all citizens can have "full access" to those critical goods and services. However, this means that the actual distribution of goods and services available to families will be less skewed than what the size distribution of income would otherwise indicate.

Generally, size distributions of income are constructed and measured so as to evaluate changes in that distribution over time, but this raises a new set of problems. First, changes in economic activity can have social and demographic consequences. An economic expansion that brings a macroeconomic move toward lower unemployment levels can actually cause an increase in measured, or reported, income inequality as those becoming reemployed will report more rapid growth in their incomes. The rise of income from the 1930s to the 1940s led elderly persons to move out of their children's homes into their own homes and apartments. Though it presumably represented a real increase in "welfare," it was reported as an increase in inequality due to the increase in the number of "low-income" families. The stronger the labor market, the earlier that young people enter the labor market, move out of their parents' homes, and establish their own homes, with similar results for measured inequality. The growing and widening scope of income taxation has increased the incentives to receive income in forms such as capital gains and stock options so as to escape the tax on current income receipts. However, these are typically excluded in tabulations of the income distribution. Much of the growth in taxation is due to government attempts to redistribute income, so the impact of this meandering pattern of government taxation and benefits should be evaluated before we can interpret simple changes in the size distribution of income through time. As tax rates and types of taxes have grown, individuals and families have increasingly resorted to tax avoidance. The growth in tax avoidance raises questions about the statistics for the size distribution of income because these statistics are primarily constructed from tax data such as income tax returns.

The available data are seriously deficient by these standards. First, these data are calculated only for the money income received by individuals. Though there were few noncash transfers in the 1940s, their numbers began to grow in the 1950s and, particularly, in the 1960s after President Johnson initiated the War on Poverty. Noncash transfers have continued to rise in the 1970s and 1980s. Because we are interested in a household's command over valuable goods and resources, the failure to include noncash transfers to lower income households understates the trend toward greater equality—or overstates the trend toward greater inequality.

In the last few years, the Census Bureau has presented some estimates adjusting for this. Table 16.1 presents such estimates for 1986, 1989, and 1990. Among other things, the adjustments count capital gains, employer contributions to health insurance plans that supplement wages or salaries, the net imputed return on the equity in the homes owned by households, and noncash transfers. They also make adjustments for the effect of federal and state income taxes and Social Security payroll taxes. Generally federal and state taxes should contribute to greater equality, while Social Security payroll taxes may not due to the fixed rate and maximum dollar contributions.

The before-tax adjustments to income subtract government money transfers (negative taxes) and add in capital gains and health insurance supplements. As can be seen, these increased inequality in each of these years. The after-tax adjustments subtract federal and state income taxes and social security payroll taxes. They add in means- and nonmeans-tested government cash and noncash transfers and the net imputed return on homeowners' equity in their homes. The result is that in all three years the Gini coefficient drops sharply, showing less inequality. Just as importantly, the change from the unadjusted to the adjusted Gini coefficients differs for these three years. The lowest unadjusted Gini coefficient is for 1986, and the highest is for 1989. The lowest adjusted Gini coefficient is for 1990, and the highest adjusted coefficient is for 1986. Thus, we cannot simply take the Gini coefficients of earlier years and adjust them downward by a constant amount (or percentage) to make the adjustments shown in Table 16.1. Because cash and noncash transfers have grown in real terms over the post-

Table 16.1 Money Income of Households: Percent Distribution by Quintile and Index of Income Concentration by Definition of Income, 1986

Definition Number	Definition of Income	Gini[1] Index		
	Income Before Taxes	1986	1989	1990
1	Money Income Excluding Capital Gains (Current) Measure[2].	.420	.429	.426
2	Definition 1 Less Government Money Transfers	.473	.481	.480
3	Definition 2 Plus Capital Gains .503	.496	.491	
4	Definition 3 Plus Health Insurance Supplements to Wage or Salary Income[3].	.500	.495	.490
	Income After Taxes			
5	Definition 4 Less Federal and State Income Taxes and Social Security Payroll Taxes	.483	.467	.463
8	Definition 7 Plus Nonmeans-Tested Gov't. Cash Transfers[4].	.434	.417	.412
9	Definition 8 Plus Nonmeans-Tested Gov't. Noncash Transfers[5].	.424	.407	.402
10	Definition 9 Plus Means-Tested Gov't. Cash Transfers[6].	.417	.407	.394
11	Definition 10 Plus Means-Tested Gov't. Noncash Transfers[7].	.408	.391	.384
12	Definition 11 Plus Net Imputed Return on Equity in Own Home[8]	.404	.392	.383

[1]A statistical measure of income equality ranging from 0 to 1. A measure of 1 indicates perfect inequality (i.e., one person having all the wealth and the rest having none). A measure of 0 indicates perfect equality (i.e., all persons having equal shares of wealth).
[2]Official definition of income based on money income before taxes and including government cash transfers.
[3]Employer contributions to the health insurance plans of employees.
[4]Includes Social Security and Railroad Retirement, Veterans payments, and unemployment and workers' compensation.
[5]Includes Medicare and subsidies from regular price school lunches.
[6]Includes AFDC or other assistance or welfare payments and Supplemental Security income. Households must meet certain eligibility requirements in order to qualify for these benefits.
[7]Includes Medicaid, food stamps, subsidies from free or reduced-price school lunches, and rent subsidies.
[8]Estimated amount of income a household would receive if it chose to shift amount held as home equity into an interest-bearing account.

Source: *Statistical Abstract of the United States* (Washington, D.C.: U.S. Government Printing Office, various years).

war period, this suggests that the Gini coefficients shown in Figure 16.10 understate the increases in equality in the size distribution of income.

As previously mentioned one of Kuznets' points is that the analysis should concentrate on incomes of those engaged in full-time, full-fledged participation in economic activity. Morton Paglin has considered this criticism. The Gini coefficient takes as its standard perfect intergenerational equality as well as perfect interfamily equality. This requires equal lifetime incomes as well as equal incomes across families at the same stage of life. In other words, as Morton Paglin notes, families that are in the period of child rearing are required to have the same incomes as families in the retirement stage of their life cycle, "when they have minimum economic responsibilities and maximum assets."[23] However, at any point in time some significant part of the income inequalities arise due to the differing ages and thus earning powers of individuals. Carolyn Shaw Bell says, "We do not expect young school graduates to receive as much income as their parents, or as they themselves will 20 years later. And we expect the senior citizen's pension income (much of which is tax-free) to be less than peak earnings."[24] Paglin adjusted the Gini coefficient by subtracting the income inequality due solely to the variation in the families' ages. This revised standard of equality, which he termed the *Paglin-Gini*, can be used to assess changes in income inequality without the complicating factor of changing income inequality due solely to the changing age structure of American families. In his 1975 study, Paglin adjusted the data for the years 1947 through 1972 to more correctly measure inequality. The Paglin-Gini in Figure 16.14 shows less income concentration in 1947 compared to the Gini requiring perfect intergenerational equality (which he termed the *Lorenz-Gini*), and it declines much more sharply. The Lorenz-Gini that Paglin used declined from 0.378 in 1947 to 0.359 in 1972, or by 5 percentage points. The Paglin-Gini declined from 0.303 in 1947 to 0.239 in 1972, or by 21.2 percentage points.

No calculations of Paglin-Gini coefficients (eliminating the requirement of intergenerational equality) have been made for the years since 1972. Paglin's adjustments understated the increase in equality because he used money income without adjusting for noncash transfers and the other financial items shown in Table 16.1. Since 1972, the

Fig. 16.14 Lorenz-Gini and Paglin-Gini Coefficients, 1947–1972

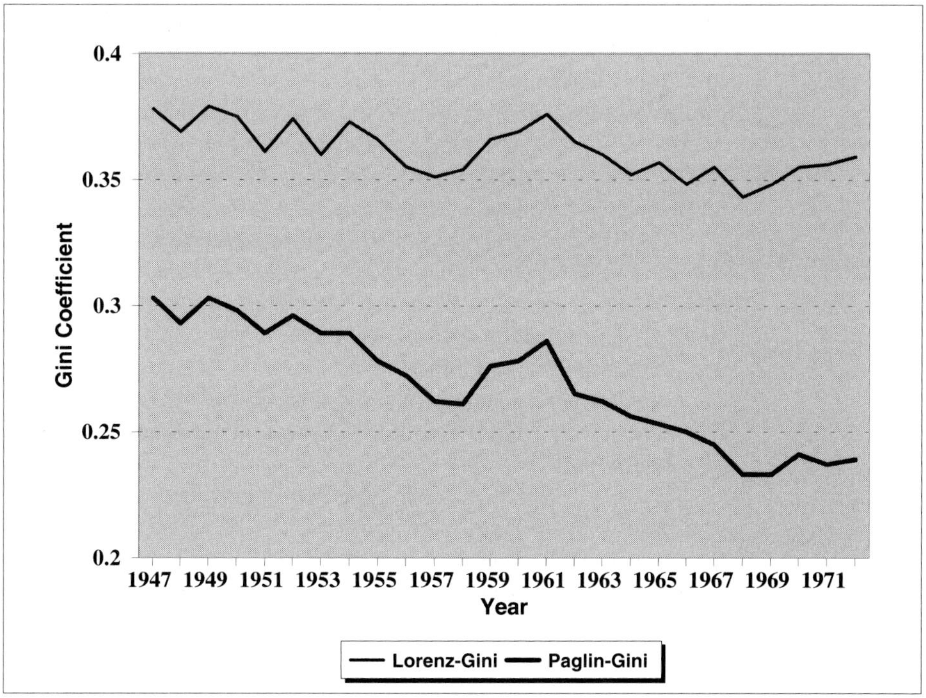

Source: Morton Paglin, "The Measurements and Trend of Inequality: A Basic Revision," *American Economic Review* 65 (September 1975): 598–609.

ending of the baby boom has reduced the number of young adult households, but the graying of the population has been increasing the number of retired households. It seems likely that if both adjustments were made, a much clearer trend of equality in the distribution of income since 1947 would be found. Unfortunately such calculations have yet to be made.

A particularly important requirement set forth by Kuznets was to construct family expenditure units by secular levels of income over long enough periods of time to form income-status groups. If this is done, then one can accurately discuss changes in the share of income going to each quintile of family expenditure units. This is not how the data reported by the federal government are organized. We know that some of the individuals in the lowest quintile are just beginning their working lives and will move up from that quintile, and some of the people fall into the lowest quintile because as they retire, their money income drops. There is movement into and out of all of the quintiles. Thus, the families in, say, the lowest quintile change over time, and we cannot discuss changes in income for the families in the lowest quintiles because these families change due to this mobility. How important is this mobility?

Several recent examinations have provided concrete evidence on this. Isabel Sawhill and Mark Condon have examined mobility for individuals who were 25 to 54 years old in the starting year. The two periods examined were 1967–76 and 1977–86.[25] Figure 16.15 summarizes the results of their findings. In both ten-year periods, nearly half of the individuals in the lowest quintile had moved to a higher quintile at the end of the period. For the three middle quintiles, about 70 percent of the individuals had moved to a higher or lower quintile by the end of the period, while for the highest quintile, about half who began the period there fell to a lower quintile by its end. Because of this mobility, in both periods those starting in the lowest quintile experienced large increases in real average incomes—72 percent in the first decade and 77 percent in the second. In contrast the real average family incomes of those starting in the top quintile grew much more slowly—6 percent in the first decade and 5 percent in the second.[26]

The Treasury's Office of Tax Analysis undertook a study of income mobility during the 1980s.[27] Their findings are reported in Table 16.2. Between 1979 and 1988, only 14.2 percent of the taxpayers who began in the lowest quintile were still there in 1988. A larger percentage, 14.4 percent, moved all the way into the highest quintile, and 0.3 percent moved into the top 1 percent of income recipients. Only in the highest quintile did more than half of those there at the beginning of the period remain there throughout the period. As Table 16.2 shows, there was considerable mobility for all of these quintiles.[28]

Even on a yearly basis it appears that there is considerable income mobility. In recent years the Census Bureau has measured income mobility with a program called the Survey of Income and Program Participation, which tracks specific families over time.[29] They found that between 1984 and 1985, 18.2 percent of the families in the lowest income quintile moved up one or more quintiles, 18.4 percent moved up between 1985 and 1986, and 17.0 percent moved up between 1987 and 1988. In the highest quintile 19.5 percent moved down one or more quintiles between 1984 and 1985, 23.7 percent moved down between 1985 and 1986, and 24.3 percent moved down between 1987 and 1988.

Fig. 16.15 Estimates of Income Mobility

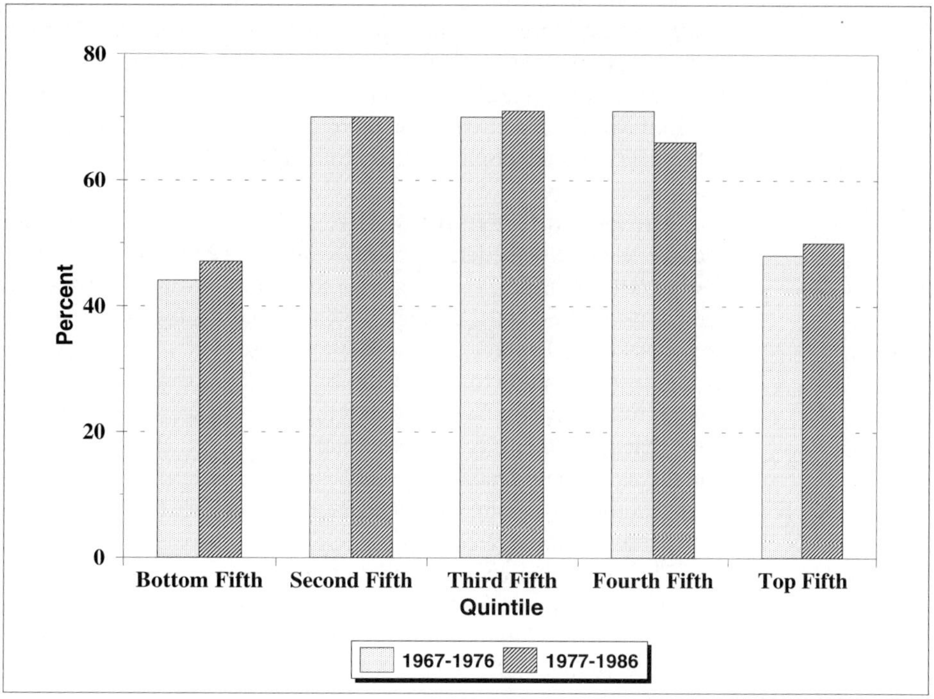

Source: The Urban Institute, *Policy Bites* (June 1992), table 1, p. 2, as cited by Cindy Kelly, "Moving Up—and Down—the U.S. Income Ladder," *The Margin* 8 (Spring 1993): 25.

Table 16.2 Income Group Mobility Between 1979 and 1988

		Status in 1988				
Status in 1979	Top 1%	Top 2% to 20%	Next Richest 20%	Middle 20%	Next Poorest 20%	Poorest 20%
Top 1%	47.3	38.6	7.7	3.8	0.4	2.2
Top 20%	5.3	59.4	20.3	9.4	4.4	1.1
Next Richest 20%	0.6	34.8	37.5	14.8	9.3	3.1
Middle 20%	0.4	14.6	32.3	33	14	5.7
Next Poorest 20%	0.3	10.8	19.5	29.6	29	10.9
Poorest 20%	0.3	14.4	25.3	25	20.7	14.2

Source: David Wessel, "Low-income Mobility Was High in the 1980s: Treasury Also Finds Those at the Top Tended to Stay There," *The Wall Street Journal* 2 June, 1992: A2.

Overall, these criticisms make it clear that the generally cited data considerably overstate the inequality in the distribution of income. If we had data that did not require perfect intergenerational income equality as the standard, included all income—not just money income—and focused on family expenditure units over long periods of time, we could accurately measure and trace the size distribution of income. Whether the more pronounced trend of increasing equality that Morton Paglin found for the 1947–1972 period would have continued is not known.

The Recent Rise in Inequality. The Gini coefficients in Figure 16.9 suggest that income inequality began to increase in the 1970s and increased much more in the 1980s. The quintile income shares and the poverty measures also show increasing inequality in the 1980s. Though we know that the levels of inequality are overstated, it is not necessarily the case that the changes over time differ. Sawhill and Condon's Urban Institute study of income mobility did not show large differences in mobility in any quintile between the 1970s and the 1980s. (See Figure 16.15.) Let us suppose, for now, that adjustments for generational changes and changes in noncash transfers, taxes, and the net imputed return on equity in owner-occupied homes would not significantly alter the trend of rising income inequality in the 1980s.[30] How can we explain the increased inequality?

There are two leading explanations for the rising income inequality in the 1980s. First, property incomes rose more than labor incomes. During the 1970s, nominal stock prices rose little, and they fell in real terms. In the 1980s nominal and real stock prices both rose dramatically. Real ex post interest rates in the 1970s were quite low and sometimes negative. In the 1980s nominal and real interest rates rose dramatically, and, though nominal interest rates fell as inflation declined, real interest rates remained relatively high. These trends increased the share of income received by property and decreased the share of income received by labor in the 1980s. All else the same, this would increase income inequality.[31]

A changing wage structure is the most generally cited explanation for the rising inequality in the 1980s.[32] Workers with more education saw sharp increases in their wage rates relative to those with less education. Real wage rates for high school dropouts with zero to nine years experience fell sharply during the 1980s, while real wage rates for college graduates with the same experience rose. The ratio of the college to dropout wage went from 1.688 in 1973 to 1.581 in 1979 to 2.195 in 1988.[33] For workers who had not completed college, the wage rates of older workers rose relative to the wage rates of younger workers, and the average wage rate of women rose by 8 percent compared to the average wage rate of men. The decline in the real wage rates of younger workers with less education was quite pronounced. This appears to have been the primary factor driving the increase in income inequality during the 1980s.

John Bound and George Johnson have recently examined the reasons for these differential changes in real wage rates in the 1990s.[34] They considered several common explanations. Some have argued that the declines in manufacturing employment and union power were a cause, but union membership had been declining for two decades prior to the 1980s, and they have found that this was, at best, a minor influence. They have also examined the suggestion that the decline in manufacturing employment may have increased the relative demand for better educated workers and have concluded that the changes were actually unfavorable to highly educated labor. Similarly, the changes in the industrial structure from higher wage industries toward lower wage industries was not an important part of the explanation. In their analysis they have found that the most powerful force driving the wage rate changes was technological change. Changes in technology were biased toward skilled labor and away from unskilled labor.

These demand shifts drove up the wage rates of skilled (more highly educated) labor and drove down the wage rates for unskilled (less highly educated) labor. Though the same shifts were occurring in the 1970s, "they did not cause major changes in the wage structure in the 1970's because of the abnormally large increases in the relative supply of educated labor during that time."[35] The primary determinant of this shift has been the growing use of computers and associated high-tech capital such as communications and photocopy equipment and instruments. Continuing growth in the use of high-tech equipment has led Bound and Johnson to speculate that unless college attendance and completion rates rise sharply, the wage differentials may widen, and income inequality may continue to increase.[36]

The Overall Picture. The unfortunate truth is that we do not know nearly as much about the size distribution of income as we would like to. We know that the conventional measures certainly overstate the amount of inequality, but we can't say exactly by how much. Neither do we have a good picture of the trend of changes in income inequality. Because the conventional measures include only money income and because nonmoney income transfers have steadily grown throughout the postwar period, we would expect that there has been a stronger increase in equality than the measures show. Similarly, when we eliminate the standard of perfect intergenerational equality, a stronger trend of equality is found, but whether this continued past the early 1970s is also not known. Finally, the failure to correct for the substantial income mobility that recent studies have shown to exist means that we cannot say what changes have occurred in the share of income received by the lowest fifth, second fifth, and so on, of the population. It is not very satisfactory to say that we still cannot answer the question of whether market economies like the United States generate greater inequalities in the distribution of income, but that is our current state of knowledge. The one thing we can say, with some certainty, is that market-oriented economies are much better at generating income.

THE UNITED STATES' PLACE IN THE WORLD ECONOMY

As early as the Revolutionary War, average incomes in the United States were among the highest in the world. By the beginning of the Civil War, the United States had *the* highest per capita incomes in the world, a position it retained through the 1960s. In the 1970s and 1980s the rate of economic growth slowed down, and imports into the

United States—as well as exports—began to grow faster. Japanese automobile companies increasingly took a larger share of the American new car market, and foreign firms began to produce most of our television sets, radios, and stereo components. Real wages grew slowly in the 1970s and the 1980s. By the late 1980s the United States no longer had the highest per capita incomes in the world. "Deindustrialization" became the newest phrase, and politicians attempted to formulate policies to restore both the industrial vigor of the United States' manufacturing sector and the higher paying industrial jobs that they thought had gone overseas.

Figures 16.16 and 16.17 present selected countries' GDP (Gross Domestic Product) per capita as a percent of the United States' GDP per capita.[37] These are the countries with the highest per capita GDPs in the world in 1990. In 1979 Switzerland and Norway had per capita incomes higher than the United States. As the international value of the dollar rose through 1985, other countries' per capita GDPs fell relative to the United States, and by 1985 the United States once again had the highest per capita income. The international exchange value of the dollar fell from 1985 through 1990, and by 1990 six countries had per capita GDPs higher than the United States.

Fig. 16.16 Selected Nations' GDP Per Capita as a Percent of U.S. GDP Per Capita

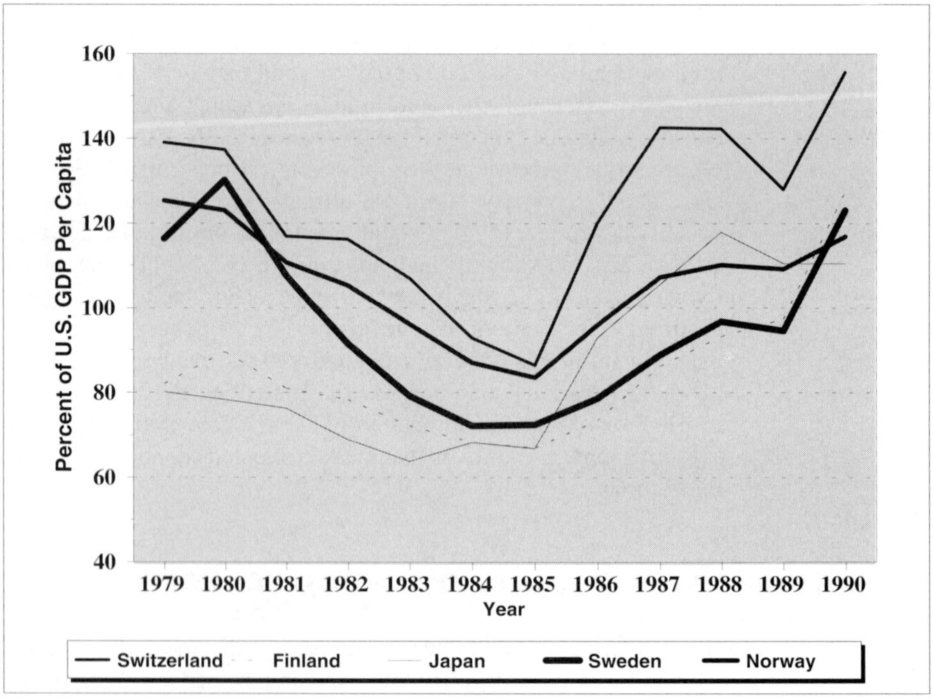

Sources: The World Bank, *World Development Report* (New York: Oxford University Press, various years).

Fig. 16.17 Selected Nations' GDP Per Capita as a Percent of U.S. GDP Per Capita

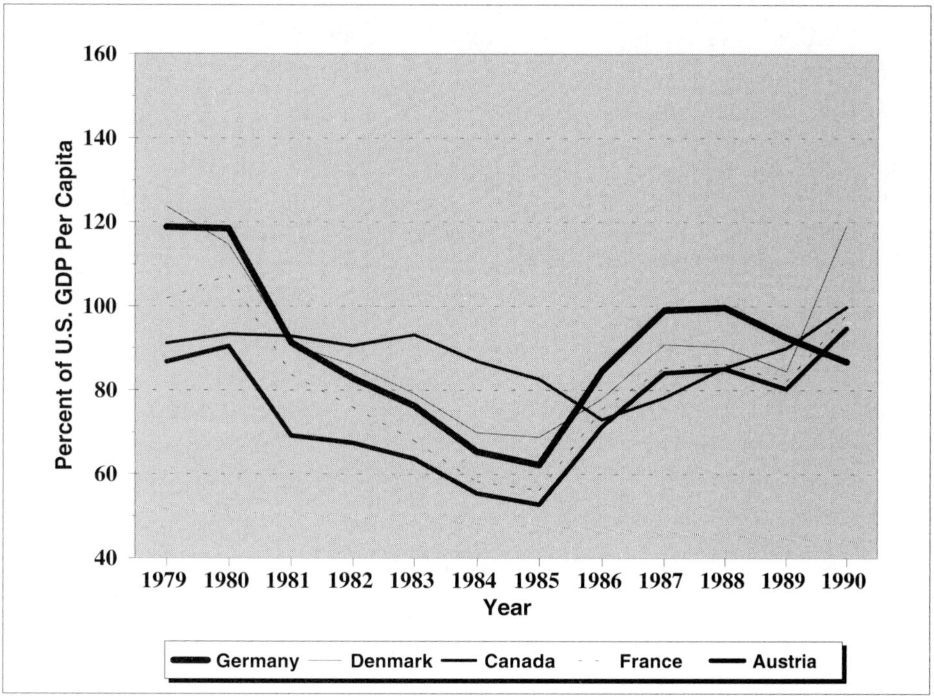

SourceS: The World Bank, *World Development Report* (New York: Oxford University Press, various years).

A general contention is that industrial activity has been exported out of the United States and replaced with service activity. Because manufacturing jobs generally have been among the highest paying jobs, this substitution has reduced (or eliminated) real wage growth and been one of the factors allowing the GDPs per capita of other industrialized countries to surpass the United States' GDP per capita. World Bank data report the share of industry and the share of manufacturing originating in GDP for 1960 and for 1989.[38] The changes in these shares are shown in Figures 16.18 and 16.19. In each figure the entry for "Average" refers to an average of all of the countries shown, excluding the United States. Though in each case the United States' share declined more than the average, it declined for most of the other countries too. The percentage decline in industry's share of GDP was larger for Germany, Denmark, France, and Austria than for the United States. For manufacturing's share, Norway's decline was as large as for the United States, and the declines for Denmark, Canada, France, and Austria were also quite large. The decline in industry's share of GDP is common to most of the high-income industrial economies, rather than being unique to the United States.

Fig. 16.18 Percentage Change of Industry's Share of GDP for Selected Countries, 1960 to 1989

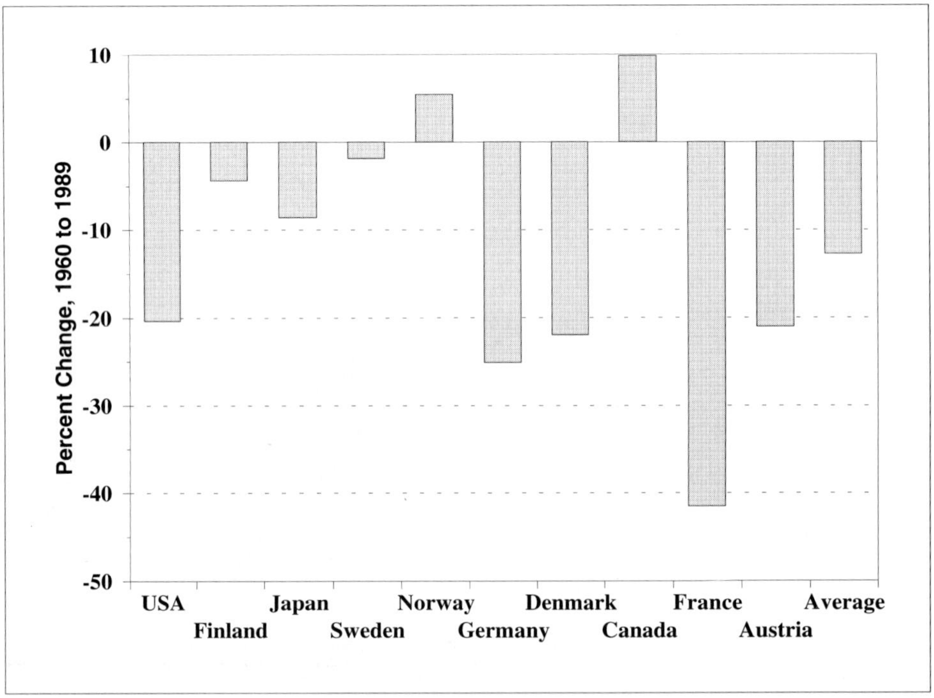

(1989 is an average of the values for 1988, and 1989, and 1990. Percentage changes are instantaneous rates of change. "Average" indicates the average for all of the countries shown, excluding the United States.)
Source: The World Bank, *World Development Report* (New York: Oxford University Press, various years).

As Figures 16.16 and 16.17 show, there is great variation in the per capita incomes of other countries relative to the United States. To compare a country's income to the United State's, it must be converted to dollar terms to provide purchasing power parity. "Purchasing Power Parity (PPP) is defined as the number of units of a country's currency required to buy the same amounts of goods and services in the domestic market as one dollar would buy in the United States."[39] For each of these years, the currencies of other countries are converted to U.S. dollars, using the current exchange rate. The variation in the per capita income ratios is clearly inverse to the variation in the international value of the dollar. The exchange rate is used for conversions to a common currency because it is readily available and because "the strong version of the Casselian Purchasing Power Parity Doctrine asserts that the equilibrium exchange rate at which the currencies of two countries will trade will be determined by the relative price levels of the countries."[40] Not only are the exchange rates not necessarily equilibrium rates, but there is clear evidence that this doctrine does not hold. Robert Summers and Alan Heston argue that exchange rates differ in a systematic and significant way from

Fig. 16.19 Percentage Change of Manufacturing's Share of GDP for Selected Countries, 1960 to 1989

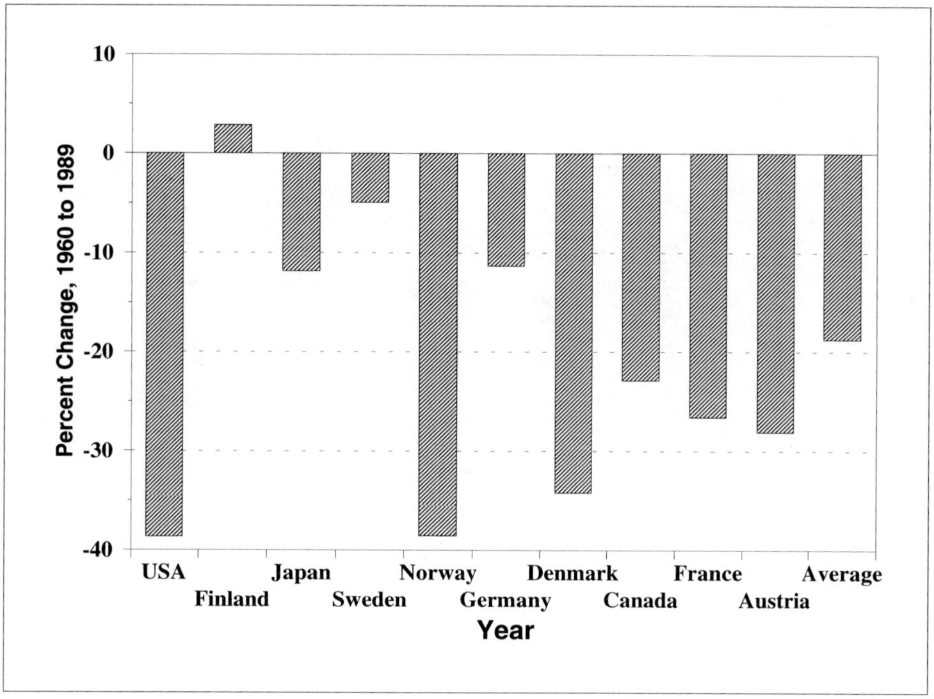

(1989 is an average of the values for 1988, 1989, and 1990. Percentage changes are instantaneous rates of change. "Average" indicates the average for all of the countries shown, excluding the United States.)
Source: The World Bank, *World Development Report* (New York: Oxford University Press, various years).

purchasing power parity (PPP). They have found that the price level of a nation, "defined as the ratio of its PPP to its exchange rate, is a rising function of the level of its income or stage of development."[41] Because this strong version of the purchasing power parity doctrine fails, it invalidates the use of exchange rates as quick, easy estimates of purchasing power parity.

The United Nations has been developing a set of studies called the International Comparison Program (ICP), which develops price comparisons among countries. Using these benchmark studies, Summers and Heston have developed alternative series that are comparable across time and space.[42] Because these series use the ICP data instead of exchange rates to estimate purchasing power parity, they provide a superior means of international comparisons. Figures 16.20 and 16.21 show real GDP per capita adjusted for changes in the terms of trade for the same set of countries as used above. A very different picture emerges. The United States remains the highest income country in the world throughout the 1950–88 period.

Fig. 16.20 Real GDP Per Capita Adjusted for Changing Terms of Trade for Selected Countries

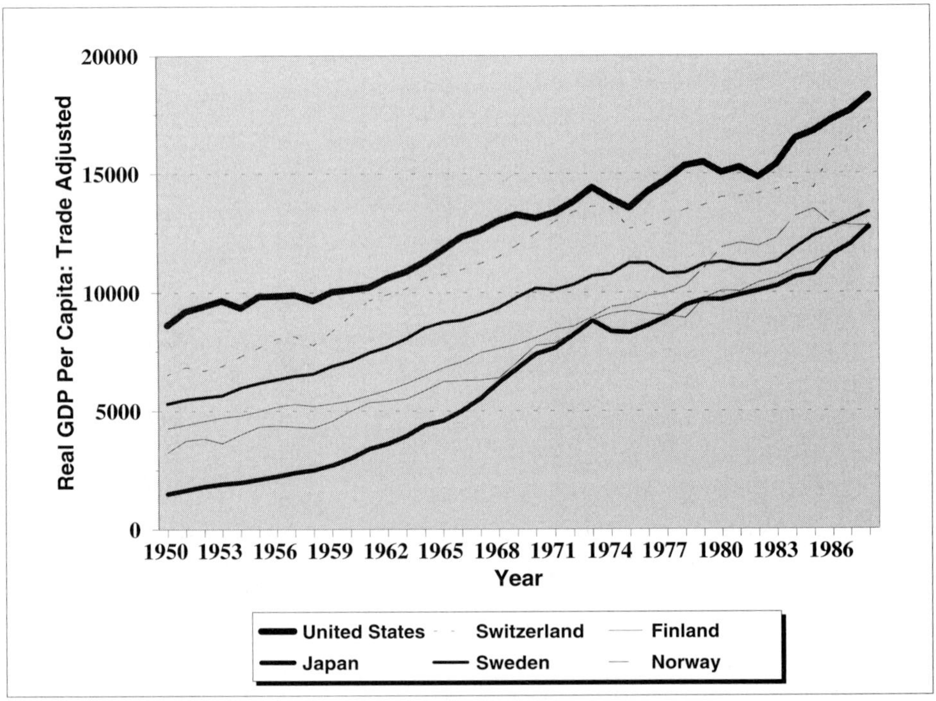

Source: Robert Summers and Alan Heston, "The Penn World Table (Mark 5): An Expanded Set of International Comparisons, 1950–1988," *Quarterly Journal of Economics* 106 (May 1991): 327–68.

It appears that the decline of the United States has been overstated. The United States has continued to have the highest per capita incomes in the world, and its industrial decline in the 1980s is not out of line with that of other industrial nations. Figure 16.22 presents average annual growth rates for 1950–70 and 1970–88 for the countries we have been comparing in this section. Except for Canada, the rate of growth for every country was slower in the latter period. For the 1970–88 period, the United States grew faster than France, Switzerland, Sweden, and Denmark—hardly the performance of a nation that has passed its peak.

Prospects. Through economic growth, the American standard of living has risen to and remained the highest in the world. Over time, economic growth has been the most important factor in reducing the incidence of poverty. There are always costs and benefits that accompany such growth. New products and services create new jobs, but some workers are displaced from jobs producing products and services that are declining in demand. Innovations—more frequent during periods of rapid growth—create the possibility of substantial wealth for successful innovators, so it is not clear that eco-

Fig. 16.21 Real GDP Per Capita Adjusted for Changing Terms of Trade for Selected Countries

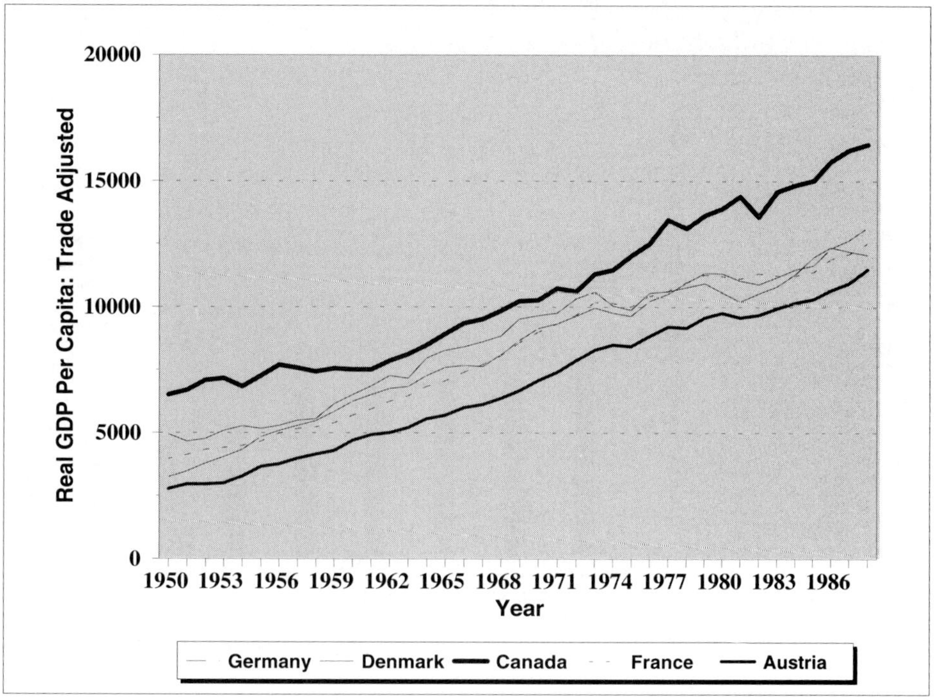

Source: Robert Summers and Alan Heston, "The Penn World Table (Mark 5): An Expanded Set of International Comparisons, 1950–1988," *Quarterly Journal of Economics* 106 (May 1991): 327–68.

nomic growth will promote equality in the size distribution of income.[43] But economic growth does open up the possibility that almost anyone can quickly move up the income levels. Will that growth continue?

There can never be a firm answer to such a question. But we can find a few clues. Economic growth does not appear to be associated with abundant natural resources.[44] An educated population and skilled labor force are much more important determinants. Though worries have surfaced about a decline in the quality of education in the United States, we still have one of the most highly skilled labor forces in the world, and this provides a foundation for growth.[45] As the evidence has shown, there is still considerable income mobility in the United States. Individuals who build the proverbial "better mousetrap" can expect to be rewarded for their efforts, and this is a great stimulus to finding better, lower cost ways to accomplish tasks and to develop new products and services—and these are the foundations of economic growth. Finally, the United States continues to have a strong system of private property rights and institutions to maintain and enforce those rights. These rights are the bedrock of a market-oriented system. As

Fig. 16.22 Average Annual Growth Rates of Real GDP Per Capita Adjusted for Changing Terms of Trade for Selected countries

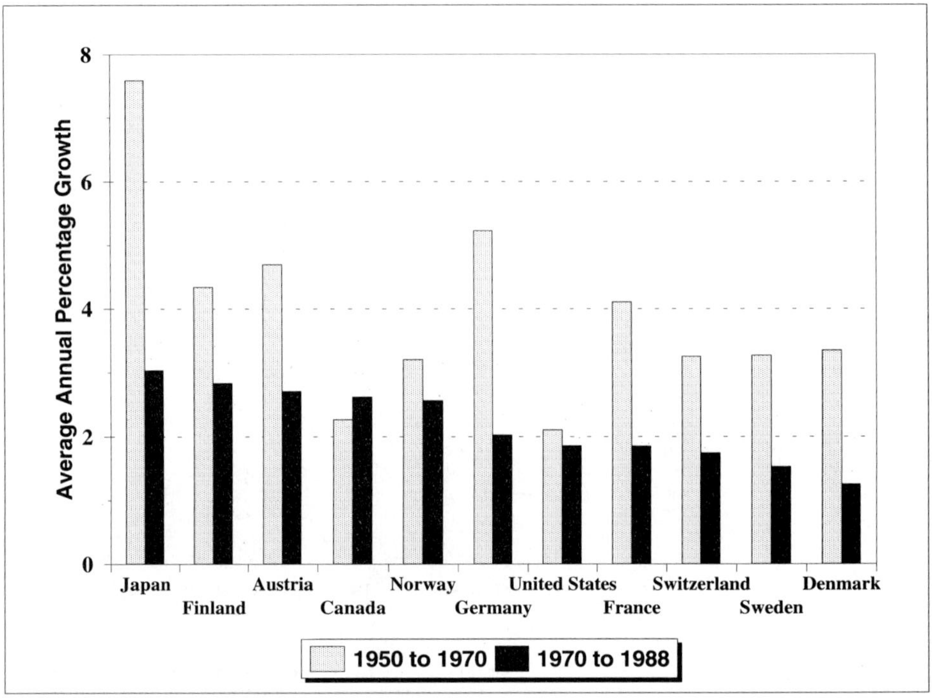

(growth rates are instantaneous rates of growth)
Source: Robert Summers and Alan Heston, "The Penn World Table (Mark 5): An Expanded Set of International Comparisons, 1950–1988," *Quarterly Journal of Economics* 106 (May 1991): 327–68.

the former communist societies will learn, without private property rights, free markets cannot arise, and the productive outpouring of goods and services will never appear. As long as the United States has institutions devoted to free choice, private property rights securely embedded in law, and economic and social mobility, then it will maintain an environment that fosters economic growth.

SELECTED REFERENCES

Bell, Carolyn Shaw. "Another Look at Distribution of Income." *The Wall Street Journal*, 23 November, 1976.

Blackburn, McKinley L.; David E. Bloom; and Richard B. Freeman. "An Era of Falling Earnings and Rising Inequality?" *Brookings Review* 9 (Winter 1990): 38–43.

Bound, John, and Georege Johnson. "Changes in the Structure of Wages in the 1980's: An Evaluation of Alterative Explanations." *American Economic Review* 82 (June 1992): 371–92.

Bartlett, Bruce. "A Class Structure That Won't Stay Put." *The Wall Street Journal*, 20 November, 1991.

Budd, Edward C. "Postwar Changes in the Size Distribution of Income in the U.S." *American Economic Review* 60 (May 1970): 247–60.

Cain, Louis P. "Discussion." *The Journal of Economic History* 43 (March 1983): 241–42.

Cutler, David M., and Lawrence F. Katz. "Macroeconomic Performance and the Disadvantaged." *Brookings Papers on Economic Activity* 2 (Winter 1991): 1–74.

__________. "Untouched by the Rising Tide." *The Brookings Review* (Winter 1992): 41–45. Reprinted in *Annual Editions: Microeconomics*. Edited by Don Cole. Guiford, CT: The Dushkin Publishing Group, 1993.

__________. "Rising Inequality? Changes in the Distribution of Income and Consumption in the 1980s." *American Economic Review* 82 (May 1992): 546–51.

Goldsmith, Selma F. "Statistical Information on the Distribution of Income by Size in the United States." *American Economic Review* 40 (May 1950): 321–41.

Holt, Charles F. "Who Benefited from the Prosperity of the Twenties." *Explorations in Economic History*, 14 (July 1977): 277–89.

Keller, Robert. "Factor Income Distribution in the United States During the 1920's: A Re-examination of Fact and Theory." *The Journal of Economic History* 33 (March 1973): 252–73.

Kelly, Cindy. "Moving Up—and Down—the U.S. Income Ladder." *The Margin* 8 (Spring 1993): 25.

Kravis, Irving B. and Lipsey, Robert. *Toward an Explanation of National Price Levels*. Princeton, NJ: Princeton Studies in International Finance, no. 52, 1983.

Kuznets, Simon. *Shares of Upper Income Groups in Income and Savings*. New York: National Bureau of Economic Research, 1953.

__________. "Economic Growth and Income Inequality." *American Economic Review* 45 (March 1955): 1–28.

__________. *Economic Growth and Structure*. New York: W. W. Norton and Co., Inc., 1965.

__________. *Modern Economic Growth: Rate, Structure, and Spread*. New Haven, CT: Yale University Press, 1966.

Lebergott, Stanley. "Income Distribution: Size." In *International Encyclopedia of the Social Sciences*, Vol. 7. Edited by David L. Sills. New York: Macmillan, 1968.

__________. *The American Economy: Income, Wealth, and Want*. Princeton: Princeton University Press, 1976.

Levy, Frank. *Dollars and Dreams: The Changing American Income Distribution*. New York: Russell Sage Foundation, 1987.

Maxwell, Nan L. *Income Inequality in the United States, 1947–1985*. Westport, CT: Greenwood Press, 1990.

Moore, Geoffrey H. "Secular Changes in the Distribution of Income." *American Economic Review* 42 (May 1952): 527–44.

Murphy, Kevin M., and Finis Welch. "Wage Premiums for College Graduates: Recent Growth and Possible Explanations." *Educational Researcher* 18 (May 1989): 17–26.

__________. "The Role of International Trade in Wage Differentials." *Workers and Their Wages*. Edited by Marvin Kosters. Washington, D.C.: American Enterprise Institute, 1991.

Osberg, Lars. *Economic Inequality in the United States*. Armonk, NY: M. E. Sharpe, Inc., 1984.

Paglin, Morton. "The Measurement and Trend of Inequality: A Basic Revision." *American Economic Review* 64 (September 1975): 598–609.

Renaghan, Thomas M. "Distributional Effects of Federal Tax Policy, 1929–1933." *Explorations in Economic History* 21 (January 1984): 40–63.

Schmitz, Mark and Fishback, Price V. "The Distribution of Income in the Great Depression: Preliminary State Estimates." *The Journal of Economic History* 43 (March 1983): 217–30.

Smiley, Gene. "Did Incomes for Most of the Population Fall from 1923 Through 1929?" *The Journal of Economic History* 43 (March 1983): 209–16.

Soltow, Lee. "Evidence of Income Inequality in the United States, 1966–1965." *The Journal of Economic History* 20 (June 1969): 279–86.

Summers, Robert, and Alan Heston. "The Penn World Table (Mark 5): An Expanded Set of International Comparisons, 1950–1988." *Quarterly Journal of Economics* 106 (May 1991): 326–68.

Wessel, David. "Low-Income Mobility Was High in 1980s: Treasury Study Also Finds Those at Top Tended to Stay There." *The Wall Street Journal*, 2 June, 1992.

Williamson, Jeffrey G. "The Sources of American Inequality, 1896–1948." *The Review of Economics and Statistics* 58 (November 1976): 387–97.

Wolff, Edward N. "Changing Inequality of Wealth." *American Economic Review* 82 (May 1992): 552–58.

World Bank. *World Development Report*. New York: Oxford University Press, various years.

NOTES

1. Stanley Lebergott, "Income Distribution: Size," in David L. Sills, ed., *International Encyclopedia of the Social Sciences* vol. 7 (New York: Macmillan, 1968), 145. See also the discussions in Stanley Lebergott, *The American Economy: Income, Wealth, and Want* (Princeton: Princeton University Press, 1976).
2. Employee compensation includes wages and salaries and supplements to wages and salaries. Proprietors' income includes the income received by farm and nonfarm proprietors. Property income includes the rental income of persons, corporate profits before taxes and after the inventory valuation and capital consumption adjustments, and net interest. Rental income, received by individuals, is difficult to link up with any particular factor. The government sector has no capital account, so the income generated in the government sector is attributed solely to labor inputs (as if capital inputs were not used or as if capital were completely unproductive). Net interest figures, along with proprietors' income and rental incomes, are also less dependable. The figures for net interest measure the excess of interest payments of the domestic business system over its interest receipts. Also included are net interest payments received from abroad. Questions about the accuracy of these figures are raised by the imputations. Included in the figures are imputed interest arising in connection with the operations of financial intermediaries. The National Income accounts assume that all interest payments received by all financial institutions are completely paid out to the depositors, bondholders, and so on, of the institutions. The depositors, and so on, then use some of the interest income to purchase checking services, savings account services, and so on. Thus, in the national income accounts, the amount of interest income received by those who have assets issued by financial intermediaries is substantially greater than what is actually received. If the financial markets actually operated this way, the interest rates and costs of providing these financial services might differ considerably from what they currently are. Therefore, there are serious questions about the accuracy of the imputations.

3. The data prior to 1930 were developed by D. Gale Johnson and are slightly different from the post-1930 data developed by the Bureau of Economic Analysis. This is the reason for the slight break in the series at the 1930–39 period.
4. Lebergott, "Income Distribution: Size."
5. Lee Soltow, "Evidence of Income Inequality in the United States, 1866–1965," *The Journal of Economic History* 29 (June 1969): 279–86.
6. Simon Kuznets, *Shares of Upper Income Groups in Income and Savings* (New York: National Bureau of Economic Research, 1953).
7. J. G. Williamson used the ratio of unskilled to skilled wages as an indicator of the distribution of income. He found that this ratio tracked Kuznets' share of the lower 93 percent of the nonfarm population relatively well, providing confirmation of the usefulness of his measure. See Jeffrey G. Williamson, "The Sources of American Inequality, 1896–1948," *The Review of Economics and Statistics* 58 (November 1976): 387–97.
8. Charles F. Holt, "Who Benefited from the Prosperity of the Twenties?" *Explorations in Economic History* 14 (July 1977): 277–89.
9. Gene Smiley, "Did Incomes for Most of the Population Fall from 1923 Through 1929?" *The Journal of Economic History* 43 (March 1983): 209–16. See also Gene Smiley, "Tax Rate Changes and Tax Avoidance: The 1915–1929 Era," Working Paper, College of Business Administration, Marquette University, Milwaukee, Wisconsin, July 1988.
10. For a more extensive discussion of changes in the *functional* distribution of income, primarily in the twenties, see Robert Keller, "Factor Income Distribution in the United States During the 1920's: A Re-examination of Fact and Theory," *The Journal of Economic History* 33 (March 1973): 252–73.
11. Mark Schmitz and Price V. Fishback, "The Distribution of Income in the Great Depression: Preliminary State Estimates," *The Journal of Economic History* 43 (March 1983): 217–30.
12. Louis P. Cain, "Discussion," *The Journal of Economic History* 43 (March 1983): 241–42.
13. Thomas M. Renaghan, "Distributional Effects of Federal Tax Policy, 1929–1933," *Explorations in Economic History* 21 (January 1984): 40–63.
14. For example, see Geoffrey H. Moore, "Secular Changes in the Distribution of Income," *American Economic Review* 42 (May 1952): 528; Selma F. Goldsmith, "Statistical Information on the Distribution of Income by Size in the United States," *American Economic Review* 40 (May 1950): 334; Edward C. Budd, "Postwar Changes in the Size Distribution of Income in the U.S.," *American Economic Review* 60 (May 1970): 247–60; and Lars Osberg, *Economic Inequality in the United States* (Armonk, NY: M. E. Sharpe, Inc., 1984), table 2.2, p. 15.
15. See Chapter 15 for more discussion of this.
16. The following discussion draws on Nan Maxwell, *Economic Inequality in the United States, 1947–1985* (Westport, CT: Greenwood Press, 1990), chapter 8.
17. Ibid., 121.
18. Ibid., 62–64.
19. Ibid., chapter 5.
20. Simon Kuznets, "Economic Growth and Income Inequality," *American Economic Review* 45 (March 1955), reprinted in Simon Kuznets, *Economic Growth and Structure* (New York: W. W. Norton and Co., Inc., 1965), 257–87; See also Simon Kuznets, *Modern Economic Growth: Rate, Structure, and Spread* (New Haven, CT: Yale University Press, 1966), 195–206.
21. Kuznets, "Economic Growth and Income Inequality," 258.
22. Lebergott, "Income Distribution: Size," 145–47.

23. Morton Paglin, "The Measurement and Trend of Inequality: A Basic Revision," *American Economic Review* 65 (September 1975): 598.
24. Carolyn Shaw Bell, "Another Look at Distribution of Income," *The Wall Street Journal*, 23 November, 1976, 12.
25. The Urban Institute, *Policy Bites* (June 1992), as cited in Cindy Kelly, "Moving Up—and Down—the U.S. Income Ladder," *The Margin* 8 (Spring 1993): 25.
26. Kelly, "Moving Up—and Down—the U.S. Income Ladder," 25.
27. David Wessel, "Low-Income Mobility Was High in 1980s: Treasury Study Also Finds Those at Top Tended to Stay There," *The Wall Street Journal*, 2 June, 1992. The study used a sample of 14,351 taxpayers.
28. It should be noted that this study does not shed much light on the very poorest Americans, those who have incomes so low that they pay no income taxes at all.
29. Bruce Bartlett, "A Class Structure That Won't Stay Put," *The Wall Street Journal*, 20 November, 1991.
30. Though we can make this assumption, it is questionable. As discussed in Chapter 9, the share of the population that is elderly and largely retired has continued to increase along with a decline in the age at which workers retire. This should have brought about a greater trend of increasing income equality after making adjustments to eliminate the requirement of perfect intergenerational equality. The income tax cuts of the 1980s reduced the absolute tax rates more for higher income taxpayers, but the *share* of income taxes paid by the higher income taxpayers rose, while the share paid by the lowest income taxpayers fell as a result of these tax cuts. This should have increased the after-tax equality trend. In contrast, Social Security tax rates and the maximum levels of income subject to Social Security taxation both rose. This tended to affect more directly the lower income taxpayers and should have increased the inequality after taxes. At present we have no way to assess the net effect of all of these adjustments on the trend of inequality in the 1970s and 1980s.
31. For a related discussion of this in the context of wealth inequality, see Edward N. Wolff, "Changing Inequality of Wealth," *American Economic Review* 82 (May 1992): 552–58.
32. See the following: John Bound and George Johnson, "Changes in the Structure of Wages in the 1980's: An Evaluation of Alternative Explanations," *American Economic Review* 82 (June 1992): 371–92; Kevin M. Murphy and Finis Welch, "Wage Premiums for College Graduates: Recent Growth and Possible Explanations," *Educational Researcher* 18 (May 1989): 17–26; Kevin M. Murphy and Finis Welch, "The Role of International Trade in Wage Differentials," in Marvin Kosters, ed., *Workers and Their Wages* (Washington, D.C.: American Enterprise Institute, 1991); McKinley L. Blackburn, David E. Bloom, and Richard B. Freeman, "An Era of Falling Earnings and Rising Inequality?" *Brookings Review* 9 (Winter 1990): 38–43; David M. Cutler and Lawrence F. Katz, "Macroeconomic Performance and the Disadvantaged," *Brookings Papers on Economic Activity* 2 (Winter 1991): 1–74; David M. Cutler and Lawrence F. Katz, "Untouched by the Rising Tide," *Brookings Review*, (Winter 1992): 41–45, reprinted in Don Cole, ed., *Annual Editions: Microeconomics* (Guiford, CT: The Dushkin Publishing Group, 1993); David M. Cutler and Lawrence F. Katz, "Rising Inequality? Changes in the Distribution of Income and Consumption in the 1980s," *American Economic Review* 82 (May 1992): 546–51.
33. Bound and Johnson, "Changes in the Structure of Wages in the 1980's," table 1, p. 373.
34. Ibid., 371.
35. Ibid., 389.
36. Ibid., 389.

37. In 1990 the U.S. Department of Commerce began to emphasize Gross Domestic Product (GDP) in place of Gross National Product (GNP). Though the two measures are closely related, Commerce officials argued that GDP is a better measure of the domestic production of goods and services. GNP and GDP differ by the amount of net factor payments. Net factor payments (NFP) equal the payments received from abroad (the earnings of domestic residents on foreign profits, loans, and worker remittances) minus the earnings of foreigners in the domestic economy.

$$GNP = GDP + NFP \quad \text{or} \quad GDP = GNP - NFP$$

Between 1980 and 1990, GNP exceeded GDP, but the difference declined throughout the decade. GNP was 1.77 percent larger than GDP in 1980 and 0.71 percent larger in 1990. The linear relationship between yearly GNP and GDP values from 1980 through 1990 was:

$$GDP = \underset{(-13.07)}{-69.5964} + \underset{(543.35)}{1.006833(GNP)} \qquad R^2 = 0.9997$$

(The t values are in parentheses.) The relationship between GNP and GDP is discussed in any recent Macroeconomics textbook.

38. The World Bank, *World Development Report* (New York: Oxford University Press, various years).
39. The World Bank, *World Development Report, 1989* (New York: Oxford University Press, 1989), 300.
40. Robert Summers and Alan Heston, "The Penn World Table (Mark 5): An Expanded Set of International Comparisons, 1950–1988," *Quarterly Journal of Economics* 106 (May 1991): 335.
41. Ibid. Extensive empirical work on this issue is reported in Irving B. Kravis and Robert Lipsey, *Toward an Explanation of National Price Levels* (Princeton, NJ: Princeton Studies in International Finance, no. 52, 1983).
42. Summers and Heston, "The Penn World Table (Mark 5)," 327–68.
43. In the 1970s and 1980s large fortunes were created for young entrepreneurs in the new personal computer industry. For example, William Gates, Jr., dropped out of college in the mid-1970s to found the software company, Microsoft. Today Microsoft is a giant in the computer field, and he is one of the richest individuals in the United States.
44. For example, Japan has little in the way of domestic natural resources, yet it has had one of the fastest growing economies in the postwar period.
45. It was sometimes suggested in the late 1970s and 1980s that American workers, especially in such basic industries as automobiles, were less productive and too highly paid and that was the root of the industry's problems. However, Japanese companies that opened up American automobile plants used American labor and paid competitive wage rates. The cars produced in these plants were as high in quality as the imported Japanese cars and were produced at essentially the same costs. The problem with the American companies was not labor but management and the internal organization of the firms. By the early 1990s Ford and Chrysler had made impressive strides toward matching the Japanese companies in productive performance.

Author Index

A

Abramovitz, Moses, 125
Alston, Lee J., 37
Anderson, Benjamin, 122
Anderson, Gary M., 120, 133
Arndt, H. W., 165
Arnold, Thurman, 54–55, 133
Arrington, Leonard, 133
Atwell, James B., 7

B

Baily, Martin N., 268
Bain, Joe, 275
Baker, George, 3
Baker, Jonathan B., 51
Baran, Paul A., 125
Barber, Clarence L., 154, 155
Barro, Robert J., 377
Baruch, Bernard, 6
Baxter, William, 274, 314
Bell, Carolyn Shaw, 408
Benjamin, Daniel K., 135
Berle, Adolf, 125
Bernanke, Ben, 159
Bernstein, Barton J., 200
Bernstein, Irving, 29
Bernstein, Michael A., 125
Blough, Roger, 216
Boeing, William E., 75
Bogue, Allan G., 42
Bolch, Ben, 154
Bork, Robert, 273
Bound, John, 412–13
Bovard, James, 250, 252
Bowles, Chester, 197, 200–201
Brown, E. Cary, 122, 123
Brown, Walter Folger, 75
Brozen, Yale, 273
Brunner, Karl, 119–20, 162, 164
Burns, Arthur, 369, 370, 371
Bush, George, 374

C

Cain, Louis P., 399
Caldwell, Roger, 163
Califano, Joseph, 378
Carter, Jimmy, 218, 252, 286, 372
Chakrabarti, Alok K., 268
Chandler, Alfred D., Jr., 49, 267
Chandler, Lester V., 20, 22, 130, 134
Cohen, Avi, 49
Cohen, Yehoshua S., 92
Condon, Mark, 410, 412
Conkin, Paul, 127, 134
Coolidge, Calvin, 44
Cullen, Michael, 92

D

Darby, Michael, 125–26, 134, 135
Dawson, Roy, 92
Degen, Robert A., 369, 371
De Long, J. Bradford, 105, 106
Demsetz, Harold, 275
Devine, Warren D., Jr., 48
Dubinsky, David, 30
Durant, W. C., 50
Dwyer, Gerald, 105

E

Easterlin, Richard A., 125, 220–23
Edwards, Richard C., 263
Eichengreen, Barry, 166–69
Eis, Carl, 52
Eisenhower, Dwight D., 215, 288
Eisner, Marc Allen, 274
Epstein, Gerald, 120–21

F

Feenstra, Robert C., 350
Feldstein, Martin, 376
Fels, Rendig, 154
Ferguson, Thomas, 120–21
Field, Alexander J., 159
Fishback, Price V., 399
Fisher, Irving, 104
Fleisig, Heywood, 166
Ford, Gerald R., 218, 252, 371
Ford, Henry, 2, 51, 72
Freeman, Richard B., 225–26, 232

Friedman, Milton, 117–19, 120, 122, 163, 164

G

Galbraith, John Kenneth, 104
Gallaway, Lowell, 149, 204–6
Gardner, Richard, 203
George, P. J., 153
Giedion, Simon, 49
Gilman, George F., 91
Goldfield, Michael, 230
Gomper, Samuel, 28–29
Gordon, Robert J., 370
Green, William, 29
Gunderson, Gerald, 104

H

Hand, Learned, 272
Hansen, Alvin H., 125
Harberger, Arnold, 276
Harl, Neil, 246
Harris, Seymour, 125
Hartford, George Huntington, 91
Hawley, Ellis W., 53, 54, 134
Hayek, Friedrich A., 148, 150, 151
Heller, Walter, 216
Heston, Alan, 416–17
Hickman, Bert G., 154, 155, 220
Hicks, John R., 165
Higgs, Robert, 198, 199, 203, 356
Hillman, Sidney, 30
Hirsch, Richard F., 292
Hitler, Adolf, 184
Holt, Charles F., 397–98
Hoover, Herbert, 81, 95, 123, 124, 149–50, 165
Hopkins, Harry, 128
Howard, E. H., 83
Hughes, Jonathan, 10, 203
Humphrey, Hubert H., 217

J

Jackson, Robert, 54–55, 132
Jerome, Harry, 48
Johnson, D. Gale, 252
Johnson, George, 412–13
Johnson, H. Thomas, 99
Johnson, Lyndon Baines, 216–17, 311, 324, 363, 368–69, 378, 407

K

Kahn, Alfred, 297
Kalecki, Michael, 125
Kendrick, John W., 157, 228–29
Kennedy, John F., 216, 368, 378
Kesselman, Jonathan R., 126
Kindleberger, Charles P., 104, 125, 165–66
Krooss, Herman, 263
Krug, Julius, 200–201
Kuznets, Simon P., 125, 198, 397–98, 399, 404–5, 410

L

Lebergott, Stanley, 392, 405–6
Levy, Frank, 403
Lewis, John L., 30, 31
Lewis, W. Arthur, 125
Lilley, William, III, 381–82
Lindert, Peter, 164
Livesay, Harold C., 50
Lorant, John, 49
Lucas, Robert E., Jr., 125
Lucia, Joseph L., 163

M

McAdoo, William G., 6
McClelland, George, 82
McMahon, Marshall, 154
McNair, Malcolm P., 92, 336
Macy, R. H., 90
Mansfield, Edwin, 265–66
Markin, Rom J., 93
Marshall, George C., 203–4
Martin, William McChesney, Jr., 368
Maxwell, Nan L., 402–3
May, Eleanor G., 92, 336
Mayer, Thomas, 155–56, 164
Means, Gardiner C., 125
Medoff, James L., 232
Meltzer, Allen, 119–20, 162, 164
Mercer, Lloyd J., 152–53, 154–55
Merganthaler, Othmar, 80
Miller, G. William, 371
Miller, James C., III, 381–82
Miron, Jeffrey, 118
Mishkin, Fredrick S., 155
Mitchell, Broadus, 15
Morgan, J. P., 2, 3, 4, 115
Morgan, W. Douglas, 152–53, 154–55
Mosco, Vincent, 308

Munnell, Alicia H., 377
Munro, Douglas, 376
Murray, Charles, 377, 378
Muth, Richard F., 154
Myers, Robert J., 228–29

N

Nelson, Daniel, 49
Nixon, Richard M., 217, 285, 287, 340, 345, 369–70, 371
Noble, Edward J., 82
Nourse, Edwin, 152

O

Oksanen, E. H., 153
Oshima, Harry T., 48
Otis, Robert, 92

P

Paglin, Morton, 408–9, 412
Peppers, Larry, 122, 123
Pilgrim, John, 154
Porter, Patrick G., 50
Pujo, Arsene, 3

R

Rapping, Leonard A., 125
Reading, Don C., 133
Reagan, Ronald, 218, 232, 252, 274, 286, 288, 372–73
Renaghan, Thomas M., 124, 399
Rockhoff, Hugh, 195, 197, 370
Roosa, Robert, 344, 345
Roose, Kenneth D., 122
Roosevelt, Franklin Delano, 11, 19, 21–22, 37, 44, 53–54, 69, 76, 95, 97, 116, 125, 126–27, 129, 130, 133, 134, 188, 194, 377, 399
Rosenberg, Nathan, 267
Ross, David, 270–71, 273, 276
Rostow, W. W., 18
Rothbard, Murray N., 104

S

Saint-Etienne, Christian, 166
Santoni, Gary J., 105
Saunders, Clarence, 91, 92
Savin, N. E., 126
Sawhill, Isabel, 410, 412
Scherer, Frederick M., 270–71, 273, 276
Schlesinger, Arthur M., Jr., 134
Schmitz, Mark, 399
Schumpeter, Joseph A., 125, 134
Schwartz, Anna, 117–19, 120, 122, 159, 163, 164
Shannon, David A., 20
Shleifer, Andre, 105
Shughart, William, 120
Sirkin, Gerald, 105
Sloan, Alfred, 50
Smiley, Gene, 398
Smith, Vernon, 106
Soltow, Lee, 397–98
Soule, George, 7, 15, 66
Stein, Herbert, 123, 124, 367
Steindl, Josef, 125
Stewart, A. T., 90
Stillman, James, 3
Strong, Benjamin, 115, 117–19
Summers, Robert, 416–17
Swanson, Joseph, 156
Sweezy, Paul M., 125

T

Taylor, Frederick W., 2, 48
Teigen, Lloyd D., 254
Temin, Peter, 104, 155–57, 159, 163–64, 169
Timoshenko, Vladimir P., 125
Tollison, Robert, 120, 133
Toma, Mark, 120
Trescott, Paul B., 118
Truman, Harry S., 201, 288, 367
Tugwell, Rexford, 126–27

U

Ulman, Lloyd, 28

V

Vatter, Harold G., 18
Vedder, Richard K., 149, 204–6
Volcker, Paul, 371, 372
von Hippel, Eric, 268
von Mises, Ludwig, 148

W

Wagner, Richard, 31, 132
Wallace, Henry, 130

Wallis, John Joseph, 133, 135
Wanniski, Jude, 104
Warren, George W., 128
Weidenbaum, Murray L., 375, 380, 382
Weinstein, Michael, 22, 135–36
Weintraub, David, 125
Welles, Orson, 81
Wells, H. G., 81
Wheelock, David C., 120
White, Eugene Nelson, 105, 163
Wicker, Elmus R., 117, 119, 120, 162, 163
Williamson, Samuel, 156
Wilson, Woodrow, 4, 6, 8, 10
Wood, Robert C., 91, 92
Woolworth, Frank W., 91
Wright, Gavin, 133
Wynn, Ed, 82

Subject Index

"5 and 10 Cent Store," 91

A

A&P stores, 91, 93, 272
A. B. Banks, 163
ABC, 82, 309
Adamson Act (1916), 6
AFL-CIO, 230
Age Discrimination in Employment Act (1967), 381
Agricultural acts, 250–51
Agricultural Adjustment acts (1933 and 1938), 44–45, 129–30, 135
Agricultural and Consumer Protection Act (1973), 251
Agricultural Marketing Act (1929), 44
Agriculture
  and crop destruction, 20–21
  and debt crisis of 1980s, 245–50
  and employment, 223, 236
  and exports, 249, 251
  farm incomes, 2, 4
  farm prices, 2, 4, 7–8, 36, 129, 135, 217, 242–45, 249, 251–53
  fertilizers, herbicides, and insecticides, 241
  foreclosures on farms, 36, 36–37, 39, 129, 249–50
  genetics and modern breeding, 242
  "golden years" of, 2, 43
  and government programs, 45–46, 250–54, 348
  meat crisis of 1973, 217, 242–45
  mechanization and technological changes in, 40–43, 238–42
  productivity of, 36, 40–41, 46, 237–40
  property values, 36, 37, 237, 238, 246–49
  size of farms, 39, 40, 236–37
  and trade policies, 348
Agriculture, Department of, 241, 250, 253, 254
Aid to Families with Dependent Children (AFDC), 361, 375, 377, 378, 379
Air Commmerce Act (1926), 75
Airline Deregulation Act (1978), 298
Airlines, 75–76, 297–98
Air Mail Act (1925), 75
Air Mail Act (1934), 75–76
Air Pollution Control Act (1962), 381
Air traffic, 294
Alcoa (Aluminum Company of America), 55, 133, 201, 272, 274
Allied Chemical Corp., 201
Allis Chalmers tractor, 41
Amalgamated Broadcasting Network, 82
Amalgamated Clothing Workers Union (ACWU), 30–31
American Airlines, 76
American Broadcasting Company (ABC), 82, 309
American Can Company, 53
American Exchange Trust, 163
American Express, 321
American Farm Bureau, 132
American Federation of Labor, 3, 10, 28–31, 184, 188, 230
American Society of Composers and Publishers (ASCAP), 82
American Tobacco Corp., 3, 53
AM radio, 83, 306–7
Amtrak, 297
"Anacostia Flats, shame of," 21
Annual Improvement Factor (AIF), 230
Anthracite railroads, 53
Antitrust
  Division of Justice Department, 54, 132–33
  laws, 6, 50, 52–54
  and AT&T, 314
  "incipiency" and antitrust policy, 272
  policies after World War II, 272–74
Apple Computer, 273
Area Redevelopment Act (1961), 378
Army Air Corps, 75
Army Corps of Engineers, 294
Artificial insemination, 242
Assembly production line, 72
Asset-substitution effect, 377
Associated Press (AP), 81
Association of American Railroads, 73
AT&T, 7, 77–79, 82, 309, 311–15
Attorney General, U.S., 6

Automobile use, 18
Automobile industry, 8, 20, 51, 152–54, 202, 269, 293, 350
  capacity utilization in, 152–53
  prices, 72, 350
  production, 18, 152, 264
  sales of imported cars during 1970s, 218
  "saturation" of, 152–53
Aviation Company (AVCO), 75

B

Baby boom, 201–2, 215, 222, 403
Backward integration, 50–51
Banco Kentucky, 163
BankAmericard, 321
Bank Board, 318
Banking, 99–101, 316–22
  "banking holidays," 19–20, 21
  branching of banks, 99
  credit cards, 321–22
  district banks, 114–15
  failures, 19, 159–61, 162–63, 219, 318–21
  and monetary policy between the world wars, 114–21
  and New Deal reform, 127
  and panics, 99–100, 116, 159–61
Banking Act (1933), 127
Banking Act (1935), 114, 128
Bank Insurance Fund (BIF), 320
Bank of America, 321
Bank of Tennessee, 163
Bank of the United States, 19, 163
Beatrice Food Corp., 270
Belgian Relief, 7
Bell Laboratories, 315
Bell Telephone companies, 314
Bendix Corp., 273
Big Bear stores, 92
Birth control, 222
Bituminous Coal Conservation Act (1937), 66
Black Thursday, 104, 325
Boeing Corp., 76, 297
Bond market crashes, 121, 372–73
Braniff Airlines, 75, 299
Bretton Woods, 203, 340, 344–45, 351, 369, 370
Brown Shoe decision, 272
Bureau of Commerce, 75, 76
Bureau of Internal Revenue, 186
Bureau of Labor Statistics (BLS), 228
Burlington Industries, 270
Buses, 73–75, 297
Businesses
  associations, 2
  ownership of, 2
  regulations of, 375, 380–82
Buy-Sell Program, 286

C

Cable television, 310
Caldwell and Company, 162–63
Capital flows, 98
Carte Blanche, 321
"Cash-and carry" grocery, 91
CBS, 81, 82, 308, 309
CCC
  See Commodity Credit Corporation
Celler-Kefauver amendment, 272
Census Bureau, 407
Chain stores, 91, 336–37
Chamber of Commerce, U.S., 2
Chase Manhattan, 321
Chicago Tribune, 82
Chrysler Corp., 20, 31–32, 152, 218, 264, 268, 269, 350
Cigarette industry, 380
Cities Service Corp., 270
Citrus industry, 39
Civil Aeronautics Act (1938), 76, 297
Civil Aeronautics Authority (CAA), 76
Civil Aeronautics Board (CAB), 76, 297–98
Civilian Conservation Corps, 128
Civil Rights Act (1964), 378, 381
Civil Works Administration, 128
Civil Works Service Program, 128
Clayton Act (1914), 3, 53, 272
Coal industry, 63–67, 290–91
Collective bargaining, 28, 31, 230
Columbia Broadcasting System (CBS), 81, 82, 308, 309
Command Economy, 5
Committee on Industrial Preparedness, 5
Commodity Credit Corporation (CCC), 11, 44–45, 127, 129, 130, 249–53, 348
Communication Act (1934), 82, 310
Communications industry, 77–83, 305–16
Communism, failure of, 392
Computer chip industry, 348
Condec Corp., 268
Congress of Industrial Organizations (CIO), 31, 184, 188, 230

Connally Act (1935), 69
Connecticut General Insurance Company, 270
Conoco Corp., 270
Construction, 157–58
Consumer Price Index (CPI), 184, 186
Consumer Products Safety Commission (CPSC), 380
Consumer protection, 380–81
Consumer spending, 16, 18, 148, 155–56, 199, 200, 204–5
Continental Airlines, 75, 299
Continental Can case, 272
Continental Trailways, 297
Convenience stores, 336
Cooperative Marketing Act (1924), 44
Corporate profits, 393–94
Corporate savings, 149
Corporate stability, 263
Cost of Living Adjustments (COLA), 230
Cost of Living Council, 286, 287
Cotton, 39
Council for National Defense, 5
Council of Economic Advisors, 367
Council on Environmental Quality (EPA), 382
Country Club Plaza, 92, 335
Cracking process to refine crude oil, 68
Credit, consumer, 19
Credit cards, 321–22
Crop and livestock destruction, 20–21, 37–38
Crosley Corp., 202
Current account balance, 341–42
Current Tax Payment Act (1943), 192
Curtiss-Wright Aircraft and Engine Company, 75

D

Dawes Plan, 95
DC-3 aircraft, 76
DDT insecticide, 189, 241
Deficit as percent of GNP, 216
Delta Airlines, 75
Department of Commerce, 81
Department stores, 90, 336–37
Depository Deregulation and Monetary Control Act (1980), 219
Depository Institutions Deregulation and Monetary Control Act (1980), 318
Deposit-to currency ratio, 159, 161, 163
Deposit-to-reserve ratio, 159, 161, 163
Depressions, economic, 146
  of 1870s, 16
  of 1893–96, 16
  of 1920–1921, 15, 22, 28, 94, 99, 117
  of 1937–1938, 22–23, 116, 121–22, 132
  See also Great Depression
Devaluation of dollar, 97–98, 116, 217, 244, 340, 370
Digital Equipment Corp., 273
Dime store, 91
Diners Club Card, 321
Discount stores, 337–38
Distribution of income, 392–413
Divorces, increase of, 24
Dollar shortage, 339–40
Douglas, Donald, 76
Dow Chemical Corp., 201
Dow Jones Index, 102–3, 104, 219, 323, 325, 326
DPC, 201
DRAM computer chips, 348
DuMont Corp., 309
Du Pont Corp., 4, 201, 270, 272
Durable goods, 18, 19, 263

E

Earnings, 27–28, 29, 188–89, 205
  See Income
Eastern Airlines, 75, 76, 299
Eastman Kodak, 53
Economic Opportunity Act (1964), 378
Economic Recovery Tax Act (1981), 372–73
Economic Stabilization Act (1970), 369–70
Electrical appliances, 18, 69
Electricity, 18, 48, 69–71
  increased use of, 63, 65
  prices, 69–70, 71, 291–93
Electric utilities, 69
Electronic funds transfers (EFTs), 322
ELF Aquitaine Corp., 270
Elkins Act (1903), 3
Emergency Banking Bill (1933), 127
Emergency Education Program, 128
Emergency Feed Grain Bill (1961), 251
Emergency Fleet Corporation, 6
Emergency Petroleum Allocation Act (1973), 286, 381
Emergency Petroleum Conservation Act (1975), 286
Emergency Tariff Act (1921), 94

Emergency Transportation Act (1933), 73
Employment
  agricultural, 39
  coal industry, 66
  coal mining, 64–65
  equal opportunity, 381
  government, 356–57
  and government responsibility, 365–67
  in retail, wholesale, and service trades, 334–35, 339
Employment Service, 185
Energy, Department of, 381
Energy industry, 63–71, 282–93
Entrepreneurial income, 392–94
Environmental regulations, 381
Equal Employment Opportunity Commission (EEOC), 378, 381
Equal opportunity, 378
Equal opportunity employment, 381
European Coal and Steel Community of 1951, 203–4
European Common Market, 203–4, 348
Exchange rates, 344–47
Export Enhancement Program, 348
Exports, 95, 341–44
  as a percent of GNP, 97
  during three interwar contractions, 156
  and government subsidization of agriculture, 348
  of food before World War I, 2
  of food during World War I, 7
  surplus of during World War I, 4
Exxon Corp., 284

F

Fairchild Corp., 75
Fair Labor Standards Act (1938), 132, 135
Fair trade laws, 337–38
Farm Bureau, 129
Farm Credit System (FCS), 248, 249–50, 252
Farmers Holiday Association, 21
Farmers Home Administration, 249–50
Farmland, value of, 36, 37
Farm size, 39, 40, 236–37
Federal Aviation Administration (FAA), 294, 297
Federal Bureau of Investigation (FBI), 5
Federal Communications Commission (FCC), 82, 307–10, 312–14
Federal Crop Insurance Corporation, 45
Federal debt as percent of GNP, 193–94
Federal deficits, 363–65, 374
Federal Deposit Insurance Corporation, 127, 128
Federal Emergency Relief Act (1933), 128
Federal Energy Administration Act (1974), 381
Federal Energy Office, 286, 287
Federal Express, 311
Federal Farm Mortgage Corporation, 127
Federal Home Loan Bank Board, 319–20
Federal Housing Administration, 127
Federal Labor Unions, 30
Federal Open Market Committee, 114, 371
Federal Power Commission (FPC), 288–89
Federal Radio Commission (FRC), 81
Federal Reserve Act (1913), 114
Federal Reserve Board, 114–15, 117
Federal Reserve System, 3, 11, 19, 97, 99, 100, 114–22, 127, 128, 148, 159–61, 162, 164, 166, 206, 217, 218, 219, 249, 318, 324, 326, 365–74, 383
Federal Road-Aid Act (1916), 75
Federal Savings and Loan Insurance Corporation, 128
Federal Trade Commission (FTC), 270, 273, 274
Federal Trade Commission Act (1914), 3, 53, 272
Federated Stores, 270
Fertility rates, 221–22
Fiat Corp., 168
Financial Institutions Competitive Equality Act (1987), 320
First World War
  See World War I
FM radio, 83, 306–7
Food Administration, 7–8
Food and Agriculture Act (1977), 252
Food and Drug Act (1962), 380
Food and Fuel Production Act (1917), 5
Food Security Act (1985), 252
Food stamps, 45, 250, 361, 379
Ford Corp., 8, 20, 31–32, 152, 264, 269, 350
Fordney-McCumber Tariff (1922), 44, 94, 166
Fordson tractor, 41
Foreclosures on farms, 36, 36–37, 39, 129, 249–50
Fox Deluxe Foods, 273
Fram Corp., 273
Franchising of retail stores, 337
FSLIC, 319–20
Full-Employment Act (1946), 203, 365–67

G

Garn-St. Germain Depository Institutions Act (1982), 318
Gasoline crisis of 1973, 287
General Accounting Office (GOA), 320
General Agreement on Tariffs and Trade (GATT), 203, 347–51
General Dynamics, 273
General Maximum Price Regulation (GMPR), 194
General Motors Corp., 20, 31–32, 152, 264, 269, 270, 272, 350
Germany, 95, 169
Getty Oil Corp., 270
G.I. Bill, 202
Gini coefficient of income distribution, 395–96, 401, 407, 412–13
Glass-Steagall Act (1932), 121
Glucose and cornstarch trust, 53
GNP, 4, 15–18, 23, 93–94, 96–98, 166, 156, 199, 204–5, 213–14
Gold exchange standard, 93–94, 96–98, 166
Gold Reserve Act (1934), 98
Gold standard, 19, 93–94, 96–98, 115, 116, 166, 169–70, 217
Gold stock, 10, 344–45
Government
- deficits, 363–65, 374
- employment, 356–57
- federal spending (1950–1990), 360–62
- fiscal and monetary policies, 365–74
- growth of after 1950, 356–65
- poverty and welfare programs, 377–80
- receipts (taxes) (1950–1990), 356–58, 359–61
- responsibility for employment, 365–67
- social policies after 1950, 374–80
- stabilization policies, 365–74
- state and local spending after 1950, 262–64
- welfare expenditures as percent of GNP, 379

Government Extension Service, 129
Government intervention
- in farming, 250–54
- in manufacturing monopolies, 272–74

Government regulation, 5–7, 19
- of airlines, 297–98
- of banking, 114–17, 127, 219
- of businesses, 2, 375, 380–82
- of coal industry, 66
- of domestic transportation, 77
- of electricity production, 69
- to protect the environment, 381
- of farm prices, 44–46, 129–30
- of mass communication, 307–10
- of monetary affairs, 11
- of monopolies, 52–54
- of natural gas industry, 288–89
- of petroleum industry, 68–69, 284–88
- of prices and wages during World War II, 193–97
- of radio, 81
- of railroads, 6, 72–73, 294–95
- of telecommunications, 311–15
- of telegraph and telephone systems, 6–7
- of television, 308–10
- of trucking, 74, 294–96
- after World War I, 10
- reaction against during 1970s, 218
- during World War I, 11

Government spending, 123
Graham Act (1921), 78
Grain embargo of 1980, 252
Gramm-Rudman Act (1985), 374
Granger laws, 2
Great Depression, 2, 10, 11, 16–17, 19–22, 23, 36, 50, 53, 64–65, 73, 78–79, 106, 116, 118–21, 146–71, 326, 96, 99–101
- Austrian explanation of, 146, 148–51
- and international disruptions, 165–70
- Keynsian explanation of, 146, 151–58
- monetarist explanation of, 146, 158–65
- and property income, 394
- and use of electricity, 69
- and war debts and reparations, 95–96

Greyhound Buslines, 74, 297
Gross Domestic Product (GDP), 414–20
Guffy-Snyder Act (1937), 66
Guffy-Vinson Act (1937), 66
Gult Corp., 270

H

Harrod-Domar growth model, 154
Hawley-Smoot Tariff (1930), 44, 95, 149–50, 166, 168–69
Health, 20, 64
Heileman Brewing Co., 273
Hepburn Act (1906), 3
Highway construction, 363
Highway system, 294
Hilton Hotel Corp., 321
Hirfindahl-Hirschman Index, 275

Home Insurance Co., 163
Homelessness, 20, 22
Home Owners Loan Corporation, 127
"Hoovervilles," 20
House Ways and Means Committee, 326
Housing construction, 8, 157–58
Hudson Corp., 31
Hybrid seed corn, 42–43

I

IBM Corp., 273
ICC
  See Interstate Commerce Commission
Immigration, 2, 8, 10, 23–25, 48–49, 222–23
Import competition, 347–48, 350, 413–14
Imports, 95, 97, 168, 341–44
INA Insurance Company, 270
"Incipiency" and antitrust policy, 272
Income, 228, 392–413
  after 1950, 228
  in coal industry, 64–65, 66
  distribution of, 27–28, 38, 396–403
  farm vs. nonfarm (1920–1940), 38
  Inverse Pareto coefficients of income distribution, 396–97
  Lorenz curve of income distribution, 395–96
  Lorenz-Gini coefficients of income distribution, 409
  Paglin-Gini coefficients of income distribution, 409
Income elasticity, 263
Income tax, 3, 10, 192–93
  See also Taxes
Industrial Workers of the World, 10
Industry
  codes of the New Deal, 130–32, 134
  rate of production (1933–1937), 22
  reforms of the New Deal, 130–33
  during World War I, 7–8
Inflation, 9, 11, 17–18, 184, 213–14
Infrastructure, maintenance of, 294
Insurance, 322
Interbank Card Association, 321
Internal Revenue Service (IRS), 275
Interest-paying checking accounts, 317–18
Interest rates, 9, 11, 160, 249
Internal combustion engine, 63
International Air Transport Association, 299
International Association of Machinists, 231
International Bank for Reconstruction and Development (IBRD), 203
International Brotherhood of Electrical Workers, 231
International Comparison Program (ICP), 417
International Harvester tractor, 41
International Ladies Garment Workers Union (ILGWU), 30–31
International Monetary Fund (IMF), 203, 371
International News Service (INS), 81
International Trade Organization (ITO), 203
Interstate Commerce Act (1887), 3, 74
Interstate Commerce Commission (ICC), 3, 4, 6, 72–73, 74, 76, 77, 294–96, 297, 380
Interstate Highway System, 294
Inverse Pareto coefficients of income distribution, 396–97
Investment tax credit, 249
Isolationism, 184

J

J.C. Penney's, 91
Jewel Tea stores, 91
Job Opportunities, 378
Jobs Corp, 378
Jones and Laughlin Steel Corp., 273
Jumbo deposits, 320
"Junk bonds," 219
Justice Department, 6, 53, 54, 132–33, 273, 314

K

Kaiser Corp., 201
Kaiser-Fraser Corp., 202
Kappel Commission, 311
KDKA radio broadcast, 81
Kelly Act (1925), 75
Kennecott Copper Co., 273
Keynsian theory, 146, 151–58, 368–69
King Kullen stores, 92
Kinney Company, 272
Knights of Labor, 3
Korean War and price controls, 215
Kresge stores, 91
Kress stores, 91
Kroger stores, 91

L

Labor force, 187, 224
  growth of, 26–28

and military personnel (1940–1950), 187
regulation of working conditions and employment, 381
during World War I, 8–9
after World War II, 223–30
Labor income, 392–94
Labor Management Reporting and Disclosure Act (1959), 230
Labor unions, 8, 10, 184, 202, 216
and airline industry, 298
"American Plan," 29
in automobile industry, 350
"Business unionism," 28
declining membership in, 232
discriminatory practices, 230
early formation of, 3
membership of after 1950, 230–31
in public sector, 231–32
in railroad industry, 6, 295
and shorter work week, 131
in steel industry, 349
between world wars, 28–32
after World War II, 230–32
during World War II, 188
"Yellow-dog" contract, 29
Laissez-faire government, 114
Landrum-Griffin Act (1959), 230
Leisure time, 18
Lerner index, 275
Lever Food and Fuel Control Act (1917), 5
Liberty League, 132
Liberty Loans, 4, 9, 11
Life insurance companies, 102
Linotype machine, 80
"Little Steel," 31–32, 184
Lorenz curve of income distribution, 395–96
Lorenz-Gini coefficients of income distribution, 409

M

McClellan hearings, 230
McCrory stores, 91
McDougall Reserve Bank, 121
Mack Corp., 73
McNary-Haugan bills (1924–1928), 44
Macy Company, R. H., 82
Madison oil cases, 133
Magnuson-Moss Warranty Act (1974), 380–81
Mail order firms, 90–91
Malls and strip malls, 335
Management-controlled company union, 29
Mandatory Oil Import Program, 284–86
Mann-Elkins Act (1910), 3
Manpower Development and Training Act (1962), 378
Manufacturing, 46–55, 259–76
developments in management, 49–50, 267–68
diversification of, 49–50
industrial concentration and economic performance, 274–76
and industrial reforms of the New Deal, 130–33
mergers and monopolies, 50–52, 269–76
patent activity, 266–67
productivity growth, 63, 264, 265, 268–69
reconversion after World War II, 200–201
regional distribution, 46–47, 260–61
research and development (R&D), 264–66
share of GNP, 260–61
shortfalls in management, 268
switch to service economy, 415
technological changes, 48–50, 264–66, 267
use of new materials, 267
Marathon Oil Corp., 270
Market extension merger, 270
Market system, 146
Marshall Plan, 203–4
Mass communications media, 305–10
MasterCard, 321
Matsushita Electrical Company, 269
MCI (Microwave Communications Inc.), 314
Medicaid, 378
Medicare, 361, 378
Mellon tax cuts, 123
Merchant Marine, 5, 8
Mergers, 219, 269–72
in airline industry, 75
and monopolies of businesses, 50–52
among newspapers, 305
Microwave transmission, 314
Migration
from cities to suburbs, 72
market-induced, 38
rural-to-urban, 9, 23–26, 187–88
"Military-industrial complex," 215
Military production, 4, 186, 215, 360
Milk subsidies, 253

Miller-Tydings Act (1937), 132, 337–38
Mobil Oil Corp., 270
Monetarist theory, 146, 158–65, 369, 371, 374
Monetary policy, 114–21, 197, 218, 340
Money Market Deposit Accounts, 318
Money market mutual funds, 317, 318
Monopolies, 216
    Alcoa decision, 201
    and AT&T, 314
    of cable television companies, 310
    of electric utilities, 69
    and mergers, 50–52
    fear of "money trusts," 114
    "monopoly capitalism," 263
    and National Recovery Administration, 132
    attacked by New Deal, 132–33
    of powerful bankers, 3
    of radio networks, 82
    and status of U.S. Postal Service, 311
    after World War II, 269–76
Monopoly rents, 298, 309
Montgomery Ward, 90–91
Motor Carrier Act (1980), 74, 296
Motorola Corp., 269
Multilateral trade-weighted value of U.S. dollar, index of, 346
Mutual Broadcasting System, 82
Mutual Corp., 309
Mutual savings banks, 102

N

National Airlines, 75
National Association of Manufacturers, 132
National Association of Railroad and Utilities Commissioners, 74
National banks, 99
National Broadcasting Company (NBC), 81, 82, 309
National Defense Act (1916), 5
National Defense Advisory Council, 184, 194
National Defense Highway System, 294
National Highway Users Conference, 294
National Industrial Recovery Act (1933), 22, 30–31, 53, 128, 130, 132
National Labor Relations Act (1935), 31, 132, 188, 202
National Labor Relations Board, 31, 135, 185
National Labor Union, 3
National Railroad Passenger Corporation, 297
National Recovery Administration, 11, 53–54, 130–33, 134–36
National Resources Planning Board, 203
National Television System Committee, 308
National Youth Administration, 128
Natural gas, 288–89
Natural Gas Policy Act (1978), 289
Naval Consulting Board, 5
NBC, 81, 82, 309
Negative Income Tax (NIT), 379
Negotiable Order of Withdrawal account (NOW), 317–18
Neighborhood Youth Corps, 378
New Careers, 378
New Deal, 10, 11, 22, 42, 53, 55, 69, 114, 125–36, 374–75, 377
Newspaper Preservation Act (1970), 305
Newspapers, 80–81, 305
New York City Federal Reserve Bank, 115, 162
New York Stock Exchange (NYSE), 2, 101–2, 104, 105, 219, 322–26
Nichols Company, J. C., 92
Northeast Airlines, 75
Northwest Airlines, 75
Nuclear power, 291–93

O

Occidental Oil Corp., 270
Occupational Safety and Health Administration (OSHA), 381, 382
Office of Emergency Management (OEM), 184
Office of Price Administration (OPA), 185, 194, 195, 200–201
Office of Price Administration and Civilian Supply, 185
Office of Production Management (OPM), 185
Office of War Mobilization (OWM), 186
Office of War Mobilization and Reconversion (OWMR), 200
Oil embargo (1973), 286, 287
Old Age, Survivors, Disability, and Hospital Insurance program, 375–76
Old-Age Assistance program (OAA), 375
Old Age Insurance (OAI) program, 375
"One-price" policy, 90
Open Market Committee, 118–19
Open shop, 29

Operation Mainstream, 378
Organization of European Economic Cooperation (OEEC), 203–4
Organization of Petroleum Exporting Countries (OPEC), 217, 284

P

Pabst Brewing Co., 272
Packard Corp., 31
Packers and Stockyards Act, 44
Paglin-Gini coefficients of income distribution, 409
Pan American Airlines, 299
Pan American Airways, 76
Panasonic, 269
Paramount Corp., 309
Parcel Post Service, 90
Payment-In-Kind (PIK), 252
Payments on goods and services, 96
Peabody Coal Co., 273
Peace Corps, 378
Peanut quota system, 253
Penn Central Railroad, 369
Petroleum industry, 67–69, 282–88
  crude oil production and prices, 282–86
  cut of price controls in 1980s, 218
  gasoline production and prices, 287–88
  improvements in distribution, 68
  prices, 68, 217–18
  rates of production, 67
Philco Corp., 309
Phillips Curve, 368
Piggly Wiggly stores, 91
Pillsbury Corp., 273
Plant-specific price-cost-margin, 275
Playboy Corp., 202
Point system of rationing, 195
Population growth, 23–26, 201–2, 220–23
Postal Savings System, 102
Postal Services, 76, 310–11
Postal Telegraph, 82
Postmaster General, 6, 75
Poverty, 378, 379, 404–6
Power Trust, 53
Price-Anderson Act (1957), 291
Price changes, 17
Price controls, 193–97, 201, 217, 369–71
  fixed consumer prices, 90
  and industrial codes of the New Deal, 131
Price-fixing, 53
Prices, consumer, 22, 23, 90
Price Stabilization Division, 194
Priorities Regulation 25 of the WPB, 200
Procter and Gamble Corp., 270
Productivity
  decline of, 225–29
  increase of, 36, 40–41, 46, 237–40, 264, 265, 268–69, 403
Product line extension, 270
Professional Air Traffic Controllers Organization (PATCO), 231–32
Profit Impact of Market Strategy (PIMS), 275
Property income, 392–94
Prorationing laws for petroleum production, 68
Protectionism in recent U.S. trade, 348–50
Public Law 480 (1954), 251, 348
Public transportation, 72
Pujo Committee, 3
Purchasing Power Parity (PPP), 416–17
Pure conglomerate merger, 270

R

Race riots, 9
Radio, 81–83
Radio Act (1927), 81
Radio Law (1912), 81
Railroads, 6, 72–73, 294–97
Rationing, 195
RCA Corp., 82, 83, 270, 308
"Reaganomics," 372–73
Real Bills Doctrine, 115
Recessions, 219, 369, 371, 372–73
Reciprocal Trade Act (1934), 95
Reconstruction Finance Committee, 116
Reconstruction Finance Corporation, 127
Red Cross, 7
Regulation Q, 317
Regulatory "capture," 380
Republic Steel Corp., 273
Resident Population, 24
Resolution Trust Corporation (RTC), 320
Retail price markups, 90, 91, 92
Retail trade, 334–39
Retirement effect, 377
Revenue Act (1934), 125
Revenue Act (1935), 125
Reynolds Corp., 201
Robinson-Patman Act (1936), 132
Rural Electrification Administration (REA), 70
Rural Free Delivery service, 90

S

Safeway Corp., 270
Safeway stores, 91
Santa Fe Railroad, 270
Savings and loans, 318
  associations, 102
  bailout of, 320–21
Savings Association Insurance Fund (SAIF), 320
Schecter Company, A. L., 130
Schlitz Brewing Co., 273
School lunch programs, 250
Schuman Plan of 1950, 203–4
Sears Roebuck, 90–91, 92
Securities Act (1933), 127–28
Securities and Exchange Act (1934), 103, 127–28, 136
Securities and Exchange Commission, 54, 128
Securities markets, 101–2, 322–26
Selective Service, 9
Selective Service Act (1940), 184
Self-service policies, 91–92
Senate Finance Committee, 368
Service economy, 415
Servicemen's Readjustment Bill (GI Bill) (1944), 202
Sherman Antitrust Act (1890), 3, 4, 53, 78, 132, 272
Shipping industry, 8, 294
Shipping Act (1916), 5
Shopping centers, 92–93, 335
Sikorsky aircraft, 76
Smith-Connally Antistrike Act (1943), 188
"Soak the rich" tax changes, 399
Socal Corp., 270
Social Security, 360, 372–73, 375–77
  coverage under, 223
  Social Security Act (1935), 129, 375
  Social Security Administration (SSA), 228
  taxes for, 125, 192
  Trust Fund, 364
Soil bank programs, 251
Soil Conservation and Domestic Allotment Act (1936), 44, 130
Southern Pacific Railroad, 270
Specialized Common Carriers decision (1971), 314
Specialty stores, 336–37
Sprint, 315
Stabilization policies, 365–74
Staggers Rail Act (1980), 295, 296
Standardization in production, 7
Standard Oil Corp., 3, 53
Steel industry, 51, 264, 349–50
Steel Workers' Organizing Committee (SWOC), 31
Stock market, 95, 99, 219, 322–26
  bull market of late twenties, 102–5
  crash of, 15, 102–6, 115–16, 159
  crash of 1937, 22
  crash of 1987, 219, 270, 325
  go-go market of 1960s, 216–17, 324
  institutional holdings of stocks, 323
  Standard and Poor's index, 103, 105, 324
  See also Securities and Exchange Commission
Stock pools, 103
Strikes, 28, 31, 36, 64, 66, 117, 188, 202, 231–32
Structuralists, 378, 379
Structure-conduct-performance paradigm, 274
Studebaker Corp., 31
Sugar Equalization Board, 7
Sugar subsidies, 253
Superior Oil Corp., 270
Supermarkets, 91, 92–93, 335–36
Supplemental Security Income program (SSI), 375
Supplementary Unemployment Benefits, 230
"Supply-side" economics, 218, 372–73
Supreme Court, U.S., 3, 6, 130, 132, 288, 338
Surplus Property Act (1944), 201, 203
Survey of Income and Program Participation, 410–12

T

Taft-Hartley Act (1947), 202, 230
Tariffs, 94–95, 166–68, 347–51
Taxes, 20, 123, 375–77
  breakdown of state and local revenues, 362–63
  Civil War income tax of 1894 revived, 3
  cuts to stimulate economy, 216–17, 218, 368, 371, 372–73
  first state gasoline tax, 75
  government receipts (taxes) (1950–1990), 356–61

increase in income taxes (1932–1936), 399
new federal income tax, 3
and Roosevelt's redistribution of wealth, 22
during World War I, 9–10
See also Social Security
Tax Reduction Act (1975), 371
Teamsters, 230
Teamsters Union, 294–96
Telecommunications, 311–15
Telegraph system, 6–7, 77–79
Telephone system, 6–7, 77–79, 311–15
Television, 306, 308–10
Temporary National Economic Committee, 54, 132–33
Tennessee Valley Administration (TVA), 69–70, 136
Texaco Corp., 270
Texas Gulf Corp., 270
Texas Railroad Commission, 68, 283
Textiles and apparel, 349
Thread trust, 53
Thrift institutions, 317–21
Tire industry, 51
Tobacco production, 39
Tobin's *q*, 275
Toyota Corp., 268, 270
Tractors, 41–42, 238–40
Trade, 90–99, 334–51, 413–20
Trade barriers, 94–95, 348–50
Traffic Safety Act (1966), 380
Tragic Tuesday, 104, 325
Trailmobile Corp., 73
Transcontinental and Western Airlines, 76
Transportation, 63, 72–77, 294–99
Transportation Act (1920), 72–73
Transradio news service, 81
Trans-World Airlines, 75, 270
Travel and Entertainment (T&E) cards, 321
Treasury Department of the, U.S., 367, 410
Trenton Potteries decision, 53
Trigger Price Mechanism (TPM), 349
Trucking, 73–75, 294–96
Truth-in-Lending Act (1968), 380
Tucker Corp., 202

U

Underwood Tariff (1913), 4
Unemployment, 20, 22, 125–26
compensation for veterans, 202
"deserving" and "undeserving" poor, 377
government programs for, 377–80
and inflation, 17–18
and the New Deal, 128–29, 135
rate of, 215
rate of and GNP, 15, 185
during World War I, 4
between world wars, 15–18. 23
during World War II, 198
after World War II, 204–5, 213–14, 224–26, 228
Unemployment Compensation, 377
Unemployment Insurance program (UI), 375
Unemployment supplements, 360–61
Union-management cooperation, 29
Unit banks, 99
United Airlines, 75, 76
United Automobile Workers (UAW), 31–32, 230, 350
United Mine Workers (UMW), 28, 30–31
United Nations, 203, 417
United Parcel Service, 311
United Press Inc. (UPI), 81
United Shoe Machinery Company, 53, 273
United Shoe Machinery decision, 272
United States
Fuel Administration, 5
Grain Corporation, 6
Housing Corporation, 6
Postal Service, 6, 75, 76, 310–11
role of in world economy, 2, 413–20
Shipping Board, 5, 8
United States Railroad Association, 6
United States Steel Corp., 28, 31, 53, 270, 349
United Steelworkers, 230
Unit system of rationing, 195
Universal Product Code (UPC), 336

V

Variable rate mortgages, 317
Vertical integration, 50–51
Veteran's benefits, 202
Victory bonds, 115, 117
Victory Liberty Loan, 9
Victory Loan, 117, 193
Visa, 321
Vista, 378
Voluntary Export Restraint (VER), 349

Voluntary Restraint Agreements (VRAs), 349–50
Von's Grocery case, 272

W

Wage controls, 193–97
Wages, 392–94
- during Great Depression, 149, 150–51
- and the New Deal, 131
- after World War II, 188–89, 205, 225–29
- during 1970s–1980s, 412–13

Wagner Act (1935), 31, 55, 132, 134, 202
Walgreen's stores, 91
Wanamaker's, 90
War Finance Corporation, 6
War Industries Board, 5–6, 11
War Labor Board, 9, 184, 185, 188
War Labor Policies Board, 9
War Loan drives, 193
War Manpower Commission, 188
The War of the Worlds, 81
War on Poverty, 217, 363, 368, 378, 407
War Production Board (WPB), 185, 200–201
WEAF radio station, 82
Welfare, 377–80
Western Electric, 315
Western Union, 82
Westinghouse Corp., 81
Wheat stocks, 251
White Corp., 73
Windfall Profits Tax on oil producers, 286
WNBC radio station, 82
Women
- entering labor force, 9, 24, 26, 223
- increased labor force participation, 403
- increased work opportunities, 187–88, 215
- new social roles and fertility rates, 222

Women's Work Program, 128
Woolworth stores, 91
Workmen's Compensation, 377
Works Progress Administration (WPA), 128
World War I
- American economy during, 4–5
- cost of, 9
- debts and reparations, 94, 95–96
- growing economy during, 2
- income distribution during, 398
- inflation during, 4
- loans to Allied governments, 4
- standardization in production during, 7
- use of trucks in, 73
- war prepartions and economic mobilization, 5–7

World War II, 45–46, 184–201

X

Xerox Corp., 273

Y

Yellow Pages publishing, 315
Young Reserve Bank, 121